THE DECLINE OF FERTILITY IN EUROPE

This book is the summary volume in
a series on the decline of fertility in Europe.
A publication of the Office of Population Research,
Princeton University.

The Decline of Fertility in Europe

The Revised Proceedings of a Conference on the Princeton European Fertility Project

EDITED BY ANSLEY J. COALE
AND SUSAN COTTS WATKINS

PRINCETON UNIVERSITY PRESS
PRINCETON, NEW JERSEY

Published by Princeton University Press,
41 William Street, Princeton, New Jersey 08540
In the United Kingdom:
Princeton University Press, Guildford, Surrey

Library of Congress Cataloging in Publication Data
will be found on the last printed page of this book

ISBN 0-691-09416-0 (cloth); 0-691-10176-0 (pbk.)

Publication of this book has been aided by a grant from
The Office of Population Research

This book has been composed in Linotron Times Roman

Clothbound editions of Princeton University Press books
are printed on acid-free paper, and binding materials
are chosen for strength and durability. Paperbacks,
although satisfactory for personal collections,
are not usually suitable for library rebinding

Printed in the United States of America
by Princeton University Press
Princeton, New Jersey

Contents

Participants in the Summary Conference of the European Fertility Project

BARBARA ANDERSON
Population Studies Center
The University of Michigan
1225 South University Avenue
Ann Arbor, Michigan 48104

ANSLEY J. COALE
Office of Population Research
21 Prospect Avenue
Princeton, New Jersey 08540

PAUL G. DEMENY
The Population Council
One Dag Hammarskjold Plaza
New York, New York 10017

RICHARD EASTERLIN
Department of Economics
University of Southern California
Los Angeles, California 90089

PATRICK FESTY
Institute National d'Etudes Démographiques
27, Rue du Commandeur
Paris 14, France

RONALD FREEDMAN
Population Studies Center
The University of Michigan
1225 South University Avenue
Ann Arbor, Michigan 48104

MICHAEL R. HAINES
Department of Economics
Wayne State University
Detroit, Michigan 48202

JOHN HAJNAL
London School of Economics
Houghton Street
Aldwych
London WC2A 2AE
United Kingdom

ANDRAS KLINGER
Hungarian Central Statistical Office
1525 Budapest 11
Keleti, Karoly u. 5–7
Budapest, Hungary

JOHN KNODEL
Population Studies Center
The University of Michigan
1225 South University Avenue
Ann Arbor, Michigan 48104

RON LESTHAEGHE
Interuniversity Programme in Demography
c/o Centrum Sociologie
Vrije Universiteit Brussel
2 Pleinlaan
1050 Brussels, Belgium

MASSIMO LIVI-BACCI
Dipartimento Statistico
Universita degli Studi di Firenze
Florence, Italy

POUL MATTHIESSEN
Institute of Statistics
University of Copenhagen
Studiestraede, 6
DK1455 Copenhagen K, Denmark

CARL A. MOSK
Department of Economics
University of California, Berkeley
Berkeley, California 94720

NORMAN RYDER
Office of Population Research
21 Prospect Avenue
Princeton, New Jersey 08544

ALLAN SHARLIN (deceased)
Department of Sociology and
Graduate Group in Demography
University of California, Berkeley
Berkeley, California 94720

MICHAEL TEITELBAUM
Sloan Foundation
630 Fifth Avenue
New York, New York 10111

ROY TREADWAY
Department of Sociology
and Anthropology
Illinois State University
Normal, Illinois 61761

DIRK J. VAN DE KAA
Nederlands Interuniversitair
Demografiscu Institut
Prinses Beatrixlaan 428
Voorburg, Netherlands

ETIENNE VAN DE WALLE
Population Studies Center
University of Pennsylvania
3718 Locust Walk
Philadelphia, Pennsylvania 19104

FRANCINE VAN DE WALLE
Population Studies Center
University of Pennsylvania
3718 Locust Walk
Philadelphia, Pennsylvania 19104

SUSAN COTTS WATKINS
Population Studies Center
University of Pennsylvania
3718 Locust Walk
Philadelphia, Pennsylvania 19104

CHRIS WILSON
The London School of Economics
and Political Science
University of London
Houghton Street, Aldwych
London WC2A 2AE

E. A. WRIGLEY
The London School of Economics
and Political Science
University of London
Houghton Street, Aldwych
London WC2A 2AE

List of Tables

CHAPTER 8

CHAPTER 9

List of Figures

CHAPTER 5

CHAPTER 6

CHAPTER 9

CHAPTER 10

List of Maps

(Maps are at back of book)

Preface

In July of 1979 a conference was held in Princeton as a culmination, although not a termination, of a research project that had been in progress since 1963. The project was a study of the decline of fertility within each of several hundred provinces in Europe.

Even before 1963, there was a long history of interest in European demography (and in particular in European fertility) at the Office of Population Research at Princeton. The first director of the OPR, Frank W. Notestein, was one of the architects of a concept called The Demographic Transition, a set of generalizations about the decline in mortality and fertility that typically accompanies the modernization of a society. Moreover, during World War II the Office of Population Research had undertaken a series of studies of the population of Europe for the League of Nations, which had transferred its Economic and Transit Section from Geneva to Princeton. This series included a book on the future population of Europe and the Soviet Union, another on the population of the Soviet Union itself, a third on the population of Europe during the interwar years, and a fourth on the economic demography of Eastern and Southern Europe. Included in these books was much analysis of the decline in fertility in Europe, and an attempt to estimate what the course in fertility would be in the post-World War II years.

A more immediate stimulus to research on the decline of fertility in Europe by province was a suggestion made by Professor Jacob Viner to a graduate student in the Economics Department at Princeton who was seeking a topic for a doctoral dissertation. Professor Viner, knowing that the student, William Leasure, was interested in demography, suggested an investigation of whether the Spaniards, who Viner felt were strict Catholics like the Irish, might have reduced their fertility in the twentieth century, as the Irish did in the late nineteenth century, by postponing marriage. Leasure found relevant data for Spain—not only national data but also data by province—and investigated the decline in fertility since the late nineteenth century in the forty-nine provinces of Spain. In doing so, he found that a reduction in marital fertility rather than a postponement of marriage accounted for the decline in Spanish fertility. He also found very interesting and puzzling aspects of changing marital fertility in the different provinces. For example, 90 percent of the interprovincial variance in the level of marital fertility in 1911 (in the middle of the transition from higher to lower marital fertility) was between regions and only 10 percent within regions. Each region, which contained several provinces, shared a common cultural heritage and a common language or dialect, but was often quite heterogeneous in other social and economic characteristics. The lowest fertility region, that of Catalonia, included provinces that were industrialized and largely urban, and other provinces that were mostly rural and agricultural, yet both categories of Catalonian provinces had attained low fertility. In short, Leasure's thesis showed that the decline in fertility in Spain was not readily explained by a simple version of the demographic transition, according to which the decline should be accounted for by increasing urbanization, increasing education, changes in occupational structure, and the like. At about the same time (1962) when Leasure was working on his dissertation, John Knodel, then also a graduate student in Princeton (in sociology), and Nathanial Iskandar, who was a visiting student in the special graduate training program in demography at Princeton, undertook a joint research project examining the change in fertility at a national level in various countries in Europe. They found a somewhat puzzling pattern in which the timing of the decline in marital fertility in England and in Hungary was only slightly different, despite the very different levels of education, mortality, and stage of industrialization in the two countries. Another puzzling parallel in marital fertility occurred in Norway and Rumania. Faced with these two interesting bodies of research, I thought to myself that the extensive historical demographic statistics of high quality in Europe should make it possible to employ a systematic extension of the approach that Leasure had used in his thesis in Spain, and to investigate fertility changes in the several hundred provinces of Europe from the predecline period through the major change in fertility that most of them seemed to have experienced. In 1963, the Population Council made a small grant to Princeton that enabled me to visit statistical authorities and demographers in Austria, Czechoslovakia, Poland, Hungary, and Yugoslavia and search for data from these countries and seek possible cooperation on the project that was then being planned. The project has subsequently enjoyed the collaboration of Etienne and Francine van de Walle, Massimo Livi-Bacci, John Knodel, Paul Demeny, Ron Lesthaeghe, Michael Teitelbaum, George Siampos, Vasilios Valaoras, Carl Mosk, Jacqui Forrest, Poul Matthiessen, Barbara Anderson, Susan Cotts Watkins, Erna Härm, Allan Sharlin, and Roy Treadway, to list only those who have published books or articles on their research. Others have made a parallel study of the decline in fertility in other countries, notably in Japan and Australia.

Before the conference in 1979, six books and a number of articles had been written as part of this project; another book is in press at the time that this preface is being written, and two more may appear at a later time. Since synthesis of all of this research exceeded a reasonable research agenda for a single individual, it was decided in 1978 to hold a conference to which would be invited those who had contributed books to the series, as well as others with a particular interest in the subject. Authors of the chapters of this book were asked to contribute papers—not, however, on the countries on which they had previously written, but on interrelations that extended to more than one country, or differed in other ways from the books in which standard indexes of fertility in a set of geographical subdivisions are analyzed. The discussion extended over five days.

Since the conference, extensive revisions have been undertaken, in large part as a result of the lively discussion at the conference itself. For example, the summary paper by Coale and Treadway, designed primarily to present the demographic story of the decline in fertility, has been substantially revised. A brief description of one of the revisions in this paper will illustrate the value of the comments made at the conference.

The first map in the special set of colored maps included in this volume shows the geographic distribution of the estimated date of the beginning of the decline of marital fertility in the provinces of Europe. A preliminary version of this map was presented by Coale and Treadway at the conference. A surprising feature of the preliminary map was the large number of provinces in Hungary with an earlier date of initiation of decline than in any other European country except France. Because of the absence of earlier information about age and marital status by county, the earliest date for the calculation of fertility indexes for the provinces of Hungary was 1880. Andras Klinger, who participated in the conference, questioned the validity of the attribution of an early decline in fertility in Hungary. He pointed out, on the basis of data that had been collected in the Hungarian Statistical Office, that at the national level fertility in Hungary had been approximately constant from early in the nineteenth century until the end. Also, he noted that the tables in the Coale/Treadway paper showed that the median level of marital fertility in Hungary was as high in 1900 as in 1880, scarcely consistent with a widespread early decline. His comments led us to reconsider the method by which we had estimated the date at which fertility had begun its fall from the premodern level. We had assumed that if fertility was below a certain point at the earliest dates of calculation, it must have started a decline at some earlier time. Reexamination showed that, in fact, premodern populations prior to the widespread practice of contraception or induced abortion could well have had unchanging fertility at a lower level than we had allowed for.

Our revised paper and revised map now incorporate a more sensible and consistent picture, including low pretransitional fertility in many parts of Hungary, and a date of decline in the provinces with low fertility that was not exceptionally early. In other words, the conference was not merely a chance for those who had worked on country studies to develop generalizations for much of Europe; it was also an occasion for interchanges that led to clarification, extension, and correction.

I wish to extend my gratitude to the many participants in this project over the years, each of whom has assembled and skillfully analyzed a large body of information—in every instance, I am sure, with a much greater expenditure of time and intellectual energy than anticipated. Those who contributed to the conference as authors or discussants also deserve a thankful acknowledgment.

The project was made possible by the generous support of the Rockefeller Foundation in 1964 for exploratory work, and in 1979 for the conference. During the years in between, the project enjoyed a two-year grant from the National Science Foundation, and six and a half years of funding by the National Institute of Child Health and Human Development of the National Institutes of Health.

Ansley J. Coale
November 1984

THE DECLINE OF FERTILITY IN EUROPE

CHAPTER 1: The Decline of Fertility in Europe since the Eighteenth Century As a Chapter in Demographic History

Ansley J. Coale

From the appearance of Homo sapiens until the present, the average rate of increase of the human population must have been very close to zero, simply because man's origin was so many years ago. If the present total is accepted as four and a half billion persons, and if the origin is taken as 100,000 years in the past, the average rate of increase has been an addition each year of a mere two persons per 100,000 population. Within each extended interval until quite recently in this long span, the average annual rate of increase was also very low. In the 90,000 years before the development of settled agriculture, the average annual rate was only about 1.6 per 100,000; from that point until some 200 years ago, the average rate was still only about 4.6 per 10,000. Since 1750, average annual increase has been much greater—about 7.4 per thousand per year. The world's population has been multiplied by about 5.5 in only 230 years. In these 230 years, growth accelerated remarkably, from an annual rate of increase of about 4 per thousand at the beginning of the nineteenth century to 7 per thousand early in the twentieth, to nearly 20 per thousand in the 1960s. In the last 15 years, the rate of increase has turned down, as it must sooner or later. Sustained growth at the rate of increase reached a few years ago is a physical impossibility, because the total population would in a surprisingly short time completely cover the surface of the earth, or even fill its volume. At the peak of two percent a year, the population would be multiplied by a thousand in 350 years, by a million in 700 years, and by a billion in 1,050 years. Since such multiplication is simply not feasible, we may conclude that from a very long perspective—looking back from a thousand or more years in the future—the rapid growth that began in the eighteenth century will be seen as a brief episode in human history, during which a much enlarged population was generated. This explosion in numbers, to a total that will reach 7 to 15 billion even if growth ceases within another 50 to 150 years, is surely a momentous as well as a unique episode in the history of our population.

This outburst of rapid increase in the world's population started at the time that the industrial revolution was beginning, as newly developed modern science and more rapid advances in technology contributed to a continuous expansion of transportation and trade, and to increased agricultural productivity, as well as to the development of mechanized manufacturing. The peoples of Europe (and of European descent in America and Oceania) grew more rapidly in number than the rest of the world's population during the early phases of accelerated growth; more recently European populations were the first to return to moderate rates of increase. The decline in fertility in Europe, which accounted for the slowdown in the rate of increase of the European population, was the subject of the conference of which this book is the *Proceedings*.

Fertility and Mortality in Pre-industrial Populations

The very low rate of increase of world population over each long interval of time before the eighteenth century implies an almost perfect balance between the birth rate and the death rate. For example, the average rate of increase of 0.46 per thousand from about 10,000 years ago until the eighteenth century implies an average death rate of 39.54 per thousand, on the hypothetical assumption that the average birth rate was 40.00 per thousand. Within each continuously occupied territory, if it did not gain or lose consequentially from migration, there must also have been near equality of average birth and death rates.[1] A difference of only five per thousand between the two rates would lead to multiplication (or division) by a factor of ten in five centuries, and there are few documented instances of such large increases in the absence of immigration before the 18th century.

Figure 1.1 shows combinations of fertility and mortality that would lead in the long run to rates of increase of minus one percent, zero, one percent, two percent, three percent, and three and a half percent.[2] Fertility is expressed as the total fertility rate (TFR), the average number of children

[1] "Average" birth and death rates, because the actual course of growth did not ordinarily approximate the same rate year after year. Irregular changes, including periods of substantial growth interrupted by setbacks, must have been the usual rule. In other words, the fertility and mortality that prevailed much of the time may have produced positive growth, which was offset by intermittent periods of loss.

[2] The equilibrium rate of increase implied by given rates of mortality and fertility is $r = \log_e(\text{NRR})/\text{T}$, where NRR is the net reproduction rate, and T is the mean length of generation. NRR, in turn, is approximately equal to $(\text{TFR}/2.05) \cdot p(\bar{m})$, where $p(\bar{m})$ is the proportion of women surviving to the mean age of childbearing. In Figure 1.1, e_0^0 is taken from a "West" female life table (Coale and Demeny, 1968) with an appropriate $p(\bar{m})$; $\bar{m} = 29$.

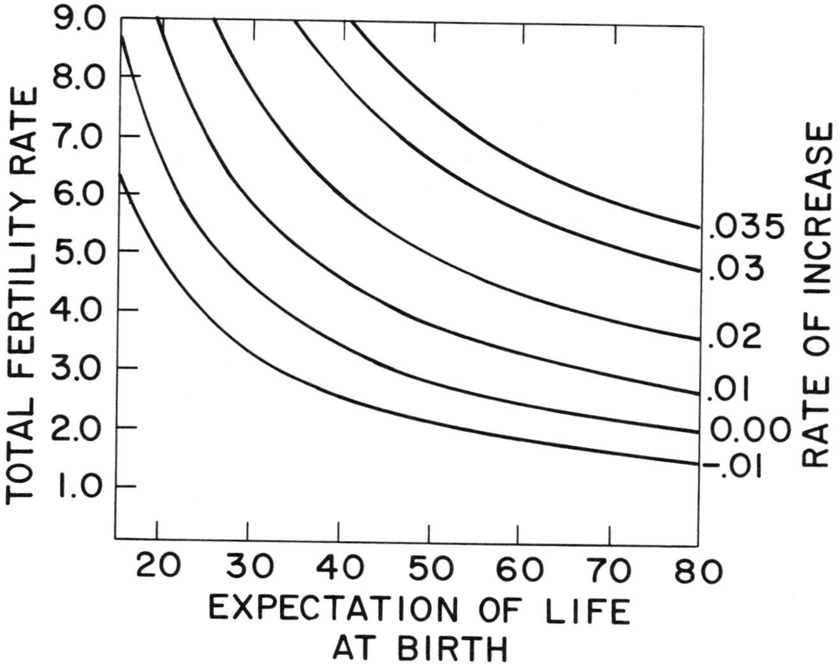

Figure 1.1. Combinations of total fertility rate and expectation of life at birth that produce long-run growth from minus one percent to three and a half percent.

born per woman reaching age 50 subject to given rates of childbearing at each age. Mortality is expressed by the average duration of life, or the expectation of life at birth e_0^0 (the length of life implied by the death rates at each age). During most of history, the world's population must have had average values of TFR and e_0^0 that in combination lay within a narrow band around the line representing combinations that lead to a growth rate of zero.

How did pre-industrial populations achieve a near-balance in birth and death rates? Logically, it seems that some form of homeostatic mechanism must be postulated to cause death rates to rise or birth rates to fall when there was an extended period of growth leading to a greatly enlarged population in a given area, and that caused death rates to fall or birth rates to rise after an extensive depletion of numbers.

It is easy to picture how death rates might increase as a result of a large increase in population. If technology is unchanging—if there is a fixed inventory of known methods of acquiring or producing useful goods, especially food and other essentials—and if the land that is accessible is limited by a combination of geography, culture, and feasible mobility, overcrowding would lower the average duration of life. After a point, a larger population means more contagion, more contamination, and less adequate nutrition.[3] Increases in mortality of this sort were what Malthus called "positive checks" to population growth. The operation of these sorts of positive checks (homeostasis through mortality that is in some degree dependent on population size within a given area) brings death rates in line with birth rates, whatever the level of fertility, provided fertility is sufficient to offset at least the minimum death rate achievable in the given cultural and technological environment. In terms of the total fertility rate and expectation of life at birth shown in Figure 1.1, if it is assumed that an average e_0^0 of 35 years is achievable, maintenance of a TFR of 4.0 would in the long run bring the average duration of life a little below 35 years, a TFR of 5.0 would lower e_0^0 to 26, and a TFR of 6.5 would in the long run drive e_0^0 down to 20 years.

Of course fertility must be high enough so that the population does not shrink even when mortality is at the lowest average level attainable. If the greatest average duration of life consistent with the achievable regularity of food supply, the unavoidable incidence of endemic disease, and the frequency and severity of epidemics is 25 years, any total fertility rate less than about 5.25 would lead to a decline in numbers and ultimate extinction.

Recognition of the necessity to maintain fertility at a level sufficient to offset mortality prompted Notestein to write:

> We may take it for granted that all populations surviving to the modern period in the face of inevitably high mortality had both the physiological capacity and the social organization necessary to produce high birth rates.

[3] Deliberately induced mortality, usually although not always infant mortality and most frequently mortality of female infants, is described by anthropologists as occurring in many populations—in Asia, among American Indians, and in the Pacific Islands, for example. The extraordinarily high mortality rates among infants in foundling homes in Europe in the eighteenth and early nineteenth centuries could also be classified, not unfairly, as a form of infanticide. Deliberate mortality can presumably have a homeostatic effect on the increase in population.

Peasant societies in Europe, and almost universally throughout the world, are organized in ways that bring strong pressures on their members to reproduce . . . .

These arrangements, which stood the test of experience throughout centuries of high mortality, are strongly supported by popular beliefs, formalized in religious doctrine, and enforced by community sanctions. (Notestein, 1953)

An unspecified component of Notestein's argument is this: How high must fertility be to offset inevitably high mortality? The general determination of how high fertility has to be is illustrated in Figure 1.1. The required total fertility rate can be found on the curve showing combinations of TFR and e_0^0 that lead to a long-run growth rate of zero, if the highest average e_0^0 achievable for a given entire population is known. In fact, the expectation of life at birth is known for few pre-industrial populations.

Lacking anything like full information, we shall consider a few examples of pre-industrial fertility and mortality in long-established societies. Figure 1.2 shows combinations of e_0^0 and TFR calculated or estimated for several European populations in the eighteenth century, for rural China about 1930, and for India in 1901 to 1911. Note that the long-run rates of increase implied for the European populations and for India are moderate positive values, and for China close to zero.

The most surprising feature of Figure 1.2 is the moderate level of fertility—TFR from about 4.1 to 6.2—in these pre-industrial populations.

The high birth rates that, according to Notestein, were an inevitable feature of pre-industrial societies were not nearly as high as can be imagined by picturing a situation in which separate high fertility characteristics reliably recorded in different populations are combined in one population. The highest reliably recorded rates of childbearing by married women are found among twentieth-century Hutterites (an Anabaptist sect settled in the north-central part of the United States, adhering to a religious prohibition of contraception or abortion), and the French Canadian population of the seventeenth century. Age of marriage was not very early in these two populations. Early marriage, and high proportions of people currently married at potentially fertile ages, *are* found, on the other hand, in many Asian and African populations. If the high marital fertility of the Hutterites were combined with the high proportions married of rural China, the total fertility rate would be over 10. No population has ever

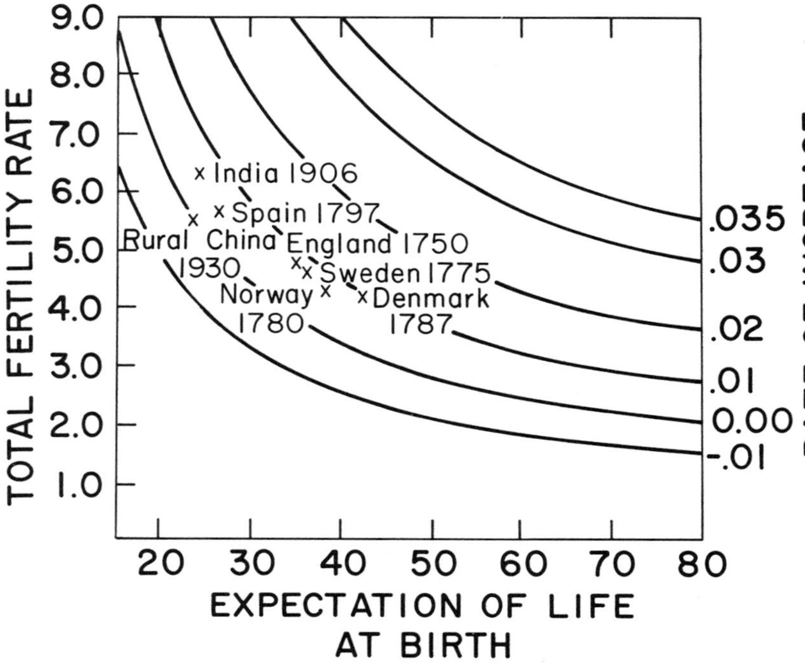

Figure 1.2. Combinations of total fertility rate and expectation of life at birth in selected pre-industrial populations—European populations in the eighteenth century, India in 1906, and rural China in 1930.

been observed to have a total fertility rate close to 10. The level of fertility actually achieved by the pre-industrial populations in Figure 1.2 is only 40 to 60 percent of what might be possible.

Although very high fertility can be imagined and could in principle be achieved, it would not be advantageous to the welfare or even to the survival of pre-industrial populations. Facing the constraints of limited technology and territory, a population with a total fertility rate of 8 to 10 would increase at annual rates of more than one percent, if its e_0^0 were over 20 years; in no more than a few centuries, overcrowding would drive its growth rate back to zero as e_0^0 fell to 13–17 years, at which point only 20 to 25 percent of women would survive to the mean age of childbearing. The long-run combination of very high fertility and very high mortality is not a combination that best enables a society to cope with adversity or rival groups. A population would have more resilience and vitality if its fertility and mortality were only moderately high. Optimal fertility in pre-industrial populations would be no higher than is consistent with zero growth at the greatest average duration of life that can be achieved in the given culture and environment. Maintenance of the lowest achievable mortality is easier if fertility responds in a homeostatic fashion to increases or decreases in the population—that is, if fertility falls when the population overfills its habitat, and rises when the population is decimated, but maintains a modest average level.

The statement that traditional societies developed customs that promoted high fertility, or faced extinction, should therefore be amended to say that traditional societies developed customs that kept fertility at *moderate* levels, avoiding both fertility so low that negative growth would make the population shrink to zero, or so high that positive growth would lead to an overcrowded habitat, and hence to higher mortality, and greater vulnerability to catastrophe or rival groups (Wrigley, 1978a).

The advantages of moderate fertility in a different context with some analogous features are known to biologists. The reproductive strategy that confers genetic advantages on animal species sometimes requires moderate rather than very high fertility. Evolutionary theorists postulate two polar strategies that are optimal for contrasting categories of animal life. Species of small body size, short life span, and short intergenerational intervals who have a limited area of foraging and a highly variable habitat survive successfully through a capacity for very rapid multiplication when their habitat is sparsely populated; species of large body size, long life span, and long intergenerational intervals who have an extensive area of foraging and a stable habitat persist successfully with limited reproduction that maintains a population of stable size, permits adequate care for a modest number of young during their long period of maturation, and avoids surpassing the capacity of the niche. The two strategies are known as *r selection* (bacteria, insects, some fish) and *K selection* (large mammals and some birds, of which the most notable is the wandering albatross, which matures only after 9 to 11 years, and lays a single egg every other year) (May and Rubenstein, forthcoming). The genetically governed reproductive strategy that is advantageous for large, slowly maturing organisms in a stable habitat has as its analog nongenetically governed reproductive strategies of human societies. In both instances, a moderate rate of reproduction rather than a very rapid rate is advantageous. Moderate reproduction is attained among larger mammals and birds by various genetically programmed restrictions on fertility, and in human populations by various social customs or practices (Dupâquier, 1972).

ANSLEY J. COALE

How Moderate Fertility Was Achieved in Pre-industrial Populations

There are two categories of constraint that kept pre-industrial fertility at moderate rather than at very high levels. One strategy consists of customs of entry into and exit from marriage that shield a large fraction of potentially fertile women from exposure to the risk of bearing children. In most pre-industrial populations, women were married within a short interval after menarche, having a mean age at first marriage of 16 to 18 years. Almost all who survived to age 25 or 30 had experienced marriage. In such populations, men may marry rather early (as in rural China in 1930, where the average age at first marriage for males was 21.3 years, compared to 17.5 for females), or rather late (as in the Uzbek Republic in the Soviet Union in 1926, where the average age at first marriage for males was 26.4, compared to 17.8 for females). Pre-industrial Europe, especially Western Europe, was exceptional in that not only males but also females married late, with a mean age of entry into first marriage of 23 to 28 years for females. The difference in age at marriage of men and women was not large; under adverse conditions marriage for both might be postponed. Moreover, again in contrast to Asian or African populations, a large fraction (10 percent or more) of women in Western Europe were still unmarried at age 50. The effect of this unusual pattern of nuptiality was to reduce fertility to less than 50 percent of its potential level if all women from 15 to 50 were currently married.[4] In contrast, the loss of potential fertility when some women between 15 and 50 years of age are not currently married is only 10 to 15 percent in many Asian and African pre-industrial populations.

Other forms of constraint that kept pre-industrial fertility moderate were various modes of behavior that limited the fertility of married couples. In almost all instances where relevant evidence exists, including (in particular) European populations, the limitation of marital fertility in pre-industrial populations is found to be nonparity-specific.

[4] Extensive marital dissolution and limitations on remarriage can also restrict exposure to childbearing. In many Western populations, divorce is quite frequent, but so is remarriage, particularly of younger women. In India early in this century, child marriage (mean age at first marriage was about 11 years), high mortality, and a tabu on remarriage of widows led to high proportions of women widowed, even at early ages. In 1901, the proportion widowed was 4.3 percent at ages 15–19, rising to 46.3 percent at 45–49. The overall reduction in fertility (compared to immediate and universal remarriage) was about 12 percent.

In this discussion, cohabitation outside marriage has been omitted for most pre-industrial populations. The argument could be readily modified to include other forms of unions.

Parity-specific and Nonparity-specific Limitation of Marital Fertility

At this point a digression is needed to describe the difference between parity-specific and nonparity-specific limitation of marital fertility, a distinction introduced by Louis Henry. Parity-specific limitation means that couples modify their behavior to avoid having more children after a certain number—the maximum desired—has been born (Henry, 1961). Parity-specific limitation typically involves contraception (folk methods, such as withdrawal, or more modern techniques, such as condoms, diaphragms, IUDs, or pills), or induced abortion. Nonparity-specific limitation includes any circumstances or forms of behavior that reduce the chance of conception or increase the interval between births—circumstances or behavior that are not modified according to the number of births that has already been experienced, but occur after the first birth as well as after the fifth or sixth. Henry proposed that parity-specific limitation be called *controlled fertility*, and that fertility affected only by behavior that is not parity-specific be called *natural fertility*. To avoid the disputes that occasionally center on the terms "natural" and "controlled," Henry's distinction will here be expressed in terms of parity-specific and nonparity-specific limitation of childbearing by married couples.

Fertility not affected by parity-related limitation varies a great deal in level because of health-related factors, such as reduced sexual activity in populations subject to chronic fevers, high rates of miscarriage for anemic women, and sterility caused by venereal disease or tuberculosis. It is also reduced by periodic separation of spouses associated with seasonal migration, or by periods spent away from home by fishermen, herdsmen, or hunters (F. van de Walle, 1975; Menken, 1979).

The most important source of differences in fertility that is not limited by parity-related measures is variation in breast-feeding. When a mother nurses an infant, postpartum resumption of menstruation and ovulation is delayed, and so is the next conception. The duration of amenorrhea varies from three or four months when the baby is not breast-fed to eighteen months in Bangladesh and Indonesia, where breast-feeding is prolonged. Very long interbirth intervals (almost four years on the average) are recorded for the !Kung tribe in Southwest Africa. A recent study provides an explanation in terms of the nursing practices in this population. Intensive observation of a number of !Kung mothers shows that nursing bouts occur all day at intervals separated by an average of only about fifteen minutes, and that the children sleep next to the mother, and have access to the breast at night. Nursing continues until the child is more than three years old. Blood samples of women with these breastfeeding routines show reduced levels of serum estriol and progesterone, hormonal changes that inhibit the return of ovulation (Konner and Worthman, 1980).

Another source of variation is tabus on sexual intercourse. A tabu found in many societies rules out sexual relations for a nursing mother. The prohibition is often reinforced by the belief that sperm poison the mother's milk—a belief reported in Africa, Asia, and Europe. The period of prescribed postpartum abstinence sometimes extends beyond the period of nursing, particularly in West Africa. It may seem odd that deliberate abstinence from intercourse is not parity-related, particularly since the couples resorting to abstinence in West Africa testify that their purpose is to postpone the next birth to protect the health of the child recently born, and of the mother. However, abstinence is practiced after the first birth as well as after the sixth—it is not in fact a parity-related measure. John Caldwell reported at a conference on natural fertility the results of a West African survey showing that couples of high parity with more of their children still living actually abstain for a somewhat *shorter* interval than those at the same parity with fewer living children (Caldwell, 1979). In contrast to parity-related control measures, West African abstinence is apparently intended to *increase* the number of surviving children. It is very different from parity-related limitation among couples who manage to avoid further childbearing after a certain number have been born.

Indications That Marital Fertility Is or Is Not Subject to Parity-specific Limitation

I will argue in the course of this essay that the decline in fertility that has been almost universal in Europe was a change from (a) moderate fertility, kept from a very high level by late marriage and permanent celibacy, and by nonparity-specific limitation of marital ferility, to (b) low fertility brought about primarily by the parity-specific practice of contraception or abortion. (Newly instituted parity-specific limitation of marital fertility is also a frequent, although in the early stages not a universal, feature of fertility reduction in those less developed countries in which a fall in fertility has occurred. In some of these countries, a rise in age at marriage for women from a mean age of 18 or less to a mean age in the twenties has also been very important in contributing to the decline and frequently precedes the widespread initiation of parity-related control.)

An essential part of the evidence sustaining the argument that there was a transition from nonparity-related to parity-related limitation of marital fertility consists of empirical indications that pre-industrial marital fertility was not limited by parity-specific behavior. This section—a further digression on parity-specific limitation—is a description of such indicators.

Direct indication of parity-specific limitation of marital fertility is obtained today in sample surveys in which women are asked to provide detailed histories of their own fertility, and to supply information about the practice of contraception or abortion following each of the births they have had. Further, they are asked questions about the number of children they want and whether births that had already occurred were wanted at the time. Direct testimony of this sort cannot be obtained about populations in the past. The presence or absence of parity-related limitation must be inferred from what has been recorded about these populations.

A very useful indirect indication of parity-related limitation of marital fertility can be derived from records of the age of women at the birth of their last child. Statistics from many populations show that in the absence of parity-related limitation, the mean value of this age is within about one year of 40. It may be slightly less because of health-related factors or nonparity-specific practices such as terminal abstinence from sexual intercourse after a married son or daughter takes up life in the household. But very low age at last birth (an average below 36, say), or large reductions in the mean age, or a lower mean age at the last birth for women married young than for those first married at a later age are good indicators of the prevalence of parity-related limitation. However, data on the age of women when they gave their last birth can be found only in detailed individual records such as have been constructed from genealogies, or from the reconstruction of life histories from the data on births, deaths, and marriages in parish registers.

A more accessible form of evidence of the existence of parity-related limitation is the age pattern of the fertility of currently married women. The age pattern of marital fertility is similar in different populations not subject to parity-related limitation. Such fertility is at its highest, almost on a plateau, from age 20 to 30, after which it declines with increasing rapidity until zero fertility is reached before age 50. With fertility at ages 20–24 set at 100, the typical sequence of rates in the successive five-year intervals is 94, 86, 70, 36, and 5. On the other hand, the presence of the widespread practice of parity-related limitation causes a different age pattern of marital fertility, a pattern of much steeper decline as age increases. This increased steepness of decline means that as age advances, marital fertility rates with parity-related control form an ever smaller ratio to the marital fertility rates of a population *not* affected by parity-related limitation.

In his original article on parity-related and nonparity-related limitation of marital fertility, Henry presented a number of schedules of marital fertility not affected by parity-related limitation (which he called natural fertility). These schedules were later the basis of model schedules of marital fertility in which the effect of parity-related limitation ranged from no effect to a very great steepening of the decline of marital fertility with age (Coale, 1971; Coale and Trussell, 1974, 1978). The model schedules of marital fertility had the following mathematical expression:

$$r(a) = Mn(a)\exp(m \cdot v(a)),$$

where $r(a)$ is marital fertility at age a, $n(a)$ is a typical schedule of marital fertility in the absence of parity-related limitation, M is ratio $r(a)/n(a)$ at ages 20–24, and $v(a)$ is a steadily decreasing function from ages 20–24 and 45–49. The value of m is a measure of the extent to which parity-related limitation affects the sequence of age-specific marital fertility rates.[5] The values of m differ by less than 0.2 from zero in the marital fertility schedules assembled by Henry in his article on natural fertility. In Norway, Sweden, and Taiwan, the value of m before marital fertility began its modern decline (in the 1880s or 1890s in Sweden and Norway; in the 1950s in Taiwan) was close to zero, and then rose monotonically to over 1.0 as marital fertility fell (Knodel, 1977b; and Knodel, 1982). If the fitted value of m is close to zero, indicating that the decline of marital fertility with age is no

[5] For computation of m, the schedule $n(a)$ is taken as the average of the ten schedules least affected by poor-quality data in Henry's original article, and $v(a)$ is taken as an average of values calculated for forty-eight schedules of parity-related control, with m in each set as 1.0 for the purpose of calculation. If m is 1.00, the ratio of limited marital fertility to fertility not affected by parity-related limitation at 20–24 to 45–49 is 1.0, 0.757, 0.513, 0.353, 0.243, 0.188. The value of m is estimated by noting that $\log(r(a)/n(a)) = \log M + mv(a)$, and fitting a straight line to $\log(r(a)/n(a))$; its slope is m. The values of $n(a)$ and $v(a)$ for five-year age intervals beginning at age 20 are as indicated in the accompanying table.

	20–24	25–29	30–34	35–39	40–44	45–49
$n(a)$	0.460	0.431	0.396	0.321	0.167	0.024
$v(a)$	0.000	−0.279	−0.667	−1.042	−1.414	−1.670

steeper than in a typical schedule not affected by parity-related limitation, the presumption that such limitation is virtually absent is a strong one, even though the level of marital fertility may be low because of nonparity-related limitation.

Evidence of the Absence of Parity-Related Limitation of Fertility in Pre-industrial Europe

There are not many national data on age-specific marital fertility rates in Europe before the sustained modern reduction in fertility began. In Norway, data on the number of legitimate births by age of mother and on the number of women classified by age and marital status are available for the years since the late 1870s, and in Sweden since 1870. The value of *m* in Norway was −0.01 in 1878 to 1880; rose to 0.18 in 1910, 0.30 in 1920, 0.56 in 1930, 0.61 in 1946, 0.79 in 1950, 0.92 in 1955, and 1.08 in 1960. Similarly, in Sweden there was a monotonic increase from an *m* of 0.078 in 1871–1880 to an *m* of 1.22 in 1951–1960 (Knodel, 1982). In both instances the rise in *m* begins at the end of a plateau of essentially constant overall marital fertility, and increasing *m* correlates closely with decreases in overall marital fertility. These two Scandinavian populations conform well to a general picture of fertility moderated by nonparity-related limitation—primarily late marriage and frequent avoidance of marriage even at the age of menopause—until a certain moment when parity-related limitation, almost certainly some form of contraception, began to have effect, and then had increasing effect until marital fertility was reduced by at least 50 percent.

At a level lower than national coverage, a number of age-specific marital fertility schedules have been calculated by reconstitution of parish registers, or by analyzing genealogies. Knodel has assembled marital fertility schedules for fourteen German villages beginning in 1750 (Knodel, 1982). For the three 25-year periods from 1750 to 1825, the age structure of marital fertility shows no evidence of a consequential degree of parity-related limitation, since the value of *m* differs from zero by less than 0.1. In his doctoral dissertation at Cambridge University, Chris Wilson (1982) has analyzed marital fertility rates of sixteen English parishes, using reconstitution of demographic data covering fifty years at a time, from 1550 to 1850. In each half century, the value of *m* differs from zero by less than 0.1. The slight positive values of *m* for these parishes are the result of high levels of marital fertility at ages 20–24 and 25–29; above age 30 the decline has a steepness virtually identical with the model schedule of nonparitylimited fertility rates. In these parishes, many of the women (in aggregate 25 percent) were pregnant at the time of marriage. Since women pregnant at marriage necessarily have a marital fertility rate of 1.0 during the first year of marriage, premarital pregnancy increases marital fertility rates in those age intervals containing a large fraction of newlyweds. The slight positive values of *m* for the English parishes are reduced even closer to zero when adjustment is made for this effect.[6]

The greatest degree of conformity to a model schedule of marital fertility not affected by parity-related limitation is found in a set of marital fertility schedules presented at an IUSSP seminar by Jacques Dupâquier (1979). These schedules were calculated by various authors who reconstituted the registers of twenty-two French parishes in the seventeenth and eighteenth centuries: when the data from these parishes are combined, the age-specific marital fertility rates are virtually the same as in the model schedule with no parity-related limitation; the ratio of one set of rates to the other from ages 20–24 to ages 40–44 falls in the very narrow range of 0.96 to 1.00, and the calculated value of *m* is less than 0.01.

Exceptional Instances of Pre-industrial Parity-related Limitation of Fertility

Parity-related limitation of marital fertility in Europe, while rare, was not completely absent before the sustained modern reduction in fertility began. A survey of early instances of parity-related limitation is found in Massimo Livi-Bacci's contribution to this volume (Chapter 3). His examples occur in special segments of the population in a number of European countries—the nobility in France, England, and Italy, the bourgeoisie of Geneva, and the Jewish population in some Italian cities. These groups were not of sufficient numerical importance to affect the national age-specific fertility rates, although they may be important in understanding factors that later led to the adoption of contraception or abortion in the national populations.

[6] Wilson also shows that among women in these sixteen parishes who bore a child after age 30 (a stipulation that minimizes the effect of secondary sterility), differences in age at birth of last child for women married at different ages were trivial. He applies other tests that show conclusively that parity-related control of fertility was not consequential. By estimating the duration of nursing-induced postpartum infertility (from the difference in interbirth intervals following infant deaths at various ages), he accounts for the modest level (about two-thirds of the Hutterites) of marital fertility in these parishes.

Two additional instances of early parity-related restriction of fertility occurred in populations that were not elite (like the nobility and the Geneva bourgeoisie) nor urbanized and restricted to special occupations (like the Jewish population in Italian cities). The most conspicuous example of the early adoption of parity-related control is in the rural population of much of France in the late eighteenth and early nineteenth centuries. Evidence for such control takes the form of very low and steadily declining marital fertility, as measured by the index I_g (see Chapter 2 by Coale and Treadway for definition of I_g). By 1830 marital fertility in many *départements* was as little as 35 to 50 percent of the Hutterite level, and steadily falling (E. van de Walle, 1974).

The second instance of precocious parity-related control of fertility, not confined to privileged classes nor to special urban populations, occurred in subgroups of the rural population in a region in southern Hungary stretching from Somogy, south of Lake Balaton, to Krassó-Szörény, bordering on Rumania (Demeny, 1968). The fraction of the population with low fertility was not large enough in all of the counties to lower the fertility of the county as a whole, but in some villages the birth rate was below 20 or even below 15 per thousand early in this century, and consistently lower than the death rate. Hungarian demographers, drawing on the parish registers in some of the villages with very early low fertility, have calculated age-specific marital fertility schedules. In Table 1.1 values of *m* are shown, which are based on reconstituted fertility data for five villages in southern Transdanubia in the eighteenth and nineteenth centuries. In all

Table 1.1. Index of fertility control (m) in selected Hungarian villages.

Village	Period	m	Village	Period	m
Besence	1747-1790	.05	Sarpilis	1760-1790	-.17
and	1791-1820	.30		1791-1820	.26
Vajszlo	1821-1850	.70		1805-1830	.82
	1851-1893	1.49			
Alsonyek	1760-1790	.33	Bakonya	1759-1779	.50
	1791-1820	.55		1780-1804	.74
	1821-1850	.75		1805-1831	1.03

Sources: Andorka, 1978; Table 3.1.

five, rising *m* clearly indicates an increasing degree of parity-related control, culminating in a marital fertility schedule little different from European populations in the middle of the twentieth century. In Besence and Vajszlo, the median size of a completed family declined from 6.0 children ever born to older women in 1747–1790 to only 2.0 in 1851–1893 (Andorka, 1978, Table 3.5).

The low fertility of certain sectors of the Hungarian population was noticed (generally with disfavor) by contemporary Hungarian observers. The chief medical officer of Baranya, the county wherein three of the villages in Table 1.1 are located, wrote in 1845: "... in most Hungarian villages of the county the young wives consider it a shame to bear in the first four or even ten years of their marriage, and even the healthiest and strongest women bear not more than two children.... Many young wives hinder birth clandestinely and sinfully in order to maintain their beauty, while many others are induced by poverty to do this, because often three or four families have to live on half a plot of land.... They are taught methods of birth control by older people ... abortions are performed, ... as is well known" (Holbing, 1845, in Andorka, 1978). According to Andorka, low marital fertility was not only well known, but was popularly called the "one child system"; in Baranya in the late nineteenth century a "one child system committee" was formed to investigate the custom.

A puzzling additional possible exception to the general absence of parity-related control before the modern decline began is Denmark. From 1787 until the 1880s, the index of marital fertility for Denmark (I_g) remained in the narrow range of 64.5 to 68.5 percent of Hutterite marital fertility. Such constancy is typical of the absence of parity-related limitation; once contraception and abortion are widely used, marital fertility usually falls steadily, as it did in Denmark beginning in the 1880s. It is only after 1868 that the availability of age-specific marital fertility rates makes possible the calculation of *m* for the rural areas and provincial towns of Denmark. The average value of *m* from 1868 to 1880 is 0.24 for the provincial towns, and 0.20 for the rural areas—values a little too high to be accepted as indications of the absence of parity-related limitation. The earliest calculated value of *m* for the capital (1875–1879) is 0.62. Thus there may have been some parity-related restriction of fertility in Denmark prior to 1880; there almost certainly was in Copenhagen. Since the positive values of *m* in the rural areas and the provincial towns are found just before the index of marital fertility began to fall, it is possible that the initiation of some kind of contraceptive practice by some older women may have occurred shortly before 1880. The slight decline in marital fertility of older married women may not have resulted, as might be expected, in a decline in I_g, because it may have been offset by small increases among younger married women—from slightly curtailed breast-feeding, for example. In the later years of the century, a sustained decline in I_g began, and it was accompanied, as expected, by a steady rise in *m* from about 0.3 in the 1880s to nearly 1.0 in the 1930s and 2.0 in the 1960s.

Further Observations on Moderate Fertility in Pre-industrial Populations

In the West European populations in which marriage was late and exposure to the risk of childbearing was less than 50 percent of the potential maximum (because of the large fraction of women not currently married), the level of marital fertility was moderately high—from 65 to 80 percent of the exceptionally high marital fertility of the Hutterites. In a number of non-European populations in which marriage is early and universal, 85 to 90 percent of potentially fertile women are exposed to the risk of childbearing by being married. In such populations the level of marital fertility is substantially lower than in Western Europe—only 50 to 60 percent of Hutterite marital fertility. Very high proportions married are rarely combined with moderately high marital fertility, even in pre-industrial populations. If Asian proportions married were combined with West European pre-industrial marital fertility, the total fertility rate would be at least 7 to 8, compatible in the long run with an average duration of life of less than 20 years. For reasons stated earlier, such combinations of high fertility and high mortality would be disadvantageous for the long-run welfare, and possibly the viability, of a pre-industrial population.

What, then, accounts for the different levels of pre-industrial fertility already noted—from a TFR of 4.1 in Denmark to 6.2 in India? And what explains the still higher fertility levels (over 7 in the United States in 1800, nearly 7 in Russia in the late nineteenth century, over 7 in Bangladesh, Pakistan, and some Latin American populations a decade ago, and about 8 in Kenya) in other pre-industrial populations? The low pre-industrial fertility in Scandinavia would be consistent with an e_0^0 of about 33 years, that of rural China with an e_0^0 of about 24 years, and the fertility in India with an e_0^0 of about 20 years. If it is assumed that an e_0^0 of 30 years or more could have been attained in India and China, as in Scandinavia, the higher fertility of these populations might simply be a less effective moderation of fertility than in Scandinavia, no matter what nonparity-related limitation was practiced, with consequent long-run higher mortality. Marital fertility was lower in the Asian populations than in pre-industrial Western Europe, but not low enough to offset the higher nuptiality in Asia than in Europe. More effective moderation of fertility in Europe thus may have permitted a more favorable equilibrium point of birth and death rates, a possibility supported to some extent by the potentially homeostatic character of limitation of fertility by late marriage.

The reconstruction of the population of England from the mid-sixteenth to the mid-nineteenth century by the Cambridge Group for the History of Population and Social Structure shows how important variation in nuptiality was in moderating the rate of increase of the English population (Wrigley and Schofield, 1981). Their estimates of total fertility rates (smoothed by a 25-year moving average) show a variation from a low of 3.9 to a high of 5.7 between 1550 and 1800; the surprisingly small variation in e_0^0 (also smoothed by a 25-year moving average) is from about 32.5 to 39 years. The annual rate of increase implied by the combinations of average TFR and e_0^0 over 25-year intervals varied from below zero in the 25-year period centered on 1670 to nearly 1.3 percent at the end of the eighteenth century. This variation was caused much more by changes in fertility than by changes in mortality; yet evidence from reconstituted parish registers shows that marital fertility was virtually constant. The dominant source of the variation in fertility, and thus in the rate of natural increase, was variation in age at marriage and variation in the proportion remaining permanently single. In terms of the fertility indexes used in the Princeton study of the modern decline of fertility in Europe, the extensive variation in English fertility from 1550 to 1870 was almost wholly a variation in I_m (the index of proportion married), with I_g (the index of marital fertility) virtually unchanging.

Wrigley and Schofield note that large-amplitude variation in fertility (caused by variation in nuptiality) provided an accommodation to the slow and varying growth in resources, not by intense spasms of elevated mortality, but by wide fluctuations in fertility. One can imagine nuptiality as an efficient homeostatic mechanism, if prospective brides and grooms felt compelled to marry later when times were bad. But Wrigley and Schofield conclude:

> It was a system capable of achieving a balance between population and resources, but it is perhaps misleading to describe it as an equilibrium

> system, since one of its striking features was the remarkable slowness of response between economic (real-wage) and demographic (fertility) changes . . . . England displayed what might be termed dilatory homeostatis, winning the war of adjustment, but doing so by employing a strategy appropriate to yesterday's circumstances. (Wrigley and Schofield, 1981, p. 451)

When marriage is early and universal, as in Asia, it is more difficult to see how restraints on marital fertility (by nonparity-related means such as prolonged breast-feeding or postpartum abstinence) would operate in a homeostatic manner—reducing fertility when population increase puts pressure on resources. It is possible, however, that the higher fertility in India and China may not have been the result of the lesser effectiveness of these practices (as compared to Western European nuptiality) in restraining fertility, but may have been the consequence of unavoidably higher mortality, resulting, for example, from a climate and a technology that made catastrophic food shortages more difficult to avoid. Under this hypothesis, the higher total fertility in India than in China would have been necessary because over the past several centuries, with possibly more contagion in a tropical climate and a less dependable food supply, an average e_0^0 of 20 years was the best that could be maintained, whereas in China the attainable average duration of life was a little greater.

When there is a large change in the availability of resources, traditional restraints on fertility are generally modified. An example is the settlement of North America by West Europeans. The settlers brought with them the technology of Europe, which was applied, with adaptation to new conditions, to extensive and very fertile land, until then sparsely settled by a population still dependent at least partly on hunting and fishing. The native population was progressively displaced; the supply of agricultural land the colonists could occupy was, by European standards, enormous. In Europe, the colonists had been accustomed to marrying late because only at an age in the late twenties or higher had men come into possession of land or qualified for the steady positions that custom dictated marriage required; custom also sanctioned only a slight difference in age between bride and groom, so that women as well as men married late. In America, the young European immigrant or his descendants could always settle at the frontier; also the plentiful supply of land meant a relatively high demand for labor, if individuals chose to work for wages. Indeed, the high fertility in the United States (TFR over 7 in 1800) was highest near the frontier, and much lower in the long-settled seaboard areas (Easterlin, 1976). Similarly, newly available land in the south of Russia and in the Asiatic part of the Russian Empire may be part of the explanation of the high total fertility rate (6.8) in European Russia in the late nineteenth century.

Another instance in which a change in environment led to partial abandonment of fertility-limiting behavior is the rise in fertility among the !Kung, whose four-year interbirth intervals, caused by nursing at fifteen-minute intervals, was described earlier. The !Kung are a people who have continued a traditional life based on hunting and gathering until today, although an increasing fraction has recently adopted a sedentary life. The birth intervals among the !Kung are, according to Richard Lee, associated with the form of child care provided, which in turn is associated with the prevalent food gathering customs.

> Women's work—gathering wild vegetable food—provides well over half of all the food consumed by a !Kung camp. . . . Subsistence work occupies two or three days of work each week for each adult woman. On each work day a woman walks from 3 to 20 kilimeters (2 to 12 miles) round trip, and on the return leg she carries loads of 7 to 15 kilograms. . . . Of course, the major burden carried by women has yet to be mentioned. On most gathering trips and on every visit and group move, a woman has to carry with her each of her children under the age of four years. Infants and young children have an extremely close relationship with their mothers. . . . For the first few years of an infant's life, mother and child are rarely separated by more than a few paces. . . .
>
> Since every child has to be carried, it is fortunate that generally the birth interval among the !Kung is as long as it is. The advantage of long birth spacing to hunter-gatherers is obvious. A mother can devote her full attention to caring for an offspring for a longer period, and the older the offspring is when the mother turns to the care of the subsequent young, the better are his chances for survival. (Lee, 1980)

Thus, the nursing of the children at intervals of fifteen minutes is not an unnatural feature of the continued close contact of mother and child. The effect of producing very long interbirth intervals is clearly functional, permitting the woman to have only one child to carry until the child is able to walk on his own.

When the !Kung adopt a sedentary life, the birth intervals are shortened. According to well-founded estimates, large increases (30 to 50 percent) in marital fertility occurred in Soviet Central Asia from 1926 to 1970, in rural Korea from 1930 to 1960, and in Taiwan from 1930 to 1956. Presumably these increases were the result of the attenuation of nonparity-related fertility-limiting factors such as prolonged nursing (Coale, Anderson, and Härm, 1979).

Why Parity-related Limitation of Fertility Is Rare in Pre-industrial Populations

The absence of a consequential extent of parity-related limitation of marital fertility in pre-industrial European populations (with a few exceptions) was described earlier. Similar evidence of age-specific marital fertility rates in a pattern by age that conforms to the absence of parity-related control exists for rural China around 1930, for Korea in 1960 (before the decline began), for Taiwan before 1956, and for Soviet Central Asia in 1959. In a number of less developed countries in which marital fertility has not yet begun to decline, women have directly reported nonuse of contraception. There seems no basis for believing that in less developed countries in the twentieth century couples stop childbearing when they have a certain number of births before an irreversible decline has begun. A corollary implication is that in these populations contraception was little practiced.

The apparent general absence of contraception and of parity-related limitation in pre-industrial populations is puzzling. Norman Himes (1963) has documented knowledge of contraception in many societies back to classical times. Surveys of modern populations have shown that often very low marital fertility was achieved when the dominant method of contraception was withdrawal, which is mentioned (and condemned) in the Old Testament. Since moderate fertility is beneficial to society as a whole, why did parity-related contraceptive practice not become a general custom in pre-industrial societies? A somewhat fanciful reason is this: parity-related fertility control is too effective and too appealing to individual self-interest. One of the empirical findings of our study of the decline of fertility in Europe is that once the reduction in marital fertility is well started—once marital fertility has fallen by at least 10 percent—the decline is not reversed until marital fertility has fallen very far, by 50 percent or more. Conventional opinion has generally condemned contraception, and beliefs about the bad physical and psychological effects of withdrawal are ubiquitous. Suppose that a segment of a pre-industrial population learns that this form of contraception is in fact harmless and finds that the burdens of childbirth and childcare can be avoided after one or two children have been born. Suppose this group also comes to feel that there is no value in the perpetuation of the family name, and no dishonor in living more confortably with a small number of children. The rate of reproduction of such a group may almost always have fallen to a point below that consistent with replacement, even given the lowest mortality achievable in a pre-industrial population. In other words, parity-related limitation may have been rediscovered and readopted repeatedly, only to die out with its practitioners. It may have been the social equivalent of a lethal mutation that appears recurrently but never persists.

The instances of pre-industrial parity-related limitation of marital fertility cited earlier are examples of how such limitation can reduce fertility below the level consistent with survival. In the villages of Baranya, known by their nineteenth-century contemporaries as addicted to the one-child family, in which marital fertility was very low and strongly restrained by parity-related measures, mortality was still high. In Besence and Vajszlo more than 20 percent of the newborns died before reaching age one until late in the nineteenth century (Andorka, 1978); many of the villages of southern Transdanubia had a negative rate of natural increase as a result of such low fertility while mortality remained high. In the French *départements* where fertility was already low in the early nineteenth century, the rate of childbearing was not adequate to replace the population. In both Lot-et-Garonne (southwest France) and Calvados (in Normandy), the population declined steadily after 1836, by a total of 20 percent in one instance, and 25 percent in the other, with no substantial out-migration (E. van de Walle, 1974).

The Transition in Europe from Moderately High Fertility and Mortality to Very Low Fertility and Mortality

If there were valid data on fertility and mortality for the countries of Europe in the seventeenth or early eighteenth century, it is a good guess that most of the points showing the total fertility rate and life expectancy for each country would have fallen in or around the region in the (TFR, e_0^0) plane delineated as pre-transitional in Figure 1.3. The points for the countries of Europe around 1980 fall in or around the region labeled

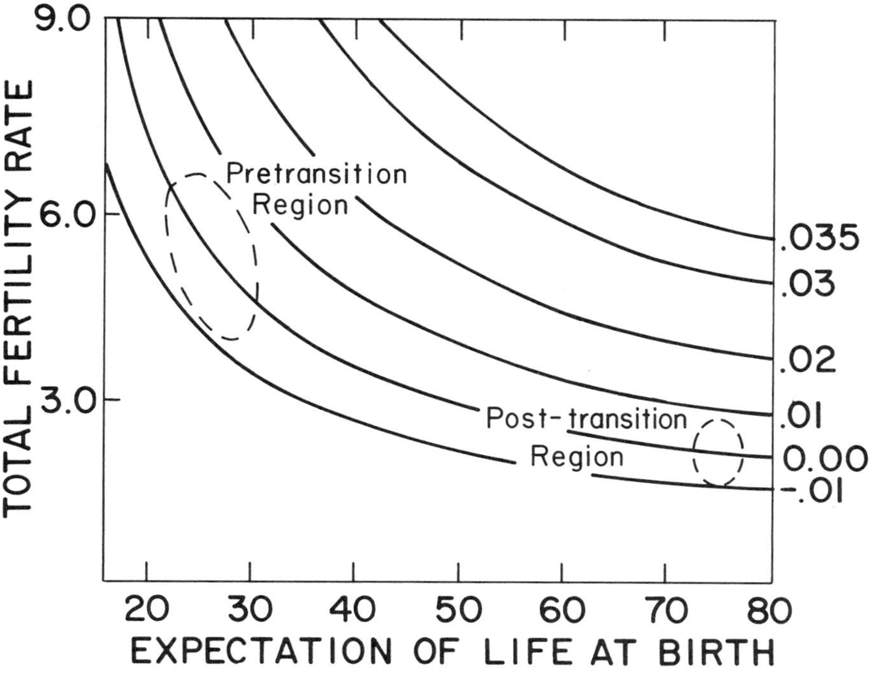

Figure 1.3. The typical locus of total fertility rate and expectation of life at birth in pre-transitional (estimated) and post-transitional (typical of contemporary Europe) populations.

post-transitional. The pre-transitional region is, obviously enough, a set of moderately high fertility and mortality combinations—e_0^0 from about 20 to 30 or 35 years, TFR from about 4 to over 6.5—that would yield near-zero growth; the post-transitional region is a set of very low fertility and mortality combinations—e_0^0 from 72 to 78, TFR from about 1.5 to 2.5—that would also yield near-zero growth.

The pre-industrial region of combinations of TFR and e_0^0 in Figure 1.3 is a region of average values consistent with moderate growth over a long time span. But the average may not have been usual, since the typical time pattern of growth was probably one of positive increase interrupted by catastrophic reductions. The prevalent values of TFR and e_0^0 may have oscillated between combinations to the right or above the delimited pre-industrial region and lower, or more leftward, combinations that led to rapid decrease in numbers.

The first combinations of TFR and e_0^0 derived from valid data are a few in the eighteenth century; all lie to the right of the pre-industrial region because e_0^0 had already begun to increase along its long climb to values above 70 years. The decline in mortality had many antecedents, beginning with the rise of modern science, the development of oceanic navigation, and the growth of world trade. The opening of the Western hemisphere to European settlement, with the consequent increase of food supplies for Europe, the interchange of plant varieties among formerly isolated civilizations, including the introduction of the potato and other nutritious crops into Europe, the construction of roads, canals, and railroads that facilitated internal transportation and the growth of national markets, improved agricultural technology, and the growth of nonagricultural output with the continuous extension of the division of labor and the introduction of mechanized mining and manufacture provided the material basis for a more certain supply of food and other components of a rise in real income, despite a steady increase in population. The development of the first effective forms of preventive medicine, especially vaccination against smallpox; improved habits of personal hygiene such as washing with soap; and the provision of purer water to some cities made possible a gradual rise in e_0^0 in the first half of the nineteenth century. Further economic progress, the discovery of the germ theory of disease and of anesthesia, and more extensive supplies of clean water to urban populations contributed to a more rapid increase in e_0^0 in the later years of the nineteenth century. A rapid increase in e_0^0 had spread to Southern and Eastern Europe by the early twentieth century. A further spurt of rising e_0^0 in the middle of the twentieth century was quite general in Europe. It accompanied unprecedented advances in scientific medicine, including the invention of effective chemotherapy and antibiotics, whcih virtually eliminated what mortality from infectious diseases still remained. By 1980 female e_0^0 was over 72 years in every European population except that of Albania; the median national figure was above 75.

Had pre-industrial fertility remained unchanged during this revolutionary reduction in mortality, the multiplication of the European population would have been prodigious. The intrinsic rate of increase would have risen to more than 2.5 percent in Western Europe and to more than 3.5 percent in most of Eastern Europe. Instead, the universal increase in life expectancy has been matched by a decrease in fertility almost as universal, a decrease in the total fertility rate so great that the intrinsic rate of increase in every European nation except Albania, the Soviet Union, Portugal, Ireland, and Northern Ireland is negative. Were it not for the momentum embodied in the age distribution, the legacy of the past trends, the population of Europe would now be diminishing.

The change from the pre-transitional region to the post-transitional region has not been along a path in which TFR and e_0^0 stayed close to the locus of combinations yielding an intrinsic rate of increase of zero, except in France. In Figure 1.4, the sequence of e_0^0 and TFR values from early data until a recent point is shown for Sweden, France, and Hungary. Points for 1800, 1830, 1850, 1870, 1890, 1910, 1930, 1960, and 1980 are shown for Sweden and France, and for all but 1800 in Hungary. (The earliest points for Hungary are estimated from birth rates and death rates provided by Andras Klinger at the 1979 conference.) In all three countries, the earliest point is on the right (higher e_0^0) of the pre-transitional region, because mortality had probably decreased from a still earlier date. In France alone, TFR fell before 1870, as France from 1800 traced a transitional path with simultaneous declines of fertility and mortality such that the intrinsic rate of increase was never far from zero. The experience of Sweden and Hungary was more typical of the European transition; mortality declined earlier than fertility, and during much of the transition the intrinsic rate of increase was above one percent. (A subtle feature of the shift from one region of zero intrinsic rate of increase to another is that the shift produces a considerable increase in population, even if the intrinsic rate of increase remains at zero, or the net reproduction rate at 1.0. To appreciate the reason for this growth, imagine that the initial population is stationary, and that each cohort exactly replaces itself—cohort net reproduction rates are all 1.0—as e_0^0 rises from 25 to 75. Under these assumptions, the annual number of births would be constant, since annual births were constant in the original stable population, and each cohort replaces itself. The initial population, with an e_0^0 of 25, is twenty-five times the annual number of births; the ultimate population is seventy-five times the annual number of births, or three times as large. If *period* intrinsic growth rates are zero as fertility and mortality decline, fertility is a little lower during the transition, so that the increase is less than the ratio of the final e_0^0 to the initial e_0^0.)

Estimates of TFR and e_0^0 can be obtained for the following countries beginning in about 1870: Austria, Belgium, Denmark, England and Wales, Finland, France, Germany, Hungary, Italy, Netherlands, Norway, Poland,

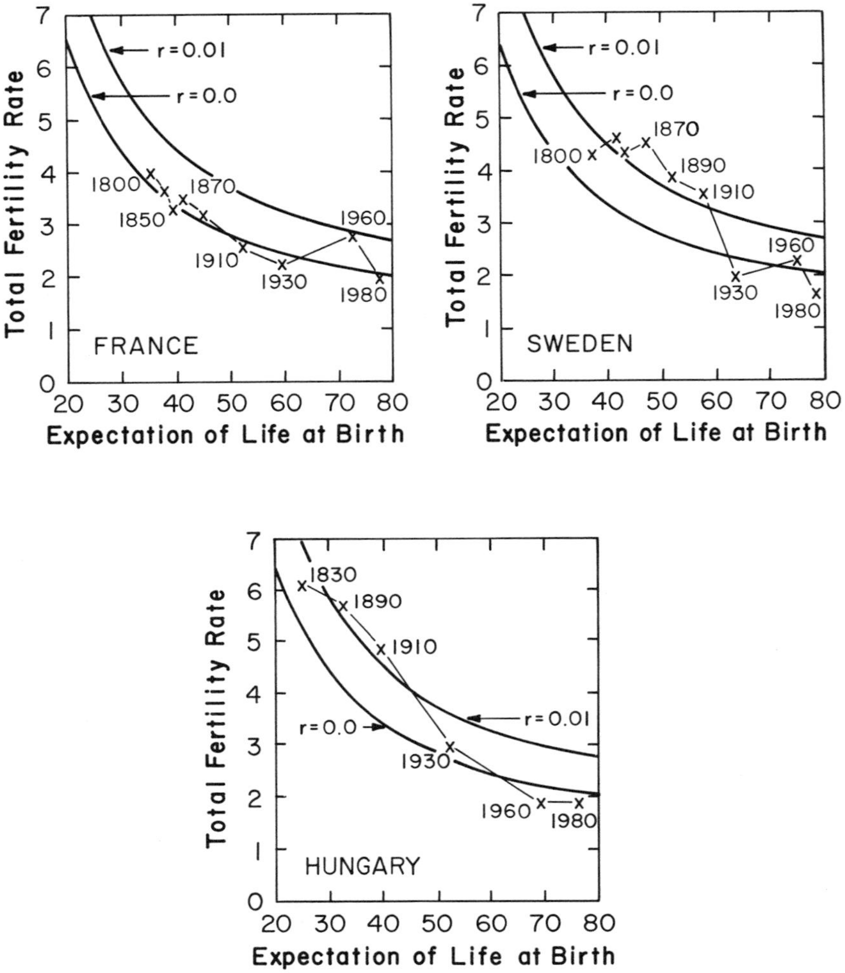

Figure 1.4. The evolution of total fertility rate and expectation of life at birth in France, Hungary, and Sweden from early in the nineteenth century to 1980.

Russia, Scotland, Spain, Sweden, and Switzerland. (For some of the countries, estimates for 1870 were made from the crude birth rate and crude death rate by the use of model stable populations.)

In Figure 1.5, the combinations of TFR and e_0^0 for these countries are shown for selected years from 1870 to 1980. In 1870 all but France and Switzerland had TFRs little if at all reduced from the average over

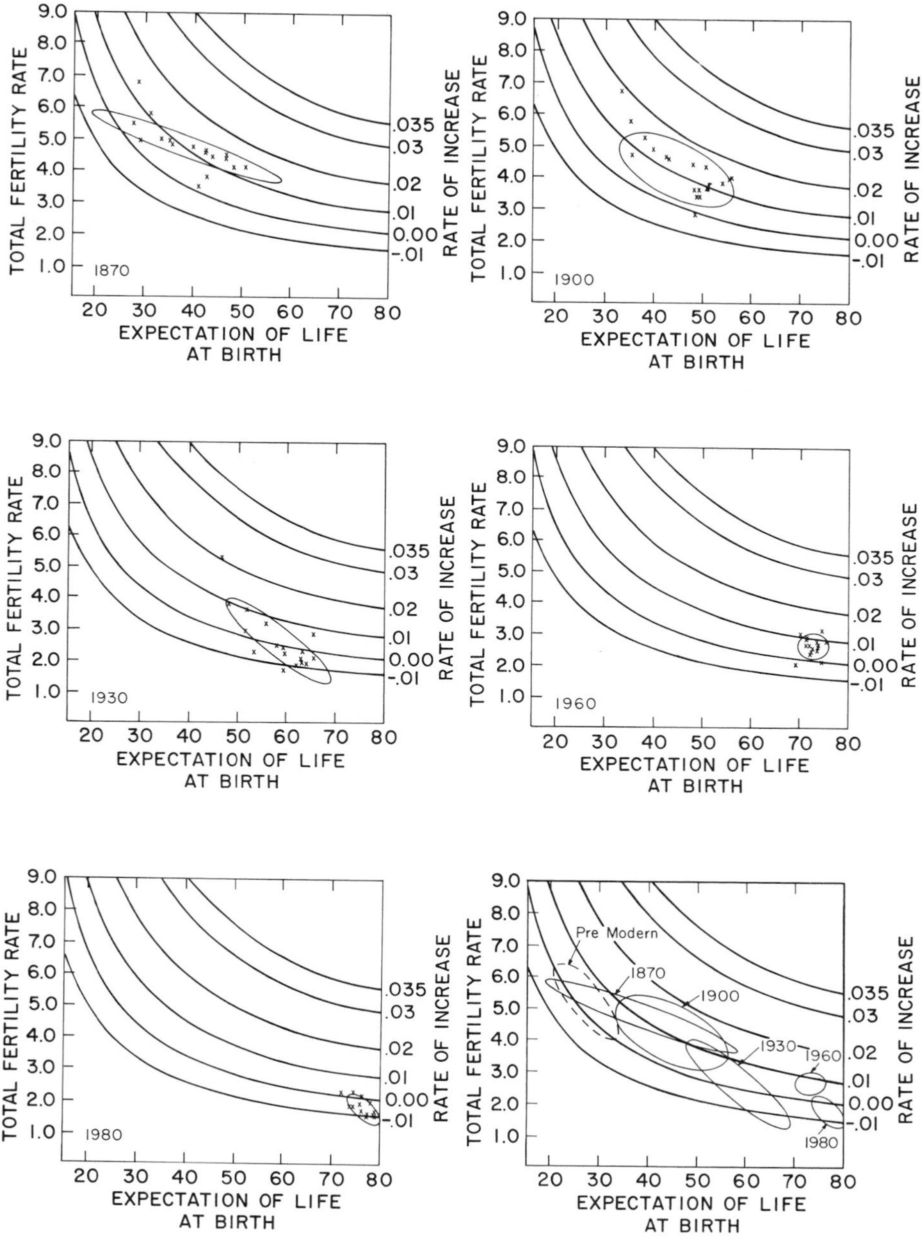

Figure 1.5 The evolution of total fertility rate and expectation of life at birth in 17 European countries, from 1870 to 1980.

an interval extending far into the past, but e_0^0's that had risen since the eighteenth century to establish intrinsic rates of increase above one percent in most countries. By 1900, further increases in e_0^0 had occurred in every country, and in most there had been at least a slight decline in TFR. The decline in TFR from 1900 to 1930 was at least 30 percent in every country except France, which had progressed so far in its transition by 1900. (Russia is also an exception, only because its estimate of TFR and e_0^0 is for 1926, as published data on births were suspended before 1930). From 1930 to 1960, TFR rose in the countries that had negative intrinsic rates of increase in 1930, indeed in all of Northwestern Europe. The principal basis of this increase was a large reduction in age at marriage—a partial abandonment of the long-established West European pattern of late marriage and avoidance of marriage. In Southern and Eastern Europe the decline in TFR continued from 1930 to 1960, creating a much more compact cluster of points at the later date. From 1960 to 1980 every country had a decline in TFR as marital fertility fell, many couples lived together without marrying (but usually with lower fertility than those at the same age who were married), and divorce rates rose sharply.

In each of the first five panels of Figure 1.5, 75 percent of points in each set (combinations of TFR and e_0^0) are encompassed by an ellipse. The ellipses are designed to summarize, graphically, the position of a collection of points in two dimensions. (The technical details of the calculation of the ellipses are given in Chapter 2 by Coale and Treadway). The reader can get his own visual impression of the relation of each ellipse to the points for which it is intended to give a sort of geometric summary. In the last panel of Figure 1.5, the five ellipses are shown in the same diagram, together with a hypothetical ellipse representing the estimated location of the seventeen countries in the mortality and fertility plane, as of the seventeenth century. This last panel provides a succinct summary of the demographic transition in Europe—a movement from fairly diverse combinations yielding low rates of intrinsic increase, with moderate fertility and mortality, through intermediate combinations with higher growth potential because of longer life and only slightly lower fertility, to rather uniform combinations, with low to negative growth potential, of very low fertility and mortality.

The demographic transition in Europe, then, was a transition from approximate balance of birth and death rates at moderately high levels to approximate balance at very low levels. Pre-industrial populations had moderately high mortality because uncertain food supplies and unavoidable disease made low mortality unachievable; fertility was only moderately high because of low proportions married and birth intervals that are extended by various nonparity-related factors. Couples married late, or postponed the next pregnancy for self-interested reasons, such as waiting until attaining the economic position to form a viable household or extending the interbirth interval until the survival of the most recently born would not be jeopardized. These actions were probably not closely linked to reaching a desired specific total number of children, since pursuit of such a goal would naturally lead to parity-related limitation—and there is good evidence that parity-related limitation occurred only in small special subpopulations in pre-industrial Europe, with the exceptions in France and Hungary discussed above. Mortality fell as agricultural and industrial productivity increased, and improved environmental conditions and better medical knowledge and facilities drastically reduced the incidence of fatal infectious disease. The fall in mortality was gradual at first, then more rapid, and cumulated to a quite uniform long average duration of life, not far from 75 years in every European population in 1980.

Except among special subpopulations, such as the nobility, fertility in most of Europe did not fall until about 1870, despite the gradual decline in mortality. The sole national exception was France, where TFR by 1870 was 20 percent lower than in 1800. After 1870, fertility fell in every country; in 1980 there was a notable concentration of TFRs, mostly at levels too low to maintain the population despite the very high e_0^0's. Nuptiality had been far from constant; but the dominant reason for the attainment of low fertility was the universal adoption of parity-related limitation of births—the effective employment of contraception and abortion in order to have no more than the small number of births each couple wishes.

One of the features of this transition is the increased uniformity of fertility and mortality among the European populations. The pre-transitional "region" of TFRs and e_0^0's consistent with near zero growth was a large region—the highest e_0^0 probably exceeded the lowest by 50 percent, and the spread of TFRs was a difference of more than two children per woman. The post-transitional region was much more compact—there is little variation in the aggregate fertility and mortality of these highly modernized populations.

The mathematics of geometric increase insures that no average rate of increase very different from zero can persist for many centuries because the cumulative effect is such a large multiplier or divisor. With fairly static technology, variation in mortality would provide much of the homestatic action required to keep growth within bounds. The revolutionary technical changes of the past two centuries have insulated modern populations from any inevitable increase in mortality as populations grow. If Europe's population had increased in the past century to half again or twice its actual size, individual real incomes might have been lower, but e_0^0 could certainly have reached 65 to 70 years (as in Sri Lanka or Hong Kong), and quite possibly the actual 75. Is the arrival at TFRs that recently have oscillated near the level required for an intrinsic rate of increase of zero an instance of homeostatic forces at work, or is it an accident? Presumably the level of fertility in recent years reflects fairly closely the aggregate outcome of the actions of individual couples, each trying, with general success, to have the fertility each couple prefers. In fact, some of the decline from 1960 to 1980 is the result of more successful avoidance of unwanted births. It would be merely a matter of luck that the population should want, as a matter of individual choice, a number of offspring that would in aggregate keep the populations at a zero rate of increase. It is more likely, in my opinion, that if marriage remains a much less than universally chosen institution, and if women continue to gain their rightful equal opportunities for rewarding lives outside of the home, the TFR will continue well below two. Whether such continuation will generate counterbalancing changes in fertility preferences, or effective pronatalist state intervention, time will tell.

Such, then, is the background of the research that underlay the Conference on European Fertility in Princeton. The research, undertaken by many of the conference participants, and some who were unable to attend, was a study of the decline of fertility by province in individual European countries. At the conference, papers were invited that summarized the data on fertility change since 1870 in the provinces of all of Europe, and that dealt with special subjects such as precursors of the modern decline; the relation of fertility to infant mortality; rural-urban differences during the transition; the relation of fertility decline to secularization and to factors particular to regional cultures. This essay has been an attempt to sketch in the broader demographic setting in which the decline occurred.

Chapter 2: A Summary of the Changing Distribution of Overall Fertility, Marital Fertility, and the Proportion Married in the Provinces of Europe

Ansley J. Coale and Roy Treadway

Introduction

The European Fertility Project was undertaken in 1963 because of the clear importance, not only for Europe, but for the world, of a basic change that had occurred in the preceding fifty to two hundred years in virtually every European province—a decline of some 50 percent in the average number of children born per woman.

The fact that a decline in human fertility had occurred in Europe was widely known; indeed, a general proposition had been formulated that fertility can be expected to fall as a result of a set of social and economic changes characterized as "modernization"; this proposition was often accepted, it seemed, on the basis of a superficial appreciation of European experience.

In particular, both sides in a continuing debate on desirable policies on population in less developed countries have based their positions in large part on impressionistic interpretations of the history of European fertility. According to one position, a reduction in fertility is the inevitable result of urbanization, lower mortality, the spread of education, and the occupational changes that accompany industrialization, so that government support of birth control is unnecessary. Others infer from their impression of European experience that reduction in mortality occurs more readily under the influence of modernization than reduction in fertility, that the consequent rapid transitional growth in population can be an impediment to progress, and that deliberate programs to speed the decline in fertility are useful or even essential.

A deeper and more detailed knowledge of the reduction of fertility in Europe thus seemed desirable. Such deeper and more detailed knowledge appeared attainable. Demographic data for Europe are unusually rich and accurate. Censuses that list the population classified by age and marital status were begun in Europe in the eighteenth century, were common by the mid-nineteenth, and were almost universal by the beginning of the twentieth. Registration of births and deaths also became quite general at similarly early dates; in most countries such registration had become almost complete in coverage by the beginning of this century. These data, appropriate for the estimation of fertility, were available not only for the national populations of Europe, but also for smaller constituent units such as provinces, *départements*, or counties. It therefore appeared feasible to trace the history of fertility in the large number of very diverse European provinces from an era in which fertility fluctuated around a virtual plateau through a period of sustained decline in which it fell to much lower levels.

The Project was designed with two principal purposes—to create a detailed quantitative record of fertility in each of the several hundred provinces of Europe during the period of major decline, and to determine the social and economic conditions that prevailed when the modern reduction in the rate of childbearing began. The mere systematic recording of fertility (and its demographic constituents of nuptiality, plus marital and nonmarital rates of childbearing) over this period promised to be a useful contribution to European social history. The record of social and economic conditions in each province in conjunction with the evolution of fertility would help, it was hoped, in establishing a better understanding of what caused the population of the different provinces to initiate and then continue the behavior that lowered the rate of childbearing.

This paper is limited to the sufficiently formidable task of summarizing the history of fertility during the period of its modern decline. "Modern decline" here means the fall in the fertility of married couples as they undertook the practice of contraception or induced abortion, at first to reduce the rate of childbearing of each couple after the desired number of children had already been born, and later to control the timing of the births they chose to have. In Chapter 1, evidence is given that such "parity-specific" control of fertility is not characteristic of pre-industrial populations, and that it was the principal component of the fall in the rate of childbearing during the sustained reduction that occurred in almost all European provinces. As we shall see, before this modern decline there were substantial differences in the overall fertility of different areas in Europe, but differences caused by earlier or later age of marriage, shorter or longer breast-feeding, and other such factors not related to the number of children already born to each couple.

The quantitative history of the fertility of more than six hundred European provinces over a time span of one hundred years or more entails an indigestible mass of numbers, especially since it has proven essential to represent the fertility of a given area at each moment by at least three numbers, rather than some single index. The three numbers are an index of overall fertility (I_f), an index of the fertility of married women (I_g), and an index of the proportion of potentially fertile women who are currently married (I_m). When (as was usually true for most of the period of interest) the contribution of the nonmarried to overall childbearing is quantitatively slight, overall fertility (I_f) is approximately equal to the product of marital fertility and the proportion married (or $I_m \cdot I_g$).

In the later parts of this chapter and in the appendixes, the large array of fertility indexes is presented in a variety of forms: in a long table that lists most of the indexes that have been calculated, in maps that show the geographical distribution at different dates of the three principal indexes, in frequency distributions, and in special graphs and diagrams. One appendix describes the indexes in technical detail, lists their advantages, and states their limitations. Other appendixes contain a list of the sources of data, methods of adjustment, etc. The extended detail and the technical features of this information will be of interest primarily to specialists. Thus most of the text of this chapter is a nontechnical discussion of some of the more important points contained in or implied by this large body of data.

Even this nontechnical discussion must begin with a definition of the indexes of fertility that are the common feature of all of the research that has been part of this project. We offer here an accurate but intuitive and minimally complex set of definitions: a full set of definitions replete with mathematical formulae is given in Appendix B of this chapter. There are three indexes of childbearing: I_f, the index of the rate of childbearing by all women regardless of their marital status; I_g, the index of the rate of childbearing by married women; and I_h, the index of the rate of childbearing by women not currently married. All three indexes incorporate the same concept: each relates the number of births produced by the women in question to the number they would have produced had they experienced the highest set of birth rates by age of mother that has been reliably recorded. These maximum rates of childbearing were experienced by married Hutterites during the years 1921–1930. The Hutterites are an Anabaptist sect living in the north-central area of the United States and in the southern part of central Canada. The Hutterites have kept accurate statistics of births, scrupulously adhere to a religious proscription of contraception and abortion, and because of early weaning of their infants have short interbirth intervals. Women married at an early age and experiencing Hutterite fertility would have an average of more than twelve births before menopause. Individual women in various populations have experienced many more than twelve births. Hutterite fertility is not the maximum fertility that is biologically achievable; it is merely the highest recorded for a population. In addition to the three indexes of childbearing for three categories of women, the Project employs an index (I_m) of proportion married among women of childbearing age as a factor helping to determine overall fertility. It is a measure of the extent to which marital status would contribute to the attainment of maximal fertility, if married women experienced fertility not subject to parity-related restriction, and nonmarried women bore no children at all. Precisely, I_m is the ratio of the number of births currently married women would experience if subject to Hutterite fertility to the number of births all women would experience if subject to Hutterite fertility.

Each of the four indexes lies between zero and one. A value of zero for one of the fertility indexes means no childbearing by the given segment of the population; a value of one means age-specific fertility at the Hutterite level. An I_m of zero means no married women at ages 15–50, and an I_m of one means all women 15–50 are married.

The four indexes are related by an identity $I_f = (I_m \cdot I_g) + (1 - I_m) \cdot I_h$. The product $I_m \cdot I_g$ expresses the contribution of married women to the attainment of maximum fertility in the population; $(1 - I_m) \cdot I_h$ expresses the contribution of nonmarried women; the resultant value of I_f expresses how closely the women of childbearing age approach the maximum potential fertility. If births to nonmarried women are a negligible proportion of the total, I_f is closely approximated by $I_m \cdot I_g$; the index of overall fertility is factored into the index of marital fertility and an index of proportion married. (See Appendix B at the end of this chapter for a further discussion of the advantages and limitations of these indexes.)

A sense of the meaning of these indexes can be gained by considering some examples. Three provinces at the bottom of the range (the lowest 10 percent in the distribution) of overall fertility (I_f) in Europe in 1900 were Lot-et-Garonne (a *département* of France), Geneva, and County Tipperary in Ireland. The overall rate of childbearing in the first two areas was only about one-sixth of the Hutterites (I_f of 0.168 and 0.164), while in Tipperary I_f was a little higher at 0.220. Since women subject to Hutterite fertility from age 15 to age 50 would bear an average of 12.4 children, the corresponding figure (the total fertility rate) of these populations was about

$12.4 \times I_f$, or 2.1, 2.0, and 2.7 children, respectively. Overall fertility in Lot-et-Garonne in 1900 was very low because its marital fertility was the lowest in Europe (I_g only 0.230). The proportion married in Lot-et-Garonne was in fact the highest in Western Europe (I_m of 0.700), higher than in any national population, even in Eastern Europe, except for Bulgaria, Rumania, and Serbia. Marital fertility in Tipperary, in contrast, was moderately high (I_g of 0.742), slightly higher than the median of the estimated predecline levels for all European provinces; but the proportion married was the lowest in Europe (I_m of 0.289). Geneva's overall fertility was the lowest of these three examples of low overall fertility as the result of a combination of low, but not extreme, values both of proportion married (I_m of 0.435) and marital fertility (I_g of 0.343). The highest fertility in any European province in 1900 was in the Serbian province of Toplica, with an overall rate of childbearing (I_f of 0.663) two-thirds as high as would have resulted if all women from 15 to 50 had borne children at the rate of married Hutterites (approximate total fertility of Toplica was 8.24 children per woman). This very high fertility was the result of the highest proportion married in Europe (I_m of 0.842) and high marital fertility (I_g of 0.781, a little higher than in Tipperary). In all of these areas, the non-married had quite low fertility, ranging from less than one percent to a little over three percent of Hutterite fertility, so that to a good approximation overall fertility could be considered the product of marital fertility and proportion married ($I_f \cong I_m \cdot I_g$).

The outline of the modern decline in fertility is expressed in this chapter in terms of these indexes. We begin with the central feature of the decline: the nearly universal reduction in marital fertility.

Changes in the Marital Fertility of European Provinces

Pre-modern populations in Europe, as elsewhere, did not restrict fertility by parity-related measures—in other words, they did not, to a degree that affected national or provincial birth rates, practice contraception or induced abortion. Marital fertility varied from one population to another because of differences in the prevalence and average duration of breast-feeding, periodic separation of spouses, etc; but such factors were usually slow to change, so that the characteristic time pattern of I_g was a plateau—little variation through time. For example, I_g calculated for fifty-year time intervals from 1600 to 1800 from the reconstitution of thirteen English parish registers, and then from censuses plus corrected registered births from 1851 to 1871, falls within the range of 0.667 to 0.682 (Wrigley and Schofield, 1983).

The Level of I_g *before the Modern Decline*

The approximate level of a pre-decline "plateau" of I_g can be estimated for 579 provinces, namely those provinces in which the first few values of I_g (at least two) that can be calculated hardly differ from one another. (When the earliest I_g's for a province are a descending sequence, one may presume that farther in the past there was a plateau, but its hypothetical level is not included in this section). The difference in level among these pre-decline plateaus is wide, from an I_g of about 0.50 to an I_g of nearly 1.00. The mean I_g of the plateaus is a moderate 0.721; the standard deviation is 0.077 (see Figure 2.1). The distribution is closely fitted by a normal (Gaussian) distribution with this mean and standard deviation. Given the normal shape of the distribution, the high and low values need not be judged anomalous, since the extremes are as expected on the basis of the mean and dispersion of the I_g's in the central part of the distribution.

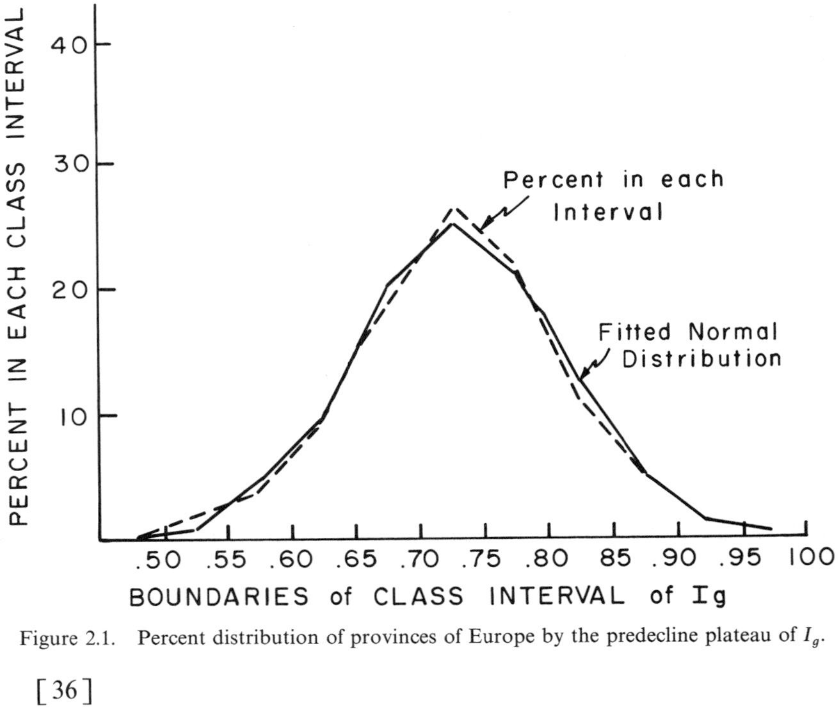

Figure 2.1. Percent distribution of provinces of Europe by the predecline plateau of I_g.

Moreover, the highest plateaus are near the level of the well-documented fertility of married Hutterites, and the lowest plateaus are matched by I_g's of non-European pre-industrial populations, including Chinese rural households in 1929–1931, rural Korea around 1930, and selected Asian populations in the Soviet Union in 1926 (Barclay et al., 1976; Coale, Anderson, and Härm, 1979). In other words, the extremes are consistent with the level of marital fertility recorded in other populations not characterized by parity-related control.

The Date of Initiation and Time Pattern of the Modern Decline in $\mathrm{I_g}$

In the typical history of marital fertility in Europe, the plateau of I_g was interrupted by a decline that began at the time of the initiation of contraception or abortion (or both) among a large enough segment of the population to affect aggregate marital fertility; I_g then continued to fall, reaching a minimum in almost all instances (Ireland a prominent exception) of at least 50 percent below the plateau. An important feature of the history of I_g within each province is the date at which a sustained decline began. The decline is characterized as *sustained* because it was generally monotonic, except for postwar reversals, and continued to fall until a greatly reduced level was reached.

The date at which a decline had clearly started was estimated for every province. To avoid the uncertainty of detecting the time of the very first downturn in a series inevitably affected by stochastic variation, what was estimated was not the moment of this downturn, but the date at which a point ten percent below a plateau level was reached, in a descent of I_g that never again returned to the plateau. (Other forms of approximate dating were employed for provinces in which I_g was already declining at the first calculated index. See Appendix D at the end of this chapter for details.) The frequency distribution of dates of decline is shown in Figure 2.2, and the date for selected national populations in Table 2.1. The bimodality of the distribution of the date of decline by province is conspicuous. The early peak in the distribution of dates is comprised entirely of early declines in I_g in *départements* of France. For France as a whole, the date of a ten percent decline is conservatively estimated as 1827; there are a number of *départements* in which the decline must have begun before 1800. In Europe, excluding France, there is a surprising concentration of the date of decline around 1900. Fifty-three percent of the dates (59 percent when France is excluded) are found in the interval from 1890 to 1920. The geographic distribution of estimated date of decline is shown on Map 2.1

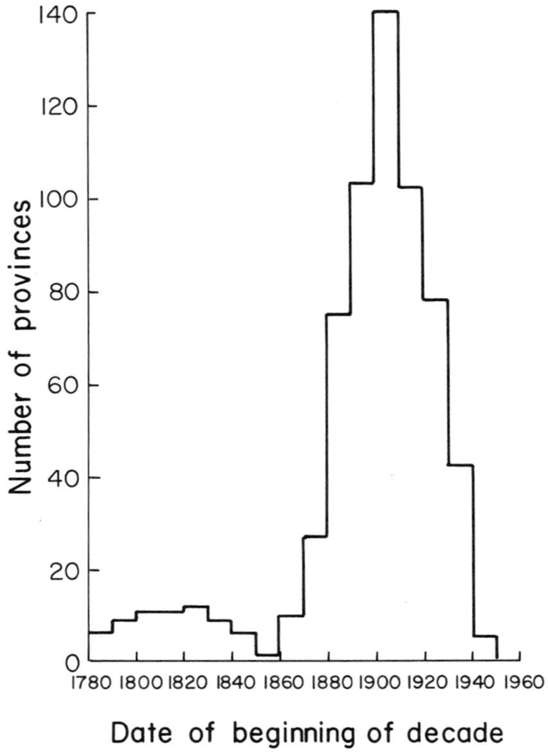

Figure 2.2. Distribution by decade of number of provinces of Europe experiencing ten percent decline in I_g.

Table 2.1. Estimated date of 10-percent decline, selected countries (1900 boundaries).

Country	Date	Country	Date	Country	Date
Austria	1907	Greece	1913	European Russia	1922
Belgium	1881	Hungary	1910	Scotland	1894
Denmark	1898	Ireland	1922	Spain	1920
England & Wales	1892	Italy	1913	Sweden	1902
Finland	1912	Netherlands	1897	Switzerland	1887
France	1827	Norway	1903	Europe (median province date)	1903
Germany	1888	Portugal	1916		

in the set of colored maps included in this book. The solid red areas (before 1830) comprise forty-nine French *départements*; outside of France there were declines in I_g before 1880 in two provinces in Catalonia (near the French border of Spain), in parts of French-speaking Belgium, in some cantons of Switzerland, in several German provinces, two small counties in Scotland, two Danish provinces, in the Russian Baltic provinces of

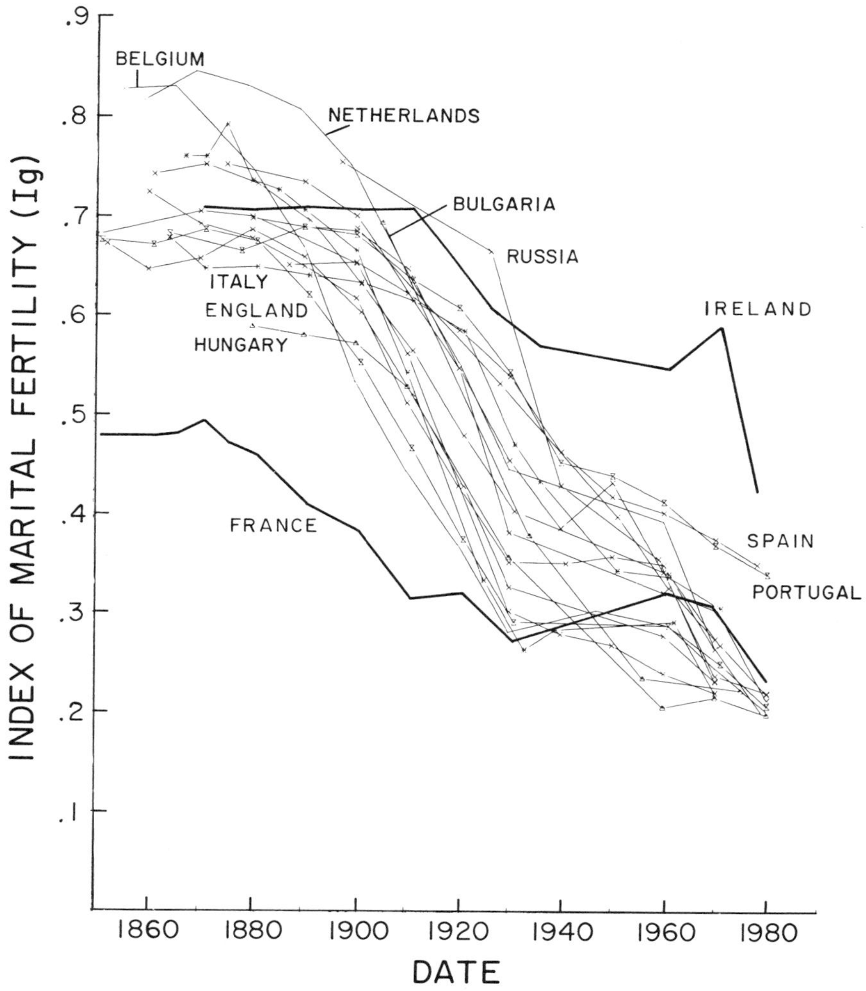

Figure 2.3. I_g in selected national populations of Europe.

Latvia and St. Petersburg, in the Swedish Island of Gotland, a few counties in Hungary, and one province in East Serbia. The declines that occurred after 1920 were in Ireland and the southern and eastern periphery of Europe (in Russia, Rumania, Albania, southern Italy, southern Greece, Spain, and Portugal).

The time sequence from 1870 to 1970 or 1980 of national I_g's for eighteen countries is shown in Figure 2.3. In 1870, the low I_g of France resulting from the very early decline and the substantial differences in natural fertility among countries still on a plateau are evident, as is the general clustering of the timing of the early stages of reduction near the turn of the century. In Figure 2.4 the decline in I_g for the same countries is shown again, but here time is measured for each population from the moment that a 10-percent decline from the plateau is reached, and the level of I_g is shown relative to the estimated plateau, set at 100. After this transformation, the slowness of the decline in I_g in France associated with its very

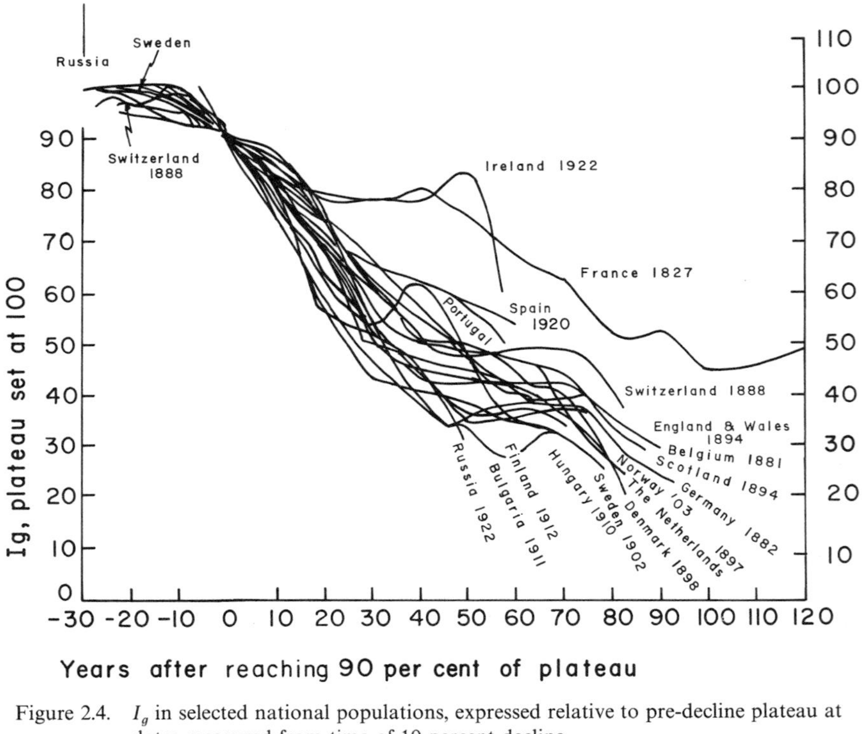

Figure 2.4. I_g in selected national populations, expressed relative to pre-decline plateau at dates measured from time of 10-percent decline.

early start stands out, as does the leveling off of I_g in Ireland at a higher value than in other populations. France and Ireland aside, the variation in time pattern of relative reduction in I_g from a plateau is surprisingly limited. Except for France, Ireland, Spain, and Portugal, the fall from 90 percent to 60 percent of the plateau level requires an interval within the limits of eighteen to thirty years. All but Ireland, Spain, and Albania (not shown) reach a point at least 50 percent below the plateau.

The Frequency Distribution of the Provinces of Europe by Level of I_g *during the Decline*

Two factors dominated in establishing geographic differentials in marital fertility in Europe since 1800: the level of pre-decline I_g (the plateau), and the date at which decline began. The differentials in the pre-decline period, which are seen in the distribution of plateau levels in 579 provinces, are those inherent in differences in natural fertility; since fertility reduction in different provinces began at different times, the differences in I_g then became greater as the early starters reached levels of I_g well below the lower limit of the distribution of plateau I_g's.

The frequency distribution of provinces classified by level of I_g at selected dates from the earliest calculations to 1960 or 1970 is shown for each of nineteen European countries in Table 2.2, which also shows the distribution for Europe (with and without France) at thirty-year intervals beginning in 1870.

Increasing differentials followed by convergence to common values form the pattern that can be expected in any new behavior that ultimately spreads through a population. Such a pattern is the expected sequence for the prevalence of parity-related limitation of fertility in a population that initially is subject to natural fertility: at first, limited segments of the population adopt a limited version of the new form of behavior, creating differentials that did not previously exist; as the pioneers intensify the practice and others begin it, differentials widen; when controlled fertility becomes universal, there is convergence at a low level. Initially widening and then narrowing differentials in fertility among groups differing in education, religion, or occupation can be expected within each province, and can in principle occur without becoming manifest as geographic differentials.

The distribution of I_g in the provinces of European Russia shown in Table 2.2 illustrates the classic sequence. As the mean I_g falls from 0.766 to 0.238, the distribution changes from a tight cluster (standard deviation 0.061) at high values, when at most a few more urbanized or Westernized

Table 2.2. Distribution of number of provinces by level of I_g for selected countries at selected dates.

I_g	AUSTRIA 1880	1890	1900	1910	1931	1960	BELGIUM 1846	1866	1880	1900	1930	1961	1970
<.180					1						1		
.180-.249					1	1					8	4	15
.250-.319					4	1					6	22	25
.320-.389					1	5				5	14	12	1
.390-.459				1	1	1				1	5	2	
.460-.529				2	0	1			2	8	2	1	
.530-.599		2	2	4					3	3	4		
.600-.669	6	4	5	3					5	4			
.670-.739	6	5	4	3			2	2	7				
.740-.809	3	4	4	3			7	3	3	6	1		
.810-.879	1	2	2	1				2	6	8			
.880+	1							2	15	6			
Number	17	17	17	17	8	9	9	9	41	41	41	41	41
Mean	.711	.707	.695	.637	.280	.358	.766	.820	.791	.666	.355	.310	.259
S.D.	.077	.074	.085	.116	.093	.072	.029	.083	.149	.193	.124	.053	.025

I_g	DENMARK 1852	1870	1890	1901	1911	1930	1960	ENGLAND AND WALES 1851	1871	1891	1911	1931	1961
<.180												2	
.180-.249						1	1					5	
.250-.319						3	15					29	45
.320-.389					1	12	6					9	
.390-.459				1	1	6					25		
.460-.529					7	1					16		
.530-.599	1	2	1	3	5					5	4		
.600-.669	9	10	10	10	3			17	8	34			
.670-.739	9	7	7	4	3			26	33	6			
.740-.809	1	1	2	2				2	4				
Number	20	20	20	20	20	23	22	45	45	45	45	45	45
Mean	.678	.662	.674	.638	.558	.361	.293	.681	.695	.635	.463	.285	.290
S.D.	.041	.050	.057	.077	.082	.061	.029	.031	.032	.031	.043	.044	.014

I_g	FRANCE 1831	1851	1871	1891	1911	1931	1961	GERMANY 1871	1880	1900	1910	1933	1962
<.180						1						2	
.180-.249				1	8	15	1					20	3
.250-.319		2	4	13	41	44	34				1	22	23
.320-.389	4	12	18	30	19	25	50				2	15	2
.390-.459	12	21	21	14	13	5	4			1	11	7	
.460-.529	17	20	13	11	3		1			4	18	1	
.530-.599	18	13	13	9	3			2	4	16	15		
.600-.669	13	11	5	4				9	16	17	10		
.670-.739	8	6	10	4				19	22	14	8		
.740-.809	5	1	2	1				22	15	10	4		
.810-.879	1		1					13	13	6	3		
.880+								7	2	4			
Number	78	86	87	87	87	90	90	72	72	72	72	67	28
Mean	.559	.497	.493	.432	.332	.295	.332	.759	.732	.674	.561	.293	.281
S.D.	.111	.109	.126	.120	.078	.054	.042	.087	.084	.114	.126	.078	.032

Table 2.2. Continued.

I_g	GREECE 1900	GREECE 1928	GREECE 1951	GREECE 1961	HUNGARY 1880	HUNGARY 1910	HUNGARY 1930	HUNGARY 1960	IRELAND 1871	IRELAND 1891	IRELAND 1911	IRELAND 1926	IRELAND 1961
<.180								3					
.180-.249								18					
.250-.319			2	5			5	3					
.320-.389			2	12		4	7						
.390-.459		2	10	1		5	10						1
.460-.529		5	3		13	17	1					1	1
.530-.599	2	8	1		28	35	2		1			2	5
.600-.669	1	2			18	12				2	5	17	23
.670-.739	5				6				26	24	13	9	1
.740-.809	2								4	4	7	2	
.810-.879										1	6		
Number	10	17	18	18	65	73	25	24	31	31	31	31	31
Mean	.683	.539	.418	.340	.583	.543	.386	.214	.714	.709	.740	.656	.612
S.D.	.065	.061	.060	.042	.064	.073	.074	.037	.032	.034	.072	.055	.052

I_g	ITALY 1871	ITALY 1891	ITALY 1911	ITALY 1931	ITALY 1951	ITALY 1961	NETHERLANDS 1859	NETHERLANDS 1879	NETHERLANDS 1899	NETHERLANDS 1909	NETHERLANDS 1930	NETHERLANDS 1960
<.180												
.180-.249					5	6						
.250-.319				2	3	2						
.320-.389				2	3	3					3	5
.390-.459				3	2	2					3	5
.460-.529			2	2	4	4				1	3	1
.530-.599	1	1	2	3	1	1				1	1	
.600-.669	8	8	4	5					2	4	1	
.670-.739	7	7	7	1			1	1	1	3		
.740-.809			1				4	4	6			
.810-.879							4	3				
.880+							2	3	2	2		
Number	16	16	16	18	18	18	11	11	11	11	11	11
Mean	.662	.664	.654	.506	.362	.354	.815	.828	.773	.678	.471	.401
S.D.	.031	.037	.090	.131	.120	.116	.064	.080	.108	.120	.094	.040

I_g	NORWAY 1875	NORWAY 1890	NORWAY 1900	NORWAY 1920	NORWAY 1930	NORWAY 1960	POLAND 1897	POLAND 1931	POLAND 1960	PORTUGAL 1890	PORTUGAL 1911	PORTUGAL 1930	PORTUGAL 1960
<.180									1				
.180-.249					1				4				1
.250-.319					1	8			3				6
.320-.389				1	6	11			12			1	4
.390-.459					9	1		4	2			2	1
.460-.529				5	2			6				5	6
.530-.599			1	7	1			4		1	2	4	1
.600-.669	2	2	4	6			1	2		6	13	5	2
.670-.739	3	8	11	1			5			9	4	2	1
.740-.809	14	10	4				3			5	2	3	
.810-.879	1						1						
.880+													
Number	20	20	20	20	20	20	10	16	22	21	21	22	22
Mean	.756	.735	.707	.565	.402	.332	.731	.515	.323	.702	.656	.577	.428
S.D.	.052	.037	.046	.078	.082	.044	.063	.061	.071	.060	.058	.113	.148

Table 2.2 Continued.

I_g	RUSSIA 1870	1897	1926	1940	1959	1970	SCOTLAND 1871	1891	1911	1931	1961
<.180											
.180-.249					3	56					
.250-.319				4	23	23				3	15
.320-.389			1	22	23	1				11	18
.390-.459			2	24	25				4	16	
.460-.529			7	21	5				6	3	
.530-.599		3	11	6	1				18		
.600-.669	3	2	17	1	1		1	9	5		
.670-.739	11	12	17				9	12			
.740-.809	32	32	18				19	11			
.810-.879	2	1	1				4	1			
.880+	1										
Number	50	50	74	78	81	80	33	33	33	33	33
Mean	.766	.746	.651	.429	.363	.238	.755	.706	.547	.396	.328
S.D.	.054	.066	.107	.078	.077	.033	.043	.059	.061	.050	.024

I_g	SPAIN 1887	1900	1910	1930	1950	1960	SWEDEN 1880	1900	1930	1950	1960
<.180											
.180-.249									2	2	17
.250-.319				1	6	8			9	22	8
.320-.389				4	8	10			11	1	
.390-.459		1	1	3	15	21					
.460-.529	2	2	5	6	19	10	1	2	2		
.530-.599	4	4	7	14	1	1	1	5			
.600-.669	23	19	19	16	1		7	6			
.670-.739	15	17	13	6			10	8			
.740-.809	3	4	3				5	2			
.810-.879	1	1					1	2			
.880+											
Number	48	48	48	50	50	50	25	25	25	25	25
Mean	.659	.662	.632	.566	.435	.408	.691	.657	.321	.277	.247
S.D.	.061	.076	.081	.104	.074	.066	.073	.096	.075	.027	.017

I_g	SWITZERLAND 1870	1888	1910	1930	1950	1960	EUROPE 1870	1900	1930	1960	EUROPE without FRANCE 1870	1900	1930	1960
<.180				1					9	4			8	4
.180-.249				2	2			3	55	60			40	59
.250-.319			1	3	4	6	4	12	129	222		1	85	188
.320-.389		1	1	7	6	6	18	42	123	175		5	98	125
.390-.459	1	1	4	3	5	7	22	17	76	77	1	4	71	73
.460-.529		1	3	3	4	5	19	40	54	37	6	29	54	36
.530-.599	2	2	7		4	1	36	101	62	14	23	93	62	14
.600-.669	4	8	3	6			63	112	68	24	96	110	68	24
.670-.739	6	5	4				186	129	26	3	176	127	26	3
.740-.809	7	5	2				135	94	23		133	94	23	
:810-.879	4	1					37	26	1	0	36	26	1	
.880+	1	1					30	13			30	13		
Number	25	25	25	25	25	25	588	589	626	616	501	502	536	526
Mean	.725	.667	.559	.418	.403	.393	.689	.631	.428	.349	.723	.671	.449	.352
S.D.	.115	.115	.133	.144	.104	.088	.124	.141	.157	.100	.084	.105	.159	.106

provinces had begun to reduce marital fertility, to a much more spread-out distribution (standard deviation of 0.107), as the first provinces to experience the decline progress toward lower fertility while the late starters remain high, to a very tight cluster at low fertility (standard deviation 0.033) as the laggards catch up.

The classic sequence of widening and then narrowing differentials in I_g is found in some countries but not in others. Belgium exemplifies divergence followed by convergence very well; in the nine Belgian provinces the range of I_g extends only from 0.717 to 0.810 in 1846, expands to the range 0.394 to 0.877 in 1900, and contracts again to only 0.224 to 0.302 in 1970. In England and Wales, on the other hand, the transition from high to low I_g, while extensive, occurred at nearly the same time in almost all the counties. The standard deviation of county I_g was 0.031 in 1851, reaching a maximum of only 0.044 in 1931 and a minimum of 0.014 in 1961. Despite the absence of large geographic differentials during the decline of I_g in England and Wales, *class* differentials in marital fertility widened and then contracted in the expected fashion, as revealed by tabulations of the fertility of marriages by duration of marriage and social class in the censuses of 1911, 1961, and 1971. It was only the geographic distribution of marital fertility in England and Wales that did not exhibit greatly expanded differentials during the transition to controlled fertility.

The frequency distribution of the provinces of all Europe according to level of I_g has a large range for differing reasons at each date of tabulation from 1870 to 1960. In 1870 there were provinces with exceptionally high natural fertility, and provinces with exceptionally low natural fertility, and French *départements* that had already greatly reduced marital fertility. In 1900, about half of the provinces of Europe had begun the reduction of I_g, and the standard deviation had increased. The standard deviation of I_g reaches a maximum in 1930, when marital fertility had fallen very low in the West, and some provinces had not yet begun, or had just begun, the reduction in marital fertility. By 1960, convergence is apparent; only a few provinces retain high marital fertility. The indexes for national populations in 1970 and 1980 indicate that variation in I_g remained slight, while the overall level was further reduced.

The Geographic Distribution of I_g

The changing geographic distribution of I_g is displayed in Maps 2.2 to 2.5, in which coded levels of I_g are shown in two colors. The codes designate twelve levels, ranging from I_g over 0.880 (deepest blue), through 0.530

to 0.660 (lightest blue), 0.460 to 0.530 (lightest red), to less than 0.180 (deepest red).

A map for a date earlier than 1870—ideally at 1800 or earlier—would have been useful, but the requisite data do not exist. For a number of countries, in fact, data for 1880 are plotted on the 1870 map, and in some instances values calculated for 1900 are used as the earliest available. In countries where later data are plotted for 1870, both the social context and demographic data (such as age composition) usually support the inference of little change in marital fertility from 1870 to 1900 (see Appendix C at the end of this chapter for details, and Figure 2.C for the actual dates of the data plotted on the 1870 maps).

The variation in I_g shown on the 1870 map is a reflection of two factors: (1) differences in natural fertility before the onset of parity related control, and (2) reduced I_g in provinces in which the decline had begun before 1870.

The lowest marital fertility in 1870 is found in the provinces listed earlier that experienced an early decline (primarily in France and in provinces bordering France) plus a few with unusually low plateaus, connoting natural fertility near the lower extreme of the distribution. I_g's above 0.880 are found in a cluster of areas in southern Germany and Austria, and in western Germany and the Low Countries. These instances of extremely high marital fertility are almost certainly associated with the virtual absence of breast-feeding, as demonstrated for some areas by Knodel and E. van de Walle (1967). Conspicuously absent in 1870 is any systematic tendency toward low I_g in areas known to be leaders in introducing universal education, in achieving low mortality, or becoming industrialized. Such relations emerged only as I_g departed from a plateau, a change that occurred mostly after 1870.

The transformation of marital fertility by the widening adoption of parity-related limitation, once such adoption had started, is seen by comparing the four I_g maps.

The maps give a visible impression of where marital fertility was highest in the early years, of where and when (such as southern England from 1900 to 1930) rapid reductions took place, of the emergence in 1930 of a loosely connected area of low fertility (encompassing France, England and Wales, southern Scotland, Belgium, Germany, western Czechoslovakia, Austria, Hungary, Switzerland, northern Italy, and the southern parts of Scandinavia), and of the much homogenized low I_g of 1960.

Proportions Married in European Provinces during the Decline in Marital Fertility

During the modern decline in fertility in Europe, overall fertility in most provinces can be considered as composed of two factors: marital fertility and proportion married. In other words, the calculated values of overall fertility (I_f) reported here can be approximated in most instances by $I_m \cdot I_g$ with little loss in accuracy, since the omitted product $(1 - I_m) \cdot I_h$ that represents the contribution to fertility of women not currently married is usually negligible. The consistent feature of the decline in fertility in the many provinces of Europe has been the large decline in I_g. We shall now consider the part played during this decline by the other factor, the proportion married, measured by I_m.

Nuptiality had a uniquely important role in determining European fertility before the late nineteenth century. As John Hajnal (1965) showed, late marriage and high proportions still single at age 50 have long been characteristic of populations west of an imaginary line from Trieste to St. Petersburg. Variation in age of first marriage and in the proportion remaining single accounts for most differences in provincial I_m.

The European pattern of marriage (as Hajnal called it) had been established well before the initiation of censuses and official vital statistics that make calculation of our standard indexes possible. Low values of I_m are found in data from very early censuses (such as in Denmark in 1787), that list marital status by age, and for still earlier dates (back to the beginning of the eighteenth century in the Bavarian village of Anhausen, and back to the middle of the sixteenth century for a sample of English parishes) from genealogies or reconstituted parish registers (Knodel, 1978c; Wrigley and Schofield, 1983). In England for three centuries, overall fertility varied substantially because of ups and downs in mean age at first marriage, and especially because of variation in the proportion remaining single, while marital fertility remained nearly constant. Malthus was no doubt influenced in his advocacy of late marriage as a "preventive check" to restrain population growth by his observation of the operation of precisely such a check in Western Europe in the late eighteenth century.

Because of the absence of data for the more remote past, it is not possible to extend our tables, maps, and figures back to the date (before 1800) when I_g began to decline in some of the pioneering French *départements*. Nevertheless, it is clear from various kinds of partial evidence that I_g was typically constant, although different in different populations because of nonparity-related customs affecting marital fertility. The reconstructed English record shows that in Western Europe, where the proportion married was low, substantial temporal variation in I_m must have occurred. Such variation was not sufficient, it seems clear, to alter the picture of much lower I_m in the west than found to the east of Hajnal's line.

If it were possible to calculate provincial I_g's and I_m's for 1800, it is a warranted conjecture that the coefficient of variation (standard deviation divided by the mean) of provincial I_m would be substantially higher than the coefficient of variation of provincial I_g. (The frequency distribution of I_m within nineteen countries and all Europe at four dates from 1870 to 1960 is shown in Table 2.3).

The first calculations of coefficient of variation that could be made were for 1870, when the coefficient of variation of I_m was 0.209 and the coefficient of variation of I_g was 0.180. Remember that by 1870 the interprovincial variability of I_g in Europe had become greatly increased by the reduction in fertility that had occurred in France. The coefficient of variation of I_g in European provinces in 1870 excluding France was 0.116. The coefficient of variation of the distribution of estimated provincial plateaus of I_g was 0.106, which is only half of the coefficient of variation of 1870 I_m. In other words, a good estimate of the relative influence on overall fertility of differences in nuptiality and differences in marital fertility before parity-related control became important is that differences in nuptiality had about twice the effect of differences in marital fertility.

The Early Geographic Pattern of $\mathrm{I_m}$

The geographic pattern of proportion married from 1870 to 1960 can be seen in Maps 2.6 to 2.9. Like the maps showing I_g, these maps of I_m have twelve coded levels, ranging from deepest blue ($I_m = 0.800$ or above) through lightest blue (0.550 to 0.599) and lightest red (0.500 to 0.549) to deepest red (I_m less than 0.300).

The pattern of I_m in 1870 (a year for which a map of provincial levels of I_m can be made, with some extrapolations back from later data) shows the remarkable validity of Hajnal's designation of a line from Trieste to St. Petersburg as the boundary west of which marriage was late and proportions remaining single high. In establishing an objective rule for assigning twelve class intervals (six red and six blue) for mapping I_m, the dividing point between red and blue fell at $I_m = 0.550$. The provinces just west of Hajnal's proposed line are red (on the low side), and those to the

Table 2.3. Distribution of number of provinces by level of I_m for selected countries at selected dates.

AUSTRIA

I_m	1880	1890	1900	1910	1931	1960
<.300	1	1				
.300-.349	3	2	1			
.350-.399	1	2	4	3	3	
.400-.449	4	4	4	4	3	
.450-.499	1	2		2	2	
.500-.549	4	3	4	4		3
.550-.599	1	2	3	3		4
.600-.649	2	1	1	1		1
.650-.699						1
.700-.749						
.750-.799						
Number	17	17	17	17	8	9
Mean	.455	.455	.468	.484	.422	.581
S.D.	.105	.099	.085	.076	.039	.052

BELGIUM

I_m	1846	1866	1880	1900	1930	1961	1970
<.300							
.300-.349	2		2				
.350-.399	3	5	10	2			
.400-.449	4	3	20	18	1		
.450-.499	0	1	5	15	4		
.500-.549			4	1	6		
.550-.599				3	17		
.600-.649				2	8	7	4
.650-.699					1	15	15
.700-.749					4	12	21
.750-.799						7	1
Number	9	9	41	41	41	41	41
Mean	.383	.400	.427	.464	.577	.697	.699
S.D.	.030	.032	.043	.056	.066	.045	.030

DENMARK

I_m	1852	1870	1890	1901	1911	1930	1960
<.300							
.300-.349							
.350-.399	4	1					
.400-.449	8	7	3	1	1		
.450-.499	8	12	13	15	8	4	
.500-.549			4	4	11	17	
.550-.599						2	1
.600-.649							1
.650-.699							18
.700-.749							2
.750-.799							
Number	20	20	20	20	20	23	22
Mean	.440	.455	.475	.480	.500	.517	.678
S.D.	.037	.033	.024	.021	.022	.022	.031

ENGLAND AND WALES

I_m	1851	1871	1891	1911	1931	1961
<.300						
.300-.349						
.350-.399			2	2		
.400-.449	10		12	14	2	
.450-.499	24	22	22	18	13	
.500-.549	8	19	8	9	28	
.550-.599	3	3	1	2	2	1
.600-.649		1				
.650-.699						14
.700-.749						27
.750-.799						3
Number	45	45	45	45	45	45
Mean	.482	.504	.471	.472	.507	.708
S.D.	.034	.037	.040	.040	.029	.031

FRANCE

I_m	1831	1851	1871	1891	1911	1931	1961
<.300							
.300-.349							
.350-.399	3	2	3				
.400-.449	12	11	9	7	1	1	
.450-.499	17	17	14	15	1	1	1
.500-.549	17	17	18	17	17	8	
.550-.599	20	20	22	18	19	20	6
.600-.649	8	16	17	27	23	34	35
.650-.699	1	3	3	2	23	25	47
.700-.749			1	1	3	1	1
.750-.799							
Number	78	86	87	87	87	90	90
Mean	.519	.534	.543	.556	.605	.616	.647
S.D.	.068	.071	.074	.070	.059	.054	.035

GERMANY

I_m	1871	1880	1900	1910	1933	1962
<.300						
.300-.349						
.350-.399	4				1	
.400-.449	19	5	8	3	7	
.450-.499	31	34	22	18	11	
.500-.549	18	26	31	34	24	1
.550-.599		7	11	16	17	1
.600-.649				1	7	7
.650-.699						6
.700-.749						12
.750-.799						1
Number	72	72	72	72	67	28
Mean	.467	.501	.508	.523	.527	.676
S.D.	.041	.035	.044	.038	.061	.057

Table 2.3. Continued.

I_m	GREECE 1900	1928	1951	1961	HUNGARY 1880	1910	1930	1960	IRELAND 1871	1891	1911	1926	1961
<.300										1	1		
.300-.349									4	24	28	13	
.350-.399									16	5	1	17	
.400-.449			1		1	1			6	1	1	1	1
.450-.499		4	6		1	1			4				19
.500-.549		5	8	2			1		1				10
.550-.599	2	3	2	10		2	6						
.600-.649	4	1	1	5	9	17	11						1
.650-.699	3	3			21	28	6	5					
.700-.749	1	1		1	29	22	1	12					
.750-.799					4	2		7					
Number	10	17	18	18	65	73	25	24	31	31	31	31	31
Mean	.637	.573	.515	.593	.688	.669	.623	.731	.399	.329	.329	.354	.495
S.D.	.047	.081	.052	.042	.057	.054	.049	.032	.048	.025	.021	.021	.032

I_m	ITALY 1871	1891	1911	1931	1951	1961	NETHERLANDS 1859	1879	1899	1909	1930	1960
<.300												
.300-.349							1					
.350-.399				1			3		2			
.400-.449				1	1		7	4	2	3		
.450-.499	1	2	8	7	5	1		5	6	6	4	
.500-.549	3	11	6	7	6	6		2	1	2	6	
.550-.599	12	3	2	2	5	6					1	1
.600-.649					1	5						7
.650-.699												3
.700-.749												
.750-.799												
Number	16	16	16	18	18	18	11	11	11	11	11	11
Mean	.558	.530	.505	.498	.519	.564	.408	.467	.454	.475	.506	.636
S.D.	.027	.030	.032	.045	.049	.045	.037	.037	.042	.039	.031	.028

I_m	NORWAY 1875	1890	1900	1920	1930	1960	POLAND 1897	1931	1960	PORTUGAL 1890	1911	1930	1960
<.300													
.300-.349	1			2	2								
.350-.399	6	5	4	2	5					3	1	1	
.400-.449	11	12	11	11	9			1		6	5	4	
.450-.499	1	2	5	4	4			2		7	6	8	3
.500-.549	1	1		1		1	1	5		2	5	6	5
.550-.599						1	1	3		3	4	3	9
.600-.649						3	3	5	3				5
.650-.699						12	5		10				
.700-.749						3			8				
.750-.799									1				
Number	20	20	20	20	20	20	10	16	22	21	21	22	22
Mean	.410	.424	.425	.421	.411	.664	.634	.558	.693	.462	.488	.485	.559
S.D.	.034	.035	.032	.042	.037	.043	.047	.066	.035	.062	.057	.046	.048

Table 2.3 Continued.

RUSSIA

I_m	1897	1926	1940	1959	1970
<.300					
.300-.349					
.350-.399					
.400-.449		1	1		
.450-.499	2	2	1	1	
.500-.549	3	3	1	13	
.550-.599	5	6	2	38	
.600-.649	6	36	24	25	30
.650-.699	9	24	46	2	47
.700-.749	13		4	2	4
.750-.799	11	2	1		
.800+	1		1		
Number	50	74	81	81	81
Mean	.682	.630	.654	.583	.661
S.D.	.091	.053	.052	.041	.021

SCOTLAND

I_m	1871	1891	1911	1931	1961
<.300	1	1			
.300-.349	6	11	10	2	
.350-.399	12	12	11	8	
.400-.449	9	6	6	16	
.450-.499	3	2	5	6	
.500-.549	1			1	
.550-.599	1	1	1		1
.600-.649					11
.650-.699					17
.700-.749					4
.750-.799					
.800+					
Number	33	33	33	33	33
Mean	.398	.379	.390	.419	.658
S.D.	.058	.057	.061	.044	.030

SPAIN

I_m	1887	1900	1910	1930	1960
<.300					
.300-.349					
.350-.399				1	
.400-.449	4	3	5	9	
.450-.499	5	5	5	8	2
.500-.549	3	9	9	14	25
.550-.599	6	7	8	15	15
.600-.649	20	19	19	1	7
.650-.699	10	5	2		1
.700-.749					
Number	48	48	48	48	50
Mean	.591	.573	.562	.513	.556
S.D.	.079	.073	.067	.061	.042

SWEDEN

I_m	1880	1900	1930	1950	1960
<.300	1				
.300-.349		1			
.350-.399	7	7	4		
.400-.449	10	10	15		
.450-.499	7	5	6		
.500-.549		2			
.550-.599				2	2
.600-.649				18	20
.650-.699				4	3
.700-.749				1	
Number	25	25	25	25	25
Mean	.420	.423	.429	.633	.629
S.D.	.049	.048	.030	.027	.025

SWITZERLAND

I_m	1870	1888	1910	1930	1950	1960
<.300						
.300-.349	3					
.350-.399	7	7		6	1	
.400-.449	11	12	7	12		
.450-.499	1	4	18	7	6	2
.500-.549	2	2			13	9
.550-.599	1				5	10
.600-.649						4
.650-.699						
.700-.749						
.750-.799						
.800+						
Number	25	25	25	25	25	25
Mean	.411	.428	.459	.427	.517	.564
S.D.	.058	.042	.022	.035	.040	.037

EUROPE

I_m	1870	1900	1930	1960
<.300	4	6		
.300-.349	19	41	15	
.350-.399	72	35	51	1
.400-.449	121	108	91	2
.450-.499	119	121	92	27
.500-.549	80	99	130	71
.550-.599	62	64	90	114
.600-.649	54	63	95	156
.650-.699	30	25	52	141
.700-.749	15	15	6	81
.750-.799	11	11	2	22
.800+	1	1		1
Number	588	589	624	616
Mean	.500	.504	.523	.627
S.D.	.104	.105	.094	.073

EUROPE without FRANCE

I_m	1870	1900	1930	1960
<.300	4	6		
.300-.349	19	41	15	
.350-.399	69	35	51	1
.400-.449	112	103	90	2
.450-.499	105	108	91	26
.500-.549	62	83	122	71
.550-.599	40	43	70	108
.600-.649	37	34	61	12
.650-.699	27	23	27	94
.700-.749	14	14	5	80
.750-.799	11	11	2	22
.800+	1	1		1
Number	501	502	533	526
Mean	.493	.494	.508	.623
S.D.	.107	.108	.090	.078

east are blue (on the high side). The separation of high from low I_m's by a dividing line at 0.550 was not perfect. There were no provinces with an I_m less than 0.550 to the east of the line, but there were provinces to the west in France and Spain with I_m's above 0.600, and in Italy and Portugal with I_m's above 0.550.

East of Hajnal's line I_m is highest to the south and east, attaining the highest levels in Europe in the Balkans and at the Caspian. To the west, the lowest proportions married occur along the western rim—in Norway and the North Sea provinces of Sweden, in Scotland and Ireland, in the Low Countries, and in Brittany, the Atlantic provinces of Spain, and Portugal. The High Alps of Austria, Switzerland, and Germany are the locus of a very low pocket of I_m; within France I_m was relatively low in the French Alps, the Central Massif, and the western Pyrenees. The incidence of marriage in Western Europe was thus especially low along the Atlantic seaboard, and in very mountainous provinces.

Changes in $\mathrm{I_m}$ *from 1870 to 1960*

There were few changes in I_m from the date of the earliest calculated values until 1930 comparable to the changes already noted in I_g. Some western populations showed a steady increase in I_m from the middle of the nineteenth century or earlier, broken only by setbacks such as those associated with major wars. Such an increase occurred in France (from 0.51 to 0.61 in the interval 1831 to 1930), in the Low Countries (from 0.38 to 0.52 in the interval 1856 to 1910 in Belgium), and in Germany, Portugal, and Denmark. In other western populations, I_m followed a very level course—notably in Austria, Switzerland, Sweden, Norway, England, and Wales and Scotland—from the mid-nineteenth century until about 1930. In still other West European countries (Finland, Ireland, Spain) I_m declined (in Finland from 0.50 to 0.40 in the interval 1851 to 1930; in Ireland from 0.41 to 0.32 in 1870 to 1900). In Eastern Europe high values of I_m were generally maintained—the major exception being Russia, where I_m fell from 0.70 in 1897 to 0.63 in 1926 and 0.58 in 1959; but the low values were largely due to the shortage of males lost in the military.

The relatively modest changes in nuptiality from 1870 to 1930 can be seen by comparing Maps 2.6, 2.7, and 2.8. The increase in I_m in many provinces in France is visible, as is the decline in Russia, where, as noted above, most of the change (which actually occurred from 1897 to 1926, the dates of the first two censuses of Russia, rather than from 1900 to 1930) can be attributed to a shortage of males in 1926 because of military losses in World War I and the Russian Civil War. The proportion married among males 20–49 in 1926 was almost as high as in 1897 (Coale, Anderson, and Härm, 1979).

After 1930 a major change occurred in the pattern of I_m as the West European populations that had the lowest proportions married began marrying earlier and no longer remained single in such large proportions. Frequency distributions of provinces by levels of I_m at selected dates are shown in Table 2.3 for nineteen countries, and for Europe as a whole (with and without France). The unweighted mean I_m for the provinces of Europe remained essentially unchanged from 1870 to 1900 as increases in some provinces was offset by declines in others, rose slightly from 1900 to 1930 (from 0.50 to 0.52), and then increased substantially from 1930 to 1960 (to 0.63). Indeed, the general rise in I_m from 1930 to 1960 just about exactly offset the further decline in I_g so that the average value of I_f for European provinces fell insignificantly (from 0.237 to 0.223).

The different trends in I_m in different provinces caused increased uniformity in the distribution. The move toward earlier and more universal marriage after 1930 in Western Europe, which was called a marriage boom by Hajnal, dramatically increased I_m where it was lowest; at the same time, in Russia, at least, I_m was reduced in the provinces where formerly it had been highest. The standard deviation of the distribution of I_m was lower in 1960 than in 1900 in most countries, and in Europe as a whole (see Table 2.3). The persistence of regional differentials within countries from 1870 to 1930 and the frequent fading of such differentials after 1930 are discussed more fully in the paper by Watkins (Chapter 8).

A comparison of the maps showing I_m in 1870, 1900, 1930, and 1960 shows that the basic pattern of differentials from high to low remained essentially unchanged through 1930, with relatively high nuptiality to the south and east and relatively low nuptiality in the north and west. By 1960, however, because of very large increases in I_m in many of the western populations, and a substantial decline in many of the areas in Russia where I_m had earlier been highest, the pattern is drastically different from the earlier dates. The Balkans remain an area of high I_m in 1960, but they now form the lower end of a strip of high I_m that extends north to the Baltic. In terms of colors, note that the red tones used to represent low proportions married, which characterized about half of the provinces in the earliest dates, are hardly to be found in the 1960 map of I_m (map 2.9).

Overall Fertility, Marital Fertility, and Proportion Married

Having considered changes in the two principal components of overall fertility in Europe (marital fertility and the proportions married), we now turn to a somewhat briefer treatment of overall fertility as measured by the index I_f. (The frequency distribution by province of this index for nineteen countries at different dates and for all Europe is given in Table 2.4.)

The Geographical Distribution of $\mathrm{I_f}$

The levels of I_f in the provinces of Europe at four dates are shown in Maps 2.10 to 2.13, where, as in the other maps, there are twelve coded categories, from over 0.590 (deep blue) to under 0.140 (deep red).

In 1870 the map of I_f (which equals, to a good approximation, the product of I_m and I_g) more closely resembles, in the general topography of the west-to-east gradation of fertility, the 1870 I_m map than the 1870 map of I_g. To be sure, the influence of low I_g in the early declining regions of France is visible in low values of I_f. In 1900 the influence of the pattern of I_g on I_f is stronger, and by 1930 I_g has become the dominant factor in variation in I_f. In 1960 the maps for I_f and I_g are visually almost indistinguishable; both are mostly red, and the patterns of lighter and darker areas are quite similar. After 1960, I_f declined further in most of Europe; national values in 1980 are less than 0.185 in most countries, and less than 0.250 in all but Albania (for which no recent data on marital status by age have been published).

The Joint Distribution of I_m, I_g, and I_f

To provide a different insight into fertility changes in the past century or so in the provinces of Europe, we shall make use of a method of presentation first used in the study of the decline in fertility in Russia that is part of the European Fertility Project (Coale, Anderson, and Härm, 1979). This form of presentation involves the simultaneous depiction of marital fertility, proportion married, and approximate overall fertility for a province or a number of provinces. The presentation is a simple one: the two principal constituent indexes (I_m and I_g) of overall fertility for a given population are plotted in a two-dimensional diagram of which the vertical dimension is I_m and the horizontal dimension is I_g. The product

Table 2.4. Distribution of number of provinces by level of I_f for selected countries at selected dates.

AUSTRIA

I_f	1880	1890	1900	1910	1931	1960
<.140					1	1
.140-.184					6	
.185-.229				1	1	1
.230-.274						7
.275-.319	5	3	3	5		
.320-.364	3	5	6	4		
.365-.409	5	4	2	2		
.410-.454	2	4	5	5		
.455-.499	2	1	1			
Number	17	17	17	17	8	9
Mean	.374	.374	.376	.354	.159	.234
S.D.	.053	.062	.058	.065	.046	.038

BELGIUM

I_f	1846	1866	1880	1900	1930	1961	1970
<.140					3		
.140-.184					12	4	18
.185-.229				3	18	30	23
.230-.274			2	13	5	5	
.275-.319	5	1	11	6		2	
.320-.364	4	6	12	2	2		
.365-.409		2	9	12	1		
.410-.454			5	5			
.455-.499			2				
Number	9	9	41	41	41	41	41
Mean	.314	.349	.354	.319	.205	.218	.185
S.D.	.017	.017	.050	.071	.053	.027	.013

DENMARK

I_f	1852	1870	1890	1901	1911	1930	1960
<.140						1	
.140-.184						5	1
.185-.229					1	13	17
.230-.274		1		1	1	4	4
.275-.319	6	7	4	9	11		
.320-.364	14	7	9	4	5		
.365-.409		5	5	6	2		
.410-.454			2				
.455-.499							
Number	20	20	20	20	20	23	22
Mean	.332	.337	.349	.333	.306	.203	.212
S.D.	.021	.035	.039	.040	.043	.029	.021

ENGLAND AND WALES

I_f	1851	1871	1891	1911	1931	1961
<.140					11	
.140-.184				4	31	
.185-.229				20	3	37
.230-.274			5	15		8
.275-.319	3	2	22	4		
.320-.364	29	16	14	2		
.365-.409	11	23	4			
.410-.454	2	2				
.455-.499		2				
Number	45	45	45	45	45	45
Mean	.353	.373	.315	.231	.152	.217
S.D.	.027	.036	.035	.036	.025	.013

FRANCE

I_f	1831	1851	1871	1891	1911	1931	1961
<.140						3	
.140-.184				2	19	31	5
.185-.229	4	10	14	29	44	49	47
.230-.274	14	39	31	36	19	7	34
.275-.319	36	24	29	14	5		4
.320-.364	21	12	11	4			
.365-.409	3	1	2	2			
.410-.454							
.455-.499							
Number	78	86	87	87	87	90	90
Mean	.301	.276	.276	.249	.212	.193	.226
S.D.	.040	.039	.041	.041	.033	.028	.026

GERMANY

I_f	1871	1880	1900	1910	1933	1962
<.140					13	1
.140-.184				1	40	3
.185-.229			1	2	10	20
.230-.274			1	13	4	4
.275-.319	4	1	7	23		
.320-.364	18	14	27	22		
.365-.409	29	34	23	5		
.410-.454	16	16	9	6		
.455-.499	5	6	4			
Number	72	72	72	72	67	28
Mean	.388	.398	.370	.318	.167	.207
S.D.	.041	.041	.051	.056	.032	.027

Table 2.4. Continued.

I_f	GREECE 1900	GREECE 1923	GREECE 1951	GREECE 1961	HUNGARY 1880	HUNGARY 1910	HUNGARY 1930	HUNGARY 1960	IRELAND 1871	IRELAND 1891	IRELAND 1911	IRELAND 1926	IRELAND 1961
<.140							0	3					
.140-.184			3	3			1	17					
.185-.229		1	8	14		1	5	4		12	2	8	
.230-.274		5	6	1			13		15	17	26	23	3
.275-.319		3	1		1	5	4		8	2	3		19
.320-.364	2	4			4	10	2		7				8
.365-.409		2			17	27							1
.410-.454	5	2			26	23			1				
.455-.499	2				9	6							
.500-.544	1				6	1							
.545-.589					1								
.590+					1								
Number	10	17	18	18	65	73	25	24	31	31	31	31	31
Mean	.442	.315	.218	.203	.433	.397	.261	.166	.293	.239	.248	.239	.307
S.D.	.058	.064	.036	.026	.055	.050	.045	.030	.039	.022	.017	.014	.026

I_f	ITALY 1871	ITALY 1891	ITALY 1911	ITALY 1931	ITALY 1951	ITALY 1961	NETHERLANDS 1859	NETHERLANDS 1879	NETHERLANDS 1899	NETHERLANDS 1909	NETHERLANDS 1930	NETHERLANDS 1960
<.140					4	2						
.140-.184				2	5	6					1	
.185-.229				5	3	4					4	
.230-.274			2	4	3	5				1	3	8
.275-.319		1	2	1	3	1	1		2	5	3	3
.320-.364	2	4	6	5			8		5	2		
.365-.409	11	9	5	1			2	8	4	3		
.410-.454	3	2	1					3				
Number	16	16	16	18	18	18	11	11	11	11	11	11
Mean	.390	.374	.348	.266	.194	.201	.344	.397	.356	.326	.241	.257
S.D.	.020	.029	.048	.070	.063	.054	.029	.025	.029	.043	.043	.018

I_f	NORWAY 1875	NORWAY 1890	NORWAY 1900	NORWAY 1920	NORWAY 1930	NORWAY 1960	POLAND 1897	POLAND 1931	POLAND 1960	PORTUGAL 1890	PORTUGAL 1911	PORTUGAL 1930	PORTUGAL 1960
<.140				1	2				2				
.140-.184				1	10	2			3				4
.185-.229				2	7	8			2			1	6
.230-.274			2	12		9		5	12	1		3	3
.275-.319	6	9	11	4	1	1		6	2	2	4	8	3
.320-.364	11	8	5					4	1	8	7	7	4
.365-.409	2	2	2	1						9	8	3	2
.410-.454	1	1					4	1		1	2		
.455-.499							3						
.500-.544							3						
Number	20	20	20	20	20	20	10	16	22	21	21	22	22
Mean	.399	.335	.323	.256	.179	.229	.480	.305	.236	.362	.355	.317	.261
S.D.	.030	.034	.036	.049	.043	.032	.039	.047	.056	.042	.043	.045	.071

Table 2.4. Continued.

RUSSIA

I_f	1870	1897	1926	1940	1959	1970
<.140					1	19
.140-.184			1	1	21	49
.185-.229			1	16	36	12
.230-.274			1	24	17	
.275-.319		3	6	19	5	
.320-.364	3	1	6	14		
.365-.409	2	1	8	2	1	
.410-.454	2	4	23	2		
.455-.499	4	5	20			
.500-.544	14	13	8			
.545-.589	13	11				
.590+	12	12				
Number	50	50	74	78	81	80
Mean	.538	.527	.420	.279	.211	.157
S.D.	.076	.090	.075	.055	.043	.023

SCOTLAND

I_f	1871	1891	1911	1931	1961
<.140				4	
.140-.184			4	12	1
.185-.229		2	14	15	19
.230-.274	3	12	9	2	13
.275-.319	10	9	5		
.320-.364	12	8			
.365-.409	5	1	1		
.410-.454	2				
.455-.499		1			
.500-.544	1				
.545-.589					
.590+					
Number	33	33	33	33	33
Mean	.335	.294	.233	.181	.226
S.D.	.059	.056	.049	.030	.018

SPAIN

I_f	1887	1900	1910	1930	1950	1960
<.140					1	
.140-.184				1	12	5
.185-.229			1	5	17	19
.230-.274		1	1	9	19	20
.275-.319	3	3	9	10	1	6
.320-.364	9	9	10	18		
.365-.409	13	16	11	7		
.410-.454	15	14	16			
.455-.499	8	5				
Number	48	48	48	50	50	50
Mean	.404	.394	.371	.306	.212	.230
S.D.	.054	.053	.055	.059	.037	.032

SWEDEN

I_f	1880	1900	1930	1950	1960
<.140			4		
.140-.184			17	6	21
.185-.229		1	3	18	4
.230-.274	2	2	1	1	0
.275-.319	10	14			
.320-.364	9	6			
.365-.409	4	1			
.410-.454		1			
.455-.499					
Number	25	25	25	25	25
Mean	.322	.311	.163	.194	.175
S.D.	.038	.048	.035	.017	.012

SWITZERLAND

I_f	1870	1888	1910	1930	1950	1960
<.140			1	5	2	
.140-.184		1	1	10	4	6
.185-.229	1	1	4	3	11	7
.230-.274	4	5	8	6	5	7
.275-.319	10	10	6	1	3	5
.320-.364	8	7	5			
.365-.409	2	1				
.410-.454						
.455-.499						
.500-.544						
.545-.589						
.590+						
Number	25	25	25	25	25	25
Mean	.309	.296	.266	.182	.214	.228
S.D.	.044	.047	.058	.055	.049	.046

EUROPE

I_f	1870	1900	1930	1960
<.140			49	10
.140-.184		7	179	107
.185-.229	15	82	168	268
.230-.274	59	102	68	157
.275-.319	108	103	40	52
.320-.364	144	96	45	16
.365-.409	128	86	22	5
.410-.454	62	51	28	
.455-.499	28	22	19	
.500-.544	19	14	8	2
.545-.589	13	14		
.590+	12	12		
Number	588	589	626	617
Mean	.364	.333	.237	.223
S.D.	.083	.098	.096	.048

EUROPE without FRANCE

I_f	1870	1900	1930	1960
<.140			46	10
.140-.184		1	148	102
.185-.229	1	41	110	221
.230-.274	28	72	61	123
.275-.319	79	96	40	48
.320-.364	133	93	45	16
.365-.409	126	86	22	5
.410-.454	62	51	28	
.455-.499	28	22	19	
.500-.544	19	14	8	2
.545-.589	13	14		
.590+	12	12		
Number	501	502	536	527
Mean	.379	.350	.244	.223
S.D.	.078	.094	.101	.051

of $I_m \cdot I_g$ (which can be designated I_f*, since it falls short of I_f by the exclusion of births to the nonmarried) can be seen on the same diagram because there is inscribed a series of contour lines representing (by rectangular hyperbolas) loci of specified values of $I_m \cdot I_g$. An example of this presentation is Figure 2.5, which displays the major fertility indexes of more than six hundred provinces of Europe in 1900. The four provinces that were used in the introduction of this chapter to illustrate the fertility indexes are labeled in Figure 2.5—Lot-et-Garonne with the lowest I_g, Tipperary with the lowest I_m, Geneva with the lowest I_f outside of France,

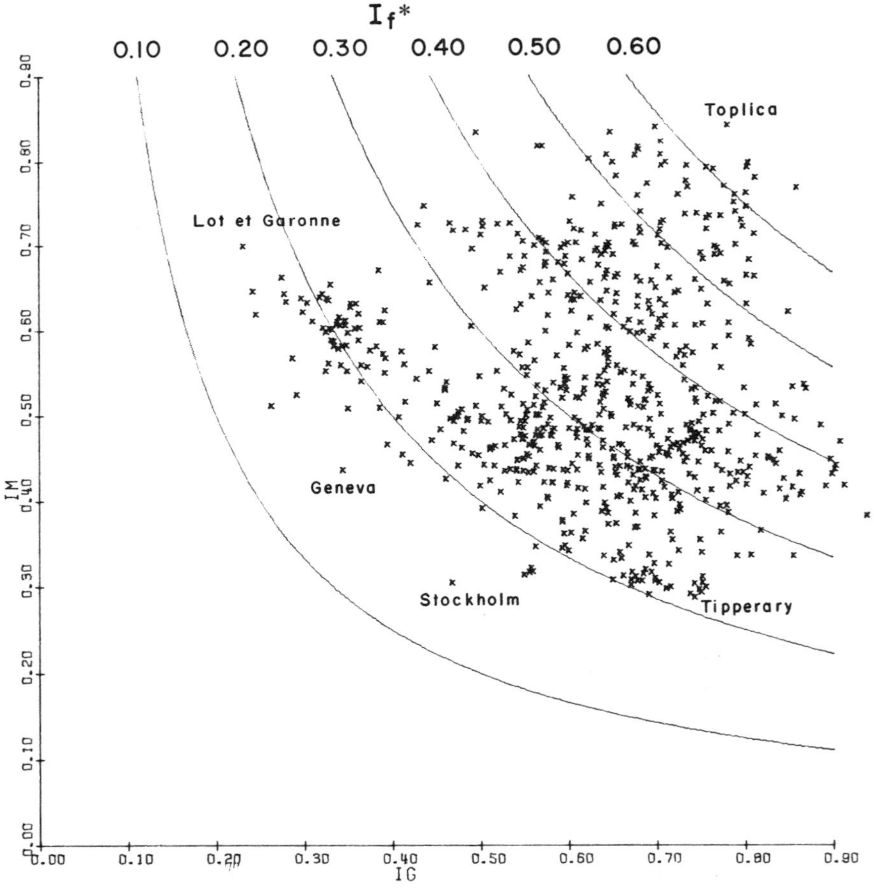

Figure 2.5. Position of provinces of Europe in 1900 in I_m, I_g plane.

and Toplica with the highest I_m. Also labeled is Stockholm, with very low I_f from a combination of minimal I_m and low I_g.

There are too many points in Figure 2.5 to allow individual labeling of all provinces or even to code provinces by country. To convey a sense of where the provinces within each country are located in the I_m, I_g plane, a further device—the use of ellipses to summarize the location of a number of points—is employed. Figure 2.6 shows I_m and I_g for the *départements* of France in 1900. Comparison of Figures 2.6 and 2.5 reveals that most of the points in the cluster to the left (low I_g) in Figure 2.5 are

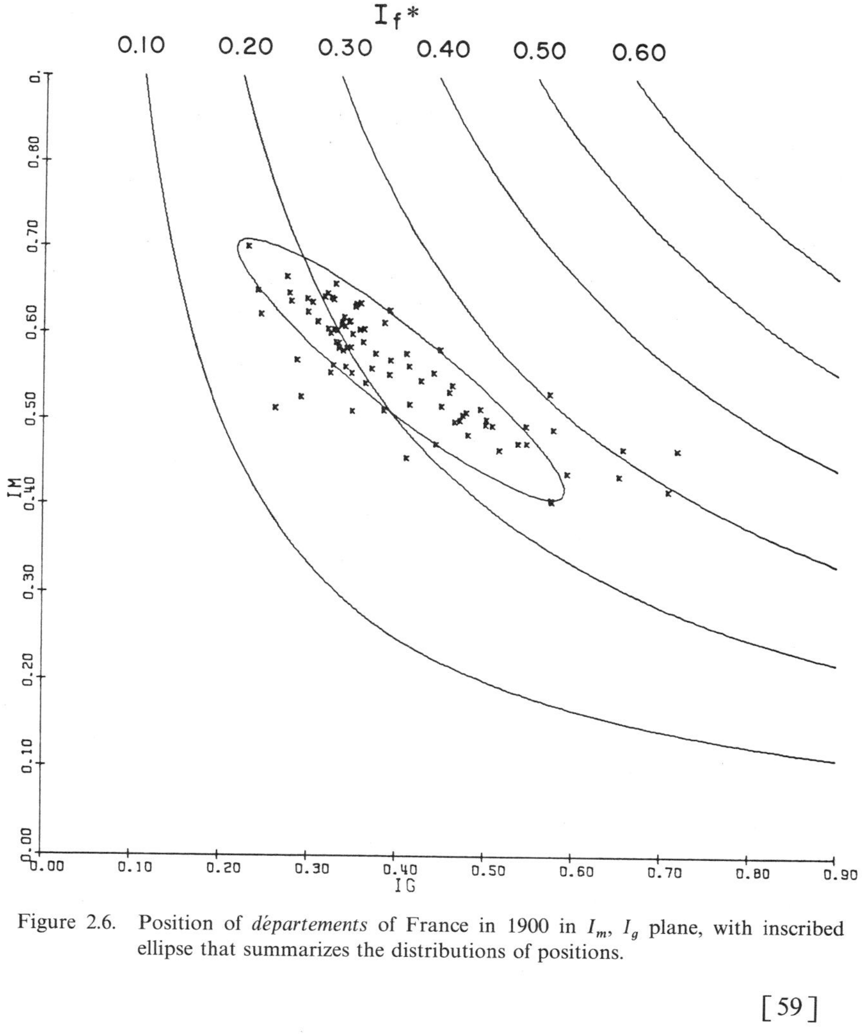

Figure 2.6. Position of *départements* of France in 1900 in I_m, I_g plane, with inscribed ellipse that summarizes the distributions of positions.

French *départements*, although Geneva, Stockholm, and a few other areas outside France also had very low I_g. An ellipse is inscribed in Figure 2.6 that summarizes the position of the eighty-seven *départements* of France in the I_m, I_g plane in 1900. The position, length, width, and orientation of the ellipse are all determined by the location of the eighty-seven *départements* in the plane. The ellipse includes 75 percent of the points whose position it summarizes.[1] From Figure 2.6, the reader can form an impression of how an ellipse represents a set of points.

In Figures 2.7 to 2.9 ellipses representing the location in the I_m, I_g plane of the provinces in most of the countries of Europe are shown for 1900, 1930, and 1960. Much information is condensed in these figures. In 1900 there appears a clumsy stack of ellipses, with Ireland (minimal I_m) on the bottom and the Balkan states (maximal I_m) on the top. The ellipse for France is semi-detached to the left (low I_g). For France and especially for Belgium, the ellipses are elongated in the I_g dimension, indicating strong interprovincial differences in I_g. In France and Germany the tilt of the ellipse indicates a negative relation between proportion married and marital fertility. Low marital fertility in Hungary (because of low plateaus of I_g) and in England and Wales (because the decline in I_g has begun) is evident in the leftward displacement of these two ellipses from the general stack. The predominantly vertical structure of the nest of ellipses shows the greater role of variation in I_m than variation in I_g in causing differences

[1] The calculation of the parameters of these ellipses is described in the following terms in the book on the fertility of Russia in which they were first used:

1. The points to be represented are divided into the top third, middle third, and bottom third with respect to position along the axis (I_m or I_g) in which the interquartile distance is the greatest.
2. The median value of I_m and the median value of I_g are found within the bottom set and the top set of points. The slope of the line connecting the I_m, I_g) doublets thus located is taken as the slope of the major axis of the ellipse; the minor axis is perpendicular to the major axis.
3. A preliminary length of each axis is calculated as the distance between the quartiles, when the points are arranged in order along each axis. The center of the ellipse is located at the median position along each axis.
4. The first three steps determine the location, direction of major axis, and shape of the ellipse. Its final size is fixed by multiplying both axes by a scale factor chosen so that the adjusted ellipse encompasses 75 percent of the points. (Coale, Anderson, and Härm, 1979)

The algorithm for calculating an ellipse of this sort was invented by Michael Stoto, who also wrote a FORTRAN program for calculating and plotting the ellipse from the listing of a set of I_m, I_g values.

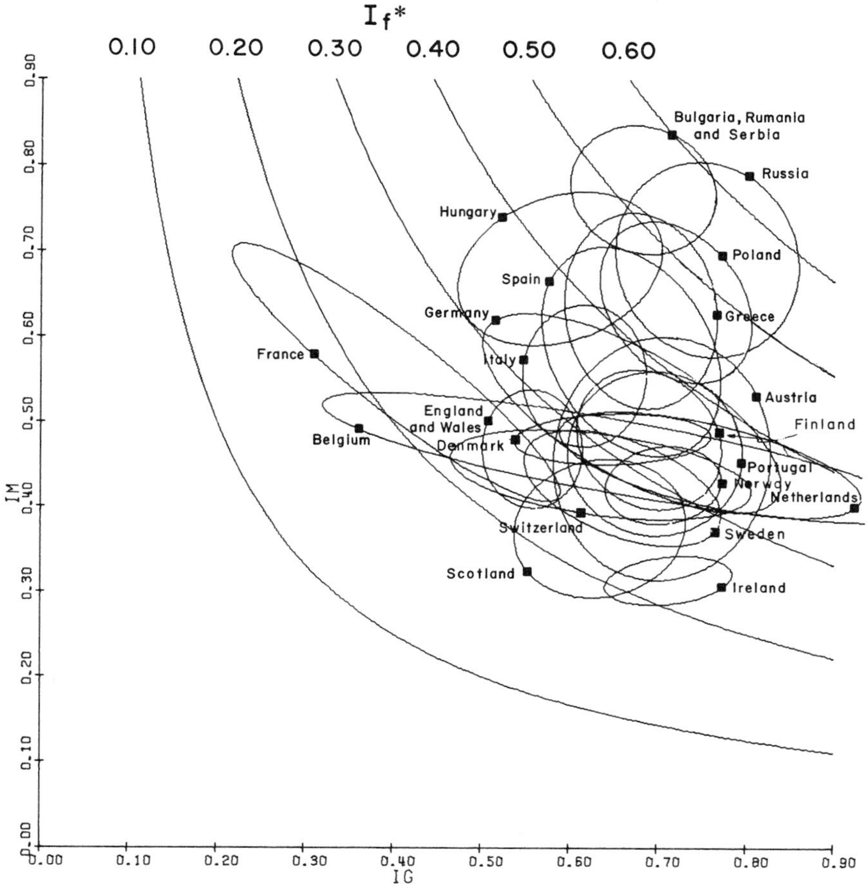

Figure 2.7. Ellipses summarizing the distribution of provinces of various countries of Europe in the I_m, I_g plane, 1900.

in overall fertility in 1900 among the provinces of Europe, except in the areas where the modern reduction had already progressed far.

In 1930 the ellipses have moved well to the left (lower I_g). The retardation of the decline in marital fertility and the continuation of low proportions married in Ireland are seen in the corner position of the Irish ellipse. The rightward extension of ellipses for Switzerland, Spain, Portugal, Italy, Russia, and the Balkans shows the delayed reduction in I_g in some provinces in these countries.

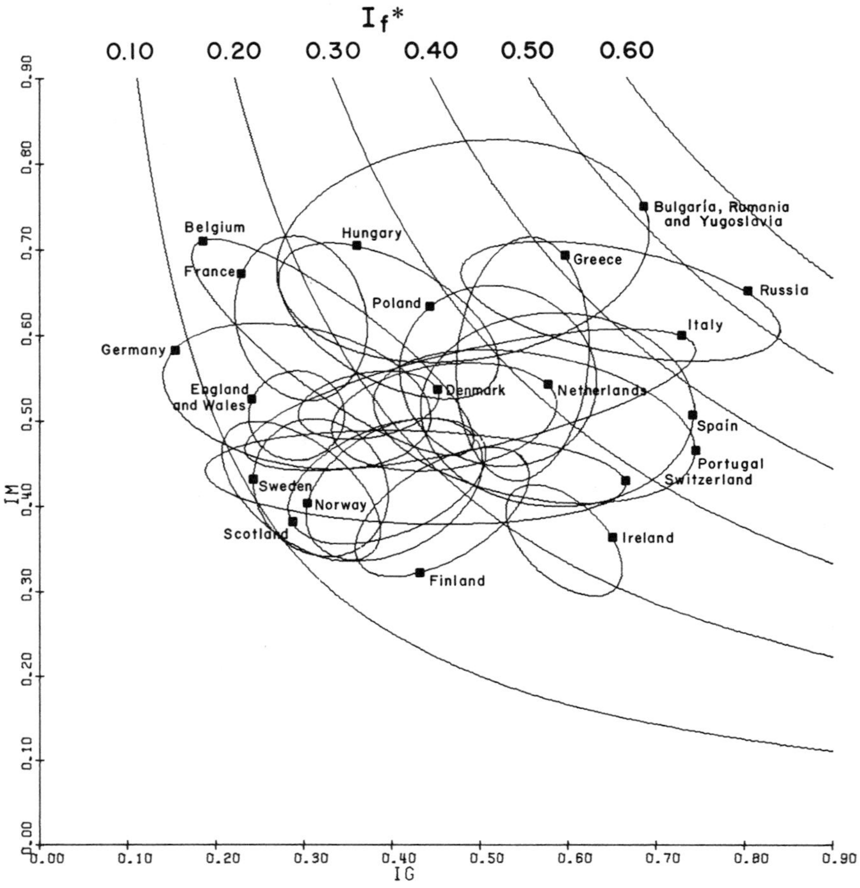

Figure 2.8. Ellipses summarizing the distribution of provinces of various countries of Europe in the I_m, I_g plane, 1930.

In 1960 most of the ellipses have shrunk (indicating more nearly uniform I_m's and I_g's within countries) and have come to center on an I_f* of about 0.200. Ireland is isolated at the highest levels of I_g and lowest I_m's; the Balkan area still has the highest proportion married; and Portugal, Italy, and the Balkans show a wide diversity in marital fertility in ellipses that have a large horizontal extension.

The same device of ellipses that summarize the distribution of provinces in the I_m, I_g plane provides a clear picture of the evolution of fertility

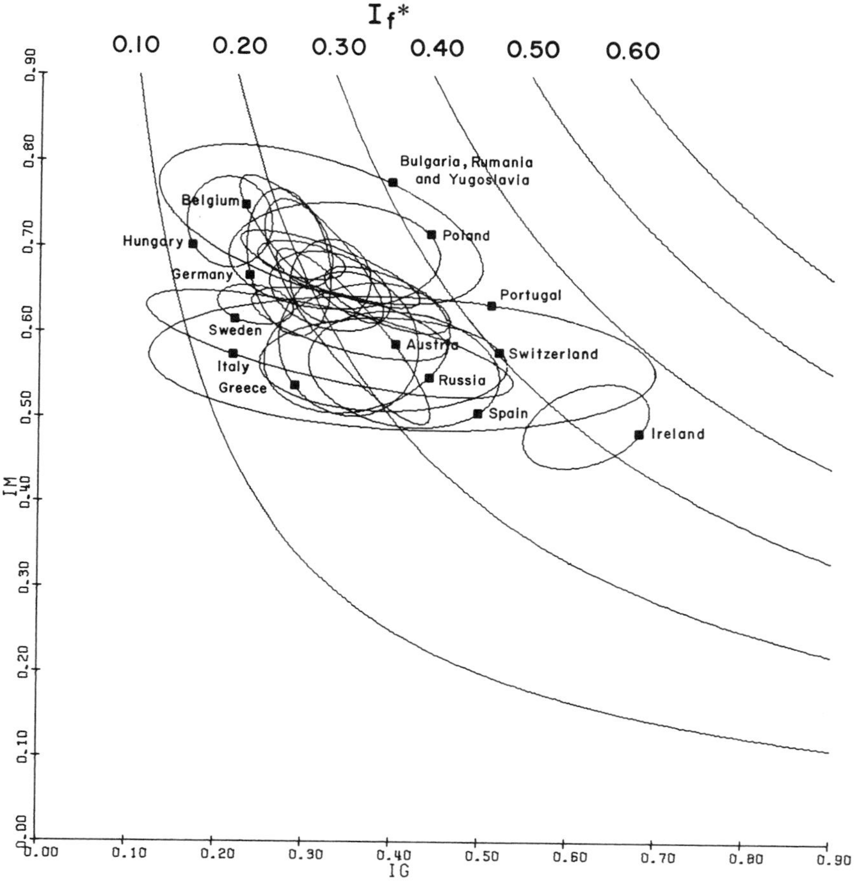

Figure 2.9. Ellipses summarizing the distribution of provinces of various countries of Europe in the I_m, I_g plane, 1960.

(including its changing interprovincial diversity) within a given country.

In Figures 2.10 to 2.28 ellipses summarizing the joint distribution of I_m, I_g, and I_f* at dates from late in the nineteenth century until about 1960 are shown for nineteen countries. These "marching ellipses" convey graphically the overall shift (movement of the center of the ellipse) in marital fertility and proportion married in each national population, and also the changing dispersion of I_m and I_g among the provinces in each country.

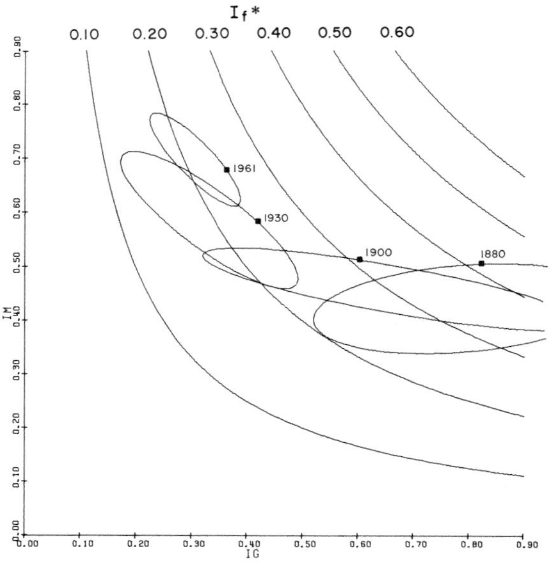

Figure 2.10. Succession of ellipses showing the distribution of the provinces of Belgium in the I_m, I_g plane at different dates.

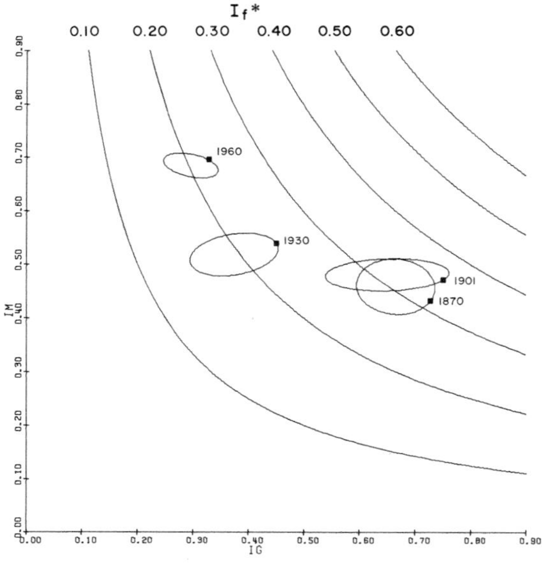

Figure 2.11. Succession of ellipses showing the distribution of the provinces of Denmark in the I_m, I_g plane at different dates.

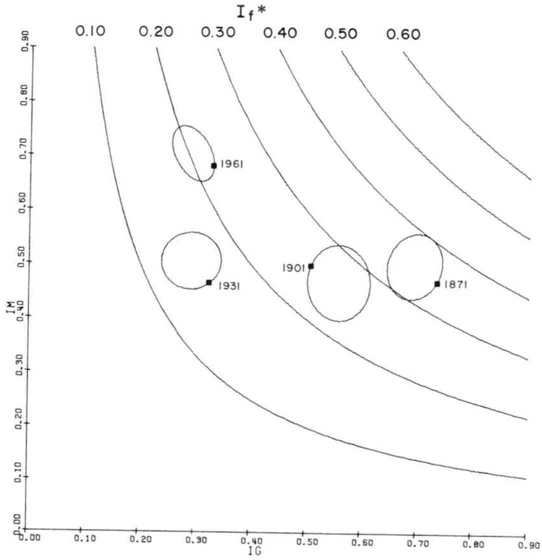

Figure 2.12. Succession of ellipses showing the distribution of the provinces of England and Wales in the I_m, I_g plane at different dates.

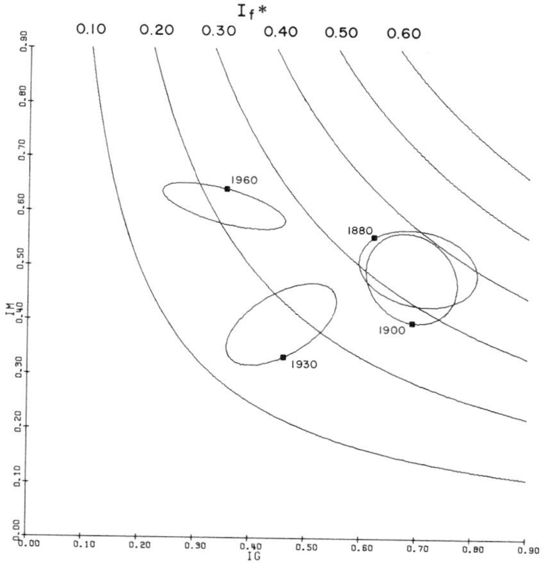

Figure 2.13. Succession of ellipses showing the distribution of the provinces of Finland in the I_m, I_g plane at different dates.

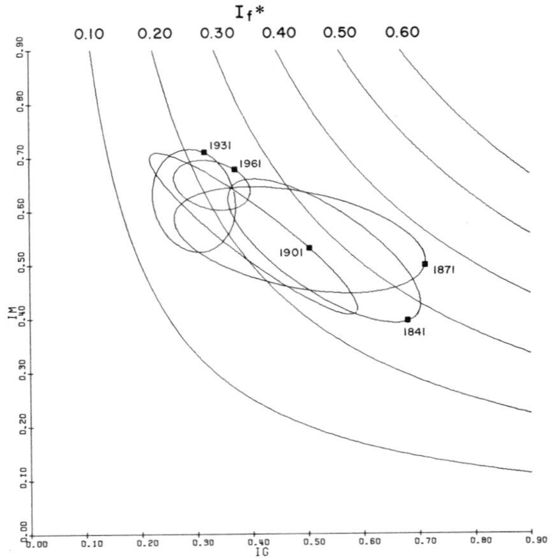

Figure 2.14. Succession of ellipses showing the distribution of the provinces of France in the I_m, I_g plane at different dates.

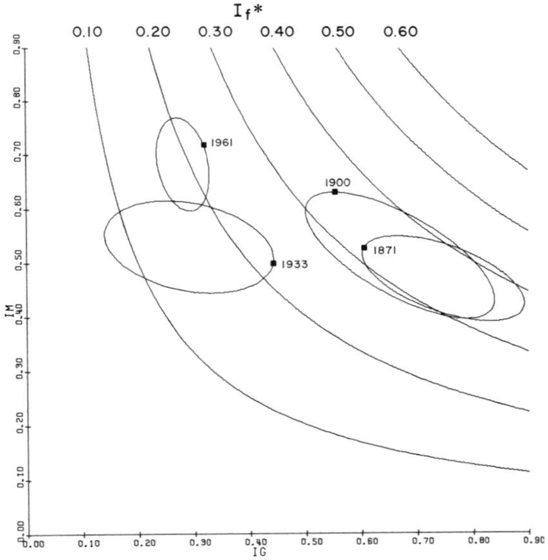

Figure 2.15. Succession of ellipses showing the distribution of the provinces of Germany in the I_m, I_g plane at different dates.

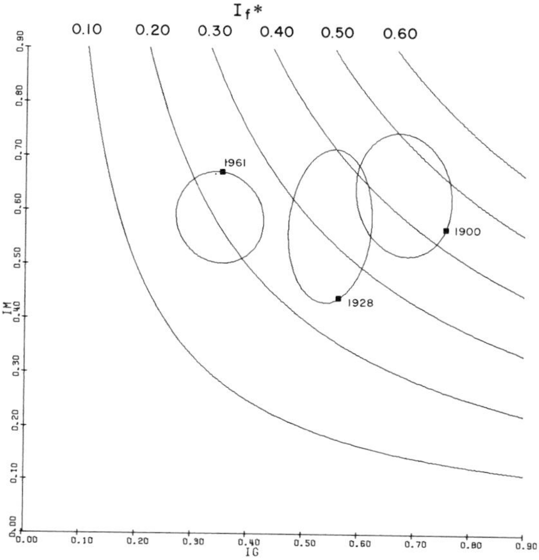

Figure 2.16. Succession of ellipses showing the distribution of the provinces of Greece in the I_m, I_g plane at different dates.

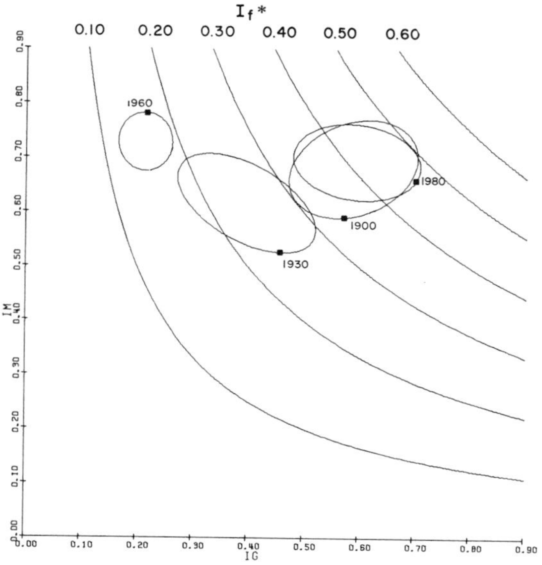

Figure 2.17. Succession of ellipses showing the distribution of the provinces of Hungary in the I_m, I_g plane at different dates.

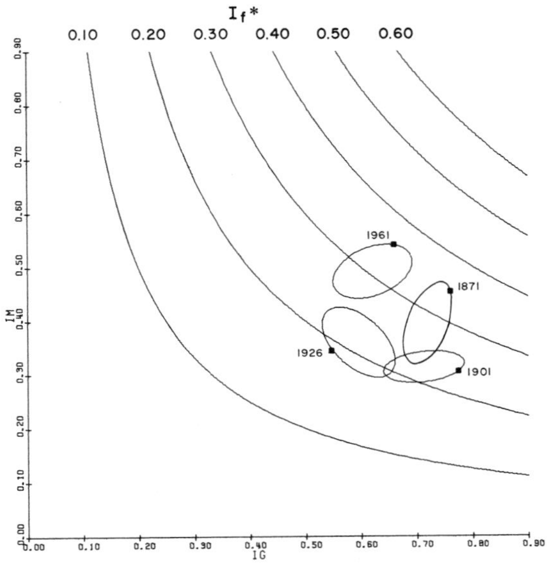

Figure 2.18. Succession of ellipses showing the distribution of the provinces of Ireland in the I_m, I_g plane at different dates.

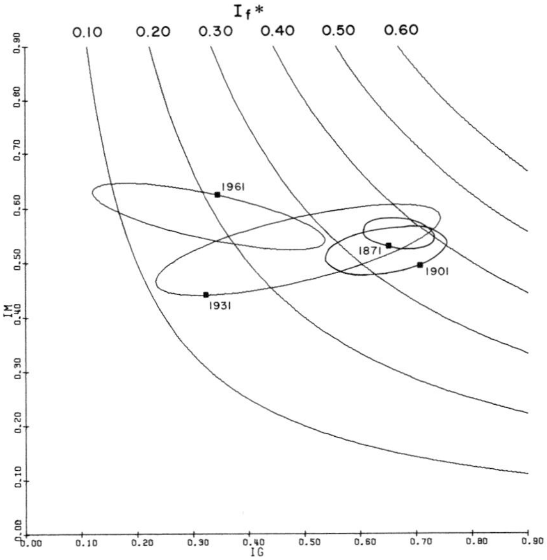

Figure 2.19. Succession of ellipses showing the distribution of the provinces of Italy in the I_m, I_g plane at different dates.

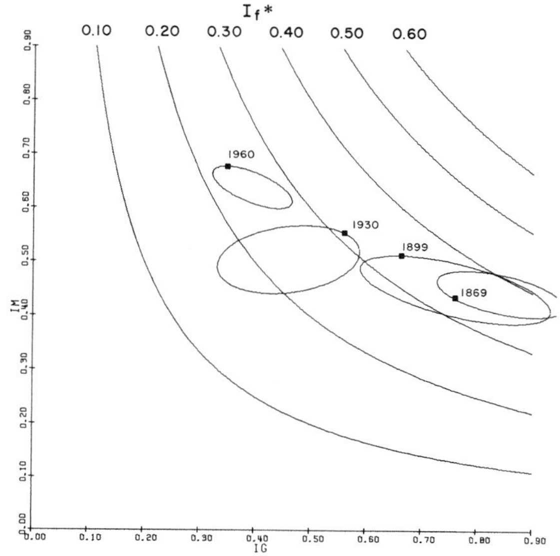

Figure 2.20. Succession of ellipses showing the distribution of the provinces of the Netherlands in the I_m, I_g plane at different dates.

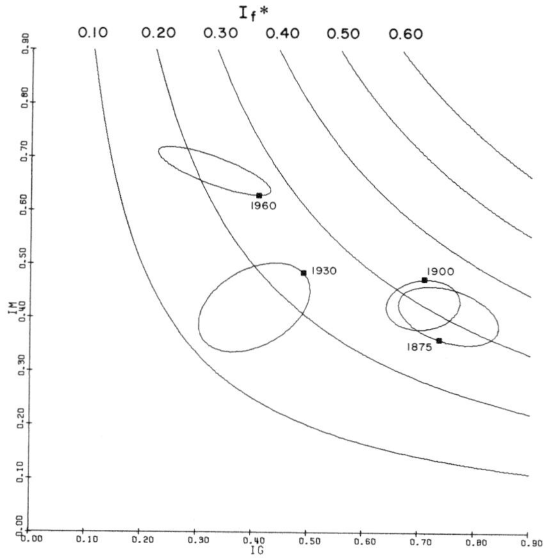

Figure 2.21. Succession of ellipses showing the distribution of the provinces of Norway in the I_m, I_g plane at different dates.

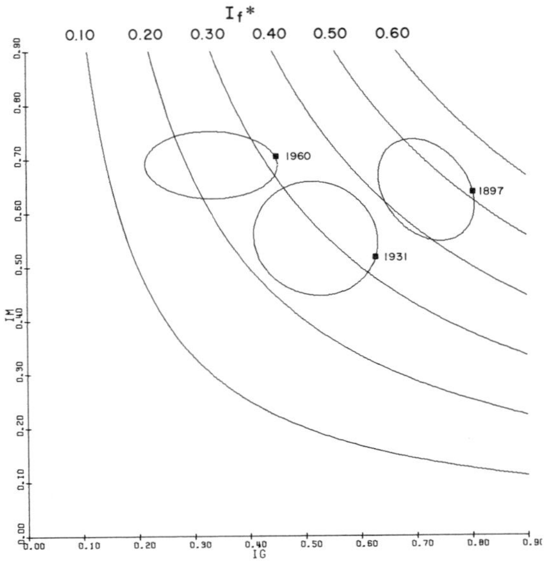

Figure 2.22. Succession of ellipses showing the distribution of the provinces of Poland in the I_m, I_g plane at different dates.

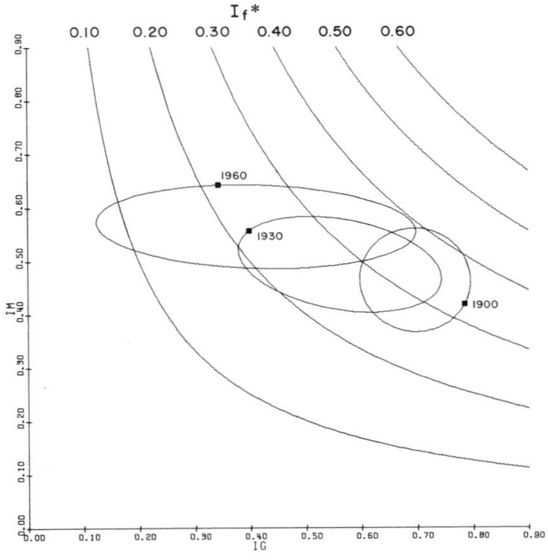

Figure 2.23. Succession of ellipses showing the distribution of the provinces of Portugal in the I_m, I_g plane at different dates.

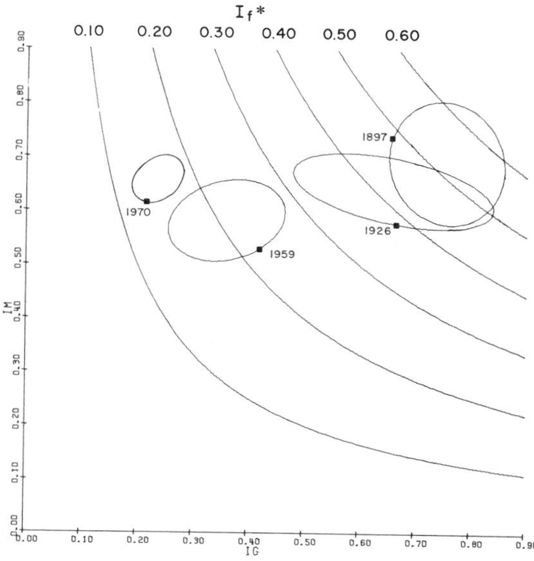

Figure 2.24. Succession of ellipses showing the distribution of the provinces of Russia in the I_m, I_g plane at different dates.

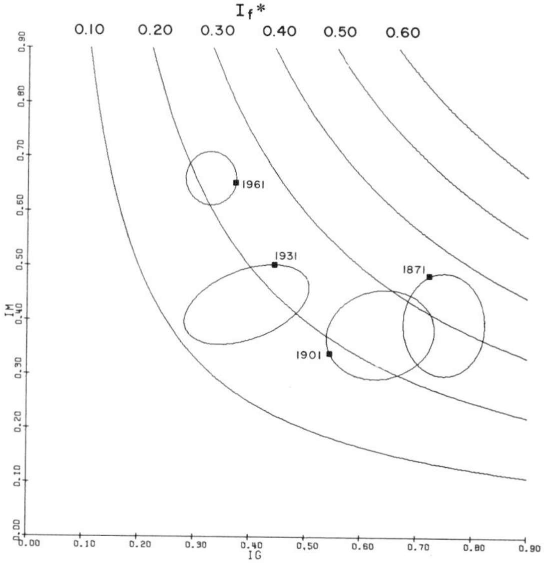

Figure 2.25. Succession of ellipses showing the distribution of the provinces of Scotland in the I_m, I_g plane at different dates.

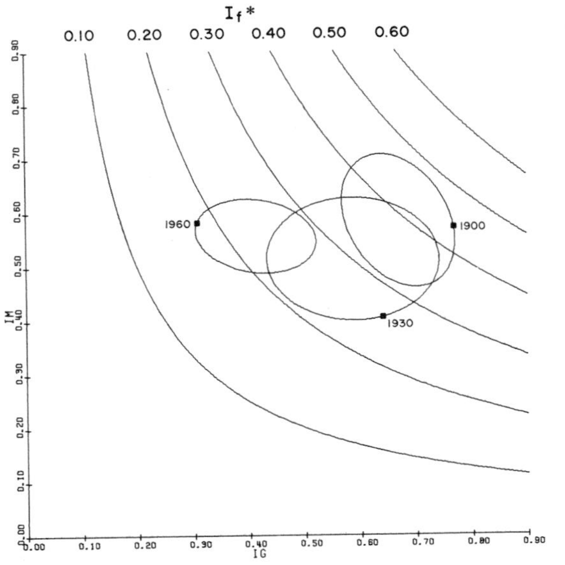

Figure 2.26. Succession of ellipses showing the distribution of the provinces of Spain in the I_m, I_g plane at different dates.

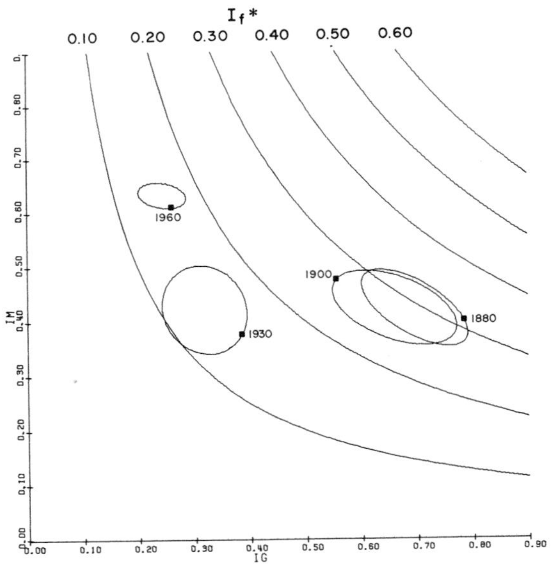

Figure 2.27. Succession of ellipses showing the distribution of the provinces of Sweden in the I_m, I_g plane at different dates.

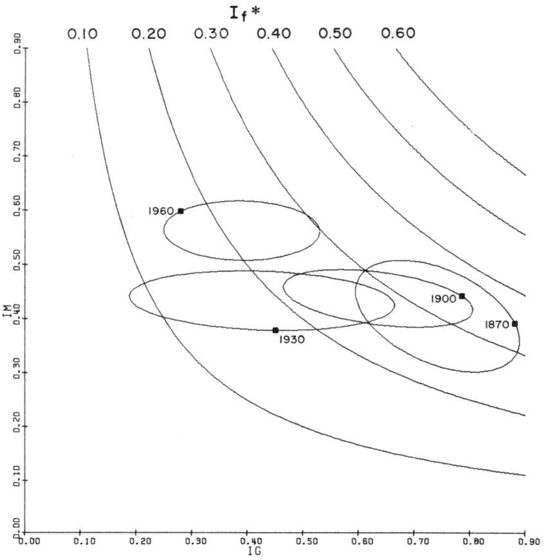

Figure 2.28. Succession of ellipses showing the distribution of the provinces of Switzerland in the I_m, I_g plane at different dates.

The contrast in the size of ellipses during the transition between Belgium and England and Wales is especially marked. There are very extended ellipses in Belgium in 1880 and 1900 (and still quite long in 1930) because of the big difference between the French-speaking and Flemish-speaking areas at the time the decline in I_g began. In England and Wales, a series of small ellipses shows how uniform the change both in marital fertility and proportion married was in the counties of England and Wales, although the change in both was quite large.

The Irish ellipses are confined to a relatively small segment of the plane; from 1871 to 1961, changes in I_m were more consequential than changes in I_g.

Illustrate Trajectories in the $I_m \cdot I_g$ *Plane*

The different trajectories of marital fertility and proportion married (in the provinces of Europe) have been listed in detailed tables, and are summarized in frequency distributions, maps, and ellipses. In conclusion, we show the trajectory in the $I_m \cdot I_g$ plane of the median I_m and the median I_g in European provinces in 1870, 1900, 1930, 1960, and 1970, and the trajectories of six populations at different dates, each population epitomizing a different feature of European fertility experience.

In Figure 2.29 the trajectory of combinations of I_m and I_g for the provinces of Europe is shown with the $I_m \cdot I_g$ combinations at selected dates for three populations that are maximally deviant in their experience from

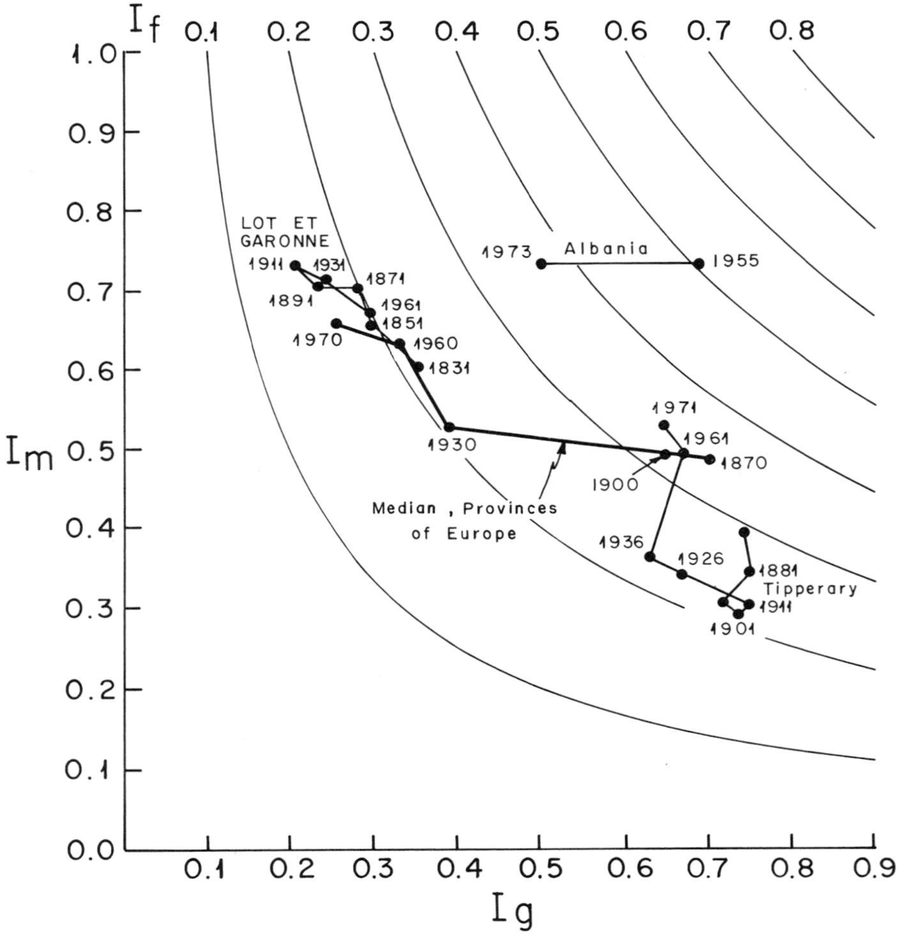

Figure 2.29. Trajectories of I_m, I_g for Europe and three exceptional populations.

the general European fertility history. One of the idiosyncratic populations is Lot-et-Garonne, a French *département* that had very low fertility very early. Note that in 1831, I_m and I_g in Lot-et-Garonne were close to the European average for 1960. By 1911, I_g in this *département* was as low as the lowest in a national population in 1960. Most of its transition to low marital fertility had occurred before 1831; after a leisurely evolution, it reached its lowest I_g and highest I_m in 1911; by 1961 it had returned to a point closely matching its I_m and I_g of 1851.

A second extreme time pattern of fertility change occurs in the Irish county of Tipperary, where, as in Lot-et-Garonne since 1831, the fertility changes have been relatively restricted.

I_m in Tipperary fell from an already low value in 1871 to an extremely low 0.289 in 1901, while I_g remained about constant. After 1911, I_m rose and I_g fell, but both changes were limited. By 1971, I_m was 80 percent higher than in 1901, and 30 percent higher than in 1871; the decline in I_g in the meantime was so modest that I_f was about 10 percent higher in 1971 than a century earlier. The third exceptional population is Albania. Data on age and marital status in Albania are available only from the single census, conducted in 1955; but subsequent information on births and data on number of marriages by age support the conclusion that I_m changed very little from 1955 to 1973, and that overall fertility and presumably marital fertility declined by about 20 percent. There was probably little decline before 1955; the registered birth rate recorded a peak in that year, with a preceding upward trend that was almost certainly the result of increased completeness of registration.

In Figure 2.30 the trajectory of $I_m \cdot I_g$ for the average of European provinces is compared with four populations that embody different patterns, each characteristic of the evolution to 1970 of fertility from different starting points. England and Wales show a horizontal movement to lower I_g (from an initial plateau just below the average plateau for Europe) and constant I_m, until after 1931, when I_m rises steeply; Turnhout, in Belgium, shows a rise in I_m from 1890 to 1970, except for postwar 1920, and a decline of I_g after 1900 from a very high plateau (about 0.90). Zala, in Hungary, shows a decline in I_g from a low plateau (less than 0.60) after 1900 and an I_m that is slightly higher in 1960 and 1970 than around 1900, after a dip in 1930. Bulgaria has a large drop in I_g from a presumed plateau in 1905 to a very low level in 1970, while maintaining a high I_m. These more representative European trajectories appear in 1970 in a common region in the $I_m \cdot I_g$ plane.

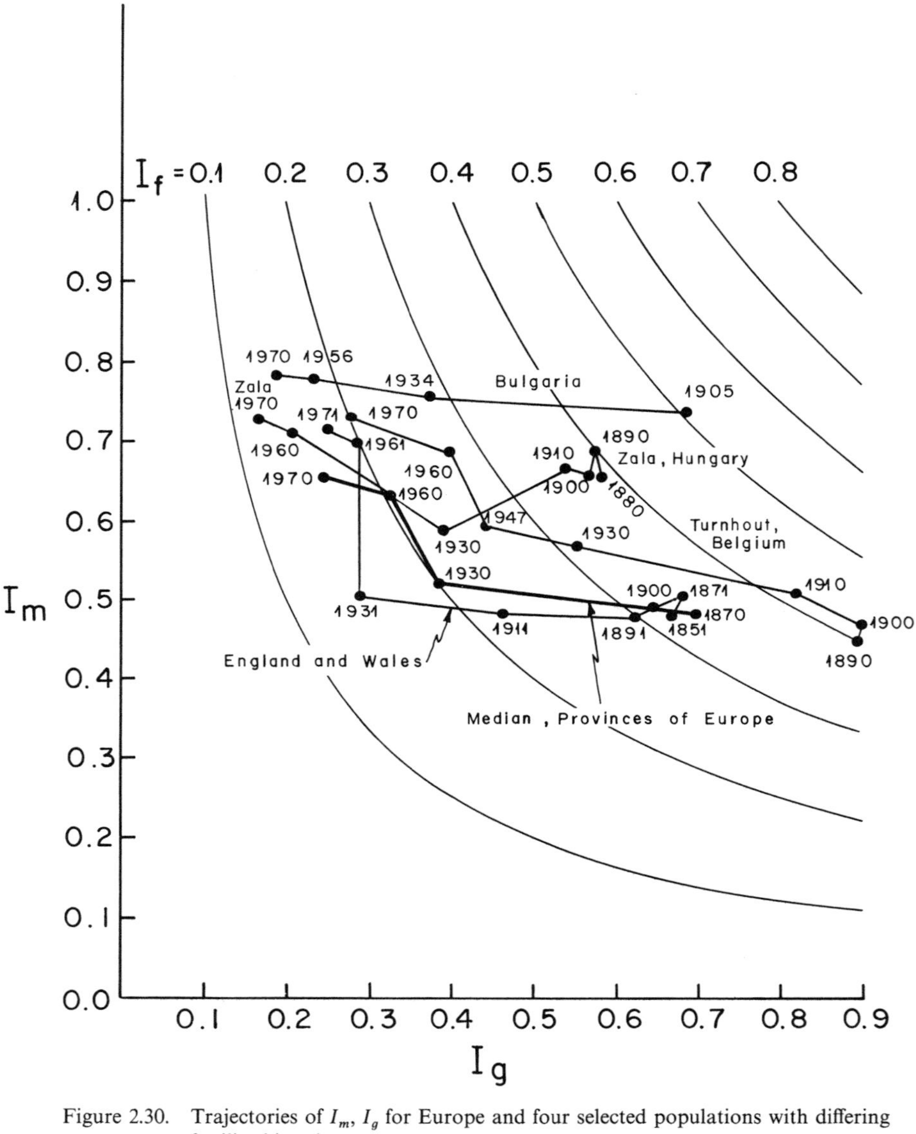

Figure 2.30. Trajectories of I_m, I_g for Europe and four selected populations with differing fertility histories.

Postscript: Recent Changes in Fertility in Europe

The four indexes (I_f, I_g, I_h, and I_m) covering most of the countries of Europe in 1960 and 1970 and a subset in 1980 are shown in Table 2.5. Values of I_m were calculated through the courtesy of the Statistics Division of the United Nations in making available a preliminary printout of tabulations of age and marital status for all populations with official data (from censuses or other sources) since 1972. These data appear in the Demographic Yearbook for 1982; the final tables may differ occasionally from the data employed in these calculations. The I_m's shown for 1980 pertain to a date in the late 1970s or early 1980s.

In countries for which there are data on age and marital status, the value of I_f could be calculated by the standard procedure utilizing the number of registered births for a period of one to three years, centered on the date of the marital status information. In other countries, an approximate value of I_f was obtained by multiplying the I_f for 1970 by the ratio TFR(80)/TFR(70). The total fertility rates were taken from Monnier (1981). Between 1960 and 1970 I_f fell in almost all countries; the median I_f declined by 15 percent. From 1970 to 1980, I_f declined again in all but four East European countries; the median I_f fell again by 16 percent. Thus 1960, which is the last date for which there are calculated fertility indexes by province in most of Europe, was not an end point for changes in fertility. From 1960 to 1970, I_g declined in all but Hungary and Ireland, whereas I_m rose in twelve countries, remained about the same in six, and declined in nine, leading to a very small increase in the median I_m.

From 1970 to 1980, I_m rose slightly in Czechoslovakia, France, Hungary, Poland, Portugal, and Spain; rose extensively in Ireland; and fell in the other thirteen countries in which the index for around 1980 can be calculated. The decrease was by 9 percent or more in England and Wales, Scotland, Norway, West Germany, Denmark, and Sweden. In Sweden, the decrease was by 23 percent, reducing I_m in Sweden to 0.461, only slightly above the Swedish I_m of 1930.

These large recent declines in I_m are part of a new pattern of nuptiality characterized by large increases in the proportion of couples cohabiting without being married, some of whom later became formally married, but at a later age than those who do not cohabit before marriage. There are also very large increases in the proportion of marriages dissolved by divorce at every duration of marriage and a reduction in remarriage rates

Table 2.5. Values of fertility indexes for countries of Europe: 1960, 1970, and 1980.

	I_f			I_g			I_h			I_m		
	1960	1970	1980	1960	1970	1980	1960	1970	1980	1960	1970	1980
Austria	.219	.180	.138	.330	.246	.197	.073	.061	.058	.588	.644	.575
Belgium	.208	.179	.145	.289	.247	.204	.015	.017	.014	.705	.703	.689
Bulgaria	.196	.162	.166	.236	.189	--	.057	.069	--	.776	.778	--
Czechoslovakia	.192	.182	.204	.254	.248	.271	.032	.032	.035	.722	.692	.716
Denmark	.199	.173	.129	.279	.234	--	.045	.058	--	.660	.651	.552
Finland	.215	.148	.138	.343	.239	.222	.022	.018	.039	.602	.587	.545
France	.222	.202	.165	.323	.305	.235	.037	.033	.048	.646	.622	.626
Germany	.202	.167	.122	.293	.222	--	.039	.034	--	.644	.704	.615
East Germany	.211	.169	.161	.267	.215	--	.071	.061	--	.713	.702	.659
West Germany	.200	.166	.111	.301	.224	.170	.032	.027	.025	.625	.704	.603
Greece	.191	.183	.172	.327	.276	--	.006	.006	--	.576	.656	--
Hungary	.158	.163	.158	.207	.217	.200	.032	.028	.042	.725	.713	.732
Ireland	.285	.294	.247	.548	.591	.425	.011	.014	.024	.513	.485	.557
Italy	.200	.193	.135	.338	.307	--	.011	.010	--	.578	.616	--
Luxembourg	.180	.181	.124	.260	.251	.184	.017	.020	.020	.670	.696	.634
Netherlands	.252	.195	.133	.394	.267	.203	.009	.015	.012	.630	.661	.632
Norway	.221	.212	.146	.322	.308	.215	.024	.034	.040	.660	.649	.586
Poland	.244	.186	.201	.335	.279	.285	.035	.024	.029	.696	.635	.674
Portugal	.255	.238	.226	.414	.370	.341	.057	.044	.042	.556	.596	.615
Roumania	.240	.152	.202	.346	.199	--	--	--	--	.694	.764	--
Spain	.228	.225	.217	.403	.376	.351	.012	.008	.012	.553	.589	.605
Sweden	.172	.167	.137	.241	.222	--	.052	.085	--	.626	.599	.461
Switzerland	.207	.172	.126	.350	.268	--	.019	.017	--	.570	.618	--
United Kingdom												
England and Wales	.214	.196	.154	.289	.251	.209	.041	.059	.049	.699	.715	.656
Scotland	.234	.201	.153	.341	.270	.221	.031	.048	.044	.656	.691	.615
Northern Ireland	.274	.277	.239	.475	.452	--	.015	.023	--	.586	.592	--
Yugoslavia	.241	.189	.168	.322	.248	--	.066	.052	--	.684	.697	--
European Russia	.207	.152	.145	.356	.233	--	--	--	--	.581	.656	--
Median	.214	.182	.153	.327	.251	--	.032	.028	--	.646	.656	--

of the divorced. Accompanying these changes are large increases in the proportion of births occurring to couples not formally married. Thus in Denmark, I_h rose from 0.058 to 0.117; the difference between the fertility of the married and the nonmarried was an I_g of 0.139 and an I_h of 0.117.

The validity of these indexes may be compromised by a different basis of classification of births by marital status in the registration of births, and the classification of the marital status of the parents in the census. Births are recorded as occurring to married persons only for those married according to a statutory definition, and the classification of those currently married at each age in the census may include those living in consensual unions. Whether or not this logically incorrect calculation occurs, the changes in nuptiality occurring in Europe, especially in Sweden and Denmark, make the analysis of fertility in terms of marital status and marital fertility obsolete.

The historic decline in fertility that was almost universal in the provinces of Europe from the late eighteenth century to 1960 (but primarily from 1870 to 1960) can be delineated, as we have attempted to do in terms of the reduction of childbearing by married couples as they undertake the use of contraception or resort to induced abortion—a delineation that includes allowance for differences and changes in nuptiality. Europe may be launched on a new fertility transition in which formal marriage becomes dramatically less relevant, and may again be a pioneer in a trend that later occurs in other parts of the world.

Appendix A: Tables of Indexes of Fertility and Proportion Married, Provinces of Europe, various dates

AUSTRIA

	I_f	I_g	I_h	I_m		I_f	I_g	I_h	I_m		I_f	I_g	I_h	I_m
Austria					Lower Austria					Upper Austria				
1880	.402	.677	.118	.509	1880	.354	.634	.158	.412	1880	.342	.683	.107	.408
1890	.392	.683	.113	.489	1890	.327	.598	.143	.405	1890	.340	.680	.109	.404
1900	.391	.670	.106	.506	1900	.302	.543	.124	.422	1900	.360	.687	.115	.428
1910	.345	.588	.085	.517	1910	.224	.397	.088	.440	1910	.321	.595	.109	.436
Salzburg					Styria					Carinthia				
1880	.318	.706	.134	.322	1880	.317	.643	.128	.367	1880	.340	.660	.218	.276
1890	.323	.688	.135	.341	1890	.324	.641	.130	.379	1890	.341	.639	.214	.298
1900	.335	.645	.141	.386	1900	.333	.641	.130	.398	1900	.360	.640	.219	.336
1910	.316	.558	.139	.422	1910	.319	.586	.128	.415	1910	.358	.604	.212	.371
Carniola					Trieste					Gorizia-Grad.				
1880	.376	.799	.055	.431	1880	.320	.605	.103	.432	1880	.416	.771	.021	.526
1890	.396	.824	.056	.443	1890	.296	.591	.084	.417	1890	.436	.787	.024	.540
1900	.396	.827	.046	.449	1900	.288	.549	.088	.435	1900	.413	.772	.029	.517
1910	.386	.812	.042	.456	1910	.283	.501	.095	.462	1910	.439	.798	.041	.524
Istria					Tyrol					Vorarlberg				
1880	.447	.756	.031	.573	1880	.305	.827	.025	.350	1880	.316	.896	.029	.330
1890	.447	.754	.030	.576	1890	.310	.814	.031	.356	1890	.286	.805	.023	.336
1900	.447	.773	.037	.557	1900	.322	.818	.036	.366	1900	.299	.773	.028	.364
1910	.440	.729	.047	.578	1910	.340	.787	.042	.399	1910	.288	.700	.029	.386
Bohemia					Moravia					Silesia				
1880	.398	.675	.102	.517	1880	.398	.703	.071	.518	1880	.379	.701	.068	.491
1890	.378	.640	.103	.512	1890	.378	.683	.078	.495	1890	.390	.739	.078	.472
1900	.365	.609	.098	.522	1900	.386	.685	.076	.510	1900	.426	.745	.087	.516
1910	.299	.492	.079	.532	1910	.341	.595	.067	.522	1910	.372	.636	.080	.523
Galicia					Bukovina					Dalmatia				
1880	.463	.659	.162	.605	1880	.459	.651	.149	.619	1880	.409	.720	.029	.550
1890	.454	.717	.137	.546	1890	.481	.668	.162	.630	1890	.451	.749	.039	.580
1900	.472	.732	.126	.571	1900	.453	.663	.132	.605	1900	.430	.711	.040	.582
1910	.433	.681	.089	.580	1910	.415	.619	.106	.602	1910	.446	.743	.041	.578
Austria					Vienna					Lower Austria				
1931	.124	.186	.073	.452	1931	.051	.086	.022	.459	1931	.152	.238	.069	.495
1960	.219	.330	.060	.588	1960	.139	.221	.030	.571	1960	.231	.335	.049	.636
Upper Austria					Salzburg					Styria				
1931	.183	.309	.086	.435	1931	.165	.274	.091	.403	1931	.168	.267	.097	.417
1960	.248	.373	.073	.584	1960	.240	.361	.097	.543	1960	.235	.341	.078	.596

Carinthia					Tyrol					Vorarlberg				
1931	.204	.312	.136	.383	1931	.180	.358	.064	.394	1931	.169	.393	.025	.391
1960	.254	.370	.091	.585	1960	.260	.428	.075	.525	1960	.269	.479	.045	.516

Burgenland				
1931	.229	.309	.107	.603
1960	.227	.317	.038	.677

ALBANIA

1955	.513	.700	.010	.728

BELGIUM

Belgium-Arrondissements				
1846	.306	.757	.036	.375
1856	.328	.827	.040	.366
1866	.359	.830	.041	.403
1880	.354	.749	.048	.435
1890	.320	.669	.050	.436
1900	.273	.534	.033	.479
1910	.244	.444	.032	.517
1920	.198	.370	.026	.501
1930	.177	.282	.018	.602
1947	.194	.304	.016	.617
1961	.208	.289	.015	.705
1970	.179	.247	.017	.703

Antwerp					Mechelen				
1880	.412	.810	.070	.463	1880	.426	.863	.056	.459
1890	.374	.713	.078	.466	1890	.406	.812	.066	.456
1900	.316	.584	.063	.485	1900	.388	.743	.060	.480
1910	.239	.419	.044	.519	1910	.331	.597	.042	.521
1920	.189	.330	.032	.527	1920	.254	.484	.034	.490
1930	.164	.251	.023	.618	1930	.216	.351	.019	.593
1947	.167	.254	.017	.631	1947	.224	.353	.011	.622
1961	.202	.276	.017	.715	1961	.210	.292	.008	.712
1970	.169	.228	.020	.714	1970	.174	.232	.011	.736

Turnhout					Brussels					Leuven				
1880	.410	.898	.028	.439	1880	.349	.673	.093	.442	1880	.397	.849	.054	.432
1890	.398	.899	.032	.422	1890	.290	.570	.079	.431	1890	.382	.806	.059	.433
1900	.443	.908	.033	.469	1900	.252	.470	.060	.467	1900	.376	.751	.051	.464
1910	.431	.823	.027	.507	1910	.180	.317	.040	.505	1910	.322	.610	.040	.495
1920	.334	.707	.027	.452	1920	.148	.263	.029	.509	1920	.260	.501	.034	.483
1930	.323	.567	.018	.556	1930	.128	.197	.024	.599	1930	.222	.369	.020	.580
1947	.268	.445	.009	.595	1947	.145	.221	.023	.617	1947	.215	.343	.010	.615
1961	.277	.400	.006	.688	1961	.173	.239	.023	.695	1961	.210	.293	.008	.709
1970	.206	.280	.008	.727	1970	.161	.226	.023	.678	1970	.181	.235	.038	.724
Bruges					Kortrijk					Diksmuide				
1880	.369	.899	.039	.383	1880	.374	.894	.032	.397	1880	.412	.967	.023	.412
1890	.355	.870	.041	.379	1890	.370	.853	.034	.410	1890	.377	.886	.026	.408
1900	.370	.839	.038	.414	1900	.385	.812	.034	.452	1900	.373	.844	.024	.426
1910	.325	.680	.028	.456	1910	.300	.618	.021	.467	1910	.323	.705	.018	.444
1920	.234	.496	.025	.444	1920	.227	.489	.018	.444	1920	.247	.590	.013	.406
1930	.210	.389	.015	.522	1930	.215	.352	.009	.600	1930	.244	.473	.008	.508
1947	.224	.383	.013	.571	1947	.215	.352	.008	.601	1947	.210	.382	.006	.542
1961	.221	.324	.009	.674	1961	.218	.310	.008	.695	1961	.225	.353	.004	.633
1970	.186	.257	.012	.709	1970	.186	.254	.010	.721	1970	.199	.285	.006	.693

BELGIUM-Arrondissements (continued)

	I_f	I_g	I_h	I_m
Veurne				
1880	.456	.921	.026	.481
1890	.384	.821	.025	.451
1900	.368	.752	.025	.472
1910	.309	.595	.017	.506
1920	.227	.453	.020	.478
1930	.211	.373	.009	.555
1947	.164	.274	.016	.575
1961	.208	.313	.007	.656
1970	.178	.256	.011	.680
Tielt				
1880	.339	.942	.017	.348
1890	.328	.903	.019	.349
1900	.373	.938	.022	.383
1910	.331	.797	.013	.405
1920	.239	.682	.012	.339
1930	.253	.552	.005	.453
1947	.191	.373	.002	.509
1961	.216	.356	.003	.603
1970	.185	.266	.005	.689
Oudenaarde				
1880	.340	.911	.034	.349
1890	.350	.880	.038	.371
1900	.369	.863	.031	.407
1910	.297	.658	.023	.431
1920	.211	.522	.019	.382
1930	.201	.379	.012	.515
1947	.202	.320	.006	.625
1961	.200	.298	.006	.665
1970	.172	.247	.004	.691
St. Niklaas				
1880	.426	1.030	.031	.395
1890	.408	.971	.039	.396
1900	.417	.902	.040	.437
1910	.359	.708	.030	.486
1920	.271	.540	.025	.477
1930	.213	.366	.013	.566
1947	.242	.388	.010	.614
1961	.211	.306	.007	.681
1970	.192	.260	.011	.728
Maaseik				
1880	.378	.930	.017	.395
1890	.369	.937	.019	.381
1900	.419	.950	.019	.429
1910	.443	.935	.012	.467
1920	.363	.857	.016	.413
1930	.391	.788	.008	.491
1947	.288	.573	.005	.498
1961	.313	.492	.004	.633
1970	.199	.286	.007	.689

	I_f	I_g	I_h	I_m
Ostend				
1880	.459	.899	.052	.481
1890	.450	.905	.055	.465
1900	.432	.800	.061	.502
1910	.360	.651	.048	.517
1920	.241	.477	.034	.468
1930	.201	.341	.020	.563
1947	.194	.305	.020	.611
1961	.216	.300	.015	.707
1970	.179	.241	.019	.721
Ypres				
1880	.390	.903	.038	.407
1890	.375	.853	.041	.411
1900	.374	.795	.035	.446
1910	.323	.659	.024	.471
1920	.231	.510	.019	.431
1930	.237	.412	.012	.563
1947	.210	.356	.006	.584
1961	.219	.322	.008	.671
1970	.202	.264	.014	.751
Eeklo				
1880	.376	.945	.031	.378
1890	.345	.875	.038	.367
1900	.359	.821	.040	.409
1910	.305	.629	.030	.459
1920	.219	.491	.022	.421
1930	.205	.358	.015	.555
1947	.205	.343	.007	.588
1961	.213	.310	.006	.681
1970	.187	.256	.012	.716
Dendermonde				
1880	.416	1.052	.028	.379
1890	.392	.950	.036	.389
1900	.417	.903	.033	.441
1910	.357	.712	.027	.482
1920	.262	.564	.025	.440
1930	.224	.390	.013	.560
1947	.221	.362	.008	.603
1961	.214	.316	.005	.671
1970	.188	.257	.011	.719
Tongeren				
1880	.363	.872	.024	.400
1890	.335	.850	.026	.376
1900	.355	.846	.025	.402
1910	.353	.788	.019	.434
1920	.306	.716	.018	.413
1930	.273	.537	.011	.499
1947	.227	.403	.007	.556
1961	.256	.384	.007	.661
1970	.201	.285	.009	.694

	I_f	I_g	I_h	I_m
Roeselare				
1880	.381	.987	.025	.370
1890	.374	.949	.026	.378
1900	.407	.945	.025	.415
1910	.341	.743	.018	.445
1920	.248	.586	.013	.410
1930	.238	.440	.006	.534
1947	.260	.460	.005	.561
1961	.216	.331	.003	.648
1970	.189	.262	.005	.717
Aalst				
1880	.355	.898	.025	.377
1890	.348	.854	.031	.385
1900	.385	.835	.028	.443
1910	.321	.661	.021	.469
1920	.240	.534	.019	.430
1930	.228	.397	.014	.559
1947	.235	.390	.007	.594
1961	.223	.314	.006	.704
1970	.183	.250	.008	.723
Ghent				
1880	.361	.846	.046	.394
1890	.340	.764	.045	.410
1900	.316	.651	.043	.449
1910	.239	.466	.030	.480
1920	.181	.364	.023	.464
1930	.168	.282	.015	.574
1947	.179	.284	.014	.611
1961	.201	.286	.013	.688
1970	.180	.246	.017	.713
Hasselt				
1880	.382	.868	.035	.418
1890	.347	.818	.037	.398
1900	.372	.865	.030	.410
1910	.369	.791	.025	.449
1920	.326	.695	.029	.446
1930	.322	.553	.020	.566
1947	.315	.538	.012	.576
1961	.274	.391	.009	.695
1970	.199	.276	.010	.709
Nivelles				
1880	.337	.707	.045	.441
1890	.322	.686	.043	.434
1900	.259	.486	.034	.497
1910	.210	.359	.025	.556
1920	.172	.296	.021	.549
1930	.151	.223	.013	.658
1947	.140	.204	.009	.674
1961	.183	.238	.015	.753
1970	.155	.210	.016	.715

Ath						Charleroi						Mons					
	1880	.275	.555	.051	.444		1880	.350	.596	.069	.534		1880	.297	.526	.063	.504
	1890	.238	.480	.048	.440		1890	.287	.478	.066	.536		1890	.276	.472	.064	.520
	1900	.223	.408	.038	.499		1900	.259	.390	.053	.611		1900	.243	.382	.048	.582
	1910	.185	.315	.028	.548		1910	.197	.277	.042	.660		1910	.202	.306	.035	.617
	1920	.176	.304	.025	.541		1920	.174	.253	.037	.633		1920	.191	.292	.033	.610
	1930	.157	.233	.016	.650		1930	.137	.180	.028	.717		1930	.157	.213	.021	.710
	1947	.174	.249	.016	.677		1947	.214	.261	.048	.777		1947	.196	.265	.025	.711
	1961	.196	.254	.020	.752		1961	.204	.252	.032	.781		1961	.203	.255	.026	.771
	1970	.179	.247	.021	.700		1970	.186	.249	.026	.719		1970	.181	.247	.020	.710
Soignies						Thuin						Tournai					
	1880	.316	.612	.050	.473		1880	.304	.539	.060	.510		1880	.283	.637	.045	.402
	1890	.277	.489	.058	.507		1890	.237	.405	.054	.523		1890	.256	.556	.043	.414
	1900	.243	.390	.045	.573		1900	.231	.347	.052	.607		1900	.242	.479	.038	.462
	1910	.207	.310	.037	.625		1910	.198	.283	.043	.645		1910	.188	.351	.025	.500
	1920	.175	.269	.033	.603		1920	.186	.283	.036	.606		1920	.174	.321	.027	.499
	1930	.154	.210	.021	.703		1930	.168	.228	.023	.706		1930	.211	.326	.022	.621
	1947	.213	.293	.026	.702		1947	.170	.235	.022	.694		1947	.194	.299	.019	.625
	1961	.209	.262	.027	.775		1961	.217	.277	.028	.761		1961	.198	.269	.019	.717
	1970	.189	.250	.020	.736		1970	.185	.251	.022	.712		1970	.189	.264	.023	.689
Huy						Liege						Verviers					
	1880	.308	.688	.032	.420		1880	.342	.688	.061	.448		1880	.313	.716	.026	.415
	1890	.261	.581	.034	.414		1890	.295	.577	.060	.454		1890	.264	.620	.023	.404
	1900	.240	.491	.031	.455		1900	.258	.470	.051	.494		1900	.219	.500	.017	.418
	1910	.191	.358	.022	.504		1910	.175	.299	.037	.526		1910	.187	.382	.017	.466
	1920	.163	.308	.023	.490		1920	.151	.262	.031	.518		1920	.177	.361	.014	.471
	1930	.146	.229	.014	.613		1930	.136	.197	.029	.639		1930	.172	.322	.007	.523
	1947	.172	.263	.016	.631		1947	.166	.244	.030	.636		1947	.187	.333	.014	.541
	1961	.198	.262	.018	.739		1961	.181	.235	.027	.741		1961	.215	.324	.011	.651
	1970	.170	.238	.020	.686		1970	.166	.228	.024	.697		1970	.193	.282	.017	.666
Waremme						Arlon						Bastogne					
	1880	.356	.805	.036	.417		1880	.339	.730	.019	.450		1880	.350	.854	.011	.402
	1890	.314	.722	.040	.402		1890	.308	.650	.017	.460		1890	.314	.804	.011	.381
	1900	.298	.637	.040	.433		1900	.289	.582	.017	.482		1900	.309	.756	.010	.401
	1910	.244	.464	.034	.490		1910	.274	.496	.018	.535		1910	.295	.651	.011	.443
	1920	.195	.379	.027	.477		1920	.205	.384	.020	.507		1920	.230	.536	.010	.419
	1930	.171	.282	.015	.586		1930	.193	.307	.012	.614		1930	.211	.469	.006	.442
	1947	.175	.270	.007	.637		1947	.164	.261	.010	.613		1947	.231	.446	.009	.508
	1961	.178	.236	.013	.741		1961	.226	.295	.013	.756		1961	.240	.385	.003	.621
	1970	.154	.213	.012	.704		1970	.177	.243	.013	.714		1970	.204	.327	.010	.611
Marche						Neufchateau						Virton					
	1880	.317	.751	.011	.414		1880	.317	.719	.014	.430		1880	.281	.643	.014	.424
	1890	.281	.702	.012	.391		1890	.288	.672	.014	.416		1890	.240	.548	.017	.419
	1900	.258	.643	.009	.392		1900	.288	.623	.015	.449		1900	.241	.541	.011	.435
	1910	.226	.523	.007	.425		1910	.257	.524	.011	.479		1910	.232	.457	.008	.498
	1920	.212	.482	.007	.431		1920	.226	.500	.010	.440		1920	.190	.407	.010	.454
	1930	.202	.402	.006	.495		1930	.207	.407	.007	.501		1930	.197	.345	.005	.565
	1947	.207	.382	.007	.533		1947	.217	.404	.005	.531		1947	.196	.338	.006	.571
	1961	.229	.349	.006	.649		1961	.236	.362	.006	.646		1961	.219	.300	.008	.724
	1970	.201	.305	.011	.645		1970	.197	.314	.007	.618		1970	.190	.279	.013	.665

BELGIUM-Arrondissements (continued)

	I_f	I_g	I_h	I_m
Dinant				
1880	.298	.663	.015	.437
1890	.257	.573	.015	.434
1900	.244	.511	.014	.462
1910	.212	.423	.009	.490
1920	.198	.423	.010	.455
1930	.188	.329	.006	.563
1947	.209	.351	.011	.582
1961	.227	.333	.010	.673
1970	.191	.290	.012	.644
Antwerp (Provinces)				
1846	.311	.786	.037	.365
1856	.318	.799	.041	.365
1866	.366	.861	.043	.395
1880	.415	.837	.059	.457
1890	.385	.761	.068	.457
1900	.349	.661	.058	.482
1910	.289	.508	.041	.518
1920	.222	.403	.032	.512
1930	.198	.313	.022	.604
1947	.197	.308	.014	.623
1961	.222	.308	.013	.709
1970	.178	.242	.013	.721
West Flanders				
1846	.295	.810	.022	.347
1856	.311	.897	.027	.326
1866	.372	.939	.027	.375
1880	.387	.918	.032	.400
1890	.373	.878	.035	.401
1900	.386	.838	.034	.437
1910	.324	.671	.024	.463
1920	.235	.518	.020	.432
1930	.222	.394	.011	.551
1947	.216	.367	.008	.579
1961	.215	.316	.008	.672
1970	.187	.260	.008	.710
Limburg				
1846	.290	.773	.018	.359
1856	.306	.839	.022	.347
1866	.335	.863	.025	.370
1880	.374	.881	.027	.406
1890	.350	.872	.029	.380
1900	.376	.877	.027	.411
1910	.380	.822	.020	.448
1920	.321	.722	.022	.427
1930	.320	.592	.015	.529
1947	.287	.508	.008	.558
1961	.281	.416	.006	.671
1970	.204	.287	.010	.700

	I_f	I_g	I_h	I_m
Namur				
1880	.308	.646	.032	.450
1890	.265	.571	.032	.432
1900	.254	.485	.028	.495
1910	.206	.356	.021	.552
1920	.182	.330	.022	.520
1930	.171	.263	.014	.632
1947	.199	.302	.018	.637
1961	.212	.284	.019	.729
1970	.188	.265	.019	.688
Brabant				
1846	.325	.737	.068	.384
1856	.329	.765	.069	.374
1866	.361	.784	.068	.408
1880	.356	.710	.079	.440
1890	.310	.626	.070	.431
1900	.273	.517	.056	.470
1910	.205	.365	.039	.509
1920	.168	.302	.029	.507
1930	.145	.226	.023	.602
1947	.158	.242	.020	.622
1961	.182	.250	.021	.703
1970	.161	.224	.020	.691
Hainaut				
1846	.319	.717	.041	.411
1856	.335	.722	.050	.424
1866	.354	.700	.053	.464
1880	.312	.577	.058	.489
1890	.269	.478	.058	.502
1900	.246	.394	.047	.572
1910	.198	.298	.036	.617
1920	.179	.277	.034	.597
1930	.155	.212	.023	.699
1947	.195	.270	.025	.694
1961	.207	.262	.027	.766
1970	.193	.259	.028	.715
Luxemburg				
1846	.334	.774	.014	.421
1856	.316	.768	.015	.400
1866	.320	.782	.015	.398
1880	.318	.733	.014	.424
1890	.284	.669	.014	.412
1900	.277	.625	.012	.432
1910	.256	.527	.011	.476
1920	.213	.462	.010	.449
1930	.203	.381	.007	.524
1947	.207	.373	.007	.547
1961	.233	.338	.008	.682
1970	.201	.302	.011	.653

	I_f	I_g	I_h	I_m
Philippeville				
1880	.255	.488	.019	.504
1890	.204	.393	.016	.499
1900	.210	.365	.013	.560
1910	.199	.318	.011	.611
1920	.200	.332	.014	.585
1930	.181	.289	.018	.601
1947	.207	.315	.012	.644
1961	.243	.329	.013	.729
1970	.196	.276	.017	.693
East Flanders				
1846	.296	.793	.033	.345
1856	.302	.923	.032	.303
1866	.356	.930	.031	.361
1880	.375	.921	.036	.384
1890	.359	.849	.039	.395
1900	.363	.780	.037	.439
1910	.295	.594	.027	.473
1920	.221	.467	.023	.446
1930	.199	.344	.014	.561
1947	.210	.345	.011	.694
1961	.208	.303	.010	.676
1970	.182	.257	.010	.696
Liege				
1846	.330	.765	.035	.404
1856	.330	.790	.036	.390
1866	.342	.791	.041	.401
1880	.311	.704	.046	.434
1890	.285	.598	.046	.433
1900	.250	.490	.039	.468
1910	.184	.333	.031	.509
1920	.161	.293	.027	.503
1930	.149	.232	.022	.605
1947	.177	.375	.022	.612
1961	.188	.252	.023	.720
1970	.171	.239	.020	.689
Namur				
1846	.325	.743	.027	.415
1856	.318	.745	.026	.405
1866	.331	.731	.027	.432
1880	.296	.618	.025	.457
1890	.252	.536	.025	.444
1900	.244	.469	.022	.497
1910	.216	.364	.018	.546
1920	.189	.350	.019	.520
1930	.178	.280	.011	.621
1947	.209	.325	.016	.625
1961	.224	.306	.016	.717
1970	.190	.271	.019	.679

BULGARIA

Bulgaria 1905	.514 .694 .009 .737	Bourgas 1905	.496 .705 .005 .701	Vratza 1905	.552 .724 .006 .760
Plovdiv 1905	.513 .704 .007 .726	Pleven 1905	.518 .707 .010 .729	Sofia 1905	.501 .701 .008 .711
Stara-Zagora 1905	.479 .637 .005 .749	Choumen 1905	.513 .654 .007 .782	Varna 1905	.542 .732 .007 .737
Vidin 1905	.521 .678 .026 .759	Kustendil 1905	.545 .756 .005 .719	Rousse 1905	.536 .689 .017 .773
Tirnovo 1905	.493 .680 .010 .721				
Bulgaria 1934	.292 .379 .030 .750	Bourgas 1934	.364 .465 .036 .765	Vratza 1934	.245 .306 .071 .740
Plovdiv 1934	.342 .454 .017 .743	Pleven 1934	.228 .297 .024 .748	Sofia 1934	.280 .407 .018 .674
Stara-Zagora 1934	.313 .383 .022 .806	Choumen 1934	.312 .381 .032 .801		
Bulgaria 1956	.196 .236 .057 .776	Blagoevgrad 1956	.274 .364 .061 .704	Bourgas 1956	.216 .257 .067 .787
Varna 1956	.201 .236 .065 .796	Vratza 1956	.158 .187 .049 .788	Kolarovgrad 1956	.215 .241 .083 .830
Pleven 1956	.167 .201 .049 .778	Plovdiv 1956	.201 .247 .055 .760	Rousse 1956	.212 .239 .081 .829
City Of Sofia 1956	.143 .188 .032 .709	Province Of Sofia 1956	.190 .245 .045 .725	Stara Zagora 1956	.185 .216 .061 .800
Tirnovo 1956	.155 .180 .052 .803	Haskovo 1956	.304 .349 .107 .814		

CZECHOSLOVAKIA

Czechoslovakia 1930	.205 .327 .050 .558	Bohemia 1930	.161 .255 .047 .546	Moravia-Silesia 1930	.192 .327 .041 .527
Slovakia 1930	.279 .421 .061 .606	Ruthenia 1930	.396 .568 .107 .627	Totczech-not Ruthenia 1930	.195 .314 .048 .555

CZECHOSLOVAKIA (continued)

	I_f	I_g	I_h	I_m		I_f	I_g	I_h	I_m		I_f	I_g	I_h	I_m
Czechoslovakia 1961	.192	.254	.032	.722	Prague 1961	.100	.142	.014	.674	Central Bohemia 1961	.155	.198	.028	.746
West Bohemia 1961	.183	.233	.033	.748	North Bohemia 1961	.167	.217	.029	.733	South Bohemia 1961	.184	.244	.030	.719
South Moravia 1961	.182	.247	.028	.705	East Bohemia 1961	.171	.224	.029	.731	North Moravia 1961	.196	.255	.034	.732
Central Slovakia 1961	.251	.331	.042	.725	West Slovakia 1961	.213	.283	.034	.716	East Slovakia 1961	.275	.365	.045	.720

DENMARK

	I_f	I_g	I_h	I_m		I_f	I_g	I_h	I_m		I_f	I_g	I_h	I_m
Denmark					Hovedstaden (Kbh. &F. B)					Copenhagen				
1852	.329	.671	.066	.436	1852	.277	.585	.095	.371	1852	.326	.661	.038	.462
1860	.339	.645	.068	.469	1860	.288	.559	.101	.407	1860	.324	.642	.041	.471
1870	.331	.656	.067	.447	1870	.263	.564	.090	.364	1870	.335	.697	.046	.443
1880	.348	.686	.064	.456	1880	.320	.636	.104	.405	1880	.315	.653	.038	.451
1890	.340	.658	.061	.468	1890	.295	.551	.104	.427	1890	.296	.612	.036	.452
1901	.315	.604	.059	.471	1901	.243	.450	.088	.429	1901	.308	.614	.041	.466
1911	.286	.522	.062	.486	1911	.210	.365	.090	.434	1911	.236	.460	.033	.475
1921	.236	.429	.051	.488	1921	.164	.291	.063	.444	1921	.227	.404	.035	.519
1930	.184	.327	.039	.505	1930	.126	.218	.045	.466	1930	.152	.260	.022	.545
1960	.199	.279	.045	.660	1960	.155	.236	.052	.564	1960	.203	.261	.049	.725
Frederiksborg Amt					Holbaek Amt					Soroe Amt				
1852	.334	.642	.060	.471	1852	.339	.640	.057	.483	1852	.352	.658	.059	.489
1860	.329	.615	.063	.483	1860	.317	.592	.056	.487	1860	.332	.629	.057	.481
1870	.309	.608	.059	.455	1870	.316	.588	.060	.486	1870	.318	.653	.053	.441
1880	.322	.629	.052	.467	1880	.335	.652	.051	.473	1880	.336	.668	.052	.461
1890	.326	.622	.049	.483	1890	.330	.641	.043	.481	1890	.339	.673	.047	.467
1901	.315	.577	.052	.501	1901	.326	.625	.039	.490	1901	.322	.620	.042	.484
1911	.282	.498	.052	.516	1911	.308	.551	.043	.522	1911	.293	.530	.045	.512
1921	.233	.415	.040	.516	1921	.259	.452	.041	.530	1921	.258	.451	.047	.523
1930	.175	.309	.028	.525	1930	.199	.346	.031	.532	1930	.199	.342	.039	.528
1960	.206	.278	.045	.693	1960	.205	.283	.043	.676	1960	.195	.266	.043	.685
Praestoe Amt					Bornholm Amt					Lolland-Falster				
1852	.346	.651	.049	.493	1852	.312	.653	.040	.443	1852	.345	.640	.062	.491
1860	.327	.623	.048	.485	1860	.314	.626	.043	.465	1860	.313	.598	.051	.479
1870	.327	.646	.049	.466	1870	.286	.619	.039	.426	1870	.312	.644	.056	.436
1880	.340	.650	.046	.487	1880	.319	.669	.041	.442	1880	.338	.653	.053	.475
1890	.324	.641	.038	.475	1890	.322	.637	.048	.465	1890	.326	.636	.050	.471
1901	.309	.598	.036	.486	1901	.306	.617	.046	.454	1901	.313	.606	.047	.475
1911	.293	.523	.040	.524	1911	.298	.552	.052	.490	1911	.311	.542	.058	.524
1921	.259	.449	.045	.530	1921	.254	.463	.041	.505	1921	.264	.444	.055	.538
1930	.196	.327	.034	.551	1930	.211	.370	.039	.519	1930	.200	.327	.040	.558
1960	.206	.268	.057	.707	1960	.229	.302	.060	.697	1960	.194	.257	.048	.697

Svendborg Amt					Odense Amt					Vejle Amt				
1852	.314	.669	.088	.389	1852	.310	.659	.085	.392	1852	.351	.728	.046	.447
1860	.326	.679	.085	.406	1860	.317	.635	.083	.424	1860	.377	.698	.051	.504
1870	.307	.633	.078	.413	1870	.311	.633	.078	.419	1870	.345	.665	.047	.481
1880	.311	.646	.065	.423	1880	.315	.661	.067	.419	1880	.341	.687	.040	.465
1890	.312	.637	.057	.440	1890	.313	.654	.056	.429	1890	.339	.665	.039	.479
1901	.300	.587	.048	.467	1901	.306	.606	.056	.455	1901	.311	.617	.035	.474
1911	.283	.525	.052	.489	1911	.288	.528	.065	.482	1911	.279	.539	.037	.481
1921	.241	.444	.046	.490	1921	.234	.424	.053	.490	1921	.232	.450	.028	.482
1930	.190	.337	.039	.507	1930	.183	.319	.044	.504	1930	.185	.351	.021	.495
1960	.212	.293	.040	.682	1960	.197	.268	.051	.676	1960	.205	.292	.035	.663

Aarhus Amt					Randers Amt					Aalborg Amt				
1852	.356	.724	.049	.455	1852	.342	.693	.066	.440	1852	.342	.691	.082	.427
1860	.373	.691	.051	.504	1860	.364	.663	.073	.494	1860	.377	.658	.095	.501
1870	.353	.692	.047	.475	1870	.355	.636	.075	.499	1870	.373	.687	.094	.471
1880	.370	.714	.045	.486	1880	.371	.714	.066	.471	1880	.399	.734	.094	.476
1890	.361	.684	.044	.495	1890	.372	.697	.061	.489	1890	.414	.733	.093	.502
1901	.323	.604	.046	.496	1901	.354	.648	.060	.500	1901	.385	.672	.084	.513
1911	.287	.513	.059	.502	1911	.331	.576	.063	.522	1911	.361	.614	.089	.518
1921	.246	.422	.067	.505	1921	.279	.486	.050	.526	1921	.289	.496	.070	.513
1930	.197	.328	.061	.507	1930	.224	.382	.039	.538	1930	.220	.368	.055	.528
1960	.188	.274	.039	.636	1960	.214	.292	.048	.681	1960	.207	.282	.053	.673

Hjoerring Amt					Thisted Amt					Viborg Amt				
1852	.365	.684	.100	.455	1852	.336	.760	.044	.408	1852	.342	.731	.060	.420
1860	.395	.673	.109	.508	1860	.380	.730	.053	.483	1860	.381	.715	.069	.484
1870	.398	.735	.106	.464	1870	.373	.721	.054	.478	1870	.385	.725	.072	.479
1880	.409	.764	.103	.463	1880	.383	.773	.043	.466	1880	.400	.755	.063	.487
1890	.414	.735	.090	.501	1890	.377	.745	.028	.486	1890	.398	.732	.050	.509
1901	.398	.736	.080	.486	1901	.367	.741	.027	.476	1901	.380	.731	.043	.490
1911	.376	.672	.077	.502	1911	.347	.672	.026	.497	1911	.352	.634	.045	.521
1921	.313	.568	.063	.495	1921	.288	.559	.023	.495	1921	.292	.538	.034	.512
1930	.246	.435	.050	.508	1930	.232	.440	.020	.505	1930	.229	.416	.028	.518
1960	.233	.313	.052	.694	1960	.229	.327	.029	.672	1960	.228	.321	.034	.678

Ringkoebing Amt					Ribe Amt					Haderslev Amt				
1852	.314	.729	.052	.388	1852	.314	.685	.024	.438	1852	--	--	--	--
1860	.357	.717	.060	.453	1860	.325	.637	.026	.490	1860	--	--	--	--
1870	.381	.747	.069	.460	1870	.362	.696	.030	.498	1870	--	--	--	--
1880	.399	.783	.057	.471	1880	.371	.721	.029	.494	1880	--	--	--	--
1890	.409	.795	.042	.487	1890	.378	.724	.027	.503	1890	--	--	--	--
1901	.404	.807	.035	.478	1901	.374	.697	.031	.515	1901	--	--	--	--
1911	.375	.730	.032	.492	1911	.329	.624	.032	.503	1911	--	--	--	--
1921	.303	.607	.025	.478	1921	.294	.559	.029	.500	1921	--	--	--	--
1930	.247	.483	.023	.487	1930	.227	.424	.022	.511	1930	.215	.411	.022	.496
1960	.242	.348	.029	.668	1960	.241	.329	.046	.689	1960	.226	.322	.025	.678

Aabenraa Soenderborg A					Toender Amt				
1852	--	--	--	--	1852	--	--	--	--
1860	--	--	--	--	1860	--	--	--	--
1870	--	--	--	--	1870	--	--	--	--
1880	--	--	--	--	1880	--	--	--	--
1890	--	--	--	--	1890	--	--	--	--
1901	--	--	--	--	1901	--	--	--	--
1911	--	--	--	--	1911	--	--	--	--
1921	--	--	--	--	1921	--	--	--	--
1930	.204	.356	.028	.536	1930	.233	.426	.021	.524
1960	.219	.307	.029	.685	1960	.237	.332	.025	.692

England And Wales	I_f	I_g	I_h	I_m
1851	.349	.675	.045	.483
1861	.359	.670	.046	.502
1871	.369	.686	.041	.509
1881	.355	.674	.034	.501
1891	.310	.621	.026	.477
1901	.273	.553	.021	.476
1911	.234	.467	.019	.479
1921	.193	.375	.018	.489
1931	.154	.292	.014	.503
1961	.214	.289	.041	.699

London	I_f	I_g	I_h	I_m
1851	.293	.603	.022	.467
1861	.304	.603	.025	.483
1871	.314	.619	.025	.486
1881	.303	.611	.022	.476
1891	.267	.559	.018	.459
1901	.234	.498	.016	.453
1911	.213	.460	.016	.444
1921	.180	.374	.015	.459
1931	.134	.282	.012	.450
1961	.204	.299	.061	.599

Surrey	I_f	I_g	I_h	I_m
1851	.332	.693	.037	.449
1861	.333	.682	.028	.466
1871	.316	.668	.023	.455
1881	.298	.676	.021	.424
1891	.252	.608	.017	.399
1901	.224	.523	.015	.411
1911	.180	.399	.013	.433
1921	.151	.326	.015	.439
1931	.124	.251	.010	.472
1961	.189	.273	.027	.658

Kent	I_f	I_g	I_h	I_m
1851	.352	.680	.041	.486
1861	.369	.683	.041	.510
1871	.366	.678	.036	.514
1881	.354	.684	.030	.495
1891	.299	.621	.022	.462
1901	.256	.528	.019	.465
1911	.215	.438	.018	.468
1921	.176	.338	.019	.492
1931	.153	.279	.014	.524
1961	.207	.277	.034	.711

Sussex	I_f	I_g	I_h	I_m
1851	.335	.675	.043	.462
1861	.327	.681	.039	.449
1871	.325	.681	.032	.451
1881	.305	.658	.028	.439
1891	.243	.584	.021	.394
1901	.207	.502	.018	.392
1911	.164	.393	.016	.393
1921	.137	.297	.018	.429
1931	.084	.175	.008	.454
1961	.194	.273	.035	.666

Hampshire	I_f	I_g	I_h	I_m
1851	.336	.647	.040	.487
1861	.347	.639	.039	.513
1871	.341	.635	.034	.512
1881	.331	.645	.028	.490
1891	.282	.588	.021	.459
1901	.245	.511	.018	.460
1911	.214	.428	.017	.479
1921	.186	.347	.021	.506
1931	.080	.145	.008	.528
1961	.220	.289	.046	.716

Berkshire	I_f	I_g	I_h	I_m
1851	.347	.675	.051	.475
1861	.356	.687	.048	.482
1871	.361	.689	.042	.493
1881	.358	.690	.035	.494
1891	.303	.627	.026	.460
1901	.254	.542	.021	.447
1911	.202	.421	.019	.452
1921	.174	.349	.020	.467
1931	.150	.292	.016	.485
1961	.235	.306	.046	.729

Middlesex	I_f	I_g	I_h	I_m
1851	.330	.707	.030	.444
1861	.341	.720	.027	.453
1871	.357	.738	.025	.466
1881	.354	.738	.023	.463
1891	.304	.650	.017	.453
1901	.271	.561	.015	.469
1911	.216	.436	.013	.480
1921	.167	.340	.013	.469
1931	.131	.249	.010	.506
1961	.193	.273	.038	.659

Hertfordshire	I_f	I_g	I_h	I_m
1851	.356	.667	.052	.495
1861	.365	.695	.049	.490
1871	.384	.750	.045	.481
1881	.364	.719	.038	.479
1891	.315	.663	.029	.453
1901	.259	.564	.019	.441
1911	.210	.455	.015	.444
1921	.161	.342	.015	.448
1931	.136	.268	.010	.486
1961	.212	.278	.037	.730

Buckinghamshire	I_f	I_g	I_h	I_m
1851	.366	.668	.052	.508
1861	.387	.692	.053	.522
1871	.384	.699	.044	.518
1881	.383	.719	.041	.504
1891	.334	.652	.030	.489
1901	.286	.566	.023	.484
1911	.231	.462	.019	.479
1921	.174	.344	.017	.479
1931	.147	.270	.012	.522
1961	.225	.291	.040	.735

Oxfordshire	I_f	I_g	I_h	I_m
1851	.353	.674	.052	.483
1861	.374	.703	.053	.493
1871	.375	.711	.047	.494
1881	.360	.710	.038	.478
1891	.305	.651	.027	.445
1901	.255	.573	.024	.422
1911	.203	.448	.021	.426
1921	.175	.368	.020	.445
1931	.151	.296	.014	.486
1961	.224	.313	.042	.672

Northamptonshire	I_f	I_g	I_h	I_m
1851	.371	.662	.049	.525
1861	.394	.672	.053	.552
1871	.403	.696	.048	.548
1881	.394	.695	.039	.541
1891	.340	.632	.028	.516
1901	.279	.524	.023	.511
1911	.206	.400	.019	.490
1921	.174	.338	.017	.489
1931	.103	.192	.010	.513
1961	.230	.294	.046	.739

Huntingdonshire				
1851	.379	.660	.042	.544
1861	.396	.700	.049	.533
1871	.381	.681	.046	.529
1881	.362	.676	.037	.509
1891	.316	.618	.033	.484
1901	.292	.581	.027	.476
1911	.265	.502	.029	.498
1921	.207	.379	.029	.509
1931	.177	.309	.020	.543
1961	.231	.290	.045	.760
Bedfordshire				
1851	.360	.673	.053	.495
1861	.350	.673	.052	.479
1871	.348	.680	.050	.472
1881	.339	.684	.043	.461
1891	.290	.622	.030	.440
1901	.248	.541	.022	.437
1911	.208	.430	.020	.459
1921	.175	.341	.020	.484
1931	.144	.267	.013	.514
1961	.245	.306	.055	.758
Cambridgeshire				
1851	.360	.652	.052	.514
1861	.380	.689	.056	.512
1871	.379	.674	.050	.527
1881	.365	.678	.041	.509
1891	.314	.616	.031	.485
1901	.274	.546	.026	.478
1911	.216	.423	.022	.483
1921	.184	.358	.023	.480
1931	.156	.288	.017	.514
1961	.207	.284	.033	.694
Essex				
1851	.377	.679	.051	.519
1861	.401	.694	.052	.543
1871	.418	.736	.042	.543
1881	.433	.761	.034	.548
1891	.390	.698	.025	.542
1901	.324	.583	.019	.539
1911	.251	.474	.015	.512
1921	.189	.368	.014	.495
1931	.149	.275	.010	.525
1961	.202	.267	.034	.721
Suffolk				
1851	.354	.648	.059	.500
1861	.376	.666	.062	.518
1871	.379	.681	.053	.519
1881	.374	.683	.045	.517
1891	.337	.652	.037	.487
1901	.293	.580	.031	.477
1911	.243	.480	.028	.474
1921	.202	.382	.026	.494
1931	.128	.239	.014	.507
1961	.213	.290	.038	.694
Norfolk				
1851	.337	.624	.068	.482
1861	.352	.632	.074	.498
1871	.357	.645	.067	.501
1881	.360	.657	.056	.505
1891	.324	.613	.043	.492
1901	.287	.563	.035	.477
1911	.233	.464	.030	.469
1921	.192	.368	.027	.483
1931	.164	.302	.019	.511
1961	.206	.270	.041	.721
Wiltshire				
1851	.350	.679	.047	.479
1861	.371	.694	.051	.499
1871	.373	.703	.042	.501
1881	.372	.704	.037	.503
1891	.322	.632	.027	.487
1901	.278	.549	.022	.486
1911	.234	.458	.020	.488
1921	.196	.372	.022	.495
1931	.164	.293	.015	.533
1961	.238	.309	.035	.740
Dorsetshire				
1851	.333	.685	.041	.453
1861	.348	.687	.042	.475
1871	.323	.638	.036	.477
1881	.333	.675	.031	.468
1891	.292	.617	.024	.451
1901	.252	.542	.018	.448
1911	.205	.437	.017	.446
1921	.176	.349	.020	.473
1931	.158	.292	.015	.514
1961	.213	.284	.038	.710
Devonshire				
1851	.313	.669	.031	.443
1861	.325	.664	.034	.461
1871	.324	.664	.034	.461
1881	.308	.663	.026	.444
1891	.268	.596	.020	.431
1901	.232	.504	.016	.442
1911	.191	.408	.016	.449
1921	.165	.329	.016	.475
1931	.143	.269	.014	.506
1961	.204	.278	.038	.693
Cornwall				
1851	.366	.761	.034	.456
1861	.367	.733	.042	.471
1871	.333	.690	.039	.452
1881	.311	.690	.034	.423
1891	.282	.628	.027	.425
1901	.242	.528	.021	.435
1911	.199	.431	.018	.438
1921	.168	.344	.017	.463
1931	.147	.277	.015	.502
1961	.198	.271	.031	.697
Somersetshire				
1851	.321	.685	.037	.438
1861	.334	.690	.036	.455
1871	.337	.694	.032	.460
1881	.331	.692	.027	.458
1891	.290	.637	.019	.440
1901	.255	.582	.016	.422
1911	.184	.418	.012	.425
1921	.161	.342	.014	.448
1931	.137	.276	.011	.478
1961	.209	.283	.033	.705
Gloucestershire				
1851	.305	.650	.033	.440
1861	.320	.668	.032	.454
1871	.327	.668	.031	.466
1881	.319	.666	.027	.457
1891	.281	.617	.020	.436
1901	.236	.516	.015	.441
1911	.211	.470	.015	.430
1921	.179	.373	.015	.459
1931	.148	.296	.011	.481
1961	.216	.292	.040	.699
Herefordshire				
1851	.330	.668	.061	.444
1861	.367	.692	.063	.483
1871	.350	.673	.052	.480
1881	.336	.677	.045	.459
1891	.303	.660	.038	.425
1901	.268	.598	.031	.418
1911	.221	.492	.026	.419
1921	.201	.414	.028	.448
1931	.172	.340	.022	.473
1961	.224	.311	.037	.685
Shropshire				
1851	.343	.690	.060	.448
1861	.369	.703	.067	.474
1871	.381	.715	.068	.484
1881	.356	.694	.055	.471
1891	.315	.672	.042	.435
1901	.305	.653	.034	.439
1911	.231	.485	.027	.446
1921	.213	.423	.027	.468
1931	.177	.334	.022	.497
1961	.213	.291	.031	.698
Staffordshire				
1851	.432	.727	.063	.556
1861	.446	.713	.065	.589
1871	.460	.746	.061	.584
1881	.436	.738	.048	.562
1891	.385	.693	.037	.531
1901	.338	.617	.028	.526
1911	.282	.516	.024	.524
1921	.237	.431	.020	.529
1931	.181	.331	.012	.528
1961	.210	.274	.035	.733

ENGLAND & WALES (continued)

	I_f	I_g	I_h	I_m		I_f	I_g	I_h	I_m		I_f	I_g	I_h	I_m
Worcestershire					Warwickshire					Leicestershire				
1851	.376	.723	.049	.484	1851	.373	.683	.043	.514	1851	.364	.679	.057	.493
1861	.368	.684	.047	.503	1861	.375	.660	.045	.536	1861	.378	.684	.061	.509
1871	.365	.698	.041	.493	1871	.383	.686	.038	.532	1871	.396	.711	.051	.523
1881	.342	.687	.032	.474	1881	.371	.682	.031	.523	1881	.387	.700	.040	.527
1891	.298	.641	.023	.443	1891	.319	.613	.024	.499	1891	.331	.640	.029	.495
1901	.261	.555	.017	.452	1901	.292	.564	.019	.501	1901	.275	.544	.021	.487
1911	.188	.399	.014	.453	1911	.277	.522	.018	.514	1911	.218	.437	.017	.478
1921	.193	.381	.016	.486	1921	.196	.375	.015	.504	1921	.179	.353	.016	.485
1931	.162	.305	.013	.510	1931	.153	.288	.011	.512	1931	.148	.273	.013	.519
1961	.201	.269	.031	.715	1961	.231	.306	.055	.701	1961	.219	.285	.044	.727
Rutlandshire					Lincolnshire					Nottinghamshire				
1851	.338	.688	.037	.464	1851	.366	.681	.053	.499	1851	.357	.665	.063	.488
1861	.368	.714	.051	.478	1861	.380	.695	.063	.502	1861	.371	.659	.070	.511
1871	.360	.695	.042	.487	1871	.383	.691	.056	.514	1871	.386	.678	.060	.528
1881	.359	.733	.033	.466	1881	.375	.674	.045	.524	1881	.393	.678	.051	.545
1891	.288	.638	.024	.430	1891	.324	.621	.036	.493	1891	.341	.625	.039	.515
1901	.257	.582	.020	.421	1901	.287	.551	.031	.494	1901	.312	.573	.032	.516
1911	.218	.458	.021	.450	1911	.255	.460	.032	.520	1911	.238	.427	.026	.528
1921	.189	.382	.024	.461	1921	.214	.372	.030	.540	1921	.203	.370	.025	.516
1931	.165	.313	.016	.503	1931	.134	.231	.018	.545	1931	.161	.288	.017	.530
1961	.231	.298	.024	.755	1961	.224	.289	.043	.738	1961	.220	.280	.052	.735
Derbyshire					Cheshire					Lancashire				
1851	.359	.667	.056	.495	1851	.340	.654	.055	.476	1851	.362	.697	.050	.482
1861	.373	.654	.060	.528	1861	.355	.673	.052	.486	1861	.358	.665	.048	.504
1871	.407	.693	.055	.551	1871	.360	.684	.043	.495	1871	.378	.699	.041	.513
1881	.397	.685	.043	.550	1881	.343	.674	.034	.483	1881	.359	.673	.033	.509
1891	.345	.629	.033	.523	1891	.297	.623	.025	.455	1891	.312	.620	.025	.482
1901	.301	.561	.026	.513	1901	.257	.549	.019	.449	1901	.270	.549	.019	.473
1911	.290	.532	.025	.522	1911	.220	.463	.016	.456	1911	.229	.460	.017	.478
1921	.218	.387	.021	.538	1921	.174	.352	.015	.472	1921	.185	.369	.016	.479
1931	.166	.291	.014	.549	1931	.142	.280	.011	.485	1931	.151	.297	.013	.486
1961	.203	.264	.033	.738	1961	.219	.295	.032	.713	1961	.233	.316	.047	.692
West Riding					East Riding					North Riding				
1851	.388	.701	.054	.514	1851	.332	.625	.046	.492	1851	.352	.700	.056	.458
1861	.387	.681	.056	.531	1861	.363	.655	.055	.513	1861	.375	.700	.067	.487
1871	.397	.684	.050	.547	1871	.374	.660	.055	.529	1871	.395	.726	.065	.499
1881	.361	.650	.039	.528	1881	.367	.646	.045	.537	1881	.396	.715	.049	.521
1891	.304	.583	.028	.496	1891	.326	.609	.036	.505	1891	.330	.636	.038	.489
1901	.277	.534	.025	.495	1901	.277	.534	.025	.495	1901	.277	.534	.025	.495
1911	.232	.438	.021	.506	1911	.251	.477	.028	.497	1911	.269	.520	.027	.489
1921	.193	.362	.020	.508	1921	.205	.383	.025	.503	1921	.219	.411	.025	.504
1931	.148	.273	.013	.520	1931	.181	.335	.020	.511	1931	.189	.343	.021	.521
1961	.215	.283	.043	.719	1961	.224	.300	.039	.709	1961	.244	.320	.048	.720

Durham				
1851	.431	.731	.057	.555
1861	.475	.757	.062	.593
1871	.499	.761	.061	.624
1881	.458	.735	.046	.598
1891	.401	.683	.035	.564
1901	.368	.641	.028	.553
1911	.324	.565	.027	.552
1921	.271	.466	.026	.557
1931	.212	.362	.019	.563
1961	.227	.304	.030	.720
Northumberland				
1851	.354	.695	.050	.471
1861	.380	.707	.058	.496
1871	.401	.729	.054	.515
1881	.384	.718	.043	.505
1891	.341	.662	.031	.490
1901	.315	.607	.025	.498
1911	.272	.519	.024	.502
1921	.232	.434	.022	.508
1931	.175	.332	.014	.507
1961	.217	.295	.033	.702
Cumberland				
1851	.341	.695	.065	.439
1861	.361	.708	.076	.452
1871	.383	.740	.072	.465
1881	.378	.721	.057	.485
1891	.330	.663	.045	.461
1901	.285	.604	.032	.443
1911	.244	.518	.027	.441
1921	.220	.439	.025	.472
1931	.182	.344	.023	.495
1961	.225	.304	.032	.711
Westmorland				
1851	.329	.722	.051	.415
1861	.347	.723	.061	.433
1871	.346	.696	.055	.454
1881	.326	.707	.041	.427
1891	.274	.633	.031	.403
1901	.221	.539	.022	.383
1911	.178	.438	.019	.381
1921	.146	.344	.016	.396
1931	.141	.302	.016	.436
1961	.199	.287	.029	.658
Monmouthshire				
1851	.387	.665	.043	.553
1861	.406	.686	.048	.561
1871	.424	.714	.043	.569
1881	.425	.732	.041	.556
1891	.392	.693	.029	.546
1901	.378	.664	.025	.553
1911	.323	.548	.021	.573
1921	.259	.430	.021	.583
1931	.193	.320	.016	.583
1961	.226	.296	.031	.735
South Wales				
1851	.366	.743	.048	.458
1861	.377	.715	.048	.492
1871	.399	.750	.045	.501
1881	.383	.726	.035	.503
1891	.361	.690	.027	.504
1901	.339	.636	.022	.516
1911	.297	.539	.021	.531
1921	.236	.428	.018	.531
1931	.131	.232	.011	.542
1961	.211	.287	.028	.707
North Wales				
1851	.351	.725	.050	.446
1861	.355	.711	.053	.459
1871	.368	.715	.053	.475
1881	.343	.670	.045	.479
1891	.308	.668	.035	.432
1901	.271	.583	.029	.437
1911	.231	.493	.027	.438
1921	.184	.389	.024	.439
1931	.163	.329	.019	.464
1961	.217	.312	.029	.664
England and Wales				
1961	.214	.289	.041	.699
Bedfordshire				
1961	.245	.306	.055	.758
Berkshire				
1961	.235	.306	.046	.729
Buckinghamshire				
1961	.225	.291	.040	.735
Cambridgeshire				
1961	.205	.290	.029	.672
Cheshire				
1961	.219	.295	.032	.713
Cornwall				
1961	.198	.271	.031	.697
Cumberland				
1961	.225	.304	.032	.711
Derbyshire				
1961	.203	.264	.033	.738
Devon				
1961	.204	.278	.038	.693
Dorset				
1961	.213	.284	.038	.710
Durham				
1961	.227	.304	.030	.720
Ely Isle				
1961	.213	.273	.042	.742
Essex				
1961	.202	.267	.034	.721
Gloucestershire				
1961	.216	.292	.040	.699
Hampshire				
1961	.221	.290	.047	.719
Herefordshire				
1961	.224	.311	.037	.685
Hertfordshire				
1961	.212	.278	.037	.730
Huntingdonshire				
1961	.231	.290	.045	.760
Kent				
1961	.207	.277	.034	.711
Lancashire				
1961	.233	.316	.047	.692
Leicestershire				
1961	.219	.285	.044	.727
Lincolnshire Kest.				
1961	.210	.280	.027	.726
Lincolnshire Linds				
1961	.234	.299	.050	.742

ENGLAND & WALES (continued)

	I_f	I_g	I_h	I_m		I_f	I_g	I_h	I_m		I_f	I_g	I_h	I_m
Lincolnshire Holl. 1961	.195	.254	.031	.733	London A. C. 1961	.204	.299	.061	.599	Middlesex 1961	.193	.273	.038	.659
Norfolk 1961	.206	.270	.041	.721	Northamptonshire 1961	.227	.294	.044	.734	Northumberland 1961	.217	.295	.033	.702
Nottinghamshire 1961	.220	.280	.052	.735	Oxfordshire 1961	.224	.313	.042	.672	Peterborough Soke 1961	.242	.298	.056	.768
Rutland 1961	.231	.298	.024	.755	Shropshire 1961	.213	.291	.031	.698	Somerset 1961	.209	.283	.033	.705
Staffordshire 1961	.210	.274	.035	.733	Suffolk East 1961	.213	.294	.041	.681	Suffolk West 1961	.213	.281	.030	.729
Surrey 1961	.189	.273	.027	.658	Sussex East 1961	.188	.269	.038	.648	Sussex West 1961	.203	.279	.030	.695
Warwickshire 1961	.231	.306	.055	.701	Westmorland 1961	.199	.287	.029	.658	Wight Isl. 1961	.199	.274	.043	.675
Wiltshire 1961	.238	.309	.035	.740	Worcestershire 1961	.201	.269	.031	.715	Yorkshire E. Riding 1961	.224	.300	.039	.709
Yorkshire No. Riding 1961	.244	.320	.048	.720	Yorkshire W. Riding 1961	.215	.283	.043	.719	Wales Anglesey 1961	.237	.334	.032	.679
Breconshire 1961	.200	.274	.019	.708	Caernarvonshire 1961	.198	.307	.029	.609	Cardiganshire 1961	.187	.290	.024	.614
Carmarthenshire 1961	.183	.252	.020	.701	Denbighshire 1961	.209	.298	.026	.670	Flintshire 1961	.233	.324	.032	.689
Glamorgan 1961	.214	.289	.029	.712	Merionethshire 1961	.220	.319	.031	.656	Monmouthshire 1961	.226	.296	.031	.735
Montgomeryshire 1961	.214	.302	.029	.679	Pembrokeshire 1961	.236	.319	.037	.705	Radnorshire 1961	.229	.326	.026	.677

FINLAND

Finland				
1865	.364	--	--	--
1875	.381	--	--	--
1880	.375	.698	.054	.499
1890	.369	.689	.048	.501
1900	.353	.685	.044	.482
1910	.320	.647	.043	.459
1920	.240	.548	.034	.400
1930	.200	.455	.027	.404
1940	.190	.387	.025	.456
1950	.259	.433	.031	.567
1960	.215	.343	.022	.602

Uudenmaa				
1865	.361	--	--	--
1875	.351	--	--	--
1880	.326	.671	.061	.434
1890	.344	.698	.059	.446
1900	.323	.673	.059	.430
1910	.267	.575	.057	.405
1920	.155	.372	.028	.370
1930	.127	.282	.022	.404
1940	.130	.266	.021	.446
1950	.183	.314	.026	.545
1960	.183	.295	.024	.586

Turi-Dori				
1865	.365	--	--	--
1875	.377	--	--	--
1880	.368	.722	.060	.466
1890	.364	.732	.050	.461
1900	.351	.711	.050	.455
1910	.299	.635	.048	.428
1920	.221	.530	.042	.367
1930	.186	.431	.033	.383
1940	.174	.354	.028	.449
1950	.224	.370	.032	.569
1960	.191	.299	.021	.610

Ahvenanmaa				
1865	--	--	--	--
1875	--	--	--	--
1880	--	--	--	--
1890	--	--	--	--
1900	--	--	--	--
1910	--	--	--	--
1920	.174	.489	.028	.317
1930	.134	.385	.016	.321
1940	.159	.322	.026	.450
1950	.199	.306	.028	.613
1960	.197	.296	.021	.639

Hame				
1865	.381	--	--	--
1875	.397	--	--	--
1880	.394	.694	.082	.509
1890	.394	.706	.071	.509
1900	.379	.716	.065	.482
1910	.325	.643	.061	.454
1920	.222	.516	.047	.372
1930	.178	.406	.034	.388
1940	.163	.331	.028	.446
1950	.220	.369	.031	.558
1960	.195	.310	.023	.598

Viipuri (Kymen)				
1865	.342	--	--	--
1875	.343	--	--	--
1880	.347	.601	.027	.558
1890	.360	.604	.029	.575
1900	.373	.622	.028	.581
1910	.349	.616	.032	.543
1920	.253	.520	.029	.456
1930	.203	.441	.021	.433
1940	.179	.356	.021	.471
1950	.232	.382	.023	.583
1960	.203	.312	.017	.631

Mikkeli				
1865	.321	--	--	--
1875	.328	--	--	--
1880	.328	.597	.059	.499
1890	.339	.611	.058	.508
1900	.345	.612	.055	.521
1910	.332	.624	.050	.492
1920	.266	.556	.044	.433
1930	.227	.494	.032	.421
1940	.223	.437	.029	.474
1950	.286	.478	.029	.573
1960	.230	.375	.018	.593

Kuopio				
1865	.368	--	--	--
1875	.395	--	--	--
1880	.382	.689	.049	.521
1890	.382	.695	.043	.520
1900	.373	.705	.039	.502
1910	.383	.719	.039	.506
1920	.306	.649	.033	.442
1930	.253	.554	.028	.428
1940	.242	.476	.027	.479
1950	.317	.521	.029	.584
1960	.249	.403	.018	.600

Vaasa				
1865	.404	--	--	--
1875	.438	--	--	--
1880	.433	.788	.047	.520
1890	.375	.714	.037	.500
1900	.328	.692	.031	.449
1910	.289	.643	.029	.424
1920	.242	.605	.025	.374
1930	.205	.513	.022	.373
1940	.203	.440	.021	.436
1950	.272	.459	.027	.567
1960	.214	.343	.019	.602

Oulu				
1865	.350	--	--	--
1875	.389	--	--	--
1880	.389	.790	.054	.455
1890	.385	.757	.048	.475
1900	.360	.768	.037	.441
1910	.358	.760	.038	.443
1920	.315	.704	.037	.417
1930	.284	.621	.037	.423
1940	.280	.580	.030	.454
1950	.357	.598	.035	.573
1960	.285	.462	.023	.595

Lapin				
1865	--	--	--	--
1875	--	--	--	--
1880	--	--	--	--
1890	--	--	--	--
1900	--	--	--	--
1910	--	--	--	--
1920	--	--	--	--
1930	--	--	--	--
1940	.308	.565	.052	.499
1950	.380	.612	.057	.582
1960	.309	.469	.038	.628

FRANCE

France

	I_f	I_g	I_h	I_m
1831	.297	.537	.044	.514
1836	.288	.518	.044	.514
1841	.286	.515	.043	.516
1846	.279	.498	.041	.520
1851	.271	.478	.041	.526
1856	.273	.478	.043	.530
1861	.275	.478	.045	.531
1866	.276	.481	.045	.530
1871	.282	.494	.044	.529
1876	.270	.471	.041	.533
1881	.267	.460	.043	.538
1886	.256	.435	.046	.541
1891	.242	.410	.045	.540
1896	.235	.396	.045	.541
1901	.228	.383	.044	.543
1911	.204	.315	.043	.591
1921	.189	.321	.039	.534
1931	.182	.273	.037	.613
1961	.222	.323	.037	.646

Ain

	I_f	I_g	I_h	I_m
1831	.319	.582	.028	.526
1836	.312	.571	.023	.527
1841	.300	.543	.025	.532
1846	.291	.517	.027	.539
1851	.275	.479	.029	.548
1856	.259	.446	.029	.551
1861	.256	.443	.027	.550
1866	.246	.428	.027	.546
1871	.241	.417	.026	.550
1876	.251	.425	.025	.564
1881	.243	.413	.022	.565
1886	.233	.390	.030	.564
1891	.228	.377	.032	.567
1896	.228	.377	.032	.568
1901	.229	.375	.030	.577
1911	.209	.323	.032	.608
1921	.194	.334	.030	.542
1931	.183	.280	.028	.613
1961	.216	.325	.023	.639

Aisne

	I_f	I_g	I_h	I_m
1831	.298	.449	.053	.619
1836	.280	.428	.052	.608
1841	.271	.420	.042	.606
1846	.272	.414	.046	.615
1851	.268	.394	.052	.630
1856	.266	.381	.064	.638
1861	.274	.386	.074	.639
1866	.270	.383	.072	.636
1871	.269	.381	.073	.637
1876	.273	.386	.073	.638
1881	.269	.378	.077	.636
1886	.261	.364	.083	.634
1891	.259	.363	.083	.630
1896	.257	.361	.082	.628
1901	.253	.353	.081	.633
1911	.231	.317	.071	.651
1921	.245	.361	.066	.607
1931	.236	.315	.068	.682
1961	.266	.365	.052	.683

Allier

	I_f	I_g	I_h	I_m
1831	.364	.610	.049	.561
1836	.331	.539	.058	.567
1841	.321	.519	.047	.582
1846	.306	.488	.041	.594
1851	.303	.476	.039	.604
1856	.287	.451	.033	.608
1861	.303	.467	.038	.617
1866	.304	.472	.036	.615
1871	.301	.456	.037	.629
1876	.282	.422	.034	.639
1881	.259	.389	.033	.636
1886	.237	.353	.036	.633
1891	.225	.341	.035	.622
1896	.216	.326	.033	.623
1901	.201	.297	.031	.639
1911	.168	.235	.029	.678
1921	.160	.249	.029	.594
1931	.163	.229	.029	.671
1961	.198	.284	.031	.663

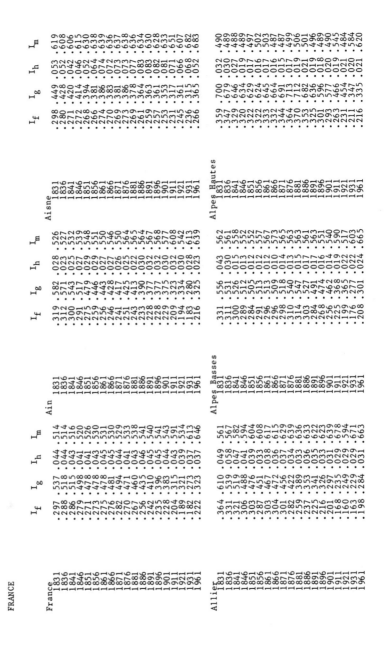

Alpes Basses

	I_f	I_g	I_h	I_m
1831	.331	.556	.043	.562
1836	.311	.531	.030	.561
1841	.300	.526	.015	.558
1846	.289	.512	.013	.552
1851	.284	.505	.012	.552
1856	.291	.513	.012	.557
1861	.296	.513	.012	.567
1866	.296	.509	.010	.573
1871	.298	.518	.014	.565
1876	.310	.540	.013	.563
1881	.314	.547	.015	.563
1886	.303	.527	.017	.561
1891	.284	.491	.017	.563
1896	.268	.474	.016	.551
1901	.256	.462	.014	.540
1911	.225	.368	.019	.590
1921	.199	.365	.022	.517
1931	.176	.277	.022	.603
1961	.208	.301	.024	.665

Alpes Hautes

	I_f	I_g	I_h	I_m
1831	.359	.700	.032	.490
1836	.347	.679	.030	.489
1841	.329	.646	.027	.488
1846	.320	.634	.019	.489
1851	.322	.629	.017	.497
1856	.322	.624	.016	.502
1861	.333	.645	.017	.503
1866	.332	.664	.016	.487
1871	.344	.691	.015	.487
1876	.364	.713	.017	.499
1881	.370	.712	.019	.506
1886	.353	.682	.021	.501
1891	.325	.636	.019	.496
1896	.301	.596	.018	.489
1901	.293	.577	.020	.490
1911	.263	.466	.019	.545
1921	.231	.454	.021	.484
1931	.211	.347	.020	.584
1961	.216	.335	.021	.620

Ardeche

1831	.341	.688	.018	.482
1836	.344	.693	.019	.482
1841	.351	.709	.023	.478
1846	.347	.712	.017	.475
1851	.338	.685	.018	.480
1856	.331	.665	.017	.485
1861	.327	.657	.016	.484
1866	.324	.666	.015	.475
1871	.324	.674	.012	.471
1876	.326	.663	.011	.484
1881	.325	.642	.014	.496
1886	.320	.624	.015	.501
1891	.311	.607	.012	.501
1896	.296	.584	.012	.497
1901	.275	.546	.011	.494
1911	.238	.425	.012	.546
1921	.202	.406	.014	.480
1931	.190	.343	.013	.535
1961	.207	.344	.013	.587

Ardennes

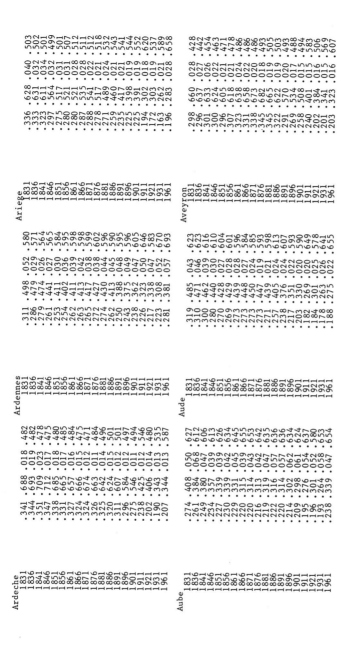

1831	.311	.498	.052	.580
1836	.286	.479	.029	.571
1841	.279	.474	.026	.564
1846	.261	.441	.027	.565
1851	.253	.411	.030	.584
1856	.254	.402	.036	.595
1861	.262	.411	.039	.598
1866	.263	.413	.042	.598
1871	.265	.417	.038	.599
1876	.272	.427	.038	.602
1881	.274	.430	.044	.596
1886	.262	.413	.045	.590
1891	.250	.388	.048	.595
1896	.243	.375	.049	.596
1901	.238	.362	.047	.605
1911	.226	.323	.050	.646
1921	.217	.338	.047	.583
1931	.223	.308	.052	.670
1961	.281	.381	.057	.693

Ariege

1831	.336	.628	.040	.503
1836	.333	.631	.032	.502
1841	.323	.611	.034	.501
1846	.297	.564	.032	.499
1851	.275	.517	.031	.501
1856	.280	.521	.031	.507
1861	.280	.521	.028	.512
1866	.287	.535	.028	.511
1871	.288	.541	.022	.512
1876	.278	.517	.021	.518
1881	.271	.489	.024	.532
1886	.259	.460	.021	.543
1891	.235	.417	.021	.541
1896	.225	.398	.019	.544
1901	.225	.391	.019	.552
1911	.194	.302	.018	.620
1921	.172	.303	.019	.537
1931	.163	.262	.021	.589
1961	.196	.283	.028	.658

Aube

1831	.274	.408	.050	.627
1836	.261	.384	.068	.612
1841	.249	.380	.047	.606
1846	.234	.357	.039	.613
1851	.227	.339	.039	.626
1856	.230	.339	.042	.634
1861	.229	.331	.045	.645
1866	.220	.315	.039	.655
1871	.220	.314	.043	.653
1876	.216	.313	.042	.642
1881	.219	.319	.047	.635
1886	.222	.316	.057	.636
1891	.220	.314	.057	.636
1896	.214	.302	.062	.634
1901	.209	.298	.061	.624
1911	.195	.276	.054	.637
1921	.196	.301	.052	.580
1931	.193	.264	.058	.653
1961	.238	.339	.047	.654

Aude

1831	.319	.485	.043	.623
1836	.310	.471	.046	.623
1841	.300	.462	.039	.616
1846	.280	.440	.030	.610
1851	.270	.428	.027	.604
1856	.269	.429	.028	.601
1861	.273	.439	.028	.596
1866	.273	.448	.027	.584
1871	.273	.450	.024	.585
1876	.273	.447	.019	.593
1881	.271	.439	.021	.598
1886	.257	.405	.024	.613
1891	.238	.376	.024	.607
1896	.217	.351	.022	.593
1901	.203	.330	.020	.590
1911	.182	.269	.020	.649
1921	.184	.301	.025	.578
1931	.178	.263	.026	.641
1961	.188	.275	.022	.655

Aveyron

1831	.298	.660	.028	.428
1836	.296	.637	.027	.442
1841	.301	.633	.026	.454
1846	.300	.624	.022	.463
1851	.296	.605	.021	.471
1856	.307	.618	.021	.478
1861	.323	.638	.024	.486
1866	.331	.658	.022	.486
1871	.338	.673	.020	.486
1876	.345	.682	.018	.493
1881	.345	.665	.019	.505
1886	.322	.622	.019	.503
1891	.291	.570	.020	.493
1896	.269	.534	.017	.488
1901	.258	.508	.015	.494
1911	.240	.401	.015	.583
1921	.202	.384	.016	.506
1931	.201	.341	.015	.569
1961	.203	.323	.016	.607

FRANCE (continued)

	I_f	I_g	I_h	I_m		I_f	I_g	I_h	I_m		I_f	I_g	I_h	I_m
Bouches Du Rhone					Calvados					Cantal				
1831	--	--	--	--	1831	.215	.397	.045	.482	1831	.278	.663	.031	.390
1836	--	--	--	--	1836	.211	.383	.048	.487	1836	.266	.621	.030	.399
1841	--	--	--	--	1841	.209	.381	.043	.492	1841	.263	.600	.029	.410
1846	--	--	--	--	1846	.202	.365	.039	.500	1846	.258	.583	.026	.417
1851	.361	.657	.064	.500	1851	.202	.355	.044	.509	1851	.257	.564	.028	.428
1856	.353	.621	.075	.510	1856	.208	.360	.045	.519	1856	.252	.541	.026	.438
1861	.367	.678	.072	.487	1861	.215	.365	.045	.531	1861	.257	.540	.029	.447
1866	.346	.629	.067	.496	1866	.219	.361	.051	.541	1866	.268	.571	.028	.442
1871	.318	.585	.062	.489	1871	.224	.365	.054	.546	1871	.277	.592	.028	.442
1876	.281	.516	.058	.488	1876	.222	.361	.053	.548	1876	.281	.588	.027	.453
1881	.251	.475	.051	.473	1881	.226	.367	.058	.545	1881	.280	.565	.030	.468
1886	.247	.455	.055	.481	1886	.229	.372	.062	.540	1886	.283	.556	.032	.478
1891	.239	.426	.057	.494	1891	.222	.361	.058	.541	1891	.274	.533	.033	.483
1896	.235	.394	.061	.522	1896	.221	.359	.058	.542	1896	.266	.510	.034	.486
1901	.220	.348	.062	.554	1901	.222	.364	.055	.542	1901	.265	.500	.033	.495
1911	.189	.287	.060	.565	1911	.221	.332	.059	.592	1911	.233	.402	.030	.547
1921	.177	.287	.050	.538	1921	.229	.363	.063	.553	1921	.214	.409	.031	.484
1931	.135	.196	.034	.623	1931	.231	.334	.064	.618	1931	.229	.382	.032	.563
1961	.199	.288	.038	.644	1961	.254	.369	.052	.638	1961	.224	.352	.023	.611
Charente					Charente Inf					Cher				
1831	.264	.437	.034	.571	1831	.281	.449	.032	.598	1831	.360	.555	.100	.572
1836	.246	.398	.039	.575	1836	.263	.425	.027	.592	1836	.339	.545	.061	.574
1841	.232	.367	.037	.590	1841	.246	.386	.039	.597	1841	.361	.577	.057	.585
1846	.229	.354	.035	.610	1846	.242	.375	.041	.603	1846	.368	.582	.051	.598
1851	.241	.363	.036	.628	1851	.247	.388	.029	.607	1851	.358	.563	.055	.597
1856	.246	.371	.029	.633	1856	.247	.388	.025	.612	1856	.348	.538	.057	.604
1861	.246	.372	.026	.636	1861	.246	.387	.022	.614	1861	.336	.528	.051	.598
1866	.248	.380	.026	.626	1866	.245	.391	.022	.603	1866	.315	.497	.047	.595
1871	.258	.398	.027	.622	1871	.248	.404	.021	.592	1871	.300	.472	.048	.594
1876	.261	.392	.032	.638	1876	.250	.404	.025	.594	1876	.285	.440	.047	.605
1881	.250	.360	.039	.657	1881	.245	.389	.021	.608	1881	.275	.417	.047	.617
1886	.230	.332	.031	.662	1886	.228	.350	.022	.626	1886	.258	.385	.047	.624
1891	.211	.311	.027	.647	1891	.206	.315	.024	.626	1891	.240	.361	.046	.617
1896	.203	.299	.028	.647	1896	.200	.308	.025	.618	1896	.225	.341	.046	.607
1901	.202	.303	.027	.635	1901	.199	.309	.025	.613	1901	.211	.321	.042	.605
1911	.197	.273	.031	.686	1911	.196	.280	.030	.666	1911	.190	.270	.041	.651
1921	.186	.291	.032	.597	1921	.195	.306	.033	.591	1921	.179	.284	.037	.575
1931	.197	.278	.034	.666	1931	.206	.291	.040	.663	1931	.172	.242	.036	.658
1961	.227	.315	.034	.685	1961	.243	.332	.046	.689	1961	.219	.304	.039	.679

Correze

1831	.351	.680	.026	.496
1836	.340	.639	.031	.509
1841	.330	.602	.032	.523
1846	.325	.582	.028	.535
1851	.318	.552	.034	.548
1856	.315	.535	.035	.559
1861	.317	.533	.038	.563
1866	.318	.549	.032	.554
1871	.334	.580	.030	.552
1876	.350	.597	.029	.565
1881	.353	.593	.025	.578
1886	.341	.552	.027	.598
1891	.317	.504	.031	.603
1896	.291	.476	.031	.585
1901	.271	.448	.025	.582
1911	.235	.344	.026	.657
1921	.202	.327	.027	.584
1931	.184	.272	.024	.647
1961	.185	.265	.024	.669

Corse

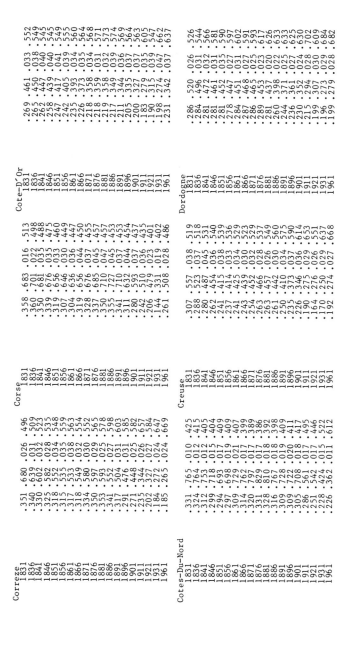

1831	.358	.683	.016	.513
1836	.360	.701	.022	.498
1841	.350	.681	.035	.488
1846	.339	.676	.035	.475
1851	.319	.656	.033	.460
1856	.307	.646	.030	.449
1861	.304	.636	.036	.447
1866	.319	.656	.044	.450
1871	.328	.676	.037	.455
1876	.337	.685	.045	.457
1881	.350	.710	.047	.457
1886	.355	.727	.045	.453
1891	.341	.710	.037	.453
1896	.311	.632	.044	.454
1901	.280	.593	.037	.437
1911	.242	.510	.036	.435
1921	.206	.479	.023	.401
1931	.144	.331	.019	.402
1961	.261	.508	.028	.486

Cote-D'Or

1831	.269	.461	.033	.552
1836	.265	.450	.038	.549
1841	.262	.447	.040	.545
1846	.258	.439	.040	.545
1851	.247	.417	.041	.549
1856	.242	.405	.039	.555
1861	.235	.393	.034	.560
1866	.226	.373	.035	.564
1871	.218	.358	.034	.568
1876	.218	.359	.031	.571
1881	.219	.358	.032	.573
1886	.217	.349	.039	.574
1891	.211	.344	.036	.569
1896	.205	.335	.037	.564
1901	.200	.327	.037	.563
1911	.183	.279	.035	.605
1921	.190	.315	.039	.547
1931	.198	.274	.047	.662
1961	.231	.342	.037	.637

Cotes-Du-Nord

1831	.331	.765	.010	.425
1836	.324	.764	.012	.415
1841	.312	.753	.012	.405
1846	.299	.718	.015	.404
1851	.294	.693	.017	.409
1856	.297	.698	.019	.409
1861	.309	.729	.021	.407
1866	.314	.762	.017	.399
1871	.320	.797	.017	.389
1876	.331	.829	.017	.386
1881	.328	.810	.018	.392
1886	.316	.767	.018	.398
1891	.309	.728	.019	.409
1896	.309	.722	.020	.411
1901	.305	.708	.018	.417
1911	.286	.561	.017	.495
1921	.251	.542	.017	.446
1931	.228	.424	.015	.522
1961	.226	.362	.011	.612

Creuse

1831	.307	.557	.038	.519
1836	.288	.523	.037	.518
1841	.280	.487	.045	.531
1846	.262	.454	.036	.540
1851	.241	.415	.038	.539
1856	.237	.414	.033	.536
1861	.241	.425	.034	.529
1866	.243	.439	.030	.523
1871	.254	.452	.032	.529
1876	.263	.466	.028	.537
1881	.263	.457	.026	.549
1886	.261	.442	.030	.560
1891	.250	.410	.034	.575
1896	.235	.373	.037	.590
1901	.226	.346	.036	.614
1911	.190	.275	.029	.653
1921	.164	.276	.026	.551
1931	.170	.250	.029	.637
1961	.192	.274	.027	.668

Dordogne

1831	.286	.520	.026	.526
1836	.284	.496	.031	.544
1841	.281	.472	.032	.566
1846	.281	.461	.031	.581
1851	.281	.452	.035	.590
1856	.278	.447	.027	.597
1861	.284	.451	.031	.602
1866	.287	.468	.027	.591
1871	.286	.465	.025	.593
1876	.289	.453	.023	.617
1881	.281	.437	.020	.626
1886	.260	.398	.022	.633
1891	.244	.371	.025	.633
1896	.236	.361	.027	.625
1901	.230	.352	.024	.630
1911	.215	.294	.028	.702
1921	.199	.307	.030	.609
1931	.196	.273	.029	.684
1961	.199	.279	.028	.682

FRANCE (continued)

Doubs

Year	I_f	I_g	I_h	I_m
1831	.303	.687	.035	.411
1836	.291	.643	.035	.421
1841	.281	.605	.037	.429
1846	.275	.587	.037	.432
1851	.273	.563	.042	.444
1856	.278	.559	.050	.447
1861	.287	.578	.048	.450
1866	.293	.592	.050	.448
1871	.297	.611	.047	.444
1876	.308	.639	.044	.444
1881	.309	.621	.048	.455
1886	.293	.584	.044	.462
1891	.277	.530	.047	.475
1896	.270	.524	.044	.470
1901	.261	.516	.040	.465
1911	.242	.417	.043	.534
1921	.215	.399	.040	.486
1931	.214	.351	.037	.565
1961	.251	.383	.028	.629

Drome

Year	I_f	I_g	I_h	I_m
1831	.299	.533	.035	.530
1836	.292	.520	.033	.532
1841	.288	.510	.034	.534
1846	.281	.497	.029	.537
1851	.270	.477	.026	.540
1856	.270	.472	.030	.543
1861	.273	.476	.033	.543
1866	.272	.477	.028	.542
1871	.275	.486	.021	.547
1876	.275	.478	.023	.553
1881	.259	.455	.022	.548
1886	.250	.441	.026	.538
1891	.238	.422	.023	.540
1896	.225	.393	.023	.546
1901	.217	.371	.022	.559
1911	.190	.312	.021	.582
1921	.177	.319	.021	.524
1931	.166	.256	.021	.616
1961	.215	.322	.029	.634

Eure

Year	I_f	I_g	I_h	I_m
1831	.213	.348	.028	.577
1836	.206	.328	.036	.581
1841	.207	.323	.043	.587
1846	.209	.323	.043	.595
1851	.213	.319	.046	.613
1856	.218	.318	.050	.626
1861	.224	.323	.052	.636
1866	.227	.320	.059	.646
1871	.223	.311	.059	.648
1876	.216	.304	.054	.649
1881	.215	.302	.055	.646
1886	.215	.303	.058	.642
1891	.219	.307	.061	.641
1896	.225	.315	.064	.641
1901	.226	.317	.063	.641
1911	.223	.302	.065	.672
1921	.225	.330	.069	.598
1931	.228	.304	.066	.682
1961	.260	.354	.062	.676

Eure-et-Loire

Year	I_f	I_g	I_h	I_m
1831	.277	.432	.047	.597
1836	.263	.419	.041	.588
1841	.256	.413	.034	.587
1846	.262	.416	.032	.599
1851	.263	.406	.033	.616
1856	.266	.399	.037	.633
1861	.269	.399	.038	.638
1866	.264	.391	.040	.638
1871	.260	.387	.042	.633
1876	.262	.389	.044	.632
1881	.260	.383	.046	.635
1886	.257	.372	.050	.642
1891	.255	.370	.050	.641
1896	.247	.362	.049	.633
1901	.244	.358	.048	.634
1911	.233	.328	.045	.665
1921	.224	.342	.049	.595
1931	.225	.313	.047	.670
1961	.239	.337	.038	.675

Finistere

Year	I_f	I_g	I_h	I_m
1831	.404	.815	.021	.483
1836	.384	.783	.020	.477
1841	.370	.760	.019	.475
1846	.353	.727	.021	.471
1851	.331	.686	.023	.466
1856	.336	.691	.026	.465
1861	.350	.727	.023	.464
1866	.361	.767	.019	.458
1871	.376	.811	.017	.452
1876	.381	.838	.014	.445
1881	.374	.819	.015	.447
1886	.374	.784	.015	.466
1891	.366	.773	.015	.464
1896	.351	.744	.016	.461
1901	.342	.718	.015	.466
1911	.303	.551	.016	.537
1921	.246	.500	.015	.476
1931	.211	.394	.012	.522
1961	.228	.371	.012	.603

Gard

Year	I_f	I_g	I_h	I_m
1831	.316	.516	.025	.593
1836	.320	.520	.026	.595
1841	.332	.542	.028	.592
1846	.340	.549	.039	.589
1851	.336	.554	.030	.585
1856	.331	.549	.028	.582
1861	.325	.548	.021	.576
1866	.306	.526	.020	.566
1871	.311	.536	.021	.564
1876	.303	.520	.016	.569
1881	.299	.500	.019	.582
1886	.272	.447	.015	.594
1891	.255	.419	.016	.593
1896	.239	.393	.016	.593
1901	.219	.361	.016	.590
1911	.183	.306	.016	.578
1921	.173	.299	.020	.547
1931	.155	.242	.018	.609
1961	.208	.303	.027	.657

Haute-Garonne

1831	.286	.518	.039	.517
1836	.270	.478	.043	.523
1841	.258	.448	.038	.537
1846	.247	.423	.033	.548
1851	.243	.414	.037	.548
1856	.228	.385	.035	.551
1861	.223	.369	.037	.561
1866	.212	.352	.034	.560
1871	.222	.367	.038	.560
1876	.220	.361	.035	.569
1881	.225	.358	.044	.575
1886	.211	.332	.040	.585
1891	.194	.304	.038	.585
1896	.184	.288	.041	.577
1901	.179	.286	.037	.569
1911	.165	.246	.038	.613
1921	.162	.260	.041	.552
1931	.160	.235	.040	.614
1961	.191	.285	.031	.630

Gers

1831	.235	.421	.031	.523
1836	.226	.395	.032	.535
1841	.221	.380	.023	.554
1846	.209	.352	.021	.569
1851	.206	.338	.023	.581
1856	.203	.328	.021	.592
1861	.202	.321	.023	.601
1866	.212	.337	.024	.601
1871	.218	.346	.025	.599
1876	.214	.333	.026	.612
1881	.207	.316	.027	.622
1886	.191	.290	.026	.626
1891	.174	.259	.022	.639
1896	.166	.247	.023	.639
1901	.163	.241	.022	.648
1911	.161	.219	.024	.700
1921	.166	.254	.031	.603
1931	.181	.257	.031	.665
1961	.206	.302	.029	.651

Gironde

1831	.278	.393	.083	.626
1836	.262	.375	.081	.618
1841	.253	.358	.085	.616
1846	.239	.333	.087	.618
1851	.239	.341	.072	.620
1856	.228	.338	.053	.614
1861	.230	.336	.063	.613
1866	.231	.338	.063	.611
1871	.216	.316	.060	.607
1876	.205	.308	.044	.609
1881	.202	.303	.040	.615
1886	.195	.287	.046	.620
1891	.186	.265	.055	.621
1896	.180	.256	.056	.622
1901	.172	.245	.053	.621
1911	.149	.212	.046	.622
1921	.168	.256	.047	.579
1931	.157	.219	.044	.644
1961	.196	.283	.040	.641

Herault

1831	.288	.508	.031	.538
1836	.286	.493	.031	.553
1841	.289	.490	.031	.561
1846	.283	.485	.024	.562
1851	.277	.472	.028	.562
1856	.265	.451	.022	.565
1861	.270	.452	.027	.573
1866	.271	.451	.028	.575
1871	.286	.467	.032	.583
1876	.267	.436	.024	.591
1881	.262	.421	.027	.596
1886	.232	.377	.027	.586
1891	.226	.372	.027	.577
1896	.225	.371	.026	.576
1901	.211	.342	.027	.583
1911	.176	.277	.023	.603
1921	.183	.306	.025	.562
1931	.152	.239	.021	.601
1961	.181	.278	.023	.619

Ille-et-Vilaine

1831	.316	.790	.017	.388
1836	.298	.751	.018	.382
1841	.292	.733	.016	.385
1846	.295	.722	.017	.394
1851	.286	.693	.014	.400
1856	.282	.680	.014	.402
1861	.282	.682	.016	.400
1866	.286	.714	.015	.388
1871	.289	.726	.016	.385
1876	.300	.731	.016	.396
1881	.307	.729	.022	.404
1886	.300	.701	.021	.410
1891	.279	.649	.023	.409
1896	.261	.601	.023	.411
1901	.245	.575	.020	.406
1911	.225	.420	.021	.512
1921	.212	.414	.024	.483
1931	.215	.374	.021	.549
1961	.225	.362	.018	.603

Indre

1831	.338	.577	.035	.558
1836	.318	.537	.043	.558
1841	.323	.529	.050	.570
1846	.317	.512	.043	.586
1851	.310	.493	.042	.594
1856	.312	.488	.043	.605
1861	.308	.482	.042	.605
1866	.293	.458	.042	.603
1871	.284	.444	.043	.602
1876	.282	.437	.039	.609
1881	.278	.425	.038	.621
1886	.266	.402	.040	.624
1891	.249	.376	.041	.620
1896	.234	.358	.038	.614
1901	.225	.345	.037	.613
1911	.202	.289	.034	.660
1921	.182	.297	.034	.564
1931	.185	.266	.040	.642
1961	.217	.303	.041	.673

FRANCE (continued)

Indre-et-Loire	I_f	I_g	I_h	I_m
1831	.252	.408	.037	.578
1836	.234	.376	.041	.574
1841	.230	.360	.045	.586
1846	.234	.364	.037	.602
1851	.227	.347	.035	.615
1856	.222	.335	.032	.625
1861	.219	.328	.033	.630
1866	.220	.333	.033	.624
1871	.226	.345	.032	.621
1876	.223	.335	.031	.630
1881	.227	.332	.037	.643
1886	.218	.316	.039	.646
1891	.207	.303	.037	.641
1896	.195	.285	.037	.637
1901	.192	.279	.040	.636
1911	.185	.255	.046	.665
1921	.188	.274	.051	.613
1931	.191	.265	.049	.660
1961	.237	.337	.044	.660

Isere	I_f	I_g	I_h	I_m
1831	.329	.614	.054	.491
1836	.321	.608	.046	.488
1841	.305	.597	.030	.485
1846	.290	.571	.027	.484
1851	.283	.549	.032	.486
1856	.287	.563	.019	.492
1861	.271	.526	.020	.496
1866	.255	.492	.020	.499
1871	.253	.487	.021	.498
1876	.250	.472	.019	.511
1881	.250	.453	.023	.527
1886	.236	.436	.021	.518
1891	.229	.432	.025	.502
1896	.217	.409	.023	.503
1901	.207	.385	.021	.511
1911	.179	.303	.023	.557
1921	.170	.313	.024	.505
1931	.170	.272	.022	.590
1961	.216	.326	.024	.635

Jura	I_f	I_g	I_h	I_m
1831	.271	.597	.019	.436
1836	.275	.584	.023	.448
1841	.277	.582	.020	.457
1846	.270	.560	.024	.460
1851	.266	.539	.026	.468
1856	.258	.513	.028	.475
1861	.260	.506	.027	.485
1866	.264	.503	.026	.499
1871	.264	.499	.028	.500
1876	.275	.526	.024	.500
1881	.280	.535	.026	.499
1886	.271	.513	.029	.501
1891	.256	.481	.030	.502
1896	.249	.473	.027	.498
1901	.248	.471	.026	.500
1911	.226	.375	.029	.570
1921	.210	.383	.029	.511
1931	.202	.325	.029	.585
1961	.230	.360	.026	.611

Landes	I_f	I_g	I_h	I_m
1831	.318	.624	.038	.477
1836	.308	.592	.047	.478
1841	.311	.585	.056	.482
1846	.306	.556	.064	.491
1851	.308	.562	.050	.505
1856	.300	.528	.059	.514
1861	.288	.511	.053	.513
1866	.285	.513	.048	.511
1871	.285	.534	.045	.490
1876	.283	.530	.046	.490
1881	.271	.506	.039	.496
1886	.256	.475	.040	.497
1891	.241	.440	.039	.504
1896	.230	.403	.032	.534
1901	.236	.392	.032	.569
1911	.210	.294	.033	.679
1921	.178	.291	.027	.572
1931	.172	.252	.027	.643
1961	.214	.304	.028	.674

Loir-et-Cher	I_f	I_g	I_h	I_m
1831	.321	.545	.048	.550
1836	.308	.521	.048	.549
1841	.300	.501	.043	.561
1846	.305	.491	.050	.580
1851	.299	.474	.046	.591
1856	.289	.453	.039	.604
1861	.289	.446	.042	.611
1866	.287	.442	.042	.612
1871	.282	.434	.043	.611
1876	.271	.413	.042	.617
1881	.259	.388	.042	.628
1886	.252	.371	.046	.633
1891	.242	.354	.047	.636
1896	.230	.334	.046	.638
1901	.222	.320	.044	.645
1911	.209	.292	.046	.665
1921	.202	.310	.047	.589
1931	.206	.288	.047	.659
1961	.233	.324	.040	.679

Loire	I_f	I_g	I_h	I_m
1831	.376	.743	.032	.483
1836	.363	.714	.031	.486
1841	.352	.684	.030	.492
1846	.341	.665	.027	.493
1851	.332	.646	.027	.492
1856	.336	.649	.028	.496
1861	.336	.642	.030	.500
1866	.326	.622	.028	.501
1871	.318	.610	.027	.500
1876	.301	.579	.025	.498
1881	.306	.592	.027	.494
1886	.269	.512	.027	.499
1891	.251	.478	.026	.498
1896	.237	.445	.025	.503
1901	.225	.414	.023	.518
1911	.187	.310	.023	.571
1921	.173	.305	.025	.529
1931	.167	.266	.018	.600
1961	.210	.320	.023	.631

Haute Loire				
1831	.321	.741	.017	.421
1836	.317	.721	.020	.424
1841	.321	.722	.018	.430
1846	.311	.698	.016	.433
1851	.301	.658	.020	.440
1856	.302	.650	.018	.449
1861	.301	.640	.020	.454
1866	.304	.640	.020	.458
1871	.318	.658	.020	.466
1876	.318	.644	.018	.479
1881	.305	.599	.016	.495
1886	.299	.592	.018	.490
1891	.288	.581	.018	.479
1896	.272	.559	.017	.471
1901	.262	.537	.016	.473
1911	.214	.399	.013	.520
1921	.186	.396	.014	.451
1931	.187	.352	.011	.516
1961	.202	.344	.013	.571

Loire Inferieure				
1831	.290	.649	.025	.425
1836	.291	.658	.025	.421
1841	.291	.645	.025	.429
1846	.289	.624	.025	.441
1851	.286	.613	.022	.446
1856	.280	.602	.023	.445
1861	.280	.608	.023	.440
1866	.272	.589	.022	.440
1871	.261	.570	.020	.438
1876	.260	.567	.023	.436
1881	.268	.603	.020	.426
1886	.258	.563	.021	.439
1891	.246	.515	.022	.454
1896	.229	.471	.021	.464
1901	.220	.444	.019	.472
1911	.192	.349	.019	.524
1921	.187	.353	.022	.498
1931	.190	.316	.021	.574
1961	.243	.375	.025	.623

Loiret				
1831	.331	.546	.056	.561
1836	.316	.515	.068	.555
1841	.318	.514	.070	.560
1846	.321	.513	.064	.572
1851	.321	.513	.052	.584
1856	.316	.485	.067	.594
1861	.305	.479	.053	.593
1866	.294	.461	.054	.589
1871	.286	.450	.054	.586
1876	.285	.441	.054	.595
1881	.277	.421	.053	.607
1886	.269	.402	.057	.614
1891	.251	.377	.052	.613
1896	.236	.356	.050	.608
1901	.223	.336	.048	.609
1911	.204	.302	.040	.628
1921	.195	.310	.041	.570
1931	.190	.274	.042	.640
1961	.226	.317	.038	.673

Lot				
1831	.262	.509	.017	.498
1836	.264	.493	.028	.509
1841	.265	.486	.025	.521
1846	.256	.465	.019	.532
1851	.249	.446	.020	.538
1856	.248	.446	.014	.542
1861	.247	.437	.018	.547
1866	.246	.435	.017	.548
1871	.240	.429	.015	.543
1876	.235	.418	.013	.548
1881	.226	.385	.015	.570
1886	.205	.331	.019	.597
1891	.195	.319	.013	.596
1896	.199	.329	.013	.589
1901	.199	.333	.011	.583
1911	.186	.271	.015	.669
1921	.182	.296	.018	.588
1931	.177	.262	.023	.642
1961	.209	.310	.025	.646

Lot-et-Garonne				
1831	.225	.351	.031	.605
1836	.221	.339	.026	.622
1841	.219	.333	.022	.634
1846	.211	.315	.025	.641
1851	.204	.298	.024	.656
1856	.201	.290	.019	.670
1861	.199	.282	.021	.683
1866	.201	.279	.020	.701
1871	.203	.280	.019	.705
1876	.198	.271	.019	.710
1881	.195	.266	.020	.713
1886	.182	.246	.022	.714
1891	.170	.232	.023	.705
1896	.166	.230	.021	.695
1901	.168	.230	.023	.700
1911	.158	.207	.025	.730
1921	.166	.240	.031	.648
1931	.178	.238	.032	.709
1961	.204	.288	.031	.674

Lozere				
1831	.315	.682	.024	.442
1836	.314	.668	.026	.449
1841	.319	.671	.024	.456
1846	.317	.672	.017	.459
1851	.319	.665	.020	.464
1856	.328	.665	.027	.472
1861	.332	.663	.030	.476
1866	.343	.688	.027	.478
1871	.357	.713	.025	.482
1876	.375	.745	.028	.484
1881	.404	.806	.029	.482
1886	.402	.799	.026	.487
1891	.368	.715	.030	.494
1896	.341	.678	.026	.483
1901	.320	.656	.025	.467
1911	.277	.530	.019	.506
1921	.215	.486	.016	.423
1931	.205	.419	.015	.470
1961	.213	.366	.014	.564

FRANCE (continued)

	I_f	I_g	I_h	I_m		I_f	I_g	I_h	I_m		I_f	I_g	I_h	I_m
Maine-et-Loire					Manche					Marne				
1831	.260	.532	.019	.470	1831	.238	.567	.021	.398	1831	.295	.450	.057	.605
1836	.246	.492	.028	.470	1836	.228	.537	.022	.399	1836	.281	.437	.053	.595
1841	.242	.499	.002	.481	1841	.223	.516	.022	.407	1841	.273	.426	.052	.593
1846	.244	.467	.026	.495	1846	.227	.511	.021	.419	1846	.272	.422	.049	.596
1851	.240	.451	.027	.502	1851	.225	.491	.025	.430	1851	.269	.407	.058	.604
1856	.229	.427	.022	.511	1856	.231	.490	.027	.440	1856	.270	.405	.061	.609
1861	.228	.418	.022	.520	1861	.238	.498	.028	.447	1861	.264	.392	.062	.610
1866	.227	.419	.022	.517	1866	.236	.507	.025	.439	1866	.256	.380	.066	.606
1871	.222	.416	.023	.506	1871	.238	.520	.027	.428	1871	.272	.397	.081	.605
1876	.220	.409	.023	.509	1876	.246	.532	.027	.434	1876	.272	.399	.071	.612
1881	.215	.394	.024	.516	1881	.246	.511	.027	.453	1881	.272	.394	.071	.624
1886	.208	.372	.027	.525	1886	.249	.496	.029	.471	1886	.273	.401	.071	.613
1891	.198	.349	.024	.535	1891	.251	.483	.033	.484	1891	.264	.393	.068	.602
1896	.192	.329	.027	.545	1896	.248	.476	.034	.484	1896	.249	.370	.066	.602
1901	.190	.324	.025	.554	1901	.249	.480	.034	.483	1901	.240	.357	.060	.604
1911	.186	.296	.025	.594	1911	.240	.407	.034	.552	1911	.221	.316	.058	.635
1921	.192	.333	.027	.537	1921	.233	.429	.033	.503	1921	.220	.330	.053	.603
1931	.204	.323	.024	.602	1931	.242	.397	.029	.580	1931	.212	.295	.057	.653
1961	.258	.399	.027	.620	1961	.249	.374	.027	.640	1961	.241	.342	.045	.662
Haute-Marne					Mayenne					Meurthe				
1831	.270	.480	.029	.534	1831	.289	.677	.018	.411	1831	--	--	--	--
1836	.257	.454	.025	.541	1836	.273	.640	.018	.411	1836	--	--	--	--
1841	.248	.436	.025	.544	1841	.267	.610	.020	.418	1841	--	--	--	--
1846	.241	.421	.023	.548	1846	.261	.575	.021	.435	1846	--	--	--	--
1851	.238	.404	.026	.559	1851	.253	.531	.021	.454	1851	.252	.496	.042	.462
1856	.242	.401	.032	.570	1856	.252	.508	.023	.472	1856	.237	.472	.042	.454
1861	.247	.406	.027	.582	1861	.255	.505	.023	.482	1861	.253	.480	.044	.480
1866	.240	.386	.026	.594	1866	.262	.525	.023	.478	1866	.265	.478	.047	.507
1871	.238	.387	.026	.588	1871	.266	.533	.024	.477	1871	.233	.409	.038	.526
1876	.244	.403	.029	.576	1876	.273	.529	.024	.494	1876	.264	.451	.041	.543
1881	.248	.408	.027	.581	1881	.272	.503	.022	.520	1881	.261	.457	.040	.529
1886	.242	.385	.033	.592	1886	.267	.496	.022	.516	1886	.262	.445	.046	.540
1891	.229	.367	.034	.586	1891	.260	.487	.022	.513	1891	.251	.426	.046	.538
1896	.220	.355	.031	.583	1896	.253	.480	.023	.503	1896	.253	.428	.050	.538
1901	.216	.347	.032	.584	1901	.250	.474	.021	.506	1901	.256	.413	.056	.562
1911	.216	.322	.037	.628	1911	.242	.394	.021	.591	1911	.260	.378	.077	.609
1921	.216	.348	.043	.568	1921	.228	.417	.022	.520	1921	.216	.350	.050	.555
1931	.229	.334	.046	.636	1931	.232	.389	.018	.578	1931	.228	.323	.054	.645
1961	.280	.393	.046	.673	1961	.240	.366	.016	.639	1961	.252	.357	.040	.668

Meuse					Morbihan					Moselle				
1831	.273	.453	.041	.564	1831	.357	.810	.013	.431	1831	--	--	--	--
1836	.268	.452	.031	.564	1836	.337	.766	.015	.429	1836	--	--	--	--
1841	.271	.460	.031	.559	1841	.325	.737	.017	.428	1841	--	--	--	--
1846	.263	.448	.032	.555	1846	.309	.700	.016	.428	1846	--	--	--	--
1851	.252	.425	.029	.562	1851	.298	.682	.016	.424	1851	.294	.644	.032	.427
1856	.245	.411	.027	.567	1856	.295	.675	.015	.424	1856	.286	.619	.031	.434
1861	.237	.398	.026	.568	1861	.307	.689	.017	.431	1861	.302	.627	.033	.452
1866	.230	.383	.029	.569	1866	.311	.716	.018	.420	1866	.306	.618	.036	.464
1871	.237	.397	.029	.566	1871	.327	.773	.018	.410	1871	--	--	--	--
1876	.249	.422	.027	.564	1876	.346	.817	.018	.410	1876	--	--	--	--
1881	.258	.433	.029	.568	1881	.343	.802	.019	.414	1881	--	--	--	--
1886	.257	.426	.033	.569	1886	.339	.779	.023	.419	1886	--	--	--	--
1891	.253	.418	.037	.568	1891	.330	.739	.024	.428	1891	--	--	--	--
1896	.253	.416	.037	.569	1896	.312	.697	.021	.430	1896	--	--	--	--
1901	.252	.410	.037	.577	1901	.296	.652	.023	.434	1901	--	--	--	--
1911	.238	.362	.042	.615	1911	.290	.551	.024	.505	1911	--	--	--	--
1921	.231	.381	.039	.563	1921	.251	.522	.023	.457	1921	.255	.451	.032	.532
1931	.236	.345	.040	.645	1931	.241	.448	.017	.518	1931	.225	.344	.036	.615
1961	.280	.399	.044	.664	1961	.244	.390	.018	.606	1961	.278	.376	.043	.705
Nievre					Nord					Oise				
1831	.361	.605	.026	.579	1831	.344	.658	.059	.476	1831	.253	.365	.049	.646
1836	.353	.574	.047	.580	1836	.351	.672	.059	.476	1836	.248	.359	.049	.642
1841	.347	.557	.044	.592	1841	.347	.676	.054	.472	1841	.251	.365	.046	.641
1846	.335	.524	.039	.610	1846	.343	.660	.056	.476	1846	.252	.363	.046	.648
1851	.317	.488	.045	.615	1851	.349	.664	.056	.483	1851	.249	.355	.047	.657
1856	.311	.479	.039	.619	1856	.360	.674	.063	.486	1856	.253	.357	.049	.663
1861	.310	.474	.039	.623	1861	.371	.684	.066	.492	1861	.255	.357	.053	.667
1866	.299	.449	.039	.635	1866	.374	.684	.073	.493	1866	.254	.350	.057	.673
1871	.284	.432	.034	.629	1871	.380	.698	.074	.491	1871	.256	.352	.057	.676
1876	.278	.418	.032	.636	1876	.368	.670	.074	.494	1876	.251	.348	.055	.671
1881	.265	.394	.033	.642	1881	.354	.640	.074	.495	1881	.249	.344	.058	.667
1886	.253	.371	.035	.647	1886	.330	.595	.074	.493	1886	.243	.339	.057	.660
1891	.241	.357	.032	.644	1891	.310	.561	.070	.488	1891	.241	.337	.063	.651
1896	.229	.339	.030	.642	1896	.293	.520	.071	.495	1896	.241	.335	.066	.651
1901	.218	.325	.028	.640	1901	.276	.478	.066	.509	1901	.238	.329	.064	.656
1911	.190	.276	.028	.655	1911	.219	.344	.055	.569	1911	.221	.299	.062	.671
1921	.181	.290	.029	.580	1921	.200	.341	.040	.531	1921	.216	.320	.054	.608
1931	.186	.255	.034	.684	1931	.193	.280	.037	.640	1931	.223	.291	.065	.699
1961	.222	.314	.040	.665	1961	.258	.354	.049	.684	1961	.263	.355	.062	.686
Orne					Pas-De-Calais					Puy-De-Dome				
1831	.226	.475	.007	.469	1831	.298	.582	.048	.469	1831	.295	.553	.024	.513
1836	.220	.455	.009	.474	1836	.300	.581	.051	.470	1836	.283	.527	.023	.515
1841	.212	.429	.010	.482	1841	.302	.583	.051	.471	1841	.278	.517	.020	.519
1846	.202	.394	.013	.497	1846	.305	.582	.048	.480	1846	.266	.492	.018	.523
1851	.202	.376	.016	.518	1851	.305	.567	.050	.493	1851	.253	.466	.018	.526
1856	.204	.364	.019	.535	1856	.313	.569	.056	.500	1856	.246	.447	.018	.532

	I_f	I_g	I_h	I_m
Orne (cont.)				
1861	.204	.352	.022	.552
1866	.209	.357	.021	.560
1871	.214	.366	.021	.560
1876	.218	.369	.023	.564
1881	.223	.376	.023	.568
1886	.224	.372	.024	.576
1891	.211	.346	.027	.579
1896	.208	.340	.028	.579
1901	.207	.338	.026	.580
1911	.208	.316	.031	.623
1921	.212	.353	.034	.559
1931	.222	.331	.035	.632
1961	.243	.359	.033	.646
Basses-Pyrenees				
1831	.276	.621	.036	.411
1836	.268	.595	.040	.411
1841	.267	.597	.036	.411
1846	.258	.576	.038	.410
1851	.254	.563	.038	.411
1856	.261	.577	.038	.415
1861	.268	.580	.039	.424
1866	.269	.566	.038	.438
1871	.278	.589	.033	.441
1876	.284	.614	.032	.433
1881	.287	.622	.034	.430
1886	.282	.620	.029	.429
1891	.269	.601	.028	.420
1896	.257	.591	.027	.408
1901	.247	.576	.024	.404
1911	.240	.444	.028	.509
1921	.198	.414	.024	.447
1931	.187	.343	.023	.512
1961	.218	.348	.024	.598
Bas-Rhin				
1831	--	--	--	--
1836	--	--	--	--
1841	--	--	--	--
1846	--	--	--	--
1851	.321	.698	.051	.417
1856	.312	.716	.050	.393
1861	.349	.764	.063	.408
1866	.356	.774	.067	.409
1871	--	--	--	--
1876	--	--	--	--
1881	--	--	--	--
1886	--	--	--	--
1891	--	--	--	--
1896	--	--	--	--
1901	--	--	--	--
1911	--	--	--	--
1921	.219	.402	.039	.495
1931	.192	.305	.043	.570
1961	.239	.357	.036	.632

	I_f	I_g	I_h	I_m
Pas-De-Calais (cont.)				
1861	.330	.593	.063	.505
1866	.334	.597	.066	.506
1871	.341	.607	.064	.512
1876	.347	.611	.069	.512
1881	.347	.611	.073	.509
1886	.342	.593	.085	.507
1891	.340	.591	.076	.514
1896	.342	.586	.077	.521
1901	.339	.573	.075	.531
1911	.298	.438	.077	.612
1921	.257	.416	.059	.555
1931	.248	.345	.052	.671
1961	.265	.362	.044	.696
Hautes-Pyrenees				
1831	.284	.630	.038	.415
1836	.269	.587	.038	.420
1841	.261	.563	.038	.425
1846	.246	.536	.030	.427
1851	.237	.500	.035	.434
1856	.233	.489	.033	.440
1861	.236	.491	.035	.440
1866	.237	.510	.031	.432
1871	.245	.531	.028	.431
1876	.257	.541	.028	.447
1881	.257	.509	.031	.474
1886	.238	.458	.029	.488
1891	.217	.433	.028	.466
1896	.206	.426	.024	.451
1901	.200	.411	.023	.455
1911	.192	.332	.028	.539
1921	.183	.341	.030	.492
1931	.182	.296	.031	.571
1961	.196	.300	.032	.613
Haut-Rhin				
1831	--	--	--	--
1836	--	--	--	--
1841	--	--	--	--
1846	--	--	--	--
1851	.312	.747	.047	.378
1856	.280	.739	.040	.344
1861	.351	.781	.060	.404
1866	.335	.770	.052	.395
1871	--	--	--	--
1876	--	--	--	--
1881	--	--	--	--
1886	--	--	--	--
1891	--	--	--	--
1896	--	--	--	--
1901	--	--	--	--
1911	--	--	--	--
1921	.193	.382	.029	.464
1931	.180	.290	.029	.578
1961	.231	.338	.036	.647

	I_f	I_g	I_h	I_m
Puy-De-Dome (cont.)				
1861	.245	.442	.016	.536
1866	.245	.444	.015	.536
1871	.247	.445	.016	.539
1876	.248	.440	.018	.545
1881	.243	.428	.016	.552
1886	.233	.407	.016	.555
1891	.217	.377	.018	.555
1896	.206	.357	.019	.555
1901	.199	.341	.019	.561
1911	.177	.274	.021	.616
1921	.166	.287	.026	.538
1931	.162	.247	.025	.615
1961	.200	.291	.031	.648
Pyr-Orient				
1831	.348	.630	.051	.513
1836	.342	.594	.067	.521
1841	.349	.603	.056	.535
1846	.362	.624	.052	.541
1851	.371	.646	.049	.539
1856	.345	.614	.038	.534
1861	.341	.609	.039	.531
1866	.339	.627	.038	.512
1871	.337	.634	.036	.504
1876	.346	.631	.028	.528
1881	.345	.594	.031	.557
1886	.318	.534	.030	.570
1891	.279	.475	.029	.560
1896	.260	.454	.026	.546
1901	.243	.427	.022	.545
1911	.216	.341	.024	.605
1921	.179	.307	.019	.555
1931	.142	.221	.019	.608
1961	.194	.280	.024	.663
Rhone				
1831	--	--	--	--
1836	--	--	--	--
1841	--	--	--	--
1846	--	--	--	--
1851	.255	.464	.067	.473
1856	.252	.438	.067	.498
1861	.249	.441	.066	.487
1866	.236	.409	.065	.497
1871	.224	.383	.063	.502
1876	.226	.392	.054	.509
1881	.216	.383	.053	.494
1886	.199	.342	.054	.505
1891	.186	.309	.051	.521
1896	.174	.291	.049	.515
1901	.177	.291	.050	.526
1911	.144	.233	.042	.536
1921	.139	.253	.035	.476
1931	.149	.213	.040	.628
1961	.204	.314	.032	.610

Haute-Saone

1831	.316	.591	.061	.481
1836	.299	.579	.044	.477
1841	.290	.578	.036	.467
1846	.270	.546	.035	.461
1851	.254	.501	.037	.468
1856	.268	.518	.041	.475
1861	.261	.501	.038	.482
1866	.254	.487	.039	.480
1871	.252	.490	.037	.476
1876	.255	.499	.031	.477
1881	.249	.480	.033	.484
1886	.240	.449	.036	.494
1891	.242	.453	.038	.492
1896	.242	.458	.035	.490
1901	.252	.465	.041	.498
1911	.223	.366	.043	.557
1921	.207	.377	.037	.501
1931	.205	.325	.038	.582
1961	.252	.379	.032	.632

Saone-et-Loire

1831	.321	.562	.035	.543
1836	.315	.541	.040	.549
1841	.310	.520	.043	.561
1846	.307	.504	.040	.575
1851	.303	.490	.040	.585
1856	.300	.477	.044	.592
1861	.308	.490	.035	.600
1866	.313	.488	.036	.613
1871	.304	.470	.034	.620
1876	.298	.457	.033	.626
1881	.290	.438	.034	.633
1886	.271	.418	.033	.618
1891	.258	.407	.032	.603
1896	.256	.405	.032	.603
1901	.247	.385	.029	.612
1911	.211	.307	.027	.658
1921	.194	.315	.027	.581
1931	.190	.278	.024	.655
1961	.228	.328	.027	.670

Sarthe

1831	.278	.516	.030	.510
1836	.249	.465	.029	.504
1841	.234	.429	.031	.510
1846	.223	.395	.033	.527
1851	.218	.364	.037	.554
1856	.219	.355	.033	.578
1861	.222	.352	.037	.590
1866	.226	.357	.039	.588
1871	.228	.366	.036	.583
1876	.231	.364	.039	.590
1881	.229	.358	.038	.597
1886	.227	.347	.043	.606
1891	.226	.341	.045	.612
1896	.227	.342	.047	.610
1901	.225	.340	.046	.608
1911	.224	.320	.048	.647
1921	.220	.344	.054	.572
1931	.226	.324	.050	.642
1961	.255	.361	.038	.672

Seine

1831	--	--	--	--
1836	--	--	--	--
1841	--	--	--	--
1846	--	--	--	--
1851	.265	.352	.161	.543
1856	.267	.363	.154	.540
1861	.264	.354	.154	.549
1866	.260	.351	.150	.545
1871	.242	.342	.129	.531
1876	.237	.332	.126	.541
1881	.237	.354	.116	.507
1886	.232	.341	.117	.512
1891	.209	.314	.103	.502
1896	.191	.287	.094	.502
1901	.178	.262	.090	.513
1911	.147	.210	.072	.543
1921	.134	.206	.059	.510
1931	.127	.180	.055	.581
1961	.180	.269	.049	.593

Seine-et-Marne

1831	.296	.426	.046	.658
1836	.284	.421	.043	.639
1841	.280	.421	.035	.636
1846	.285	.427	.031	.642
1851	.283	.416	.036	.651
1856	.282	.409	.043	.652
1861	.283	.411	.044	.651
1866	.270	.390	.044	.653
1871	.255	.370	.041	.649
1876	.248	.366	.037	.642
1881	.245	.361	.040	.639
1886	.242	.353	.042	.641
1891	.237	.345	.041	.644
1896	.232	.339	.041	.642
1901	.223	.327	.039	.638
1911	.201	.280	.041	.670
1921	.191	.289	.042	.603
1931	.196	.261	.055	.686
1961	.228	.306	.052	.692

Seine-et-Oise

1831	--	--	--	--
1836	--	--	--	--
1841	--	--	--	--
1846	--	--	--	--
1851	.267	.393	.046	.636
1856	.268	.396	.053	.625
1861	.273	.403	.054	.628
1866	.265	.377	.059	.648
1871	.253	.370	.055	.627
1876	.249	.366	.050	.629
1881	.245	.369	.047	.613
1886	.236	.379	.045	.570
1891	.223	.350	.043	.587
1896	.220	.351	.042	.576
1901	.215	.328	.044	.604
1911	.182	.266	.043	.621
1921	.161	.252	.037	.577
1931	.143	.191	.041	.681
1961	.214	.287	.047	.696

Seine-Infer

1831	.298	.580	.054	.462
1836	.279	.538	.056	.463
1841	.278	.540	.054	.461
1846	.273	.521	.056	.467
1851	.272	.499	.059	.483
1856	.278	.491	.066	.498
1861	.298	.519	.072	.505
1866	.305	.531	.075	.504
1871	.324	.573	.079	.497
1876	.322	.569	.079	.497
1881	.328	.574	.080	.503
1886	.331	.572	.085	.506

Deux-Sevres

1831	.286	.560	.012	.499
1836	.277	.528	.020	.506
1841	.271	.498	.020	.525
1846	.270	.475	.026	.544
1851	.265	.455	.029	.554
1856	.259	.433	.032	.566
1861	.263	.431	.036	.575
1866	.270	.452	.027	.572
1871	.275	.460	.025	.574
1876	.279	.453	.024	.595
1881	.277	.436	.026	.612
1886	.266	.417	.028	.611

Somme

1831	.271	.471	.040	.536
1836	.268	.463	.044	.536
1841	.268	.458	.044	.541
1846	.270	.450	.047	.552
1851	.266	.434	.050	.562
1856	.262	.420	.054	.568
1861	.260	.409	.058	.573
1866	.254	.398	.064	.569
1871	.252	.390	.068	.571
1876	.249	.379	.069	.579
1881	.248	.371	.072	.588
1886	.244	.357	.079	.594

FRANCE (continued)

	I_f	I_g	I_h	I_m
Seine-Infer (cont.)				
1891	.315	.539	.083	.508
1896	.301	.514	.080	.509
1901	.291	.494	.076	.513
1911	.257	.397	.072	.570
1921	.229	.364	.068	.543
1931	.214	.310	.058	.619
1961	.248	.345	.053	.667
Tarn				
1831	.290	.523	.020	.537
1836	.287	.499	.021	.555
1841	.290	.489	.025	.569
1846	.285	.478	.021	.577
1851	.271	.452	.019	.582
1856	.261	.431	.019	.586
1861	.268	.441	.020	.590
1866	.279	.461	.018	.590
1871	.283	.456	.019	.605
1876	.283	.441	.018	.627
1881	.270	.417	.018	.632
1886	.246	.383	.016	.627
1891	.227	.361	.016	.612
1896	.218	.349	.016	.607
1901	.216	.339	.016	.618
1911	.190	.277	.015	.666
1921	.179	.294	.017	.583
1931	.175	.262	.017	.647
1961	.194	.285	.019	.657
Vaucluse				
1831	.321	.527	.041	.577
1836	.315	.519	.042	.572
1841	.320	.532	.042	.569
1846	.323	.546	.035	.564
1851	.321	.546	.034	.560
1856	.321	.555	.030	.554
1861	.311	.547	.029	.544
1866	.291	.520	.028	.536
1871	.287	.518	.027	.529
1876	.264	.477	.025	.529
1881	.238	.428	.024	.529
1886	.216	.392	.020	.526
1891	.204	.365	.020	.535
1896	.202	.340	.021	.565
1901	.207	.333	.026	.589
1911	.194	.303	.032	.597
1921	.179	.304	.034	.539
1931	.172	.262	.033	.607
1961	.208	.292	.043	.663

	I_f	I_g	I_h	I_m
Deux-Sevres (cont.)				
1891	.247	.390	.027	.607
1896	.232	.368	.028	.599
1901	.219	.349	.025	.599
1911	.212	.321	.024	.634
1921	.203	.340	.024	.566
1931	.213	.319	.024	.641
1961	.251	.363	.022	.671
Tarn-et-Garonne				
1831	.236	.390	.019	.586
1836	.228	.364	.022	.603
1841	.226	.351	.025	.617
1846	.219	.337	.024	.623
1851	.214	.329	.020	.628
1856	.218	.330	.018	.642
1861	.221	.328	.020	.652
1866	.222	.328	.016	.663
1871	.220	.325	.016	.663
1876	.216	.316	.014	.672
1881	.208	.299	.014	.679
1886	.196	.283	.016	.674
1891	.188	.274	.018	.666
1896	.187	.273	.019	.662
1901	.189	.274	.020	.664
1911	.176	.242	.020	.705
1921	.184	.282	.026	.615
1931	.187	.265	.032	.665
1961	.211	.306	.032	.655
Vendee				
1831	.334	.685	.018	.474
1836	.317	.630	.019	.487
1841	.317	.601	.018	.513
1846	.310	.575	.016	.526
1851	.294	.543	.015	.528
1856	.284	.521	.018	.529
1861	.283	.523	.017	.525
1866	.284	.534	.017	.516
1871	.289	.545	.018	.514
1876	.301	.552	.017	.530
1881	.303	.540	.019	.546
1886	.293	.516	.021	.550
1891	.281	.483	.022	.561
1896	.265	.462	.021	.555
1901	.253	.441	.019	.554
1911	.234	.382	.017	.595
1921	.219	.413	.017	.510
1931	.229	.374	.015	.596
1961	.259	.395	.014	.643

	I_f	I_g	I_h	I_m
Somme (cont.)				
1891	.240	.349	.080	.594
1896	.238	.344	.083	.596
1901	.233	.331	.085	.603
1911	.212	.289	.084	.626
1921	.214	.321	.071	.571
1931	.214	.284	.077	.665
1961	.255	.356	.058	.661
Var				
1831	.294	.470	.044	.585
1836	.285	.459	.037	.587
1841	.285	.458	.037	.590
1846	.271	.437	.033	.590
1851	.264	.427	.031	.588
1856	.269	.442	.026	.585
1861	.276	.456	.026	.582
1866	.282	.460	.035	.580
1871	.275	.454	.031	.577
1876	.254	.421	.027	.577
1881	.240	.398	.024	.577
1886	.232	.378	.030	.581
1891	.222	.352	.033	.593
1896	.208	.325	.035	.597
1901	.210	.324	.039	.600
1911	.177	.265	.040	.611
1921	.167	.268	.031	.572
1931	.154	.226	.032	.628
1961	.202	.285	.035	.669
Vienne				
1831	.301	.525	.012	.563
1836	.295	.507	.024	.562
1841	.287	.480	.029	.571
1846	.280	.459	.033	.578
1851	.268	.435	.036	.583
1856	.263	.418	.031	.600
1861	.260	.409	.032	.604
1866	.264	.420	.031	.601
1871	.269	.429	.034	.595
1876	.270	.429	.034	.598
1881	.268	.422	.029	.609
1886	.260	.400	.029	.622
1891	.245	.382	.028	.612
1896	.230	.358	.028	.611
1901	.216	.337	.025	.612
1911	.208	.306	.027	.651
1921	.195	.322	.027	.569
1931	.202	.299	.030	.638
1961	.235	.339	.033	.659

Haute-Vienne				
1831	.388	.598	.059	.610
1836	.361	.557	.058	.608
1841	.356	.537	.057	.622
1846	.345	.518	.054	.628
1851	.322	.480	.053	.630
1856	.302	.450	.049	.631
1861	.307	.464	.050	.622
1866	.313	.485	.044	.610
1871	.332	.509	.041	.621
1876	.343	.509	.042	.645
1881	.333	.491	.040	.650
1886	.317	.466	.042	.648
1891	.295	.441	.042	.634
1896	.275	.416	.044	.621
1901	.260	.391	.042	.626
1911	.219	.307	.036	.673
1921	.182	.294	.028	.579
1931	.170	.244	.027	.656
1961	.178	.254	.022	.672

Vosges				
1831	.300	.635	.028	.448
1836	.291	.588	.036	.463
1841	.287	.563	.041	.472
1846	.273	.536	.038	.473
1851	.259	.493	.041	.483
1856	.270	.497	.047	.495
1861	.278	.501	.053	.502
1866	.285	.515	.052	.504
1871	.301	.532	.050	.521
1876	.292	.529	.042	.513
1881	.288	.516	.045	.515
1886	.273	.490	.047	.510
1891	.271	.478	.048	.517
1896	.264	.465	.050	.516
1901	.269	.459	.053	.532
1911	.242	.385	.052	.572
1921	.206	.386	.038	.482
1931	.203	.330	.036	.568
1961	.244	.370	.033	.625

Yonne				
1831	.281	.467	.026	.578
1836	.276	.457	.030	.576
1841	.276	.444	.034	.589
1846	.280	.443	.033	.602
1851	.271	.424	.031	.610
1856	.265	.410	.028	.619
1861	.255	.390	.030	.626
1866	.241	.359	.032	.638
1871	.232	.342	.033	.644
1876	.225	.335	.028	.643
1881	.219	.322	.031	.645
1886	.210	.309	.032	.642
1891	.206	.305	.030	.639
1896	.195	.289	.030	.637
1901	.191	.277	.033	.645
1911	.183	.260	.032	.661
1921	.188	.290	.039	.592
1931	.197	.266	.046	.688
1961	.236	.324	.058	.669

Belfort, Territoire De				
1831	--	--	--	--
1836	--	--	--	--
1841	--	--	--	--
1846	--	--	--	--
1851	--	--	--	--
1856	--	--	--	--
1861	--	--	--	--
1866	--	--	--	--
1871	.280	.671	.041	.379
1876	.308	.738	.038	.386
1881	.301	.668	.042	.413
1886	.301	.612	.053	.444
1891	.277	.558	.052	.446
1896	.273	.494	.060	.491
1901	.263	.450	.065	.516
1911	.228	.345	.076	.564
1921	.175	.300	.044	.512
1931	.200	.302	.043	.604
1961	.237	.330	.044	.674

Alpes-Maritimes				
1831	--	--	--	--
1836	--	--	--	--
1841	--	--	--	--
1846	--	--	--	--
1851	--	--	--	--
1856	--	--	--	--
1861	.291	.538	.025	.518
1866	.297	.519	.033	.544
1871	.305	.502	.042	.572
1876	.285	.493	.038	.543
1881	.297	.550	.050	.495
1886	.282	.521	.043	.500
1891	.217	.383	.041	.515
1896	.206	.369	.041	.504
1901	.199	.349	.043	.510
1911	.168	.280	.047	.519
1921	.138	.254	.033	.475
1931	.121	.191	.033	.558
1961	.156	.235	.031	.615

Savoie				
1831	--	--	--	--
1836	--	--	--	--
1841	--	--	--	--
1846	--	--	--	--
1851	--	--	--	--
1856	--	--	--	--
1861	.301	.723	.019	.401
1866	.315	.709	.021	.427
1871	.320	.698	.021	.442
1876	.322	.660	.022	.471
1881	.295	.663	.020	.428
1886	.280	.652	.021	.411
1891	.269	.567	.025	.450
1896	.263	.548	.027	.453
1901	.265	.501	.028	.501
1911	.240	.415	.029	.546
1921	.210	.403	.028	.485
1931	.208	.345	.026	.572
1961	.221	.343	.024	.619

Savoie-Haut				
1831	--	--	--	--
1836	--	--	--	--
1841	--	--	--	--
1846	--	--	--	--
1851	--	--	--	--
1856	--	--	--	--
1861	.298	.735	.027	.382
1866	.303	.689	.031	.414
1871	.320	.680	.030	.446
1876	.333	.670	.030	.474
1881	.310	.657	.026	.451
1886	.286	.624	.026	.435
1891	.263	.584	.026	.424
1896	.262	.634	.023	.390
1901	.272	.547	.025	.473
1911	.250	.450	.031	.523
1921	.213	.435	.025	.458
1931	.195	.348	.025	.528
1961	.221	.353	.028	.593

GERMANY

	I_f	I_g	I_h	I_m
Germany-Contemporary Bounds				
1867	.389	.760	.079	.454
1871	.396	.760	.071	.472
1875	.428	.791	.073	.495
1880	.404	.735	.072	.501
1885	.395	.726	.073	.494
1890	.386	.706	.070	.497
1895	--	--	--	--
1900	.373	.664	.066	.513
1905	--	--	--	--
1910	.312	.542	.059	.524
1925	--	--	--	--
1933	--	--	--	--
Marienwerder				
1867	.470	.820	.064	.537
1871	.467	.838	.060	.523
1875	--	--	--	--
1880	.474	.833	.068	.531
1885	.482	.861	.075	.518
1890	.479	.844	.072	.528
1895	.485	.861	.067	.527
1900	.491	.868	.060	.533
1905	.468	.841	.054	.526
1910	.438	.802	.052	.515
1925	.237	.433	.057	.480
1933	.222	.366	.053	.538
Frankfurt/O.				
1867	.383	.693	.084	.491
1871	.390	.704	.084	.493
1875	--	--	--	--
1880	.398	.685	.089	.518
1885	.394	.675	.092	.518
1890	.391	.666	.088	.524
1895	.374	.640	.086	.521
1900	.358	.595	.082	.538
1905	.327	.536	.074	.548
1910	.292	.472	.073	.549
1925	.188	.306	.049	.539
1933	.163	.236	.045	.616
Posen				
1867	.430	.787	.058	.510
1871	.443	.789	.059	.526
1875	--	--	--	--
1880	.446	.792	.060	.527
1885	.439	.803	.062	.508
1890	.436	.797	.058	.512
1895	.442	.823	.053	.506
1900	.454	.834	.051	.515
1905	.445	.814	.046	.519
1910	.409	.778	.042	.498
1925	.221	.382	.040	.527
1933	.237	.458	.043	.467

	I_f	I_g	I_h	I_m
Ostpreussen				
1867	.403	.744	.071	.494
1871	.403	.790	.069	.464
1875	--	--	--	--
1880	.410	.794	.077	.464
1885	.420	.800	.085	.469
1890	.431	.794	.085	.488
1895	.432	.800	.084	.486
1900	.423	.781	.078	.491
1905	.391	.739	.069	.481
1910	.364	.692	.068	.475
1925	.251	.476	.055	.465
1933	.226	.384	.050	.527
Berlin				
1867	.328	.648	.082	.434
1871	.314	.636	.074	.427
1875	.355	.662	.087	.467
1880	.320	.594	.080	.467
1885	.283	.535	.069	.459
1890	.258	.494	.060	.456
1895	.238	.448	.062	.455
1900	.217	.394	.061	.467
1905	.204	.356	.065	.477
1910	.183	.303	.073	.479
1925	.085	.147	.028	.477
1933	.090	.152	.024	.512
Stettin-Str.				
1867	.392	.713	.085	.489
1871	.393	.733	.083	.478
1875	--	--	--	--
1880	.402	.709	.090	.505
1885	.401	.706	.093	.501
1890	.397	.690	.089	.511
1895	.392	.674	.092	.515
1900	.384	.638	.091	.537
1905	.346	.572	.081	.539
1910	.308	.501	.080	.542
1925	.206	.336	.073	.506
1933	.185	.278	.058	.579
Bromberg				
1867	.466	.806	.064	.542
1871	.466	.817	.059	.537
1875	--	--	--	--
1880	.471	.821	.065	.536
1885	.477	.852	.069	.521
1890	.471	.833	.066	.528
1895	.479	.855	.064	.525
1900	.483	.853	.058	.535
1905	.465	.832	.050	.531
1910	.428	.790	.046	.514
1925	--	--	--	--
1933	--	--	--	--

	I_f	I_g	I_h	I_m
Danzig				
1867	.438	.815	.086	.483
1871	.420	.806	.076	.471
1875	--	--	--	--
1880	.434	.806	.082	.486
1885	.436	.821	.084	.478
1890	.438	.807	.079	.493
1895	.446	.820	.076	.497
1900	.452	.812	.072	.514
1905	.431	.775	.066	.515
1910	.402	.730	.065	.506
1925	--	--	--	--
1933	--	--	--	--
Potsdam				
1867	.380	.674	.075	.508
1871	.379	.680	.073	.504
1875	--	--	--	--
1880	.400	.669	.083	.541
1885	.390	.652	.085	.538
1890	.380	.623	.081	.552
1895	.350	.573	.076	.551
1900	.302	.498	.064	.548
1905	.257	.430	.054	.540
1910	.209	.347	.048	.537
1925	.163	.263	.049	.532
1933	.156	.225	.045	.613
Koslin				
1867	.410	.762	.073	.489
1871	.415	.786	.073	.479
1875	--	--	--	--
1880	.422	.783	.078	.488
1885	.425	.801	.081	.478
1890	.421	.782	.078	.487
1895	.419	.785	.077	.484
1900	.421	.763	.073	.504
1905	.395	.723	.065	.502
1910	.366	.670	.062	.501
1925	.236	.446	.050	.468
1933	.210	.349	.048	.537
Bresslau				
1867	.388	.740	.095	.453
1871	.398	.749	.092	.466
1875	--	--	--	--
1880	.391	.724	.093	.472
1885	.384	.720	.096	.461
1890	.382	.715	.094	.464
1895	.382	.704	.098	.468
1900	.379	.680	.094	.486
1905	.352	.625	.087	.492
1910	.321	.569	.087	.487
1925	.206	.371	.065	.461
1933	.178	.289	.053	.530

Liegnitz				
1867	.351	.660	.087	.460
1871	.358	.671	.086	.466
1875	--	--	--	--
1880	.373	.662	.094	.491
1885	.372	.654	.098	.492
1890	.371	.641	.096	.505
1895	.363	.623	.093	.510
1900	.360	.597	.091	.531
1905	.334	.552	.083	.536
1910	.312	.512	.081	.536
1925	.206	.342	.064	.512
1933	.173	.258	.058	.574

Oppeln				
1867	.447	.820	.061	.509
1871	.457	.827	.055	.521
1875	--	--	--	--
1880	.426	.806	.053	.495
1885	.437	.836	.057	.488
1890	.452	.842	.057	.503
1895	.481	.870	.057	.521
1900	.491	.866	.054	.538
1905	.472	.846	.048	.532
1910	.441	.816	.049	.511
1925	.271	.568	.042	.436
1933	.244	.442	.035	.512

Magdeburg				
1867	.384	.669	.075	.520
1871	.383	.673	.071	.518
1875	--	--	--	--
1880	.400	.649	.085	.557
1885	.404	.646	.091	.564
1890	.390	.622	.087	.567
1895	.375	.590	.092	.569
1900	.351	.544	.091	.573
1905	.310	.488	.082	.563
1910	.283	.427	.088	.577
1925	.176	.269	.065	.544
1933	.151	.212	.055	.614

Merseburg				
1867	.417	.731	.089	.511
1871	.421	.736	.089	.514
1875	--	--	--	--
1880	.449	.734	.101	.550
1885	.456	.733	.106	.559
1890	.448	.711	.103	.568
1895	.426	.678	.103	.562
1900	.410	.644	.102	.568
1905	.371	.580	.093	.570
1910	.335	.506	.097	.581
1925	.212	.316	.075	.566
1933	.168	.225	.063	.648

Erfurt				
1867	.396	.732	.062	.499
1871	.410	.741	.058	.515
1875	--	--	--	--
1880	.410	.704	.062	.542
1885	.402	.700	.063	.532
1890	.387	.669	.059	.538
1895	.369	.651	.057	.525
1900	.356	.617	.058	.533
1905	.332	.574	.054	.534
1910	.298	.508	.053	.538
1925	.187	.323	.039	.519
1933	.155	.245	.034	.575

Schleswig				
1867	.354	.686	.066	.464
1871	.348	.680	.059	.465
1875	--	--	--	--
1880	.374	.673	.069	.505
1885	.372	.664	.071	.508
1890	.372	.651	.070	.521
1895	.373	.640	.072	.530
1900	.356	.595	.068	.547
1905	.336	.546	.067	.561
1910	.305	.487	.068	.565
1925	.174	.297	.039	.524
1933	.165	.259	.035	.580

Hannover				
1867	.359	.679	.071	.473
1871	.356	.677	.062	.478
1875	--	--	--	--
1880	.360	.651	.063	.505
1885	.352	.643	.064	.497
1890	.342	.616	.064	.503
1895	.341	.608	.068	.506
1900	.327	.562	.067	.524
1905	.288	.491	.058	.530
1910	.248	.420	.054	.531
1925	.143	.255	.031	.497
1933	.129	.210	.026	.560

Hildesheim				
1867	.362	.650	.085	.490
1871	.364	.661	.065	.503
1875	--	--	--	--
1880	.374	.651	.061	.530
1885	.367	.645	.060	.526
1890	.366	.635	.056	.536
1895	.361	.628	.055	.534
1900	.351	.598	.056	.545
1905	.322	.546	.051	.546
1910	.292	.492	.051	.545
1925	.190	.335	.042	.506
1933	.163	.264	.032	.565

Luneburg				
1867	.319	.567	.063	.508
1871	.319	.573	.050	.514
1875	--	--	--	--
1880	.329	.554	.051	.553
1885	.332	.562	.055	.546
1890	.330	.552	.055	.552
1895	.339	.557	.061	.561
1900	.334	.537	.058	.577
1905	.316	.503	.056	.581
1910	.297	.465	.057	.588
1925	.185	.313	.039	.532
1933	.167	.259	.033	.591

Stade				
1867	.373	.681	.053	.509
1871	.379	.688	.046	.519
1875	--	--	--	--
1880	.392	.678	.047	.546
1885	.396	.676	.052	.552
1890	.390	.660	.049	.557
1895	.394	.667	.049	.559
1900	.389	.643	.048	.573
1905	.379	.611	.048	.587
1910	.348	.548	.051	.598
1925	.203	.348	.032	.541
1933	.177	.280	.027	.593

Osnabruck				
1867	.344	.744	.027	.442
1871	.358	.746	.021	.464
1875	--	--	--	--
1880	.369	.737	.025	.484
1885	.372	.742	.028	.481
1890	.362	.730	.028	.475
1895	.367	.749	.028	.469
1900	.370	.737	.027	.483
1905	.366	.719	.025	.491
1910	.354	.686	.024	.498
1925	.245	.529	.017	.444
1933	.209	.444	.012	.457

Aurich				
1867	.328	.719	.034	.429
1871	.337	.743	.027	.433
1875	--	--	--	--
1880	.364	.743	.026	.471
1885	.373	.760	.029	.470
1890	.379	.752	.026	.486
1895	.379	.765	.027	.478
1900	.371	.747	.024	.479
1905	.363	.726	.024	.483
1910	.350	.680	.025	.496
1925	.246	.499	.023	.469
1933	.219	.411	.019	.510

GERMANY (continued)

	I_f	I_g	I_h	I_m
Munster				
1867	.320	.827	.014	.377
1871	.329	.829	.012	.388
1875	--	--	--	--
1880	.371	.835	.016	.434
1885	.384	.862	.016	.435
1890	.395	.858	.014	.451
1895	.414	.886	.016	.458
1900	.442	.885	.017	.490
1905	.459	.870	.018	.517
1910	.447	.811	.021	.539
1925	.268	.527	.021	.489
1933	.196	.364	.013	.520
Kassel				
1867	.363	.724	.069	.449
1871	.374	.731	.054	.473
1875	--	--	--	--
1880	.381	.702	.048	.510
1885	.361	.675	.046	.501
1890	.356	.673	.045	.496
1895	.344	.660	.043	.489
1900	.339	.634	.042	.502
1905	.326	.591	.038	.522
1910	.294	.530	.036	.523
1925	.197	.366	.028	.500
1933	.164	.284	.021	.545
Dusseldorf				
1867	.406	.853	.023	.461
1871	.420	.872	.022	.469
1875	--	--	--	--
1880	.430	.841	.025	.496
1885	.420	.835	.026	.487
1890	.407	.802	.025	.491
1895	.399	.784	.026	.492
1900	.400	.743	.028	.521
1905	.381	.677	.029	.543
1910	.325	.569	.029	.549
1925	.170	.314	.020	.510
1933	.140	.243	.013	.552
Aachen				
1867	.373	.903	.015	.403
1871	.386	.931	.014	.405
1875	--	--	--	--
1880	.395	.915	.016	.422
1885	.388	.917	.016	.413
1890	.389	.918	.017	.412
1895	.385	.913	.016	.411
1900	.381	.891	.015	.418
1905	.362	.827	.014	.429
1910	.331	.737	.014	.439
1925	.215	.456	.014	.455
1933	.172	.332	.010	.504

	I_f	I_g	I_h	I_m
Minden				
1867	.384	.796	.035	.459
1871	.386	.798	.028	.465
1875	--	--	--	--
1880	.401	.783	.030	.493
1885	.397	.787	.030	.485
1890	.389	.768	.028	.487
1895	.386	.772	.028	.482
1900	.379	.739	.030	.492
1905	.356	.683	.029	.499
1910	.319	.619	.024	.496
1925	.198	.442	.016	.427
1933	.161	.330	.011	.470
Wiesbaden				
1867	.340	.700	.049	.447
1871	.343	.688	.038	.469
1875	--	--	--	--
1880	.329	.642	.033	.486
1885	.307	.627	.031	.464
1890	.292	.599	.032	.460
1895	.290	.592	.033	.459
1900	.289	.566	.035	.477
1905	.274	.513	.037	.499
1910	.237	.435	.035	.506
1925	.149	.285	.021	.483
1933	.123	.218	.016	.526
Koln				
1867	.368	.846	.035	.410
1871	.380	.872	.035	.412
1875	--	--	--	--
1880	.401	.850	.042	.445
1885	.390	.823	.045	.443
1890	.390	.803	.048	.452
1895	.375	.774	.050	.449
1900	.374	.734	.053	.471
1905	.350	.665	.050	.488
1910	.298	.554	.048	.493
1925	.173	.328	.029	.483
1933	.135	.245	.017	.517
Sigmaringen				
1867	.386	.868	.091	.379
1871	.411	.888	.080	.409
1875	--	--	--	--
1880	.422	.814	.064	.478
1885	.380	.764	.056	.458
1890	.352	.748	.051	.432
1895	.347	.776	.044	.414
1900	.360	.801	.041	.420
1905	.355	.764	.032	.442
1910	.334	.689	.026	.465
1925	.202	.474	.021	.400
1933	.177	.399	.023	.409

	I_f	I_g	I_h	I_m
Arnsberg				
1867	.445	.818	.026	.529
1871	.471	.839	.023	.549
1875	--	--	--	--
1880	.487	.815	.029	.583
1885	.482	.817	.028	.575
1890	.477	.811	.026	.575
1895	.474	.810	.027	.571
1900	.477	.781	.029	.595
1905	.461	.741	.030	.607
1910	.404	.644	.034	.606
1925	.205	.364	.022	.536
1933	.150	.253	.013	.571
Koblenz				
1867	.361	.769	.021	.454
1871	.372	.799	.019	.453
1875	--	--	--	--
1880	.387	.783	.021	.481
1885	.372	.761	.022	.474
1890	.366	.750	.020	.474
1895	.363	.755	.020	.467
1900	.360	.739	.019	.474
1905	.345	.691	.017	.487
1910	.314	.626	.016	.488
1925	.213	.439	.014	.469
1933	.173	.345	.011	.486
Trier				
1867	.401	.826	.024	.470
1871	.404	.844	.021	.465
1875	--	--	--	--
1880	.423	.835	.023	.492
1885	.412	.832	.024	.480
1890	.414	.828	.024	.484
1895	.423	.844	.025	.486
1900	.433	.841	.025	.501
1905	.423	.793	.023	.520
1910	.386	.713	.023	.526
1925	.262	.599	.013	.425
1933	.197	.442	.010	.433
Oberbayern				
1867	.406	.842	.158	.363
1871	.418	.839	.140	.398
1875	.461	.838	.147	.454
1880	.434	.786	.144	.452
1885	.409	.762	.139	.433
1890	.388	.732	.136	.423
1895	--	--	--	--
1900	.368	.680	.126	.437
1905	--	--	--	--
1910	.292	.534	.100	.442
1925	.170	.323	.061	.416
1933	.144	.275	.049	.419

Niederbayern				
1867	.415	.923	.161	.334
1871	.439	.921	.134	.388
1875	.479	.931	.135	.431
1880	.477	.913	.135	.440
1885	.468	.916	.134	.427
1890	.453	.906	.128	.417
1895	--	--	--	--
1900	.455	.912	.125	.419
1905	--	--	--	--
1910	.425	.835	.112	.433
1925	.283	.574	.089	.401
1933	.240	.473	.080	.409

Pfalz				
1867	.374	.735	.072	.455
1871	.409	.776	.062	.487
1875	.454	.789	.053	.545
1880	.424	.736	.050	.545
1885	.406	.720	.048	.533
1890	.388	.707	.049	.516
1895	--	--	--	--
1900	.395	.690	.053	.538
1905	--	--	--	--
1910	.345	.568	.050	.569
1925	.210	.373	.035	.517
1933	.171	.288	.026	.553

Oberpfalz				
1867	.414	.888	.152	.357
1871	.439	.889	.117	.417
1875	.484	.907	.107	.471
1880	.472	.880	.103	.475
1885	.464	.886	.101	.462
1890	.444	.876	.095	.447
1895	--	--	--	--
1900	.449	.896	.086	.449
1905	--	--	--	--
1910	.414	.803	.070	.469
1925	.281	.572	.059	.433
1933	.234	.455	.051	.453

Oberfranken				
1867	.365	.717	.144	.386
1871	.379	.714	.116	.439
1875	.412	.732	.113	.483
1880	.384	.688	.107	.477
1885	.374	.679	.102	.471
1890	.357	.666	.092	.462
1895	--	--	--	--
1900	.363	.664	.077	.487
1905	--	--	--	--
1910	.325	.565	.066	.519
1925	.214	.397	.046	.479
1933	.178	.305	.037	.526

Mittelfranken				
1867	.385	.759	.147	.388
1871	.401	.762	.130	.428
1875	.437	.765	.134	.480
1880	.408	.717	.130	.474
1885	.390	.694	.127	.464
1890	.371	.663	.121	.460
1895	--	--	--	--
1900	.362	.624	.116	.484
1905	--	--	--	--
1910	.292	.483	.094	.509
1925	.167	.297	.052	.471
1933	.144	.247	.044	.494

Unterfranken				
1867	.367	.782	.090	.400
1871	.377	.781	.073	.430
1875	.411	.789	.066	.477
1880	.376	.726	.062	.473
1885	.352	.711	.058	.450
1890	.339	.704	.053	.439
1895	--	--	--	--
1900	.349	.711	.047	.455
1905	--	--	--	--
1910	.327	.617	.039	.497
1925	.229	.459	.031	.463
1933	.189	.355	.025	.498

Schwaben				
1867	.399	.948	.100	.353
1871	.424	.942	.091	.391
1875	.469	.934	.094	.447
1880	.454	.880	.092	.460
1885	.428	.845	.088	.449
1890	.402	.814	.083	.436
1895	--	--	--	--
1900	.382	.782	.078	.432
1905	--	--	--	--
1910	.339	.669	.065	.453
1925	.200	.418	.047	.413
1933	.165	.345	.040	.407

Dresden				
1867	.362	.640	.107	.478
1871	.369	.651	.105	.484
1875	--	--	--	--
1880	.385	.639	.110	.520
1885	.377	.625	.110	.519
1890	.366	.604	.102	.526
1895	--	--	--	--
1900	.349	.552	.100	.549
1905	--	--	--	--
1910	.247	.394	.080	.531
1925	.145	.237	.054	.496
1933	.119	.186	.046	.524

Leipzig				
1867	.394	.717	.110	.468
1871	.403	.730	.104	.478
1875	--	--	--	--
1880	.423	.715	.107	.519
1885	.419	.698	.111	.524
1890	.406	.665	.110	.533
1895	--	--	--	--
1900	.353	.564	.107	.537
1905	--	--	--	--
1910	.256	.403	.090	.532
1925	.144	.230	.057	.501
1933	.119	.179	.048	.540

Zwickau				
1867	.475	.778	.138	.527
1871	.482	.786	.131	.537
1875	--	--	--	--
1880	.485	.761	.133	.562
1885	.486	.760	.135	.562
1890	.467	.728	.124	.567
1895	--	--	--	--
1900	.415	.640	.112	.575
1905	--	--	--	--
1910	.296	.463	.091	.553
1925	.158	.256	.056	.509
1933	.119	.181	.045	.547

Neckarkreis				
1867	--	--	--	--
1871	.420	.846	.075	.448
1875	.467	.849	.069	.511
1880	.425	.781	.065	.503
1885	.384	.744	.064	.471
1890	.355	.710	.062	.452
1895	--	--	--	--
1900	.340	.660	.062	.466
1905	--	--	--	--
1910	.285	.505	.056	.510
1925	.156	.302	.030	.463
1933	.138	.263	.023	.475

Swarzwalkreis				
1867	--	--	--	--
1871	.454	.892	.083	.458
1875	.483	.893	.068	.504
1880	.448	.836	.068	.495
1885	.415	.814	.071	.464
1890	.394	.799	.067	.446
1895	--	--	--	--
1900	.391	.780	.064	.458
1905	--	--	--	--
1910	.350	.642	.054	.503
1925	.193	.417	.034	.416
1933	.167	.355	.027	.427

GERMANY (continued)

	I_f	I_g	I_h	I_m
Jagstkreis				
1867	--	--	--	--
1871	.452	.859	.112	.454
1875	.486	.876	.097	.499
1880	.454	.826	.089	.495
1885	.424	.801	.086	.473
1890	.394	.774	.082	.451
1895	--	--	--	--
1900	.373	.746	.074	.446
1905	--	--	--	--
1910	.345	.651	.057	.484
1925	.217	.459	.035	.430
1933	.185	.389	.031	.431
Freiburg				
1867	--	--	--	--
1871	.351	.742	.073	.415
1875	--	--	--	--
1880	.348	.700	.053	.456
1885	.328	.677	.055	.440
1890	.315	.657	.049	.437
1895	--	--	--	--
1900	.318	.650	.044	.452
1905	--	--	--	--
1910	.286	.549	.039	.485
1925	.199	.412	.033	.440
1933	.174	.343	.029	.462
Starkenburg				
1867	--	--	--	--
1871	.408	.763	.066	.492
1875	--	--	--	--
1880	.392	.695	.057	.525
1885	.365	.679	.056	.496
1890	.353	.666	.054	.488
1895	.354	.667	.053	.490
1900	.365	.641	.054	.529
1905	.351	.583	.052	.561
1910	.306	.498	.053	.569
1925	.181	.320	.035	.514
1933	.148	.238	.025	.580
Mecklenburg				
1867	.307	.616	.073	.431
1871	.325	.598	.086	.467
1875	.349	.612	.092	.496
1880	.337	.579	.092	.503
1885	.338	.574	.093	.508
1890	.339	.566	.091	.522
1895	--	--	--	--
1900	.326	.518	.087	.554
1905	--	--	--	--
1910	.287	.440	.091	.561
1925	.212	.323	.090	.524
1933	.187	.272	.067	.583
Donaukreis				
1867	--	--	--	--
1871	.441	.921	.096	.418
1875	.480	.922	.090	.470
1880	.455	.868	.084	.474
1885	.422	.834	.080	.453
1890	.387	.793	.073	.437
1895	--	--	--	--
1900	.381	.791	.065	.434
1905	--	--	--	--
1910	.342	.678	.050	.466
1925	.200	.453	.033	.399
1933	.169	.388	.027	.392
Karlsruhe				
1867	--	--	--	--
1871	.422	.851	.062	.456
1875	--	--	--	--
1880	.405	.770	.050	.493
1885	.377	.746	.051	.469
1890	.356	.722	.049	.456
1895	--	--	--	--
1900	.361	.689	.052	.485
1905	--	--	--	--
1910	.308	.545	.051	.519
1925	.191	.365	.037	.468
1933	.154	.284	.029	.491
Oberhessen				
1867	--	--	--	--
1871	.356	.614	.071	.525
1875	--	--	--	--
1880	.346	.578	.061	.551
1885	.326	.560	.058	.533
1890	.310	.539	.055	.527
1895	.310	.542	.058	.521
1900	.307	.526	.058	.533
1905	.297	.489	.054	.562
1910	.275	.443	.050	.574
1925	.197	.346	.034	.522
1933	.162	.261	.023	.584
Thuringen				
1867	--	--	--	--
1871	.380	.644	.088	.526
1875	.412	.679	.091	.546
1880	.390	.634	.090	.553
1885	.392	.635	.095	.549
1890	.384	.621	.092	.552
1895	--	--	--	--
1900	.374	.586	.091	.572
1905	--	--	--	--
1910	.307	.477	.082	.570
1925	.193	.309	.057	.538
1933	.151	.220	.048	.602
Konstanz				
1867	--	--	--	--
1871	.397	.848	.094	.402
1875	--	--	--	--
1880	.395	.774	.071	.461
1885	.362	.720	.066	.453
1890	.343	.695	.059	.447
1895	--	--	--	--
1900	.339	.694	.046	.452
1905	--	--	--	--
1910	.310	.599	.034	.489
1925	.208	.437	.029	.440
1933	.177	.356	.027	.456
Mannheim				
1867	--	--	--	--
1871	.413	.787	.073	.476
1875	--	--	--	--
1880	.414	.750	.056	.516
1885	.396	.731	.057	.503
1890	.385	.719	.060	.493
1895	--	--	--	--
1900	.388	.686	.065	.520
1905	--	--	--	--
1910	.330	.556	.068	.537
1925	.196	.357	.045	.484
1933	.153	.267	.032	.515
Rheinhessen				
1867	--	--	--	--
1871	.367	.759	.061	.438
1875	--	--	--	--
1880	.366	.705	.047	.485
1885	.345	.683	.046	.470
1890	.329	.663	.041	.462
1895	.315	.634	.043	.460
1900	.320	.609	.048	.485
1905	.302	.551	.044	.508
1910	.264	.471	.043	.515
1925	.175	.331	.032	.479
1933	.146	.255	.023	.532
H. Oldenburg				
1867	.332	.695	.026	.457
1871	.329	.691	.022	.459
1875	.362	.731	.025	.478
1880	.353	.689	.028	.491
1885	.350	.694	.029	.483
1890	.355	.693	.030	.491
1895	.372	.710	.034	.499
1900	.381	.689	.035	.530
1905	.373	.649	.039	.547
1910	.349	.603	.040	.549
1925	.234	.437	.031	.499
1933	.206	.367	.023	.534

F. Lubeck				
1867	.367	.644	.108	.483
1871	.365	.648	.099	.484
1875	.390	.678	.102	.501
1880	.385	.651	.100	.517
1885	.404	.672	.109	.523
1890	.395	.655	.103	.529
1895	.390	.646	.105	.527
1900	.385	.618	.105	.546
1905	.375	.595	.097	.558
1910	.350	.545	.099	.564
1925	.198	.352	.051	.487
1933	.171	.282	.041	.540

Birkenfeld				
1867	.365	.652	.038	.532
1871	.376	.704	.035	.510
1875	.404	.729	.035	.532
1880	.389	.708	.037	.525
1885	.386	.694	.048	.523
1890	.383	.691	.046	.522
1895	.375	.700	.041	.506
1900	.385	.700	.038	.525
1905	.377	.673	.036	.535
1910	.352	.618	.035	.544
1925	.231	.434	.020	.511
1933	.173	.291	.015	.571

Braunschweig				
1867	--	--	--	--
1871	.360	.623	.088	.509
1875	.395	.676	.082	.527
1880	.372	.608	.084	.550
1885	.369	.602	.087	.547
1890	.366	.595	.085	.550
1895	.356	.580	.084	.548
1900	.340	.547	.079	.558
1905	.301	.486	.071	.555
1910	.263	.420	.069	.553
1925	.169	.277	.050	.521
1933	.142	.214	.041	.587

Anhalt				
1867	--	--	--	--
1871	.383	.672	.072	.518
1875	.415	.682	.086	.553
1880	.402	.646	.085	.565
1885	.405	.639	.088	.575
1890	.398	.621	.084	.584
1895	--	--	--	--
1900	.359	.554	.082	.587
1905	--	--	--	--
1910	.275	.416	.080	.578
1925	.192	.287	.071	.561
1933	.161	.217	.057	.647

Shmbrg/Lippe				
1867	--	--	--	--
1871	.361	.717	.030	.481
1875	--	--	--	--
1880	.357	.641	.030	.535
1885	.354	.648	.023	.530
1890	.328	.589	.017	.544
1895	--	--	--	--
1900	.321	.553	.029	.558
1905	--	--	--	--
1910	.270	.467	.023	.557
1925	.161	.291	.012	.533
1933	.139	.222	.011	.607

Lippe				
1867	--	--	--	--
1871	.380	.767	.040	.467
1875	--	--	--	--
1880	.397	.732	.043	.514
1885	.393	.726	.049	.507
1890	.393	.726	.044	.512
1895	--	--	--	--
1900	.374	.685	.039	.519
1905	--	--	--	--
1910	.329	.595	.031	.529
1925	.198	.415	.020	.451
1933	.161	.305	.013	.509

Lubeck				
1867	.307	.651	.052	.425
1871	.315	.643	.044	.453
1875	.345	.669	.053	.473
1880	.340	.635	.053	.493
1885	.332	.606	.055	.503
1890	.324	.582	.056	.509
1895	--	--	--	--
1900	.309	.534	.059	.526
1905	.293	.488	.058	.546
1910	.252	.417	.058	.541
1925	.154	.254	.045	.523
1933	.131	.201	.034	.576

Bremen				
1867	.319	.746	.035	.400
1871	.334	.728	.034	.433
1875	.366	.769	.035	.452
1880	.340	.668	.037	.481
1885	.305	.619	.034	.463
1890	.290	.603	.033	.450
1895	.285	.592	.013	.470
1900	.283	.550	.039	.477
1905	.279	.504	.043	.512
1910	.241	.417	.047	.525
1925	.144	.252	.031	.510
1933	.129	.220	.022	.542

Hamburg				
1867	.292	.666	.054	.389
1871	.315	.662	.053	.430
1875	.349	.672	.061	.471
1880	.340	.630	.061	.491
1885	.322	.594	.065	.485
1890	.321	.582	.069	.491
1895	.313	.561	.072	.493
1900	.270	.474	.065	.501
1905	.238	.406	.062	.513
1910	.210	.346	.060	.526
1925	.118	.205	.028	.511
1933	.114	.192	.024	.536

Germany-not Alsace/Lorraine				
1867	.389	.760	.079	.454
1871	.398	.760	.072	.474
1875	.430	.792	.073	.496
1880	.406	.736	.073	.502
1885	.397	.727	.074	.495
1890	.388	.707	.070	.498
1895	--	--	--	--
1900	.374	.665	.067	.514
1905	--	--	--	--
1910	.313	.543	.060	.524
1925	.185	.334	.041	.490
1933	.157	.264	.033	.534

Unterelsass				
1867	--	--	--	--
1871	.378	.793	.064	.430
1875	--	--	--	--
1880	.379	.729	.063	.475
1885	.366	.704	.067	.469
1890	.344	.666	.064	.465
1895	--	--	--	--
1900	.330	.619	.059	.484
1905	--	--	--	--
1910	.275	.484	.052	.516
1925	--	--	--	--
1933	--	--	--	--

Oberelsass				
1867	--	--	--	--
1871	.364	.802	.051	.417
1875	--	--	--	--
1880	.359	.762	.047	.437
1885	.348	.740	.049	.432
1890	.337	.710	.048	.436
1895	--	--	--	--
1900	.326	.638	.048	.471
1905	--	--	--	--
1910	.249	.462	.036	.498
1925	--	--	--	--
1933	--	--	--	--

GERMANY (continued)

	I_f	I_g	I_h	I_m		I_f	I_g	I_h	I_m		I_f	I_g	I_h	I_m
Lothringen														
1867	--	--	--	--										
1871	.326	.695	.035	.441										
1875	--	--	--	--										
1880	.337	.670	.034	.476										
1885	.329	.656	.034	.475										
1890	.321	.637	.034	.476										
1895	--	--	--	--										
1900	.344	.639	.038	.509										
1905	--	--	--	--										
1910	.328	.557	.037	.558										
1925	--	--	--	--										
1933	--	--	--	--										
Deutshereich 1939	.179	.284	.033	.583	Ostpreussen 1939	.253	.401	.051	.578	Berlin 1939	.145	.224	.037	.578
Schles. Slub. 1939	.238	.353	.045	.626	Sigmaringen 1939	.228	.503	.021	.429	Pfalz 1939	.195	.304	.027	.607
Mecklenburg 1939	.247	.346	.072	.638	Thuringen 1939	.200	.281	.051	.647	Braunschweig 1939	.188	.291	.040	.590
Anhalt 1939	.219	.290	.064	.685	Shmbrg/Lippe 1939	.203	.299	.022	.656	Lippe 1939	.203	.335	.020	.581
Bremen 1939	.193	.295	.032	.612	Hamburg 1939	.168	.254	.037	.604	P. Brandenburg 1939	.206	.287	.052	.654
P. Pommern 1939	.250	.368	.059	.618	P. Schlesien 1939	.241	.375	.046	.591	P. Sachsen 1939	.206	.283	.059	.659
P. Hannover 1939	.220	.343	.032	.604	P. Westfalen 1939	.207	.343	.018	.582	P. Hessen/Nas 1939	.187	.299	.024	.592
P. Rheinland 1939	.185	.307	.019	.576	K. Bayern R. Rh. 1939	.219	.368	.051	.529	K. Sachsen 1939	.159	.232	.045	.606
K. Wuerttemberg 1939	.209	.367	.031	.532	Gh. Baden 1939	.202	.347	.029	.546	Gh. Hessen 1939	.186	.280	.026	.628
Gh. Oldenburg 1939	.269	.426	.027	.605	Sr Saarland 1939	.188	.305	.016	.595					
Germany (East & West) 1962	.202	.293	.039	.644	Berlin West 1962	.133	.213	.039	.537	Schleswig 1962	.201	.310	.032	.608
Bremen 1962	.178	.263	.033	.633	Hamburg 1962	.154	.244	.028	.581	Rheinl-pf 1962	.220	.320	.031	.656
Bayern 1962	.208	.315	.044	.605	Hessen 1962	.192	.278	.030	.653	Saarland 1962	.220	.309	.029	.681

Neid-Sach					Nordr-Wes					Bad-Wurtt				
1962	.209	.316	.028	.629	1962	.197	.291	.024	.645	1962	.213	.333	.032	.601
Hauptstadt Berlin					Rostock					Schwerin				
1962	.195	.254	.076	.671	1962	.246	.312	.083	.711	1962	.249	.320	.070	.717
Neubrandenburg					Potsdam					Frankfurt				
1962	.263	.325	.085	.742	1962	.229	.287	.073	.726	1962	.234	.286	.083	.747
Cottbus					Magdeburg					Halle				
1962	.227	.277	.072	.756	1962	.219	.277	.069	.724	1962	.205	.257	.070	.721
Erfurt					Gera					Suhl				
1962	.214	.276	.059	.712	1962	.201	.258	.064	.709	1962	.205	.256	.053	.749
Dresden					Leipzig					Karl-Marx-Stadt				
1962	.200	.257	.077	.686	1962	.194	.250	.073	.685	1962	.178	.223	.064	.718
Brbundesrep					East Germany									
1962	.200	.301	.032	.625	1962	.211	.267	.071	.713					

GREECE

Greece					Attica (inc. Athens)					Central Greece East				
1900	.440	.688	.015	.632	1900	.361	.600	.024	.584	1900	.546	.810	.023	.665
1928	.307	.535	.009	.566	1928	.210	.398	.010	.515	1928	.271	.490	.012	.543
1951	.203	.399	.005	.502	1951	.147	.303	.005	.477	1951	.204	.404	.005	.500
1961	.191	.327	.006	.576	1961	.153	.281	.006	.537	1961	.200	.343	.004	.577
Central Greece Middle					Central Greece West					Peloponnesus North				
1900	.455	.703	.018	.638	1900	.438	.694	.016	.621	1900	.463	.751	.012	.610
1928	.256	.481	.011	.523	1928	.242	.450	.010	.526	1928	.297	.592	.007	.496
1951	.187	.397	.004	.465	1951	.253	.546	.006	.457	1951	.224	.487	.005	.453
1961	.194	.338	.004	.571	1961	.256	.447	.005	.569	1961	.214	.373	.006	.568
Peloponnesus South					Ionian Islands					Epirus				
1900	.443	.690	.012	.636	1900	.338	.594	.016	.557	1900	.477	.673	.010	.705
1928	.326	.637	.008	.505	1928	.263	.522	.010	.493	1928	.346	.533	.009	.643
1951	.199	.448	.004	.438	1951	.185	.378	.007	.481	1951	.259	.467	.006	.547
1961	.219	.380	.006	.569	1961	.187	.311	.008	.589	1961	.220	.364	.006	.598
Thessaly					Macedonia West					Macedonia Middle				
1900	.448	.641	.009	.694	1900	--	--	--	--	1900	--	--	--	--
1928	.323	.542	.006	.590	1928	.420	.575	.013	.723	1928	.410	.594	.012	.683
1951	.231	.460	.004	.497	1951	.220	.403	.006	.541	1951	.234	.428	.006	.539
1961	.196	.341	.005	.570	1961	.226	.367	.008	.606	1961	.200	.330	.007	.598
Macedonia Salonica					Macedonia East					Thrace				
1900	--	--	--	--	1900	--	--	--	--	1900	--	--	--	--
1928	.293	.512	.009	.568	1928	.415	.603	.012	.681	1928	.389	.558	.007	.694
1951	.160	.314	.004	.504	1951	.219	.397	.006	.544	1951	.262	.409	.004	.636
1961	.151	.281	.004	.529	1961	.202	.324	.007	.613	1961	.222	.311	.005	.710

GREECE (continued)

	I_f	I_g	I_h	I_m		I_f	I_g	I_h	I_m		I_f	I_g	I_h	I_m
Aegean Islands					Cyclades					Dodecanesus				
1900	--	--	--	--	1900	.455	.677	.013	.664	1900	--	--	--	--
1928	.258	.518	.008	.491	1928	.341	.591	.005	.575	1928	--	--	--	--
1951	.197	.364	.006	.533	1951	.232	.406	.007	.565	1951	.293	.488	.009	.591
1961	.175	.272	.005	.637	1961	.216	.336	.006	.644	1961	.226	.367	.005	.609
Crete														
1900	--	--	--	--										
1928	.290	.575	.007	.498										
1951	.212	.418	.005	.503										
1961	.202	.348	.005	.574										

HUNGARY

	I_f	I_g	I_h	I_m		I_f	I_g	I_h	I_m		I_f	I_g	I_h	I_m
Hungary					Baranya					Fejer				
1880	.442	.589	.111	.692	1880	.415	.518	.119	.743	1880	.494	.651	.106	.713
1890	.453	.580	.137	.713	1890	.368	.442	.131	.761	1890	.469	.617	.101	.715
1900	.422	.572	.118	.670	1900	.345	.429	.124	.724	1900	.464	.632	.083	.695
1910	.388	.529	.107	.665	1910	.301	.366	.117	.739	1910	.430	.583	.071	.701
Gyor					Komarom					Moson				
1880	.449	.651	.113	.625	1880	.475	.647	.093	.689	1880	.483	.703	.102	.633
1890	.464	.684	.087	.632	1890	.488	.664	.094	.691	1890	.496	.711	.126	.631
1900	.428	.651	.068	.619	1900	.481	.645	.096	.702	1900	.474	.705	.120	.606
1910	.377	.583	.057	.608	1910	.462	.615	.096	.706	1910	.444	.661	.111	.606
Somogy					Sopron					Tolna				
1880	.429	.557	.102	.717	1880	.444	.663	.088	.620	1880	.463	.586	.085	.755
1890	.411	.517	.102	.744	1890	.460	.681	.094	.624	1890	.405	.506	.084	.760
1900	.380	.500	.084	.712	1900	.443	.684	.084	.598	1900	.384	.502	.069	.729
1910	.332	.423	.077	.735	1910	.404	.613	.076	.610	1910	.338	.425	.063	.759
Vas					Veszprem					Zala				
1880	.425	.610	.118	.624	1880	.467	.631	.097	.692	1880	.424	.586	.120	.654
1890	.438	.617	.122	.638	1890	.438	.593	.087	.694	1890	.436	.578	.124	.687
1900	.420	.624	.093	.615	1900	.430	.596	.067	.686	1900	.415	.582	.092	.659
1910	.392	.581	.080	.623	1910	.383	.533	.059	.684	1910	.383	.541	.071	.663
Arva					Bars					Esztergom				
1880	.390	.620	.041	.603	1880	.439	.590	.081	.704	1880	.487	.654	.117	.690
1890	.426	.649	.048	.630	1890	.433	.584	.088	.696	1890	.483	.636	.127	.700
1900	.401	.603	.048	.636	1900	.442	.599	.074	.702	1900	.481	.650	.109	.688
1910	.340	.544	.030	.604	1910	.406	.542	.069	.712	1910	.434	.578	.082	.709
Hont					Lipto					Nograd				
1880	.376	.497	.086	.706	1880	.414	.583	.067	.673	1880	.422	.543	.107	.724
1890	.357	.457	.092	.726	1890	.453	.648	.067	.664	1890	.424	.528	.120	.747
1900	.361	.465	.083	.726	1900	.447	.643	.051	.669	1900	.416	.533	.106	.726
1910	.317	.408	.069	.733	1910	.383	.570	.057	.636	1910	.401	.520	.092	.723

Nyitra					Pozsony					Trencsen				
1880	.487	.666	.093	.688	1880	.435	.637	.092	.629	1880	.405	.599	.078	.629
1890	.486	.671	.093	.680	1890	.437	.647	.104	.613	1890	.446	.644	.106	.632
1900	.500	.701	.083	.674	1900	.438	.670	.092	.598	1900	.451	.681	.092	.610
1910	.453	.640	.069	.672	1910	.394	.600	.079	.605	1910	.390	.614	.075	.584
Turoc					Zolyom					Bacs-Bodrog				
1880	.375	.541	.070	.648	1880	.441	.591	.101	.694	1880	.554	.707	.117	.741
1890	.431	.613	.093	.648	1890	.431	.579	.094	.695	1890	.501	.610	.133	.773
1900	.408	.599	.066	.642	1900	.429	.595	.080	.678	1900	.431	.566	.100	.709
1910	.387	.565	.069	.641	1910	.396	.550	.069	.680	1910	.393	.510	.095	.717
Csongrad					Heves					Jasz Nk Sz				
1880	.478	.622	.100	.725	1880	.513	.653	.121	.737	1880	.517	.637	.132	.764
1890	.475	.595	.106	.753	1890	.529	.671	.124	.739	1890	.506	.613	.138	.773
1900	.412	.573	.075	.676	1900	.476	.630	.095	.713	1900	.471	.614	.109	.718
1910	.375	.525	.070	.671	1910	.439	.578	.075	.724	1910	.443	.577	.096	.722
Pest					Abauj					Bereg				
1880	.521	.666	.138	.725	1880	.403	.561	.114	.647	1880	.407	.558	.096	.672
1890	.516	.654	.148	.728	1890	.417	.557	.143	.662	1890	.515	.636	.187	.730
1900	.477	.637	.123	.689	1900	.409	.558	.141	.641	1900	.518	.675	.151	.700
1910	.438	.580	.109	.698	1910	.367	.500	.125	.645	1910	.461	.651	.115	.645
Borsod					Gomor					Saros				
1880	.432	.558	.128	.707	1880	.377	.482	.103	.723	1880	.430	.587	.075	.694
1890	.442	.561	.150	.710	1890	.401	.505	.121	.731	1890	.452	.614	.124	.669
1900	.430	.561	.124	.700	1900	.394	.502	.112	.723	1900	.452	.624	.122	.657
1910	.406	.525	.123	.704	1910	.363	.467	.110	.708	1910	.402	.562	.098	.654
Szepes					Ung					Zemplen				
1880	.455	.639	.083	.669	1880	.397	.559	.071	.669	1880	.393	.556	.076	.660
1890	.449	.619	.114	.663	1890	.484	.624	.139	.711	1890	.458	.588	.157	.700
1900	.462	.642	.102	.666	1900	.464	.608	.122	.703	1900	.439	.574	.135	.692
1910	.421	.588	.100	.658	1910	.392	.530	.109	.673	1910	.385	.525	.108	.664
Bekes					Bihar					Hajdu				
1880	.544	.674	.105	.771	1880	.443	.559	.157	.712	1880	.451	.578	.137	.712
1890	.518	.642	.103	.769	1890	.500	.589	.219	.758	1890	.464	.596	.148	.705
1900	.458	.606	.077	.720	1900	.459	.588	.184	.680	1900	.437	.599	.112	.667
1910	.436	.575	.072	.722	1910	.440	.573	.178	.664	1910	.414	.586	.099	.646
Maramaros					Szabolcs					Szatmar				
1880	.432	.574	.091	.700	1880	.438	.605	.110	.661	1880	.381	.538	.085	.655
1890	.514	.600	.272	.739	1890	.570	.720	.191	.717	1890	.490	.628	.134	.720
1900	.486	.630	.163	.693	1900	.535	.712	.130	.697	1900	.454	.615	.106	.683
1910	.473	.630	.171	.659	1910	.463	.659	.097	.653	1910	.424	.595	.097	.656
Szilagy					Ugosca					Arad				
1880	.367	.492	.093	.686	1880	.377	.513	.077	.689	1880	.482	.603	.169	.720
1890	.480	.571	.176	.770	1890	.502	.629	.129	.745	1890	.494	.586	.210	.756
1900	.445	.570	.145	.706	1900	.497	.652	.094	.722	1900	.434	.550	.178	.687
1910	.436	.571	.128	.695	1910	.462	.622	.095	.696	1910	.382	.481	.167	.684
Csanad					Krasso Sz.					Temes				
1880	.593	.713	.150	.786	1880	.346	.466	.042	.716	1880	.446	.565	.156	.708
1890	.570	.673	.170	.796	1890	.354	.419	.184	.726	1890	.422	.477	.276	.725
1900	.484	.642	.118	.700	1900	.327	.384	.211	.671	1900	.349	.442	.171	.657
1910	.438	.569	.101	.722	1910	.305	.357	.205	.658	1910	.311	.378	.168	.679

HUNGARY (continued)

	I_f	I_g	I_h	I_m		I_f	I_g	I_h	I_m		I_f	I_g	I_h	I_m
Torontal					Also-Feher					Beszterce N.				
1880	.534	.676	.145	.732	1880	.417	.551	.100	.702	1880	.359	.478	.077	.702
1890	.495	.583	.189	.777	1890	.452	.562	.136	.742	1890	.373	.449	.121	.768
1900	.422	.533	.176	.687	1900	.425	.574	.108	.680	1900	.375	.483	.102	.719
1910	.394	.479	.165	.731	1910	.421	.578	.108	.665	1910	.364	.482	.098	.694
Brasso					Csik					Fogaras				
1880	.414	.586	.082	.659	1880	.524	.651	.169	.737	1880	.414	.552	.059	.720
1890	.415	.584	.084	.662	1890	.525	.631	.176	.767	1890	.426	.531	.111	.751
1900	.366	.540	.075	.626	1900	.513	.652	.146	.725	1900	.420	.548	.111	.705
1910	.348	.517	.067	.624	1910	.500	.659	.118	.707	1910	.366	.502	.090	.669
Haromszek					Hunyad					Kis-Kukullo				
1880	.440	.580	.150	.675	1880	.351	.473	.045	.715	1880	.424	.549	.120	.708
1890	.451	.577	.163	.696	1890	.374	.452	.131	.757	1890	.451	.539	.177	.759
1900	.423	.577	.142	.645	1900	.377	.469	.144	.718	1900	.420	.548	.155	.674
1910	.419	.576	.137	.642	1910	.333	.419	.127	.704	1910	.411	.554	.161	.635
Kolozs					Maros Torda					Nagykukullo				
1880	.403	.513	.120	.719	1880	.417	.556	.103	.693	1880	.394	.496	.111	.736
1890	.422	.507	.161	.755	1890	.450	.557	.148	.739	1890	.391	.477	.129	.752
1900	.401	.522	.158	.669	1900	.423	.567	.148	.657	1900	.381	.490	.131	.696
1910	.405	.531	.158	.662	1910	.430	.573	.163	.652	1910	.369	.486	.130	.673
Szeben					Sz. Doboka					Torda Ar.				
1880	.387	.546	.077	.661	1880	.375	.491	.068	.726	1880	.403	.527	.100	.709
1890	.388	.532	.077	.683	1890	.429	.505	.127	.799	1890	.459	.547	.170	.765
1900	.372	.545	.075	.632	1900	.409	.519	.116	.726	1900	.439	.573	.155	.680
1910	.354	.523	.076	.622	1910	.409	.531	.104	.713	1910	.448	.599	.139	.672
Udvarhely					Bjelovar K.					Lika Krbava				
1880	.450	.549	.177	.732	1880	--	--	--	--	1880	--	--	--	--
1890	.476	.553	.224	.767	1890	.367	.444	.084	.786	1890	.550	.759	.095	.686
1900	.457	.574	.180	.703	1900	.345	.436	.074	.748	1900	.517	.743	.078	.660
1910	.450	.574	.169	.694	1910	.329	.411	.074	.756	1910	.378	.608	.062	.579
Modrus Rij.					Pozega					Srijem				
1880	--	--	--	--	1880	--	--	--	--	1880	--	--	--	--
1890	.476	.664	.059	.689	1890	.468	.567	.130	.773	1890	.472	.588	.082	.770
1900	.438	.653	.064	.634	1900	.418	.542	.109	.714	1900	.472	.601	.126	.729
1910	.379	.572	.067	.619	1910	.423	.547	.120	.709	1910	.456	.571	.132	.737
Varazdin					Virovitica					Zagreb				
1880	--	--	--	--	1880	--	--	--	--	1880	--	--	--	--
1890	.441	.632	.071	.659	1890	.499	.606	.177	.750	1890	.448	.575	.114	.725
1900	.436	.643	.056	.647	1900	.462	.591	.165	.697	1900	.398	.545	.098	.671
1910	.423	.637	.048	.636	1910	.453	.576	.161	.704	1910	.362	.501	.097	.656
Fiume City					Budapest									
1880	.346	.680	.062	.460	1880	.309	.465	.182	.447					
1890	.408	.702	.104	.508	1890	.297	.472	.154	.451					
1900	.354	.617	.104	.487	1900	.256	.420	.125	.444					
1910	.312	.522	.112	.489	1910	.202	.340	.093	.442					

Hungary	1930	.235	.357	.053	.598
Gyor, Moson Es Pozsony	1930	.253	.417	.050	.554
Sopron	1930	.257	.426	.046	.555
Veszprem	1930	.277	.417	.052	.616
Bekes	1930	.236	.356	.048	.611
Csongrad	1930	.207	.328	.047	.570
Pest-Pilis-Solt-Kiskun	1930	.170	.276	.044	.539
Abauj-Torna	1930	.310	.442	.070	.646
Nograd Es Hont	1930	.268	.372	.053	.673
Baranya	1930	.213	.272	.080	.692
Komarom Es Esztergom	1930	.265	.378	.057	.648
Tolna	1930	.219	.292	.049	.699
Zala	1930	.250	.391	.045	.591
Bihar	1930	.297	.410	.084	.654
Hajdu	1930	.274	.430	.072	.563
Szabolcs Es Ung	1930	.364	.552	.066	.613
Borsod, Gomor Es Kishon	1930	.265	.381	.064	.633
Zemplen	1930	.307	.467	.063	.604
Fejer	1930	.270	.392	.054	.639
Somogy	1930	.218	.294	.062	.673
Vas	1930	.253	.423	.045	.551
Bacs-Bodrog	1930	.213	.277	.053	.713
Csanad, Arad, Es Torron.	1930	.234	.336	.053	.640
Jasz-Nagykon-Szolnok	1930	.272	.398	.059	.628
Szatmar, Ugocsa, Es Ber.	1930	.362	.540	.090	.605
Heves	1930	.266	.372	.053	.669

Hungary	1960	.158	.207	.032	.725
Miskolo	1960	.141	.182	.029	.732
Baranya	1960	.192	.227	.076	.773
Borsod-Abauj-Zemplen	1960	.206	.258	.051	.747
Gyor-Sopron	1960	.167	.232	.016	.699
Komarom	1960	.173	.215	.036	.767
Somogy	1960	.162	.198	.047	.761
Tolna	1960	.167	.205	.050	.754
Zala	1960	.174	.232	.031	.710
Budapest	1960	.092	.129	.014	.675
Pecs	1960	.134	.171	.028	.741
Bacs-Kiskun	1960	.165	.209	.038	.739
Csongrad	1960	.152	.196	.029	.732
Hajdu-Bihar	1960	.218	.282	.047	.727
Nograd	1960	.171	.211	.030	.777
Szabolcs-Szatmar	1960	.228	.300	.047	.715
Vas	1960	.172	.243	.019	.681
Debrecen	1960	.142	.196	.026	.684
Szeged	1960	.113	.161	.021	.664
Bekes	1960	.159	.204	.036	.732
Fejer	1960	.185	.236	.033	.750
Heves	1960	.153	.186	.038	.776
Pest	1960	.157	.200	.033	.746
Szolnok	1960	.170	.220	.039	.727
Veszprem	1960	.181	.239	.028	.725

ICELAND

	I_f	I_g	I_h	I_m
1850	.392	.943	.087	.357
1860	.386	.871	.081	.385
1870	.338	.778	.094	.357
1880	.306	.829	.089	.294
1890	.310	.753	.090	.332
1901	.315	.701	.076	.383
1910	.297	.681	.063	.378
1920	.288	.638	.063	.392
1930	.263	.530	.074	.415
1940	.244	.442	.102	.418
1950	.308	.454	.162	.498
1960	.335	.414	.215	.602

IRELAND

Ireland	I_f	I_g	I_h	I_m
1871	.295	.708	.014	.405
1881	.268	.706	.011	.370
1891	.245	.709	.010	.336
1901	.235	.707	.009	.324
1911	.247	.708	.010	.339
1926	.229	.610	.012	.362
1936	.218	.570	.013	.369
1961	.287	.548	.011	.513

Carlow County	I_f	I_g	I_h	I_m
1871	.278	.721	.018	.371
1881	.260	.722	.013	.347
1891	.229	.703	.013	.314
1901	.224	.684	.011	.316
1911	.234	.702	.011	.323
1926	.236	.629	.018	.357
1936	.233	.583	.019	.379
1961	.368	.707	.020	.507

Dublin County All	I_f	I_g	I_h	I_m
1871	.237	.597	.008	.388
1881	.251	.633	.008	.388
1891	.244	.658	.009	.362
1901	.230	.657	.010	.341
1911	.232	.643	.012	.349
1926	.226	.603	.011	.364
1936	.216	.596	.009	.352
1961	.271	.582	.009	.457

Kildare County	I_f	I_g	I_h	I_m
1871	.274	.672	.013	.396
1881	.271	.704	.010	.376
1891	.248	.690	.011	.348
1901	.261	.717	.010	.356
1911	.273	.660	.013	.402
1926	.259	.623	.020	.396
1936	.278	.636	.021	.419
1961	.349	.631	.018	.540

Kilkenny County	I_f	I_g	I_h	I_m
1871	.261	.739	.014	.340
1881	.256	.745	.011	.334
1891	.231	.727	.010	.308
1901	.227	.750	.009	.295
1911	.250	.754	.010	.322
1926	.250	.680	.016	.352
1936	.235	.628	.020	.353
1961	.299	.606	.013	.482

Offaly County-Kings	I_f	I_g	I_h	I_m
1871	.267	.701	.009	.372
1881	.252	.694	.007	.358
1891	.240	.705	.006	.335
1901	.214	.682	.005	.308
1911	.235	.726	.008	.316
1926	.239	.640	.010	.364
1936	.236	.616	.013	.365
1961	.349	.659	.011	.522

Longford County	I_f	I_g	I_h	I_m
1871	.287	.717	.006	.395
1881	.251	.680	.006	.364
1891	.229	.690	.005	.327
1901	.224	.693	.005	.318
1911	.254	.758	.006	.329
1926	.255	.678	.007	.369
1936	.231	.616	.013	.362
1961	.323	.646	.011	.491

Louth County	I_f	I_g	I_h	I_m
1871	.266	.705	.009	.368
1881	.253	.695	.007	.357
1891	.232	.680	.007	.334
1901	.212	.661	.007	.314
1911	.236	.706	.008	.327
1926	.241	.628	.011	.373
1936	.224	.613	.012	.354
1961	.297	.626	.006	.469

Meath County	I_f	I_g	I_h	I_m
1871	.248	.699	.009	.348
1881	.248	.728	.007	.334
1891	.216	.675	.008	.311
1901	.217	.710	.007	.299
1911	.230	.696	.006	.324
1926	.235	.638	.012	.356
1936	.235	.611	.018	.366
1961	.320	.620	.011	.507

Laoighis Co.-Queens	I_f	I_g	I_h	I_m
1871	.262	.703	.010	.364
1881	.258	.761	.008	.333
1891	.227	.721	.007	.308
1901	.220	.715	.006	.301
1911	.241	.733	.006	.323
1926	.241	.640	.013	.364
1936	.236	.615	.018	.370
1961	.331	.649	.012	.502

Westmeath County	I_f	I_g	I_h	I_m
1871	.273	.727	.010	.368
1881	.278	.786	.008	.348
1891	.232	.710	.006	.321
1901	.211	.670	.005	.309
1911	.232	.693	.006	.328
1926	.248	.648	.010	.372
1936	.238	.625	.016	.365
1961	.335	.668	.011	.493

Wexford County	I_f	I_g	I_h	I_m
1871	.263	.737	.015	.343
1881	.250	.726	.012	.334
1891	.226	.711	.011	.307
1901	.223	.702	.011	.306
1911	.240	.715	.014	.322
1926	.238	.649	.018	.348
1936	.234	.613	.018	.362
1961	.312	.613	.017	.496

Wicklow County				
1871	.268	.710	.014	.366
1881	.252	.711	.010	.345
1891	.224	.679	.009	.321
1901	.221	.650	.008	.332
1911	.223	.628	.009	.347
1926	.229	.582	.016	.376
1936	.218	.552	.018	.373
1961	.301	.581	.017	.502

Kerry County				
1871	.418	.782	.011	.529
1881	.351	.797	.007	.435
1891	.298	.816	.007	.360
1901	.277	.806	.006	.338
1911	.286	.854	.006	.330
1926	.256	.768	.008	.326
1936	.215	.654	.009	.319
1961	.293	.613	.007	.474

Waterford County				
1871	.296	.704	.020	.402
1881	.275	.726	.017	.364
1891	.240	.723	.013	.319
1901	.225	.697	.014	.308
1911	.238	.695	.014	.330
1926	.226	.652	.012	.335
1936	.236	.636	.013	.358
1961	.294	.603	.009	.482

Cavan County				
1871	.305	.738	.008	.406
1881	.258	.677	.006	.375
1891	.225	.682	.006	.324
1901	.217	.671	.005	.318
1911	.248	.762	.006	.320
1926	.248	.675	.010	.358
1936	.239	.636	.017	.359
1961	.309	.617	.010	.492

Londonderry County				
1871	.265	.718	.018	.353
1881	.244	.691	.016	.339
1891	.234	.702	.015	.319
1901	.225	.737	.013	.293
1911	.240	.706	.017	.325
1926	.244	.632	.017	.368
1936	.251	.601	.019	.394
1961	.335	.605	.018	.540

Galway County				
1871	.342	.694	.008	.487
1881	.302	.698	.005	.429
1891	.274	.736	.004	.369
1901	.268	.790	.003	.337
1911	.281	.863	.004	.323
1926	.267	.779	.006	.337
1936	.258	.747	.008	.338
1961	.302	.657	.007	.454

Clare County				
1871	.343	.732	.012	.460
1881	.300	.768	.007	.385
1891	.257	.764	.006	.332
1901	.239	.751	.006	.313
1911	.249	.790	.006	.309
1926	.233	.685	.010	.330
1936	.228	.648	.011	.341
1961	.303	.631	.009	.475

Limerick County				
1871	.315	.726	.014	.423
1881	.280	.747	.011	.365
1891	.241	.750	.011	.312
1901	.234	.755	.010	.301
1911	.258	.797	.012	.314
1926	.259	.706	.011	.357
1936	.243	.663	.014	.352
1961	.309	.639	.012	.473

Antrim-Down-Belfast				
1871	.295	.726	.027	.383
1881	.277	.717	.022	.366
1891	.292	.693	.021	.404
1901	.245	.650	.015	.362
1911	.243	.602	.017	.386
1926	.218	.512	.016	.407
1936	.193	.433	.015	.425
1961	.255	.414	.016	.602

Donegal County				
1871	.259	.681	.006	.375
1881	.251	.701	.005	.352
1891	.229	.719	.005	.313
1901	.233	.751	.005	.306
1911	.268	.853	.006	.310
1926	.243	.729	.014	.320
1936	.216	.659	.013	.315
1961	.263	.582	.011	.442

Monaghan County				
1871	.267	.688	.012	.377
1881	.228	.683	.008	.324
1891	.201	.649	.008	.301
1901	.208	.670	.006	.303
1911	.238	.723	.006	.323
1926	.225	.648	.008	.339
1936	.220	.610	.013	.346
1961	.313	.641	.011	.479

Leitrim County				
1871	.321	.729	.004	.436
1881	.284	.714	.003	.395
1891	.257	.699	.003	.365
1901	.235	.713	.002	.327
1911	.263	.813	.002	.321
1926	.238	.691	.004	.341
1936	.221	.629	.006	.344
1961	.304	.623	.007	.482

Cork County All				
1871	.336	.710	.011	.465
1881	.290	.738	.006	.386
1891	.252	.744	.006	.333
1901	.230	.742	.006	.305
1911	.234	.710	.007	.323
1926	.203	.608	.008	.325
1936	.198	.590	.009	.326
1961	.289	.617	.007	.463

Tipperary County				
1871	.301	.744	.012	.394
1881	.264	.750	.009	.345
1891	.228	.721	.010	.306
1901	.220	.742	.009	.289
1911	.237	.750	.010	.307
1926	.239	.667	.013	.345
1936	.238	.633	.015	.361
1961	.338	.667	.013	.497

Armagh County				
1871	.287	.706	.023	.386
1881	.245	.673	.017	.349
1891	.237	.687	.016	.329
1901	.237	.696	.014	.328
1911	.240	.663	.014	.349
1926	.230	.591	.016	.372
1936	.222	.514	.017	.412
1961	.287	.520	.015	.539

Fermanagh County				
1871	.262	.681	.019	.365
1881	.235	.689	.015	.328
1891	.216	.673	.015	.306
1901	.219	.675	.012	.313
1911	.251	.725	.011	.336
1926	.231	.611	.016	.362
1936	.225	.578	.017	.371
1961	.301	.572	.013	.517

Tyrone County				
1871	.263	.728	.017	.346
1881	.228	.682	.013	.322
1891	.209	.700	.012	.286
1901	.209	.690	.011	.292
1911	.239	.709	.013	.325
1926	.239	.631	.016	.363
1936	.240	.598	.018	.383
1961	.324	.605	.016	.523

Mayo County				
1871	.357	.732	.005	.485
1881	.301	.696	.003	.430
1891	.274	.742	.002	.367
1901	.257	.750	.002	.341
1911	.294	.878	.002	.333
1926	.243	.732	.003	.329
1936	.222	.676	.005	.324
1961	.289	.608	.006	.470

IRELAND (continued)

Roscommon County

	I_f	I_g	I_h	I_m
1871	.336	.755	.005	.442
1881	.275	.711	.003	.384
1891	.244	.728	.003	.332
1901	.218	.697	.002	.311
1911	.249	.789	.002	.314
1926	.248	.707	.006	.346
1936	.209	.603	.006	.340
1961	.278	.553	.007	.497

Sligo County

	I_f	I_g	I_h	I_m
1871	.326	.742	.005	.435
1881	.269	.687	.004	.388
1891	.233	.687	.002	.337
1901	.224	.747	.002	.298
1911	.258	.852	.003	.300
1926	.220	.669	.005	.324
1936	.207	.609	.008	.331
1961	.291	.604	.009	.475

ITALY

Italy-Regions

	I_f	I_g	I_h	I_m
1864	.399	.677	.044	.560
1871	.389	.646	.050	.568
1881	.384	.648	.063	.549
1891	.376	.640	.055	.549
1901	.369	.633	.048	.549
1911	.346	.616	.037	.534
1921	.304	.585	.029	.495
1931	.255	.471	.027	.513
1936	.236	.434	.022	.519
1951	.192	.344	.014	.538
1961	.200	.338	.011	.578

Piemonte

	I_f	I_g	I_h	I_m
1864	.375	.642	.041	.557
1871	.372	.631	.030	.570
1881	.369	.642	.029	.556
1891	.344	.617	.024	.539
1901	.319	.592	.020	.522
1911	.251	.478	.017	.508
1921	.184	.374	.010	.478
1931	.160	.299	.015	.511
1936	.148	.264	.014	.535
1951	.122	.209	.008	.567
1961	.145	.228	.009	.621

Liguria

	I_f	I_g	I_h	I_m
1864	.375	.658	.033	.547
1871	.368	.630	.033	.562
1881	.339	.615	.036	.523
1891	.314	.581	.034	.512
1901	.293	.551	.033	.502
1911	.251	.488	.025	.488
1921	.179	.368	.016	.462
1931	.149	.294	.018	.474
1936	.134	.261	.015	.483
1951	.106	.189	.009	.539
1961	.135	.222	.010	.591

Lombardia

	I_f	I_g	I_h	I_m
1864	.396	.668	.046	.562
1871	.389	.657	.032	.572
1881	.384	.664	.025	.562
1891	.383	.674	.022	.554
1901	.382	.683	.020	.547
1911	.343	.619	.022	.537
1921	.257	.517	.018	.479
1931	.211	.407	.019	.495
1936	.195	.373	.016	.501
1951	.155	.286	.009	.526
1961	.168	.286	.008	.576

Trentino Alto Adige

	I_f	I_g	I_h	I_m
1864	--	--	--	--
1871	--	--	--	--
1881	--	--	--	--
1891	--	--	--	--
1901	--	--	--	--
1911	--	--	--	--
1921	.290	.700	.025	.393
1931	.230	.528	.030	.401
1936	.218	.493	.029	.407
1951	.206	.430	.019	.454
1961	.222	.419	.018	.508

Veneto

	I_f	I_g	I_h	I_m
1864	--	--	--	--
1871	.412	.682	.028	.586
1881	.379	.651	.051	.546
1891	.400	.698	.050	.540
1901	.419	.743	.049	.534
1911	.400	.738	.046	.512
1921	.348	.704	.049	.457
1931	.265	.527	.033	.470
1936	.251	.492	.026	.484
1951	.192	.358	.016	.515
1961	.197	.340	.010	.567

Venezia Giulia

	I_f	I_g	I_h	I_m
1864	--	--	--	--
1871	--	--	--	--
1881	--	--	--	--
1891	--	--	--	--
1901	--	--	--	--
1911	--	--	--	--
1921	.273	.518	.053	.473
1931	.201	.372	.046	.474
1936	.189	.335	.037	.510
1951	.105	.178	.019	.540
1961	.130	.212	.014	.585

Emilia

	I_f	I_g	I_h	I_m
1864	.401	.648	.036	.597
1871	.381	.597	.079	.584
1881	.370	.595	.117	.530
1891	.375	.616	.105	.528
1901	.380	.638	.094	.527
1911	.389	.646	.090	.537
1921	.300	.535	.069	.494
1931	.220	.386	.049	.508
1936	.194	.340	.034	.523
1951	.141	.237	.018	.560
1961	.152	.237	.012	.623

Toscana

	I_f	I_g	I_h	I_m
1864	.426	.733	.053	.548
1871	.410	.662	.086	.563
1881	.371	.634	.079	.526
1891	.357	.613	.065	.533
1901	.345	.595	.052	.539
1911	.313	.550	.038	.538
1921	.255	.473	.023	.516
1931	.191	.341	.017	.538
1936	.173	.308	.013	.545
1951	.136	.235	.008	.566
1961	.148	.233	.007	.623

Marche				
1864	.381	.683	.027	.540
1871	.352	.620	.087	.498
1881	.372	.660	.103	.483
1891	.373	.645	.090	.511
1901	.374	.632	.075	.538
1911	.375	.652	.053	.538
1921	.324	.600	.033	.514
1931	.262	.475	.020	.531
1936	.239	.436	.013	.535
1951	.172	.299	.006	.567
1961	.169	.270	.004	.621
Umbria				
1864	.370	.627	.055	.550
1871	.363	.600	.097	.529
1881	.361	.590	.144	.487
1891	.361	.590	.122	.511
1901	.361	.590	.099	.534
1911	.318	.614	.046	.478
1921	.326	.558	.039	.553
1931	.267	.439	.036	.572
1936	.235	.391	.022	.577
1951	.160	.256	.010	.609
1961	.157	.239	.007	.645
Lazio				
1864	--	--	--	--
1871	.385	.610	.080	.575
1881	.350	.539	.157	.503
1891	.340	.533	.145	.503
1901	.333	.528	.135	.503
1911	.329	.557	.092	.509
1921	.283	.517	.042	.507
1931	.259	.465	.035	.520
1936	.234	.426	.027	.519
1951	.177	.314	.016	.540
1961	.193	.356	.013	.524
Abruzzi				
1864	.393	.669	.035	.565
1871	.388	.638	.041	.581
1881	.393	.644	.045	.582
1891	.386	.626	.039	.590
1901	.378	.609	.033	.599
1911	.349	.595	.019	.573
1921	.369	.666	.020	.541
1931	.322	.553	.024	.564
1936	.298	.504	.022	.571
1951	.205	.361	.012	.553
1961	.194	.316	.008	.605
Campania				
1864	.390	.689	.039	.539
1871	.387	.667	.037	.555
1881	.382	.671	.037	.545
1891	.372	.652	.035	.546
1901	.361	.634	.032	.547
1911	.357	.667	.023	.518
1921	.354	.771	.021	.444
1931	.338	.647	.025	.504
1936	.308	.600	.022	.494
1951	.252	.496	.016	.492
1961	.270	.490	.013	.538
Puglia				
1864	.430	.744	.046	.550
1871	.423	.701	.040	.580
1881	.444	.720	.048	.588
1891	.430	.697	.041	.594
1901	.419	.677	.034	.598
1911	.406	.703	.025	.561
1921	.407	.735	.022	.541
1931	.358	.643	.023	.540
1936	.335	.612	.019	.533
1951	.272	.501	.013	.530
1961	.264	.470	.009	.552
Basilicata				
1864	.417	.678	.050	.584
1871	.402	.645	.025	.608
1881	.429	.642	.063	.632
1891	.415	.625	.049	.635
1901	.399	.606	.033	.638
1911	.415	.649	.019	.628
1921	.419	.716	.019	.573
1931	.386	.624	.022	.604
1936	.370	.590	.022	.613
1951	.276	.474	.015	.569
1961	.266	.425	.010	.618
Calabria				
1864	.379	.640	.066	.546
1871	.392	.639	.070	.566
1881	.373	.610	.075	.558
1891	.370	.590	.067	.580
1901	.367	.573	.058	.601
1911	.374	.610	.046	.581
1921	.388	.704	.033	.528
1931	.346	.595	.041	.550
1936	.329	.566	.039	.549
1951	.281	.496	.026	.543
1961	.279	.463	.018	.586
Sicilia				
1864	.441	.705	.068	.585
1871	.421	.696	.065	.564
1881	.419	.679	.080	.566
1891	.398	.647	.065	.573
1901	.380	.618	.052	.579
1911	.356	.606	.030	.566
1921	.340	.624	.020	.530
1931	.304	.531	.024	.553
1936	.281	.492	.019	.552
1951	.239	.416	.016	.557
1961	.249	.413	.012	.592
Sardegna				
1864	.377	.642	.022	.572
1871	.390	.631	.066	.573
1881	.388	.648	.087	.537
1891	.367	.648	.065	.519
1901	.349	.647	.047	.503
1911	.346	.671	.029	.493
1921	.343	.714	.018	.466
1931	.323	.662	.026	.467
1936	.309	.632	.022	.469
1951	.294	.589	.019	.483
1961	.272	.547	.011	.487

ITALY (continued)

	I_f	I_g	I_h	I_m
Italy-Regions (adjusted)				
1864	.399	--	--	--
1871	.389	--	--	--
1881	.384	--	--	--
1891	.376	--	--	--
1901	.369	--	--	--
1911	.346	--	--	--
1921	.304	--	--	--
1931	.255	--	--	--
1936	.236	--	--	--
1951	.192	--	--	--
1961	.200	--	--	--
Lombardia				
1864	.396	.669	.046	.561
1871	.389	.659	.032	.570
1881	.384	.648	.026	.576
1891	.383	.680	.022	.549
1901	.382	.691	.020	.541
1911	.343	.641	.021	.519
1921	.257	.526	.018	.471
1931	.211	.416	.019	.484
1936	.195	.382	.016	.489
1951	.155	.289	.009	.521
1961	.168	.286	.008	.576
Venezia Giulia				
1864	--	--	--	--
1871	--	--	--	--
1881	--	--	--	--
1891	--	--	--	--
1901	--	--	--	--
1911	--	--	--	--
1921	.273	.518	.053	.473
1931	.201	.383	.045	.460
1936	.189	.346	.036	.494
1951	.105	.227	.015	.423
1961	.130	.223	.013	.556
Marche				
1864	.381	.711	.026	.519
1871	.352	.709	.026	.478
1881	.372	.763	.033	.465
1891	.373	.725	.038	.488
1901	.374	.685	.052	.509
1911	.375	.702	.049	.500
1921	.324	.621	.032	.497
1931	.262	.490	.019	.515
1936	.239	.455	.012	.513
1951	.172	.299	.006	.567
1961	.169	.275	.004	.610

	I_f	I_g	I_h	I_m
Piemonte				
1864	.375	.657	.040	.544
1871	.372	.643	.029	.559
1881	.369	.655	.028	.545
1891	.344	.631	.023	.527
1901	.319	.608	.019	.508
1911	.251	.494	.016	.492
1921	.184	.382	.010	.468
1931	.160	.304	.015	.503
1936	.148	.268	.014	.527
1951	.122	.228	.007	.520
1961	.145	.228	.009	.621
Trentino Alto Adige				
1864	--	--	--	--
1871	--	--	--	--
1881	--	--	--	--
1891	--	--	--	--
1901	--	--	--	--
1911	--	--	--	--
1921	.290	.703	.025	.391
1931	.230	.543	.029	.390
1936	.218	.493	.029	.407
1951	.206	.430	.019	.454
1961	.222	.420	.018	.507
Emilia				
1864	.401	.653	.036	.592
1871	.381	.629	.043	.577
1881	.370	.664	.050	.521
1891	.375	.668	.060	.518
1901	.380	.673	.069	.515
1911	.389	.653	.089	.531
1921	.300	.538	.069	.491
1931	.220	.393	.048	.499
1936	.194	.352	.033	.505
1951	.141	.240	.018	.553
1961	.152	.239	.012	.618
Umbria				
1864	.370	.628	.055	.549
1871	.363	.640	.052	.529
1881	.361	.693	.048	.485
1891	.361	.661	.053	.506
1901	.361	.601	.094	.527
1911	.318	.638	.044	.460
1921	.326	.562	.039	.549
1931	.267	.443	.036	.567
1936	.235	.399	.021	.565
1951	.160	.256	.010	.609
1961	.157	.243	.007	.634

	I_f	I_g	I_h	I_m
Liguria				
1864	.375	.696	.031	.517
1871	.368	.649	.032	.546
1881	.339	.639	.035	.503
1891	.314	.601	.033	.495
1901	.293	.567	.032	.488
1911	.251	.489	.025	.487
1921	.179	.370	.016	.460
1931	.149	.296	.018	.471
1936	.134	.267	.015	.472
1951	.106	.226	.008	.451
1961	.135	.222	.010	.591
Veneto				
1864	--	--	--	--
1871	.412	.688	.028	.581
1881	.379	.683	.048	.520
1891	.400	.712	.049	.529
1901	.419	.760	.048	.522
1911	.400	.809	.042	.467
1921	.348	.712	.049	.452
1931	.265	.565	.031	.438
1936	.251	.525	.025	.454
1951	.192	.358	.016	.515
1961	.197	.346	.010	.557
Toscana				
1864	.426	.737	.053	.545
1871	.410	.690	.052	.561
1881	.371	.683	.042	.513
1891	.357	.647	.042	.521
1901	.345	.610	.047	.529
1911	.313	.565	.037	.524
1921	.255	.477	.023	.512
1931	.191	.348	.017	.527
1936	.173	.318	.013	.528
1951	.136	.235	.008	.566
1961	.148	.235	.007	.618
Lazio				
1864	--	--	--	--
1871	.385	.594	.102	.575
1881	.350	.609	.088	.503
1891	.340	.590	.087	.503
1901	.333	.540	.124	.503
1911	.329	.562	.091	.504
1921	.283	.517	.042	.507
1931	.259	.467	.035	.518
1936	.234	.435	.026	.508
1951	.177	.358	.014	.474
1961	.193	.360	.013	.518

Abruzzi					Campania					Puglia				
1864	.393	.711	.033	.532	1864	.390	.689	.039	.539	1864	.430	.744	.046	.550
1871	.388	.680	.038	.545	1871	.387	.672	.037	.551	1871	.423	.701	.040	.580
1881	.393	.704	.040	.532	1881	.382	.680	.036	.538	1881	.444	.720	.048	.588
1891	.386	.701	.034	.527	1891	.372	.679	.033	.524	1891	.430	.697	.041	.594
1901	.378	.699	.028	.522	1901	.361	.678	.030	.512	1901	.419	.677	.034	.598
1911	.349	.720	.015	.474	1911	.357	.716	.021	.483	1911	.406	.723	.024	.545
1921	.369	.738	.018	.488	1921	.354	.797	.020	.430	1921	.407	.743	.022	.535
1931	.322	.618	.021	.505	1931	.338	.667	.024	.489	1931	.358	.653	.023	.532
1936	.298	.566	.019	.508	1936	.308	.627	.021	.473	1936	.335	.630	.018	.518
1951	.205	.361	.012	.553	1951	.252	.508	.016	.480	1951	.272	.501	.013	.530
1961	.194	.348	.007	.549	1961	.270	.509	.012	.518	1961	.264	.490	.009	.529
Basilicata					Calabria					Sicilia				
1864	.417	.690	.049	.574	1864	.379	.651	.065	.537	1864	.441	.705	.068	.585
1871	.402	.663	.024	.591	1871	.392	.653	.068	.554	1871	.421	.696	.065	.564
1881	.429	.681	.057	.596	1881	.373	.632	.072	.539	1881	.419	.679	.080	.566
1891	.415	.682	.043	.582	1891	.370	.649	.060	.527	1891	.398	.647	.065	.573
1901	.399	.679	.028	.569	1901	.367	.667	.048	.516	1901	.380	.624	.051	.573
1911	.415	.721	.016	.565	1911	.374	.734	.037	.483	1911	.356	.619	.029	.554
1921	.419	.747	.018	.549	1921	.388	.766	.030	.485	1921	.340	.624	.020	.530
1931	.386	.654	.021	.576	1931	.346	.673	.036	.486	1931	.304	.541	.023	.543
1936	.370	.628	.020	.576	1936	.329	.648	.034	.480	1936	.281	.512	.018	.530
1951	.276	.474	.015	.569	1951	.281	.515	.025	.523	1951	.239	.425	.016	.545
1961	.266	.461	.009	.570	1961	.279	.518	.016	.524	1961	.249	.422	.012	.579
Sardegna														
1864	.377	.642	.022	.572										
1871	.390	.631	.066	.573										
1881	.388	.648	.087	.537										
1891	.367	.648	.065	.519										
1901	.349	.647	.047	.503										
1911	.346	.672	.029	.492										
1921	.343	.714	.018	.466										
1931	.323	.663	.026	.466										
1936	.309	.633	.022	.468										
1951	.294	.589	.019	.483										
1961	.272	.551	.011	.483										
Italy-Provinces					Alessandria					Asti				
1864	--	.677	--	.560	1864	--	.564	--	.686	1864	--	.564	--	.686
1871	--	.646	--	.568	1871	--	.575	--	.668	1871	--	.575	--	.668
1881	--	.648	--	.549	1881	--	.594	--	.649	1881	--	.631	--	.663
1911	--	.616	--	.534	1911	--	.480	--	.558	1911	--	.497	--	.610
1931	--	.471	--	.513	1931	--	.287	--	.532	1931	--	.299	--	.600
1936	--	.434	--	.519	1936	--	.242	--	.528	1936	--	.251	--	.598
1951	--	.344	--	.538	1951	--	.191	--	.558	1951	--	.207	--	.590
1961	--	.338	--	.578	1961	--	.219	--	.609	1961	--	.213	--	.641
Cuneo					Novara					Vercelli				
1864	--	.696	--	.545	1864	--	.658	--	.541	1864	--	.658	--	.541
1871	--	.673	--	.573	1871	--	.641	--	.557	1871	--	.641	--	.557
1881	--	.690	--	.566	1881	--	.662	--	.533	1881	--	.629	--	.550
1911	--	.621	--	.517	1911	--	.463	--	.526	1911	--	.384	--	.475
1931	--	.439	--	.493	1931	--	.291	--	.517	1931	--	.254	--	.510
1936	--	.387	--	.514	1936	--	.266	--	.549	1936	--	.228	--	.548
1951	--	.290	--	.528	1951	--	.225	--	.573	1951	--	.198	--	.580
1961	--	.264	--	.576	1961	--	.245	--	.619	1961	--	.204	--	.625

ITALY-Provinces (continued)

	I_f	I_g	I_h	I_m		I_f	I_g	I_h	I_m		I_f	I_g	I_h	I_m
Torino					Aosta					Genova				
1864	--	.659	--	.496	1864	--	.659	--	.496	1864	--	.658	--	.554
1871	--	.643	--	.514	1871	--	.643	--	.514	1871	--	.627	--	.569
1881	--	.644	--	.556	1881	--	.644	--	.556	1881	--	.611	--	.504
1911	--	.433	--	.470	1911	--	.433	--	.470	1911	--	.474	--	.474
1931	--	.254	--	.506	1931	--	.333	--	.502	1931	--	.272	--	.455
1936	--	.231	--	.527	1936	--	.280	--	.541	1936	--	.246	--	.459
1951	--	.179	--	.574	1951	--	.264	--	.595	1951	--	.185	--	.523
1961	--	.224	--	.633	1961	--	.232	--	.626	1961	--	.220	--	.576
Savona					La Spezia					Imperia				
1864	--	.658	--	.554	1864	--	.658	--	.554	1864	--	.657	--	.505
1871	--	.627	--	.569	1871	--	.627	--	.569	1871	--	.648	--	.521
1881	--	.620	--	.549	1881	--	.628	--	.604	1881	--	.609	--	.509
1911	--	.529	--	.505	1911	--	.537	--	.530	1911	--	.443	--	.488
1931	--	.322	--	.478	1931	--	.330	--	.528	1931	--	.321	--	.500
1936	--	.291	--	.500	1936	--	.293	--	.545	1936	--	.259	--	.521
1951	--	.191	--	.554	1951	--	.199	--	.574	1951	--	.195	--	.560
1961	--	.216	--	.598	1961	--	.226	--	.618	1961	--	.231	--	.625
Bergamo					Brescia					Como				
1864	--	.711	--	.530	1864	--	.589	--	.555	1864	--	.710	--	.516
1871	--	.731	--	.548	1871	--	.619	--	.567	1871	--	.692	--	.504
1881	--	.743	--	.537	1881	--	.609	--	.541	1881	--	.735	--	.514
1911	--	.837	--	.533	1911	--	.745	--	.513	1911	--	.640	--	.513
1931	--	.669	--	.472	1931	--	.584	--	.490	1931	--	.422	--	.465
1936	--	.631	--	.474	1936	--	.545	--	.503	1936	--	.389	--	.497
1951	--	.453	--	.492	1951	--	.393	--	.516	1951	--	.317	--	.500
1961	--	.378	--	.548	1961	--	.346	--	.564	1961	--	.290	--	.547
Varese					Cremona					Mantova				
1864	--	.710	--	.516	1864	--	.655	--	.595	1864	--	--	--	--
1871	--	.692	--	.504	1871	--	.608	--	.617	1871	--	.576	--	.655
1881	--	.734	--	.569	1881	--	.611	--	.563	1881	--	.558	--	.609
1911	--	.570	--	.556	1911	--	.627	--	.536	1911	--	.583	--	.554
1931	--	.312	--	.487	1931	--	.427	--	.506	1931	--	.354	--	.540
1936	--	.300	--	.488	1936	--	.401	--	.529	1936	--	.318	--	.566
1951	--	.258	--	.542	1951	--	.310	--	.533	1951	--	.254	--	.594
1961	--	.294	--	.587	1961	--	.283	--	.575	1961	--	.256	--	.635
Milano					Pavia					Sondrio				
1864	--	.693	--	.562	1864	--	.627	--	.640	1864	--	.763	--	.487
1871	--	.683	--	.561	1871	--	.616	--	.634	1871	--	.760	--	.499
1881	--	.671	--	.570	1881	--	.628	--	.614	1881	--	.762	--	.475
1911	--	.552	--	.552	1911	--	.491	--	.536	1911	--	.719	--	.481
1931	--	.326	--	.497	1931	--	.296	--	.517	1931	--	.592	--	.484
1936	--	.298	--	.496	1936	--	.259	--	.531	1936	--	.539	--	.500
1951	--	.221	--	.526	1951	--	.208	--	.547	1951	--	.438	--	.515
1961	--	.259	--	.578	1961	--	.221	--	.604	1961	--	.405	--	.578

Bolzano				
1864	--	--	--	--
1871	--	--	--	--
1881	--	--	--	--
1911	--	--	--	--
1931	--	.574	--	.373
1936	--	.517	--	.388
1951	--	.422	--	.440
1961	--	.449	--	.498
Trento				
1864	--	--	--	--
1871	--	--	--	--
1881	--	--	--	--
1911	--	--	--	--
1931	--	.500	--	.421
1936	--	.476	--	.424
1951	--	.437	--	.467
1961	--	.391	--	.518
Belluno				
1864	--	--	--	--
1871	--	.778	--	.541
1881	--	.757	--	.502
1911	--	.724	--	.576
1931	--	.471	--	.489
1936	--	.426	--	.495
1951	--	.352	--	.549
1961	--	.321	--	.569
Padova				
1864	--	--	--	--
1871	--	.685	--	.621
1881	--	.623	--	.575
1911	--	.758	--	.519
1931	--	.597	--	.468
1936	--	.538	--	.475
1951	--	.392	--	.482
1961	--	.370	--	.554
Rovigo				
1864	--	--	--	--
1871	--	.675	--	.674
1881	--	.631	--	.613
1911	--	.713	--	.563
1931	--	.525	--	.534
1936	--	.474	--	.555
1951	--	.328	--	.545
1961	--	.310	--	.614
Treviso				
1864	--	--	--	--
1871	--	.713	--	.620
1881	--	.682	--	.556
1911	--	.823	--	.520
1931	--	.582	--	.452
1936	--	.549	--	.465
1951	--	.401	--	.495
1961	--	.368	--	.558
Udine				
1864	--	--	--	--
1871	--	.676	--	.543
1881	--	.668	--	.506
1911	--	.738	--	.548
1931	--	.439	--	.466
1936	--	.414	--	.499
1951	--	.296	--	.563
1961	--	.283	--	.588
Venezia				
1864	--	--	--	--
1871	--	.633	--	.558
1881	--	.598	--	.521
1911	--	.714	--	.506
1931	--	.542	--	.479
1936	--	.507	--	.496
1951	--	.341	--	.526
1961	--	.327	--	.583
Verona				
1864	--	--	--	--
1871	--	.630	--	.573
1881	--	.614	--	.550
1911	--	.665	--	.500
1931	--	.478	--	.465
1936	--	.459	--	.465
1951	--	.358	--	.499
1961	--	.335	--	.558
Vicenza				
1864	--	--	--	--
1871	--	.715	--	.594
1881	--	.685	--	.564
1911	--	.747	--	.433
1931	--	.571	--	.449
1936	--	.545	--	.457
1951	--	.401	--	.491
1961	--	.386	--	.537
Gorizia				
1864	--	--	--	--
1871	--	--	--	--
1881	--	--	--	--
1911	--	--	--	--
1931	--	.460	--	.443
1936	--	.404	--	.460
1951	--	.223	--	.530
1961	--	.253	--	.579
Trieste				
1864	--	--	--	--
1871	--	--	--	--
1881	--	--	--	--
1911	--	--	--	--
1931	--	.270	--	.463
1936	--	.244	--	.508
1951	--	.159	--	.544
1961	--	.192	--	.588
Bologna				
1864	--	.625	--	.594
1871	--	.597	--	.562
1881	--	.601	--	.501
1911	--	.585	--	.504
1931	--	.325	--	.502
1936	--	.282	--	.510
1951	--	.199	--	.552
1961	--	.209	--	.618
Ferrara				
1864	--	.660	--	.606
1871	--	.589	--	.637
1881	--	.534	--	.561
1911	--	.633	--	.538
1931	--	.374	--	.509
1936	--	.333	--	.547
1951	--	.224	--	.591
1961	--	.224	--	.661
Forli				
1864	--	.668	--	.612
1871	--	.569	--	.577
1881	--	.586	--	.515
1911	--	.673	--	.544
1931	--	.445	--	.544
1936	--	.413	--	.558
1951	--	.297	--	.574
1961	--	.283	--	.617
Modena				
1864	--	.663	--	.618
1871	--	.616	--	.602
1881	--	.625	--	.554
1911	--	.689	--	.566
1931	--	.421	--	.528
1936	--	.361	--	.544
1951	--	.241	--	.575
1961	--	.245	--	.643
Parma				
1864	--	.637	--	.563
1871	--	.612	--	.575
1881	--	.614	--	.537
1911	--	.656	--	.541
1931	--	.368	--	.489
1936	--	.330	--	.505
1951	--	.226	--	.555
1961	--	.230	--	.604
Piacenza				
1864	--	.616	--	.627
1871	--	.577	--	.620
1881	--	.592	--	.579
1911	--	.676	--	.554
1931	--	.461	--	.447
1936	--	.399	--	.443
1951	--	.263	--	.477
1961	--	.254	--	.548

ITALY-Provinces (continued)

	I_f	I_g	I_h	I_m		I_f	I_g	I_h	I_m		I_f	I_g	I_h	I_m
Ravenna					Reggio Dell'Emilia					Arezzo				
1864	--	.634	--	.566	1864	--	.692	--	.593	1864	--	.753	--	.528
1871	--	.569	--	.521	1871	--	.635	--	.595	1871	--	.667	--	.547
1881	--	.587	--	.465	1881	--	.623	--	.553	1881	--	.669	--	.517
1911	--	.550	--	.503	1911	--	.727	--	.576	1911	--	.642	--	.553
1931	--	.330	--	.529	1931	--	.404	--	.509	1931	--	.429	--	.580
1936	--	.300	--	.540	1936	--	.353	--	.529	1936	--	.381	--	.586
1951	--	.236	--	.559	1951	--	.243	--	.572	1951	--	.264	--	.600
1961	--	.247	--	.640	1961	--	.228	--	.630	1961	--	.245	--	.648
Firenze					Pistoia					Grosseto				
1864	--	.758	--	.550	1864	--	.758	--	.550	1864	--	.710	--	.628
1871	--	.679	--	.565	1871	--	.679	--	.565	1871	--	.661	--	.620
1881	--	.622	--	.526	1881	--	.691	--	.557	1881	--	.644	--	.499
1911	--	.509	--	.504	1911	--	.597	--	.544	1911	--	.550	--	.612
1931	--	.299	--	.504	1931	--	.340	--	.528	1931	--	.341	--	.624
1936	--	.274	--	.506	1936	--	.307	--	.553	1936	--	.306	--	.630
1951	--	.214	--	.546	1951	--	.219	--	.596	1951	--	.224	--	.659
1961	--	.233	--	.597	1961	--	.227	--	.628	1961	--	.213	--	.677
Livorno					Lucca					Massa-Carrara				
1864	--	.657	--	.504	1864	--	.738	--	.514	1864	--	.720	--	.524
1871	--	.545	--	.506	1871	--	.680	--	.537	1871	--	.694	--	.582
1881	--	.527	--	.462	1881	--	.664	--	.499	1881	--	.651	--	.532
1911	--	.454	--	.532	1911	--	.583	--	.490	1911	--	.637	--	.556
1931	--	.306	--	.551	1931	--	.383	--	.484	1931	--	.439	--	.544
1936	--	.279	--	.547	1936	--	.357	--	.497	1936	--	.380	--	.561
1951	--	.199	--	.622	1951	--	.371	--	.389	1951	--	.269	--	.577
1961	--	.226	--	.641	1961	--	.279	--	.580	1961	--	.255	--	.623
Pisa					Siena					Ancona				
1864	--	.727	--	.575	1864	--	.693	--	.594	1864	--	.700	--	.547
1871	--	.647	--	.578	1871	--	.628	--	.585	1871	--	.624	--	.527
1881	--	.625	--	.543	1881	--	.602	--	.555	1881	--	.650	--	.510
1911	--	.511	--	.572	1911	--	.518	--	.600	1911	--	.628	--	.550
1931	--	.315	--	.556	1931	--	.319	--	.596	1931	--	.433	--	.530
1936	--	.286	--	.566	1936	--	.280	--	.598	1936	--	.390	--	.531
1951	--	.215	--	.599	1951	--	.202	--	.621	1951	--	.278	--	.567
1961	--	.226	--	.636	1961	--	.194	--	.660	1961	--	.258	--	.613
Ascoli Piceno					Macerata					Pesaro e Urbino				
1864	--	.679	--	.500	1864	--	.676	--	.530	1864	--	.672	--	.584
1871	--	.653	--	.434	1871	--	.626	--	.487	1871	--	.584	--	.535
1881	--	.704	--	.433	1881	--	.662	--	.471	1881	--	.633	--	.512
1911	--	.681	--	.505	1911	--	.681	--	.523	1911	--	.629	--	.569
1931	--	.522	--	.501	1931	--	.482	--	.517	1931	--	.475	--	.576
1936	--	.484	--	.504	1936	--	.461	--	.517	1936	--	.427	--	.591
1951	--	.329	--	.533	1951	--	.296	--	.567	1951	--	.297	--	.603
1961	--	.290	--	.611	1961	--	.256	--	.629	1961	--	.279	--	.635

Perugia				
1864	--	.627	--	.550
1871	--	.600	--	.529
1881	--	.594	--	.476
1911	--	.630	--	.442
1931	--	.452	--	.573
1936	--	.401	--	.581
1951	--	.265	--	.607
1961	--	.245	--	.647
Roma				
1864	--	--	--	--
1871	--	.610	--	.575
1881	--	.513	--	.501
1911	--	.541	--	.473
1931	--	.430	--	.501
1936	--	.380	--	.486
1951	--	.289	--	.515
1961	--	.323	--	.563
Viterbo				
1864	--	--	--	--
1871	--	.610	--	.575
1881	--	.606	--	.494
1911	--	.587	--	.514
1931	--	.444	--	.564
1936	--	.400	--	.564
1951	--	.286	--	.608
1961	--	.262	--	.642
Pescara				
1864	--	.665	--	.586
1871	--	.617	--	.618
1881	--	.642	--	.564
1911	--	.625	--	.543
1931	--	.575	--	.534
1936	--	.523	--	.540
1951	--	.355	--	.525
1961	--	.326	--	.582
Avellino				
1864	--	.690	--	.567
1871	--	.766	--	.551
1881	--	.762	--	.600
1911	--	.672	--	.558
1931	--	.663	--	.563
1936	--	.610	--	.574
1951	--	.448	--	.522
1961	--	.405	--	.586
Napoli				
1864	--	.717	--	.526
1871	--	.678	--	.537
1881	--	.666	--	.520
1911	--	.657	--	.488
1931	--	.641	--	.479
1936	--	.601	--	.462
1951	--	.528	--	.480
1961	--	.543	--	.514

Terni				
1864	--	.627	--	.550
1871	--	.600	--	.529
1881	--	.604	--	.488
1911	--	.583	--	.536
1931	--	.403	--	.569
1936	--	.363	--	.568
1951	--	.235	--	.615
1961	--	.225	--	.641
Frosinone				
1864	--	--	--	--
1871	--	.610	--	.575
1881	--	.599	--	.525
1911	--	.617	--	.613
1931	--	.590	--	.566
1936	--	.529	--	.578
1951	--	.383	--	.588
1961	--	.324	--	.652
Campobasso				
1864	--	.665	--	.624
1871	--	.649	--	.621
1881	--	.634	--	.627
1911	--	.567	--	.623
1931	--	.540	--	.604
1936	--	.498	--	.617
1951	--	.365	--	.586
1961	--	.334	--	.631
L´Aquila				
1864	--	.679	--	.532
1871	--	.652	--	.548
1881	--	.671	--	.547
1911	--	.594	--	.565
1931	--	.544	--	.561
1936	--	.480	--	.557
1951	--	.367	--	.536
1961	--	.323	--	.585
Benevento				
1864	--	.655	--	.557
1871	--	.665	--	.594
1881	--	.672	--	.595
1911	--	.642	--	.556
1931	--	.619	--	.542
1936	--	.580	--	.551
1951	--	.417	--	.509
1961	--	.390	--	.573
Salerno				
1864	--	.669	--	.543
1871	--	.594	--	.588
1881	--	.630	--	.554
1911	--	.694	--	.542
1931	--	.666	--	.528
1936	--	.605	--	.525
1951	--	.474	--	.499
1961	--	.437	--	.565

Rieti				
1864	--	.627	--	.550
1871	--	.600	--	.529
1881	--	.597	--	.522
1911	--	.634	--	.561
1931	--	.523	--	.541
1936	--	.462	--	.560
1951	--	.332	--	.571
1961	--	.285	--	.617
Latina				
1864	--	--	--	--
1871	--	.610	--	.575
1881	--	.601	--	.513
1911	--	.614	--	.553
1931	--	.590	--	.565
1936	--	.551	--	.615
1951	--	.399	--	.600
1961	--	.355	--	.639
Chieti				
1864	--	.665	--	.586
1871	--	.617	--	.618
1881	--	.615	--	.621
1911	--	.562	--	.593
1931	--	.526	--	.582
1936	--	.488	--	.590
1951	--	.344	--	.576
1961	--	.279	--	.617
Teramo				
1864	--	.668	--	.490
1871	--	.633	--	.518
1881	--	.682	--	.496
1911	--	.670	--	.497
1931	--	.623	--	.497
1936	--	.569	--	.518
1951	--	.376	--	.518
1961	--	.328	--	.598
Caserta				
1864	--	.680	--	.533
1871	--	.656	--	.554
1881	--	.659	--	.530
1911	--	.684	--	.522
1931	--	--	--	--
1936	--	--	--	--
1951	--	.508	--	.490
1961	--	.492	--	.542
Bari				
1864	--	.775	--	.558
1871	--	.744	--	.593
1881	--	.740	--	.592
1911	--	.704	--	.564
1931	--	.645	--	.535
1936	--	.607	--	.527
1951	--	.514	--	.532
1961	--	.491	--	.549

	I_f	I_g	I_h	I_m		I_f	I_g	I_h	I_m		I_f	I_g	I_h	I_m
Foggia					Lecce					Brindisi				
1864	--	.725	--	.566	1864	--	.717	--	.530	1864	--	.717	--	.530
1871	--	.669	--	.586	1871	--	.670	--	.560	1871	--	.670	--	.560
1881	--	.693	--	.605	1881	--	.714	--	.549	1881	--	.718	--	.581
1911	--	.650	--	.579	1911	--	.762	--	.527	1911	--	.733	--	.562
1931	--	.620	--	.574	1931	--	.690	--	.516	1931	--	.624	--	.517
1936	--	.608	--	.576	1936	--	.640	--	.505	1936	--	.595	--	.504
1951	--	.513	--	.560	1951	--	.506	--	.480	1951	--	.472	--	.524
1961	--	.485	--	.575	1961	--	.464	--	.518	1961	--	.443	--	.572
Taranto					Potenza					Matera				
1864	--	.717	--	.530	1864	--	.678	--	.584	1864	--	.678	--	.584
1871	--	.670	--	.560	1871	--	.645	--	.608	1871	--	.645	--	.608
1881	--	.711	--	.608	1881	--	.634	--	.627	1881	--	.669	--	.652
1911	--	.699	--	.571	1911	--	.645	--	.623	1911	--	.662	--	.644
1931	--	.616	--	.560	1931	--	.615	--	.606	1931	--	.646	--	.600
1936	--	.606	--	.552	1936	--	.589	--	.614	1936	--	.592	--	.611
1951	--	.464	--	.556	1951	--	.471	--	.572	1951	--	.482	--	.563
1961	--	.421	--	.565	1961	--	.423	--	.623	1961	--	.428	--	.607
Catanzaro					Cosenza					Reggio di Calabria				
1864	--	.642	--	.560	1864	--	.638	--	.542	1864	--	.639	--	.534
1871	--	.646	--	.573	1871	--	.619	--	.577	1871	--	.658	--	.545
1881	--	.611	--	.575	1881	--	.602	--	.554	1881	--	.618	--	.543
1911	--	.578	--	.586	1911	--	.583	--	.581	1911	--	.675	--	.575
1931	--	.598	--	.560	1931	--	.587	--	.568	1931	--	.601	--	.520
1936	--	.577	--	.562	1936	--	.552	--	.567	1936	--	.571	--	.520
1951	--	.520	--	.563	1951	--	.475	--	.545	1951	--	.492	--	.519
1961	--	.496	--	.603	1961	--	.434	--	.592	1961	--	.457	--	.558
Agrigento					Caltanissetta					Enna				
1864	--	.718	--	.624	1864	--	.711	--	.629	1864	--	.711	--	.629
1871	--	.717	--	.605	1871	--	.712	--	.618	1871	--	.712	--	.618
1881	--	.671	--	.612	1881	--	.706	--	.619	1881	--	.667	--	.620
1911	--	.657	--	.627	1911	--	.699	--	.651	1911	--	.570	--	.630
1931	--	.588	--	.590	1931	--	.619	--	.608	1931	--	.537	--	.600
1936	--	.543	--	.594	1936	--	.568	--	.604	1936	--	.526	--	.639
1951	--	.424	--	.568	1951	--	.469	--	.574	1951	--	.437	--	.609
1961	--	.401	--	.593	1961	--	.482	--	.602	1961	--	.400	--	.626
Catania					Messina					Palermo				
1864	--	.719	--	.565	1864	--	.684	--	.537	1864	--	.685	--	.572
1871	--	.695	--	.535	1871	--	.619	--	.540	1871	--	.716	--	.561
1881	--	.654	--	.531	1881	--	.657	--	.519	1881	--	.685	--	.578
1911	--	.553	--	.573	1911	--	.615	--	.535	1911	--	.629	--	.523
1931	--	.499	--	.584	1931	--	.518	--	.514	1931	--	.578	--	.509
1936	--	.462	--	.582	1936	--	.464	--	.504	1936	--	.526	--	.503
1951	--	.416	--	.569	1951	--	.390	--	.507	1951	--	.462	--	.529
1961	--	.436	--	.615	1961	--	.375	--	.552	1961	--	.451	--	.560

Siracusa					Ragusa					Trapani				
1864	--	.692	--	.621	1864	--	.692	--	.621	1864	--	.761	--	.617
1871	--	.712	--	.567	1871	--	.712	--	.567	1871	--	.715	--	.565
1881	--	.665	--	.575	1881	--	.693	--	.562	1881	--	.745	--	.548
1911	--	.535	--	.604	1911	--	.604	--	.554	1911	--	.615	--	.521
1931	--	.443	--	.613	1931	--	.459	--	.585	1931	--	.500	--	.496
1936	--	.431	--	.613	1936	--	.433	--	.605	1936	--	.483	--	.505
1951	--	.359	--	.624	1951	--	.326	--	.623	1951	--	.391	--	.545
1961	--	.366	--	.652	1961	--	.333	--	.662	1961	--	.389	--	.579

Cagliari					Sassari					Nuoro				
1864	--	.625	--	.565	1864	--	.671	--	.584	1864	--	.671	--	.584
1871	--	.620	--	.562	1871	--	.649	--	.591	1871	--	.649	--	.591
1881	--	.625	--	.534	1881	--	.669	--	.560	1881	--	.673	--	.513
1911	--	.698	--	.468	1911	--	.676	--	.497	1911	--	.657	--	.501
1931	--	.656	--	.479	1931	--	.638	--	.459	1931	--	.710	--	.448
1936	--	.630	--	.484	1936	--	.607	--	.464	1936	--	.677	--	.447
1951	--	.603	--	.502	1951	--	.531	--	.478	1951	--	.634	--	.441
1961	--	.554	--	.502	1961	--	.513	--	.486	1961	--	.577	--	.449

LUXEMBURG

1900	.337	.704	.023	.461
1930	.187	.319	.019	.561
1960	.180	.260	.017	.670

NETHERLANDS

Netherlands					Noordbrabant					Gelderland				
1859	.345	.816	.023	.406	1859	.293	.892	.012	.319	1859	.336	.822	.020	.394
1869	.384	.845	.024	.438	1869	.349	.931	.013	.366	1869	.365	.830	.021	.425
1879	.402	.831	.023	.469	1879	.388	.941	.012	.404	1879	.382	.836	.019	.445
1889	.375	.808	.022	.450	1889	.370	.954	.013	.379	1889	.369	.828	.019	.432
1899	.347	.752	.016	.450	1899	.374	.954	.010	.385	1899	.354	.797	.015	.434
1909	.312	.652	.012	.469	1909	.374	.882	.009	.418	1909	.328	.710	.012	.452
1920	.273	.554	.011	.482	1920	.351	.797	.010	.434	1920	.292	.619	.012	.461
1930	.227	.446	.008	.499	1930	.304	.660	.006	.456	1930	.248	.509	.008	.479
1960	.252	.394	.009	.630	1960	.277	.468	.006	.588	1960	.265	.422	.009	.619

Zuidholland					Noordholland					Zeeland				
1859	.390	.860	.035	.431	1859	.337	.766	.025	.421	1859	.400	.884	.029	.434
1869	.429	.894	.036	.458	1869	.372	.798	.026	.448	1869	.449	.919	.031	.470
1879	.447	.877	.032	.491	1879	.400	.790	.029	.486	1879	.436	.879	.028	.480
1889	.407	.836	.028	.469	1889	.360	.737	.028	.468	1889	.392	.830	.025	.456
1899	.357	.754	.020	.459	1899	.305	.638	.018	.463	1899	.360	.742	.020	.471
1909	.308	.634	.015	.473	1909	.255	.524	.013	.473	1909	.304	.613	.012	.485
1920	.249	.505	.011	.482	1920	.220	.433	.011	.494	1920	.254	.501	.011	.496
1930	.197	.387	.008	.500	1930	.181	.344	.009	.512	1930	.203	.389	.006	.515
1960	.234	.356	.011	.647	1960	.232	.358	.014	.632	1960	.245	.356	.006	.681

NETHERLANDS (continued)

	I_f	I_g	I_h	I_m		I_f	I_g	I_h	I_m		I_f	I_g	I_h	I_m
Utrecht					Friesland					Overyssel				
1859	.351	.866	.028	.385	1859	.327	.717	.015	.444	1859	.335	.775	.017	.419
1869	.388	.884	.030	.419	1869	.375	.771	.017	.474	1869	.364	.786	.017	.452
1879	.414	.891	.029	.446	1879	.369	.703	.016	.514	1879	.377	.777	.015	.476
1889	.399	.866	.028	.443	1889	.333	.685	.015	.475	1889	.376	.777	.012	.476
1899	.365	.804	.020	.440	1899	.314	.633	.012	.486	1899	.369	.755	.009	.483
1909	.304	.676	.012	.440	1909	.287	.550	.009	.514	1909	.329	.653	.007	.497
1920	.265	.566	.010	.458	1920	.271	.512	.008	.521	1920	.283	.581	.006	.482
1930	.217	.449	.008	.475	1930	.241	.445	.008	.533	1930	.239	.474	.004	.500
1960	.253	.408	.013	.608	1960	.279	.429	.006	.644	1960	.277	.440	.006	.625
Groningen					Drenthe					Limburg				
1859	.330	.751	.028	.419	1859	.347	.751	.024	.444	1859	.337	.876	.015	.374
1869	.368	.786	.031	.446	1869	.373	.750	.023	.481	1869	.367	.897	.016	.399
1879	.382	.752	.031	.487	1879	.385	.742	.021	.505	1879	.383	.921	.013	.408
1889	.352	.744	.024	.455	1889	.392	.759	.021	.502	1889	.370	.951	.013	.380
1899	.335	.699	.019	.465	1899	.405	.757	.017	.524	1899	.377	.968	.011	.382
1909	.311	.609	.014	.499	1909	.392	.707	.015	.545	1909	.389	.900	.010	.426
1920	.273	.522	.012	.512	1920	.367	.646	.012	.560	1920	.351	.738	.011	.468
1930	.219	.408	.009	.528	1930	.301	.521	.011	.568	1930	.297	.590	.007	.497
1960	.236	.357	.008	.653	1960	.265	.390	.005	.677	1960	.267	.424	.008	.624

NORWAY

	I_f	I_g	I_h	I_m		I_f	I_g	I_h	I_m		I_f	I_g	I_h	I_m
Norway					Ostfold Co Smaelenene					Akershus County				
1875	.334	.752	.049	.406	1875	.351	.769	.053	.416	1875	.300	.655	.053	.411
1890	.333	.735	.042	.420	1890	.361	.763	.040	.443	1890	.328	.725	.042	.420
1900	.317	.701	.040	.420	1900	.362	.729	.039	.468	1900	.312	.665	.034	.441
1920	.245	.548	.029	.416	1920	.254	.522	.030	.456	1920	.226	.476	.028	.441
1930	.168	.382	.020	.408	1930	.162	.348	.017	.438	1930	.144	.300	.016	.451
1960	.221	.322	.024	.660	1960	.204	.279	.019	.709	1960	.215	.292	.019	.717
Oslo Kristiana					Hedmark County					Oppland Kristians				
1875	.352	.869	.081	.344	1875	.350	.789	.077	.384	1875	.321	.754	.054	.382
1890	.308	.705	.071	.373	1890	.365	.787	.066	.416	1890	.347	.754	.046	.425
1900	.260	.592	.059	.377	1900	.360	.782	.056	.418	1900	.342	.736	.042	.432
1920	.130	.347	.025	.325	1920	.307	.645	.045	.438	1920	.277	.627	.028	.416
1930	.069	.197	.010	.318	1930	.221	.443	.038	.452	1930	.207	.457	.022	.427
1960	.162	.269	.017	.573	1960	.206	.289	.026	.683	1960	.211	.306	.023	.667
Buskerud County					Vestfold Co Jarls/Larv					Telemark Co Bratsberg				
1875	.348	.784	.047	.408	1875	.327	.731	.040	.415	1875	.316	.757	.026	.397
1890	.349	.755	.038	.434	1890	.316	.691	.031	.432	1890	.326	.725	.025	.430
1900	.349	.733	.033	.451	1900	.312	.678	.029	.437	1900	.305	.687	.021	.427
1920	.263	.532	.027	.468	1920	.244	.502	.023	.463	1920	.252	.529	.022	.453
1930	.157	.336	.016	.441	1930	.156	.327	.015	.451	1930	.153	.336	.013	.434
1960	.200	.281	.019	.693	1960	.219	.298	.016	.720	1960	.202	.285	.012	.697

Aust-Agder Co Nedened				
1875	.320	.748	.020	.412
1890	.305	.698	.018	.422
1900	.296	.695	.019	.410
1920	.240	.572	.014	.405
1930	.173	.418	.012	.397
1960	.233	.343	.017	.662

Vest-Agder Co List/Man				
1875	.317	.773	.014	.399
1890	.316	.745	.014	.413
1900	.305	.724	.012	.411
1920	.236	.583	.011	.394
1930	.179	.430	.008	.404
1960	.243	.353	.013	.676

Rogaland Co Stravanger				
1875	.339	.778	.024	.418
1890	.334	.768	.021	.419
1900	.320	.745	.020	.413
1920	.265	.581	.019	.438
1930	.186	.438	.011	.409
1960	.248	.363	.012	.672

Hordaland Co Bergen				
1875	.329	.776	.026	.405
1890	.326	.762	.021	.412
1900	.302	.725	.023	.397
1920	.239	.566	.018	.404
1930	.171	.420	.010	.392
1960	.267	.385	.013	.684

Bergen				
1875	.339	.808	.039	.390
1890	.297	.729	.030	.382
1900	.265	.653	.033	.375
1920	.180	.472	.022	.350
1930	.121	.329	.011	.346
1960	.181	.322	.012	.544

Sogn Og Fjordan				
1875	.324	.796	.033	.382
1890	.319	.801	.022	.381
1900	.315	.780	.020	.388
1920	.259	.686	.013	.366
1930	.207	.538	.010	.372
1960	.275	.424	.012	.639

More Og Romsdal County				
1875	.324	.727	.051	.404
1890	.309	.732	.037	.391
1900	.309	.717	.032	.404
1920	.261	.607	.024	.407
1930	.185	.454	.015	.386
1960	.256	.376	.020	.663

Sor-Trondelag County				
1875	.314	.649	.078	.413
1890	.306	.668	.064	.400
1900	.304	.669	.060	.401
1920	.251	.552	.048	.403
1930	.168	.385	.031	.385
1960	.220	.323	.029	.651

Nord-Trondelag County				
1875	.310	.671	.059	.411
1890	.304	.658	.048	.420
1900	.310	.654	.049	.431
1920	.266	.589	.033	.419
1930	.198	.436	.027	.420
1960	.248	.353	.033	.671

Nordland County				
1875	.378	.765	.069	.444
1890	.397	.744	.063	.491
1900	.370	.723	.060	.468
1920	.295	.611	.050	.437
1930	.218	.449	.044	.429
1960	.249	.341	.056	.675

Troms County				
1875	.388	.768	.064	.460
1890	.375	.736	.058	.468
1900	.360	.715	.054	.463
1920	.301	.629	.049	.434
1930	.224	.476	.045	.416
1960	.262	.371	.067	.641

Finnmark County				
1875	.427	.753	.083	.514
1890	.421	.747	.077	.513
1900	.410	.747	.082	.494
1920	.380	.665	.090	.504
1930	.277	.521	.073	.455
1960	.278	.381	.091	.646

POLAND

Poland 1897	.472	.720	.050	.631
Warshau 1897	.441	.695	.071	.594
Kalissk 1897	.545	.848	.044	.624
Kelitsk 1897	.487	.714	.039	.663
Louizinsk 1897	.469	.693	.036	.660
Ljublinsk 1897	.443	.633	.043	.678
Petrokovsk 1897	.454	.720	.041	.608
Plotsk 1897	.501	.757	.059	.633
Radomsk 1897	.545	.772	.037	.691
Suvalsk 1897	.445	.798	.040	.534
Sidletsk 1897	.470	.681	.062	.659

Poland 1931	.290	.501	.038	.544
Warszawa 1931	.261	.460	.032	.536
Lodz 1931	.272	.475	.028	.546
Kielle 1931	.321	.532	.028	.581
Lublin 1931	.315	.491	.046	.603
Bialystok 1931	.331	.551	.026	.580
Wilno 1931	.284	.509	.026	.535
Nowogrodek 1931	.349	.579	.029	.582
Polesie 1931	.426	.632	.059	.641

POLAND (continued)

	I_f	I_g	I_h	I_m		I_f	I_g	I_h	I_m		I_f	I_g	I_h	I_m
Wolyn 1931	.305	.457	.037	.639	Poznan 1931	.245	.526	.039	.424	Pomorze 1931	.306	.602	.051	.463
S´lask 1931	.251	.456	.037	.511	Krakow 1931	.304	.567	.044	.496	Lwow 1931	.276	.485	.048	.521
Stanistawow 1931	.365	.518	.068	.650	Tarnopol 1931	.265	.400	.044	.621					
Poland 1960	.244	.335	.035	.696	M. St. Warszawa 1960	.130	.187	.014	.669	Warszawskie 1960	.249	.342	.021	.710
Bydgoskie 1960	.270	.377	.037	.685	M. Poznan 1960	.157	.231	.020	.647	Poznanskie 1960	.271	.380	.029	.690
M. Lodz 1960	.131	.179	.020	.698	Lodzkie 1960	.230	.314	.022	.714	Kieleckie 1960	.259	.355	.021	.713
Lubelskie 1960	.241	.329	.020	.715	Bialostockie 1960	.279	.395	.025	.686	Olsztynskie 1960	.323	.423	.069	.718
Gdanskie 1960	.253	.345	.038	.700	Koszalinskie 1960	.312	.382	.107	.743	Szczecinskie 1960	.255	.305	.101	.753
Zielonogorskie 1960	.274	.345	.077	.737	M. Wroclaw 1960	.160	.222	.037	.667	Wroclawskie 1960	.258	.323	.075	.736
Opolskie 1960	.264	.387	.041	.644	Katowickie 1960	.203	.280	.028	.693	M. Krakow 1960	.152	.235	.016	.621
Krakowskie 1960	.264	.388	.025	.658	Rzeszowskie 1960	.259	.381	.027	.655					

PORTUGAL

	I_f	I_g	I_h	I_m		I_f	I_g	I_h	I_m		I_f	I_g	I_h	I_m
Portugal					Braganca					Vila Real				
1864	.329	.682	.079	.424	1864	--	--	--	.440	1864	--	--	--	.388
1878	.341	.664	.079	.452	1878	--	--	--	.448	1878	--	--	--	.407
1890	.358	.689	.075	.456	1890	.407	.738	.137	.438	1890	.358	.714	.126	.389
1900	.353	.681	.073	.460	1900	.369	.686	.113	.438	1900	.345	.686	.108	.405
1911	.344	.636	.083	.471	1911	.371	.663	.114	.468	1911	.334	.646	.101	.427
1920	.318	.609	.075	.455	1920	.401	.780	.114	.432	1920	.354	.708	.111	.408
1930	.304	.544	.088	.474	1930	.393	.749	.104	.448	1930	.409	.758	.129	.445
1940	.257	.453	.076	.481	1940	.351	.601	.108	.494	1940	.328	.567	.115	.471
1950	.255	.440	.059	.513	1950	.319	.572	.047	.518	1950	.346	.598	.091	.503
1960	.255	.414	.057	.556	1960	.329	.499	.112	.562	1960	.352	.590	.072	.540

Viano de Castelo					Braga					Porto				
1864	--	--	--	.345	1864	--	--	--	.372	1864	--	--	--	.386
1878	--	--	--	.358	1878	--	--	--	.387	1878	--	--	--	.447
1890	.282	.704	.050	.354	1890	.339	.749	.059	.403	1890	.358	.669	.092	.461
1900	.258	.615	.059	.357	1900	.316	.675	.055	.418	1900	.372	.713	.087	.453
1911	.276	.655	.062	.361	1911	.308	.647	.054	.428	1911	.343	.639	.094	.457
1920	.278	.685	.063	.347	1920	.316	.714	.056	.396	1920	.297	.593	.074	.430
1930	.294	.671	.070	.374	1930	.348	.730	.061	.429	1930	.309	.569	.088	.460
1940	.250	.553	.058	.388	1940	.330	.652	.053	.463	1940	.268	.484	.072	.475
1950	.280	.583	.051	.431	1950	.376	.741	.046	.470	1950	.302	.533	.063	.508
1960	.264	.523	.034	.469	1960	.381	.714	.032	.511	1960	.314	.524	.058	.557
Guarda					Viseu					Aveiro				
1864	--	--	--	.459	1864	--	--	--	.383	1864	--	--	--	.381
1878	--	--	--	.486	1878	--	--	--	.412	1878	--	--	--	.421
1890	.407	.760	.068	.489	1890	.361	.744	.100	.401	1890	.337	.724	.057	.418
1900	.398	.770	.049	.483	1900	.352	.705	.080	.435	1900	.356	.742	.058	.428
1911	.390	.721	.047	.509	1911	.320	.636	.082	.430	1911	.333	.676	.056	.447
1920	.373	.725	.039	.487	1920	.336	.699	.078	.416	1920	.313	.665	.055	.423
1930	.336	.622	.048	.511	1930	.325	.618	.078	.457	1930	.310	.612	.057	.455
1940	.318	.568	.034	.533	1940	.307	.552	.070	.482	1940	.284	.520	.054	.494
1950	.299	.522	.024	.553	1950	.313	.551	.056	.519	1950	.297	.510	.044	.543
1960	.265	.460	.015	.562	1960	.298	.514	.040	.544	1960	.307	.491	.039	.594
Castelo Branco					Coimbra					Leiria				
1864	--	--	--	.492	1864	--	--	--	.406	1864	--	--	--	.474
1878	--	--	--	.518	1878	--	--	--	.426	1878	--	--	--	.441
1890	.406	.735	.040	.525	1890	.316	.670	.049	.429	1890	.371	.738	.040	.474
1900	.413	.766	.033	.518	1900	.282	.598	.036	.436	1900	.365	.669	.044	.514
1911	.390	.719	.027	.524	1911	.281	.555	.046	.463	1911	.344	.658	.049	.484
1920	.359	.702	.028	.491	1920	.271	.561	.040	.444	1920	.326	.618	.053	.484
1930	.332	.619	.027	.516	1930	.251	.484	.039	.477	1930	.324	.555	.075	.519
1940	.293	.512	.024	.551	1940	.220	.406	.035	.497	1940	.282	.478	.075	.515
1950	.261	.441	.018	.574	1950	.219	.391	.031	.524	1950	.260	.429	.058	.545
1960	.224	.378	.014	.575	1960	.218	.360	.029	.572	1960	.240	.376	.046	.586
Santarem					Lisbon					Portalegre				
1864	--	--	--	.506	1864	--	--	--	.510	1864	--	--	--	.556
1878	--	--	--	.470	1878	--	--	--	.460	1878	--	--	--	.550
1890	.371	.691	.048	.501	1890	.322	.552	.108	.471	1890	.393	.650	.060	.563
1900	.368	.669	.045	.518	1900	.339	.559	.135	.468	1900	.392	.658	.061	.552
1911	.328	.605	.053	.499	1911	.331	.540	.165	.441	1911	.388	.634	.062	.570
1920	.319	.567	.047	.524	1920	.263	.427	.132	.445	1920	.355	.608	.060	.539
1930	.303	.491	.063	.561	1930	.213	.332	.124	.432	1930	.315	.520	.065	.551
1940	.239	.384	.061	.551	1940	.150	.230	.091	.422	1940	.247	.381	.076	.561
1950	.206	.344	.020	.574	1950	.149	.236	.069	.476	1950	.203	.314	.057	.570
1960	.205	.302	.050	.615	1960	.178	.260	.076	.552	1960	.189	.274	.058	.606
Evora					Setubal					Beja				
1864	--	--	--	.496	1864	--	--	--	--	1864	--	--	--	.534
1878	--	--	--	.510	1878	--	--	--	--	1878	--	--	--	.582
1890	.347	.610	.080	.498	1890	--	--	--	--	1890	.399	.639	.080	.566
1900	.395	.691	.093	.497	1900	--	--	--	--	1900	.402	.672	.081	.538
1911	.385	.622	.112	.534	1911	--	--	--	--	1911	.405	.640	.092	.571
1920	.352	.596	.112	.497	1920	--	--	--	--	1920	.369	.602	.098	.538
1930	.320	.500	.134	.509	1930	.330	.445	.221	.489	1930	.314	.542	.100	.484
1940	.252	.385	.136	.467	1940	.245	.314	.189	.448	1940	.253	.429	.110	.449
1950	.207	.316	.100	.497	1950	.195	.246	.142	.515	1950	.231	.375	.114	.447
1960	.175	.254	.085	.536	1960	.165	.197	.121	.519	1960	.203	.300	.114	.466

PORTUGAL (continued)

	I_f	I_g	I_h	I_m
Faro				
1864	--	--	--	.541
1878	--	--	--	.601
1890	.428	.702	.068	.565
1900	.401	.654	.076	.560
1911	.390	.617	.093	.566
1920	.338	.544	.087	.549
1930	.270	.419	.097	.537
1940	.220	.317	.113	.525
1950	.203	.284	.093	.576
1960	.172	.250	.072	.566
Ponta Delgada				
1864	--	--	--	.477
1878	--	--	--	.481
1890	.388	.794	.023	.474
1900	.360	.853	.014	.417
1911	.431	.753	.013	.565
1920	.423	.739	.008	.568
1930	.351	.621	.011	.556
1940	.306	.562	.018	.535
1950	.324	.580	.010	.550
1960	.388	.639	.010	.601

	I_f	I_g	I_h	I_m
Angra				
1864	--	--	--	.337
1878	--	--	--	.376
1890	.331	.711	.058	.418
1900	.356	.725	.041	.461
1911	.372	.713	.018	.510
1920	.335	.659	.024	.490
1930	.295	.563	.020	.506
1940	.259	.472	.021	.527
1950	.294	.480	.023	.593
1960	.336	.503	.028	.649
Funchal				
1864	--	--	--	.448
1878	--	--	--	.514
1890	.409	.800	.033	.485
1900	.405	.786	.010	.504
1911	.417	.784	.014	.523
1920	.353	.729	.013	.475
1930	.373	.757	.015	.487
1940	.332	.643	.017	.503
1950	.300	.623	.018	.467
1960	.323	.649	.015	.486

	I_f	I_g	I_h	I_m
Horta				
1864	--	--	--	.353
1878	--	--	--	.341
1890	.274	.650	.043	.379
1900	.304	.726	.033	.391
1911	.322	.651	.027	.473
1920	.280	.593	.022	.452
1930	.257	.507	.027	.478
1940	.235	.415	.031	.530
1950	.231	.383	.027	.573
1960	.226	.353	.017	.622

RUMANIA

	I_f	I_g	I_h	I_m
Rumania 1899	.528	.645	.216	.727
Oltenia 1899	.493	.604	.148	.758
Rumania 1930	.363	.489	.111	.667
Dobrogea 1930	.439	.568	.115	.715
Bucovina 1930	.314	.468	.064	.619
Crisana-Maramures 1930	.298	.397	.109	.656

	I_f	I_g	I_h	I_m
Moldova 1899	.501	.645	.167	.698
Dobrogea 1899	.681	.858	.093	.769
Oltenia 1930	.357	.480	.119	.659
Moldova 1930	.416	.582	.104	.653
Transilvania 1930	.353	.472	.115	.667

	I_f	I_g	I_h	I_m
Muntenia 1899	.520	.660	.151	.725
Muntenia 1930	.360	.484	.134	.646
Basarabia 1930	.415	.558	.083	.699
Banat 1930	.235	.276	.140	.699

Rumania 1956	.240	.346	--	.694	Bacau 1956	.305	.466	--	.654	Baia Mare 1956	.273	.390	--	.699
Bucuresti 1956	.219	.290	--	.754	Cluj 1956	.251	.355	--	.707	Constanta 1956	.307	.419	--	.732
Craiova 1956	.213	.301	--	.708	Galati 1956	.300	.434	--	.690	Hunedoara 1956	.205	.280	--	.731
Iasi 1956	.327	.502	--	.650	Oradea 1956	.225	.300	--	.750	Pitesti 1956	.230	.348	--	.660
Ploesti 1956	.246	.363	--	.678	Stalin 1956	.226	.347	--	.653	Suceava 1956	.285	.449	--	.634
Timisoara 1956	.182	.246	--	.741	Autonoma Maghiara 1956	.261	.373	--	.699	City Of Bucuresti 1956	.140	.212	--	.659
RUSSIA														
European Russia (Czarist Boundaries) 1897	.540	.755	.048	.696	Archangel 1897	.459	.709	.053	.619	Astrakhan 1897	.589	.704	.102	.809
Bessarabia					Vilna 1870	.516	.870	.047	.570	Vitebsk 1870	.502	.883	.024	.568
1897	.514	.680	.037	.742	1897	.428	.722	.038	.570	1897	.444	.751	.040	.568
Vladimir 1897	.546	.765	.035	.700	Vologda 1897	.494	.781	.043	.611	Volhynia 1897	.515	.703	.032	.720
Voronezh					Vyatka					Grodno 1870	.498	.752	.030	.648
1897	.648	.803	.032	.799	1897	.573	.804	.073	.684	1897	.479	.724	.028	.648
Don 1897	.598	.733	.071	.796	Ekaterinoslav 1897	.610	.776	.048	.772	Kazan 1897	.530	.749	.038	.692
Kaluga					Kiev 1870	.559	.787	.063	.685	Kovno 1870	.432	.825	.036	.502
1897	.568	.745	.064	.740	1897	.534	.752	.060	.685	1897	.394	.752	.033	.502
Kostroma 1897	.525	.776	.040	.659	Kurland 1897	.295	.548	.026	.515	Kursk 1897	.590	.789	.018	.742
Livonia 1870	.335	.670	.043	.466	Minsk					Mogilev				
1897	.290	.580	.036	.467	1897	.501	.750	.039	.650	1897	.524	.795	.029	.646
Moscow 1870	.531	.781	.150	.604	Nizhni Novgorod					Novgorod				
1897	.439	.645	.125	.604	1897	.575	.759	.059	.737	1897	.487	.806	.039	.584
Olonets 1897	.516	.801	.027	.632	Orenburg 1897	.646	.802	.048	.793	Orel 1897	.590	.795	.033	.731
Penza 1897	.606	.788	.026	.761	Perm 1897	.606	.797	.107	.723	Podolsk 1897	.497	.681	.035	.715

RUSSIA (continued)

	I_f	I_g	I_h	I_m
Poltava 1897	.549	.768	.045	.697
Samara 1897	.641	.811	.035	.781
Simbirsk 1897	.561	.756	.026	.733
Tambov 1897	.572	.735	.026	.770
Ufa 1897	.576	.772	.030	.736
Chernigov 1870	.586	.833	.039	.689
1897	.537	.764	.034	.689
European Russia (1926 Boundaries) 1926	.428	.665	.028	.628
North Dvina 1926	.512	.785	.033	.637
Novgorod 1926	.455	.742	.032	.596
Komi ASSR 1926	.500	.793	.032	.615
Ivanov 1926	.422	.764	.017	.542
Kostroma 1926	.429	.777	.019	.541
Smolensk 1926	.480	.732	.026	.643
Nizegorod 1926	.470	.747	.035	.611
Samara 1926	.456	.685	.011	.660
Voronezh 1926	.461	.691	.011	.662
Orel 1926	.499	.762	.021	.645
Votyak ASSR 1926	.540	.808	.040	.651
Pskov 1897	.500	.804	.061	.591
St. Petersburg 1870	.393	.659	.119	.507
1897	.330	.553	.101	.507
Smolensk 1897	.592	.810	.048	.714
Tver 1897	.542	.801	.028	.665
Kharkov 1897	.622	.801	.046	.763
Estonia 1870	.348	.669	.053	.479
1897	.310	.596	.032	.493
Archangel 1926	.448	.701	.046	.614
Leningrad 1926	.272	.424	.066	.575
Pskov 1926	.445	.707	.033	.611
Briansk 1926	.521	.767	.024	.669
Cherepovets 1926	.476	.769	.033	.602
Moscow 1926	.325	.507	.082	.572
Tula 1926	.508	.778	.017	.645
Tver 1926	.429	.717	.016	.589
Chuvash ASSR 1926	.472	.761	.016	.612
Kursk 1926	.483	.724	.009	.663
Tambov 1926	.445	.697	.008	.634
Vyatka 1926	.504	.795	.035	.617
Ryazan 1897	.576	.733	.029	.777
Saratov 1897	.617	.764	.061	.791
Tavrida 1897	.612	.801	.054	.747
Tula 1897	.599	.787	.029	.752
Kherson 1897	.572	.789	.063	.701
Yaroslavl 1870	.442	.740	.040	.574
1897	.442	.740	.040	.574
Vologda 1926	.486	.787	.029	.603
Murmansk 1926	.444	.564	.072	.756
Karelian ASSR 1926	.490	.741	.018	.653
Vladimir 1926	.458	.783	.016	.576
Kaluga 1926	.494	.789	.015	.619
Riazan 1926	.467	.726	.007	.640
Yaroslavl 1926	.412	.719	.031	.554
Marii ASSR 1926	.539	.847	.019	.628
Volga ASSR (Germans) 1926	.479	.748	.013	.634
Stalingrad 1926	.362	.566	.013	.631
Astrakhan 1926	.417	.609	.022	.673
Penza 1926	.517	.780	.015	.656

Saratov					Ulianovsk					Tatar ASSR				
1926	.448	.664	.015	.667	1926	.478	.747	.010	.635	1926	.469	.736	.018	.628
Ural					Kalmyk ASSR					Orenburg				
1926	.522	.778	.021	.662	1926	.335	.441	.017	.750	1926	.502	.728	.011	.685
No. Caucasian Terr.					Belo-Russia					Kazak ASSR				
1926	.407	.601	.013	.670	1926	.430	.686	.028	.611	1926	.494	.614	.017	.799
Bashkir ASSR					Crimea ASSR					Estonia				
1926	.537	.771	.028	.685	1926	.348	.531	.018	.643	1926	.202	.411	.025	.458
Moldavia					Lithuania					Latvia				
1926	.462	.666	.036	.676	1926	.292	.561	.028	.498	1926	.167	.359	.026	.423
European Russia (1959 Boundaries)					Archangel					Vologda				
1940	.279	.430	--	.649	1940	.342	.530	--	.645	1940	.305	.477	--	.639
1959	.207	.356	--	.581	1959	.253	.415	--	.609	1959	.243	.441	--	.550
1970	.152	.233	--	.656	1970	.156	.238	--	.655	1970	.143	.223	--	.639
Kaliningrad					Leningrad					Murmansk				
1940	--	--	--	--	1940	.265	.426	--	.622	1940	.320	.431	--	.743
1959	.187	.264	--	.707	1959	.126	.233	--	.540	1959	.197	.277	--	.713
1970	--	--	--	.701	1970	.114	.187	--	.612	1970	.133	.190	--	.699
Novgorod					Pskov					Karelian ASSR				
1940	.221	.350	--	.632	1940	.217	.338	--	.641	1940	.292	.434	--	.672
1959	.183	.331	--	.554	1959	.173	.300	--	.577	1959	.256	.419	--	.610
1970	.125	.193	--	.647	1970	.128	.194	--	.662	1970	.154	.235	--	.654
Komi ASSR					Briansk					Vladimir				
1940	.412	.638	--	.645	1940	.304	.445	--	.683	1940	.285	.461	--	.618
1959	.281	.438	--	.642	1959	.235	.421	--	.560	1959	.188	.332	--	.568
1970	.165	.243	--	.679	1970	.159	.246	--	.648	1970	.133	.209	--	.638
Ivanov					Kalinin					Kaluga				
1940	.290	.489	--	.594	1940	.228	.363	--	.627	1940	.265	.409	--	.648
1959	.165	.311	--	.533	1959	.167	.301	--	.553	1959	.203	.356	--	.569
1970	.131	.212	--	.616	1970	.118	.185	--	.640	1970	.136	.208	--	.653
Kostroma					Moskow					Riazin				
1940	.297	.499	--	.594	1940	.271	.440	--	.615	1940	.259	.390	--	.663
1959	.220	.396	--	.554	1959	.142	.249	--	.569	1959	.198	.347	--	.571
1970	.130	.203	--	.638	1970	.117	.185	--	.630	1970	.135	.207	--	.653
Smolensk					Tula					Yaroslavl				
1940	.221	.333	--	.665	1940	.252	.378	--	.666	1940	.283	.469	--	.603
1959	.188	.343	--	.548	1959	.171	.275	--	.624	1959	.171	.319	--	.534
1970	.136	.210	--	.645	1970	.123	.184	--	.666	1970	.132	.212	--	.624
Gorkii					Kirov					Mari ASSR				
1940	.297	.463	--	.641	1940	.339	.524	--	.647	1940	.363	.554	--	.654
1959	.202	.348	--	.580	1959	.228	.409	--	.558	1959	.277	.510	--	.543
1970	.139	.214	--	.649	1970	.137	.213	--	.645	1970	.166	.258	--	.643
Mordavian ASSR					Chuvash ASSR					Belgorod				
1940	.329	.488	--	.674	1940	.335	.521	--	.643	1940	.289	.426	--	.679
1959	.270	.512	--	.527	1959	.285	.575	--	.496	1959	.211	.383	--	.552
1970	.164	.255	--	.642	1970	.207	.329	--	.630	1970	.143	.219	--	.654

RUSSIA-1959 boundaries (continued)

	I_f	I_g	I_h	I_m
Voronezh				
1940	.272	.400	--	.678
1959	.199	.354	--	.563
1970	.141	.217	--	.648
Orel				
1940	.229	.344	--	.666
1959	.208	.374	--	.557
1970	.135	.209	--	.647
Volgograd				
1940	.285	.433	--	.657
1959	.211	.344	--	.613
1970	.153	.232	--	.660
Saratov				
1940	.341	.502	--	.679
1959	.194	.329	--	.590
1970	.150	.232	--	.646
Rostov				
1940	.284	.424	--	.670
1959	.194	.312	--	.622
1970	.141	.213	--	.664
Perm				
1940	.383	.582	--	.658
1959	.242	.409	--	.593
1970	.161	.247	--	.649
Bashkir ASSR				
1940	.354	.510	--	.694
1959	.315	.519	--	.607
1970	.192	.289	--	.665
Donets				
1940	.283	.419	--	.676
1959	.186	.288	--	.647
1970	.136	.197	--	.689
Poltava				
1940	.285	.437	--	.653
1959	.142	.255	--	.556
1970	.147	.220	--	.671
Vinnitza				
1940	.214	.316	--	.678
1959	.163	.289	--	.565
1970	.159	.232	--	.683
Trans-Carpathian				
1940	--	--	--	--
1959	.263	.410	--	.641
1970	.224	.314	--	.711

	I_f	I_g	I_h	I_m
Kursk				
1940	.271	.399	--	.679
1959	.229	.406	--	.563
1970	.143	.220	--	.653
Tambov				
1940	.315	.478	--	.659
1959	.231	.418	--	.553
1970	.152	.235	--	.646
Kuibishev				
1940	.310	.458	--	.677
1959	.202	.322	--	.626
1970	.148	.224	--	.664
Ulianov				
1940	.331	.501	--	.659
1959	.226	.375	--	.604
1970	.152	.228	--	.666
Kalmyk ASSR				
1940	.436	.590	--	.739
1959	.375	.616	--	.609
1970	.211	.314	--	.673
Sverdlov				
1940	.358	.519	--	.689
1959	.204	.330	--	.620
1970	.142	.216	--	.656
Udmurt ASSR				
1940	.378	.580	--	.652
1959	.282	.498	--	.565
1970	.171	.266	--	.643
Zaporczhie				
1940	.285	.435	--	.655
1959	.168	.268	--	.626
1970	.152	.220	--	.687
Sumy				
1940	.194	.294	--	.659
1959	.161	.289	--	.559
1970	.149	.222	--	.671
Volhynia				
1940	.217	.333	--	.652
1959	.203	.323	--	.629
1970	.196	.276	--	.708
Ivan-Franco				
1940	--	--	--	--
1959	.229	.407	--	.563
1970	.199	.292	--	.683

	I_f	I_g	I_h	I_m
Lipetsk				
1940	.259	.393	--	.659
1959	.224	.406	--	.552
1970	.151	.232	--	.649
Astrakhan				
1940	.328	.478	--	.686
1959	.250	.413	--	.606
1970	.156	.238	--	.655
Penza				
1940	.326	.484	--	.674
1959	.221	.397	--	.556
1970	.154	.239	--	.644
Tatar ASSR				
1940	.353	.540	--	.654
1959	.270	.490	--	.551
1970	.168	.263	--	.640
Orenburg				
1940	.355	.519	--	.684
1959	.269	.434	--	.618
1970	.172	.257	--	.667
Cheliabinsk				
1940	.348	.508	--	.685
1959	.217	.339	--	.639
1970	.155	.232	--	.665
Dnepropetrovsk				
1940	.260	.400	--	.651
1959	.184	.290	--	.634
1970	.149	.217	--	.689
Lugansk				
1940	.192	.277	--	.692
1959	.191	.289	--	.660
1970	.139	.200	--	.698
Kharkov				
1940	.218	.325	--	.672
1959	.143	.249	--	.576
1970	.141	.213	--	.660
Zhitomir				
1940	.215	.323	--	.666
1959	.186	.331	--	.564
1970	.180	.265	--	.679
Kiev				
1940	.234	.356	--	.656
1959	.166	.302	--	.549
1970	.152	.232	--	.656

Kirov					Lvov					Rovensk				
1940	.245	.370	--	.662	1940	.228	.399	--	.572	1940	.235	.360	--	.652
1959	.171	.280	--	.611	1959	.222	.399	--	.555	1959	.244	.418	--	.584
1970	.163	.235	--	.694	1970	.183	.274	--	.667	1970	.207	.299	--	.691
Ternopol					Khmelnitskii					Cherkassy				
1940	.210	.327	--	.641	1940	.273	.409	--	.667	1940	.264	.402	--	.656
1959	.205	.369	--	.556	1959	.191	.351	--	.544	1959	.173	.317	--	.547
1970	.181	.266	--	.681	1970	.168	.248	--	.677	1970	.157	.234	--	.670
Chernigov					Chernovits					Crimean				
1940	.233	.355	--	.655	1940	.195	.306	--	.637	1940	.264	.402	--	.656
1959	.175	.328	--	.534	1959	.198	.344	--	.577	1959	.174	.279	--	.625
1970	.146	.219	--	.665	1970	.181	.265	--	.682	1970	.154	.223	--	.690
Nikolaev					Odessa					Kherson				
1940	.317	.477	--	.665	1940	.241	.376	--	.640	1940	.309	.478	--	.647
1959	.187	.292	--	.640	1959	.177	.288	--	.612	1959	.199	.326	--	.610
1970	.164	.234	--	.701	1970	.151	.221	--	.680	1970	.169	.247	--	.684
Brest					Vitebesk					Gomel				
1940	.252	.354	--	.712	1940	.253	.409	--	.619	1940	.255	.385	--	.661
1959	.230	.378	--	.608	1959	.231	.424	--	.545	1959	.233	.406	--	.574
1970	.187	.272	--	.689	1970	.162	.250	--	.649	1970	.191	.288	--	.664
Grodno					Minsk					Mogilev				
1940	.255	.414	--	.617	1940	.240	.375	--	.640	1940	.262	.407	--	.642
1959	.233	.429	--	.544	1959	.220	.393	--	.560	1959	.239	.426	--	.561
1970	.188	.282	--	.666	1970	.158	.245	--	.646	1970	.179	.272	--	.658
Moldavia					Lithuania					Latvia				
1940	.272	.359	--	.757	1940	.222	.535	--	.416	1940	.200	.398	--	.502
1959	.275	.422	--	.651	1959	.216	.391	--	.551	1959	.161	.282	--	.569
1970	.201	.306	--	.657	1970	.187	.289	--	.645	1970	.152	.236	--	.642
Estonia														
1940	.159	.334	--	.475										
1959	.164	.282	--	.580										
1970	.168	.266	--	.634										

SCOTLAND

Scotland					Shetland					Orkney				
1861	.346	.742	.056	.422	1861	.241	.767	.014	.302	1861	.267	.712	.019	.357
1871	.359	.752	.060	.432	1871	.232	.724	.015	.306	1871	.280	.703	.025	.376
1881	.350	.733	.052	.438	1881	.230	.782	.016	.279	1881	.276	.676	.028	.382
1891	.317	.696	.042	.420	1891	.228	.750	.014	.292	1891	.247	.660	.025	.349
1901	.288	.632	.033	.425	1901	.209	.649	.013	.308	1901	.220	.595	.020	.348
1911	.260	.565	.031	.428	1911	.194	.563	.015	.326	1911	.205	.532	.020	.361
1921	.224	.480	.028	.433	1921	.149	.466	.014	.298	1921	.205	.485	.025	.392
1931	.192	.404	.024	.441	1931	.137	.393	.017	.321	1931	.173	.395	.020	.409
1961	.234	.341	.031	.656	1961	.224	.351	.026	.609	1961	.218	.318	.030	.654

SCOTLAND (continued)

	I_f	I_g	I_h	I_m
Caithness				
1861	.303	.793	.036	.352
1871	.320	.807	.050	.356
1881	.316	.792	.053	.356
1891	.305	.769	.055	.351
1901	.298	.748	.051	.355
1911	.268	.653	.048	.364
1921	.232	.557	.042	.369
1931	.219	.465	.047	.412
1961	.271	.366	.044	.706
Inverness				
1861	.267	.750	.031	.328
1871	.279	.769	.035	.333
1881	.286	.773	.034	.340
1891	.259	.746	.030	.320
1901	.237	.659	.026	.333
1911	.217	.608	.026	.327
1921	.194	.523	.025	.341
1931	.187	.459	.027	.370
1961	.231	.359	.034	.608
Banff				
1861	.371	.774	.098	.403
1871	.361	.755	.099	.398
1881	.370	.763	.102	.406
1891	.351	.766	.084	.392
1901	.319	.673	.070	.413
1911	.288	.591	.066	.423
1921	.260	.512	.058	.446
1931	.234	.441	.059	.459
1961	.231	.333	.039	.651
Angus Forfar				
1861	.321	.720	.062	.393
1871	.327	.727	.061	.399
1881	.312	.697	.052	.402
1891	.274	.650	.042	.381
1901	.244	.592	.033	.378
1911	.220	.523	.030	.385
1921	.196	.454	.028	.393
1931	.176	.388	.024	.417
1961	.232	.324	.041	.676
Kinross				
1861	.314	.701	.058	.398
1871	.310	.711	.053	.391
1881	.284	.711	.045	.358
1891	.282	.712	.035	.364
1901	.268	.577	.028	.438
1911	.240	.533	.034	.413
1921	.205	.461	.029	.407
1931	.172	.382	.027	.410
1961	.209	.309	.011	.663

	I_f	I_g	I_h	I_m
Sutherland				
1861	.239	.772	.015	.295
1871	.239	.782	.022	.285
1881	.272	.796	.027	.318
1891	.270	.788	.024	.322
1901	.246	.690	.020	.337
1911	.215	.631	.020	.319
1921	.186	.505	.022	.339
1931	.177	.453	.027	.353
1961	.238	.351	.029	.649
Nairn				
1861	.297	.770	.040	.352
1871	.296	.769	.042	.350
1881	.292	.770	.047	.339
1891	.232	.629	.038	.328
1901	.227	.599	.033	.342
1911	.202	.550	.034	.325
1921	.202	.487	.035	.368
1931	.192	.462	.035	.368
1961	.216	.316	.026	.655
Aberdeen				
1861	.346	.744	.089	.393
1871	.361	.749	.091	.411
1881	.362	.748	.085	.418
1891	.327	.742	.069	.383
1901	.299	.654	.057	.405
1911	.258	.549	.056	.411
1921	.224	.470	.047	.419
1931	.201	.405	.041	.440
1961	.209	.305	.030	.649
Perth				
1861	.295	.707	.050	.373
1871	.297	.710	.050	.374
1881	.283	.692	.042	.371
1891	.258	.684	.036	.342
1901	.221	.592	.026	.345
1911	.194	.496	.025	.357
1921	.163	.404	.024	.366
1931	.155	.356	.023	.395
1961	.214	.320	.030	.634
Clackmannan				
1861	.380	.738	.067	.467
1871	.373	.772	.059	.441
1881	.359	.790	.046	.421
1891	.259	.609	.024	.402
1901	.244	.605	.019	.385
1911	.217	.533	.022	.382
1921	.206	.449	.022	.430
1931	.173	.363	.018	.448
1961	.236	.310	.044	.722

	I_f	I_g	I_h	I_m
Ross & Cromarty				
1861	.288	.768	.018	.360
1871	.279	.760	.020	.350
1881	.278	.783	.020	.339
1891	.275	.787	.020	.332
1901	.259	.724	.018	.342
1911	.227	.667	.019	.321
1921	.204	.573	.019	.334
1931	.180	.504	.021	.329
1961	.234	.373	.024	.600
Moray Elgin				
1861	.343	.776	.071	.385
1871	.330	.754	.079	.371
1881	.335	.758	.082	.374
1891	.325	.759	.073	.367
1901	.275	.644	.056	.373
1911	.247	.567	.056	.373
1921	.227	.484	.053	.404
1931	.204	.414	.048	.428
1961	.249	.336	.045	.701
Kincardine				
1861	.351	.746	.083	.404
1871	.370	.749	.091	.424
1881	.370	.765	.080	.423
1891	.348	.760	.073	.401
1901	.310	.634	.054	.441
1911	.278	.556	.050	.451
1921	.224	.485	.040	.413
1931	.192	.378	.037	.454
1961	.210	.307	.022	.659
Fife				
1861	.347	.749	.047	.428
1871	.352	.767	.048	.423
1881	.339	.743	.040	.425
1891	.309	.694	.031	.420
1901	.279	.609	.024	.436
1911	.270	.532	.026	.482
1921	.223	.429	.026	.490
1931	.191	.366	.023	.489
1961	.228	.312	.032	.701
Stirling				
1861	.410	.780	.067	.481
1871	.435	.812	.069	.492
1881	.415	.759	.056	.511
1891	.376	.740	.044	.477
1901	.346	.673	.032	.489
1911	.307	.587	.031	.498
1921	.246	.495	.029	.466
1931	.205	.404	.024	.476
1961	.225	.328	.020	.667

Dunbarton				
1861	.364	.765	.047	.441
1871	.392	.840	.045	.437
1881	.359	.774	.033	.439
1891	.323	.706	.027	.436
1901	.304	.669	.019	.438
1911	.282	.591	.022	.457
1921	.229	.478	.020	.456
1931	.190	.410	.017	.440
1961	.248	.356	.024	.674

Argyll				
1861	.307	.763	.033	.375
1871	.302	.763	.037	.365
1881	.295	.752	.035	.363
1891	.283	.779	.033	.335
1901	.238	.686	.027	.320
1911	.204	.567	.028	.327
1921	.134	.337	.021	.357
1931	.157	.389	.027	.358
1961	.217	.335	.035	.604

Bute				
1861	.244	.735	.024	.309
1871	.241	.692	.030	.319
1881	.253	.682	.026	.347
1891	.217	.619	.020	.329
1901	.187	.555	.016	.317
1911	.153	.433	.016	.329
1921	.059	.138	.008	.393
1931	.119	.285	.015	.385
1961	.210	.314	.046	.613

Renfrew				
1861	.365	.760	.047	.446
1871	.372	.753	.047	.460
1881	.350	.730	.038	.452
1891	.334	.738	.030	.430
1901	.301	.680	.022	.424
1911	.255	.573	.020	.424
1921	.232	.499	.020	.441
1931	.195	.428	.017	.433
1961	.245	.354	.026	.666

Ayr				
1861	.406	.766	.069	.484
1871	.432	.821	.073	.481
1881	.404	.778	.059	.480
1891	.359	.741	.047	.450
1901	.318	.666	.034	.450
1911	.273	.589	.032	.433
1921	.211	.438	.026	.451
1931	.191	.397	.023	.449
1961	.229	.325	.028	.676

Lanark				
1861	.384	.734	.057	.483
1871	.410	.751	.067	.501
1881	.401	.741	.054	.505
1891	.355	.680	.043	.490
1901	.325	.635	.034	.484
1911	.299	.598	.033	.471
1921	.259	.527	.029	.461
1931	.210	.428	.024	.461
1961	.251	.372	.032	.644

West Lothian Linlith				
1861	.484	.786	.084	.569
1871	.517	.846	.099	.559
1881	.486	.794	.085	.566
1891	.498	.828	.072	.563
1901	.439	.726	.050	.576
1911	.380	.634	.041	.573
1921	.307	.551	.034	.529
1931	.237	.436	.025	.515
1961	.230	.329	.021	.678

Midlothian Edinburg				
1861	.304	.706	.043	.394
1871	.319	.690	.047	.422
1881	.312	.678	.041	.425
1891	.278	.647	.034	.397
1901	.239	.567	.026	.394
1911	.210	.498	.024	.391
1921	.188	.437	.023	.400
1931	.158	.359	.017	.411
1961	.217	.326	.029	.633

East Lothian Hadding				
1861	.351	.777	.052	.412
1871	.339	.740	.053	.416
1881	.329	.732	.044	.414
1891	.296	.697	.036	.393
1901	.264	.619	.029	.398
1911	.254	.540	.030	.438
1921	.206	.442	.025	.434
1931	.190	.392	.023	.453
1961	.216	.316	.014	.671

Berwick				
1861	.318	.762	.051	.376
1871	.323	.765	.056	.376
1881	.294	.715	.048	.368
1891	.261	.682	.042	.343
1901	.216	.562	.032	.347
1911	.191	.464	.028	.373
1921	.182	.399	.028	.415
1931	.157	.327	.023	.443
1961	.182	.259	.023	.673

Peebles				
1861	.336	.750	.056	.403
1871	.323	.716	.052	.407
1881	.288	.699	.038	.378
1891	.235	.642	.029	.335
1901	.195	.557	.024	.322
1911	.162	.444	.019	.337
1921	.136	.337	.019	.367
1931	.134	.317	.015	.393
1961	.214	.318	.024	.646

Selkirk				
1861	.352	.736	.064	.428
1871	.301	.657	.048	.416
1881	.305	.655	.043	.427
1891	.239	.615	.029	.358
1901	.192	.559	.020	.318
1911	.151	.419	.018	.331
1921	.139	.356	.017	.359
1931	.127	.297	.014	.401
1961	.200	.303	.014	.643

Roxburgh				
1861	.339	.713	.065	.422
1871	.353	.801	.066	.391
1881	.303	.687	.054	.394
1891	.238	.611	.038	.350
1901	.189	.549	.025	.314
1911	.166	.452	.024	.333
1921	.157	.391	.023	.366
1931	.141	.335	.019	.386
1961	.203	.293	.024	.668

Dumfries				
1861	.341	.755	.080	.387
1871	.327	.746	.080	.371
1881	.310	.712	.073	.372
1891	.278	.677	.057	.356
1901	.246	.602	.044	.363
1911	.223	.525	.041	.377
1921	.219	.469	.041	.417
1931	.184	.371	.037	.439
1961	.225	.313	.038	.679

Kirkcudbright				
1861	.328	.759	.072	.373
1871	.332	.750	.083	.374
1881	.313	.698	.074	.382
1891	.289	.690	.062	.362
1901	.242	.594	.042	.362
1911	.207	.504	.037	.363
1921	.194	.447	.038	.381
1931	.218	.445	.046	.432
1961	.241	.339	.032	.680

SCOTLAND (continued)

Wigtown	I_f	I_g	I_h	I_m
1861	.315	.726	.074	.370
1871	.322	.774	.083	.346
1881	.331	.746	.084	.373
1891	.304	.714	.076	.356
1901	.269	.667	.057	.348
1911	.246	.554	.057	.380
1921	.217	.472	.054	.389
1931	.213	.408	.064	.434
1961	.249	.344	.066	.659

SPAIN

Spain-Regions	I_f	I_g	I_h	I_m
1887	.391	.650	.041	.575
1900	.383	.653	.041	.559
1910	.356	.623	.036	.545
1920	.314	.586	.038	.504
1930	.291	.540	.038	.504
1940	.208	.464	.021	.422
1950	.203	.419	--	--
1960	.228	.403	.012	.553

Andalucia	I_f	I_g	I_h	I_m
1887	.392	.622	.057	.593
1900	.411	.632	.067	.609
1910	.391	.620	.059	.592
1920	.355	.598	.060	.548
1930	.344	.591	.061	.534
1940	.250	.521	.033	.445
1950	.228	.482	--	--
1960	.262	.476	.017	.536

Aragon	I_f	I_g	I_h	I_m
1887	.424	.647	.026	.641
1900	.403	.639	.023	.617
1910	.365	.593	.017	.604
1920	.330	.587	.021	.546
1930	.297	.517	.019	.558
1940	.185	.422	.012	.422
1950	.178	.358	--	--
1960	.201	.346	.005	.575

Asturias	I_f	I_g	I_h	I_m
1887	.351	.794	.024	.425
1900	.387	.832	.027	.447
1910	.363	.804	.018	.439
1920	.349	.780	.013	.439
1930	.296	.692	.023	.408
1940	.151	.443	.009	.327
1950	.172	.402	--	--
1960	.203	.336	.007	.598

Baleares	I_f	I_g	I_h	I_m
1887	.325	.581	.013	.549
1900	.296	.570	.011	.510
1910	.270	.508	.018	.514
1920	.228	.472	.009	.473
1930	.200	.403	.006	.489
1940	.155	.366	.003	.418
1950	.148	.298	--	--
1960	.192	.315	.005	.603

Canarias	I_f	I_g	I_h	I_m
1887	.429	.899	.058	.441
1900	.498	1.012	.069	.455
1910	.439	.911	.050	.452
1920	.309	.660	.037	.437
1930	.368	.772	.039	.449
1940	.322	.669	.046	.443
1950	.261	.575	--	--
1960	.279	.504	.014	.541

Castilla La Nueva	I_f	I_g	I_h	I_m
1887	.403	.651	.072	.572
1900	.370	.629	.062	.543
1910	.357	.627	.055	.528
1920	.317	.588	.050	.496
1930	.289	.534	.045	.499
1940	.191	.431	.021	.415
1950	.191	.402	--	--
1960	.229	.423	.012	.529

Castilla La Vieja	I_f	I_g	I_h	I_m
1887	.451	.712	.036	.614
1900	.440	.739	.032	.577
1910	.420	.701	.009	.594
1920	.378	.700	.033	.517
1930	.362	.680	.027	.513
1940	.246	.581	.011	.412
1950	.235	.487	--	--
1960	.232	.428	.006	.535

Cataluna	I_f	I_g	I_h	I_m
1887	.330	.534	.024	.600
1900	.282	.486	.018	.564
1910	.259	.453	.017	.555
1920	.222	.411	.018	.519
1930	.183	.323	.018	.541
1940	.126	.263	.012	.454
1950	.145	.288	--	--
1960	.187	.303	.009	.606

Extremadura	I_f	I_g	I_h	I_m
1887	.477	.688	.039	.675
1900	.438	.690	.032	.617
1910	.521	.754	.041	.673
1920	.361	.612	.031	.568
1930	.342	.605	.028	.544
1940	.255	.552	.014	.448
1950	.244	.496	--	--
1960	.252	.458	.008	.542

Galicia	I_f	I_g	I_h	I_m
1887	.324	.695	.046	.428
1900	.343	.719	.050	.438
1910	.320	.646	.046	.457
1920	.265	.634	.045	.373
1930	.282	.601	.062	.408
1940	.216	.526	.034	.370
1950	.197	.407	--	--
1960	.196	.357	.025	.515

Leon	I_f	I_g	I_h	I_m
1887	.424	.689	.043	.590
1900	.408	.705	.038	.555
1910	.381	.665	.034	.550
1920	.346	.667	.039	.489
1930	.351	.660	.038	.503
1940	.268	.606	.020	.423
1950	.240	.482	--	--
1960	.234	.425	.009	.540

Murcia				
1887	.411	.622	.053	.629
1900	.432	.643	.060	.638
1910	.437	.596	.200	.598
1920	.342	.575	.056	.551
1930	.288	.512	--	--
1940	.237	.467	.030	.474
1950	.243	.473	--	--
1960	.266	.427	.012	.611
Spain-Provinces				
1887	.391	.650	.041	.575
1900	.383	.653	.041	.559
1910	.356	.623	.036	.545
1920	.314	.586	.038	.504
1930	.291	.540	.038	.504
1940	.208	.464	.021	.422
1950	.203	.419	--	--
1960	.228	.403	.012	.553
Alicante				
1887	.378	.608	.009	.616
1900	.361	.576	.012	.619
1910	.280	.488	.013	.562
1920	.260	.477	.013	.532
1930	.251	.437	.015	.559
1940	.183	.373	.012	.474
1950	.189	.374	--	--
1960	.225	.376	.006	.592
Badajoz				
1887	.464	.684	.031	.663
1900	.405	.640	.030	.614
1910	.391	.623	.028	.609
1920	.356	.623	.012	.563
1930	.324	.597	.021	.526
1940	.245	.567	.015	.417
1950	.239	.506	--	--
1960	.251	.457	.007	.543
Burgos				
1887	.453	.716	.022	.621
1900	.459	.743	.020	.607
1910	.431	.706	.015	.602
1920	.411	.726	.024	.551
1930	.387	.695	.021	.543
1940	.274	.628	.010	.427
1950	.248	.503	--	--
1960	.236	.435	.002	.540
Castellon				
1887	.443	.667	.010	.659
1900	.394	.606	.009	.645
1910	.314	.516	.008	.602
1920	.264	.468	.006	.558
1930	.223	.383	.007	.574
1940	.166	.348	.005	.469
1950	.167	.316	--	--
1960	.189	.308	.004	.607

Valencia				
1887	.398	.640	.016	.612
1900	.375	.609	.017	.605
1910	.303	.525	.015	.565
1920	.262	.490	.012	.523
1930	.235	.426	.013	.538
1940	.169	.365	.009	.449
1950	.173	.349	--	--
1960	.211	.362	.007	.576
Alava				
1887	.415	.697	.029	.578
1900	.408	.731	.026	.542
1910	.377	.710	.016	.520
1920	.355	.720	.019	.479
1930	.303	.636	.014	.465
1940	.184	.494	.007	.363
1950	.194	.433	--	--
1960	.240	.440	.003	.543
Almeria				
1887	.401	.616	.036	.629
1900	.439	.640	.045	.662
1910	.413	.622	.060	.628
1920	.363	.589	.066	.568
1930	.362	.585	.069	.568
1940	.235	.464	.024	.479
1950	.272	.498	--	--
1960	.277	.437	.029	.608
Baleares				
1887	.325	.581	.013	.549
1900	.296	.570	.011	.510
1910	.270	.508	.018	.514
1920	.228	.472	.009	.473
1930	.200	.403	.006	.489
1940	.155	.366	.003	.418
1950	.148	.298	--	--
1960	.192	.315	.005	.603
Caceres				
1887	.496	.694	.053	.691
1900	.463	.709	.042	.631
1910	.443	.693	.039	.618
1920	.369	.608	.043	.577
1930	.371	.615	.044	.573
1940	.270	.534	.011	.495
1950	.251	.481	--	--
1960	.254	.460	.011	.542
Ciudad Real				
1887	.475	.716	.029	.649
1900	.444	.678	.026	.641
1910	.435	.690	.028	.615
1920	.405	.674	.021	.588
1930	.344	.597	.028	.555
1940	.216	.475	.014	.438
1950	.237	.470	--	--
1960	.263	.449	.007	.580

Vascongadas y Navarra				
1887	.363	.679	.025	.517
1900	.368	.695	.054	.490
1910	.341	.688	.023	.478
1920	.311	.663	.022	.451
1930	.262	.574	.013	.444
1940	.170	.476	.008	.346
1950	.184	.430	--	--
1960	.239	.443	.004	.536
Albacete				
1887	.424	.631	.068	.632
1900	.448	.654	.075	.644
1910	.411	.633	.077	.601
1920	.381	.591	.080	.589
1930	.341	.532	--	--
1940	.260	.510	.043	.465
1950	.251	.468	--	--
1960	.276	.466	.012	.581
Avila				
1887	.469	.674	.047	.673
1900	.449	.691	.042	.627
1910	.454	.671	.052	.645
1920	.398	.669	.040	.569
1930	.388	.653	.038	.570
1940	.297	.638	.012	.455
1950	.246	.498	--	--
1960	.234	.442	.008	.522
Barcelona				
1887	.304	.508	.034	.570
1900	.257	.459	.026	.533
1910	.225	.414	.022	.518
1920	.209	.409	.021	.485
1930	.173	.314	.018	.524
1940	.121	.249	.016	.451
1950	.140	.284	--	--
1960	.185	.305	.010	.594
Cadiz				
1887	.370	.606	.084	.548
1900	.372	.639	.079	.523
1910	.357	.614	.059	.537
1920	.340	.590	.060	.528
1930	.340	.590	.060	.528
1940	.279	.574	.051	.436
1950	.248	.484	--	--
1960	.282	.504	.031	.532
Cordoba				
1887	.412	.626	.060	.622
1900	.409	.642	.052	.605
1910	.406	.623	.056	.617
1920	.384	.649	.047	.560
1930	.343	.609	.042	.531
1940	.245	.511	.033	.443
1950	.232	.495	--	--
1960	.258	.484	.010	.524

SPAIN–Provinces (continued)

	I_f	I_g	I_h	I_m
Coruna(La)				
1887	.313	.688	.047	.415
1900	.350	.702	.055	.456
1910	.314	.633	.049	.454
1920	.270	.661	.048	.362
1930	.298	.618	.063	.423
1940	.224	.536	.038	.373
1950	.200	.351	--	--
1960	.194	.356	.026	.510
Granada				
1887	.418	.625	.063	.632
1900	.422	.612	.071	.649
1910	.413	.644	.055	.608
1920	.376	.620	.070	.556
Granada (cont.)				
1930	.366	.591	.081	.559
1940	.249	.486	.048	.459
1950	.238	.455	--	--
1960	.282	.483	.023	.563
Huelva				
1887	.365	.643	.039	.540
1900	.365	.643	.039	.540
1910	.350	.609	.036	.548
1920	.289	.522	.036	.521
1930	.251	.483	.028	.490
1940	.202	.467	.017	.411
1950	.209	.442	--	--
1960	.236	.441	.012	.523
Leon				
1887	.410	.710	.037	.554
1900	.410	.739	.038	.531
1910	.378	.687	.031	.529
1920	.338	.695	.038	.457
1930	.357	.684	.036	.495
1940	.253	.588	.022	.408
1950	.234	.501	--	--
1960	.235	.408	.009	.566
Lugo				
1887	.372	.824	.053	.414
1900	.373	.802	.052	.428
1910	.328	.665	.075	.429
1920	.260	.684	.040	.342
1930	.277	.673	.046	.368
1940	.206	.533	.026	.355
1950	.183	.444	--	--
1960	.178	.323	.023	.518

	I_f	I_g	I_h	I_m
Cuenca				
1887	.439	.646	.035	.661
1900	.444	.652	.035	.663
1910	.415	.629	.038	.638
1920	.386	.626	.041	.590
1930	.353	.615	--	.574
1940	.257	.500	.023	.491
1950	.247	.445	--	--
1960	.250	.415	.008	.594
Guadalajara				
1887	.445	.643	.069	.655
1900	.436	.677	.027	.629
1910	.415	.662	.015	.618
1920	.373	.638	.012	.577
Guadalajara (cont.)				
1930	.347	.613	.021	.551
1940	.222	.526	.007	.414
1950	.219	.438	--	--
1960	.208	.380	.005	.543
Huesca				
1887	.427	.624	.020	.674
1900	.399	.613	.017	.641
1910	.370	.584	.016	.623
1920	.305	.569	.016	.523
1930	.285	.484	.015	.576
1940	.164	.374	.006	.429
1950	.175	.348	--	--
1960	.184	.315	.004	.579
Lerida				
1887	.345	.528	.007	.649
1900	.330	.504	.005	.651
1910	.303	.478	--	.633
1920	.270	.441	.010	.603
1930	.223	.354	.027	.599
1940	.150	.316	.005	.466
1950	.168	.309	--	--
1960	.207	.321	.005	.640
Madrid				
1887	.327	.589	.101	.463
1900	.291	.560	.085	.434
1910	.277	.556	.071	.425
1920	.242	.506	.059	.409
1930	.233	.462	.054	.439
1940	.158	.366	.025	.390
1950	.155	.356	--	--
1960	.222	.427	.013	.504

	I_f	I_g	I_h	I_m
Gerona				
1887	.354	.564	.013	.619
1900	.321	.561	.009	.565
1910	.285	.477	.008	.591
1920	.238	.420	.010	.556
1930	.196	.351	.007	.550
1940	.124	.272	.006	.443
1950	.148	.284	--	--
1960	.180	.277	.006	.641
Guipuzcoa				
1887	.341	.708	.017	.469
1900	.343	.729	.022	.454
1910	.320	.693	.021	.445
1920	.278	.646	.026	.406
Guipuzcoa (cont.)				
1930	.238	.548	.014	.419
1940	.165	.497	.007	.323
1950	.187	.451	--	--
1960	.244	.485	.002	.502
Jaen				
1887	.441	.654	.045	.650
1900	.472	.698	.050	.651
1910	.433	.629	.067	.651
1920	.408	.627	.085	.596
1930	.399	.606	.094	.596
1940	.244	.481	--	.507
1950	.202	.474	--	--
1960	.284	.482	.018	.573
Logrono				
1887	.441	.684	.022	.633
1900	.431	.700	.021	.604
1910	.413	.658	.025	.613
1920	.347	.647	.025	.518
1930	.324	.600	.021	.523
1940	.212	.486	.006	.429
1950	.203	.469	--	--
1960	.206	.372	.003	.551
Malaga				
1887	.405	.619	.039	.631
1900	.398	.603	.058	.624
1910	.377	.585	.058	.605
1920	.366	.602	.056	.568
1930	.327	.576	.048	.528
1940	.255	.544	.035	.432
1950	.222	.476	--	--
1960	.232	.434	.014	.518

Murcia					Navarra					Orense				
1887	.406	.620	.046	.627	1887	.384	.669	.014	.565	1887	.344	.667	.041	.484
1900	.425	.636	.056	.636	1900	.353	.667	.013	.520	1900	.324	.666	.037	.456
1910	.449	.571	.268	.597	1910	.349	.685	.014	.499	1910	.330	.660	.035	.472
1920	.324	.565	.048	.534	1920	.334	.700	.016	.465	1920	.258	.592	.030	.406
1930	.264	.498	--	--	1930	.297	.654	.011	.445	1930	.266	.584	.032	.424
1940	.226	.446	.024	.479	1940	.208	.592	.011	.339	1940	.213	.525	.017	.386
1950	.239	.475	--	--	1950	.205	.487	--	--	1950	.194	.415	--	--
1960	.261	.411	.012	.625	1960	.227	.472	.004	.476	1960	.168	.309	.009	.529
Oviedo					Palencia					Palmas(Las)				
1887	.351	.794	.024	.425	1887	.497	.776	.030	.626	1887	--	--	--	--
1900	.367	.782	.025	.452	1900	.456	.765	.028	.581	1900	--	--	--	--
1910	.363	.804	.018	.439	1910	.429	.778	.023	.538	1910	--	--	--	--
1920	.349	.780	.013	.439	1920	.424	.765	.036	.532	1920	--	--	--	--
1930	.296	.692	.023	.408	1930	.385	.717	.027	.519	1930	.325	.651	.020	.483
1940	.151	.443	.009	.327	1940	.269	.648	.016	.400	1940	.336	.733	.023	.441
1950	.172	.402	--	--	1950	.262	.556	--	--	1950	.302	.630	--	--
1960	.203	.336	.007	.598	1960	.246	.456	.006	.533	1960	.313	.575	.010	.536
Pontevedra					Salamanca					Sta. Cruz De Tenerife				
1887	.281	.619	.046	.410	1887	.446	.684	.054	.622	1887	--	--	--	--
1900	.322	.716	.053	.406	1900	.427	.692	.047	.589	1900	--	--	--	--
1910	.313	.637	.051	.447	1910	.396	.662	.039	.573	1910	--	--	--	--
1920	.265	.597	.053	.390	1920	.369	.666	.046	.521	1920	--	--	--	--
1930	.275	.543	.090	.408	1930	.350	.656	.042	.502	1930	.284	.616	.042	.422
1940	.214	.509	.044	.366	1940	.275	.624	.015	.427	1940	.308	.611	.065	.445
1950	.205	.451	--	--	1950	.243	.443	--	--	1950	.225	.450	--	--
1960	.229	.414	.036	.511	1960	.242	.474	.011	.499	1960	.248	.441	.017	.545
Santander					Segovia					Sevilla				
1887	.375	.749	.028	.481	1887	.476	.682	.036	.681	1887	.390	.615	.074	.584
1900	.399	.838	.030	.457	1900	.475	.720	.032	.644	1900	.390	.644	.069	.558
1910	.392	.806	.032	.465	1910	.443	.690	.030	.626	1910	.364	.626	.060	.537
1920	.314	.747	--	.420	1920	.402	.664	.028	.588	1920	.323	.583	.057	.506
1930	.302	.686	.022	.422	1930	.403	.669	.026	.586	1930	.318	.581	.056	.499
1940	.177	.497	.010	.343	1940	.292	.612	.008	.470	1940	.246	.591	.013	.403
1950	.209	.447	--	--	1950	.250	.483	--	--	1950	.221	.504	--	--
1960	.231	.416	.010	.545	1960	.230	.419	.006	.543	1960	.251	.492	.008	.502
Soria					Tarragona					Teruel				
1887	.444	.666	.032	.650	1887	.372	.583	.011	.631	1887	.449	.671	.016	.661
1900	.442	.702	.030	.613	1900	.299	.489	.008	.605	1900	.441	.655	.016	.665
1910	.417	.678	.019	.604	1910	.362	.577	.011	.620	1910	.384	.570	.010	.668
1920	.369	.648	.021	.555	1920	.219	.382	.010	.562	1920	.362	.574	.015	.621
1930	.358	.647	.015	.543	1930	.190	.323	.007	.579	1930	.338	.531	.012	.628
1940	.260	.594	.008	.430	1940	.142	.294	.007	.470	1940	.215	.434	.045	.437
1950	.221	.445	--	--	1950	.158	.299	--	--	1950	.202	.370	--	--
1960	.202	.391	.004	.511	1960	.197	.299	.006	.651	1960	.198	.309	.003	.637
Toledo					Valencia					Valladolid				
1887	.477	.697	.052	.659	1887	.392	.648	.021	.592	1887	.473	.725	.067	.617
1900	.424	.668	.039	.612	1900	.376	.632	.018	.583	1900	.430	.729	.053	.558
1910	.420	.678	.038	.597	1910	.313	.549	.019	.555	1910	.410	.732	.045	.531
1920	.379	.624	.052	.572	1920	.264	.507	.015	.506	1920	.364	.693	.048	.490
1930	.351	.581	.049	.568	1930	.231	.434	.013	.518	1930	.343	.662	.039	.488
1940	.242	.524	.020	.440	1940	.164	.365	.011	.432	1940	.250	.579	.018	.414
1950	.231	.438	--	--	1950	.167	.345	--	--	1950	.243	.498	--	--
1960	.229	.390	.013	.575	1960	.209	.367	.007	.561	1960	.248	.468	.007	.523

SPAIN-Provinces (continued)

	I_f	I_g	I_h	I_m		I_f	I_g	I_h	I_m		I_f	I_g	I_h	I_m
Vizcaya					Zamora					Zaragoza				
1887	.342	.670	.040	.479	1887	.420	.666	.042	.606	1887	.408	.647	.034	.610
1900	.387	.692	.043	.530	1900	.385	.673	.034	.549	1900	.384	.644	.029	.577
1910	.340	.682	.033	.473	1910	.369	.639	.034	.554	1910	.354	.612	.024	.561
1920	.307	.634	.026	.462	1920	.333	.627	.039	.500	1920	.327	.604	.026	.521
1930	.248	.529	.014	.454	1930	.344	.627	.041	.517	1930	.284	.524	.023	.521
1940	.147	.388	.011	.361	1940	.283	.611	.020	.445	1940	.182	.435	.015	.398
1950	.166	.381	--	--	1950	.245	.501	--	--	1950	.171	.357	--	--
1960	.241	.409	.006	.583	1960	.221	.401	.007	.544	1960	.208	.369	.006	.556

SWEDEN

	I_f	I_g	I_h	I_m		I_f	I_g	I_h	I_m		I_f	I_g	I_h	I_m
Sweden					Stockholms Lan					Uppsala Lan				
1880	.319	.700	.054	.409	1880	.331	.630	.065	.472	1880	.309	.610	.063	.450
1900	.302	.652	.058	.411	1900	.320	.563	.076	.501	1900	.284	.552	.063	.453
1930	.152	.303	.043	.422	1930	.137	.241	.043	.477	1930	.153	.276	.051	.452
1950	.187	.269	.048	.629	1950	.191	.258	.056	.667	1950	.194	.275	.052	.639
1960	.172	.241	.052	.626	1960	.189	.259	.056	.654	1960	.187	.262	.057	.632
Sodermanlands Lan					Ostergotlands Lan					Jonkopings Lan				
1880	.327	.616	.063	.478	1880	.302	.650	.050	.419	1880	.315	.721	.032	.410
1900	.316	.566	.064	.500	1900	.284	.598	.057	.420	1900	.300	.698	.032	.402
1930	.147	.259	.042	.487	1930	.152	.288	.047	.439	1930	.152	.346	.024	.398
1950	.194	.261	.051	.681	1950	.191	.265	.052	.652	1950	.190	.293	.027	.613
1960	.178	.241	.056	.660	1960	.171	.236	.052	.646	1960	.171	.257	.026	.627
Kronobergs Lan					Kalmar Lan					Gotlands Lan				
1880	.337	.775	.038	.405	1880	.322	.691	.044	.429	1880	.243	.496	.043	.441
1900	.323	.771	.033	.393	1900	.303	.667	.040	.420	1900	.241	.474	.057	.440
1930	.176	.389	.030	.408	1930	.170	.342	.036	.439	1930	.191	.350	.057	.459
1950	.197	.299	.031	.619	1950	.193	.279	.039	.644	1950	.225	.315	.070	.631
1960	.165	.247	.026	.629	1960	.172	.248	.039	.637	1960	.203	.288	.064	.619
Blekinge Lan					Kristianstads Lan					Malmohus Lan				
1880	.357	.771	.077	.403	1880	.306	.717	.049	.385	1880	.321	.706	.054	.410
1900	.350	.761	.063	.412	1900	.293	.675	.054	.385	1900	.289	.610	.061	.414
1930	.185	.376	.048	.418	1930	.188	.365	.052	.434	1930	.142	.274	.046	.420
1950	.194	.274	.049	.643	1950	.194	.285	.043	.624	1950	.175	.251	.048	.627
1960	.169	.244	.043	.623	1960	.169	.244	.042	.629	1960	.165	.232	.050	.629
Hallands Lan					Goteborgs Lan					Alvsborgs Lan				
1880	.304	.734	.038	.382	1880	.289	.714	.049	.362	1880	.282	.725	.034	.360
1900	.303	.722	.038	.387	1900	.297	.696	.050	.382	1900	.278	.715	.029	.363
1930	.163	.371	.027	.395	1930	.135	.279	.032	.416	1930	.150	.345	.027	.388
1950	.192	.298	.029	.605	1950	.173	.257	.037	.621	1950	.181	.278	.032	.606
1960	.173	.260	.027	.625	1960	.173	.247	.046	.632	1960	.167	.249	.033	.620
Skaraborgs Lan					Varmlands Lan					Orebro Lan				
1880	.302	.748	.032	.377	1880	.290	.718	.049	.360	1880	.310	.698	.056	.395
1900	.270	.674	.034	.368	1900	.282	.677	.050	.369	1900	.300	.638	.061	.415
1930	.165	.361	.032	.404	1930	.158	.308	.046	.427	1930	.122	.235	.039	.423
1950	.197	.295	.039	.617	1950	.181	.257	.055	.623	1950	.180	.245	.052	.663
1960	.180	.262	.041	.629	1960	.169	.232	.057	.638	1960	.165	.225	.054	.646

Vastmanlan Lan					Kopparbergs Lan					Gavleborgs Lan				
1880	.336	.628	.073	.475	1880	.336	.661	.051	.467	1880	.357	.633	.091	.491
1900	.319	.571	.083	.484	1900	.332	.648	.063	.459	1900	.336	.621	.090	.464
1930	.152	.260	.054	.478	1930	.144	.272	.044	.442	1930	.163	.276	.076	.435
1950	.199	.253	.071	.705	1950	.191	.262	.063	.644	1950	.192	.252	.085	.644
1960	.185	.240	.068	.682	1960	.182	.243	.068	.648	1960	.175	.224	.091	.633
Vasternorr Lan					Jamtlands Lan					Vasterbottens Lan				
1880	.393	.744	.074	.476	1880	.371	.686	.089	.473	1880	.369	.795	.047	.430
1900	.361	.730	.067	.444	1900	.336	.657	.086	.439	1900	.393	.825	.039	.450
1930	.183	.325	.073	.439	1930	.185	.347	.077	.402	1930	.230	.461	.041	.451
1950	.191	.260	.074	.632	1950	.211	.290	.096	.594	1950	.212	.315	.045	.617
1960	.164	.220	.072	.622	1960	.172	.238	.085	.568	1960	.176	.252	.053	.616
Norrbottens Lan					Stockholm									
1880	.395	.826	.045	.448	1880	.253	.593	.114	.290					
1900	.454	.855	.061	.495	1900	.206	.467	.092	.304					
1930	.261	.526	.050	.444	1930	.079	.165	.031	.361					
1950	.243	.355	.054	.628	1950	.158	.241	.042	.584					
1960	.204	.287	.064	.629	1960	.150	.233	.046	.558					

SWITZERLAND

Switzerland					Zurich					Bern				
1860	.300	.724	.032	.388	1860	.278	.618	.025	.427	1860	.337	.766	.043	.407
1870	.305	.692	.028	.418	1870	.276	.596	.024	.441	1870	.353	.747	.038	.445
1880	.317	.677	.027	.446	1880	.277	.572	.027	.459	1880	.371	.746	.038	.470
1888	.295	.649	.024	.433	1888	.248	.528	.025	.443	1888	.360	.739	.034	.462
1900	.288	.618	.023	.445	1900	.253	.512	.032	.461	1900	.344	.693	.027	.475
1910	.249	.513	.021	.463	1910	.201	.396	.029	.468	1910	.289	.574	.022	.484
1920	.188	.429	.013	.420	1920	.139	.314	.016	.414	1920	.215	.467	.015	.443
1930	.160	.352	.012	.437	1930	.124	.261	.013	.449	1930	.170	.355	.012	.460
1941	.176	.351	.012	.483	1941	.147	.281	.014	.499	1941	.181	.355	.012	.493
1950	.195	.358	.015	.525	1950	.165	.305	.017	.515	1950	.208	.366	.015	.551
1960	.207	.350	.019	.570	1960	.184	.309	.021	.567	1960	.211	.344	.018	.593
Lucerne					Uri					Schwyz				
1860	.236	.873	.040	.235	1860	.277	.972	.008	.279	1860	.318	.871	.024	.347
1870	.280	.809	.040	.312	1870	.370	.990	.011	.366	1870	.353	.814	.020	.420
1880	.311	.704	.026	.420	1880	.348	.760	.022	.442	1880	.335	.723	.016	.451
1888	.272	.660	.021	.393	1888	.345	.906	.013	.371	1888	.298	.697	.012	.417
1900	.309	.705	.019	.422	1900	.392	.898	.011	.430	1900	.309	.697	.010	.434
1910	.286	.613	.018	.451	1910	.357	.767	.011	.457	1910	.284	.615	.010	.453
1920	.229	.564	.013	.392	1920	.302	.691	.010	.429	1920	.240	.585	.009	.401
1930	.219	.520	.013	.407	1930	.260	.609	.008	.419	1930	.231	.530	.010	.424
1941	.222	.480	.012	.449	1941	.259	.574	.008	.442	1941	.233	.492	.010	.462
1950	.241	.484	.015	.483	1950	.295	.545	.012	.533	1950	.260	.499	.012	.508
1960	.267	.474	.019	.545	1960	.306	.505	.015	.593	1960	.289	.496	.017	.569

SWITZERLAND (continued)

	I_f	I_g	I_h	I_m		I_f	I_g	I_h	I_m		I_f	I_g	I_h	I_m
Obwalden					Nidwalden					Glarus				
1860	.243	.899	.015	.258	1860	.255	.869	.017	.279	1860	.369	.713	.014	.508
1870	.294	.874	.016	.324	1870	.310	.831	.016	.361	1870	.308	.550	.009	.552
1880	.315	.770	.012	.399	1880	.340	.769	.014	.432	1880	.258	.488	.009	.520
1888	.290	.755	.013	.373	1888	.318	.744	.012	.417	1888	.230	.460	.009	.488
1900	.312	.778	.009	.394	1900	.339	.773	.006	.434	1900	.224	.454	.009	.483
1910	.329	.724	.010	.447	1910	.332	.704	.007	.467	1910	.205	.412	.012	.483
1920	.282	.722	.009	.383	1920	.294	.721	.008	.400	1920	.181	.397	.011	.441
1930	.243	.607	.009	.391	1930	.266	.645	.008	.405	1930	.162	.334	.009	.471
1941	.261	.626	.009	.409	1941	.274	.578	.011	.464	1941	.182	.340	.009	.523
1950	.291	.582	.013	.488	1950	.304	.533	.015	.558	1950	.204	.360	.021	.540
1960	.293	.530	.015	.540	1960	.295	.494	.016	.583	1960	.211	.348	.018	.585
Zug					Fribourg					Solothurn				
1860	.251	.804	.012	.301	1860	.296	.841	.036	.323	1860	.314	.805	.047	.352
1870	.266	.710	.014	.361	1870	.320	.816	.032	.368	1870	.347	.786	.040	.412
1880	.292	.669	.011	.427	1880	.368	.854	.038	.404	1880	.359	.763	.030	.449
1888	.244	.605	.010	.392	1888	.366	.842	.035	.410	1888	.341	.762	.023	.431
1900	.273	.658	.010	.405	1900	.389	.861	.032	.430	1900	.346	.712	.019	.471
1910	.248	.568	.013	.424	1910	.362	.774	.024	.451	1910	.314	.610	.019	.499
1920	.189	.514	.008	.358	1920	.299	.709	.018	.407	1920	.233	.507	.012	.447
1930	.181	.453	.008	.388	1930	.259	.612	.016	.408	1930	.188	.386	.009	.475
1941	.200	.444	.009	.438	1941	.239	.525	.016	.438	1941	.192	.368	.011	.508
1950	.216	.459	.009	.459	1950	.245	.464	.020	.506	1950	.220	.389	.015	.549
1960	.229	.448	.012	.498	1960	.248	.436	.021	.547	1960	.226	.362	.020	.603
Basel-Stat					Basel-Land					Schaffhausen				
1860	.210	.700	.018	.282	1860	.364	.839	.035	.409	1860	.326	.758	.038	.400
1870	.244	.667	.037	.328	1870	.348	.806	.030	.409	1870	.338	.729	.030	.440
1880	.258	.594	.044	.388	1880	.352	.779	.020	.437	1880	.345	.695	.029	.474
1888	.236	.579	.036	.369	1888	.338	.760	.018	.431	1888	.306	.640	.025	.456
1900	.237	.510	.037	.423	1900	.313	.680	.020	.444	1900	.282	.588	.021	.461
1910	.178	.360	.028	.453	1910	.275	.563	.021	.468	1910	.255	.487	.026	.496
1920	.107	.255	.014	.388	1920	.195	.444	.013	.422	1920	.197	.410	.019	.456
1930	.096	.206	.016	.422	1930	.156	.324	.012	.461	1930	.156	.306	.013	.488
1941	.121	.221	.015	.515	1941	.164	.321	.009	.497	1941	.187	.335	.015	.538
1950	.138	.240	.020	.534	1950	.196	.348	.012	.548	1950	.203	.335	.018	.586
1960	.156	.263	.026	.550	1960	.224	.337	.019	.645	1960	.208	.326	.020	.614
Appenzell A.					Appenzell I.					St. Gall				
1860	.323	.622	.023	.500	1860	.379	.784	.021	.469	1860	.299	.715	.023	.400
1870	.332	.633	.025	.505	1870	.400	.773	.015	.508	1870	.300	.666	.018	.434
1880	.363	.664	.026	.528	1880	.376	.710	.016	.518	1880	.311	.665	.019	.453
1888	.335	.615	.021	.529	1888	.362	.683	.014	.521	1888	.284	.621	.018	.441
1900	.279	.569	.016	.476	1900	.355	.761	.014	.457	1900	.265	.618	.017	.413
1910	.247	.495	.017	.482	1910	.304	.700	.013	.423	1910	.248	.538	.018	.441
1920	.178	.397	.011	.433	1920	.248	.682	.009	.356	1920	.189	.461	.011	.395
1930	.150	.329	.010	.438	1930	.233	.627	.007	.364	1930	.171	.418	.010	.393
1941	.188	.370	.011	.492	1941	.234	.578	.011	.393	1941	.200	.448	.010	.434
1950	.204	.381	.011	.521	1950	.226	.560	.008	.396	1950	.225	.444	.013	.492
1960	.208	.373	.020	.532	1960	.276	.544	.013	.495	1960	.241	.437	.020	.531

Grisons					Aargau					Thurgau				
1860	--	--	--	.374	1860	.292	.802	.035	.335	1860	.314	.741	.025	.403
1870	.274	.695	.017	.379	1870	.302	.754	.027	.379	1870	.324	.723	.021	.432
1880	.274	.670	.018	.393	1880	.313	.717	.019	.421	1880	.320	.665	.022	.464
1888	.263	.653	.017	.386	1888	.286	.691	.015	.401	1888	.279	.596	.021	.450
1900	.254	.637	.013	.387	1900	.309	.695	.014	.434	1900	.270	.567	.019	.458
1910	.252	.598	.013	.409	1910	.283	.593	.014	.465	1910	.245	.487	.021	.481
1920	.219	.542	.012	.391	1920	.225	.520	.010	.422	1920	.186	.412	.012	.436
1930	.178	.474	.010	.363	1930	.193	.409	.010	.458	1930	.170	.377	.010	.435
1941	.207	.484	.011	.414	1941	.199	.392	.010	.495	1941	.191	.393	.011	.471
1950	.223	.458	.014	.471	1950	.231	.413	.013	.544	1950	.219	.407	.014	.523
1960	.238	.438	.021	.519	1960	.247	.394	.019	.607	1960	.242	.400	.020	.583
Ticino					Vaud					Valais				
1860	--	--	--	.386	1860	.303	.621	.033	.459	1860	.329	.816	.019	.388
1870	.261	.675	.006	.381	1870	.301	.607	.032	.467	1870	.324	.770	.020	.406
1880	.295	.695	.016	.412	1880	.315	.628	.031	.477	1880	.335	.806	.021	.400
1888	.285	.695	.012	.399	1888	.293	.605	.029	.459	1888	.335	.800	.022	.402
1900	.290	.682	.014	.412	1900	.274	.561	.026	.463	1900	.345	.789	.021	.422
1910	.270	.576	.015	.453	1910	.217	.436	.022	.470	1910	.343	.723	.021	.459
1920	.185	.452	.012	.392	1920	.162	.352	.014	.437	1920	.316	.697	.016	.440
1930	.147	.379	.009	.373	1930	.132	.278	.012	.448	1930	.285	.610	.013	.455
1941	.148	.346	.008	.413	1941	.146	.273	.013	.512	1941	.256	.541	.011	.462
1950	.148	.306	.008	.471	1950	.155	.266	.016	.554	1950	.265	.495	.011	.524
1960	.170	.317	.012	.518	1960	.163	.269	.020	.574	1960	.265	.454	.013	.570
Neuchatel					Geneva									
1860	.329	.730	.028	.428	1860	.203	.458	.031	.403					
1870	.316	.695	.023	.435	1870	.196	.420	.039	.413					
1880	.316	.713	.023	.424	1880	.207	.421	.040	.439					
1888	.297	.659	.024	.430	1888	.177	.377	.032	.419					
1900	.249	.554	.017	.432	1900	.164	.343	.027	.435					
1910	.193	.416	.013	.446	1910	.130	.256	.027	.449					
1920	.137	.315	.008	.420	1920	.091	.194	.014	.426					
1930	.107	.232	.006	.446	1930	.082	.171	.011	.445					
1941	.131	.255	.008	.497	1941	.110	.201	.012	.520					
1950	.154	.269	.012	.551	1950	.115	.211	.012	.518					
1960	.166	.271	.017	.589	1960	.145	.256	.015	.539					

YUGOSLAVIA

Yugoslavia-Serbia Only					Belgrade					Valjevo				
1900	.530	.649	.031	.808	1900	.595	.698	.050	.840	1900	.553	.675	.044	.807
Vranja					Kragujevac					Krajina				
1900	.570	.710	.014	.799	1900	.524	.643	.024	.808	1900	.473	.570	.033	.818
Krusevac					Morava					Nis				
1900	.583	.704	.020	.823	1900	.543	.647	.019	.834	1900	.521	.650	.011	.799

YUGOSLAVIA (continued)

Pirot 1900	.601 .756 .006 .793	Podrinje 1900	.568 .705 .034 .795	Pozarevac 1900	.471 .565 .050 .818
Rudnik 1900	.561 .678 .039 .817	Smederevo 1900	.511 .623 .053 .803	Timok 1900	.415 .495 .015 .834
Toplica 1900	.663 .781 .033 .842	Uzice 1900	.560 .680 .032 .814	La Ville De Belgrade 1900	.241 .362 .043 .621
Yugoslavia 1931	.367 .509 .061 .682	Dravska 1931	.281 .572 .058 .433	Drinska 1931	.425 .558 .037 .745
Dunavska 1931	.299 .369 .110 .729	Moravska 1931	.383 .468 .068 .788	Primorska 1931	.379 .611 .052 .585
Savska 1931	.312 .436 .082 .652	Vardarska 1931	.509 .663 .023 .759	Vrbaska 1931	.458 .580 .064 .763
Zetska 1931	.453 .689 .019 .648	Beograd 1931	.167 .269 .045 .545		
Yugoslavia 1960	.241 .322 .066 .684	Bosna I Hercegovina 1960	.340 .486 .061 .657	Crna Gora 1960	.300 .482 .014 .611
Hrvatska 1960	.194 .269 .043 .669	Makedonia 1960	.346 .454 .064 .723	Slovania 1960	.189 .295 .041 .583
Uze-Podrucje In Serbia 1960	.177 .218 .071 .721	Aut.Pokrajina Vojvodin 1960	.176 .212 .090 .707	Kosovsko In Serbia 1960	.500 .575 .268 .755
Serbia Total 1960	.211 .256 .095 .722				

Appendix B: Definition, Advantages, and Limitations of the Fertility Indexes Employed in the European Fertility Project

The fertility indexes used in the European Fertility Project were designed with two major considerations in mind. First, it was essential to make explicit allowance for the effect of nuptiality on the overall fertility of the populations because in most of Europe during the period considered, childbearing was largely, although not wholly, restricted to married couples, and there were big differences among European populations in the proportion of women subject to the risk of childbearing because they were currently married. Second, the frequent absence of detailed information about recorded births (such as age or duration of marriage of the mother, or order of birth) made it necessary to employ measures that can be calculated from the simplest information: the overall number of births, the number occurring to married women, the number occurring to others, and the number of women and the number of married women in each five-year age interval from 15 to 50.

Conventional measures of overall fertility, marital fertility, and proportion married are readily calculated from such data. The general fertility rate (the number of births divided by the number of women 15 to 49), the general marital fertility rate (the number of births divided by the number of women 15 to 49), and the general nonmarried fertility rate (births to nonmarried women divided by the number of nonmarried women 15 to 49) are obvious possibilities. There would have been little difference in the findings of our research if these conventional measures had been used. The European fertility indexes differ from the conventional measures by the incorporation in their definition of a maximum age-specific fertility schedule. The maximum schedule provides a natural upper limit or standard with which the childbearing of a population or population segment is compared. The fertility schedule considered as a maximum is the fertility schedule of married Hutterites during the period from 1921 to 1930. The Hutterites are a Protestant religious sect (Anabaptist) founded in the sixteenth century. To avoid religious persecution, they moved from Western Europe to Russia in the eighteenth century and then migrated to the north-central United States and south-central Canada in the nineteenth century. Hutterite fertility is high because the sect adheres scrupulously to precepts forbidding the practice of contraception or abortion, and mothers do not nurse their infants more than a few months. Their fertility rates have been accurately recorded since the latter part of the last century; the schedule for the decade 1921 to 1930 is representative of the highest rates of Hutterite childbearing.

This maximal fertility schedule includes the following rates by five-year age intervals from ages 20–24 to 45–49: 0.550, 0.502, 0.447, 0.406, 0.222, and 0.061. Women marrying at age 20 and remaining married until age 50 would produce an average of 10.94 children if subject to these rates. In formulating the indexes, an arbitrary fertility rate of 0.300 is assigned to ages 15–19.[1]

The European fertility indexes, then, are measures of the rate of childbearing in a given population (or a defined segment of a given population) relative to the maximum fertility the population in question might achieve. Maximum is defined as the births that would occur if women at each age experienced the rate of childbearing at that age in the most prolific population reliably recorded. I_f is a measure of the fertility of all women in the population; it is the ratio of the actual number of births to the hypothetical number if women were subject to the Hutterite fertility schedule. I_g is the ratio of the number of births occurring to married women to the number that would occur if married women were subject to maximum fertility; and I_h is the ratio of the number of births occurring to nonmarried women to the number that nonmarried women would have if subject to the maximum fertility schedule. I_m is a measure of the contribution of marital status to the overall rate of childbearing; strictly speaking, it is a measure for a hypothetical population in which only married women are fertile, and in which married women are subject to maximum fertility rates at each age. I_m is the ratio of the number of births produced by married women in such a population to the number that would be produced if all women were married. It measures the extent to which

[1] Most populations with recorded marital fertility for women ages 15–19 show rates much higher than 0.300. However, most recorded marital fertility occurs in late-marrying populations, and married women less than 20 years old are usually 18 or 19. Many of the married teenagers in these populations are already pregnant when married so that marital fertility rates are artificially high. In populations in which marriage is very early, the lower capacity of adolescents to reproduce would lead to lower marital fertility at 15–19 than at 20–24, but there are few data from such populations. The choice of 0.300 was probably an excessive allowance for the lower fertility of teenagers. Since in most European populations few women less than 20 years old are married, the use of a low rate at 15–19 in constructing the indexes does not have important consequences.

marital status would limit childbearing if marital fertility were "natural"[2] and nonmarital fertility were zero.

Mathematical Formulation of the Indexes

The four indexes are expressed in mathematical form in equations (1) to (4):

$$I_f = B \Big/ \int_\alpha^\beta h(a)w(a)da, \tag{1}$$

$$I_g = B_m \Big/ \int_\alpha^\beta h(a)m(a)da, \tag{2}$$

$$I_h = B_u \Big/ \int_\alpha^\beta h(a)u(a)da, \tag{3}$$

$$I_m = \int_\alpha^\beta h(a)m(a)da \Big/ \int_\alpha^\beta h(a)w(a)da, \tag{4}$$

in which B is the total number of births, B_m the number of births to married women, and B_u the number of births to nonmarried women (single, widowed, or divorced); $w(a)$ is the number of women, $m(a)$ the number of married women, and $u(a)$ is the number of nonmarried women at age a; and $h(a)$ is the rate of childbearing of married Hutterites at age a.

It follows from these definitions that

$$I_f = I_m \cdot I_g + (1 - I_m) \cdot I_h.$$

The product $I_m \cdot I_g$ is the fraction of the maximum attainable fertility contributed by married women, and $(1 - I_m) \cdot I_h$ is the fraction contributed by nonmarried women. The sum of these two contributions is I_f—the fraction of the maximum attainable fertility that the population achieves. When the contribution of the nonmarried is negligible, as it has been in most provinces in Europe during the period covered by our study,

[2] Natural fertility (Henry, 1961) is defined as the fertility of married women in a population in which practices that might limit fertility are not followed in different degrees according to the number of children already born. Birth intervals may be lengthened by practices such as prolonged breast-feeding or postpartum abstinence, but if these practices are followed after every birth, rather than initiated after a certain number of births have already occurred in order to limit further fertility, fertility is considered natural rather than controlled. Henry shows that the age pattern of natural fertility in different populations (among them the Hutterites) is rather uniform, although the level differs extensively from one population to another.

the index of overall fertility is conveniently factored into two multiplicative components: the index of proportion married and the index of marital fertility. Each index has the intuitively appealing property of ranging between zero and one. The indexes I_f, I_g, and I_h would be zero if the population (or the segment in question) experienced no childbearing and would be 1.0 if the rate of childbearing were the highest ever reliably recorded. I_m would be zero if no one in the childbearing age were married, and it would be 1.0 if all were married.

Dependence of Indexes on Age Distribution

Coale (1969) asserted somewhat misleadingly that the fertility indexes (I_f, I_g, and I_h) embody a form of indirect standardization for age. For example, I_g can be defined as

$$\frac{\int_\alpha^\beta m(a)r(a)da}{\int_\alpha^\beta m(a)h(a)da},$$

where $r(a)$ is marital fertility at age a; and since the same age distribution occurs in the numerator and denominator, some sort of age standardization seems to take place. However, incorporation of $h(a)$ in the definition is really fertility-schedule standardization, not age standardization, because when I_g is calculated for different populations, no standard age distribution is involved—only a standard fertility schedule. The proper interpretation of the indexes is what has been presented above: that they express the fertility of a population (or of a segment) relative to the maximum that might be attained.

In fact, different populations subject to the same fertility schedule may have different values of a fertility index if the age distributions are different: the fertility indexes are not independent of the age distributions of the populations under observation.

The indexes are, in particular, affected by the interaction between the age structure of the population between the limits of 15 to 50 and the age schedule of proportions married or of fertility (in the calculation of I_m or of I_f, respectively). The dependence of the indexes on age composition is readily seen when each index is reexpressed as a weighted average. The conventional aggregate measures (the general fertility rate, the general marital fertility rate, and the overall proportion married from 15 to 50) can also be viewed as weighted averages.

In equations (5) through (7), weighted average expressions for I_f, I_g, and I_m are compared with weighted average expressions for the general fertility rate, the general marital fertility rate, and the overall proportion married among women of childbearing age.

$$I_f = \int_\alpha^\beta R'(a)(f(a)/h(a))da;\ \text{GFR} = \int_\alpha^\beta R(a)f(a)da \tag{5}$$

$$I_g = \int_\alpha^\beta S'(a)(r(a)/h(a))da;\ \text{GMFR} = \int_\alpha^\beta S(a)r(a)da \tag{6}$$

$$I_m = \int_\alpha^\beta S'(a)(m(a)/w(a))da;\ \text{PM} = \int_\alpha^\beta S(a)(m(a)/w(a))da, \tag{7}$$

where $f(a)$ is fertility, $r(a)$ is marital fertility, $h(a)$ is Hutterite marital fertility, $w(a)$ is the number of women, and $m(a)$ is the number of married women at age a. The weighting function $R(a)$ is $w(a)/\int_\alpha^\beta w(a)da$; $R'(a)$ is $w(a)h(a)/\int_\alpha^\beta w(a)h(a)da$; $S(a)$ is $m(a)/\int_\alpha^\beta m(a)da$; and $S'(a)$ is $m(a)h(a)/\int_\alpha^\beta m(a)h(a)da$. In each instance the index differs from the corresponding conventional measure because the weights used in calculating the index combine the Hutterite marital fertility schedule as a multiplier of the age distribution of women (or married women), whereas the conventional measures use the age distribution itself as weights. The fertility indexes (I_f and I_g) are the weighted average of the rates of observed fertility to $h(a)$; the corresponding conventional measures are the weighted average of the observed fertility schedule itself.

The dependence of the measures or indexes on age composition results from the interaction between the weights (which always include the number of women or the number of married women at each age) and the function—the fertility schedule, the ratio of the fertility schedule to the Hutterite schedule, or the proportion married—that is weighted. Because of this interaction, different populations with the same proportions married at every age (but different distributions) do not necessarily have the same overall proportion married or the same I_m; different populations with the same age-specific fertility schedule do not necessarily have the same general fertility rate or the same I_f; and different populations with the same marital fertility schedules do not necessarily have the same general marital fertility rate or the same I_g.

Variation in $\mathrm{I_m}$ *with Age Distribution*

From Equation (7), it is evident that I_m and the proportion married at ages 15 to 50 are weighted averages of the proportion married in each age interval. When the weighting function declines steeply with age from

15 to 50, more weight is given to the proportion married at young ages than if the weighting function does not fall steeply. When age at marriage is late, the proportion married at ages under 25 is low; thus a weighting function that assigns a large weight to young ages yields a lower number (for proportion married or I_m) than a weighting function that assigns moderate weight to young ages. A steeply declining age distribution from age 15 to age 50 occurs in populations in which fertility was high 15 to 50 years earlier; when fertility has been low for a long time, the age distribution is relatively flat. With late marriage (Ireland, 1900) the overall proportion married at ages 15 to 50 would be 20 percent lower with a steep age distribution (that of Russia in 1897) than with a flat age distribution (that of Norway in 1960).

In the calculation of I_m, the weights are modified by the incorporation of the Hutterite fertility schedule, which has its highest values from 20 to 34, and falls rapidly to its lowest level at 45 to 49. When combined with an age distribution, it yields lower weights at ages 15 to 19 and above 40 than the age distribution alone. The net effect on I_m is this: given the proportions married of Ireland in 1900 as in the above example, I_m would be 16 percent lower with a steep age distribution than with a flat one. Differences in age distribution affect I_m, but the effect is less than the effect on the overall proportion married.

When marriage is very early (as in Toplica Province in Serbia in 1900), differences in age distribution have a much smaller effect. With proportions married at each age as in Toplica, the overall proportion married at ages 15 to 50 would be only 1.8 percent lower if the age distribution sloped steeply (Russia, 1897) than if it were flat (Norway, 1960). The corresponding difference in I_m is only 0.7 percent.

To summarize: both the proportion married from 15 to 50 and I_m are affected by the age distributions of women within the span of childbearing ages, as well as by the proportion married at individual ages. I_m is slightly less affected by age distribution than is the conventional measure; the influence of age distribution is least when marriage is early and most when marriage is late.

The effect of age distribution on I_m is insignificant in most comparisons of different provinces of Europe before World War I, because with few exceptions, the age distributions of women from 15 to 50 were broadly similar (tapering rather steeply) in the different provinces. This similarity was the consequence of the general prevalence of high (or moderately high) fertility during most of the nineteenth century. Recalculating I_m for

Ireland in 1900 with the Russian age distribution in place of the Irish age distribution produces a value of 0.329 rather than 0.316; the Irish age distribution was actually slightly steeper, partly because of migration. If the higher fertility of Eastern Europe had caused generally steeper age distributions than in Western Europe, the difference in age distributions would have *lessened* the east-west differences in I_m. In fact, such an influence was nonexistent or negligible, with the single prominent exception of the flat age distributions from 15 to 50 to be found in many *départements* of France due to the low fertility that had existed in France throughout much of the nineteenth century. The French *département* of Lot-et-Garonne had especially low fertility from a very early date, and the age distribution of women in 1900 from 15 to 50 was nearly uniform. I_m in Lot-et-Garonne (0.700) was the highest in Western Europe; with the age distribution of Russia it would have been 0.669. Without the special age distribution generated by its history of especially low fertility, the I_m of Lot-et-Garonne would still have been the highest (or nearly so) in Western Europe.

The decline in fertility that is the principal subject of that conference ultimately produced age distributions throughout Europe that tapered less steeply than earlier distributions. The change would have led to an increase in I_m even if proportions married at each age had remained fixed, and did cause a larger increase in I_m than would have occurred from changing proportions married alone. In Norway, for example, I_m rose from 0.419 in 1900 to 0.660 in 1960. If the age distribution had not changed, I_m would have risen only to 0.620.

Variation in I$_g$ *with Age Distribution*

When general marital fertility and I_g are expressed as weighted averages (GMFR $= \int_\alpha^\beta S(a)r(a)da$; $I_g = \int_\alpha^\beta S'(a)(r(a)/h(a))da$, where $r(a)$ is marital fertility, $h(a)$ is Hutterite marital fertility, $S(a)$ is $m(a)/\int_\alpha^\beta m(a)da$, and $S'(a)$ is $h(a)m(a)/\int_\alpha^\beta h(a)m(a)da$), the age distribution of currently married women ($m(a)$) either constitutes the weights or is a factor (with $h(a)$) in forming the weights. As in the determination of I_m (compared to the overall proportion married), the incorporation of $h(a)$ in the weights when I_g is calculated yields weights with a slightly greater slope over the central childbearing ages, and diminishes the weights at 15 to 19 and over 40. The big difference in the interaction between the age distribution of married women and marital fertility in calculating GMFR and I_g arises from dividing $r(a)$ by $h(a)$ in calculating I_g.

Before the significance of a weighted average of $r(a)/h(a)$ instead of $r(a)$ is considered, it should be noted that variations in the age distributions of married women are more extreme than variations in the overall age distribution of women. The structure of the distribution of married women at ages from 15 to 50 is dominated by variations in the proportion married with age. When marriage is early (as in Toplica Province), the proportion married is high among women at ages from 15 to 25; when marriage is late (as in Ireland), the proportion married among younger women is very low.

The GMFR is certainly affected by these differences in the age composition of married women. When marriage is early (as in Russia), more weight is given to ages 20 to 29, where marital fertility is high. When marital fertility follows the natural fertility schedule, GMFR is 0.415 with the Toplica age distribution of married women, and only 0.339 with the Irish age distribution. The different weights associated with early or late marriage affect the general marital fertility rate much more strongly when marital fertility falls steeply with age, as it does when marital fertility is highly controlled. Swedish marital fertility of 1970 yields a GMFR of 0.133 with the Toplica age distribution of married women, and only 0.065 with the Irish age distribution. The late marriage in Ireland assigns large weights to the fertility of older married women, and their fertility is very low in the Swedish marital fertility schedule.

We now return to the calculation of I_g as the weighted average of $r(a)/h(a)$ rather than just the weighted average of $r(a)$. The effect of division by $h(a)$ is virtually to eliminate the effect of the age distribution of married women on I_g when marital fertility is natural, and to make the effect less when marital fertility is controlled. Controlled marital fertility departs increasingly from natural fertility as age increases. To be more specific, marital fertility in most populations can be approximated as $r(a) = \mathrm{M}n(a)\exp(m \cdot v(a))$ (Coale, 1971; Coale and Trussell, 1974; Knodel, 1977b), where $v(a)$ is a negative function such that $(-v(a))$ increases in an approximately linear fashion from the early twenties to about age fifty. Thus $r(a)/n(a)$ follows an exponential function of the form (constant) $\cdot \exp(-m'(a - \alpha))$, where m' is a parameter that varies directly with the extent of control of marital fertility, and α is an age near 20. Since $h(a)$ is itself an exemplar of natural fertility, $r(a)/h(a)$ has approximately the same value at all ages in natural fertility populations, and approximates a declining exponential in populations in which fertility is controlled. The different weights assigned at different ages in the calculation of I_g for populations of married women with different age distributions yield about the same I_g when the marital fertility schedule is natural, but quite different values when the marital fertility schedule is controlled and $r(a)/h(a)$ declines steeply.

If the married women of Ireland in 1900 had the Hutterite fertility schedule, I_g would be 1.00; the same schedule experienced by Toplica married women would also yield an I_g of 1.00. If these two age distributions of married women experienced the Swedish marital fertility schedule of 1970, I_g would be 0.189 for the Irish women, and 0.330 for the Toplica women. The ratio of I_g's is 1.75; the ratio of the corresponding GMFRs is 2.04.)

Clearly, when fertility is highly controlled, I_g is higher with a given age schedule of marital fertility in an early marrying population than in a late marrying population; the variation in GMFR under these conditions is still greater.

Cross-sectional differences in I_g are affected by the age distribution of married women when fertility is highly controlled, as it was in western Europe in 1930, for example. Thus the difference in I_g in 1930 between Sweden (0.303) and Vladimir Oblast (0.783) was substantially larger than it would have been if Sweden had combined its marital fertility schedule with the age distribution of married women found in Vladimir. Also, the fall in I_g in Sweden to 0.241 in 1960 would have been greater had the age schedule of marital fertility of 1960 occurred with an age distribution of married women the same as in 1930.

Thus it seems that the interpretation of both cross-sectional and intertemporal differences in I_g is muddied by the effect on I_g of differences in age distribution, with a given age schedule of marital fertility.

There is a simple escape this conclusion. It is to fall back on the direct operational meaning of the index: I_g measures how closely the married population approaches the maximum fertility it might experience. With a given age schedule of marital fertility, the closeness of the approach depends on the age distribution of married women.

Summary

1. The fertility indexes I_f, I_g, I_h, and I_m are readily calculated from summary data on the total number of births (to all women and to married women) and on the population classified by age and marital status. Their meaning is simple: the indexes of fertility proper (I_f, I_g, and I_h) measure how closely a given population (or population segment) approaches a

clearly defined maximum fertility; the index of proportion married measures the extent to which the marital status distribution permits the attainment of maximum fertility if married women experienced natural fertility, and nonmarried women bore no children at all.

2. Although less affected by the age composition of the population (or population segment) than conventional measures that can be calculated from the same data, none of the indexes is independent of age composition. In interpreting cross-sectional or intertemporal differences, the effect of differences in age composition on the indexes must be borne in mind.

3. Age distribution differences can be ignored in looking at differences in I_m prior to World War I, with the exception of the *départements* of France, wherein the flatter age distribution contributed slightly to higher values of $I_m \cdot I_m$'s. Values of I_m were slightly higher in 1960 in many areas relative to the value they would have had if age distribution had not changed.

Appendix C: Sources and Adjustments of the Fertility Indexes

Many of the indexes presented in Appendix A and in the maps, tables, and figures of this paper are taken from the individual country studies that are part of the European Fertility Project. These have been previously published in books, articles, or Ph.D. dissertations on individual countries, or are being prepared for publication. Other indexes were calculated especially for this summary or for earlier presentations. As we assembled the data for the construction of the maps and figures that form a major part of this paper, occasional errors were discovered in indexes prepared by other investigators, and we have made corrections, going back to the original raw data where possible. The purpose of this appendix, then, is to outline the sources of the data, describe any corrections or adjustments made in the data, and discuss the procedures used in the calculations made especially for this paper, including determining the date of decline for Map 2.1.

Calculations and Adjustments of Data

Fertility indexes were generally calculated on the basis of registered births over a period of three to ten years, centered on the date of the census. Underregistration of births, differences in the geographical classification of births and the population in censuses (including classification of births by place of occurrence rather than by residence of the mother), and in some instances misclassification of the population by marital status, required special adjustments in many situations. Many of the special techniques and procedures have been described in detail in the original sources. Only for those indexes constructed originally for this paper will we discuss the procedures in detail.

For each province (or country) at each date by each residence (urban, rural, and total), we checked for the internal consistency of the indexes by the identity $I_f = (I_g \cdot I_m) + (I_h(1 - I_m))$. Furthermore, where possible, we tested the rural and urban indexes for consistency of each index over time; where there were unlikely changes over time, we checked the original data for possible inaccuracy. The indexes used in this paper reflect the corrections and adjustments in the country-by-country description below.

Source and Adjustment of Data by Country

In the following listing for those countries in which the fertility indexes have been published or will be published by other authors, the secondary sources are given with little or no detail on the adjustments to the data (except for the indexes computed originally for this paper). In this situation, a reference is given to a book, dissertation, monograph, or journal article in which the indexes appear. The reader can refer to these sources for further details.

For indexes presented here for the first time, the sources are indicated along with a description of any special problems and adjustments in the calculations of the indexes.

1. *Austria.* Data from 1880 to 1910 were supplied by Paul Demeny and were presented by Jacqueline Forrest in *Fertility Decline in Austria, 1880 to 1910* (1975). Data for 1931 were also supplied by Jacqueline Forrest. The 1960 indexes were computed by Erna Härm from births for three years, 1960, 1961, and 1962 from *Die Natürliche Bevölkerungsbewegung* (1962), Tables 3 and 45.

2. *Belgium.* Ronald J. Lesthaeghe prepared all the data and calculated the fertility indexes. These are discussed in full in Lesthaeghe's *Decline of Belgian Fertility 1880–1970* (1977).

3. *Denmark.* The fertility indexes from 1852 to 1930 were calculated by Poul C. Matthiessen and are described in a paper by Matthiessen (forthcoming). Alan Minkoff calculated the 1960 indexes using contemporary birth registration from *Befolkningens bevaegelser 1958–1962* and census data. Data on marital status for 1960 by province were supplied by Matthiessen for the calculation of I_g and I_h. Births were taken from the years 1958–62. Three *Amt* or provinces were split between 1930 and 1960, but indexes were calculated for the combined provinces in 1960 to provide indexes for essentially constant areas from 1852 to 1960. Roskilde was split from København, Assens from Odense, and Skanderborg from Aarhus. For statistical reasons, indexes are also presented for the combined areas of Aabenraa and Soenderborg.

4. *England and Wales.* Michael Teitelbaum supplied the indexes for all the counties of England and Wales from 1851 to 1931. Adjustments for underregistration of births (and apparent overregistration of births in London) from 1841 to 1910 were described in detail in Teitelbaum's article, "Birth Underregistration in the Constituent Counties of England and

Wales" (Teitelbaum, 1974), and in *The British Fertility Decline: The Demographic Transition in the Crucible of the Industrial Revolution* (Teitelbaum, 1984). Erna Härm calculated the 1961 indexes from 1961 census data and 1960 and 1961 births obtained from the Registrar General's Statistical Review of England and Wales. Between 1930 and 1961, boundaries of many counties were changed somewhat and a few counties, especially in Wales, were split. For some statistical calculations, 1961 indexes for the recombined counties were used; for the maps, indexes for the 1961 counties were used so that complete detail could be given.

5. *Finland.* Erna Härm calculated the indexes for Finland from 1865 to 1960 in conjunction with the study of fertility in Russia by Coale, Anderson, and Härm, *Human Fertility in Russia since the Nineteenth Century* (1979). The Finnish data were of good quality and did not require adjustment. Some changes in the boundaries of provinces after World War I and during World War II required minor adjustments.

6. *France.* Etienne van de Walle calculated all the indexes from 1831 to 1931. The procedures for adjustment of the data, especially by age and residence of mother, and the sources of data from 1831 to 1901 are discussed in detail in his *The Female Population of France in the Nineteenth Century* (E. van de Walle, 1974).

Erna Härm calculated the 1961 indexes without adjustments. Data on births were obtained from *Mouvement de la Population* for 1961 with the use of an average of the 1961 and 1962 births. Population data came from the 1961 census.

The indexes were computed for each *département* according to the boundaries as of the date for which the indexes are given. The fertility indexes are not given for most years for the urban centers—Marseilles (Bouches-du-Rhône), Paris (Seine, Paris, Seine-et-Oise), and Lyons (Rhône)—because of the unreliability of birth data and the large number of births in urban hospitals. Annexations from Italy in 1860 and loss of territory in 1871 to Germany made reconstruction of the *départements* of Moselle, Meurthe-et-Moselle, the Territory of Belfort, Alpes-Maritimes, Savoie, and Haute-Savoie difficult. Indexes for these *départements* have been included in this study despite gaps and also possible inaccuracies in the data for the nineteenth century.

7. *Germany.* Indexes for Germany from 1871 to 1939 were calculated by John Knodel and are described in *The Decline of Fertility in Germany, 1871–1939* (1974). Most of the German data for these years were taken

directly from census or vital registration, and some of the data needed major adjustments. In some years special estimates of marital status or age of women or legitimacy status of births had to be made. These adjustments are indicated in Appendix 2B, pp. 276–278, of Knodel's book (1974). Knodel also supplied the fertility indexes for West Germany for 1961; these were taken from standard birth records and the census, without adjustment.

Alan Minkoff calculated the indexes for East Germany for 1964. Birth data were averaged for 1962–1965. The census data for 1964 gave the number of females by nontraditional age categories below age 25; age by marital status had to be allocated to traditional five-year intervals proportionately before the East German indexes could be calculated.

8. *Greece.* All the indexes were prepared by George S. Siampos and Vasilios G. Valaoras and presented in their article "Long-Term Fertility Trends in Greece" (1960). Underenumeration of births constituted the major problem for the Greek indexes, and "reverse projection" was used to adjust the fertility data. Changes in the boundaries of Greece also created minor problems, especially in the early 1900s. Specific details are discussed on pp. 601–602 of their article.

9. *Ireland.* Teitelbaum calculated preliminary indexes for Ireland as part of his study of fertility in the British Isles. Since a number of these indexes were inconsistent, Edith Pantelides recalculated the indexes for 1871 and 1881; these are discussed in detail in a manuscript by Pantelides and Coale (1979), "Two Sets of County Boundaries, and Erroneous Figures for County Vital Rates in Nineteenth-Century Ireland," which is incorporated in Teitelbaum's book (1984). Fertility indexes for 1871 and 1881 as calculated from registered births changed very erratically over time and were very inconsistent among spatially contiguous counties. Investigation by Pantelides and Coale revealed that in 1871 and 1881 the county areas for registering births were not the same as for the counties proper by which the census was recorded. Corrected fertility indexes for each county in 1871 and 1881 were obtained by multiplying the number of registered births by the ratio: population of county proper to population of registration county.

Teitelbaum calculated indexes for 1891, 1901, and 1911 based on vital statistics and censuses without adjustment. New estimates of the fertility indexes for 1926, 1936, and 1961 were made by Pantelides, using three-year averages of births, centered on the census data. Except for the 1926

I_m indexes calculated by Pantelides and the 1961 I_m indexes computed by Erna Härm, all the I_m indexes were calculated by Teitelbaum. Because of boundary changes between the counties of Antrim and Down and the city of Belfast, the fertility and marriage indexes were presented for a combination of all three areas at each date to ensure consistency over time.

10. *Italy*. Indexes for *regions* of Italy from 1861 to 1961 were used in this study, adjusted for reporting of illegitimacy and migration of married males. Data for these indexes were all taken from Massimo Livi-Bacci's *A History of Italian Fertility during the Last Two Centuries* (1977). Indexes for the smaller *provinces* were not used since only I_g and I_m were available.

The indexes in this study were adjusted for inappropriate calculation of illegitimacy, because "a large but unknown share of the children classified as illegitimate were borne by parents married solely with a religious ceremony (which the state did not recognize). It is almost certain, however, that the great majority of the parents of these children were classified as married in 1871 as well as in later censuses" (Livi-Bacci, 1977, p. 77). Thus, I_g without correction would be too low and I_h too high.

Livi-Bacci has estimated I_g values corrected for illegitimacy for the five regions of the center most affected by the misclassification (Emilia, Marche, Umbria, Lazio, and Toscana) from 1861 to 1911. These corrected I_g indexes are given on page 80, Table 2.11, of his Italian book (1977) and were substituted for the uncorrected I_g indexes for those regions and dates. Corrected I_h indexes were then calculated from the corrected I_g indexes by the identity $I_h = (I_f - (I_g \cdot I_m))/(1 - I_m)$.

In addition, many Italian regions experienced a disproportionate out-migration of males over females during much of the time of this study, thus leaving a number of females in all regions formally married but not living with their husbands. Marital fertility would be lower than would be expected if the husbands were present, and the proportion married, measured by I_m, would be higher. Thus, Livi-Bacci estimated values of I_g adjusted for migration of males, called I_g', by multiplying I_g by a ratio (R) of married females of all ages to married males of all ages. R in effect deflates or inflates the weighted sum of married women in the denominator of I_g, $\sum_i F_i m_i$. These adjusted marital fertility indexes, I_g', are given on page 84 of Livi-Bacci's study of Italian fertility (1977).

Since $R = I_g'/I_g$, appropriately adjusted values of I_m, called I_m', were calculated by $I_m' = I_m/R$. (The previously adjusted I_g values for misreporting of illegitimacy and the corresponding adjusted values of I_h were substituted for the original values of I_g and I_h before R was calculated.) Finally, the corresponding adjusted value of unmarried fertility, I_h', was computed by the identity given above. Thus, the I_g', I_h', and I_m' indexes, all adjusted for illegitimacy and migration of married males, were used in the maps and tables in this paper along with the I_f for each region at all dates. Unadjusted values are listed in the table of indexes in Appendix A as well. These and other issues involved in the adjustments are discussed at greater length in Livi-Bacci's Italian book, especially in Appendix A (1977, pp. 284–297).

11. *Luxembourg.* Alan Minkoff calculated the indexes for 1900, 1930, and 1960 from the census and vital registration without adjustment.

12. *The Netherlands.* Etienne van de Walle calculated all indexes from standard vital registration and census sources. No adjustments of the data were needed.

13. *Norway.* Etienne van de Walle calculated indexes from Norway from 1875 to 1930. Erna Härm computed the 1960 indexes, using an average of births from 1960 and 1961. The population data for 1960 came from the census in *Folktelling, 1960.* Births by marital status of mother were taken from *Folkemengdens Bevegelse* for 1960 and 1961. No adjustments of the original data were needed for any of the indexes.

14. *Poland.* Erna Härm calculated all the indexes for Poland. The 1897 and 1931 indexes were prepared for Coale, Anderson, and Härm's study of *Human Fertility in Russia since the Nineteenth Century* (1979); sources of data are given in Appendix D therein. For the 1960 indexes, population data came from the 1960 Census and *Glowny Urzad Statystycny, Rocznik Demographiczny 1945–1966*, no. 10 (1968). Birth data were taken from *Glowny Urzad*, nos. 78 and 94, averaged for 1960 and 1961, and from *Przegled Ruchu Naturalnego Ludnosci w Polsce w Latach 1948–1969*, although the percentages of births to unmarried women were derived for 1960 only. Adjustments to any of the indexes were not necessary. Changes in boundaries of the provinces of Poland after each world war made three series of provinces necessary.

15. *Portugal.* Massimo Livi-Bacci prepared all the indexes from 1864 to 1960 for Portugal. These are given in his *A Century of Portuguese Fertility* (1971). Adjustment for the underregistration of births by the "backward projection" technique was the principal correction needed for the Por-

tuguese data, and the details are given in the Appendix to his book, pp. 133–135.

16. *Russia.* All the indexes for the provinces of Russia (either for the prerevolutionary boundaries or the 1959 boundaries) were taken from Coale, Anderson, and Härm's *Human Fertility in Russia since the Nineteenth Century* (1979) and were originally calculated by Erna Härm. Calculations for 1926 on 1926 boundaries were made by Hannah Kaufman from the worksheets of Erna Härm. Problems with underregistration of births, lack of requisite tabulations of the female population by age and marital status for some populations and certain dates, and inaccurate classification of the population by marital status in certain circumstances were among the difficulties encountered in preparing the Russian data. The adjustment procedures are discussed in detail in Appendix A to the 1979 book.

Fertility indexes were assumed to remain unchanged between 1897 and 1870 except in Moscow, St. Petersburg, and those provinces, as defined in 1897, in which the birth rate (BR), as calculated by Raschin (1956), was lower for 1896–1900 than in 1860–1870 or in 1871–75 *and* in which the birth rate in 1906–1910 was lower by ten percent than the birth rate in 1896–1900. In these provinces, I_g for 1870 was assumed to be equal to I_g for 1897 times BR in 1865–1874 divided by BR in 1896–1900; similarly I_f in 1870 was assumed to be equal to I_f in 1897 times BR in 1865–1874 divided by BR in 1896–1900. The marriage index (I_m) for 1870 was assumed to be the same as in 1897 for each province because the mean age at marriage did not change much from 1870 until the early 1900s, as indicated in Coale, Anderson, and Härm (1979, Figure 5.3). I_h for 1870 was calculated from the other indexes in 1870.

17. *Scotland.* Michael Teitelbaum prepared the 1861 to 1931 indexes without any adjustment of the raw data as given in *The British Fertility Decline: Demographic Transition in the Crucible of the Industrial Revolution* (1984). Erna Härm calculated the 1961 indexes, using population data from the 1961 census and birth data from Scotland's *General Register* for 1960 and 1961. The number of births were averaged for 1960 and 1961.

18. *Spain.* Massimo Livi-Bacci calculated all the indexes for districts from 1878 to 1950 and discussed some of the results in "Fertility Changes in Spain, 1887–1950: Summary Report" (1968a) and in "Fertility and Nuptiality Changes in Spain from the Late Eighteenth to the Early Twentieth

Century" (1968b). Registration of vital events in Spain appeared to be defective until the twentieth century, and a backward projection of the census population was used to correct for underenumeration, as reported in Livi-Bacci (1968a, pp. 1–4; and 1968b, pp. 232–233). Because of unlikely temporal and spatial relationships and internal inconsistencies of the indexes, a number of the indexes were recalculated from original sources by Edith Pantelides, and these revised indexes have been used in this study.

Erna Härm calculated the 1960 indexes, using the 1960 Population Census for Spain for the population data and *Movimiento Natural de la Poblacion de España* for 1960 and 1961 for birth data by marital status. The fertility indexes were based on an average of 1960 and 1961 births.

19. *Sweden.* Carl Mosk calculated all the indexes from 1880 to 1960 as presented in his *Rural-Urban Differentials in Swedish Fertility, 1880–1960* (1978). Although five-year averages, centered on the census years, were used for 1930, 1950, and 1960, the birth data are only for the single year of the census for 1880 and1900. Alan Minkoff supplied the indexes for the entire country of Sweden in 1880. Because of the high quality of data for Sweden in all years, the indexes did not need to be adjusted. For a discussion of the Swedish data, see pp. 5–7 of Mosk's book.

20. *Switzerland.* Francine van de Walle prepared all the indexes based on vital statistics and censuses from 1880 to 1960, without adjustment (F. van de Walle, manuscript).

21. *Albania.* Alan Minkoff calculated the indexes for Albania in 1955 from the census and vital registration, unadjusted.

22. *Bulgaria.* Alan Minkoff prepared all the indexes for Bulgaria in 1905, 1934, and 1956. In Bulgaria (and in Rumania and Czechoslovakia, as indicated below), incomplete registration of births was suspected, and a test for completeness (yielding an approximate estimate of the extent of underregistration) was applied. When underregistration was revealed, I_f, I_g, and I_h, as calculated from registered births, were corrected for underregistration. The test was a comparison of the birth rate derived from registered births with that estimated by a form of reverse projection of the population under age 5 in the census. The reverse projection was accomplished by choosing a model stable population at a specified level of mortality so that the proportion under age 5 matched the proportion in the given population. Because in a stable population, the proportion

under age 5 is given by

$$C(5) = {}_5P_0/P = be^{-2.5r}({}_5L_0/l_0),$$

it follows that

$$b = {}_5P_0(l_0/{}_5L_0)/Pe^{-2.5r}.$$

Hence the birth rate in the stable population equals the average number of births during the preceding 5 years that would be estimated by reverse projection, divided by the population 2.5 years earlier that would be estimated by assuming that the population grew, for 2.5 years, at the stable rate. There is really no implication of stability other than the ascription of this rate of increase. Even if the actual rate of increase differed by the unlikely margin of 0.01 from the ascribed rate, the error of estimation of the birth rate would be only 2.5 percent.

For Bulgaria in 1905, births were averaged from 1904 to 1907, because these years were the only ones in which births were available by province. The West model stable populations with given C(5) for $e_0^0 = 35$ were used. The registered birth rate was higher than the stable population birth rate, so that no underregistration was indicated.

In 1934, births were averaged for 1933–1936 because the provincial boundaries before 1933 were different. The West model stable populations with C(5) for $e_0^0 = 50$ were used, but the estimated crude birth rate was only about 0.4 per thousand greater than the calculated crude birth rate, so that no correction for underregistration was employed. In Bulgaria in 1956, registered births by province were unavailable. The registered births for Bulgaria (average 1953–1960) were allocated to the provinces in the same proportion as the population at age less than 1.0 in the census. This figure was multiplied by the proportion of legitimate and illegitimate births for all of Bulgaria to get estimates of provincial births for married and unmarried women, respectively.

23. *Czechoslovakia.* Czechoslovakia was part of Austria or Hungary until the 1920s; thus, no indexes are given for Czechoslovakia proper until 1930, and fertility indexes before 1930 for present-day Czechoslovakia can be found in Austria and Hungary. Alan Minkoff prepared the 1930 and 1961 indexes.

In 1930, no underregistration was assumed, and the births were averaged from 1931 to 1933. Data sources were 1936. *Státni Urad Statistický,*

Czechoslovakia Republic, no. 12, Prague, 1957; *Statisticka rockenka Republiky Ceskoslovenské, 1934, Statisticka rockenka Republiky Ceskoslovenské, 1932, Czechkoslovak Republic Statistics Manual #4*; and 1938, *The League of Nations Statistical Yearbook, 1937–38.*

In 1961, complete registration was also assumed. Birth statistics were available for only two agglomerations (regions) of the eleven provinces, so that a procedure similar to that for Bulgaria in 1956 was employed. The proportions of infants in each province to the total number of infants in their respective region were used to allocate the births in each region to each province. The average number of live births from 1959 to 1963 was used. Marital status of mother was not available for each province; thus, the proportion of legitimate and illegitimate births for the entire country in 1961–1963 was assumed to apply to each province.

24. *Hungary.* Paul Demeny prepared the 1880–1910 indexes from registered births and population censuses (with minor corrections by Roy Treadway to adjust indexes for which the rural, urban, and total indexes were not consistent). In the provinces with more than one city, the data for the cities were combined to give one set of indexes for the urban areas.

Alan Minkoff prepared the 1930 indexes. Data were drawn from the 1930 census, and births were averaged from 1929 to 1932. No adjustments were made to the data. Volumes published in 1932, 1936, and 1941 of the *Magyar Statisztikai Kozlemének Uj Sorozut*, Budapest, were used as the source of some of the data.

Erna Härm calculated the 1960 indexes without adjustment to the data. Births were averaged from 1960 and 1961, obtained from *Kozponti Statistica Hivital* for 1960 and 1961. Proportions of illegitimate births were taken from 1961 data only. Females by marital status and age came from census provincial volumes, and the totals for Hungary were obtained from *1960 Evi*, no. 5, *Demographic Adatok.*

25. *Rumania.* Alan Minkoff calculated the 1899, 1930, and 1960 indexes. In 1899, East model stable populations with the same proportion under age 5 and the same death rate as for 1898–1900 were used to test for underregistration of 1898–1899 births; extensive underregistration was found. Average births from 1898 and 1899 were used to calculate preliminary values of I_g and I_f. A correction factor to adjust for underregistration was calculated by finding a model stable population with the given proportion under age five and the given death rate; the birth rate in this stable population was then ascribed to the province. The ascribed

birth rate was divided by the preliminary birth rate to determine the correction factor for inflating I_f and I_g.

In 1930, the West model stable populations, with $e_0^0 = 45$ and the corresponding C(5), were used to test for underenumeration in comparison with average rates in 1929–1931. Significant underregistration of births was indicated, so that the ratio of the predicted birth rate to the measured birth rate was used to adjust I_f and I_g for each province. Births by legitimacy status were not given by province in 1930, but were given in 1938. The proportion of legitimate births in 1930 for each province was estimated by assuming that the relative change in the proportion legitimate in each province from 1930 to 1938 was the same as in all of Rumania.

The Rumanian census of 1930 did not contain a cross-tabulation of women by marital status and age for each province, although it did have tabulations of the population by marital status and sex, and by age and sex (for the rural and urban population of each province as well as for the total). Marital status by age for the rural and urban population of the provinces of Rumania was estimated by selecting a model schedule of proportions ever married by age, with the earliest age at first marriage set at 15, the proportions ever married at age 50 set at 0.985 for rural females and 0.970 for urban females, and the pace of first marriage determined (by successive approximation) to match the recorded total number of ever-married women (including a proportionate allocation of women with marital status unknown). A similar indirect procedure was used to estimate the proportion of the ever-married at each age who were widowed or divorced, given the overall number. The rural and urban populations were combined to give the number of females by age and marital status for the total province.

In 1956, births were not available by province, so that the methods of estimating births by province for Bulgaria in 1956 was used. Total births for all of Rumania were taken for the interval 1954–1958; no adjustments for underenumeration were made. Because there were no data on illegitimacy, all births were assumed to be legitimate, and all provincial I_h values were 0.000.

26. *Yugoslavia.* Alan Minkoff prepared estimates of the indexes for both 1900 and 1931. In 1900, some of the area of present-day Yugoslavia was in either Austria or Hungary, and thus the 1900 indexes are given under those countries. For 1900, indexes could in fact be computed only for Serbia. Births were taken from 1896–1905 and averaged. To test for un-

derregistration of births, West model stable populations with $e_0^0 = 35$ and corresponding C(5) were used; significant underregistration was found. The ratio of the predicted birth rate (using the stable population with mortality level 7) to the computed birth rate was used to adjust I_f and I_g.

Legitimate and illegitimate births were not given directly, but were broken down as:

b_1 = total live births (both legitimate and illegitimate);
b_2 = illegitimate births (both live and dead); and
b_3 = stillbirths (both legitimate and illegitimate).

From this tabulation the number of live illegitimate births was estimated.

In 1931, birth data were unavailable, so the birth rates given for Yugoslavia in Dudley Kirk's *Europe's Population in the Interwar Years* (1946) were used. These were tested for underenumeration by use of West model stable populations with given C(5) and matching the death rate for 1930–1931 estimated by Kirk. In comparison with the calculated birth rates of 1930–1931, underregistration was significant in three provinces. The I_f and I_g values calculated from raw data were adjusted by multiplying each of them by the ratio of the estimated birth rate to the calculated birth rate, respectively. Since there were no birth data, no proportions of births by marital status of mother were available either. Thus, the proportion legitimate was assumed to be equal in each province to the proportion legitimate in each province in 1934 (the nearest year for which data were available). Population data came from 1937, *Opsta Drzavna Statistika Definitivni: Ṛezultati Popisa Stanov nistra od 31 marta 1931 godine* (Belgrade: Drzavna Stamparija).

Erna Härm calculated the 1960 indexes. Births were averaged for 1960 and 1961 and were assumed to be accurately registered. Data on births, including legitimacy status of births, came from *Savezni Zavod za Statistiku, Demografska Statistika.* The number of females by age and marital status by province came from the 1960 Census, vol. 1.

27. *Iceland.* Poul C. Matthiessen supplied the indexes for Iceland from 1850 to 1960. In general, births were averaged for a ten-year period centered on the decennial census. Because 1870 census data were not available, they were interpolated from 1860 and 1880 population data. The statistical publications of Iceland give the total number of live births, stillbirths, and the total number of births (live plus stillbirths) for unmarried women but not for all women or for married women. Thus, the total number of live births by marital status of mother was estimated by assuming the same

proportion of stillbirths and live births inside and outside of marriage. Adjustments for underregistration of births were not needed.

Sources and Assumptions for the 1870 Indexes

A number of countries did not have sufficiently accurate or detailed censuses or vital registration to compute fertility or marital indexes in 1870, the earliest year analyzed in this study and presented on the maps; this was true for Spain and most of the countries of Eastern Europe. For these countries, we assumed that it was unlikely that fertility declined very much from 1870 until the date of the first good source of data (except possibly in some urban areas). Thus, we assumed that the 1870 indexes were the same for each province as the indexes in the year of the first available suitable data, if that year were 1900 or earlier. Although by using this assumption we probably estimated fertility indexes for 1870 slightly lower than they actually were, the assumption does allow the preparation of maps for 1870 that, for most areas, are approximately correct.

For the other dates—1900, 1930, and 1960—we assigned the indexes for the actual date (such as 1901, 1931, and 1961 in England and Wales) that was closest to the target data as long as that date was within five years of the target data. Thus, Albania's indexes for 1955 were presented on the maps and used in the analyses as the indexes for 1960.

The actual dates of the data used for 1870 and other pertinent notes about the indexes for each country are as follows (see Figure 2.C):

1. Austria: 1880 data from the Austrian portion of the Austrian-Hungarian Empire. (I_g and I_h were nearly the same in 1880 and 1890, although I_m declined in that decade, to recover by 1900).
2. Belgium: 1866 data.
3. Denmark: 1870 data.
4. England and Wales: 1871 data.
5. Finland: 1880 data (1875 had I_f values only).
6. France: 1871 data.
7. Germany: 1871 data. (The 1960 data are from 1961 for West Germany and from 1964 for East Germany.)
8. Greece: 1900 data.
9. Ireland: 1871 data. (Ireland includes both Northern Ireland and the Republic of Ireland.)
10. Italy: 1871 data.

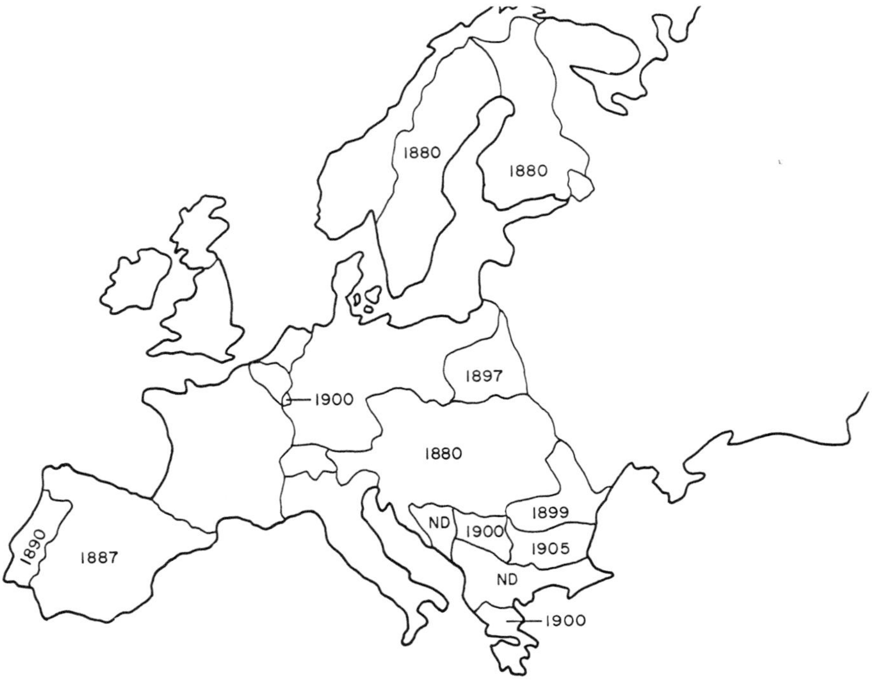

Figure 2.C. Real date of I_q, I_m, and I_f values plotted on Maps 2.2, 2.6, and 2.10 (nominal date is 1870). For Russia, data are for 1897, except in 11 provinces where fertility indexes are adjusted for higher birth rate in 1870.

11. Luxembourg: 1900 data.
12. Netherlands: 1869 data.
13. Norway: 1875 data.
14. Poland: 1897 data. (There was little change in birth rate from 1866 to the end of the century.)
15. Portugal: 1890 data. (1864 and 1878 had I_m indexes only.)
16. Russia: 1870 data, where the 1870 fertility and marriage indexes were derived from 1897 indexes corrected for changes in the birth rate as explained above under "Source and Adjustments of Data by County" for Russia.
17. Scotland: 1871 data.
18. Spain: 1887 data. (All indexes were presented for Spanish districts and not for the larger regions.)

19. Sweden: 1880 data.
20. Switzerland: 1870 data.
21. Albania: Data available only for 1955, shown on 1960 map.
22. Bulgaria: No data available for 1870. (1905 data used for 1900.)
23. Czechoslovakia: No data available for 1870 and 1900. Some current Czechoslovakian provinces were part of Austria, Hungary, and Poland in 1870 and 1900.
24. Hungary: 1880 data, except that 1890 data were used for eight southern provinces for which 1880 data were missing.
25. Rumania: 1899 data.
26. Yugoslavia: 1900 data. The 1900 data included Serbia only; portions of current Yugoslavia were also part of Austria and Hungary in 1870 and 1900.
27. Iceland: 1870 data.

APPENDIX D: Notes on the Date of Decline

The date coded on Map 2.1 and the distribution of dates in Figure 2.2 relate to the decade within which I_g in each province fell below 90 percent of a previous plateau. The plateau was taken as the highest value of I_g from an early sequence of approximately constant I_g's. If I_g declined and rose again to about its earlier level, the first decline was ignored. In other words, the date was intended to signal the approximate time of an early point in a sustained decline.

In some provinces (notably, many *départements* in France) I_g was at a low level and declining at the first dates at which the index could be calculated. In these provinces, if the earliest I_g was less than 0.67 but above 0.60, the date at which I_g fell below 0.60, never to recover, was accepted as the date of initiation of sustained decline. In provinces in which the first calculated values of I_g were less than 0.60, and showed a downward trend, our rule was to estimate the time at which I_g had fallen below 0.60 by extrapolation backward using the earliest date of decline, or by assuming a drop in I_g of 0.05 per decade, whichever gave the later date.

The basis for estimating the date of decline is illustrated by the following examples of different procedural rules for four hypothetical provinces, in which I_g is shown at eight dates from 1850 to 1930.

Values of I_g

	1850	1860	1870	1880	1890	1900	1910	1930
Province A	.783	.792	.786	.721	.662	.593	.501	.386
Province B	.652	.637	.582	.531	.507	.482	.420	.307
Province C	.571	.540	.506	.471	.452	.430	.390	.320
Province D	.551	.562	.545	.557	.560	.548	.487	.416

In Province A, the plateau is taken as 0.792; the value 10 percent below the plateau is 0.713, a value reached, as determined by linear interpolation, in 1881. In province B, the date of decline is taken as the date when an I_g of 0.600 is reached, estimated as 1867. In C, on the assumption that before the earliest date the decline was 0.05 per decade, I_g passed through 0.600 in 1844. In D, the plateau is estimated at the low level of 0.562, and the 90 percent of plateau level as 0.506, reached at an estimated date of 1907.

We now describe some special problems and their resolution:

1. Province boundaries changed, so that I_g for the same geographical unit could not be traced in establishing a date. This difficulty proved less than we had feared. It proved possible with minor special calculations to estimate the date using the provincial boundaries in Europe of 1900. In Belgium, Denmark, England and Wales, France, Ireland, Italy, the Netherlands, Norway, Portugal, Scotland, Spain, Sweden, and Switzerland, there were no boundary changes after 1900, or the decline had occurred before boundaries were altered. The most severe problems of changed boundaries were in Eastern Europe. We reached the following solutions:

a. In Austria, I_g in eight provinces had declined according to our criteria before 1910, and in three others would have reached the date of decline between 1910 and 1920, on the basis of extrapolation of the trend from 1900 to 1910.

   A date was determined for Carmiola and Gorizia combined by interpolation from 1910 using the value of I_g in the province of Drav in Yugoslavia (1931), and Venezia Giulia and Trentino-Alto Adige in Italy (1921).

b. Dates for Bromberg and Posen (combined) in Germany were calculated by equating their combined territory with that of Poznan in Poland in 1931.

c. Dates for the Polish provinces of 1897 were calculated by equating the following:

Provinces in 1897	*Provinces in 1931*
Warsaw Podolsk	Warsaw
Kalissk	Lodz
Louizinisk	Bialystok
Ljublinsk Sedlesk	Lublin
Kelitsk Petrokovsk Radomsk	Kielle

d. Dates for Russian provinces as of 1897 were determined by using the values of I_g calculated for 1926 according to czarist boundaries (Coale, Anderson, and Härm, 1979);

e. In Hungary, there were forty countries (1900 boundaries) in which the 10-percent decline in I_g did not occur before 1910. Twenty-one of these counties had calculated I_g's always below 0.600 from the earliest date (1880). The date of decline of twenty-four of the forty was estimated to occur in the decade 1910 to 1920. Of these, fourteen were calculated to fall below 90 percent of the estimated plateau by extrapolating the change from 1900 to 1910; in the other ten counties and in the sixteen estimated to experience the 10-percent decline after 1920, the date was calculated by interpolation between I_g for 1930 in the territory in Hungary, Rumania, or Yugoslavia, with the greatest overlap with the county's territory as of 1900.

f. I_g in the provinces of Bulgaria was interpolated between 1905 and 1934 with these equivalents:

1905	1934
Boorgas	Boorgas
Vidin and Vratza	Vratza
Plovdiv	Plovdiv
Tirnovo and Pleven	Pleven
Rustandel and Sofia	Sofia
Stara-Zagora	Stara-Zagora
Rousse and Varna and Choumen	Choumen

g. I_g in the provinces of Serbia in 1900 was interpolated with I_g for areas in Yugoslavia in 1931 with these equivalents:

1900	1931
Belgrade, Krajina, Smederevo	Dunavska
Valtevo, Podrinje, Uzice	Drinska
Vranja	Vardarska
Krusevac, Morava, Nis, Pirot, Toplica	Moravska

In Krajina, Pozarevac, and Timok, the estimated date of decline was before 1900.

2. In Ireland (after adjustment of births in 1871 and 1881 for apparent mismatch in the areas of registration and census enumeration), many counties had an unaccountably high value of I_g in 1911. If the 1911 I_g was well above earlier values, it was ignored in estimating the plateau. In all but a few instances a decline to 90 percent of the 1891–1911 plateau would be attributed, by interpolation, to the 1920s. But in twenty-four counties I_g was above 0.600 in 1961; in ten instances I_g in 1961 was greater than 90 percent of the estimated plateau, or only slightly below this point. In these ten counties it was assumed that the 10-percent decline had not occurred before 1961.

CHAPTER 3: Social-Group Forerunners of Fertility Control in Europe

Massimo Livi-Bacci

INTRODUCTION

During the last two decades, demographic research has collected an extraordinary wealth of statistical data concerning fertility and nuptiality trends in Europe during the nineteenth and twentieth centuries. We now have a precise geography of the onset of fertility decline throughout the provinces of Europe; we know how and where a substantial fall from high and relatively stable levels of fertility has taken place, mostly in the late nineteenth and early twentieth centuries; we know also that after the initial fall a continuous and irreversible decline has taken place until very low levels of family size have been reached. A relatively detailed picture of rural and urban fertility is also available, and a good deal of information on mortality and on social and economic differentials helps in the causal interpretation of demographic changes.

Some important questions, however, are still in need of answers. The first concerns the nature of stable high fertility, compatible with natural fertility patterns, prevailing before the onset of an irreversible decline. Indeed, stating that the irreversible decline of fertility started during a given period does not imply that fertility control was previously unknown. Pre-transition populations may have included a small proportion of couples effectively controlling their fertility, or a somewhat larger proportion of couples less effectively controlling their fertility, so that aggregate levels of marital fertility remained high; the transition may then represent an increase in the proportion of couples intentionally planning their fertility, or an increase in the degree of control exerted. Although some couples may have indeed been more or less effectively limiting their families well before the transition, in a stable society where social and economic change was relatively slow, and where contacts between different social strata may have been limited, fertility control may not easily spread through the population, or increase its hold on the already controlling couples. As a consequence, fertility may have remained relatively high and apparently constant, and lack of detectable change at the aggregate level may be mistaken for uniform behavior within the population.

The history of European populations before the onset of the irreversible decline shows that there were some more or less extended pockets of low fertility. I shall call these fertility-controlling groups "forerunners." Indeed, they are forerunners of a behavior that will be imitated or rediscovered decades or even centuries later by the rest of the population.

In this paper, I shall assemble and comment on the existing demographic data on the "forerunners" in the hope that this may increase our understanding of the complex transition of the populations of Western Europe from high to low fertility. My task would be impossible if historical demographers had not accumulated a significant although heterogeneous body of data on the demographic characteristics of some small groups. Most of these groups are geographically limited populations—the society of a valley, district, village, or parish—where the behaviors of different social groups are mixed and therefore indistinguishable. Sometimes, however, the microscope of the demographer has been focused on a specific social group because of its prominence or because of the existence of adequate documentation. I will consider these groups in this paper—the aristocracies; a minority religious group, the Jews; and some urban populations.

The Aristocracies

Aristocracies have been extensively studied by demographers because of their social prominence and well-established genealogies (Fahlbeck, 1903; Sundbärg, 1909; Savorgnan, 1923 and 1925). As we shall see, I have given an extensive connotation to the term aristocracy: for my purposes they are the wealthy—high officers and prominent bourgeois—as well as the nobility. The great majority of aristocrats attained their status through birth; unlike other social characteristics, one's genealogy remains immutable throughout life.

The aristocracies to be considered here differ from one another in several respects. The nobility of Venice comprised a large segment of the population of the city (4 or 5 percent), while dukes and peers of France in the ancien régime were but a handful of highly placed families (Beltrami, 1954; Henry and Levy, 1960). The aristocracies of Milan, Genoa, and Florence consisted primarily of families who had founded their fortune on trade, and resembled the bourgeois families of Geneva more than the European ruling families of royal blood (Zanetti, 1972; Greppi, 1970; Litchfield, 1969;

Henry, 1956; Peller, 1965). They differed also in behavior. For example, the British peerage had no strong incentive to marry within the limited circle of the nobility (Hollingsworth, 1964), while most of the European nobility was strongly endogamic. In short, demographic dimensions and marriage strategies, social and political prominence and the nature of their privileges, and the origin of their fortunes and levels of personal wealth are all highly variable characteristics of the aristocracies considered here.

Table 3.1 presents some measures of the fertility and nuptiality of these aristocracies. There are two indicators of family size (the sum of legitimate fertility rates from age 20, or 25, to age 50, or $TLFR_{20}$ and $TLFR_{25}$), two indicators of fertility control (the mean age at birth of the last child and Coale and Trussell's *m*), and two measures of nuptiality (the mean age at first marriage and the proportion remaining single at age 50.)

These series show a substantial decline from the seventeenth to the eighteenth centuries, the most extreme case being that of the French dukes and peers, where $TLFR_{20}$ falls from 5.08 in 1650–1699 to 2.4 in the eighteenth century. This fall of fertility is confirmed by other evidence. In Venice, the birth rate of the nobility falls from 34–39 per thousand in the sixteenth century to 27.6 in 1642 and 20–24 between 1755 and 1790 (Beltrami, 1954). In Lyon, a study of three generations of prominent citizens (the *echevins*, or city council members, their fathers, and their children) reveals a continuous fall of marital fertility from the first generation (married between 1650 and 1730) to the second (married between 1680 and 1770), and to the third (married between 1720 and 1810 (Garden, 1977). In some instances, a first phase of the decline, leading to relatively low levels in the eighteenth century, is followed by a recovery; this is the case for the British peerage and for Milan's airstocracy. In others, fertility remains low. Figure 3.1 offers a visual impression of the decline in family size of the aristocracies from the seventeenth to the nineteenth centuries.

Family size is an indirect measure of family limitation, because it can be affected by behavior that is not parity-specific. For some of the groups I have presented two more direct indicators of fertility control: Coale and Trussell's *m*, and the mean age of mothers at the birth of their last child. As can be seen in Figures 3.2 and 3.3, the first of the two measures declines and the second increases in all groups, paralleling the decline in family size. Signs of the existence of control are evident as early as the seventeenth century for some groups, namely the French dukes and peers, the bourgeoisie of Geneva, and the aristocracies of Milan and Genoa.

Table 3.1. Fertility and nuptiality of the aristocracies, seventeenth to nineteenth centuries.

Cohort	$TLFR_{20}$	$TLFR_{25}$	Mean Age at Birth of Last Child	Measure of Fertility Control m	Mean Age at First Marriage		Percent Remaining Single	
					Males	Females	Males	Females
			Florence's Aristocracy[a]					
1600-99	6.86	4.60	--	.597	35.4	19.7	60	55
1700-99	6.03	3.61	--	.960	30.7	21.0	38	14
1750-99	5.44	2.74	--	1.784	28.2	20.8	--	--
			Milan's Aristocracy					
Before 1650	9.47	6.74	38.4	.227	30.8	19.6	49	75
1650-99	8.32	5.36	34.2	.708	30.9	19.7	56	49
1700-49	6.62	4.09	34.2	.831	33.4	21.2	51	34
1750-99	5.52	3.34	35.2	1.003	30.8	20.4	37	13
1800-49	5.69	3.62	33.7	.819	31.5	22.3	18	8
1850-99	4.03	2.50	34.2	.822	32.3	24.4	12	25
			Genoa's Families[b]					
Before 1600	6.82	4.73	35.5	.473	32.1	19.6	--	--
1600-49	6.04	4.29	34.6	.235	30.8	20.3	--	--
1650-99	5.54	3.59	33.2	.698	31.4	21.1	--	--
1700-74	5.01	3.28	30.5	.668	31.6	21.4	--	--
			Belgian Aristocracy[c]					
1680-1750	7.88	5.73	38.6	.117	29.5	24.3	--	--
1750-1830	6.91	4.67	35.8	.422	29.3	23.7	--	--
1650-1830	7.27	5.06	--	.312	--	--	--	--
			French Dukes and Peers[d]					
1650-99	5.08	3.13	31.2	.829	25.5	20.0	17-27	--
1700-99	2.40	1.27	25.9	1.537	22.5	18.9	17-27	--

Sources:

Florence:	Litchfield, 1969
Milan:	Zanetti, 1972
Genoa:	Greppi, 1970
Belgian aristocracy:	Vandenbroeke, 1977
French Dukes:	Henry and Lévy, 1960
Geneva:	Henry, 1956
Ghent:	Vandenbroeke, 1977
British Peerage:	Hollingsworth, 1964
European ruling families:	Peller, 1965

Notes:

a) Median age at first marriage.
b) Mean age at birth of last child for women married before age 30.
c) Mean age at birth of last child for 1750-1830 refers to 1800-20.
d) Mean age at birth of last child for women married before age 20.
e) The two measures of family size are the sum of the duration specific marital fertility rates for women married before age 25 and between ages 25 and 35.
f) The measure of family size is the mean number of births per married man.

Table 3.1. (continued)

Cohort	$TLFR_{20}$	$TLFR_{25}$	Mean Age at Birth of Last Child	Measure of Fertility Control m	Mean Age at First Marriage		Percent Remaining Single	
					Males	Females	Males	Females
			Geneva's Bourgeoisie					
Before 1600	7.47	5.53	38.7	.023	27.2	22.0	10.6	2
1600-49	9.42	6.79	38.2	.120	29.1	24.9	17.0	7
1650-99	6.54	4.07	34.4	.759	32.6	25.2	18	26
1700-49	4.83	2.86	31.9	1.084	31.9	27.0	31	29
1750-99	4.87	2.92	31.9	.976	31.5	24.4	20	32
1800-49	3.79	2.07	31.7	1.380	29.4	22.7	22	25
1850-99	3.99	2.32	31.7	.976	29.2	24.7	--	17
			Ghent's Industrial Families					
1790-1850	6.07	3.86	33.7	.656	27.6	22.1	--	--
			British Peerage[e]					
1550-99	7.08	3.58	--	--	25.5	20.0	19	7
1600-49	6.33	3.54	--	--	26.7	21.3	23	16
1650-99	6.15	3.29	--	--	27.5	22.1	24	20
1700-49	5.52	3.35	--	--	29.9	23.9	25	24
1750-99	6.33	3.88	--	--	29.4	24.7	22	24
1800-49	5.46	3.62	--	--	30.8	25.5	19	22
1850-99	3.28	2.39	--	--	31.0	25.9	18	24
			European Ruling Families[f]					
1500-49	5.8	--	--	--	25.2	20.2	29.7	24.1
1550-99	6.0	--	--	--	25.2	20.2	29.7	24.1
1600-49	6.2	--	--	--	27.5	22.7	24.3	24.9
1650-99	5.9	--	--	--	27.5	22.7	24.3	24.9
1700-49	5.0	--	--	--	27.3	21.7	20.4	13.2
1750-99	4.6	--	--	--	27.3	21.7	20.4	13.2
1800-49	4.6	--	--	--	28.4	22.2	17.4	12.3
1850-99	4.0	--	--	--	29.9	22.5	17.4	12.3

Because nuptiality is so closely related to family size, it deserves some attention. The mean age at first marriage of females is almost without exception between the ages of 20 and 25. For males, the mean age at first marriage is between 27 and 33 with only two exceptions, the early cohorts of the British peerage, and the early-marrying French dukes and peers. The age differences between males and females are greater than those usually found in the general population, but members of the aristocracy married at ages well within the range prevailing in Western populations.

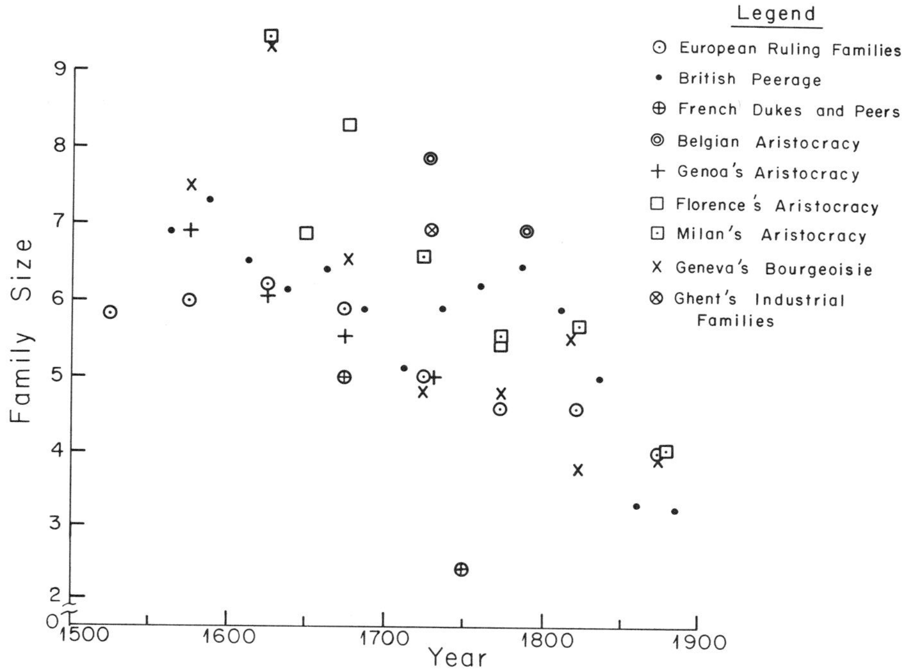

Figure 3.1. Family size measures, European aristocracies, sixteenth to eighteenth centuries.

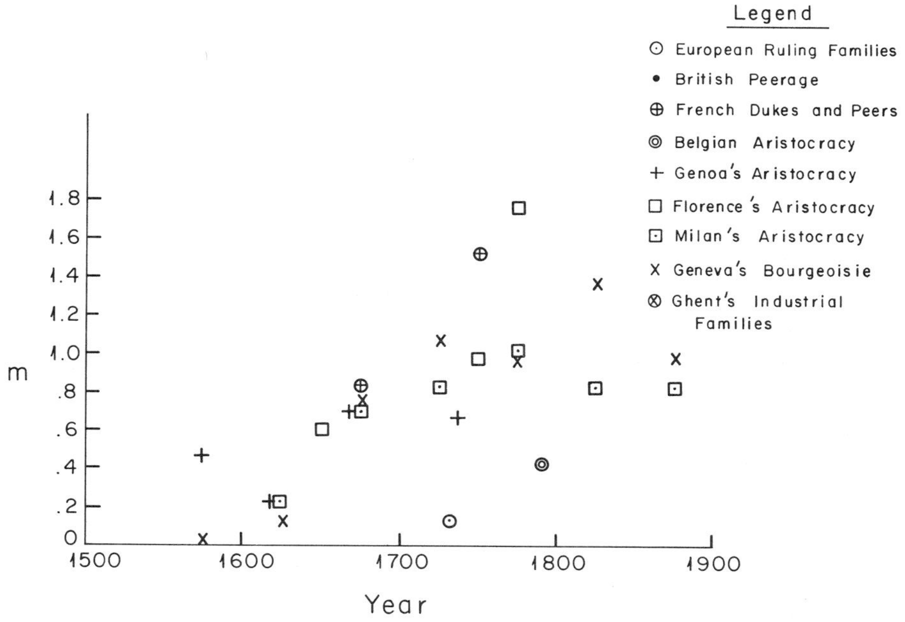

Figure 3.2. Values of *m*, European aristocracies, sixteenth to eighteenth centuries.

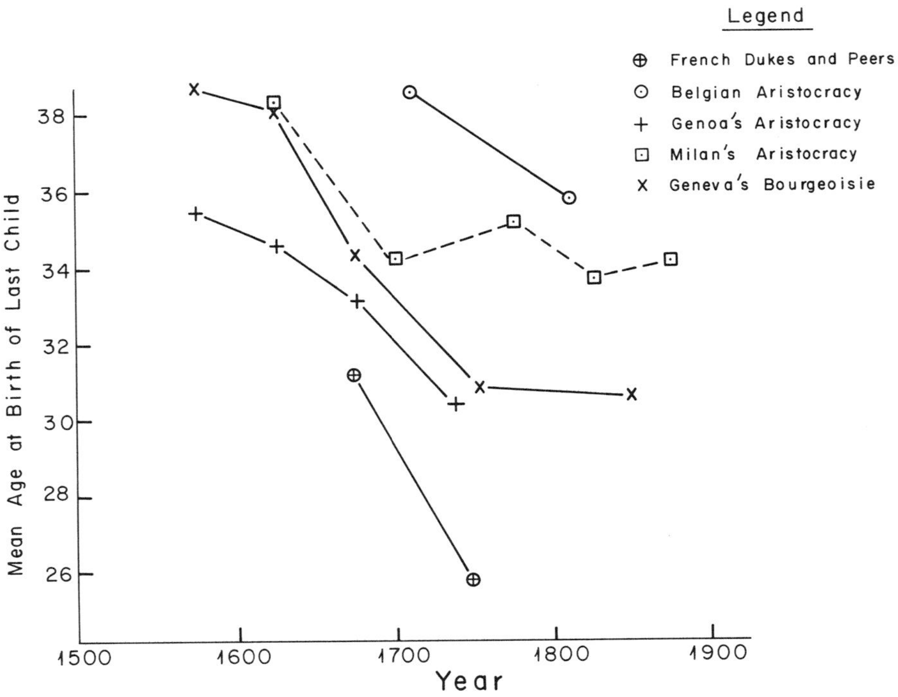

Figure 3.3. Mean age at birth of last child, European aristocracies sixteenth to eighteenth centuries.

Although delayed marriage and family limitation may be alternative ways of achieving small families, both approaches were used by these aristocracies, and there is no evidence that the adoption of family limitation led to a fall in the age of female marriage during the period examined.

The peculiarity of the marriage strategies of privileged groups is evident when the proportion remaining single at age 50 is considered. This proportion is usually high (in some cases perhaps extremely high) and varies over time. Time trends are neither clear nor uniform: the proportion remaining single goes up among the British peers and the bourgeois Genevan families, while it goes down until 1800–1849 among the European ruling families and in Milan's aristocracy.

Mortality, and particularly child mortality, is the other important demographic variable often associated with the course of fertility (F. van de Walle, Chapter 4). Couples aiming at a given family size may try to "replace" a dead child; when child mortality falls, children are replaced with lower frequency, and thus fertility goes down. Only with special tabulations of the data derived from family reconstitution is it possible to put to a test historically the theory of the child-replacement effect. We shall limit ourselves, therefore, to seeing whether the decline of fertility has taken place in a context of mortality decline.

In the case of Geneva's bourgeoisie and of Milan's aristocracy, mortality of the young (measured by l_{20}/l_0) and of the general population (e_0^0) falls from the seventeenth century (Henry, 1956; Zanetti, 1972); for the ruling families there is a fall of ${}_5q_0$ and of e_0^0 after the mid-seventeenth century, but mortality in the eighteenth century was higher than in the sixteenth (Peller, 1965). In the case of the British peerage, there is a continuous fall in mortality (${}_5q_0$) after the mid-seventeenth century; before that date, a maximum level was reached in the cohorts born in the second and third quarters of the seventeenth century (Hollingsworth, 1964). For the other groups, data on mortality are not available, or they are quite defective.

In the few well-documented cases, therefore, the fall of fertility takes place in a context of declining mortality, although it is difficult to understand the sense of the relation between the two variables without further analysis.

Privileged groups—ruling families, nobility, bourgeoisie—although heterogeneous in nature, are certainly forerunners of the fertility decline. All show evidence of family limitation in the eighteenth century, and in some instances in the seventeenth. The fertility decline of these groups occurs in the context of a marriage pattern characteristic of Western Europe at that time, and of declining mortality. Although the forerunners that we know most about are French, Italian, Flemish, and British, I suspect that the aristocracies of other countries could be easily added if the appropriate documentation existed.

The Jews

Privileged groups such as aristocracies are not the only ones to show an early decline of fertility. Discrimination, rather than privilege, defines another group, the Jews, whose fertility declines much earlier than that of other populations in Western Europe.

Historians and demographers have speculated that the level of fertility must have been very high among the Jews before the eighteenth and nineteenth centuries. Religious and social norms favored early and universal marriage and channeled sexual life within the family, and great value was attached to children while the misfortune of childlessness was stressed (Katz, 1959; Livi, 1920; Bachi, 1981). For the Jews of Eastern Europe and of the Pale of Settlement, a pattern of high fertility and high nuptiality can be found until the end of the nineteenth century; we do not know, however, whether the same pattern was typical of Western European Jews, since by the time that satisfactory data first became available the transition to low fertility has already begun.

Jewish populations were characterized by a strict adherence to religious and social norms, by a marked professional specialization in commerce and trade, and by a deep emphasis on religious education. They were concentrated in urban communities and often physically confined within the walls of a ghetto, their separation from the rest of the population enforced by discriminatory legislation. Jewish communities thus had a unique social life and a well-defined identity, supported by a high degree of endogamy. Emancipation, initiated by the French Revolution and reinforced by the waves of liberalization in the mid-nineteenth century, weakened the demographic cohesion of the Jews. Since migration and mixed marriage make the identification of the Jews as a population (in demographic terms) problematic, I shall limit my analysis to the period before emancipation, although data from the second half of the nineteenth century may well be helpful in the interpretation of long-term trends.

In many areas of Western Europe, during the eighteenth and the first part of the nineteenth centuries, the birth rate of the Jews was conspicuously lower than that of the gentile majority. This early decline in the birth rate may have been the consequence of a gradual departure of marriage patterns from the traditional norms of universal and early marriage, as Jews gradually assimilated and adopted the Western European marriage pattern. The birth rates found around the time of emancipation are all so low, however, that they can probably be ascribed to family limitation.

Table 3.2 reports birth rate series for seven large Jewish communities in Italy from the end of the seventeenth to the end of the nineteenth centuries. While the data cover different time spans, they all point to an early decline of Jewish fertility, a decline that appears to be under way in all communities by the beginning of the nineteenth century. The decline is more gradual for the community of Rome, whose social and economic level was notoriously much lower than that of the other communities.

If the birth rate of the Jews is compared with that of the total or the Catholic population, its lower level is evident in every case known to me.

Table 3.2. Jewish birth rate, selected communities: 1669-1675 to 1901-1915.

Date	Florence	Leghorn	Modena	Padua	Rome	Trieste	Verona
1669-1675	43.8[a]	54.8	--	--	--	--	--
1675-1700	45.9[b]	42.3	--	--	--	--	--
1701-1725	--	28.1	--	--	--	--	--
1726-1750	39.4[c]	27.5	--	--	--	--	--
1751-1775	30.6	25.2	27.1[g]	--	41.6[j]	--	--
1776-1800	26.7	21.6	28.5	--	44.1	51.0[l]	--
1801-1825	27.2[d]	22.6	27.0	23.9[i]	36.4	44.4	25.9[m]
1826-1850	24.3[e]	25.5	26.9	28.0	36.8	35.3	26.0[n]
1851-1875	--	29.5[f]	22.1[h]	26.7	35.3	29.6	22.9[o]
1876-1900	--	--	--	16.4	29.3[k]	20.7	16.6[p]

Sources: Livi (1920) for Florence, Leghorn, Modena, Padua, and Rome; Livi-Bacci (1977) for Trieste and Verona.

Notes:
a) 1675
b) 1676-1685
c) 1741-1750
d) 1801-1807
e) 1826-1844
f) 1851-1860
g) 1756-1775
h) 1851-1865
i) 1816-1825
j) 1771-1775
k) 1776-1807
l) 1786-1800
m) 1816-1825
n) 1826-1845
o) 1846-1875
p) 1876-1895

Table 3.3 reports the data for three Jewish communities of Tuscany. In each the Jewish birth rate is significantly lower than that of the total population. For the years 1838–1842, a more detailed analysis for the community of Leghorn (the second in size in Italy, after Rome) shows beyond any doubt the spread of fertility control, with a marital fertility rate of 0.170 and an I_g around 0.400. A nominative family reconstitution done for Florence's Jews (Table 3.4) during the period 1818–1850, gives a hypothetical number of children per woman marrying at the age of 25 ($TLFR_{25}$) of 4.37 (for a mean age at first marriage of women of 24.4); the shape of the fertility curve, the level of family size, and the value of *m*

Table 3.3. Jewish and total or Catholic birth rate, Florence, Leghorn and Pitigliano: 1801-1805 to 1846-1850.

	Florence		Leghorn		Pitigliano	
Date	Jewish	Total	Jewish	Total	Jewish	Catholic
1801-1805	27.7	--	21.3	42.8	--	--
1806-1810	24.4[a]	39.0	22.5	35.4[d]	--	--
1811-1815	27.6[b]	40.2	19.2	38.8	47.2	55.9
1816-1820	26.8	42.7	21.5	39.8	47.2	55.9
1821-1825	28.3	43.9	28.6	38.4	42.1	53.9
1826-1830	23.1	42.0	27.0	36.7	42.1	53.9
1831-1835	25.1	39.4	26.3	34.4	34.9	46.9
1836-1840	24.0	37.8	25.8	33.7	34.9	46.9
1841-1845	25.1[c]	37.5	23.7	35.6	36.9	42.1
1846-1850	--	--	24.5	36.3	36.9	42.1

Sources: Livi Bacci, 1977.

Notes: a) 1806-1807; b) 1815; c) 1841-1844; d) 1810.

indicate the existence of a high degree of control fully compatible with the low birth rate. It is only in the rural community of Pitigliano (a rare instance of a Jewish community living in a rural environment in Italy) that there is little evidence from family reconstitution of fertility control, although the birth rate was significantly lower than that of the Catholic population. Outside Tuscany, the Jewish birth rate was also low in Mantua (28.1, compared with 44.2 for the total population in 1791–1795).

The analysis of the Italian case leads to the following conclusions: (1) the birth rate of the Jews at the end of the eighteenth century was at moderate levels almost everywhere, and a decline, perhaps imputable in part to a change in the marriage pattern, had already taken place; (2) the birth rate of the Jews was generally much lower than that of the Catholics living in the same city; (3) the moderate level of the birth rate (around

Table 3.4. Fertility and nuptiality of some Jewish communities, eighteenth to nineteenth centuries.

Period	$TLFR_2$	$TLFR_{25}$	Age at Birth of Last Child	Measure of Fertility Control m	Mean Age at First Marriage	
					Males	Females
			Bayonne			
1751-1787	7.02[a]	5.01[a]	--	.259	27.0	23.4
			Pitigliano			
1808-1865	8.44	6.05	40.6	.273	25.2	22.0
			Florence			
1818-1850	6.50	4.37	--	.664	28.0	24.4
			Nonnenweier			
1800-1849	9.71	7.27	41.5	.068	32.1	26.6
1850-1879	8.03	5.67	37.8	.293	30.8	25.7
			Altdorf			
1800-1839	9.55	7.50	40.9	--	29.2[b]	25.5[b]
1840-1869	9.92	7.33	39.3	.066	29.3[b]	27.4[b]
1870-1899	7.34	4.97	35.8	.541	29.4[b]	24.7[b]

Sources: Bayonne: Nahon, 1976; Pitigliano: Livi-Bacci, 1980; Florence: Sardi Bucci, 1976; Nonnenweier: Goldstein, 1981; Altdorf: Goldstein, 1985.

Notes: a) Fertility of families with at least one child.
b) Median age at marriage.

25 per 1,000) and of other appropriate indicators where these are available confirm the existence of a deeply rooted fertility control. In Italy, then, the decline of Jewish fertility preceded that of the Italian population by at least a century.

For other countries, demographic data are poorer and inconclusive, although in agreement with the findings for the Italian Jews. A relative abundance of information is available for the second half of the nineteenth century, but by that time emancipation of the Jews had already been achieved throughout Western Europe. The economic, social, educational, and professional progress of the Jews was so rapid after emancipation that their identification as a separate population becomes quite problematic. I shall make some reference to data prior to that of the mid-nineteenth century with the understanding that almost everywhere after that date, the fertility of the Jews is found to be sensibly lower than that of their Christian urban counterparts.

Germany at mid-nineteenth century appears to be similar to Italy, in that the birth rate for Jews has already fallen while that for other denominations has not. In Prussia, between 1822–1844 and 1857–1862, the birth rate of the Jews declines from 37.2 to 33.9, while the birth rate of Catholics and Protestants remains constant around 40. For Jews, the transition thus precedes unification, while it is only after 1880 than an irreversible decline in fertility occurs among Protestants, and only after 1910 among Catholics (Knodel, 1974). Data for a later period (the 1870s) for Bavaria and Hesse give a birth rate for the Jews around 31–33 per 1,000, 9 to 10 points below that of the Catholics and 5 to 6 below that of the Protestants (Knodel, 1974). Although part of this difference was probably due to the higher urban concentration of the Jews, data for later dates and for urban areas, as well as the results of two village studies in rural Baden, show that in a similar environment (whether urban or rural) Jews have preceded non-Jews in the process of fertility decline (Goldstein, 1981 and 1985; see also Table 3.4).

In the German-speaking Jewish community of Prague, the birth rate was significantly below that of the rest of the population at the end of the eighteenth century (34.4 against 45.0 per 1,000 in 1791–1792), not unlike the Italian case; differences increase during the nineteenth century as the Jewish birth rate continues to decline (24.7 in 1830–1833 and 22.1 in 1881–1885) while that of the rest of the population remains constant (39.5 and 42.7 in 1830–1833 and 1881–1885) (Herman, 1980). An early fertility decline among Bohemia's and Moravia's Jews is confirmed by the census of Czechoslovakia of 1930: parity progression rates for Jewish women born before 1860 rapidly decrease after the fourth child (Bachi, 1981).

Little is known for other countries. The official survey made in France for 1855–1859 gives a birth rate of 24.9 per 1,000 for the Jews, compared to 26.5 for the total population of France (Szajkowski, 1946). In France, however, emancipation already had a long history and the small difference is not meaningful. More interesting, if supplemented by further research, could be the results of a partial reconstitution of Jewish families in Bayonne in the second half of the eighteenth century, showing the existence of a moderate degree of control (Nahon, 1976).

In the second half of the nineteenth century, for which information is relatively abundant, Jewish fertility is much lower everywhere than that of the gentile population (Livi, 1920; Hersch, 1948). However, at this relatively late stage of European demographic history, differences related to religion tend to share the nature of differences related to social or economic status, rather than reflecting the impact of values and norms typical of well-identified and homogeneous groups.

The nuptiality pattern of Western Jewish communities before emancipation was not, as far as we know, significantly different from that of the gentile population. Many have argued that this similarity of the Jewish marriage pattern was due to a preceding profound change away from the traditional norms of early and universal marriage. This may be so, and what fragmentary evidence there is does not contradict this hypothesis.

Much more is known about mortality. Everywhere, that of the Jews was lower than that of the Christian population. The reasons for this lower mortality, relatively well documented at the end of the eighteenth and beginning of the nineteenth centuries, are very complex, and include the hygienic norms prescribed by religion, a traditional habit of moderation in eating and drinking, the low incidence of venereal diseases, and a better than average economic level—not to mention the controversial speculations concerning the possibility of selective mechanisms related to differential mortality (Livi, 1920; Bachi, 1981). Evidence of the lower mortality of the Jews is overwhelming and conclusive; it was lower in communities where Jewish fertility was under control; it was lower in those where differences of fertility between Jews and gentiles were not evident, as in some rural communities; and it was lower in some Polish and Russian communities where socioeconomic conditions were extremely poor (Schmelz, 1971). It is this low mortality, coupled with high nuptiality and fertility, that has permitted the Jewish groups in Eastern Europe and in the Pale of Settlement to increase at an extremely high rate between the end of the eighteenth and the beginning of the twentieth centuries (Bachi, 1981).

MASSIMO LIVI-BACCI

Urban Populations

In past times, the birth rate in the cities has generally been lower than that in the countryside. Traditionally, the balance of births and deaths has contributed very little to urban growth; in many instances, urban growth has taken place only because of immigration. Arrays of pre-nineteenth-century urban birth rates consistently show them to be lower than those of the surrounding rural population (Mols, 1955). This finding is of little consequence, however, since the demographic and social structure of the cities was radically different from that of the rest of the population. Because of the exchange of populations between rural and urban areas—due to the influx of young women who delivered their children in the cities in order to escape the reprobation for their illegitimate status in their village of origin, parents from rural areas who abandoned their children to the care of charitable institutions in the cities, and well-to-do mothers who entrusted their children to the care of women in the countryside—and because of the high frequency of nonmarriage in peculiar sectors of the urban populations (such as the religious and the militaries, inmates in hospitals and prisons, domestic servants, paupers, vagrants, prostitutes), any interpretation of the comparison of aggregate measures of fertility in rural and urban areas is extremely difficult (Livi-Bacci, 1977; Bardet, 1974; Lachiver, 1973).

Two basic questions must be answered: (1) Is the lower birth rate of the cities the consequence of a different nuptiality pattern, with later marriage and higher proportions single? (2) If the marriage pattern cannot explain all the differences between urban and rural birth rates, is the lower urban fertility the consequence of fertility control or of other factors, social or biological (such as higher mobility and frequent separation of couples, health and nutritional patterns, and so forth)?

Only a detailed demographic analysis can give an answer to these questions. Fortunately, demographers have already started to put their skills to the very hard test of the nominative study of urban populations. Bardet is the first to complete a family reconstitution for a large urban population, that of Rouen, for the seventeenth and eighteenth centuries. I will draw upon the results that he graciously made available to me. Four categories of families can be reconstituted: the prominent (merchants, officers), the less prominent (small merchants and officers of lower rank), the *maîtres artisans*, and the proletariat. Figure 3.4 shows the period

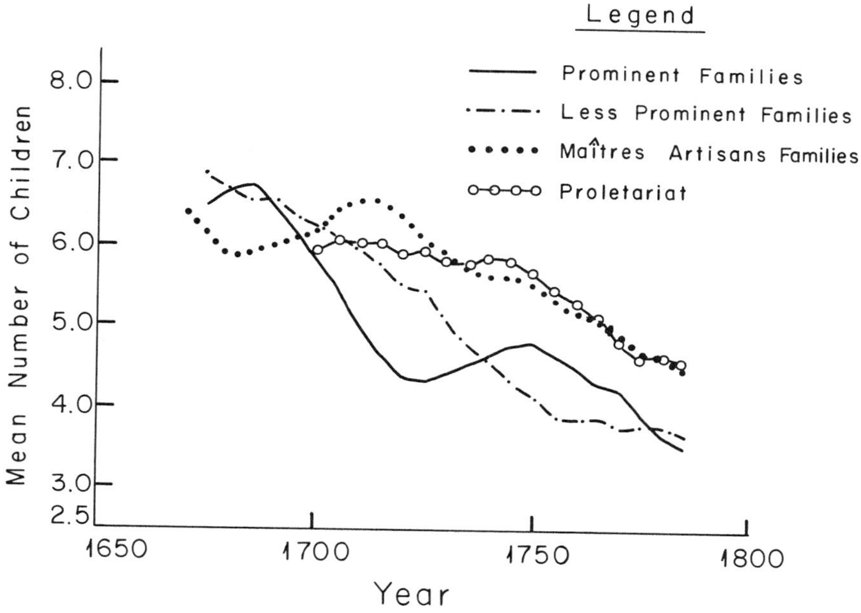

Figure 3.4. Period marital fertility by social class, Rouen, 1670–1785.

measures of marital fertility for the four categories of families from 1670 to 1800.

The results are of the utmost interest. In the total population, the mean number of children falls below six after 1710, below five after 1760, and approaches four in 1800; the decline of fertility is already on its way at the beginning of the eighteenth century. The higher the social status, the earlier and faster the decline: among the prominent, the mean number of children falls below five after 1710, while among the proletariat the same threshold is reached around 1770, or sixty years later. At the onset of the Revolution, the prominent and less prominent had a family size of one unit lower than the *maîtres artisans* and the proletariat. However, the decline of fertility is also evident in the proletariat after the mid-eighteenth century.

In Rouen, fertility control is almost certainly practiced by the beginning of the eighteenth century, almost a century before that in the rest of the population of Normandy. Fertility control becomes rooted in the various social strata with a gradual movement, from top to bottom, suggesting the existence of a typical diffusion model.

A similar pattern seems to be suggested by another important urban study, that of Calvinist Geneva, studied by Perrenoud (Perrenoud, 1974 and 1979). The detailed data on fertility are impatiently waited for by historians and demographers, but some partial results show unequivocally that fertility was already being controlled at the beginning of the eighteenth century. According to Perrenoud, the decline of fertility of Geneva's population takes place on a parallel with that of the bourgeois families of the same city studied by Henry. Moreover, evidence of control can be found in the different social strata of Geneva's population during the first half of the eighteenth century.

Later on, during the nineteenth century, urban-rural differentials, measured with more refined tools than the birth rate, are evident throughout Europe. Urban populations precede the rest of the population in the transition from high to low fertility, and by the second half of the century a clear dichotomy in fertility patterns is solidly established (Sharlin, Chapter 5). But not unlike the Jews after emancipation, urban populations of the nineteenth century are of scarce interest in the economy of this paper. Their social identity, after centuries of stability, rapidly changes; they grow in size and in power, and the influx of immigrants changes the relation between town and countryside. Urban populations cannot be forerunners of change; they are themselves the prime movers of change.

Conclusions

Well before the widespread decline of fertility in the provinces of Europe, a few social groups had already—often a century or more ahead of the general population—begun the process of controlling fertility. The groups reviewed in this paper are certainly not exhaustive of all known examples of early fertility control, although I have done my best to assemble the relevant cases. It is likely that historical demography will gradually unveil other interesting cases.

Aristocracies, in the extended sense adopted in this paper, and many Jewish communities are certainly forerunners of fertility control: the time spans separating them from the general population can be estimated in decades in some instances, in centuries in others. In the aristocracies and in the prominent social classes, the decline begins to be evident by the end of the seventeenth century. For the Jews we have less conclusive evidence, although for some Italian communities the decline could have taken place during the first part of the eighteenth century. Even in France, where the decline becomes general at the time of the Revolution, the fall of fertility in the high aristocracy or among the prominent citizens of Rouen takes place at least a century before.

In the groups for which we have sufficient detail, the decline takes place in a context of patterns of age at marriage similar to those of the general population. For the Jews there is some well-grounded speculation that a rise in the age at marriage might have preceded or accompanied the first phase of the decline. The proportion remaining single was more variable: very high in the aristocracies, very low among the Jews, and often high in the urban populations. Differences in marriage strategies are reflected more in the variable proportion of those excluded from marriage rather than by the age at marriage: aristocracies tended to maximize the chances of transmitting an undivided patrimony, while Jewish minorities fought the dangers of their small numerical size by maximizing the opportunities for marriage and, therefore, for reproduction.

Mortality among the forerunners was generally relatively moderate and lower than in the general population; this is true for the aristocracies and for the Jews, though doubts remain for the urban populations (which in many cases had higher mortality than the rest of the population). The higher mortality in the urban population was probably caused (at least in part) by the "marginal" population formed by paupers, vagrants, inmates in institutions, and the like, more so than by the "stable" sector formed by the normal families. Whether, however, a fall of mortality preceded or followed the decline of fertility we cannot yet tell, and the child-replacement hypothesis (or any equivalent one) remains in need of validation.

One common aspect of the forerunners is their urban residence or urban connection, although there is at least one case of early rural decline—in Calvinist Ormansag in Hungary, which deserves attention (Andorka, 1971 and 1972; Demeny, 1968). This is certainly true for the aristocracies and for the Jewish communities. The few rural Jewish communities studied in Germany and in Italy do not show evidence of early control. The relevance of the urban factor is therefore evident, but an unsolved question remains: are these groups forerunners of fertility control because they live in the special cultural, social, and economic environment of the city, or is the city environment special because of the existence and role of the forerunners? This question can be addressed, but there is little hope that empirical evidence will be able to give a satisfactory answer.

Forerunners had a variety of religious affiliations. We have reviewed Calvinist Geneva and Catholic Rouen; Calvinist, Catholic, and Anglican aristocracies; and Jewish minorities. The various groups seem to be ready to adopt new strategies irrespective of their religious affiliation. The contraposition, advanced by some writers (Burguière, 1972; Perrenoud, 1974), of a Calvinist and Protestant strategy, which is adaptable to the change of external conditions and able to adjust the degree of fertility control according to necessity, against a Catholic strategy, which is less flexible but whose transition to control is irreversible, is interesting but needs documentary evidence.

Forerunners had similarities and differences. The urban connection and the context of moderate mortality are points in common, and also in common is an above-average economic level. Different are their marriage strategies, their religious affiliation, and the cultural context. Further generalizations cannot be made, but a few final remarks are in order.

First, fertility control is evident in some groups beginning in the seventeenth century. It may have existed before, but there is little hope that well-grounded evidence will be found for earlier periods. Second, the evidence we have concerns prominent or easily defined groups. Other groups that have adopted a similar strategy may exist, but they will appear only when larger studies, such as the one on Rouen, are undertaken. Last, we have discussed the forerunners as groups, not as individuals. Small groups cannot modify the aggregate behavior of large populations; similarly, individual couples, who control fertility, cannot affect the aggregate fertility of a group and their existence may never become known.

Chapter 4: Infant Mortality and the European Demographic Transition

Francine van de Walle

> What is the use of reducing infant mortality when it is precisely that reduction which imposes the greatest restraint on us in the begetting of children, so that, taken all round, we nevertheless rear no more children than in the days before the reign of hygiene, while at the same time we have created difficult conditions for our sexual life in marriage.
>
> Freud, *Civilization and Its Discontents*, p. 35

Fundamental changes have taken place in both mortality and fertility during the nineteenth and the twentieth centuries. The dramatic reduction in the death rates was largely independent of the decision of individuals: improvements in the standards of living and in environmental sanitation, medical progress, and a better understanding of disease. The decrease in family size, by contrast, was the result of the deliberate choice of couples to limit childbearing. Since in many instances mortality started to fall before fertility, theorists emphasized the causal link between the drop in mortality and the decline in fertility. Today the relation between fertility and mortality is considered an important area of policy-oriented research in less-developed countries.

Theories of the demographic transition have paid special attention to infant mortality. The reduction of infant and child mortality has often been singled out as the decisive factor that initiated the decline in fertility. "It is reasonable to suppose that parents bear children not for the rewards accruing from the birth itself but principally for the rewards expected to accrue from surviving children" (Preston, 1978, p. 9). If a high birth rate is functional adjustment to the high risks of dying in infancy and childhood, then it loses its justification when the replacement of the generations is assured with fewer births.

In his 1961 review of the studies of the fertility decline in industrial countries, Ronald Freedman expressed the opinion that then prevailed:

> Most sociologists and demographers would probably agree . . . that [one of the two] basic causes of the general decline [was] . . . a sharp

reduction in mortality which reduced the number of births necessary to have any desired number of children. (Freedman, 1961–1962, p. 53)

How well has this generalization withstood the test of time and the accumulation of additional evidence by recent studies and particularly by the Princeton European Fertility Project? Before turning to the evidence on the levels and trends of infant mortality during the demographic transition, and their relation to the levels and trends of fertility, let us provide a framework for this study by reviewing some of the theories on the subject.

Forms of the Relation between Infant Mortality and Fertility

To explicate the relation between infant and child mortality and fertility, it is convenient to rely on Preston's introduction to a volume devoted to this issue (Preston, 1978). Preston reviews the different effects and summarizes the theories, the empirical findings, and their plausible interpretations. Four mechanisms have been isolated in theory: (1) the child replacement effect; (2) the insurance effect; (3) the physiological effect; and (4) the societal effect.

To establish the existence of these effects and to measure their importance is not an easy task, particularly with aggregate data in which they are confounded. A multitude of additional influences—cultural, socioeconomic, and demographic—confuse the picture further by acting jointly on both mortality and fertility. Still, the study of the decline of fertility in Europe must include an investigation of the possible mechanisms, distinguishing between the situation prior to the fertility decline and after it has begun.

1. *The first type of relation between infant mortality and fertility is in the absence of birth control.* Natural fertility is defined as fertility in the absence of family limitation, where family limitation is a behavior that appears when a certain family size has been reached that the couple does not want to exceed (Henry, 1961). Under conditions of natural fertility, we should not expect to find a strong relation between marital fertility and infant mortality because fertility is not within the calculus of conscious choice (Coale, 1973). Since there is no definite number of children at which the couple aims, *the concept of the replacement child* when an elder has died is illusory. So is the *insurance effect* which would result from parents anticipating the death of a child as they perceive that infant mortality is

high, and as they bear more children to hedge against future losses. When couples are not conscious of family-size goals, the hoarding strategy cannot apply. In sum, before contraception appears within marriage, fertility is not something that can be turned on and off at will in function of experienced or expected parental losses.

There are, however, other reasons to expect to find a relation between infant mortality and marital fertility prior to the exercise of voluntary control. One such reason is the *physiological effect.* A number of writers (among them Gautier and Henry, 1958; Knodel and E. van de Walle, 1967; Van Ginneken, 1978) have emphasized the importance of breast-feeding as an intervening variable connecting the frequency of infant deaths and births. Since breast-feeding tends to delay the return of ovulation, a surviving child should postpone the arrival of a sibling; conversely, a child's death will interrupt lactation, ovulation will resume, and the woman will be once again at risk of pregnancy.

Cultural and institutional practices may reinforce the physiological effect. Medical doctors from antiquity to the nineteenth century recommeded that mothers or wet nurses practice sexual continence during lactation in order to protect the health of the woman and the child (E. van de Walle and F. van de Walle, 1972). Today, postpartum abstinence (sometimes longer than the period of lactation) is regarded as necessary to ensure survival of the child in many traditional African societies (Page and Lesthaeghe, 1981). In some cultures the mother returns to her parents' home while she is nursing. Even when abstinence is not enjoined or the spouses are not separated, breast-feeding and the mere presence of an infant in the home may alter the reproductive behavior of the couples. "Often, mothers allow their baby to sleep at their breast during a part of the night," says a nineteenth-century observer (Struve, 1802). In other words, women may forego their wifely duty because they give priority to their mother's role or because they are tired and overburdened with work taking care of the infant. If the child dies, normal relations with the husband and the risk of pregnancy are resumed. In short, in breast-feeding populations, physiological and behavioral effects link the death of a young child to shorter birth intervals. Among some premodern populations, social customs rejected breast-feeding. For example, in most of Bavaria during the last half of the nineteenth century, nursing was avoided and high mortality and high fertility went hand-in-hand (Knodel, 1968).

Other biological characteristics of a population may also influence the relationship between fertility and mortality. Poor health, which was associated with high mortality in pre-industrial Europe, may have an effect on coital frequency, extend the length of amenorrhea, or lead to a high incidence of pregnancy wastage and pathological sterility. In these situations, high infant mortality may coexist with low fertility.

It should also be considered that fertility may influence mortality, rather than vice versa. Infants of high parity experience higher risks of dying, and infants born after short intervals are subject to higher mortality. An additional complication is provided by infanticide or, at the very least, child neglect. Infanticide is the result of a deliberate decision to kill or let die, but death may also follow from the parents' indifference. Braun alleges that in the eighteenth century, landless cottage workers in the canton of Zurich were not unhappy to see some of their numerous offspring die (Braun, 1978). In a study on abandoned children in Belgium in the same epoch, Hélin calls the trip to the Foundling Hospital a "deferred infanticide" (1973, p. 227). In 1846 in Paris the infant mortality rate of abandoned children was 660 per 1,000 (Armengaud, 1973, p. 308). Among urban and poor populations concealed infanticide may have been a way to control fertility and eliminate illegitimate children (Bergues, 1960; Sauer, 1978; Scrimshaw, 1978; Ware, 1977).

In sum, it seems plausible that natural fertility variations were related to differences in infant mortality through a combination of physiological and behavioral mechanisms. In addition, some authors have referred to a *societal effect*. The community has its own functional norms and customs to ensure the balance between its fertility and mortality levels. "An unconscious rationality," as Wrigley calls it, guarantees the welfare of the group. For example, in a regime of high mortality, to prevent a fall in population a community may need to develop marriage rules which ensure that men (and still more women) marry soon after reaching sexual maturity, regardless of whether their parents are living or not (Wrigley, 1978a, p. 143). The population does not need to be aware of any association between these social customs and their results. Various studies have found a correlation between nuptiality and fertility. From a review of a number of early West European communities, Daniel S. Smith concludes that "this relationship supports Ohlin's hypothesis (1961) linking male age at marriage to mortality through the age of inheritance" (D. S. Smith, 1977, p. 37). And T. Paul Schultz generalizes from the experience of Taiwan to diverse premodern societies:

> To perpetuate society and maintain family lines, in the face of heavy child mortality couples are encouraged to marry and start bearing chil-

dren at an early age. This institutionalized adaptation to the regionally *anticipated* level of mortality relieves individual couples of some of the burden of controlling their fertility within marriage in response to actual child mortality. (Schultz, 1980, p. 230)

But nuptiality is not the sole response to a high mortality environment. Other authors have referred to societal effects without seeming to agree on the definition. Friedlander examined the alternative societal responses to a change in infant mortality (Friedlander, 1977). Migration opportunities, changes in household structure or in the level of economic production may occur and obviate the need to limit fertility. Thus, alternative societal responses, he states, tend to weaken the intensity of the fertility response. For Singarimbum and Hull, the societal effect involves any mechanism by which infant and child mortality encourages high fertility[1] (Singarimbum and Hull, 1977).

At the aggregate level, a relation between nuptiality and infant mortality might be expected to constitute a long-term adaptation mechanism through which population growth can be adjusted to compensate for mortality levels. Thus, the West European pattern of marriage might be interpreted as the ultimate consequence of relatively favorable historical characteristics of the health environment (see Coale, Chapter 1).[2]

2. *An entirely new set of relations between fertility and mortality should prevail after the initiation of controlled fertility.* This is a standard component of the transition theory. Modernization brings a reduction in infant mortality; more children survive, and this creates pressure for fertility control. Awareness of a decline in mortality may not reach the parents immediately, however, and couples may find themselves with more children surviving than they had expected. The theory postulates a time lag of fertility decline behind mortality decline: the time required for parents to adjust to the new conditions of mortality. They become conscious of a desirable size of the family and set for themselves a target number of

[1] Their empirical analysis in Java, however, fails to show any causal relation between high mortality and the social norms related to marriage and fertility.

[2] There is also a link between age at marriage and mortality through the ratio of males to females. Changes in mortality may result in a shortage or an influx of partners. For example, if grooms are typically five years older than their brides, a sudden drop in infant mortality will result in a larger cohort of women. The excess of women in the marriage market will face the choice of being left single or marrying men closer to their own age. Thus, the age at marriage of males will decline. This appears to be an important phenomenon in contemporary developing countries.

children, which they do not want to exceed. Some of the factors that affected natural fertility (such as the effects of lactation, health, abstinence, and social customs) coexist with a new factor, the desire to control fertility. Couples may now choose to replace an infant who died.

If a societal effect has determined marital customs, nuptiality patterns could survive long after mortality differentials have disappeared. If the two are still linked toward the end of the period considered, one would think that they are so through a rather stable and well-established system of customs, affecting both nuptiality and the care of children.

The Choice of the Indexes

1. *Infant mortality.* What indexes of fertility and mortality should we correlate in a study of the relation? Recently Matthiessen and McCann (1978, p. 52) have criticized the use of the infant mortality rate as an index of the survival of children. They note that in most European countries child mortality between 1 and 14, or between 0 and 15, fell before infant mortality, and in certain important cases this preceded the onset of change in infant mortality by as much as a generation. Wrigley (1969) is of the same opinion when he states that infant mortality showed no tendency to fall in most parts of Western Europe until the last years of the century, whereas there were substantial falls in mortality among children and teenagers. For example, in England and Wales the matter seems established: the infant mortality rate is about 150 in 1840 when statistics become available and is still so in 1901; during the same period mortality between 1 and 14 declines steadfastly. Thus, it may have been the decline in child rather than infant mortality that is implicated in the decline of European marital fertility. Although this line of reasoning is valid, some points remain to be clarified.

First, changes in infant mortality may have occurred before the universal inception of vital statistics. Although the data used by Matthiessen and McCann show that a ten percent decline in infant and child mortality usually occurred at the end of the nineteenth century, the possibility of an earlier decline must be considered. Figure 4.1 shows the trend in the probability of dying between birth and age one and between age one and age five (${}_1q_0$ and ${}_4q_1$, respectively, in life table notation) for four countries. France and Sweden, with the longest series of mortality data, experience simultaneous declines in infant and child mortality. In Sweden, child mortality fluctuates more than infant mortality. In France from the first date

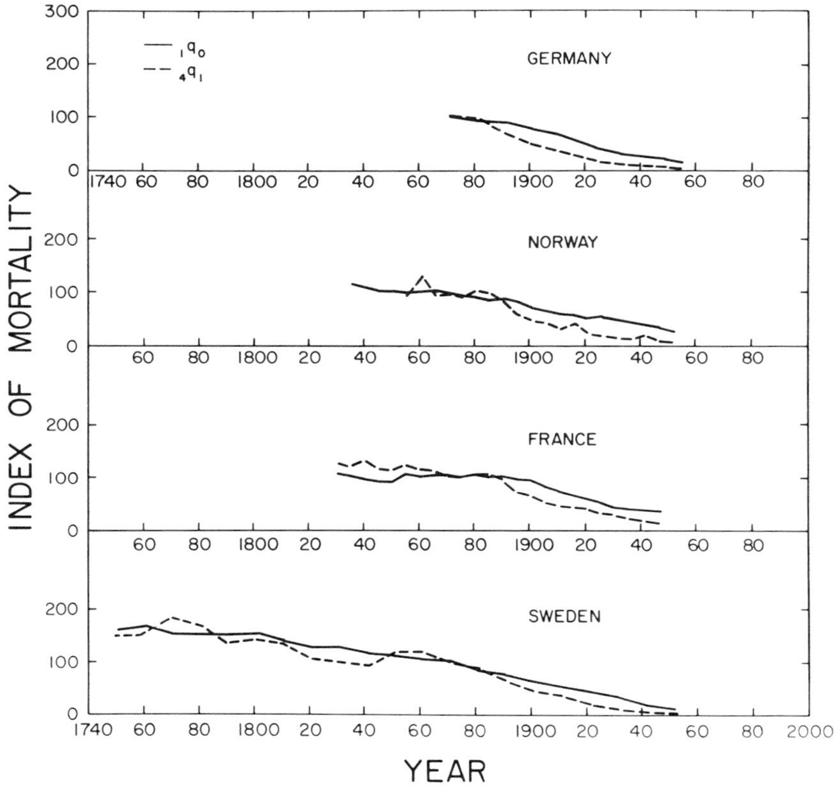

Figure 4.1. Index of infant mortality ($_1q_0$) and child mortality ($_4q_1$), four countries with extended series.

that data are available, the drop in the two measures is significant but the amount of decline in child mortality is larger than that of infant mortality; the same is true for Norway after 1890, and for Germany after 1880. There seems to be unassailable evidence that the decline of child mortality was faster than the decline in infant mortality during the last quarter of the nineteenth century; before that time the evidence is mixed, and the situation may have differed from country to country. One could, at least, speculate on prestatistical era declines in other countries by analogy with France and Sweden.

Second, we must note that the initial levels of infant mortality, and therefore the extent of its early decline, may have been underestimated because of underregistration in the statistics at the time. Infant deaths occurring during the period of heaviest mortality in the first days of life are more likely than any others to slip through unrecorded. In many countries the rates tend to rise during the early era of vital registration. This seems to be true primarily in high-mortality countries; there could well be a relation between the levels of infant mortality and statistical backwardness. A conspicuous example of underregistration occurs in the prov-

Table 4.1. Index of death rates under one year and between one and four years, provinces of the Netherlands: 1840 to 1899 (1875-1879 = 100).

Provinces		1840-51	1850-59	1860-75	1875-79	1880-84	1885-89	1890-94	1895-99
Groningen	A	72	81	91	100	80	69	70	67
	B	118	114	118	100	82	82	71	57
Friesland	A	73	88	98	100	84	73	65	57
	B	115	115	107	100	89	89	70	44
Drente	A	83	95	98	100	93	88	90	90
	B	121	134	124	100	107	103	93	72
Overijssel	A	83	92	98	100	96	94	94	90
	B	112	112	115	100	100	100	88	64
Gelderland	A	78	84	96	100	94	92	90	92
	B	123	119	131	100	88	100	92	73
Utrecht	A	78	89	101	100	94	84	75	66
	B	155	145	145	100	103	107	83	69
Noord-Holland	A	91	100	100	100	96	82	68	56
	B	122	119	111	100	108	92	69	56
Zuid-Holland	A	90	99	104	100	89	75	64	54
	B	126	131	133	100	97	82	72	54
Zeeland	A	113	124	116	100	83	70	68	65
	B	178	163	137	100	85	78	67	52
Noord-Brabant	A	65	71	88	100	101	96	96	96
	B	113	104	117	100	100	104	92	79
Limburg	A	62	85	96	100	96	92	100	106
	B	93	111	111	100	96	71	82	64
Total	A	82	92	99	100	93	82	72	76
	B	123	123	123	100	100	90	77	61

Source: Computed from E. W. Hofstee, 1978a, pp. 213, 214.

Notes: A refers to the number of deaths under one year per mid-year population under one year. B refers to the number of deaths between one and four per mid-year population between one and four years.

inces of the Netherlands (Table 4.1). In the two more socioeconomically advanced provinces of north and south Holland, infant mortality is more or less at a standstill before 1875, and after 1875 its decline matches that of child mortality. In Noord Brabant and Limburg, two rural high-fertility provinces, infant mortality appears to be, respectively, 35 and 38 percent lower in 1840 than in 1875; and after 1875, the apparent decline of child mortality continues to be faster than that of infant mortality.

In view of the uncertainty of the evidence, are there a priori reasons why child mortality should have declined earlier than infant mortality? The impact of smallpox vaccination remains to be measured, but it is likely that it effectively removed, during the nineteenth century, one of the most prevalent causes of mortality in childhood.[3] For infants, however, who benefit from their mother's immunity, vaccination did not have the same impact. Improvements in the quality of food and in hygiene, changes in behavior, and education may also account for the decreases in child mortality. Well-fed children are better able to resist intestinal or pulmonary diseases, while sanitary practices reduce the incidence of infections and illness. In the *département* of Seine in the nineteenth century, child mortality from ages one to four seems an index of sanitary conditions, whereas mortality under one year is a reflection of customs that rule infant feeding (E. van de Walle and Preston, 1974). Improvements in nutrition and in sanitation (mostly water supply and sewage disposal) thus would have a larger effect on child mortality than on infant mortality.

Levels and trends of the two rates may also depend on local customs concerning breast-feeding and the timing of weaning. The age of weaning is a period of heavy risks and may influence the age pattern of mortality under four years. A comparison in the accompanying table between Bavaria and Italy for the period 1876–1885 suggests the respective influences of breast-feeding and of diarrheal diseases due to poor sanitation.

	$_1q_0$	$_4m_1$
Italy	.271	.064
Bavaria	.425	.031

[3] The study of this problem by McKeown (1976) from vital registration statistics starting in 1837 tends to underestimate the possible steep decline following Jenner's discovery prior to that date.

In parts of Bavaria, breast-feeding was practically nonexistent, and nearly half the children died before reaching age one (Knodel, 1970). In Italy breast-feeding was customary, and the timing of weaning was late, according to Livi-Bacci (1977, p. 261). Mortality was high when children gave up suckling and became highly vulnerable to their environment.

Thus, the evolution of infant and child mortality may diverge depending on the factors responsible for regional differences and the responsiveness of these factors to modernization. Survival through childhood, and not just past the first year of life, is what matters to parents. It therefore remains possible that the decline of child mortality has a role in the demographic transition. Unfortunately, statistics on child mortality are rarely available in the nineteenth century at the provincial level. Although infant mortality remains a proxy for juvenile mortality in general, deaths before age one are by far the most important component of survival through childhood.

Beginning here, this paper will deal only with infant mortality.

2. *Marital fertility* (I_g) is an appropriate index to relate to infant mortality. The index of marital fertility (I_g), the index of total fertility (I_f), and the index of the proportion married (I_m) are explained by Coale and Treadway in Chapter 2. In short,

$$I_g = \frac{B_1}{\sum m_i f_i} \qquad I_f = \frac{B}{\sum w_i f_i} \qquad I_m = \frac{\sum m_i f_i}{\sum w_i f_i}$$

where B_1 = annual legitimate births,

B = annual total births,

f_i = the fertility of married Hutterite women in age interval i,

m_i = the number of married women in age interval i,

w_i = the total number of women in age interval i.

First, changes in fertility caused by family limitation are best measured with an index free of the effect of the proportion married. Second, when fertility is controlled, couples make the decision to replace a child who died in order to attain a certain family size and thus the outcome of that decision is appropriately captured by a measure of marital fertility. To test the hypothesis of a societal mechanism linking infant mortality levels and nuptiality patterns, I will subsequently use the indexes of overall fertility (I_f) and the proportion married (I_m).

Levels and Trends of Marital Fertility and Infant Mortality

Schematically, the history of marital fertility in most European countries can be summarized as follows. Prior to a clearly recognizable date of decline, I_g is characterized by a plateau of high level—typically between 70 and 80 percent of the fertility of the married Hutterites, who provide the standard of comparison. Variations among provinces in I_g tended to increase as changes occurred and to decrease when the transition was completed. The decline took place with remarkable simultaneity in the various European countries. With the exception of the forerunner France, and a few latecomers such as Ireland and Albania, most European provinces began the transition to lower marital fertility, signaled by a 10-percent decline in I_g, during a thirty-year span between 1890 and 1920 (Coale and Treadway, Chapter 2). One can plausibly infer that the decline of marital fertility coincided with the appearance of wide-scale family limitation.

Once statistics become available, it is evident that there was great variety in the levels of infant mortality.[4] In about 1870 the range is between 449 in an urban administrative area of Bavaria and 72 in a rural district of Norway. At the end of the nineteenth century, rates were still over 300 in the predominantly Great Russian provinces, while in Scandinavia rates over 100 had by then become the exception. Levels of infant mortality thus differed widely among countries and within countries. Table 4.2 presents the territorial variability of infant mortality among administrative areas in eleven countries at three different dates.

Figure 4.2 shows the diversity of levels and the different slopes of declines in selected European countries after national data become available during the nineteenth century. Some of these countries also have data at the provincial level and appear in Table 4.2. It is noticeable that the national trends hide wide regional differences in levels of infant mortality. Still, national figures illustrate some clear-cut trends:

1. After about 1890 the fall in infant mortality is fast, massive, and irreversible in most countries (whether shown in Figure 4.2 or not). In some Eastern European countries the decline occurs later, about 1920.

2. The decline was steeper in the countries where infant mortality was high to start with and more moderate or later in the countries experiencing a low mortality at early dates. As a result, levels start to converge around

[4] Throughout the entire study the infant mortality rate is the average number of deaths under one year per 1,000 live births during the same period (usually five years).

Table 4.2. Territorial variability in infant mortality rate, selected countries: Around 1870, 1900, and 1930.

		Levels					Variation	
Country	Year	Number of Prov.	Mean	High	Low	Range	Standard Deviation	Coefficient of Variation
Belgium	1900	41	159	286	100	186	49	.308
Denmark	1850	19	129	225	92	133	30	.233
	1901	19	119	162	96	66	19	.160
	1930	22	78	93	63	30	8	.103
England and Wales	1871	45	140	183	106	77	20	.143
	1901	45	130	171	96	75	22	.169
	1931	43	52	74	38	36	9	.173
France	1866	89	178	296	96	200	36	.202
	1901	87	136	207	82	125	25	.184
	1931	90	77	103	51	52	12	.156
Germany	1867	64	237	428	115	313	77	.325
	1900	71	192	312	94	218	49	.255
	1933	66	70	137	45	92	16	.229
Netherlands	1879	11	181	258	122	136	46	.254
	1899	11	141	191	98	93	28	.199
	1930	11	51	70	38	32	11	.216
Norway	1875	20	115	184	77	107	27	.255
	1900	20	98	163	71	92	24	.245
	1930	20	51	92	35	57	13	.256
Russia	1897	50	260	415	147	268	.067	.258
Spain	1900	49	189	270	102	168	.036	.191
Sweden	1870	25	148	253	96	157	.031	.209
	1900	25	100	169	74	95	.022	.220
	1930	25	55	80	44	36	10	.182
Switzerland	1870	25	210	357	142	215	.050	.238
	1900	25	137	197	84	113	.026	.190
	1930	25	53	85	38	47	.013	.245
Total Provinces	1870	298	175	428	77	351	.058	.331
	1900	394	159	415	71	344	.062	.390
	1930	302	65	137	35	102	.017	.262

Sources: The infant mortality rates for the Netherlands, Norway, Spain, Sweden and England and Wales (in 1931) were computed by the author from national vital statistics. The infant mortality rates for the other countries were computed in the course of the European Fertility Project.

Notes: The infant mortality rate is the ratio of deaths under one year in a given time period for 1,000 live births in the same period. Spain is not included in the total.

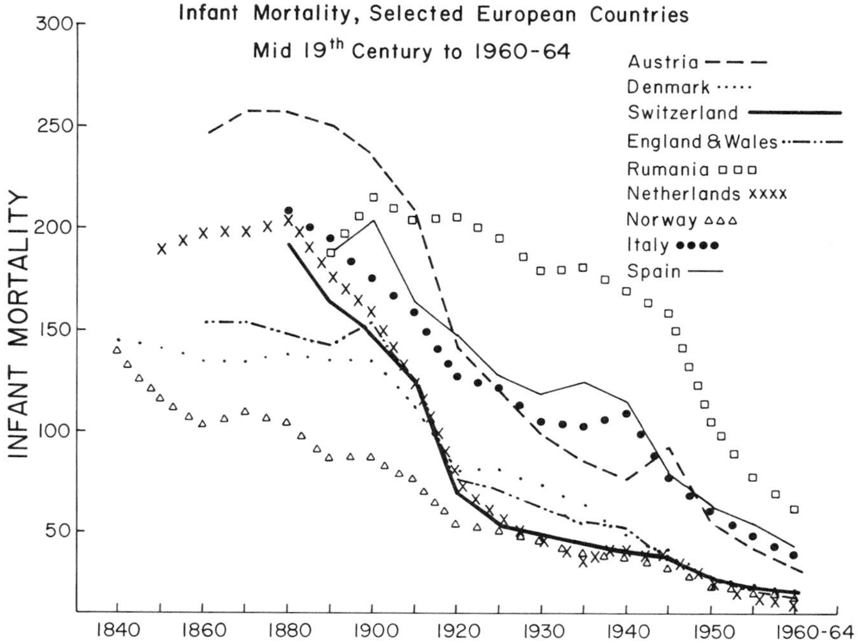

Figure 4.2. Infant mortality, selected European countries; mid-nineteenth century to 1960–1964.

the turn of the century and converge definitively in the 1950s. Typically, the absolute decline in infant mortality was between 150 and 220 points in the high mortality group, compared to 115 to 130 in the low mortality group.

3. Before 1890 the trends differ widely among countries. In several countries, the curve of infant mortality shows an upward trend in the beginning, which strongly suggests improving registration. (As noted before, infant deaths are commonly among the least completely reported vital events.) The three countries with the lowest rates experience plateaus interrupted by short declines. In Austria, Belgium, and the Netherlands there is no recorded decline before the dramatic fall; by contrast, in Italy and in Switzerland the decline is steep since the beginning of published statistics.

In most instances we are left ignorant of past trends: the data do not allow us to go back in time and the existence of an earlier decline cannot be ascertained. Yet data on infant mortality are available for three countries since the middle of the eighteenth century and for Prussia since 1806;

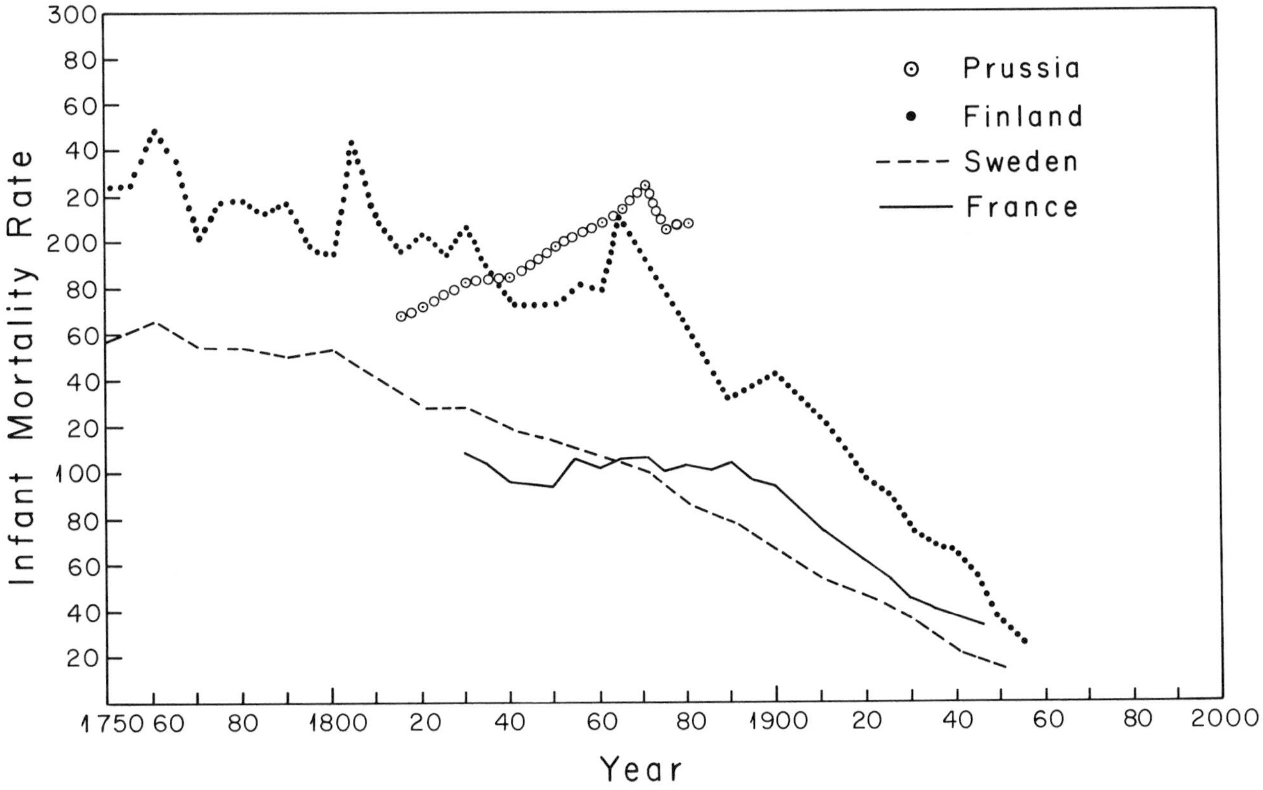

Figure 4.3. Infant mortality rates for four countries with extended series.

these are shown in Figure 4.3. In pre-industrial Europe, infant mortality rates were subject to large fluctuations: epidemics, famines, and wars caused sudden rises in mortality even in the first year of life. In France, infant mortality started to decline at the end of the Old Regime, ca. 1790; by 1850, however, the trend leveled off, and no further change occurred until 1880. In Sweden, the decline was continuous since the beginning of the nineteenth century. Finland illustrates a slow, hesitant kind of decline between the mid-eighteenth and mid-nineteenth centuries, with peaks in time of war (1808–1809) or famine (1832). The last crisis, a combination of crop failure and epidemics, ravaged Finland during the years 1867–1868; the crude death rate reached an extraordinary 78 per 1,000, but infant mortality rose less than adult mortality. Overall, Finland shows a net tendency toward declining infant mortality since 1750. In Prussia, by contrast, the infant mortality rate shows a rather steady increase lasting for more than half a century. John Knodel (1974, p. 160) discusses the genuineness of this increase in view of past underregistration of infant deaths and of contemporary arguments such as the worsening situation of the working class. Knodel concludes that the available evidence contains no indication that infant mortality really declined in Prussia between 1816 and 1875. Apart from Prussia, the existing evidence on infant mortality reveals declines before 1850. There are not enough data for other countries to judge whether mortality was declining or not.

In sum, the exact date of decline in infant mortality is difficult to pinpoint because of irregularities in its course and because of scarcity of documents prior to the last decades of the nineteenth century. Before the general massive drop in this century, there were wide differences in levels and trends of infant mortality among European regions, among countries, and within each country.

Urban versus Rural Mortality

An important and widespread differential that exists at the provincial level is the urban-rural one, for which documentation is generally available. Infant mortality was higher in towns and cities than in the countryside, a trend that reverses itself at the time of the abrupt fall in infant mortality. Urbanization occupies a special place in theories of the fertility decline (see Sharlin, Chapter 5). On the one hand, marital fertility in most provinces declines first in the cities; on the other hand, mortality levels in the cities—particularly infant and child mortality levels—were generally higher than in the countryside in the nineteenth century. Thus, the theory must resolve this apparent contradiction.

The issue is tackled by Gosta Carlsson (1966, pp. 166–169). In Sweden, the survival chances to age 15 were "appallingly bad" in Stockholm before 1860; but they improved dramatically thereafter, and by 1920 they were better than in rural areas.[5] Carlsson explains the earlier decline of fertility in the cities not so much by the levels of infant mortality, which should have resulted in higher urban fertility during the entire period, as by the speed of the decline. It is not the precise demographic impact of mortality on family size that counted, but the strength of the psychological stimulus. But the evidence in Table 4.3 on urban-rural differentials in infant mortality suggests that they were not drastically reduced before the twentieth century. Even if we trust Carlsson's data for Stockholm, it is unlikely that urban parents would have interpreted a change in the probability of surviving to age 15 from 0.5 to 0.6 as a powerful signal to limit their family size. (Out of five children born in an average family in Stockholm, the number of survivors may have jumped between 1870 and 1890 from 2.5 to 3.0, hardly a spectacular change.) One should look for more powerful causes for the early decline in urban fertility. At this stage, I suggest that factors associated with urbanization influenced both fertility and infant mortality, but that there was no clear direct causal link between the two variables.

There are several intriguing aspects of urban versus rural infant mortality. First, there are differences in age-specific mortality under one year. During the first month of life and particularly during the first week, differences are small and, when they exist, it is to the advantage of the urban population. After the first month, however, the risks of dying are much higher in the cities (Ulmer, 1927, p. 85; Knodel, 1974). These differences can be attributed to the different causes of neonatal and postneonatal deaths. It would seem that the older infants would be more vulnerable to the poor hygiene of the city and to density-related diseases. Second, illegitimacy, which was far more widespread in the cities, may be blamed for a part of the urban-rural differences. In Germany in the 1870s, the illegitimate infant mortality was 62 percent higher than the legitimate rate and the difference increased by the turn of the century (Knodel, 1974, p. 167). Third, the larger the city, the higher the infant mortality rate. Fourth,

[5] It should be noted that Carlsson's survival rates are derived directly from the infant mortality rate.

Table 4.3. Index of urban infant mortality rate, selected countries (Rural = 100).

Date	Sweden	Finland	Norway	Prussia	Bavaria	Date
1811-20	137	--	--	--	--	--
1821-30	139	--	--	--	--	--
1831-40	142	--	--	--	--	--
1841-50	151	--	--	--	--	--
1851-60	160	--	142*	--	--	--
1861-70	152	--	136	116	104	1862-70
1871-80	162	--	148	121	103	1876-77
1881-90	146	125	149	118	102	1878-82
1891-00	137	125	152	113	96	1888-92
1901-10	126	124	145	108	96	1898-02
1911-20	113	112	136	96	86	1908-12
1921-30	98	89	115	94	75	1923-27
1931-40	82	77	105	102	72	1928-32
1941-50	86	88	93	--	76	1933-37
1951-60	89	--	86	--	--	--

*1856-60.

Sources:

Sweden: Historik Statistik for Sverige, Part One, Population, 1720-1967. National Bureau of Statistics, 1969.
Norway: Trend of Mortality and Causes of Death in Norway, 1856-1955. Central Bureau of Statistics of Norway, 1961.
Finland: Statistiksk Arsbok for Finland, NY Serie-LXVIII-AR 1952. Utgiven av Statistiska Centralbyran, 1953, p. 52.
Prussia and Bavaria: Knodel, 1974, p. 169.

earlier and steeper declines in the cities reversed the differentials in high mortality regions (Bavaria) by the turn of the century, and in low mortality regions (Scandinavia) by around 1900–1920.

The pre-decline differences in urban and rural infant mortality seem due less to the healthiness of the rural environment than to the disadvantages of the urban environment. The crowded nineteenth-century cities were nests of infections, where physical contacts made the transmission of airborne and contagious diseases easy and where epidemics spread quickly. Hygiene and the quality of water were poor, sewage disposal systems were nonexistent. Mothers worked long hours outside the home, infants were weaned early or, as in France, sent to be fed and often to die in the neighboring countryside. The custom of using mercenary wet nurses gave way during the late nineteenth century at the time of the invention of pasteurization of milk.

It would be interesting to trace the course of infant or child mortality in the cities of Europe to study their determinants, but that is not the object of this paper. It is certain, however, that infant mortality was higher in urban than in rural areas at the beginning of the period under review, while marital fertility (I_g) was usually lower. By the end of the period, both infant mortality and marital fertility were lower in urban than in rural areas. Where cities and towns account for a substantial proportion of the administrative units involved, and where sharp differentials in fertility and mortality exist between cities and countryside, this may strongly influence the sign and the degree of the correlation coefficients computed in the next sections.

We shall now consider two essential questions. The first concerns the relation between levels of infant mortality and either marital or overall fertility. The second question asks whether the fall in infant mortality preceded the decline in fertility and therefore can be considered to have induced the desire for family limitation.

Relation between Levels of Infant Mortality and Fertility

1. *Marital fertility.* Earlier we suggested that the levels of infant mortality and marital fertility (I_g) should not be strongly related in the pretransitional era. As the decline progresses (perhaps by 1900) and as family limitation becomes widespread, we would expect couples to adjust their fertility to the levels of mortality prevailing in the area: this would lead

to a positive relation between mortality and marital fertility. Finally, as infant mortality reaches low levels by 1930, its effect on desired family size should disappear, although high fertility and high mortality might survive together in some more backward provinces of Europe.

Figure 4.4 shows the relation between marital fertility (I_g) and infant mortality, in a series of European countries, at three dates: 1870, 1900, and 1930. In the nineteenth century, national levels of marital fertility were generally not related to levels of infant mortality; this absence of significant correlation reflects the scatter of points in the left part of Figure 4.4. In 1870 there was a wide variety of infant mortality levels; national levels of marital fertility show little impact of family limitation. Alone in Europe, France has reduced its marital fertility and stands isolated on the graph. The next two graphs in Figure 4.4 lead us into a new era: changing values of both indexes can be observed. By 1900 about half of the countries had started their long-term decline in marital fertility; by 1930 substantial reductions had been attained in almost every country. As noted earlier, the fall in infant mortality in most countries began after 1890,

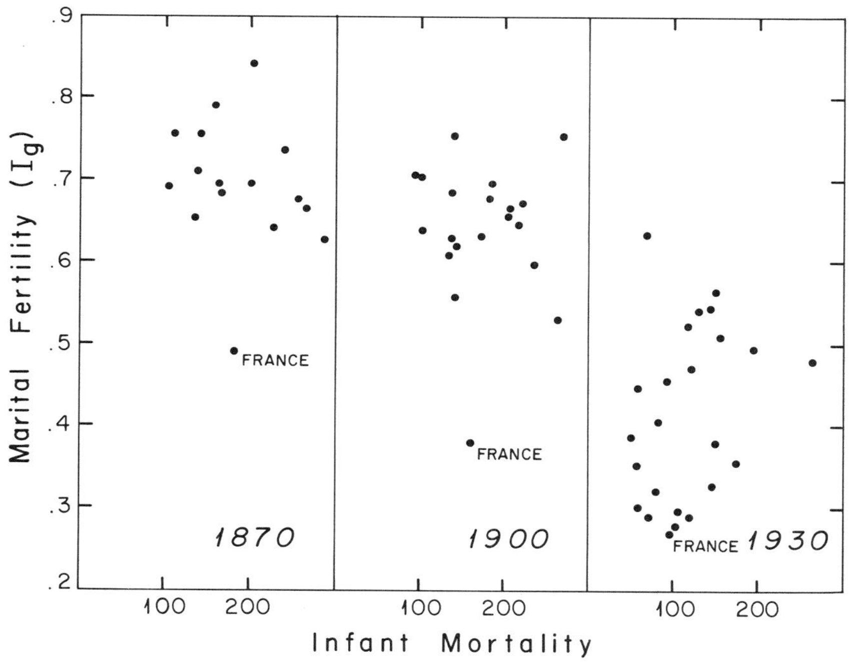

Figure 4.4. Scattergram relating I_g to infant mortality, selected countries of Europe.

which clearly suggests that the two are related. Nonetheless, these graphs show no clear relation between the level of the two variables among countries at a point in time; infant mortality was not lowest in those countries where marital fertility was also lowest. An extreme case would be Ireland, where marital fertility did not decline before the 1920s, despite relatively low infant mortality. Zero-order correlations at the national level are weak, although in the expected direction: $r = 0.22$ in 1870, 0.07 in 1900, and 0.25 in 1930.

At the provincial level, correlations are sometimes stronger and sometimes weaker than at the national level, but they are not always in the expected direction. It is most interesting that the correlations generally become larger and more significant over time. Correlations for selected countries at the provincial level are shown in Table 4.4. In the first column, under the heading 1870, are the correlations for the earliest dates for which I_g and infant mortality could be computed by province. Except in France, they are assumed to represent an era prior to, or at the very beginning of, the decline of fertility. In general, the correlations are weak. Only Germany and the Netherlands show a significant positive correlation, one that will hold consistently through time. In a special study of Bavarian districts, Knodel and E. van de Walle found a strong positive correlation, which they attributed in part to breast-feeding customs, what we can call the physiological effect of interrupted nursing (Knodel and E. van de Walle, 1967). However, the correlation persisted even when restricted to those districts where breast-feeding was uncommon, suggesting that the relation between infant mortality and marital fertility may sometimes be independent of the physiological mechanism. Correlations in the Netherlands grow stronger with time, but the lower coefficient of 1870 may be an artifact of underregistration of infant deaths. The highest fertility in the country was, in the nineteenth century, coupled with low rates of infant mortality in the two most isolated and socioeconomically backward provinces. Infant mortality increased in these areas thereafter and became the highest in the Netherlands in 1900 (see Table 4.1).

Under the headings 1900 and 1930 correlations are usually significant, although sometimes negative. The Scandinavian countries repeatedly exhibit negative correlations, quite strong in Denmark and Norway in 1900, although there is a reversal in 1930, which is especially striking for Sweden. The existence of one large capital city, where infant mortality was especially high in 1900 but especially low by 1930, accounts for this reversal. In Scandinavia, capital cities constitute the most populous administrative

Table 4.4. Infant mortality rate, correlations with marital fertility (I_g), selected countries, by province: Around 1870, 1900, and 1930.

	1870		1900		1930	
Country	N	r	N	r	N	r
Belgium	--	--	41	.575***	--	--
Denmark	19	-.134	19	-.677**	22	-.025
England & Wales	45	.090	45	.174	43	.614**
France	89	.007	87	.281**	90	.310**
Germany	64	.545**	71	.219*	66	.473**
Netherlands	11	.634*	11	.798**	11	.910**
Norway	20	.327	20	-.409*	20	.166
Russia	--	--	50	.399**	--	--
Spain	--	--	49	.110	--	--
Sweden	25	.126	25	-.027	25	.523**
Switzerland	25	-.038	25	.209	25	.557**
Total Provinces	298	.156**	443	.383**	302	.078

* Significant at the .05 level.
** Significant at the .005 level.

Notes: For each set of correlations, the infant mortality index refers to the same period as that of the marital fertility index; there are few exceptions when infant deaths and births were not available for the same period. In those instances, the registration period for infant mortality precedes that of the marital fertility index.

Between countries there is a variability of dates as fertility indexes were, as a rule, computed around census years. These dates are as follows:

Belgium: 1900
Denmark: 1850, 1901, 1930
England & Wales: 1871, 1901, 1931
France: 1866, 1901, 1931
Germany: 54 units in 1867 and 10 in 1880, 1900, 1933
Netherlands: 1879, 1899, 1930
Norway: 1875, 1900, 1930
Russia: 1897
Spain: 1900
Sweden: 1880, 1900, 1930
Switzerland: 1870, 1900, 1930

Spain is not included in the total.

areas. As with other cities, they show low marital fertility and a changing infant mortality rate, high in 1870, low in 1930. In the rural districts the range in infant mortality is small (for example, in 1870 the range in Denmark with Copenhagen is 133 and without Copenhagen it is 53). Consequently, the drastic changes in urban infant mortality after 1900 heavily influence the sign of the correlation coefficients. In Sweden, Stockholm has, in 1870, one of the lowest levels of I_g coupled with an infant mortality of 253, nearly three times higher than in the rural districts; in 1930 the infant mortality rate in Stockholm is 44, one of the lowest of the country.

Belgium in 1900 deserves a special comment. The correlation is positive and significant among Belgian administrative areas (*arrondissements*), but it dwindles to insignificance in each of the two linguistic regions ($r =$ 0.135 in French-speaking areas, and -0.005 in the Dutch-speaking areas) (Lesthaeghe, 1977, p. 176). The clustering of areas by linguistic regions is responsible for the correlation.

Infant mortality was comparatively low in the western provinces of Russia, even though it was high by European standards: 214 per thousand births as late as 1908–1910; there had been no decline since 1867–1881 (Coale, Anderson and Härm, 1979, p. 67). The western provinces are also those where marital fertility declined first. These two variables do not have a clear causal connection between themselves; rather, both variables may have a common association with another factor, in this instance a cultural one.

As the decline of marital fertility progressed, more and more countries experienced a positive relation between infant mortality and I_g, which became increasingly significant as high mortality areas also preserved high fertility. Switzerland illustrates this fact. A number of isolated Alpine and economically backward cantons retained exceptionally high levels of fertility and infant mortality up to the 1960s. On the other hand, more highly modernized regions had reached low levels of both variables, very likely because of the common influence of economic factors. As an example, in 1960 the canton of Uri still had a marital fertility index of 0.505 and an infant mortality rate of 31, while the canton of Basel had reached low rates of 0.263 and 18, respectively. By 1930, the cities in all countries that had long experienced higher infant mortality have both low infant mortality and low marital fertility; this contributed to consistently positive, and usually significant correlations.

2. *Overall fertility and the proportion married.* Let us now investigate the relation between infant mortality and overall fertility (I_f) independent of marital fertility (I_g). This, in the system of fertility indexes used in the Princeton European Fertility Project and discussed in Chapter 2, is tantamount to investigating the earlier-mentioned hypothesis of a societal effect that would operate through a relation between the proportion married (I_m) and infant mortality. Table 4.5 reports the findings on this point. The positive relation between nuptiality and mortality surfaces occasionally, but no more frequently than an inverse relation that is difficult to explain a priori.

Finally and most importantly, Table 4.6 highlights the relation between overall fertility (I_f) and infant mortality, which is generally positive with the exception of Denmark. Where, as in Germany and the Netherlands, high levels of mortality coexist with high marital fertility, this is somehow complemented by low proportions married (I_m). In England and Wales the positive, long-lasting relation is carried on through nuptiality. Switzerland provides an interesting evolution from positive to negative relation between nuptiality and mortality, but overall fertility and infant mortality

Table 4.5. Infant mortality rate, correlations with proportion married (I_m), selected countries, by province: Around 1870, 1900, and 1930.

Country	1870 N	1870 r	1900 N	1900 r	1930 N	1930 r
Belgium	--	--	41	-.231	--	--
Denmark	19	-.299	19	-.322	22	.433*
England & Wales	45	.521**	45	.659**	43	.344*
France	89	.178*	87	-.207*	90	-.184*
Germany	64	-.460**	71	-.280*	66	-.232*
Netherlands	11	-.166	11	-.800**	11	-.330
Norway	20	.083	20	.026	20	.368
Russia	--	--	50	.305*	--	--
Spain	--	--	49	.310*	--	--
Sweden	25	-.313	25	.015	25	.380*
Switzerland	25	.526**	25	.199	25	-.485*
Total Provinces	298	-.021	443	.491**	302	.408**

Note: See Table 4.4.

Table 4.6. Infant mortality rate, correlations with overall fertility (I_f), selected countries, by province: Around 1870, 1900, and 1930.

	1870		1900		1930	
Country	N	r	N	r	N	r
Belgium	--	--	41	.668**	--	--
Denmark	19	-.329	19	-.528*	22	.117
England & Wales	45	.438**	45	.514**	43	.671**
France	89	.125	87	.342**	90	.297**
Germany	64	.413**	71	.255*	66	.588*
Netherlands	11	.878**	11	.369	11	.853**
Norway	20	.287	20	-.050	20	.420**
Russia	--	--	50	.423**	--	--
Spain	--	--	49	.656**	--	--
Sweden	25	.086	25	.209	25	.721**
Switzerland	25	.472*	25	.301	25	.499*
Total Provinces	298	.232**	443	.685**	302	.439**

Note: See Table 4.4.

retain the strong positive correlation throughout, thanks to the evolution of marital fertility (Table 4.7). The nature of the mechanisms involved is mysterious, but they appear to be powerful. For most European countries, then, the correlations between I_f or I_m on one hand and infant mortality on the other, are very strong in 1900 and 1930 at the provincial level.

The relations are evident even at the level of nations, as shown in Figures 4.5 and 4.6. The distribution of I_m along the vertical axis in Figure 4.5 reflects a well-known geographical distribution between Eastern and Western Europe in the age pattern of female marriage. All we are really saying here is that countries in Eastern and Southern Europe were characterized in 1870, 1900, and 1930 both by early marriage and by a high infant mortality. (Countries of Southern and Eastern Europe are conspicuously absent from the tables showing correlations at the provincial level.) Whether there is a causal relation between the two is by no means certain. It would be fascinating to discover that the Western and Eastern European patterns of marriage were ultimately adaptations to the levels of mortality, but there is hardly sufficient evidence for such a sweeping statement.

3. *Relation between declines in infant mortality and in marital fertility.* I now return to our theoretical relation between infant mortality and

Table 4.7. Infant mortality rate, correlations with demographic indexes, by canton, Switzerland: 1870 to 1960.

	Correlation Coefficients between Infant Mortality and ...		
Census Date	Overall Fertility I_f	Marital Fertility I_g	Proportion Married I_m
1870	.472	-.038	.526
1880	.396	.092	.449
1888	.445	.140	.469
1900	.301	.209	.119
1910	.348	.384	-.255
1920	.544	.589	-.317
1930	.499	.557	-.485
1941	.444	.562	-.711
1950	.295	.439	-.508
1960	.432	.483	-.288

Source: F. van de Walle, manuscript.

marital fertility. Although the test of the relation between levels of the two variables is not conclusive, some countries show an association that strengthened as the decline progressed.

Table 4.8 compares relative changes in infant mortality and marital fertility during two periods, before 1900 and from 1900 to 1930 (1910 for Belgium). If the declines of the two variables were parallel, there should be a correlation in each period. Results are inconsistent, to say the least. The various correlation coefficients are low, and when they are significant they are sometimes difficult to explain. Before 1900 the only significant coefficient is found in the Netherlands. Others are very weak or negative.

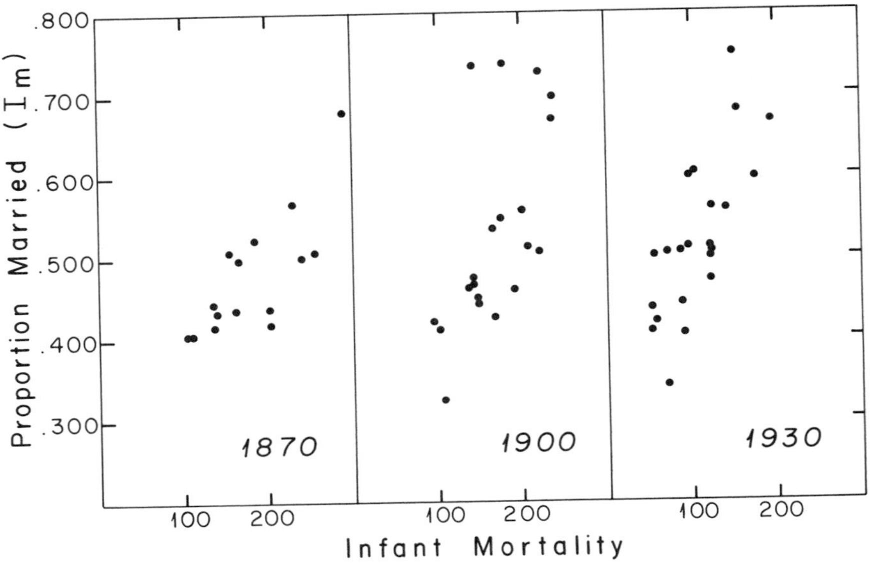

Figure 4.5. Scattergram relating I_m to infant mortality, selected countries of Europe.

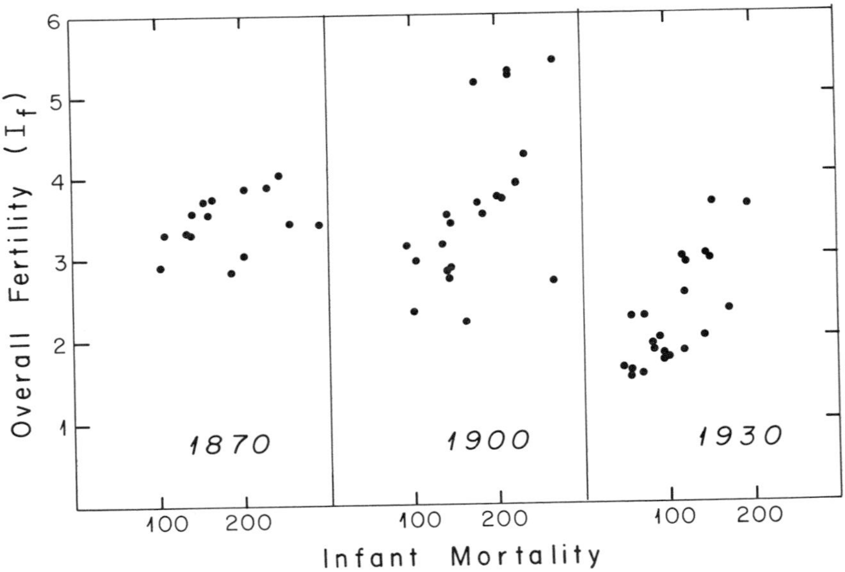

Figure 4.6. Scattergram relating I_f to infant mortality, selected countries of Europe.

Table 4.8. Relative change in infant mortality rate, correlation with relative change in marital fertility (I_g), selected countries, by province: 1870 to 1930.

Country	Δ IMR Exact Date	Correlation Coefficients Δ I_g First Period	Second Period
Belgium			
Flanders	1890-1900	-.168	+.125
	1900-1910	-.007	+.086
Wallonia	1890-1900	-.296	-.325
	1900-1910	-.283	-.443
Denmark	1850-1900	-.013	-.251
	1900-1930	+.660**	+.082
England	1871-1901	-.068	-.060
	1901-1931	+.146	+.308*
France	1866-1901	+.154	-.188
	1901-1931	+.034	+.043
Germany	1867-1901	+.165	-.444**
	1901-1933	+.160	+.415**
Netherlands	1879-1899	+.909**	-.809
	1899-1929	+.176	-.077
Norway	1875-1900	-.151	+.371
	1900-1930	+.320	-.163
Sweden	1880-1900	-.030	+.325
	1900-1930	+.389*	+.175
Switzerland	1870-1900	-.030	-.389*
	1900-1930	+.325	+.175

*Significant at the .05 level.
**Significant at the .005 level.

After 1900, when the stage is set for a precipitous drop in both mortality and fertility for most countries, only England and Germany show a significant relation. Besides, in three countries there is a relation between the reduction in infant mortality before 1900 and the decrease in fertility in the period 1900–1930 (Norway, Sweden, and Switzerland). This raises the question of antecedence. A few remarks on different countries might add some insight to our conclusions.

Table 4.9 presents for three countries the order of the onset of infant mortality and fertility declines, given by the dates at which the indexes decline by 10 percent from their pre-transition plateau, never to recover to their previous level. In Switzerland infant mortality dropped first in a majority of the districts. The mean dates of decline were, respectively, 1883 for infant mortality and 1899 for marital fertility, or a lag of sixteen years. Moreover, various time indicators of the decline of infant mortality (dates of 10-percent decline, 50-percent decline, and date when infant mortality reached 100 per thousand) are consistently correlated with the date of the 10-percent decline of marital fertility (r is respectively 0.364, 0.498, and 0.437). The relation does not wash out when cultural or socio-economic variables are taken into account (F. van de Walle, manuscript). In sum, we find in Switzerland the kind of textbook case we were looking for: no relationship before the onset of family limitation, a decline of infant mortality that precedes and therefore also possibly causes the decline of marital fertility, and a positive relation that becomes increasingly significant as the decline progresses.

In Germany, infant mortality declines first in 36 administrative areas (Knodel, 1974, p. 180) and marital fertility declines first in 34. Therefore,

Table 4.9. Order of the onset of the infant mortality and marital fertility declines.

Country	Number of Units	Infant Mortality Declines First	Marital Fertility (I_g) Declines First	Both at the Same Time
Switzerland	181	172	8	1
Germany	71	36	34	1
Belgium	9	1	8	-

Note: Units are "districts" in Switzerland and Germany and "provinces" in Belgium.

the comparison of the dates indicates that the decline in infant mortality could not have been an initiating cause of fertility decline in over half the provinces. On the other hand, during the entire period, correlations between levels of infant mortality and marital fertility were positive. In Prussia a strong association in the amount of change between each variable appears in the correlation between the decline in marital fertility by 10 percent and (1) the decline in infant mortality by 10 percent ($r = 0.379$), and (2) its decline by 50 points ($r = 0.542$) (Knodel, 1974, p. 184).

In Belgium and in England (not in the table) the situation is clear-cut. In the former, with the exception of the province of Limburg, the decline in marital fertility preceded the change in infant mortality. Moreover, correlations between levels of the two indexes are nonexistent or negative and no association can be found between the changes in both variables. Lesthaeghe concludes that infant mortality played a rather insignificant role in the history of the marital fertility transition in Belgium (Lesthaeghe, 1977, p. 175). In England, Teitelbaum notes, "The really substantial decline in both infant and child mortality took place in the decades after the turn of the century long after the onset of the decline in marital fertility" (Teitelbaum, 1984).

In comparison, Sweden and the Netherlands experience the opposite situation: an earlier decline in infant mortality. Yet, is it possible to argue from antecedence to causality? In Sweden infant mortality started to fall almost a century before marital fertility—why, then, did not fertility decline sooner if it is the number of surviving children that counts? In the Netherlands both rates were high at the end of the nineteenth century and both declines were late. Infant mortality started to fall a decade before fertility, around the turn of the century. We suspect that both declines were a consequence of modernization and that in 1910 Dutch fertility was ready to fall independently of infant mortality.

The problem of finding an appropriate index to measure the sequence of the declines is complex at the European level. The date at which infant mortality and marital fertility decline by 10 percent from their pretransition plateau is a relevant index in some countries: in Germany and in Switzerland, for example, it works because statistics are reliable and there is little fluctuation in the fall of infant mortality. But in other countries data are often of poor quality and irregularities exist in the course of the infant mortality rate. Besides, the dates of the creation of a civil registration system vary widely among countries (from mid-eighteenth century to World War II) and we do not know about past levels of mortality or eventual declines. An alternative is to use the date at which a certain level of infant mortality and marital fertility were reached. In Table 4.10 the dates at which infant mortality reaches 100 are correlated with those at which marital fertility (I_g) fell to 0.600. These dates often correspond approximately to the time at which both infant mortality and marital fertility undergo their transitional fall to lower modern levels. The results are far from conclusive. Except for the recurrent negative coefficients found in the Scandinavian countries, correlations coefficients are usually positive. Only three countries show a significant relationship between the dates of the declines, as measured by the time when the above levels were reached.

To conclude this section, Table 4.11 gives dates of decline at the national level for nineteen countries. We call attention to two points. First, all countries except France and Hungary reached an I_g of 0.600 during a 34-year span, while the 100-points mark in infant mortality was reached during a span of 71 years. Southern and eastern countries experience a later decline in infant mortality while sharing more or less the same dates of decline in marital fertility with the northern and western countries. Second, there is no clear relation between the two declines. The dates in the marital fertility column are not consecutive. Infant mortality falls to 100 before marital fertility falls to 0.600 in only three countries. The issue of a causal relationship between the decline in infant mortality and marital fertility remains unresolved. This does not mean that the indexes were not related at some point during the course of the decline. Sometimes infant mortality was the forerunner in the decline, sometimes it was

Table 4.10. Correlations between dates of decline in infant mortality and marital fertility (I_g), selected countries.

Denmark	-.496*	Netherlands	.728*
England	.085	Norway	-.275
France	.146	Sweden	.213
Germany	.220*	Switzerland	.331*

*Significant at the 0.5 level.

Note: The dates are those at which infant mortality reaches 100 and marital fertility (I_g) = .600.

Table 4.11. Dates of decline in infant mortality and in marital fertility (I_g), selected countries.

Country	Infant Mortality Falls to 100	Marital Fertility (I_g) Falls to .600
Norway	1882	1913
Sweden	1896	1904
Ireland	1900	1928
Switzerland	1912	1901
Denmark	1913	1901
Netherlands	1913	1914
England & Wales	1914	1894
Finland	1921	1914
France	1925	1831
Germany	1926	1905
Belgium	1928	1895
Austria	1932	1908
Greece	1940	1916
Italy	1944	1916
Spain	1944	1916
Portugal	1950	1921
Bulgaria	1951	1914
Rumania	1953	1908

Sources: Infant Mortality: Institut national de la statistique et des études économiques, 1966.
I_g: Table 2.5, Chapter 2 (Coale and Treadway).

marital fertility. In other circumstances the declines were synchronous. Yet characteristically the massive declines of this century occurred simultaneously in infant mortality and in marital fertility in all countries. No systematic causal relation can be posited, but modern western nations sooner or later witnessed both declines.

Conclusions

In view of this uncertain statistical evidence, it is interesting to ask where the general opinion reflected by Freedman's quote, given at the beginning of this paper, might have originated. Why the widespread assumption that fertility came down as a result of the mortality decline?

It may well be a generalization based on the behavior and motivation of contemporary populations. In modern contracepting populations, it is reasonable to expect that couples will replace a child who dies. This notion may have been extrapolated to the past, despite the possible anachronism involved. There was also, of course, a coincidence between the trends in marital fertility and in infant mortality. That irreversible changes in levels of the two rates occurred during the same relatively short time span may have prompted theoreticians to look for a causal relation.

On the other hand, the argument is old. Early population theorists stressed the dependence of births upon deaths. In the 1770s, J. L. Muret, minister of Vevey, made a laborious search in the registers of different parishes in the Pays de Vaud that left him perplexed. "But whence comes it that the country where children escape the best from dangers of infancy . . . should be precisely that in which fertility is the smallest?" (Muret, 1766, p. 68). Muret conjectured that a special providence was called into action to render women less prolific in healthy countries. A quarter of a century later Malthus retorted to Muret that ". . . as experience warrants, the smaller mortality of healthy and improved countries is balanced by the greater prevalence of the prudential restraint on marriage and population" (Malthus, [1830] 1960, p. 48). Since population size has to be kept within bounds, he concluded that the most healthy countries, because their fecundity is lower, will not be overpopulated; the unhealthy countries would be able to sustain their population by their extraordinary fecundity (Malthus, [1830] 1960, p. 68). Stressing continence as the first element of the law of compensation reflects the moral and socioeconomic thought of the early nineteenth century.

The time of inception of vital registration coincided with a general recognition of a need for statistical information. In mid-nineteenth-century Europe a more rational concept of life and a quest for national efficiency convinced statisticians that high levels of infant mortality were a national disgrace. Swiss statisticians, for example, were very concerned with the causes of the numerous deaths occurring among children. They thought remedies were not to be found in medical treatment but in a better quality of life. The relation between numbers of births and numbers of deaths was routinely acknowledged; in the 1870s people were told that "if more infants survive, fewer infants will be begot and the capital spent on the deceased will be used more efficiently" (*Statistique de la Suisse* [1878], p. XIX), or that "it is less important to aim at a large number of births than to endow society with a new generation, strong and healthy" (*Statis-*

tique de la Suisse [1901], p. 34). This literature is indicative of the ambiguity that existed concerning the relation between infant mortality and fertility. Did the level of infant mortality influence fertility? Or did high parity lead to numerous infant deaths? The *Statistique de la Suisse* (1878) reports that medical doctors were concerned that inadequate nutrition or housing, and lack of hygiene and education were among the causes of high infant mortality; but it concluded that repeated pregnancies were the primary factor, because mothers of high parity were weak and gave birth to unhealthy babies.

Rightly or wrongly, Swiss statisticians and medical doctors believed in a close relation between births and infant deaths. They tested their theory by comparing birth rates and infant mortality rates. When the cantons were ranked according to the level of infant mortality, the birth rate fell in the right order, with a few exceptions (industrial cantons experienced exceptionally high rates, and some Alpine agricultural cantons exceptionally low rates). Table 4.7 confirms the view of the Swiss statisticians. Infant mortality and overall fertility are continuously related, thanks to the proportion married in the nineteenth century, and to marital fertility after 1900.

The Swiss statisticians, however, did not distinguish betweeen marital fertility and overall fertility. They argued about the spacing of childbearing in marriage, but when it came to providing statistical evidence, they relied on the relation between the birth rate and infant mortality. These early theoreticians of the demographic transition were not concerned with marital fertility: they discussed societal survival rather than the motivation of couples. They were looking for global mechanisms through which the institutions might adapt to the level of mortality by insuring that enough children would be produced to fill the gaps created by the losses due to epidemics, famines, and the generally poor level of hygiene and child care. In general, our results are in line with this view. In most countries, we find that infant mortality retains a relation through time with overall fertility. In 1900 the relation is stronger with nuptiality than with marital fertility.

At the end of this quest, we cannot report that the historical evidence confirms that the declines of infant mortality led to the decline of fertility. High mortality as well as high fertility are incompatible with the standard of living and the rational approach to the problems of health that now prevail in developed countries; both declines occurred in the course of modernization.

CHAPTER 5: Urban-Rural Differences in Fertility in Europe during the Demographic Transition

Allan Sharlin

> The urban population is still a concept in search of application . . . .
>
> Massimo Livi-Bacci, *A History of Italian Fertility*, p. 214

ACKNOWLEDGMENTS

I would like to thank Mary Ellen Wortham-Krimmer and Dana Takagi for research assistance. The Institute of Urban and Regional Development of the University of California, Berkeley, provided financial assistance. I am grateful to Michael Teitelbaum and Ansley Coale for comments.

INTRODUCTION

Traditional demographic transition theory posited a role for urban places in the passage from high to low fertility. Demographers initially included urbanization among the causes of the demographic transition (Notestein, 1953). Urbanization usually meant the process by which increasing proportions of the population lived in urban areas, but in the modern period, it also stood for a fundamental revolution in the economic basis of the city—from guilds to capitalism and from artisanal production to industrial production. These changes altered the economic role of the family, including decreasing the economic incentive for large numbers of children. And as traditional values were replaced by modern urban values, the virtues of small families were emphasized. Empirical evidence provided support for this general scheme. In most countries of Western Europe, the massive shifts in population from rural to urban areas occurred at roughly the same time as striking declines in marital fertility.

Recent research has chipped at many of the pillars of demographic transition theory, and urbanization has not gone untouched. For example, an account of the rough coincidence of timing does not encompass France

Editors' note: The untimely death of our colleague, Allan Sharlin, preceded the publication of this volume. Thus only minor editorial changes were made in this chapter.

and England. France began its demographic transition in the late eighteenth century, long before the emergence of the modern city, while the decline in fertility in England only got underway decades after cities like Birmingham and Manchester had become grimy industrial centers. When the timing of the fertility decline is measured more precisely by the date of a 10-percent fall in I_g, countries varied widely in the proportion of their population living in urban areas when the fertility transition began. In Finland, Hungary, Bulgaria, France, and Sweden, more than 80 percent of the population was still rural when the fertility transition began, while in the Netherlands, Scotland, and England and Wales less than 30 percent was still rural when I_g declined by 10 percent (Knodel and E. van de Walle, Chapter 10).

While the causal relationships are thus not quite so direct or simple as was once thought, it is hard to reject the idea that there is a relationship between urban-rural differences and the demographic transition. Surely the perspective of kind or size of place can still be expected to provide valuable insights into the transition from high to low fertility.

Issues of measurement raise the most fundamental problems for any analysis of the relation between urban places and the fertility transition. What is urban and what is rural? Can urban places number as small as 5,000 or 10,000 in population, and does this change over time? What criteria can serve to determine a cutoff point? If official definitions are adopted, as is usually the case, how does one adjust for the fact that official definitions change over time, or differ from country to country? Problems of measurement quickly shade over into problems of conceptualization. Do we mean by urban a purely demographic phenomenon of a large population agglomeration, or do we mean an urban way of life? Moreover, the very nature of urban life, regardless of definition, changes over time. A short walk by foot would take an inhabitant of a medieval city into the countryside while a resident of a contemporary metropolis can travel for tens of miles to reach rural areas. With changes in the nature of work, in the scale of production, and in ecological patterns, the sources of rural-urban differences in fertility probably vary over time. Changes in the nature of the urban environment are all the more problematic in that they occur, give or take several decades, at the same time as the decline in fertility. The timing is too inexact to impute a causal relationship, but close enough to raise serious conceptual problems in the measurement of rural-urban differences. For a comparative project drawing data from more than six hundred provinces in Europe over one hundred years, finding a standardized definition looms on the horizon as a gargantuan obstacle.

In the absence of a single, satisfying solution, three conceptual distinctions are useful—defining the urban as opposed to the rural population, examining what it is about urban places that makes for lower fertility, and allowing for the dynamic phenomenon of urbanization (population agglomeration). These distinctions are combined into two approaches—an end-run around the problems of concept and measurement and a direct march into the quagmire. Here an end-run means a search for empirical regularities in urban-rural differences that hold true regardless of both varying definitions and the stage of urbanization. Thus, official government definitions of urban and rural are used even though they vary over time and place. The march into the quagmire involves an effort to make distinctions between different kinds of rural and urban places—by size and by social and economic characteristics. Neither approach is fully satisfactory. The end-run does not generate an explanation, and the march into the quagmire inevitably rests on the consideration of scattered rather than systematic evidence. Together the two approaches offer some useful insights into two separate but related problems—the causes of urban-rural differences in fertility and how urban-rural differences contribute to an understanding of the demographic transition. Ultimately, since the urban-rural distinction is virtually a code phrase for an array of social, economic, and cultural differences and changes, urban-rural differentials in fertility are only of limited utility.

Urban-Rural Differences in I_m and I_g

The single most comprehensive generalization about urban-rural fertility differentials in Western Europe is that urban fertility is lower than rural fertility at virtually every date for which data were collected by the European Fertility Project. The generalization is most comprehensive with respect to marital fertility, and only slightly less comprehensive for overall fertility, the product of marriage patterns and marital fertility.

Figures 5.1 through 5.7 show rural I_g minus urban I_g on the horizontal axis and rural I_m minus urban I_m on the vertical axis. Thus, points in the upper right quadrant indicate that rural I_m and I_g were both higher than urban I_m and I_g. The figures cover seven countries: Germany, Switzerland, Hungary, Russia, Norway, Finland, and Sweden. The upper left-hand corner of each figure shows urban-rural differences at the first date for which data are available. Before 1880 very few provinces outside of France had begun a major sustained decline in I_g: two provinces in Catalonia and parts of French-speaking Belgium, a few cantons in Switzerland, several German provinces, two counties in Scotland, Latvia, and St. Petersburg, two Danish provinces, the Swedish Island of Gotlands, a few counties in Hungary, and one province in East Serbia (Coale and Treadway, Chapter 2). The size of these pre-decline differentials is usually relatively small. The differences between rural and urban I_g vary from slightly more than 0 to about 0.2, and only rarely does rural I_g exceed urban I_g by more than 0.2. The exceptions in the other direction (urban exceeds rural) seem to stem from either inaccurate data or definitions of urban that include places so small as to be more rural than urban in character. Germany (Figure 5.1) provides examples of both. John Knodel reports that rural-urban fertility indexes for 1867 "appear to be unreasonable for many administrative areas" because "apparently the definition of urban areas or city boundaries used by the census did not match the definition used by the vital statistics" (1974, pp. 94–95). After eliminating areas where discrepancies in the definition led to errors, Knodel still finds a number of administrative areas in which rural marital fertility was exceeded by urban marital fertility prior to the onset of a general decline in German fertility. However, when large cities are separated from small urban areas, "large cities were generally characterized by lower marital fertility than either the corresponding rural or urban sectors" (Knodel, 1977c, p. 365). Looking at the provinces of Europe as a whole, the differential usually operates in the expected direction. Given the variations in definition and the very different kinds of areas encompassed by both rural and urban, this consistency is quite impressive.

Not only do the cities have lower marital fertility but they also have lower levels of nuptiality as measured by I_m. There are even fewer exceptions to this rule than with marital fertility. The social mechanism behind this differential in pre-industrial cities seems relatively clear. Since employment for women as servants usually precluded marriage, higher concentrations of servants are related to lower levels of female nuptiality. The percentage of the population employed as servants increases with size of place while the proportion married decreases (Sharlin, 1978). For Prussian cities over 20,000 in 1880, there was a high correlation between the proportion of women who were servants and both the proportion single at ages 45–49 and the female singulate mean age at marriage (Knodel and Maynes, 1976, pp. 150–151). For men, the relationship between urban

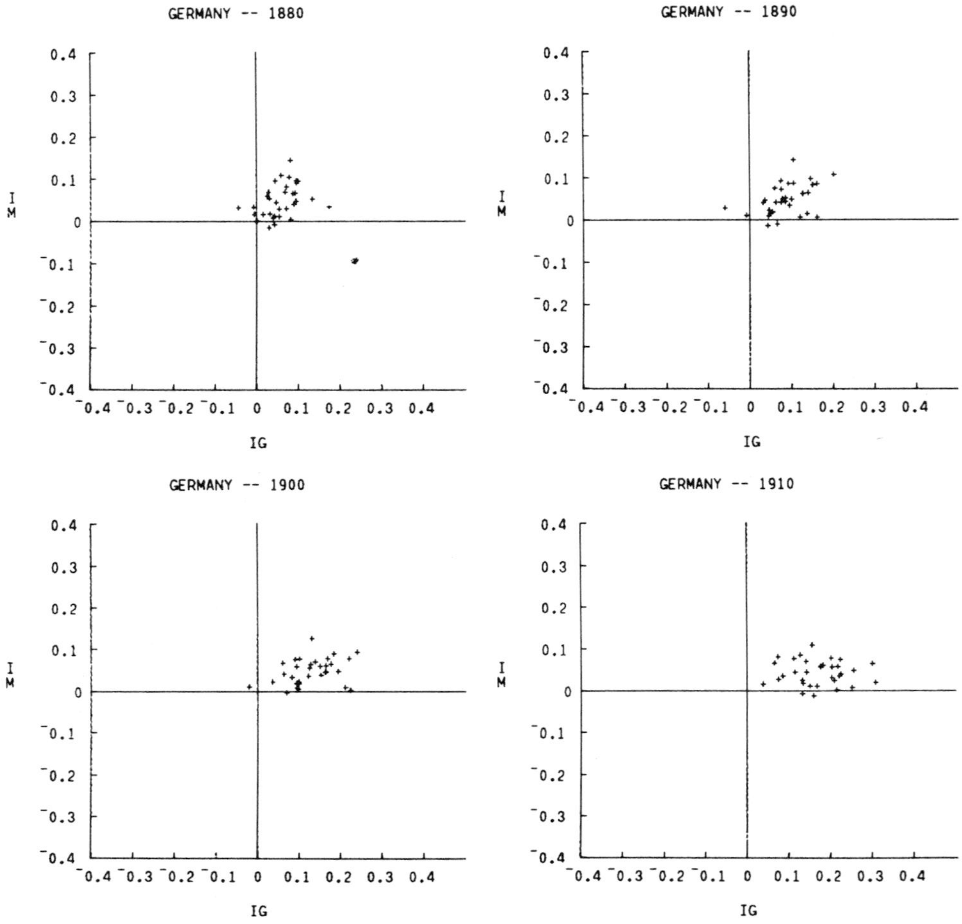

Figure 5.1. Rural minus urban I_g and I_m, Germany.

and rural occupational structures and nuptiality is not as straightforward. Some urban occupations made earlier marriage feasible, while others delayed marriage. The net effect, however, was later marriage and higher proportions remaining single in cities as compared to the countryside, for both men and women.

Both marital fertility and nuptiality work in the same direction to create relatively large differences in overall fertility. Only in the few instances in which urban marital fertility is higher than rural do differences in nuptiality result in higher overall fertility for urban areas. The usual lower levels of urban overall fertility provide a good part of the explanation for the natural decrease typically found in early modern cities (Sharlin, 1978).

Although pre-decline differentials in nuptiality do not seem especially problematical, the explanation for these pre-decline differentials in marital fertility remains a puzzle in historical demography. Insights into this problem would add much to our understanding of pre-modern fertility as well as the demographic transition. At least two distinct explanations can account for the differentials, and each has evidence on its side.

First, variations in levels of natural fertility could cause the differentials in marital fertility. In this version neither city nor country couples practiced family limitation, and fertility differentials thus resulted solely from behavior, such as breast-feeding, which was not parity-specific. So far the evidence does not permit us to determine whether fertility in the populations of entire cities was natural, and the measures used in the European Fertility Project cannot distinguish natural fertility populations from populations practicing family limitation at relatively high levels of fertility. Nevertheless, variation in levels of natural fertility in rural areas are known to have been of such magnitude that they could easily account for urban-rural fertility differences around 1870 (Henry, 1961; Leridon and Menken, 1979). To conclude, however, that the differentials are not the result of family limitation in the urban areas requires us to believe that the factors affecting natural fertility combined purely fortuitously to produce the same urban-rural fertility differentials as those seen subsequently, when fertility was controlled. And if family limitation was practiced in neither urban nor rural areas, we might have expected that some factors affecting natural fertility such as infant mortality and breast-feeding would have acted to increase urban fertility relative to rural.[1] A variant on this theme would be the possibility that couples acted consciously to space (birth control) but not to terminate childbearing (family limitation).[2] Under such a fertility regime couples would act to limit the number of children over time to reach a lower total number or to control childbearing during periods of crisis, but would not attempt to cease childbearing entirely after reaching some desired number of children. Birth

[1] On urban-rural differences in breast-feeding for a later period, see Livi-Bacci (1977), pp. 257–260. On urban-rural differentials in infant mortality, see F. van de Walle, Chapter 4.

[2] Knodel (1978c) presents these definitions. Also see Knodel, 1977b.

control of this sort would be indistinguishable in a statistical sense from natural fertility, since it would appear as a slightly lower level of natural fertility.[3] No European evidence supports this explanation, but African data lend evidence to the possibility (Page and Lesthaeghe, 1981).

A second more likely explanation is that urban populations practiced family limitation on a scale large enough to affect urban fertility levels before the onset of the demographic transition on a national level (Livi-Bacci, Chapter 3). Indeed, it is just this expectation—that urban dwellers have reason to want fewer children—that is embedded in classic demographic transition theory. Research on marital fertility in London and Geneva suggests how this might have worked in the era before the national declines in fertility. Recent research by Finlay (1981) suggests that London had very high marital fertility in the first half of the seventeenth century. Using birth interval data, Finlay finds an average interval of just under 27 months for four parishes in London; the two wealthy parishes had mean birth intervals of only 23 months. Although this kind of data is not ideal, the 23-month interval is "close to the shortest recorded, and equivalent to an age-specific marital fertility rate of at least 500 live births per thousand woman-years lived" (p. 134). Equivalent intervals for four English rural parishes were much longer. This evidence then suggests that urban marital fertility was in fact higher than rural marital fertility. How can these results be squared with the European Fertility Project findings that urban I_g was lower than rural I_g prior to the onset of the demographic transition? Research on Geneva by Henry (1956) and Perrenoud (1979) indicates how these seemingly contradictory results might be consistent. In his pioneering study of the Genevan bourgeoisie, Henry found that marital fertility declined among this elite group beginning at the end of the seventeenth century and continuing on until the end of the eighteenth century. Perrenoud finds for a sample of the entire Genevan population extraordinarily short birth intervals for two time periods in the eighteenth century. This suggests that at the same time as one group within the population was practicing effective family limitation, other groups had very high marital fertility.

While this scattered evidence cannot be considered conclusive, it does indicate that the lower urban I_g found in the European Fertility Project may reflect the fact that the first national censuses in Europe did not take place prior to the onset of limited contraceptive practice. Certain urban

[3] T. C. Smith (1977) presents this argument for infanticide.

groups like the Genevan bourgeoisie may have already been limiting their fertility even though the mass of both the urban and the rural population was not practicing family limitation. These elite groups may have done enough to reduce the overall urban marital fertility levels to somewhat below rural marital fertility by the time of the first national censuses but prior to the beginning of the general decline in fertility. Although this thesis is certainly plausible, it does require us to believe that family limitation was practiced by certain urban groups in almost all cities across Europe at the time of the first national censuses; this is possible, but prudence would suggest the accumulation of more evidence before fully accepting the thesis.

With the onset of the demographic transition, problems about the immediate cause of fertility differentials disappear. Fertility differences can be attributed to the proportion of couples practicing family limitation, and the degree of this limitation. In examining urban-rural differentials in the transition, it is essential to distinguish between earlier onsets of fertility decline and preexisting fertility differentials. Once done, however, two generalizations hold true remarkably well. First, when it is possible to perceive a difference between urban and rural areas, the decline in fertility always begins first in urban areas. Second, during the course of the demographic transition the urban-rural difference widens as urban fertility declines more rapidly in the initial stages. An examination of the data from individual European countries supports these generalizations.

For Germany, John Knodel (1974) concludes that "the decline began first in the urban populations but was followed after a short time lag by a parallel decline in the rural population" (pp. 109–110). Moreover, "the earlier declines in urban areas resulted in accentuating the differences in levels of fertility between rural and urban areas as the decline took place" (p. 100). Also, rural values of nuptiality and marital fertility are consistently higher than urban values. Figure 5.1 graphs rural minus urban I_m versus rural minus urban I_g for each decade between 1880 (when the first provinces in Germany had experienced a 10 percent decline in I_g) and 1910 (when virtually all provinces in Germany had experienced a 10-percent decline). This format provides a ready means for examining the distribution of rural-urban differences by province in each country. The provinces in this instance refer to the Prussian administrative areas of Germany. Although the conformity to the generalizations is the most striking feature of the graphs, the exceptions to the rule require some comment. In 1880, three provinces had higher urban than rural values of I_g; in 1890, two; and in 1900, one. These exceptions constitute three provinces; for two of these provinces information survives on urban values of I_g broken down by cities with populations greater than 20,000 and other urban areas. In each instance cities in the over-20,000 category have lower values of I_g than the others (Knodel, 1974, pp. 279–287). In other words, the higher total urban values of I_g are caused by the preponderance of small urban areas that may very well have been rural in character. With respect to nuptiality, the exceptions occur at one or two of the four dates for each of four provinces. More detailed information is available for 1880, and the urban areas have lower singulate mean age at marriage, but still consistently higher proportions permanently celibate (Knodel and Maynes, 1976).

Belgian data are also consistent with these findings. Lesthaeghe (1977) undertook an analysis of urban and rural parts of individual *arrondissements.* He reports that marital fertility was generally higher in the rural areas than in the urban areas (pp. 114–119).

It might seem that France is an exception. The fertility of peasants in France began to decline in the late eighteenth century, but the fertility behavior of urban dwellers at this time remains unknown. Thus, no evidence disproves the assertion that urban fertility in France declined even earlier. For one small town, Meulan, the beginning of the decline can be traced back to the first half of the eighteenth century (Dûpaquier and Lachiver, 1969). At least after 1861, it appears that urban fertility declined faster than rural fertility (E. van de Walle, 1979).

In Switzerland the earliest separate urban and rural data stem from 1880, when the total I_g for the nation was 0.677, down from 0.724 in 1860. From 1880 through 1960 in each canton, urban values of marital fertility are always lower than rural values (except for one canton in 1960). The same holds true for nuptiality, although with a few more exceptions that require investigation. Figure 5.2 records these results in the same fashion as for Germany. Urban marital fertility in Switzerland declined more rapidly than rural marital fertility. In 1880, rural areas overall had an I_g value of 0.704 while the corresponding urban value was 0.549. Over the next four decades the size of the urban-rural difference grew, reaching a maximum in 1920 (urban $I_g = 0.264$ and rural $I_g = 0.507$) followed by an attenuation of the differences back to more or less the same level as pre-fertility decline differences. However, Francine van de Walle (Chapter 4) finds it impossible to detect "a marked lead" in the start of fertility decline. It may be that the decline started simultaneously in urban and rural areas,

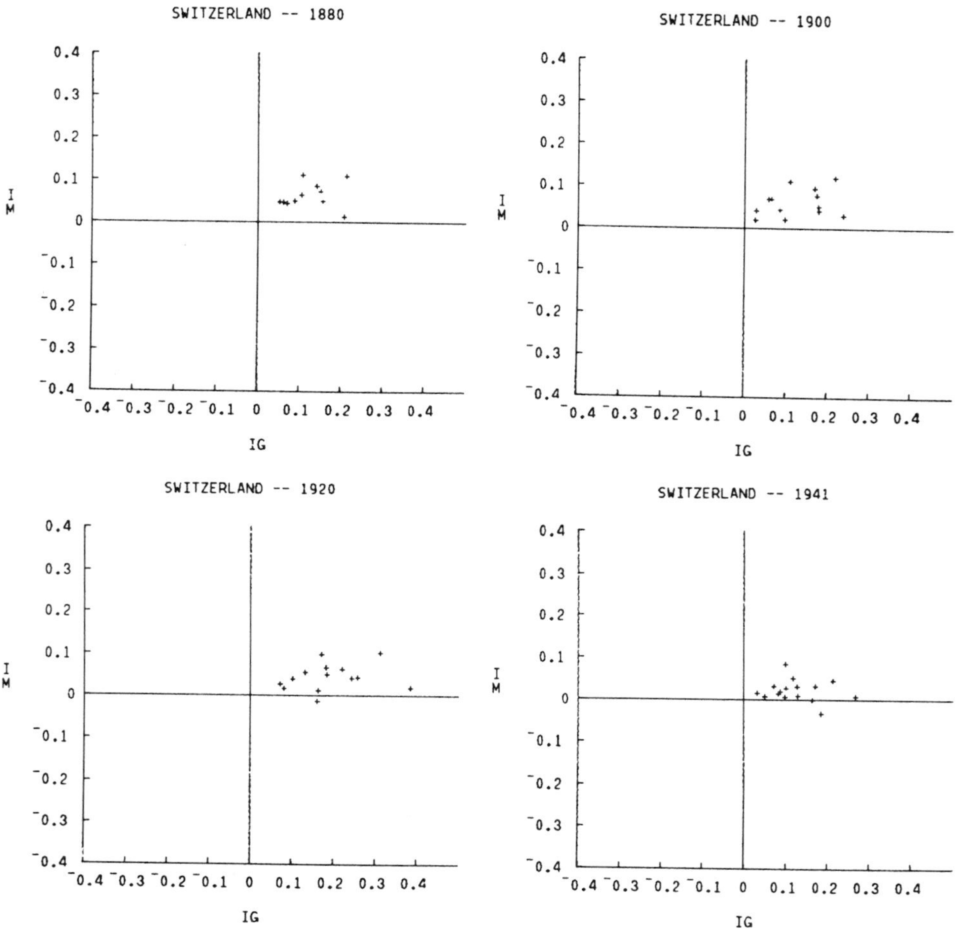

Figure 5.2. Rural minus urban I_g and I_m, Switzerland.

but the faster urban decline suggests the possiblity of simply a failure to detect a difference in the timing of the onset of fertility decline. In any case, whether a simultaneous initiation or the failure to detect a difference, the general thesis is not contradicted.

In Italy and Portugal it appears that cities began their fertility decline earlier than the neighboring rural areas (Livi-Bacci, 1971 and 1977). In Italy, Massimo Livi-Bacci (1977) concludes that "marital fertility experienced a dramatic decrease in the large cities of the North and of the Center, widening the gap between urban and rural patterns of demographic behavior" (p. 125). The same thing happened in southern Italy at a later date. The pattern repeats itself in Portugal when comparing Lisbon and Porto with their surrounding rural areas (Livi-Bacci, 1971, p. 110).

Data for Hungary between 1880 and 1910 also appear consistent with the generalizations. The mean of urban I_g in 1880 was 0.538, compared with 0.593 for rural. In succeeding decades, urban I_g declined to 0.519 and then to 0.482 and 0.422. In contrast, rural values were 0.585, 0.580, and 0.540, indicating that the rural decline in fertility had scarcely begun

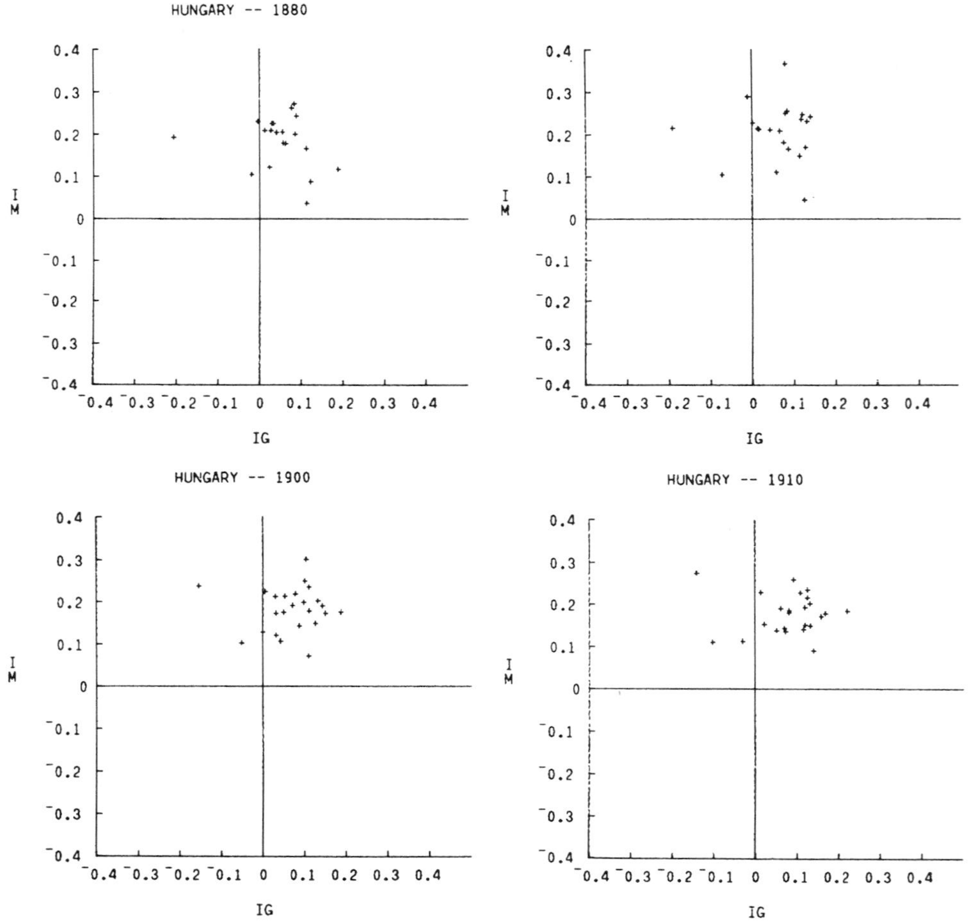

Figure 5.3. Rural minus urban I_g and I_m, Hungary.

by 1910. The results for individual provinces are reported in Figure 5.3. The exceptions—where rural I_g is lower—occur in just three provinces, although some provinces do not have urban areas (Demeny, 1968).

For the European provinces of Russia, the earliest evidence (1897) shows that urban fertility had already begun to decline everywhere, but the same had happened only in a few rural provinces. After 1897, the fall in urban marital fertility continues steadily, but by 1926, nearly one-half of the European provinces had not begun a decline in rural fertility (Figure 5.4) (Coale, Anderson, and Härm, 1979, pp. 41–47).

For Scandinavian countries, urban-rural data have been collected for Norway, Finland, and Sweden. Norway presents a contradictory case, because there is no consistent relationship between urban and rural marital fertility before 1920 (Figure 5.5). This could, however, be due to faulty data (note the wide dispersion similar to what Knodel [1974, p. 94] found for Germany in 1867) or to the fact that the officially defined urban areas are so small as to be scarcely different from the rural areas. Finland, however, does conform to the generalizations (Figure 5.6). Urban fertility declines from the earliest data (1890), and I_g falls below 0.3 by 1930. Sweden provides an interesting case because of Carlsson's (1966, p. 152) claim that urban and rural fertility began their decline at the same time. From Carlsson's own data, however, it appears that urban fertility began to decline after 1890, ten years before rural fertility. In any case, urban

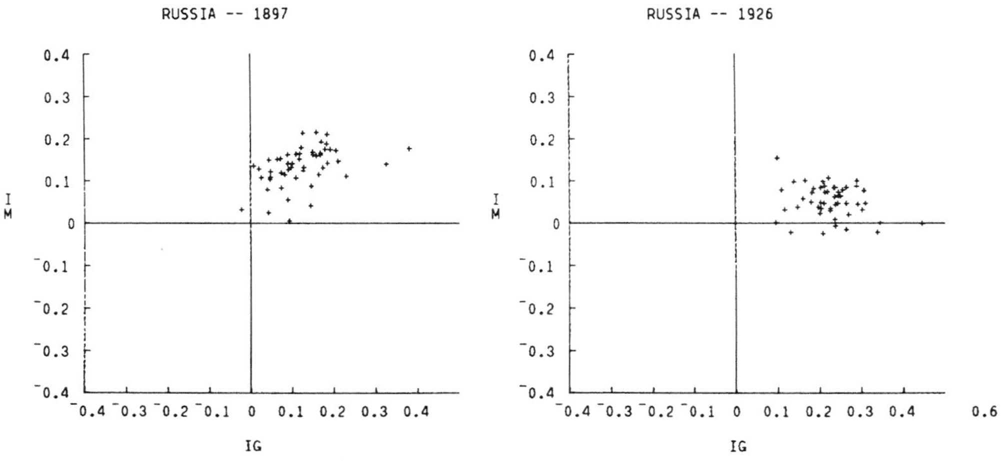

Figure 5.4. Rural minus urban I_g and I_m, Russia.

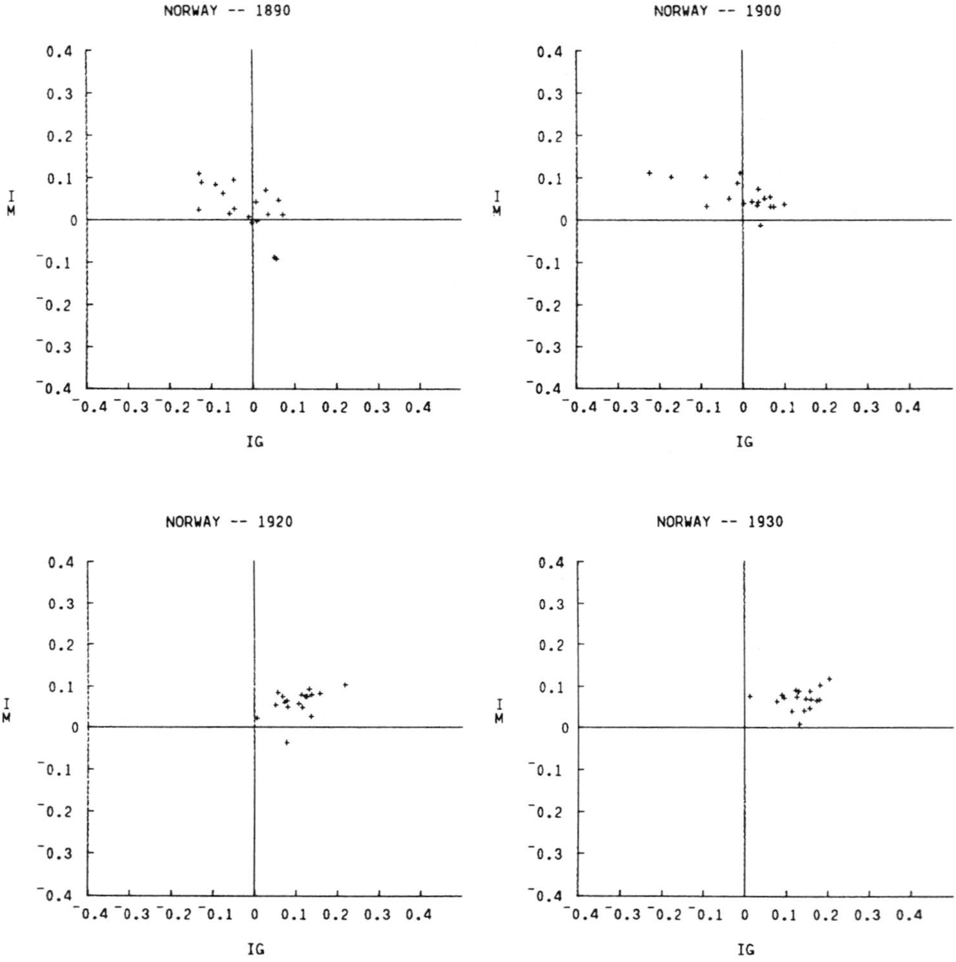

Figure 5.5. Rural minus urban I_g and I_m, Norway.

fertility fell faster, and rural fertility always exceeded urban fertility (Figure 5.7) (Mosk, 1978).

After the completion of the transition from high fertility to a low one, urban marital fertility remains lower than rural marital fertility. The differentials declined in size, but nonetheless continued to exist. In the fourth graph of each of the figures, the points fall largely in the upper right quadrant, indicating higher rural marital fertility and higher rural nuptiality.

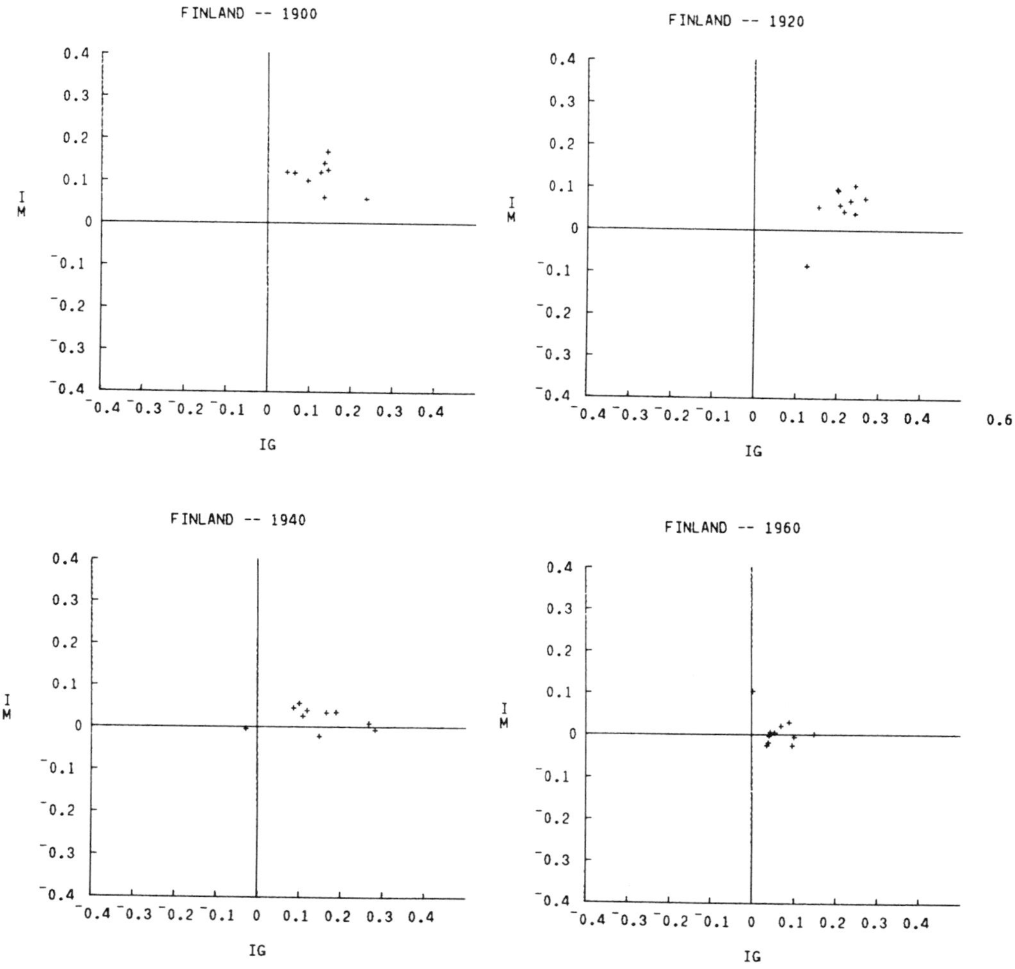

Figure 5.6. Rural minus urban I_g and I_m, Finland.

Despite the satisfaction one might derive from arriving at empirical regularities on urban-rural differences in fertility in the demographic transition, it is best to be quite explicit about what these regularities do and do not mean. The regularities do not provide any support for the proposition that urbanization played a causal role in the transition. They do not indicate that the decline spread from urban to rural areas, although this possibility is not contradicted. The generalizations do not mean that all

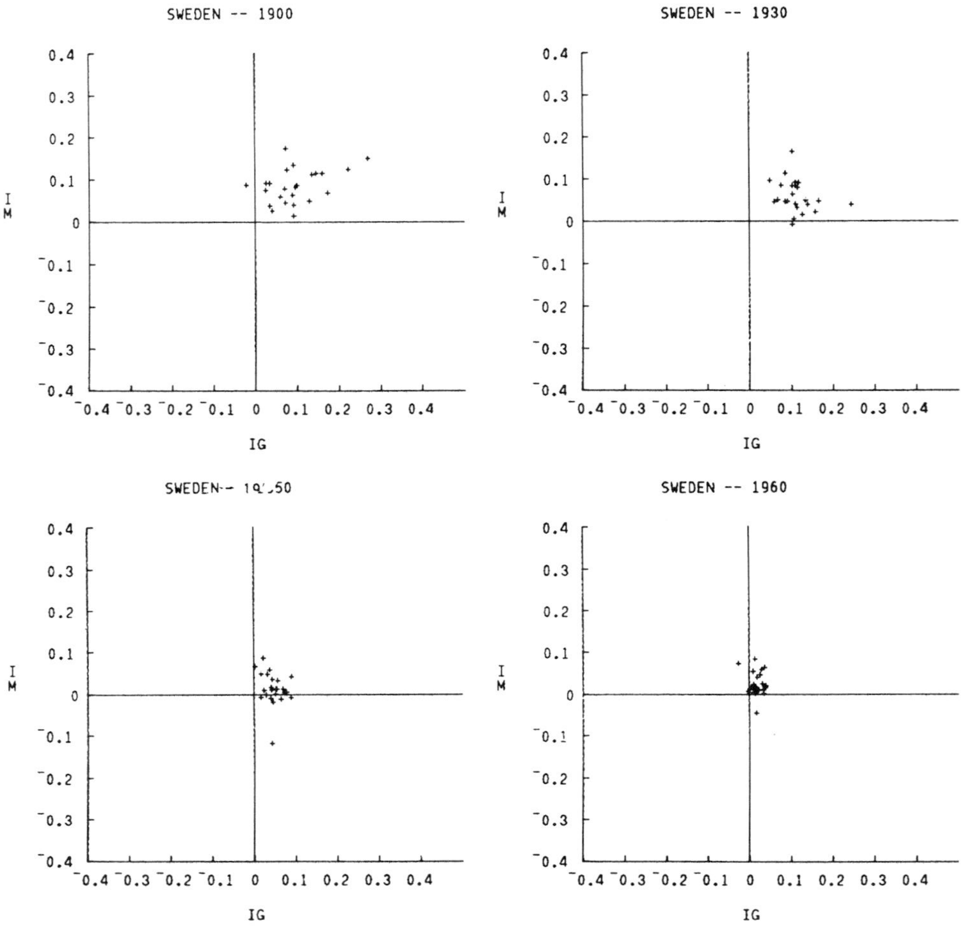

Figure 5.7. Rural minus urban I_g and I_m, Sweden.

segments of the urban population began their fertility decline before all segments of the rural population. It would be consistent with these findings if fertility declined in some rural groups before any decline in the cities, or if some urban groups began their fertility decline before urban decline in the aggregate is apparent. Moreover, there is no evidence of any instance in which the transition was completed in cities before it started in the countryside; urban and rural declines overlapped. Nonetheless, when all the different groups composing the various urban and rural populations in Europe are put together on the province level, the results are similar: urban marital fertility was lower than rural marital fertility just prior to the general decline in fertility; where a difference is detectable, urban marital fertility began to decline earlier than rural; urban fertility declined faster, increasing the gap; and in the post-transition period, rural marital fertility exceeded the urban by only a small amount. Given the variation in definitions, the generality makes the results impressive; but since the data are for relatively large aggregates, we must be very sensitive to differentials within urban and rural populations.

Variations in Urban-Rural Fertility Differentials by Region and Size of Place

This section explores variations in urban-rural fertility differentials. No claim can be made to a systematic compilation of evidence, and these data by themselves do not provide an explanation for urban-rural differences in fertility in the course of the demographic transition. However, each kind of information provides a different perspective on the same basic question. Given the empirical regularities across time and place found in the previous section, what kinds of variations occur in the relationship between urban and rural fertility? Specifically, this section examines whether rural and urban fertility vary together, whether urban-rural fertility differentials vary by region within a given country, and whether there are variations in fertility depending on size of place and kind of place. Even though these factors are examined separately, the possibility that they are different ways of looking at the same thing must be kept in mind. Collectively, the data in this section and the previous section provide only pieces of a puzzle; in the last section, I will attempt to fit the pieces into a coherent picture.

One way of looking at fertility differences is to compare rural and urban I_g for the provinces within a given country. Figures 5.1 to 5.7 allowed us to look only at the size of the differences. Plotting urban I_g against rural I_g lets us look at whether urban and rural I_g vary together. Where urban I_g is relatively high or low, is rural I_g also high or low? If so, that might be taken as an indication that the same influences on fertility operate in both rural and urban contexts within a given area. These factors might consist of similar beliefs and traditions within a given cultural region and/or common social and economic developments, causing a quite rapid diffusion. If there is a negative relationship or no relationship, then perhaps factors operating in urban areas do not carry over directly to rural areas. We might also postulate the possibility that the nature of the relationship changes during the course of the demographic transition—that a positive relationship, for example, might give way to none at all. These possibilities must be seen within the context of the regularities postulated in the previous section—rural marital fertility is higher than urban marital fertility, and the urban decline generally begins before the rural.

With notable exceptions, urban and rural I_g's appear to be highly correlated. In Germany the correlation is quite distinct over the period 1880-1910 (see Figure 5.8). The same thing can be said of Switzerland from 1880 to 1960 (see Figure 5.9). For Russia, a weak correlation in 1897 becomes a strong one by 1926 (Figure 5.10). Finland (Figure 5.11) and Sweden (Figure 5.12) offer moderately strong correlations, while Norway gives a weak one at best (Figure 5.13). Finally, there appears to be no relationship between rural and urban I_g for Hungary between 1880 and 1910

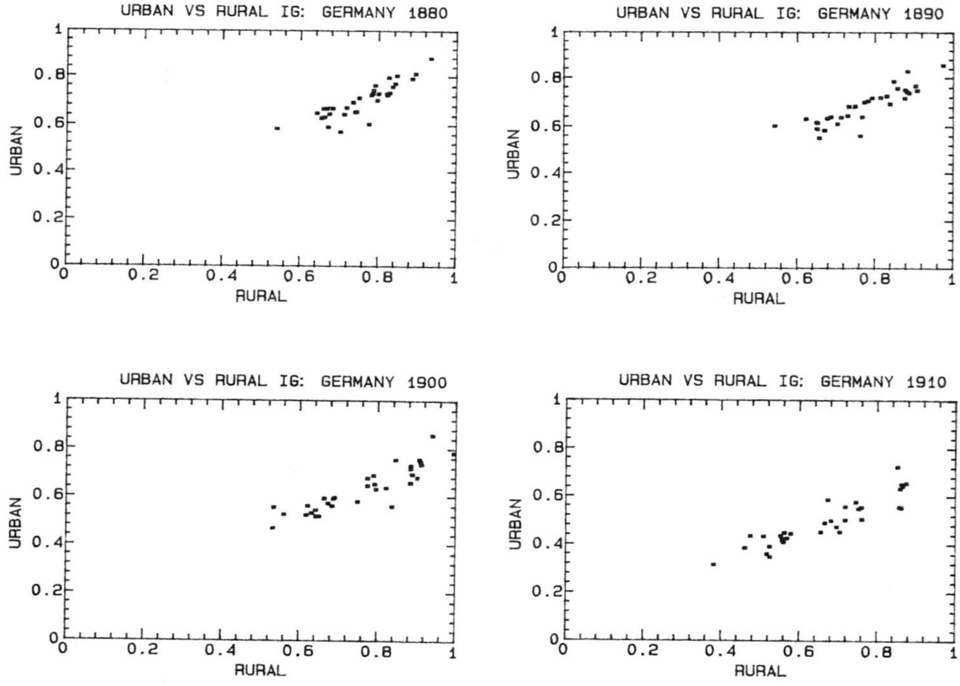

Figure 5.8. Urban and rural I_g, Germany.

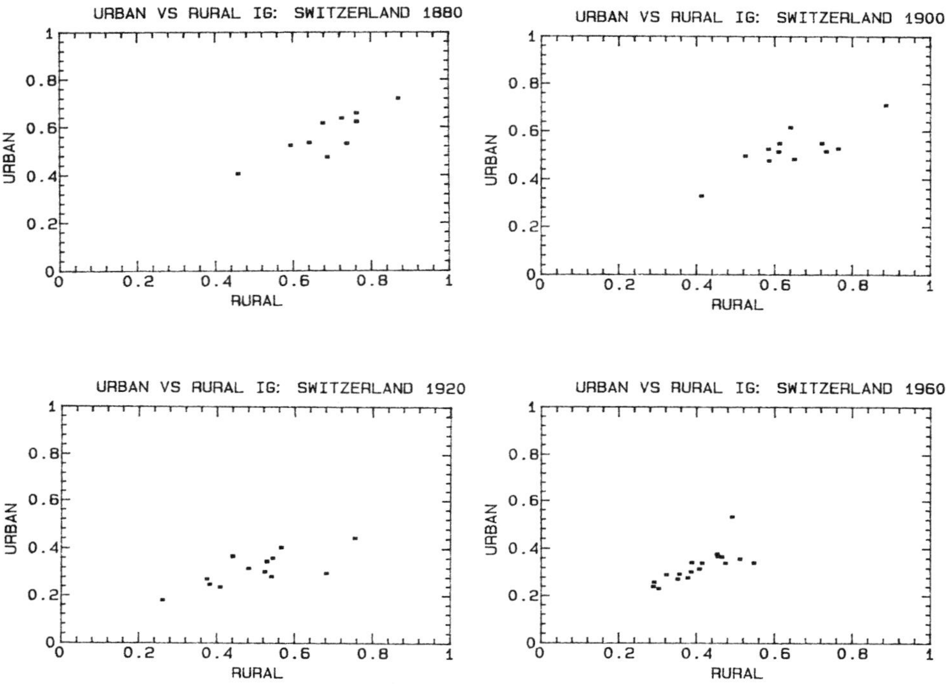

Figure 5.9. Urban and rural I_g, Switzerland.

(Figure 5.14). One might surmise that the absence of a strong correlation might stem from the predominance of very small urban localities in Scandinavia and Hungary, but the data do not permit the testing of this hypothesis. If the weak or nonexistent correlations can indeed be attributed to the absence of substantial cities, then the strong correlations certainly can be considered a piece of the puzzle.

Just as urban-rural differentials in fertility vary between countries, so they also vary across regions in a given country. The urban-rural differential itself can virtually disappear. Thus, Massimo Livi-Bacci (1977) reports that the inverse relationship between fertility and size of community in the north and center of Italy does not hold in the south. In addition, the size of the urban-rural differential is considerably attenuated in the south (pp. 122–125). Similarly, urban-rural differences in fertility are negligible in the north of Portugal but considerable in the south (Livi-Bacci, 1971, p. 107). In Belgium, Ron Lesthaeghe (1977) observes very different

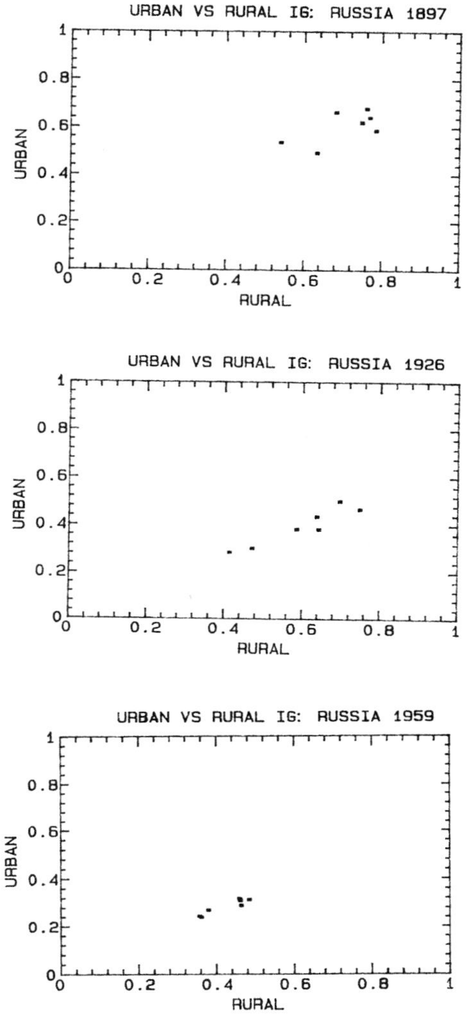

Figure 5.10. Urban and rural I_g, Russia.

patterns of urban-rural differentials in Flanders and Wallonia. Urban-rural fertility differences were small in Wallonia but large in Flanders. Urban areas in Wallonia "behaved more or less as one unit" while urban areas in Flanders differed by size in level of fertility and in the timing of the decline (p. 119).

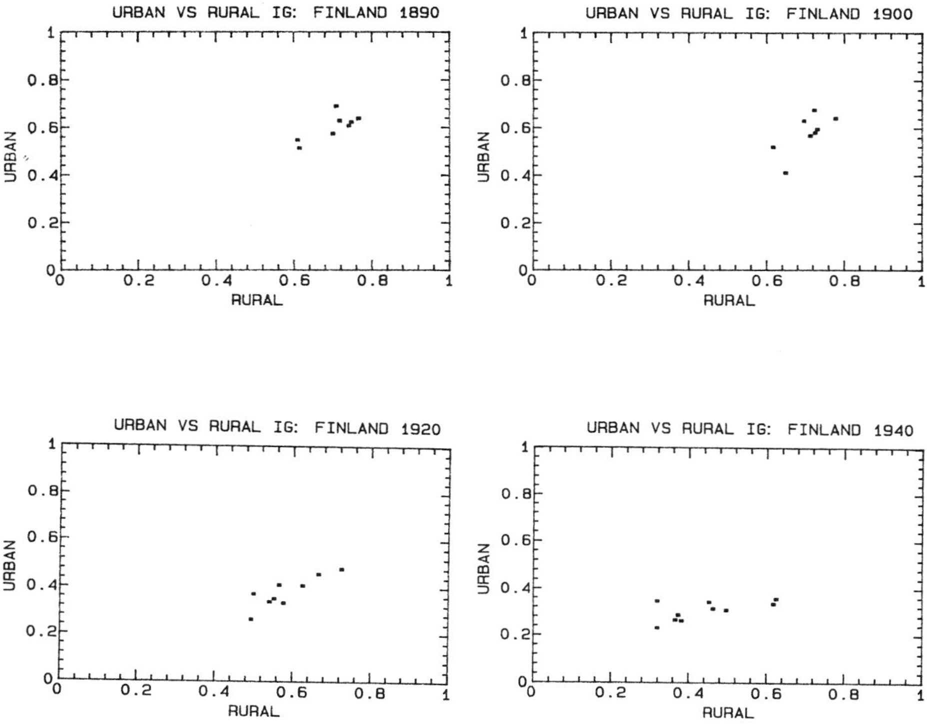

Figure 5.11. Urban and rural I_g, Finland.

The level of marital fertility in cities within a given country seems to vary by size of the city. The largest cities have the lowest fertility. For Prussia, "larger cities have lower fertility and are located in areas where rural fertility is also low" (Knodel, 1974, p. 98). The large cities begin a decline in fertility several years before the small cities, which in turn begin a decline several years before rural areas. Moreover, the process can sometimes be followed in an even way from cohort to cohort in each size of place (Knodel, 1974, pp. 98–109). In Switzerland, Francine van de Walle (manuscript) found "a constant inverse relationship between the size of city and the level of marital fertility." Geneva had the lowest level of I_g followed by the other four large cities and then the remaining cities; rural areas had the highest level of I_g (see ms., Chap. 5). An inverse relationship between size of city also occurs in France in the mid-nineteenth century (E. van de Walle, 1979). In Belgium, the provincial towns had higher

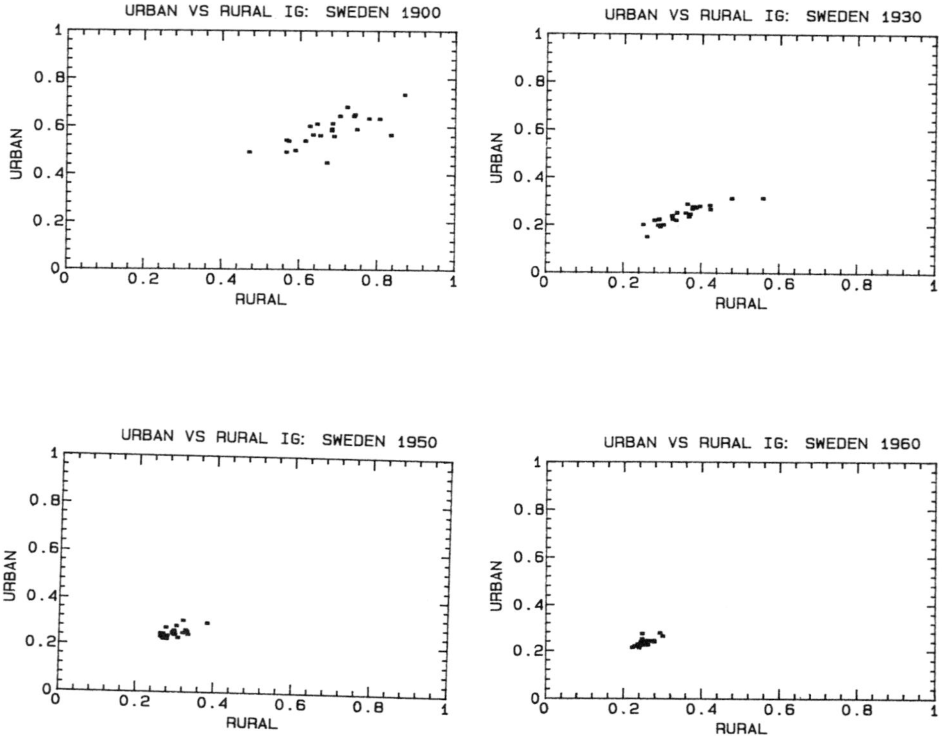

Figure 5.12. Urban and rural I_g, Sweden.

marital fertility than the four large cities—Antwerp, Brussels, Ghent, and Liège (Lesthaeghe, 1977, p. 116). Marital fertility was inversely correlated with size of place in northern and central Italy (Livi-Bacci, 1977, pp. 123–125). For 1897 in Russia, Coale, Anderson, and Härm (1979) compare the marital fertility in the largest city of each province with the remainder of the urban population combined. In forty-five out of fifty provinces, marital fertility was lowest in the largest city. They conclude that "size of city was a significant determinant of urban marital fertility" (p. 51). Moreover, in a multivariate analysis, urban I_g by province in 1897 and 1926 had a negative correlation with a measure of city size (p. 64).

In short, size of city seems to bear a consistent inverse relationship to the level of marital fertility. The decrease in marital fertility with increases in size of urban place seems to hold consistently throughout the period of the European demographic transition. The data, however, are not

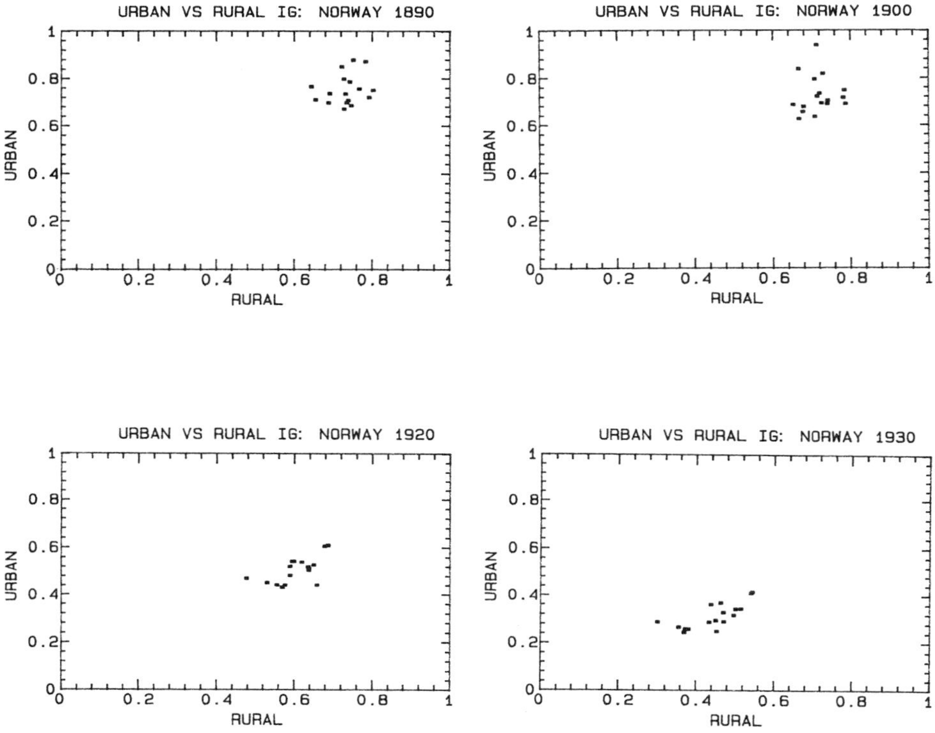

Figure 5.13. Urban and rural I_g, Norway.

detailed enough to permit an investigation into the exact quantitative nature of this relationship. Moreover, it is also worth noting that we do not know whether the size of rural places or the nature of rural settlements bears any relationship to marital fertility.

Finally, rural-urban fertility differentials can be examined from the perspective of kind of place. For example, do small cities have higher fertility if they are heavily industrialized? Is the fertility of rural areas affected by the presence of industry? In the cities, the fertility varies according to social and economic structures. For example, Francine van de Walle (manuscript) concludes for Switzerland that "the more urban the area, the lower the marital fertility." Yet she notes "spots of very low fertility in small cities." Three of these small cities were centers of metallurgical industry, and one can easily infer that fertility in these places was "associated with a strong industrial environment" (see Chapter 5). On the other hand,

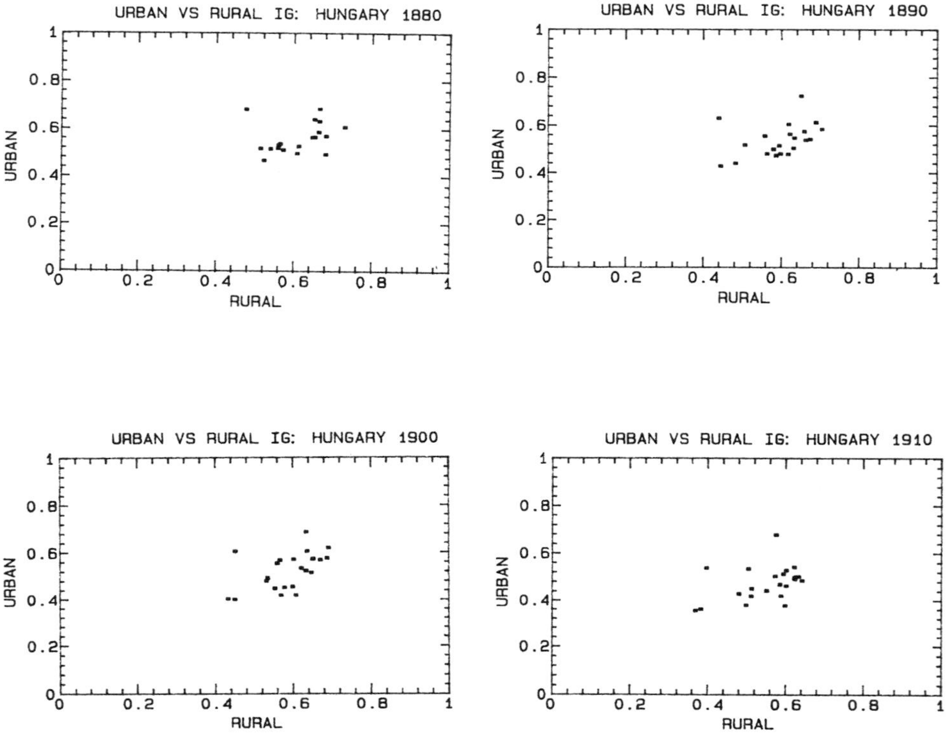

Figure 5.14. Urban and rural I_g, Hungary.

Etienne van de Walle (1979) finds in France that "towns with a high proportion in industry (70 percent and over) are often characterized by heavy industry practiced in manufactures. In those cities, the crude marital fertility rates are specially high.'' Other studies by Michael Haines (1979), Dov Friedlander (1973), and E. A. Wrigley (1961) indicate that miners had relatively high fertility. It seems clear that occupational structure affects fertility independently of size of place, but industry per se does not have an effect in one direction. The data are simply not systematic enough to work out a coherent and complete explanation. Rural areas also varied in character. Some had an industrial base, and agricultural areas varied enormously in their systems of labor and land tenure. Moreover, the countryside did not remain the same during the nineteenth century. The countryside became more rural as small places lost functions to larger ones. The European Fertility Project did not collect information on rural occupational structures. However, local studies by Rudolph Braun (1978) of the canton of Zurich and David Levine (1977) of two villages in Leicestershire demonstrate marked differences in rural fertility depending on the presence or absence of rural industry.

It is not at all clear whether all these bits of evidence tell different stories or reflect different aspects of the same thing. Large cities have lower marital fertility, and they also tend to be located in provinces with lower fertility. Should one perceive the phenomena in terms of size or region? Could they be independent phenomena or are they simply indicators of one underlying mechanism? Similarly, how should we understand the correspondence between size of place and kind of place and their correlations with variations in fertility? Do these differentials have anything at all to do with the regularities found earlier?

Beyond Description

How can we weave all these disparate pieces of evidence into a coherent story or series of stories? How can we move from empirical description to explanation? It may seem self-evident, but it is first necessary to elucidate the elements of the demographic transition that require explanation. Only then is it possible to consider the role of urban-rural differentials in any explanation. In brief, I shall argue that urban-rural fertility differences cannot be of much help in answering the large questions, but they do provide insights into some of the smaller ones.

Perhaps the largest question is: Why did the demographic transition occur? One approach to this question would be to regard the demographic transition as one aspect of the larger process of modernization along with commercialization, bureaucratization, the nation-state, and industrialization. Fertility decline would then appear as a necessary part of the adjustment process to a new order of things. This can surely be explained in a variety of ways; one common perspective argues that the value of children changes. To go beyond a general statement of this sort and delineate a specific list of factors forming a causal mechanism for the general process of European fertility decline is almost certainly an illusory quest. Other social scientists such as economists, historians, sociologists, and anthropologists have grappled unsuccessfully with specific explanations for other aspects of modernization. The failure may lie with insufficient data or it may simply be in the nature of social phenomena.

Another big question is: Why does the fertility transition happen in some places before others, in France before England, in Wallonia before Flanders, in Lot-et-Garonne before Morbihan? The European Fertility Project has uncovered a series of detailed ad hoc arguments, rather than confirmed or generated specific but general mechanisms. Nonetheless, this means failure at even retrospective predictive insight into the geographical progression of the fertility transition. However, just as economic historians cannot offer a general model for the progression of industrialization in Europe, it does not seem that fertility decline poses a more tractable problem in this respect. A different set of circumstances combined to initiate the industrial revolution in England in the late eighteenth century, and to foster industrialization in France and Belgium in the first half of the nineteenth century or in Germany in the second half of the century. Traditionally, economic historians point to such factors as natural resources, indigenous technical training, foreign and domestic capital, availability of markets, and economic and labor organization. Industrialization does not even necessarily occur first in urban places. No one expects the same combination of factors to create industrialization in each country. Why should fertility decline be any different? Thus, urbanization or urban-rural differentials may or may not play a role in determining or explaining the onset of a decline in fertility. For example, we could examine whether rapid urbanization precedes fertility decline. France and England clearly present two different cases. The goal of finding a general explanation for the timing of this fertility decline in Europe was probably an illusory quest.

In terms of smaller questions, the urban-rural perspective can provide insights into the process by which the demographic transition occurs in particular places. Perhaps a useful beginning point is a comparison of urban-rural differentials with other differentials. The most striking comparison is between regional and urban-rural differentials. The same story appears consistently. Regional differentials are always larger than urban-rural differentials. What this suggests is not simply the obvious—that regional differentials are more important than urban-rural—but that fertility decline occurs in discrete cultural areas (regions) and that urban-rural differentials are subsidiary differences within given regions. Hence we would expect fertility decline to begin in a particular cultural area within a country and that the particular pattern of urban-rural differentials need not be duplicated in other areas within the same country. Thus, Flanders and Wallonia form distinct cultural regions within Belgium, begin their fertility declines at different times, and have quite distinct patterns of urban-rural differentials. The same is true of the north and south of Italy and also of the north and south of Portugal. Where we do not find significant regional differentials in fertility, we would not expect to find different patterns of urban-rural differentials.

If we take as given that fertility decline begins within particular cultural regions, then urban-rural differentials can make a distinct contribution to understanding the demographic transition in fertility. First, where it is possible to detect a difference between urban and rural areas, the fertility of urban areas declines first. For whatever reason urban places are more receptive to initiating family limitation. However, rural areas follow quickly. In no instance do urban areas complete their fertility decline before the onset of fertility decline in rural areas.

So far as scattered and incomplete evidence can suggest, urban-rural fertility differences may be imputed to variations in size *and* to variations in social and economic characteristics. This corresponds to several empirical observations. Occupational composition of the population accounts for some but not all of the difference between urban and rural fertility. Marital fertility varies inversely with size of place, with certain exceptions. The exceptions seem related to variations in occupational structures across urban places and across rural places. Thus, cities of the same size vary according to how industrial they are. Similarly, one of the major determinants of rural fertility seems to be the presence or absence of cottage industry.

This piecing together of the various bits of evidence into a story is less than satisfactory. Even if the data were complete for all the European provinces on these issues, it is most unlikely that size and occupational structure could account for all the variance in urban-rural fertility differentials. There are two ways of looking at this lack of fit. First, the effects of size and occupational structure do not act in a simple and direct way. The process can be understood in terms of interaction effects—for example, *a* causes *b* if *c* but not if not *c*. It would be necessary then to have knowledge of a series of other factors and of their collective interaction in producing a given level of fertility. To figure out the causal lines in a complete way is almost certainly an impossibility. Second, the measures used in this paper are really very inexact. For example, size of place does not directly affect fertility, but rather it acts through a series of other unknown factors. Aggregated data compound these problems further. Only with detailed local studies which reconstruct the social environment is it possible to work out the particular mechanisms affecting fertility. In an analogous way one can think of comparative studies on the development of representative government or on the demise of guilds in Western Europe.

In conclusion, the examination of urban-rural differences in fertility offers some useful insights into the demographic transition. As much as authors would like to claim importance for their subjects, urban-rural fertility differentials have limited value for the study of the demographic transition. Other differentials are larger, and urban-rural differentials are indicators of complex processes rather than factors acting directly on fertility.

Chapter 6: Modes of Production, Secularization, and the Pace of the Fertility Decline in Western Europe, 1870–1930

Ron Lesthaeghe and Chris Wilson

> Economic circumstance has a dominant influence on social attitudes in the poor society because, for those who are poor, nothing is so important as their poverty and nothing is so necessary as its mitigation. In consequence, among the poor only religion, with its promise of a later munificence for those who endure privation with patience, has been competitive with economic circumstance in shaping social attitudes.
>
> —J.K. Galbraith

Acknowledgments

The authors wish to thank the following persons for their help with the data collection, methodological suggestions, and substantive comments: M. Elchardus, E. W. Hofstee, J. Knodel, M. Livi-Bacci, P. C. Matthiessen, H. Moors, K. Schwarz, R. Van Malderghem, F. van de Walle, H. Wander, and the second-year sociology students of the Vrije Universiteit in Brussels. An earlier version of this paper appeared in *Bevolking en Gezin*, no. 3 (Brussels, 1978), under the title "Productievormen, Stemgedrag en Vruchtbaarheidstransitie in Westeuropees Perspectief, 1870–1930."

Introduction

Fertility is no exception to Galbraith's general rule that economics and religion are the main determinants of social attitudes. The move from high to low fertility that occurred in Europe over the last century or so—termed the fertility transition—was heavily influenced by just such considerations of economic well-being and religious belief. As A. J. Coale (1973) has suggested, the conditions necessary for a major fall in marital fertility were, first, that "fertility must be within the calculus of conscious choice"; second, that "perceived social and economic circumstances must make reduced fertility seem advantageous to individual couples"; and third, that "effective techniques of fertility reduction must be available."

In this paper we shall ignore the third condition, the availability of contraceptive techniques, and instead concentrate on the first two, those of perceived advantage and moral acceptability.[1] In doing so our purpose is to formulate a framework for analysis that incorporates these two conditions and expresses them in a manner suitable for quantification, which is then used to check their validity. It is *not* our intention to present a *complete* picture of the marital fertility transition in any country; rather, we wish to offer a general framework of *indispensable elements* central to several cases. To this end we shall begin with an elaboration of Coale's first two conditions, starting with the second.

Perceived Social and Economic Circumstances Must Make Reduced Fertility Seem an Advantage to Individual Couples

The statement that fertility limitation within wedlock must be perceived as advantageous is not immediately understandable. A plethora of economic and social forces impinge upon the process of decision making: the separation of the most important from the secondary is never easy and always implies a loss of information and precision. It is our contention, however, that such a separation is useful and that from it three factors emerge as central in calculating the advantage of fertility limitation.

1. The familial nature of most units of economic production;
2. The dominant factor of production at the disposal of households in each particular occupational category;
3. The direction and strength of intergenerational flows of goods, money, and services of all types, including power and influence within the household.

Bearing these factors in mind, let us examine the society of Western Europe as it appeared before the onset of the demographic transition. We will consider the countries of central continental Europe, from Scandinavia to Italy, during the first half of the nineteenth century.

[1] We feel that Coale's third condition, that is, the availability of methods of fertility limitation, takes the form of an enabling mechanism whereby the motives implied in the first two conditions are realized. As such, we feel it does not possess explanatory power of the same order compared with the first two conditions.

As a host of local studies have shown, the formation of a new household through marriage was countenanced by society only if and when the potential members of that new household could establish *independent* and *sufficient* means to support themselves.[2] In such circumstances, potential grooms and brides remained within their families of origin for a long time and contributed a substantial portion of their economically productive years to the parentally controlled unit. However, not everyone stayed in the parental household until marriage: many joined other households as unmarried servants. But it is likely that a portion of the wages was remitted to the parental household and another portion was saved for a future marriage.

In pre-transition Europe the overlap of the household and the production unit was characteristic not only of agriculture but also of industry. This is vividly illustrated by the expansion during the eighteenth and early nineteenth centuries of the number of households involved in cottage industries of various kinds in addition to, or even to the exclusion of, agricultural activity. This expansion of the early industrial sector resulted from the steadily rising pressure on resources in agriculture caused by slight but sustained population growth. It implies that the group of wage earners was far from negligible and that the degree of geographical mobility of labor should not be underestimated. It is noteworthy, however, that the growth of cottage industries (whether or not in combination with seasonal wage labor in agriculture or subsistence farming) indicates that wage labor as well as industrial production were not incompatible with the persistence and even enhancement of the familial production unit.[3] Finally, as already shown with lodgers and servants, marked regional differences were also apparent in the employment of these mixed agricultural and early (or proto) industrial sectors.

In general, the possibility of household members finding employment in other households and their engagement in early industrial activities clearly indicate that the economy was capable of absorbing some population growth. This means that employment could be generated to sustain family incomes even in the presence of natural fertility, provided that

[2] See J. Dupâquier (1972) for an elegant formulation of the Malthusian system.

[3] The phenomenon of expanding domestic industry is well documented for the Low Countries, Switzerland, and Germany; the trend also extended to the British Isles.

the population as a whole did not make full use of its entire reproductive capacity.[4]

These features of seventeenth and early eighteenth-century Western European societies have a number of implications. First, with the apparently low cost of raising children and with the additional possibility for unmarried persons to find employment outside the parental home or within the household of origin but outside agriculture, it is likely that net transfers of resources from the younger to the older generations took place.[5] Second, returns from additional children might have diminished, but the pace at which this occurred was probably low, especially because employment outside the home or within the home but outside agriculture was available. In other words, the marginal gain to the parents of an additional child was likely to remain positive as long as those working away from home also remitted a part of their earnings to their families. In this perspective, the rational reproductive strategy for the heads of such labor-intensive familial production units—who themselves utilized only a portion of their reproductive capacity because of delayed marriage—would generally not use further restraint in marital fertility. Third, if the demographic system operated via controls on nuptiality and not on marital fertility, a moral code and mechanisms of social control must have existed, legitimizing and enforcing such a system. Hence, what would be needed at the next stage, that is, the onset of the marital fertility transition, was not only a major change with respect to the parameters of household economies, but also a change in the cultural domain through which any new forms of fertility behavior would be legitimized. A regime of the type just outlined is more typical of the households of tenant farmers and workers in cottage industries—i.e., for those whose means of production is familial labor—than for those who can also rely on capital (including land). To see the argument in its proper perspective, we must examine the situation of other social and professional groups. Table 6.1 provides a summary and should prove useful as a first sketch.

In broad outline, four relevant categories can be identified in Western Europe just before the onset of the marital fertility decline. The first comprises what we have already termed the group of rural workers who predominantly rely on their families and who possess little or no capital.

[4] The term "natural fertility" as it is used here is discussed by Coale in Chapter 1.

[5] Caldwell (1976) terms such flows "wealth flows." We prefer the more general "support flows" since much more than purely financial transactions are involved.

Table 6.1. Socio-professional groupings in the nineteenth century: The bases of fertility behavior.

Socio-Professional Group	Mode of Production	Predominant Factor of Production	Optimal Fertility Strategy
A. Rural workers (Day laborers, workers in cottage industry, tenant farmers and combinations thereof)	Familial production. Net support flows from younger to older generations.	Labor	Natural fertility
B. Farmers, independent craftsmen	Familial production. Net support flows as in A but complicated by the problem of inheritance	Labor and capital	Either natural fertility or fertility control depending on trade-off between factors
C. Urban and rural bourgeoisie, aristocracy	Familial ownership with problems of inheritance uppermost. Net support flows probably from older to younger generations	Capital	Fertility control
D. Urban/industrial proletariat and workers on large scale agricultural enterprises	Non-familial production. 1. With no real income growth, net transfers from younger to older generations 2. With real income increase, possible reversal of flows	Labor	1. Natural fertility 2. Fertility control

The second group is composed of landowning farmers and independent artisans and craftsmen. The third is the bourgeoisie and aristocracy, and the fourth consists of the urban-industrial proletariat and workers in large-scale extensive agricultural enterprises.

For the landowning farmers and craftsmen (group B in Table 6.1), much of the logic of support flows[6] outlined for the first group also applies: labor remains an important element in a familial production unit and children provide that labor from about age 10 until they marry. From this point of view a rational fertility strategy would again be natural fertility. However, while the first group possessed only labor as a factor of production, the farmers and independent craftsmen of group B also had capital, and as a result had to consider the intergenerational transmission of their capital through inheritance. In a stationary population (for example, Europe in 1600–1750) this problem would not arise because a surfeit of male heirs in one family would be balanced by a deficit in another. By the early nineteenth century, however, Western Europe had long since ceased to be a stationary population, and a tendency toward lower fertility could be anticipated in an attempt to avoid the manifold division of capital in any society where primogeniture was not applied. For them, it seems likely that considerations of inheritance would be overridden by the advantages of the labor provided by children. In any case, by the nineteenth century many transfers of land occurred through the market rather than through inheritance. Thus the centrality of inheritance to the process of fertility transition seems dubious. Nevertheless, as argued by Habakkuk (1955), the trade-off between the opposing strategies of family building does seem to have produced a greater diversity of levels of fertility among farmers than among workers in cottage industries, who almost universally demonstrated high fertility.

For the third major division of society, the bourgeoisie—either rural or urban—and the small number of nobility and gentry (group C in Table 6.1),

[6] The strength and direction of intergenerational transfers of goods, services, money, and so on has over the last decade become a central and controversial theme in economic anthropology. An early application of such concepts to the problem of demographic transition was made by J. C. Caldwell in his article in *Population and Development Review*, "Towards a Restatement of Demographic Transition Theory" (1976). He assembled evidence from a number of contemporary developing countries to support the view that the direction of net intergenerational flows in traditional settings was from younger to older generations, while the converse was true in post-transitional societies. Unfortunately, detailed work of this nature on the European historical data has not yet been undertaken. For further references see Caldwell (1976, 1977).

the determination of an optimal fertility strategy was different again. For these groups the key was ownership rather than production. Capital was their predominant means of production; thus the arguments over inheritance given for independent farmers also apply to the bourgeoisie—indeed even more so because the amounts of capital involved are greater. Furthermore, children served little or no direct economic purpose until a relatively advanced age. Because parents in this group were expected to educate their children, the direction of net support flows probably went from parents to children, or perhaps weakly in the opposite direction. It is not surprising, therefore, that the earliest evidence of family limitation refers to just such elite groups (see Chapter 3 by M. Livi-Bacci).

The last group in Table 6.1 is made up of the urban and industrial proletariat and rural wage earners in large-scale, quasi-industrial agricultural enterprises (group D). Here was a group for whom the family was no longer the unit of production and for whom labor was the only factor of production at its disposal. The implications of this combination are, we think, likely to be highly dependent on trends in real income. Without an increase in real income and without any opening up of socioprofessional stratification, social perceptions are unlikely to view an investment in a child's education as a profitable investment. However, as the nineteenth century progressed and real incomes grew markedly (especially after 1850–1860) and education came to be seen as the key to betterment and intergenerational social mobility, such perceptions changed. With this change, a weakening of the links between the generations occurred first and then came a reversal of the support flows within the households of the urban workers. We suggest that once these changes took place, family limitation would become the most suitable fertility strategy for this group as well.

We now turn to an elaboration of these questions of social change and the role of education and social mobility, since they are central to an understanding of perceptions of economic and social advantages of the time.

In nineteenth-century Western Europe, the system of social status and associated income levels was gradually replaced with a new hierarchy: the traditional status system based on ascribed status yielded reluctantly to a newer one based more on achieved status. One must state this with caution, since the amount of vertical social mobility during the establishment of the new social order was limited. Rather, we can characterize the changes as a process whereby one social hierarchy was translated into another with little change at the time in the relative positions of groups or individuals. In other words, the changes could probably be better described by "lateral mobility" rather than "vertical mobility." By lateral mobility we refer to individuals or children with parents who were at the bottom of the social stratification system in the traditional sectors and then moved to new types of work provided by the growth of urban and industrial sectors, but stayed at the lower echelons of these new sectors. By the same token, those who were in the middle or at the top of the stratification system in the traditional sector moved laterally to approximately corresponding positions in the new sectors.[7]

The most disadvantaged by the shift to the new hierarchy were those left at the bottom of the traditional social scale: landless agricultural laborers, small tenants, and workers in the cottage industry. This lack of mobility was due to their lack of access to an education, which was essential to the emerging urban-industrial social system after 1860 and was the key to whatever limited opportunity for upward social mobility it could provide. Its importance is reflected in its rapid growth throughout the nineteenth century; the legal provisions for universal primary education from the 1860s onward represent the culmination and codification of a process that was already well established.

As suggested above, in certain circumstances the urban-industrial proletariat could be fairly responsive to opportunities such as education. The rural proletariat and cottage workers, however, were less likely to take advantage, partly because their real income barely increased and partly because they retained the familial, labor-intensive modes of production. This implied that parents were less likely to view education of children beyond some primary or vocational schooling as an advantage. Such households were thus denied the same degree of accessibility to the new social status system and remained a visible reminder of a disappearing social order.

Groups in society unhindered by the constraints of such a mode of production were increasingly likely to see an investment in childrens' education as positive step, even though it required the foregoing of current income and possible fees. And, as the societies of Western Europe prospered, education became increasingly affordable. An initial, intermediate

[7] For a more elaborate description of this process of the translation of one social order into another, see W. Kollmann (1976), where the author details the process for Germany between 1870 and 1910.

position could also have played a major role: parents could have invested income from their older children in the education of the younger.

In sum, then, as industrialization advanced it entailed a progressive diminution in the proportion of households organized along the lines of a familial labor-intensive mode of production. This implied a progressively greater proportion of the population that would view an investment in "high-quality children" as advantageous; this in turn produced more parents who saw an advantage in limiting the number of children. However, we must be careful to retain an accurate time perspective: we are discussing phenomena that work themselves out over more than one generation. Moreover, these phenomena are not characterized by sudden and rapid changes. Caldwell speaks of a "great divide, a point where the compass (indicating the direction of support flows) hesitatingly swings around 180 degrees" (1976, p. 345). It is a point more visible with the benefit of hindsight than to individuals who are enmeshed in the complexities of day-to-day existence.

Perhaps the most important corollary of the modernization of the modes of economic production was not so much the presumed reversal of "net support flows" between the generations as the growing independence and self-orientation of each. Unmarried children became less pressured by parents to conform to traditional patterns of behavior, not because they were more likely to be more educated than their parents, but because the father was no longer the manager of the familial unit of production and was losing economic control over wage-earning sons and daughters. This increasing independence of the younger generation was reflected in the trend toward earlier and more universal marriage, and especially in the increase in premarital conceptions and births. Since births were frequently recognized by both parents and "legitimized" afterwards, this increase can be interpreted not as measuring an increase in casual unions, but rather as a decrease in parental control over the timing of the wedding.

The picture presented so far of the structural changes of the nineteenth century leading to a marital fertility decline is a rather classic one: the gradual decline of the familial mode of production, the rising aspirations with respect to intergenerational mobility, the role of education in a situation where parents can increasingly afford it, and the increasing degree of independence between the generations all lead to much faster diminishing returns from children. The problem with such classic explanations is not that they are false, but that they are largely incomplete. The missing ingredient is cultural, not structural, as we shall now try to show.

Fertility Must Be within the Calculus of Conscious Choice

Any discussion of the moral and intellectual climate within which individuals reached their decisions in the nineteenth and early twentieth centuries inevitably revolves around the Christian moral and ethical system and its transformation. We propose that this moral system can be viewed as an excellent intellectual adaptation to, and buttress of, the traditional familial mode of production in Western Europe. The intergenerational solidarity between members of the family, so necessary for the smooth operation of such familial economic units of production, was a central concern of Christian teaching. The paternal control of this unit was thoroughly legitimized by the prevailing moral code, for which the Christian churches acted as guardians.

The eighteenth and nineteenth centuries, however, witnessed a turning away from the Christian ethic and a movement toward secular ideals. During a first phase, this secularization involved the elaboration of a fundamentally individualistic philosophy, one which drew more and more facets of a person's life into the realm of personal decision making, leaving a dwindling number in the field of social compulsion.[8] The French Revolution may have begun from such secularizing propositions, but it went much further than the mere amendment of the role of the Catholic Church: it released a "total" attack on it as an institution by devastating its roots in the economy and class structure. The Catholic Church in France would never entirely recover from this setback, not even at the time of the Second Empire.

The second wave of secularization was a corollary to a major attack on the prevailing social and economic structures of the mid-nineteenth century. Now the dominant concern was no longer to specify the indivi-

[8] Peter L. Berger has discussed the development of secularization at length in *The Social Reality of Religion* (1973). Following his definition, we have taken secularization to mean "the process by which sectors of society and culture are removed from the domination of religious institutions and symbols" (p. 113). Berger also points to the centrality of the breakdown of the traditional mode of production: "The original carrier of secularization is the modern economic process, that is, the dynamic of industrial capitalism" (p. 115) and to "a cultural lag between the secularization of the economy on the one hand and that of the state and family on the other"; this latter observation has implications for the date of the onset of fertility decline.

dual's rights and privileges within the limits of social contracts (which mimicked the patriarchy of family governance) but rather to insist on the political rights and power of a presumably homogeneous proletarian group. By 1860, such un-Christian demands, justified by sheer power relations and promising material rather than spiritual rewards, had become a major threat to the moral authority of the Church. By the end of the century, the challenge was intensified: less orthodox orientations of socialism, and more social-reformist factions of Liberal parties, had succeeded in building a network of social provisions in Western Europe, which extended an alternative system of patronage to a much larger section of the population than any organization besides the churches had ever done.

Inevitably, the impact of such changes depended on whether these waves of secularization existed on Protestant or Catholic shores. In Protestant areas, where the ideals of individual responsibility had been enshrined at the time of the Reformation, extensions of individualism produced no major shocks during the first half of the nineteenth century. Later, Protestant churches were either sufficiently decentralized to accommodate shifts in emphasis or, where a cleavage was felt, new churches could be formed. By the end of the century, the range of orientations had expanded, varying from the Methodist churches to "official," state-linked Protestant churches and further to fundamentalist ones (for example, the "black stocking" churches in some Calvinist areas of the Netherlands).

In contrast, in Catholic countries and regions the trauma of social change was more strongly felt, beginning as early as the 1850s or 1860s. In Flanders, for instance, Catholic politicians had clearly become the patrons of the domestic industries after the crises of the late 1840s, and their economic policy until the 1880s remained one of protection of the small-scale units of production (that is, their clients) against the free-market policy of the Liberal entrepreneurs. This spirit was still very much alive as late as 1919, when the Belgian Primate, Cardinal Mercier, proclaimed in his well-known letter that the solidarity and the sense of sacrifice generated by the large, hard-working Catholic family was the cornerstone on which the nation had to be rebuilt after the devastations of World War I. Another important element of the Catholic reaction—perhaps the term "backlash" would be appropriate—is the fundamentalist orientation of Pius IX in the 1860s. From that point on-ward, not only did Catholic doctrine rigidify but the Church also made a deliberate attempt to cultivate a wider basis of popular support, especially among those groups where the familial mode of production remained predominant. As a result, a "populist" movement organized around pilgrimages and devotions opposed its own symbols to those of the growing "red" urban-industrial proletariat. The proclamation of the encyclical Rerum Novarum in 1891 consolidated this movement by adding some social reformist ideals, but in fact it added momentum to the movement toward further *verzuiling*[9] in Catholic and mixed Catholic-Protestant areas of Western Europe.[10]

The first clash that impinged upon the daily life of families in the villages of Belgium, Holland, Switzerland, and Germany centered on the control of a most basic institution in any society: the schools. The "school wars" of the 1880s and 1890s and the German *Kulturkampf* indicate quite clearly that the cleavages of *verzuiling* were growing along moral, ethical, and ideological divisions. They foreshadowed the fact that few people would be able to organize any basic aspect of life without a link to these increasingly competitive factions and that the degree of *verzuiling* would come to further prominence in the 1920s and especially in the 1930s.

The decline of marital fertility, generated by the economic and social changes described earlier, continued during this period of growing polarization and expanding ethical patronage. Under such conditions, calculations of economic advantage associated with higher or lower fertility were far from being solely determined by the nature of household production. Rather, ideological, moral, and religious convictions gained importance in the atmosphere of increasing polarization. As a consequence, it is reasonable to ask whether the moral acceptability of fertility control might have become an important explanation (over and above the effect of changes in the occupational structure) for leads and lags in areas and among various population segments with respect to the actual speed of the marital fertility transition.

[9] The Dutch word *verzuiling*, derived from *zuil*, meaning pillar or column, implies a societal organization where all aspects of life are organized within a series of parallel ethical and political factions. Each of them would, for instance, patronize hospital services, news media, educational facilities, labor unions, and other social amenities.

[10] A comprehensive and thoughtful discussion of the twin processes of radicalization and democratization within the Catholic Church is found in H. Verbist (1971). The matter of changes in philosophy of the Catholic Church during the nineteenth century with respect to fertility control has been very extensively discussed by J. Stengers (1971) and the reaction of the socialist parties and neo-Malthusian groups in the Low Countries by Ph. Van Praag (1978).

Hypotheses

We are now in a position to outline the main hypotheses derived from the preceding discussion. As mentioned earlier, our intention in this paper is to provide only the framework for a model of fertility transition; our proposals will be stated simply and briefly.

First, we hypothesize that the speed of the fertility transition in an area, restricted to countries for which we will present data later, depends on the nature of the economic circumstances of the households in that area. Specifically, we suggest that where the prevailing situation is one of dependence on a familial, labor-intensive mode of production—as is characteristic among farmers, tenants and owners, and workers in cottage industries—the onset of a fertility transition will be late or the pace of the transition will be slow. Conversely, where such a mode of production has been replaced in urban-industrial settings by nonfamilial labor, where real wage increases occurred, where the advantages of education as a vehicle for lateral and, to a lesser extent, upward social mobility are perceived, and where the younger generation achieves greater independence, we suggest that the conditions exist at the beginning of the transition and progresses at a more rapid pace.

Second, we hypothesize that the moral and ethical milieus of the household can accelerate or retard the fertility decline. In areas marked by high degrees of secularization, we suggest that fertility is likely to be perceived as yet another aspect of life that is under individual control, while in areas where traditional moral codes remain strong, fertility decisions will not be allowed to come into the sphere of the "calculus of conscious choice."

Third, we hypothesize that the nature of the relationship between these two major factors will depend on the prevailing religious affiliation. In homogeneous Protestant regions the intellectual adjustments to secularization produced only limited reaction from the guardians of traditional morality, the churches, and thus led to little polarization of society along ideological or attitudinal lines, whereas in Catholic or mixed regions the hostility of the Church to any modification of morality and the sometimes century-old militancy of its opponents created a marked division of society along just such lines. In these circumstances, questions of moral acceptability can be expected to carry much more significance than in the relatively homogeneous and more flexible moral climates of Protestant countries.

Now we can turn to the problems of operationalization. However, before doing so it is interesting to note that, although some of the ideas expressed in the present work—especially those related to hypothesis 2—may appear less familiar to those concerned with the question of the demographic transition, they are not in essence novel. Julius Wolf already published an article in 1912 in which he drew attention to the correlation between secularization and fertility decline.[11]

Operationalization and Specification

The hypotheses outlined above cannot be tested at the household level, since data are not available. Therefore, operationalization must take place at a higher level of aggregation, in this case in the provinces of Europe. In the Netherlands, however, no convenient administrative unit existed: the eleven provinces were composed of a thousand or so communities. To overcome this problem, we took a stratified sample of 136 communities to get as reasonable a cross-section of the nation as possible. Given the much smaller populations of such units, one can inevitably expect more variation and hence lower correlations between variables. Nevertheless, structural relations should still be apparent even if the scatter of individual points is greater.

A Measure of Fertility Transition

Since we hope to explain here the precocity and speed of the marital fertility transition in the regions under study, it is preferable to use as the

[11] J. Wolf's work "Kinderzahl and Sozialdemokratie in Deutschland" was brought to our attention by K. Schwarz. In it Wolf presents statistics suggestive of a relationship between birth rates and the percentage of votes cast for the Socialist party. He himself notes, however, that in many cases the relationship is hidden by other factors and cannot be "isolated." Moreover he refers to symmetry between Socialist votes and the birth rate, since both are the result of a common cause, namely changes in *Weltanschauung*. In our study we take the voting patterns as a proxy for such changes and thus hypothesize an asymmetrical relationship where fertility is the dependent variable and voting patterns the independent. The quote that summarizes Wolf's point of view is as follows: "Natürlich ist nicht die Parteizugehörigkeit das Primare und die Geburtenziffer das Sekundare oder umgekehrt. Viel mehr haben die Geburtenfrequenz und die Parteizugehörigkeit die gleiche Quelle. Ganz im Sinne des von mir entwickelten Bevölkerungsgesetzes wird und kann der Repräsentant einer atheistischen, auf ökonomische bzw. egoistische Motivationen gestützten, nach jeder Richtung emanzi-pierten Weltanschauung keiner grossen Familie das Leben geben, während der Repräsentant einer religiosen, auf das kirchliche Sittengebot gestützten Kultur einer grosseren Zahl Kinder günstig ist."

dependent variable some indication of the precocity and speed of fertility decline rather than a simple measure of fertility level. This is especially true in countries characterized by great variation in pre-transition—that is, natural—fertility levels. The measure we chose was the amount of marital fertility decline that occurred during a certain period, expressed as a proportion of the whole drop in marital fertility eventually experienced by each area. This we termed ΔI_g and defined it as follows:

$$\Delta I_g(t_0, t_1) = \frac{I_g(t_0) - I_g(t_1)}{I_g(t_0) - 0.2}.$$

I_g stands for the usual standardized index of marital fertility as defined in Chapter 2, while t_0 and t_1 are dates defined, respectively, as the last date before any area experienced a sustained drop in marital fertility (usually around 1870 in the countries that concern us here) and the date at which any particular country reaches mid transition (usually around 1910).[12] Thus ΔI_g values indicate how much of the whole transition in marital fertility occurred between t_0 and t_1. To take an example, a value of ΔI_g (1880–1910) = 0.65 would indicate that in a particular region 65 percent of the whole fertility transition occurred between 1880 and 1910, while 35 percent took place after 1910, assuming that the final I_g is 0.20.

Unfortunately, for the Netherlands, data on the sex and marital status distributions are not available by five-year age groups for small units with populations below 10,000. Thus, because I_g's could not be calculated, we had to rely on marital fertility rates (number of legitimate live births per 1,000 married women aged 15–45) and define a measure of change as:

$$\Delta \text{ marital fertility rate (15–45)} = \frac{\text{rate 1879} - \text{rate 1908/11}}{\text{rate 1879} - \text{rate 1971/72}}.$$

Although analogous to ΔI_g, this measure is affected by age structure distortions especially in smaller communities, and so a much greater degree of "noise" can be anticipated in it than in the ΔI_g values for other countries.

[12] More exactly, t_1 is the date at which, given t_0, the variance of ΔI_g is at a maximum, that is, when the greatest regional differences are found in terms of how far along the road of transition each region has come.

Independent Variables

Our first hypothesis was that the decline of marital fertility depended on the extent to which households were still operating along the lines of the familial, labor-intensive mode of production (FLIMP). This we have attempted to operationalize by making use of the data on occupational category from the various censuses. Whenever possible, we have taken the proportion of active population (or active male population) engaged in the sectors of the economy where such a mode of production was prevalent—that is, in agriculture and cottage industry. For certain countries (Italy, Denmark, the Netherlands), however, it did not prove possible to separate those employed in cottage industry from persons engaged in nonfamilially organized industrial concerns; for these countries the proportion engaged in agriculture and in the rest of the primary sector was used as a proxy. The exact specifications are given in Table 6.3.

Our second hypothesis was that moral factors, especially the degree of secularization, also play a role in explaining the fertility transition. We posited that, given the considerable overlap in the decades around 1900 between political behavior and wider attitudinal factors, the votes cast for parties of a nonconfessional or social-reformist slant could be taken as a suitable proxy for the degree of secularization. In this analysis, we measured secularization by the proportion of votes cast for such parties in the first national elections held under universal male suffrage. Most of these elections occurred in the four years after World War I, the only exception to this being the Netherlands, where suitable results for small communities were not available until the 1933 elections. The relevant political parties are indicated in Table 6.2, and the variable computed from their summed support was termed V1.

The relationship between the mode of production (FLIMP) and the secularization variable (V1) is of course not negligible, as any student of European history would know: the zero-order correlation coefficient between them ranges from -0.32 in the subsample of predominantly Protestant Dutch communities to not less than -0.80 in the twenty-five Swiss cantons. Obviously, areas with large proportions of the active population in agriculture and small domestic industries were not attracted by the Socialist programs, largely for the following three reasons:

1. Socialist doctrines were predominantly oriented toward wage earners in larger enterprises;

Table 6.2. Non-confessional and/or social-reformist parties taken for the definition of the variable V1.

Country	Date of Election	Parties
Belgium	1919	Werkliedenpartij (Socialists), Liberale Partij, Communistische Partij
Denmark	1918	Social Arbejder Parti, Social Demokrat Parti, Radicale Venstre, Independent Socialists
Germany	1920-1922*	Sozial Demokratische Partei, Kommunistische Partei, Unabhängige Sozial Demokratische Partei
Italy	1921	Socialista Ufficiale, Communiste, Socialista riforma, Socialista independente
Netherlands	1933	Communistische Partij, Revolutionaire Socialistische Partij, Sociaal-Democratische Arbeiders-Partij, Vrijzinnig Democratische Bond
Switzerland	1922	Liberal-demokratische Fraktion, Sozial-demokratische Partei, Kommunistische Partei, Jungfreisinnigen und Jungradicalen, Grutlianen (Independent Socialists)

*Elections in 3 Wahlkreise, Ostpreussen, Oppeln and Schleswig-Holstein took place in the two years following the 1920 General Election.

Sources:

Belgium: R. De Smet, R. Evalenko and W. Fraeys, Atlas des Elections Belges 1919-1954, Institut de Sociologie Solvay, Université Libre de Bruxelles, 1958.

Denmark: Danmarks Statistik, Rigdagsvalgene 1918, 4. Raekke - 57.Bind 1. Haefte, pp. 119-123.

Germany: Statistischen Reichsamt, Statistik des Deutschen Reichs, Band 291, I, pp. 114-129; III, pp. 17-23; IV, pp. 19-21. Berlin, 1920, 1921, 1922.

Italy: Direzione Generale della Statistica, Statistica delle Elezione Generale Politiche per la XXVI Legislatura, Rome, 1923.

Netherlands: Centraal Bureau voor de Statistiek, Statistisch Overzicht van de Verkiezingen 1933, Inhoudende Gegevens omtrent de Verkiezingen voor de 2e Kamer der Staten Generaal, Serie A, No. 2, pp. 24-28, 1935.

Switzerland: Eidgenossischen Statistischen Amt - Statistik der Nationalratswahlen 1919-1928, Statistische Mitteilungen, Vol. XI, Heft 1, pp. 24-35, 1929.

Table 6.3. The definition of the variable representing the familial labor-intensive mode of production (FLIMP).

Country	Date	Definition
Belgium	1900	Proportion of active males in agriculture and cottage industry
Denmark	1880	Proportion of active population in agriculture
Germany	1907	Proportion of active population in agriculture and cottage industry
Italy	1921	Proportion of active males in agriculture
Netherlands	1909	Proportion of active males in agriculture
Switzerland	1910	Proportion of active population in agriculture and cottage industry

Sources:

Belgium: Ministère de l'Industrie et du Travail, Office du Travail, L'Industrie a Domicile en Belgique, Vol. X, Etudes Statistiques des Familles Ouvrieres, Societé Belge de Librairie, Brussels, 1909.
Institut National de la Statistique, Population Census 1900.

Denmark: Folketaellingen i Kongeriget Danmark den 1 Feb. 1880, Statistik Tabelraek, 4. Raekke, Litra A. No. 3, Copenhagen, 1883.

Germany: Statistischen Reichsamt, Statistik des Deutschen Reichs, Population Census 1907, Hausindustrie in Deutschland.

Italy: O. Vitali, Aspetti della Sviluppo Economico Italiana alla Luce della Riconstruzione della Popolazione Attiva, Rome, 1970.

Netherlands: Centraal Bureau voor de Statistiek, Population Census 1910.

Switzerland: Eidgenossischen Statistischen Amt, "Die Hausindustrie in der Schweiz nach der Volkzahlung von 1. Dec. 1910," Statistiche Mitteilungen, 1919, Heft 2.

2. The family as such in the Socialist doctrine is merely a consumption unit, not a cell of production;
3. Both Catholic and Protestant churches were succeeding, especially in rural areas, in replacing the old patronage network based on "village notables" by their own new form of particratic patronage, which could easily compete with the new welfare organizations that the Socialist parties were creating elsewhere.

The net result of this fragmentation is that Socialist parties (or later the Social Democrats) would largely remain secularized "class parties": their cement is the solidarity among those in a similar economic position (that is, the wage earners). The confessional parties (later the Christian Democrats) would form "Standen-parties,"[13] which integrate diverse occupational strata under the umbrella of common religious values. There the protection of the Christian family as a dynamic unit of production is the cement of the integration. Hence, the underlying meaning of the strong negative relation between FLIMP and V1 is that the changes in the economic structure not only produced a broader array of occupations, but also far more clear-cut distinctions with respect to political ideology and degree of secularization. In other words, the causality runs from the mode of the production (or occupational) variable to the secularization variable, and not the other way around.

This feature has important implications for any further multivariate statistical analysis. The problem of multicollinearity generated by high zero-order correlation coefficients between FLIMP and V1 stems from the fact that in reality FLIMP can be taken as a causal antecedent of V1. Any common variance between them (that is, $r^2_{\mathrm{FLIMP\,V1}}$) ought to be assigned to FLIMP. This can be done in a variety of ways. The use of stepwise regression, for instance, would show the effect of V1 through the increment in r^2, after FLIMP has been introduced at an earlier step. The same can be accomplished by first regressing V1 on FLIMP and by working with a new variable, V2, which is the residual of V1 in the regression:

$$\mathrm{V1} = a + b\,\mathrm{FLIMP} + \varepsilon_{\mathrm{V1}} \tag{1}$$

$$\mathrm{V2} = \varepsilon_{\mathrm{V1}}. \tag{2}$$

The values of V2 are sociologically directly meaningful, as V2 now indicates the excess or deficit of votes for secularized parties compared to the vote that one would expect on the basis of the degree of employment

[13] The German word *Standen* refers to the fact that different social strata would be integrated in one political party. *Standen* parties typically draw support from such diverse occupational groups as farmers, wage earners, the self-employed, entrepreneurs, or managerial cadres. The structure of the overall organization is therefore composed of various smaller organizations that defend the interest of each of these occupational groups. Economic tensions between these groups are often reduced through internal negotiations, since a common ethical basis and hence also the defense of Christian family values is of paramount importance to all of them.

in the FLIMP sectors. We have chosen the second procedure because we were also interested in seeing what the values of V2 would be in each of the areas. The equations with which we can now work are simply:

$$\Delta I_g = A + B_1 \text{ FLIMP} + B_2 \text{ V2} + \varepsilon, \tag{3}$$

or in z-scores:

$$z_{\Delta I_g} = \beta_1 z_{\text{FLIMP}} + \beta_2 z_{\text{V2}} + \text{u}. \tag{4}$$

Since FLIMP and V2 are orthogonal variables, the multiple correlation coefficient $r^2_{\Delta Ig \cdot \text{FLIMP V2}}$ is nothing else but

$$r^2_{\Delta I_g \text{ FLIMP}} + r^2_{\Delta I_g \text{ V2}}, \tag{5}$$

or $\beta_1^2 + \beta_2^2$ in equation (4). Moreover, β_2 will be equal to the part correlation coefficient of ΔI_g on V1, controlling for FLIMP.[13] Finally, a model incorporating an interaction term between FLIMP and V2 was tried, but the improvement in explained variance was trivial. Hence, equations (3) and (4) will be used as simple devices for subsequent empirical analysis.

Empirical Results

Before discussing in detail the results obtained from the multivariate model just outlined, it might be of interest to first make a few more simple observations. First, with reference to Table 6.4, the suggestion that Protestant areas or countries experienced a relatively homogeneous fertility transition while Catholic areas saw more heterogeneity can be readily confirmed. The figures presented there indicate that in Prostestant regions of Germany and Switzerland and in Denmark, the standard deviations of the ΔI_g-series ranged from 0.109 to 0.145, whereas Catholic areas evinced considerably greater variance with standard deviations from 0.151 to 0.264.

Another indication of the soundness of the present formulation comes from a consideration of the variable FLIMP. We pointed out that wherever possible this was calculated as a combination of the proportions engaged in agriculture and in cottage industry, rather than as simply the proportion engaged in agriculture (a more conventional indicator of urbanization-industrialization), because the mode of production in cottage industry and agriculture was the same. The advantage of doing this is apparent as soon as one examines the strength of the relationship between

Table 6.4. Means and standard deviations of ΔI_g in selected Catholic and Protestant regions of Europe.

Country	Dates of ΔI_g	Mean	S.D.	N of areas
Italy	1880–1931	.335	.264	16
Belgium	1880–1910	.465	.206	41
Catholic Germany	1869–1912	.280	.151	18
Catholic Switzerland	1860–1910	.307	.175	13
Protestant Germany	1869–1912	.419	.145	45
Protestant Switzerland	1860–1910	.450	.138	12
Denmark	1880–1911	.271	.109	19
Sweden	1881–1919/22	.378	.142	25

FLIMP and ΔI_g. In Switzerland, for example, the correlation coefficient between ΔI_g and the proportion engaged in agriculture ($r_{\Delta I_g \text{ Agric}}$) stood at -0.779. With the addition of cottage workers, this figure rose to -0.893. The Belgian data also indicate a marked rise from -0.759 to -0.811, while the German data showed the smallest improvement, from -0.676 to -0.712. Observations such as these suggest that the present approach is formulated on a sound basis, as is the evidence of the zero-order correlations between ΔI_g and V1 presented in the graphs of Figure 6.1. The visual impression of close correlation given by these scattergrams is confirmed by the figures of Table 6.5. Not only are the correlation coefficients noticeably high, ranging from 0.706 in Germany to 0.880 and 0.890 in Switzerland and Belgium, respectively, but all the data also reveal approximately the same slope and intercept, with B close to unity and A almost at zero. This line of exact proportionality between the percentage vote for secularized/social-reformist parties and the percentage of the fertility transition already realized is presented on the scattergrams of Figure 6.1 rather than the individual regression lines. Thus it is evident that one percentage point extra in nonconfessional voting was accompanied by a one-percentage-point advance along the road of fertility transition. Such a consistent pattern, found even in the Dutch data with

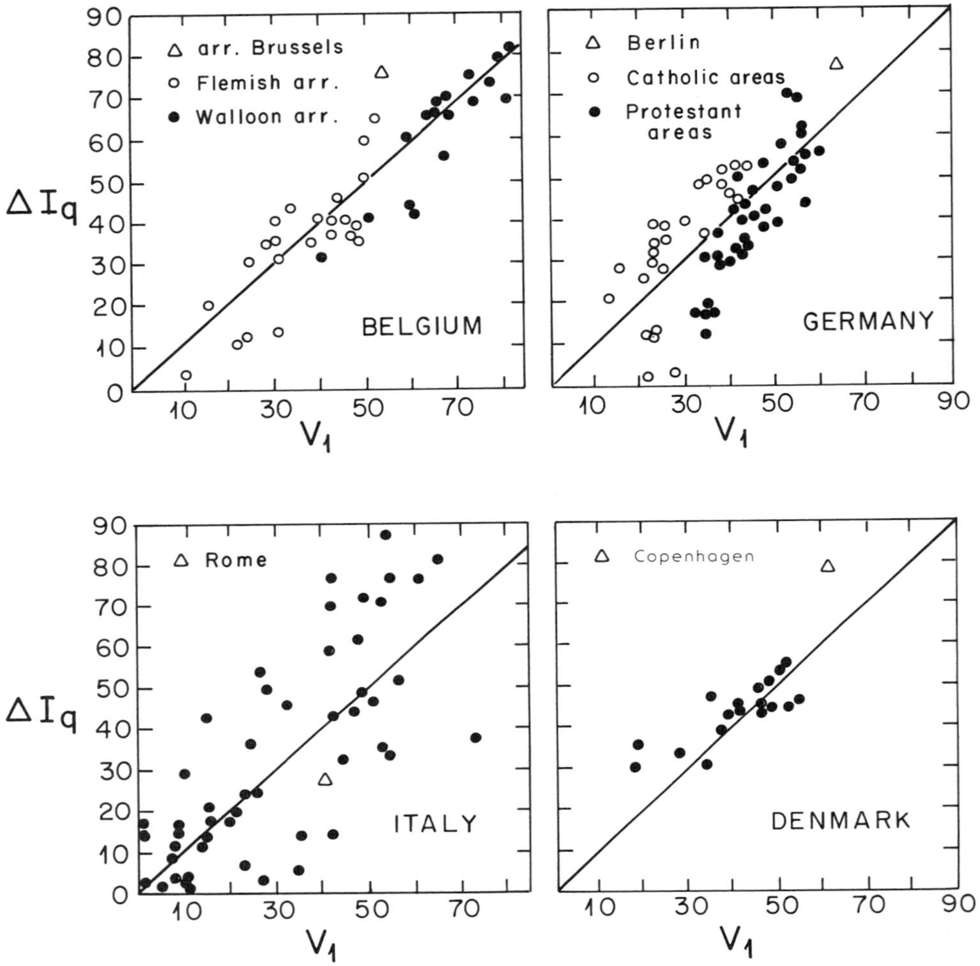

Figure 6.1. Relationship between the relative speed of the marital fertility decline and the percentage of votes for secularized social-reformist parties.

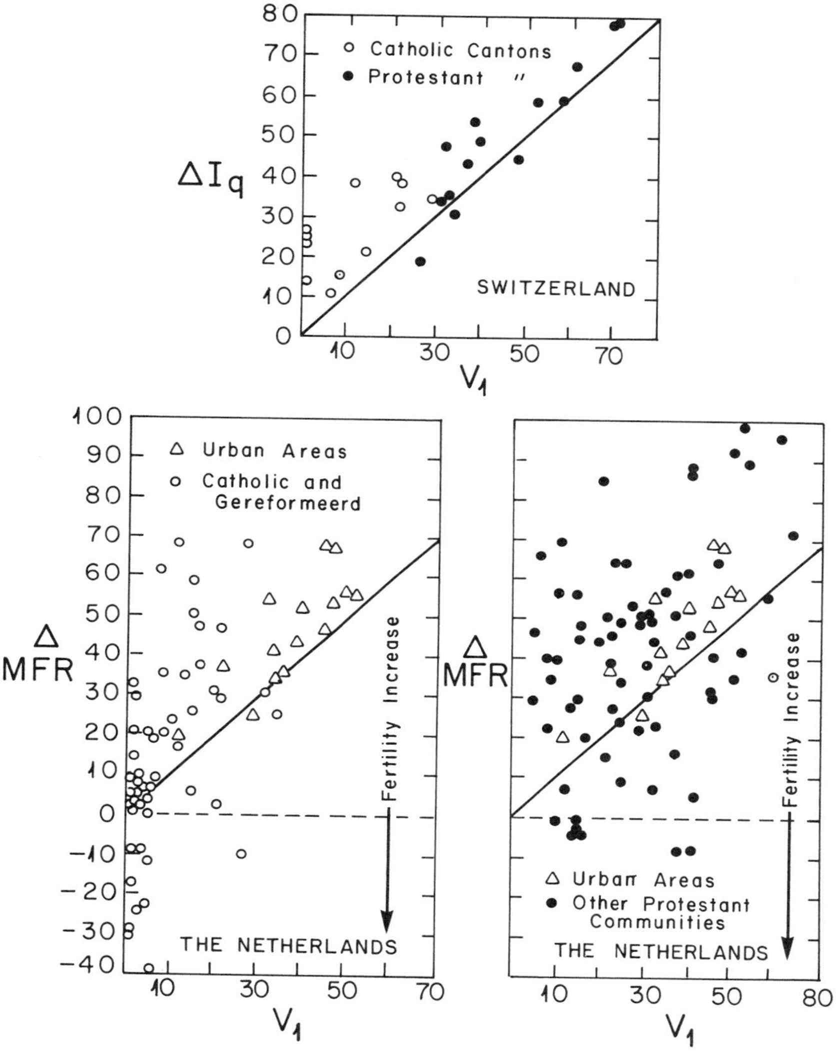

Country	Date of ΔI_g	V1, Percentage of Votes for Parties
Belgium	1880–1910	Communist, Socialist, and Liberal—1919
Italy	1881–1931	Three Socialist parties—1918
Germany	1869–1912	SPD, USPD, KPD—1920
Denmark	1880–1921	Three Socialist parties, Radicale Venstre—1918, 1920
Switzerland	1860–1920	KP, SPD, DAF, JuJ, Grut—1919–1922
Netherlands	1879–1911	CPH, SDAP, RSP, VDP—1933

Note: The names of the parties are given in full in Table 6.2. The units in each country are given in Table 6.6. I_g has been multiplied by 100.

all its extra "noise," goes a long way toward confirming our belief that around the turn of the century, political affiliation, with its ethical and ideological connotations, was indeed strongly related to regional lags and leads with respect to demographic behavior.[14]

Moving now to the simple multivariate model specified above we can complete the picture in a more thorough fashion. Table 6.6 presents the important results of the multiple regression; these results may best be understood by giving an example.

If we examine the first case, that of Italy, we can reconstruct the nature of the relationship between independent and dependent variables with

[14] If FLIMP is not taken as a causal antecedent to V1 (which in our view is a far less plausible assumption than the one defended in the text), the variance common to them cannot be assigned to FLIMP. This implies that partial instead of part correlation coefficients should be used, and that the relative impact of FLIMP will be reduced. These are given in the accompanying tables, once controlling for FLIMP and once for V1.

	r	r	r	r
Country	ΔI_g V1	ΔI_g V1, FLIMP	ΔI_g FLIMP	ΔI_g FLIMP, V1
Belgium (N = 41)	+.89	+.72	−.81	−.47
Switzerland (N = 25)	+.88	+.62	−.89	−.56
Italy (N = 16)	+.87	+.79	−.53	−.12
Denmark (N = 19)	+.80	+.58	−.94	−.81
Germany (N = 63)	+.71	+.43	−.72	−.47
Dutch Cath. and Ref. Communities (N = 54)	+.31	+.23	−.26	−.15
Dutch other Prot. Communities (N = 82)	+.42	+.38	−.23	−.11

Note again that the dependent variable for the Dutch communities is the change in the general marital fertility rate rather than in I_g. As expected, the correlation between the speed of the fertility decline and V1 remains largely resistant to the control for FLIMP in Belgium, Switzerland, Italy, and among the Dutch communities and less so in Germany and Denmark. Conversely, the drop in the relationship between ΔI_g and FLIMP due to a control for V1 is weakest in the latter two countries and strongest in the former four. On the whole, however, both FLIMP and V1 clearly have their own explanatory power, which is independent of that of the other. This again substantiates our conclusion that the speed of the marital fertility decline was not solely a function of modernization of the economic structure of the areas but also one of changes in the moral code. It should be noted, however, that the use of the procedure described in equations (1) through (4) gives a far more conservative impression of the role of the secularization variable than the procedure used here. As the main aim of the paper is to show that the secularization variable is indeed an important one, one additional reason is added for preferring the procedure used in the text to the use of partial correlations coefficients.

Table 6.5. Zero-order regression for the relationship between the relative speed of the marital fertility decline (ΔI_g) and the proportion of votes for secularized/social-reformist parties.

Country	Dependent Variable	Independent Variable	Regression Constant A	Regression Coefficient B	r	N
Belgium	ΔI_g 1880–1910	V1 1919	–.036	1.021	.890	41
Denmark	ΔI_g 1880–1921	V1 1918–1920	.271	.786	.802	19
Germany	ΔI_g 1870–1910	V1 1920	.027	.918	.706	62
Italy	ΔI_g 1881–1931	V1 1918	.059	.905	.731	53
Switzerland	ΔI_g 1860–1910	V1 1919–1922	.164	.761	.880	25
Netherlands	ΔMFR 1879–1911	V1 1933	.038	.945	.511	134

reference to the various columns of Table 6.6. Thus using the unstandardized regression coefficients, the *B*'s of column 4, we can see what the value of ΔI_g would have been given any combination of FLIMP and V2. If, for example, 44.7 percent of the male labor force in a particular Italian province worked in agriculture and it had an excess vote for the secularized parties that was 10.7 percent above expectations, given this level of agricultural involvement, we can calculate that it would already have undergone 65.5 percent of its marital fertility transition by 1931. That is to say,

$$\begin{gathered} A + B_1 \text{ FLIMP} + B_2 \text{ V2} = \Delta I_g' \\ 98.3\% + (-1.122 * 44.7\%) + (1.62 * 10.7\%) = 65.5\% \end{gathered} \tag{6}$$

Re-expressing this same example in terms of the standardized regression coefficients, the betas of column 5, we can say that a region with 1 σ below the mean value of FLIMP ($55.7\% - 13.0\% = 44.7\%$), and with 1 σ above the mean value for V2 ($0 + 10.7\%$) would have had a ΔI_g-value higher than the mean by $(\beta_1 + \beta_2) * \sigma_{\Delta I_g}$. That is,

$$\begin{gathered} \beta_1 z_{\text{FLIMP}} + \beta_2 z_{\text{V2}} = z_{\Delta I_g} \\ (-0.553 * -1) + (0.658 * 1) = 1.211. \end{gathered} \tag{7}$$

And a $z_{\Delta I_g}$-value of 1.211 corresponds to the mean value of ΔI_g (33.5%) plus $1.211 * \sigma_{\Delta I_g}$ (32.0%), or 65.5%.

Table 6.6. Parameters of equation [7].

Country + Variables	Mean X	Standard Deviation σ	Regression Constant A	Regression Coefficients B	Standardized Regression Coefficients β	Multiple Coefficients of Determination r^2
Italy (N=16)						
ΔI_g 1880–1931	.335	.264	.983			.739
FLIMP 1921	.577	.130		−1.122	−.553	
V2 1921	.000	.107		+1.620	+.658	
Belgium (N=41)						
ΔI_g 1880–1910	.465	.206	.940			.837
FLIMP 1900	.382	.134		−1.244	−.811	
V2 1919	.000	.126		+ .740	+.424	
Germany (N=63)						
ΔI_g 1871–1910	.379	.159	.704			.626
FLIMP 1907	.393	.137		− .826	−.712	
V2 1920	.000	.087		+ .625	+.345	
Germany Catholic areas (N=18)						
ΔI_g 1871–1910	.280	.151	.521			.347
FLIMP 1907	.451	.125		− .533	−.442	
V2 1920	.000	.052		+1.127	+.388	
Germany Protestant areas (N=45)						
ΔI_g 1871–1910	.419	.145	.726			.671
FLIMP 1907	.370	.135		− .830	−.776	
V2 1920	.000	.059		+ .641	+.262	
Switzerland (N=25)						
ΔI_g 1860–1910	.376	.171	.754			.862
FLIMP 1900	.383	.155		− .989	−.893	
V2 1922	.000	.121		+ .359	+.253	
Swiss Catholic areas (N=13)						
ΔI_g 1860–1910	.307	.175	.724			.833
FLIMP 1900	.434	.156		− .961	−.856	
V2 1922	.000	.105		+ .530	+.317	

Swiss Protestant areas (N=12)						
ΔI_g 1860–1910	.450	.138	.748			.858
FLIMP 1900	.328	.139		– .908	–.917	
V2 1922	.000	.071		+ .260	+.134	
Dutch Communities (N=136)*						
ΔMFR 1879–1911	.318	.282	.464			.299
FLIMP 1909	.456	.260		– .321	–.297	
V2 1933	.000	.159		+ .814	+.459	
Dutch Com. Catholic + Gereformeerd dominant (N=54)*						
ΔMFR 1879–1911	.166	.254	.302			.115
FLIMP 1909	.518	.247		– .263	–.256	
V2 1933	.000	.095		+ .598	+.223	
Dutch Com. Hervormd + other denominations dominant (N=82)*						
ΔMFR 1879–1911	.418	.254	.510			.186
FLIMP 1909	.414	.261		– .222	–.228	
V2 1933	.000	.147		+ .633	+.366	
Denmark (N=19)						
ΔI_g 1880–1911	.271	.109	.583			.885
FLIMP 1880	.358	.117		– .871	–.938	
V2 1918	.000	.062		+ .139	+.079	

*We feel that the operationalization of those engaged in familial labor-intensive modes of production for the Dutch communities through the mere proportions engaged in agriculture and horticulture is weak. The Dutch socioprofessional structure was highly diversified within and across villages (and more in the Protestant than in the Catholic ones) at the turn of the century so that FLIMP-units were probably present in large quantities in many types of activities of the secondary and even tertiary sector. Hence, a much more careful and detailed village per village operationalization of FLIMP, as suggested by more qualitative analyses of E. W. Hofstee, for instance, seems absolutely necessary. We feel that such a study would boost the values of R^2 and of B_1 and β_1 (of FLIMP) considerably, thereby bringing the Dutch results even more in line with the results for the other countries. We would also expect the values of β_2 of V2 for the communities with Hervormden and other Protestant denominations predominant to shrink below that of β_2 for the Catholic plus Gereformeerde communities. This expectation is based on the fact that a better measurement of FLIMP would lead to a more marked increase of $r^2_{FLIMP-V1}$ in the former set than in the latter, thereby boosting its β_1 and reducing β_2 of V2.

The beta coefficients squared also indicate the relative contribution of each of the independent variables to the multiple R^2. In this case V2 contributed 0.658^2, that is, 0.433, while FLIMP contributed 0.553^2, that is, 0.306. In other words, of the 73.9 percent of the variance of ΔI_g "explained" by the two variables in conjunction, 43.3 percent came from V2 and 30.6 percent from FLIMP. Thus for Italy, even when all the common variance between secularization and socioeconomic structure is given to FLIMP, V2 still retains its importance; indeed, it contributes more to predicting the regional pattern of ΔI_g than does FLIMP. A glance down column 5 to see the betas will confirm that as one moves to Protestant regions and countries, V2 increasingly loses importance relative to FLIMP.

Table 6.7. Increase in the proportion of total marital fertility transition realized before a specified date as a result of 10 percentage points reduction in proportions engaged in familial labor-intensive modes of production and of a 10 percentage points excess of votes for secularized/social-reformist parties.

	Effect of 10 percentage points drop in FLIMP	Effect of 10 percentage points excedent in non-confessional votes (V2=.10)	Percent of variance of ΔI_g explained by FLIMP	V2	Both
<u>Protestant</u>					
Denmark	+ 8.7%*	+ 1.4%*	88.0	0.6	88.5
Protestant Germany	+ 8.3	+ 6.4	60.2	6.9	67.1
Protestant Switzerland	+ 9.1	+ 2.6	84.0	1.8	85.8
<u>Mixed</u>					
All Germany	+ 8.3	+ 6.3	50.7	11.9	62.6
All Switzerland	+ 9.9	+ 3.6	79.7	6.5	86.2
<u>Catholic</u>					
Catholic Switzerland	+ 9.6	+ 5.3	73.3	10.0	83.3
Catholic Germany	+ 5.3	+11.3	19.5	15.1	34.7
Belgium	+12.4	+ 7.4	65.8	17.9	83.7
Italy	+11.2	+16.2	30.6	43.3	73.9

*The %-sign should be read here as "percentage points," i.e., the unit in which ΔI_g is expressed.

This point is examined in Table 6.7, where the effects of a 10-percent drop in FLIMP and a 10-percent excess of secularized votes are presented, and the proportions of the variance of ΔI_g are "explained" by each independent variable. The individual cases are again arranged according to religion, and the differences between the Catholic and Protestant examples stand out at once. In Protestant regions of Germany and Switzerland as well as in Denmark, the beta coefficients for V2 are tiny compared with those for FLIMP. In Catholic Germany and Switzerland, and in Belgium and Italy, the relative impact of secularization was considerable, in Italy exceeding the impact of FLIMP.

This great variability in the impact of secularization is further seen in the effects that, given the observed regression lines, a 10-percent change in FLIMP and V2 would have entailed. While the effect of a decrease in FLIMP of 10 percent would have been similar in all areas (with the exception of Catholic areas of Germany, it would have entailed between 7 and 12 percent increase in ΔI_g), an equal increase in V2 would have produced only a 1.4 percent increase in ΔI_g in Denmark but a 16.2 percent rise in Italy. To sum up, these results confirm all three hypotheses derived from our initial theory. Both the survival of a familial, labor-intensive mode of production and the relative level of secularization are related to the speed with which different regions moved along the road of demographic transition, and the importance of the two independent variables differs markedly between societies with a Catholic and a Protestant tradition.

Conclusions

We have proposed that two factors are fundamental to an understanding of the decline of marital fertility. We realize that we are not doing full justice to the complexity of the past: we have by no means explained all that we would wish to explain, but rather have articulated a model, a skeleton that must be enlarged, amended, and refined when applied in each specific case. Nevertheless, in its simplicity and unambiguous formulation of the central issues, we feel it offers a fruitful approach to understanding the early fertility transition in Western Europe.

Our first contention has been that fertility behavior was heavily influenced by the nature of the economic circumstances of the households; we suggest in particular that where a familial, labor-intensive mode of production existed there was little movement in the direction of family limitation. A mode of production was replaced or "corrupted" from within by parents' expectations of the prospective lateral mobility of their children into the wage-earning sectors, and as the younger generation increased its independence, the social and economic functions of sustained high fertility were weakened. With the further opening up of the occupational structure, greater investment per child became feasible and the greater cost of children redirected the flows of support between the younger and parental generations. The growing cost of raising children could at least partially be met—probably implying inequality between siblings—in a situation of rising real income, and a further incentive to family limitation was added.

We perceive this mechanism as being neither sufficient nor necessary; it is merely a powerful incentive for a fertility decline. It is not sufficient because there must be a concomitant alteration in the moral code, and not necessary because at least a certain amount of fertility control can be generated as an alternative or supplement to a Malthusian nuptiality control. Given that such behavior would be ethically tolerated in a "laxist" atmosphere, a very early fertility decline, such as the one witnessed in parts of France, could occur. The detailed mechanisms of such a decline are not fully understood, but it is likely, judging from the behavior of the bourgeoisie and larger farmers, that elements associated with capital possession would play an important role. In this way, it appears to us that the gradual fertility decline in France, spread over the entire nineteenth century, could be viewed as a concatenation of two distinct but overlapping transitions. The first of these, taking over in part the function of Malthusian limits to nuptiality, would occur largely within a social structure dominated by a familial mode of production; the second segment would be more contingent upon the microeconomic changes associated with industrialization and urbanization, and therefore have more in common with the countries examined in detail in this paper.

Any sustained reduction in fertility, whether related to an early adaption of the Malthusian system or to the alterations in household economics wrought by the expansion of industrial capitalism, requires a concurrent development of moral acceptability. This factor is essential to give meaning to the ranking in which areas that were originally Catholic but experienced secularization at an early date tend to have the earliest marital fertility decline, followed by Protestant countries, frequently less differentiated along dimensions of secularization, and last, by Catholic areas where secularization was more a phenomenon of the twentieth century than of the nineteenth. In all these groups, secularization, whether of long standing or newly emergent, seems to have been a necessary condition.

It is essential to note that the process of secularization during the second half of the nineteenth century was markedly different in Catholic and Protestant areas. In the latter, secular adaptions occurred even within the churches and produced a fundamentalist reaction in only a limited number of cases (for example, in Dutch Gereformeerden). Moreover, in Protestant countries secularization became pronounced only as a result of or parallel with the growth of Socialism and social reform. Given this later secularization and the lack of resistence to it from the institutional guardians of Christian morality, the apparently late onset of fertility decline and its relative homogeneity can be accounted for. Furthermore, the lack of polarization in homogeneous Protestant countries explains the lesser impact of secularization variables, given the statistical control for the prevailing economic organization.

Catholic areas and countries that did not experience marked secularization before the mid-nineteenth century were caught up in a process of fundamentalist reaction and concomitant political and ideological polarization. In this environment of emerging cleavages, areas characterized by high levels of industrialization (or of involvement in large-scale, quasi-industrial agriculture) moved to levels of secularization beyond those anticipated on the strength of the overall relationship between industrialization and secularization. In contrast, areas characterized by high levels of familial labor-intensive production during the second half of the eighteenth century remained under the control of traditional forms of institutional patronage, and as such witnessed levels of secularization below those expected, given the same overall relationship with industrialization. These areas, for example Münster in Germany, the Vierwaldstatter See cantons in Switzerland, northern Brabant, Limburg in the Low Countries, the Mezzogiorno, the Veneto in northern Italy, and northern Portugal, were most resistant to a marital fertility decline.

Countries of mixed religious affiliation that had not developed an institutional framework suitable for the defusing of potential ideological and religious friction, as had Switzerland, were subject to processes of polarization similar to those experienced in Catholic countries. Indeed, the ensuing multiplicity of distinct factions (for example, *verzuiling* in the Netherlands) led to assertions of traditional ideologies among those groups sensing the cultural dominance of other factions. This, in its turn, could produce a subculture within which the ethical legitimization of nontraditional reproductive behavior would not be readily forthcoming; see the notion of "asymmetrical tolerance" proposed by E. W. Hofstee (1978b), and the development of "front-mentalities" among Dutch population segments (F. Van Heek, 1973).[15]

The European historical experience discussed so far makes two clear points:

1. The moral and ethical acceptability of fertility control is embedded in a much broader ideological development, not necessarily concurrent with economic modernization.
2. Reactions to such changes may occur in such a way that more fundamentalist views are juxtaposed to secular ones; these divergences have proved to be closely associated with the acceleration or retardation of the marital fertility transition.

These observations from the European Fertility Project may prove to be of considerable importance in understanding early and late transitions in contemporary developing societies. The fact that the modernization of the economic and value systems could proceed at different speeds implies that fertility transitions can take other courses than those predicted on the strength of economic reasoning alone.

[15] Another interesting fact is the persistence through time of regional variations in political and ethical attitudes. It seems apparent that the character of different regions remains remarkably constant over time. This is suggested by the close correlation between various referendum results of the 1970s and indications of demographic change at much earlier dates. For example, M. Livi-Bacci found that in Italy the votes on the 1974 divorce referendum were the single best indicator of the regional pattern of I_g's in 1931, when Italy was at mid-transition. Equally in Switzerland, the correlation between the regional distribution of votes on the abortion referendum of 1977 and ΔI_g (1860–1910) was very high, $r = 0.881$. In Belgium at the time of the second "school war" in 1958, the voting results correlate with ΔI_g (1880–1910) at a level of 0.879. Divorce rates in Belgium in 1977 also correlate highly with ΔI_g (1880–1910): 0.848. It seems that, in certain countries at least, matters of outlook regarding family life are regionally differentiated in very much the same way in the 1970s as they were at the turn of the century, despite considerable socioeconomic alteration.

Chapter 7: Regional and Cultural Factors in the Decline of Marital Fertility in Europe

Barbara A. Anderson

Acknowledgment

I would like to thank Sally Findley, Calvin Goldscheider, Frances Kobrin, B. Lindsey Lowell, and Brian Silver for helpful comments.

A major result of the European Fertility Project may be that demographers and other social scientists will think more seriously about the meaning of regional and cultural factors than they have in the past. Quantitative social scientists prefer socioeconomic variables that appear easy to interpret such as education, income, and occupation, to nonsocioeconomic variables, such as religion, language, and region, which are not easily expressed as interval-level measures and which do not lend themselves to straightforward interpretations.

The Theory of the Demographic Transition posits that socioeconomic variables, such as the level and change in infant mortality, education, and percent urban, lead to the decision by a substantial portion of the population to control their marital fertility. The European Fertility Project showed that several of the proposed factors are important, and it specified some of the ways these socioeconomic factors operate.

The Theory of the Demographic Transition does not discuss the role of regional or cultural factors in marital fertility decline. However, a consistent finding of the European Fertility Project is that a large part of the decline in marital fertility cannot be explained by socioeconomic variables. Moreover, nonsocioeconomic variables, such as religion, language, ethnicity, and region, explain much of the variability in marital fertility decline, even after conventional socioeconomic variables have been taken into account. There are many different definitions of "culture." In this chapter, "cultural" factors will refer to nonsocioeconomic variables such as religion, ethnicity, language, and region.

When cultural and regional variables are found to be important, how should they be interpreted? This is related to the classic question of validity, which is: What empirical, measurable indicator fairly represents some underlying theoretical concept (Blalock, 1968)? The problem with interpretation of regional and cultural variables is the inverse of the validity problem. Thus, the question becomes: Given an observed relation between behavior and a regional or cultural variable, what underlying theoretical concept is being manifested?

When a relation between behavior and a *socioeconomic* variable is observed, the validity/inverse validity question usually is not considered problematic, since researchers typically think they know what underlying concept a socioeconomic variable, such as education, stands for. However, the European Fertility Project studies and other research demonstrate that the reasonable interpretation of socioeconomic variables is not always straightforward.

This is illustrated for urbanization, education, and mortality. For each of the socioeconomic variables the relation to marital fertility or marriage has often been thought to be obvious:

Urbanization. Researchers have proposed that as people move to urban places in the course of economic development, the age of marriage in rural areas of origin of the migrants will decrease. They expect this to happen because competition for land and other resources in rural areas lessens as people migrate to cities (Friedlander, 1969). At the same time, age at marriage in the urban destinations should increase, due to increased competition among migrants.

For European Russia in 1897, Coale, Anderson, and Härm (1979) found that although the urban population of a province usually had a later age at marriage than the rural population of the province, those provinces with a relatively late age at marriage in the urban population also had a relatively late age at marriage in the rural population. Marriage age tended to be late for both the rural and urban populations of provinces in which the rate of rural-urban migration was high. Thus, migration to cities from the rural part of a province did not act as a "safety-valve" that allowed age at marriage to drop for the rural population of the province.

While researchers often have seen urbanization as an indication of decreased pressure on rural people, urbanization may instead stand for something very different. Coale, Anderson, and Härm argue that in European Russia, high rates of rural-urban migration and a relatively late age at marriage were both the result of characteristics of the social structure in the premodern period that encouraged both temporary labor migration and late marriage. The extent to which this social structure was present was related to climate and the productivity of agriculture. Physical differences among regions—climate and soil characteristics—appear to have led to differences in the social structure that in turn led to differences among regions in the level of socioeconomic variables, such as the extent of urbanization, and in demographic variables, such as the average age of marriage.

Education. Education, especially female education, is typically expected to have a negative relation to fertility. Education is expected to increase the extent to which all activities, including childbearing, are planned and also to lead to an increased emphasis on child quality rather than on child quantity. Higher income-producing opportunities also are thought to lead to reduced fertility because of an increased taste for market activity over childraising. (See Bouvier et al. [1976] for a discussion of different interpretations of the role of education in migration.)

In many Moslem societies, the welfare of women is dependent on support and protection by men. Widows with surviving sons typically have a better life than widows without any surviving sons, even if the women were formerly fairly well off. In this kind of situation, women would rationally want to have many children, even if they were future-oriented and even if they played a substantial role in family decision making (Chaudhury and Ahmed, 1979).

Also, education will lead women to higher-paying jobs outside the home only if it is possible for women to hold such jobs. Many studies show that educated women in developing countries are denied well-paying jobs for which they are qualified when norms maintain that it is inappropriate for women to work in settings in which they would interact with men or strangers, which would often be true in high-paying, modern-sector jobs (Boserup, 1970).

Coale, Anderson, and Härm (1979) found that in European Russia in 1897, for the rural population of provinces, female literacy and female age at marriage had a strong positive relation in the cross-section. In the late nineteenth and early twentieth centuries in European Russia, both female literacy and female age at marriage tended to increase. However, there was no relation between an increase in literacy and an increase in age at marriage. Thus, literacy and age at marriage had a spurious relation in the cross-section, even though a plausible argument could be made as to why they should have been related in the manner observed for 1897. As for the relation between urbanization and marriage age, Coale, Anderson, and Härm argue that differences in pre-modern social structure in different areas of European Russia led to differences in *both* female literacy and female age at marriage.

Mortality. A decrease in mortality, especially infant mortality, is thought to spur a decline in fertility. The argument is that as parents and prospective parents realize that they do not need to have as many children as previously in order for a given number of children to survive to adulthood, they decide to limit the number of children they bear.

The empirical relation between mortality and voluntary fertility control is not that simple. Knodel (1974) found for Germany that sometimes an infant mortality decline preceded a marital fertility decline, sometimes a marital fertility decline preceded an infant mortality decline, and sometimes they declined together. However, he found that the timing of marital fertility decline was related to the timing of the decline in *child* mortality. For Denmark, Matthiessen (1985) similarly found that although marital fertility decline was unrelated to decline in infant mortality, it was related to the increase in the chance of surviving to age fifteen.

Possibly either parents in some parts of Europe did not invest heavily emotionally in children until they had survived about one year or else there was disguised infanticide (neglect) of children who were born at a time when it was difficult to support them. If so, changes in infant mortality in these settings did not represent changes in exogenous mortality conditions, as researchers previously assumed, but rather were combined with a volitional component on the part of parents. Other mortality measures, such as child mortality or child and young adolescent mortality, more validly represented the underlying concept—changing exogenous mortality conditions to which parents might respond.

Findings of the European Fertility Project Studies

Table 7.1 summarizes the findings related to regional and cultural factors in the monograph-length studies of Portugal, Germany, Austria, Italy, Belgium, Russia, Switzerland, and Great Britain.

There are three kinds of hypotheses about how to interpret relations of regional or cultural variables to behavior. They are: (1) the characteristics hypothesis; (2) the particularized ideology or particularized culture hypothesis; and (3) the social milieu hypothesis. (See Goldscheider [1971] for a discussion of various kinds of hypotheses relating ethnicity and religion to fertility.)

Researchers usually test the characteristics hypothesis first. This hypothesis contends that any empirical relation of behavioral differences among groups to differences in regional or cultural variables, such as religion or ethnic group membership, will disappear once the proper socioeconomic variables are taken into account. Thus, it posits that any apparent relation between behavior and cultural or regional variables is spurious.

Table 7.1. Cultural and regional factors related to marital fertility after various socioeconomic variables are controlled.

	Region and Terrain	Religion	Religiosity	Ethnicity	Language
Portugal	level and date of decline (especially percent Catholic marriage)		level 1960 (percent Catholic)		
Germany	maximum level and date of decline (especially language)	highest level (percent Catholic)		level (by ethnic composition: Poles, Danes)	
Austria				percent decline by ethnic composition (Germans, Czechs, Poles-Ukrainians)	
Italy	level	Jews as a group early decline	level 1931-61 (divorce vote 1961)		

Note: Terms in parentheses refer to probable basis of regional classification for region and to indicators used for other categories.

Table 7.1. (continued)

	Region and Terrain	Religion	Religiosity	Ethnicity	Language
Belgium	date of decline (especially language)		level 1910 (percent non-Catholic vote 1910)		level, change in, (language homogeneity); level in districts of Brussels 1910, (percent only French-speaking)
Russia	date of decline, level 1926			date of decline, level 1926 (ethnic composition); level 1959 (ethnic groups)	
Switzerland	level (language, religion, altitude)	level (percent Protestant)			level (percent German-speaking)
Great Britain		date of decline (percent Catholic for England and Wales)		date of decline (percent born Ireland for Scotland, percent born France for England and Wales, percent born England, Wales and Ireland for Great Britain)	

For example, imagine that people with low socioeconomic status have higher fertility than people with high socioeconomic status. Suppose that on average Catholics have both higher fertility and lower socioeconomic status than Protestants. If Protestants and Catholics with the *same* socioeconomic status did not differ in fertility, then the higher fertility of Catholics as a group would be presumed to result from the compositional effect of a higher proportion of Catholics than of Protestants having low socioeconomic status.

It is conventional to consider socioeconomic variables as causally prior to regional or cultural variables. Thus, in the above example, most researchers would conclude that religion in itself had no effect on fertility. Even when group differences according to cultural variables, such as religion, region, or ethnic group membership, remain after some socioeconomic variables have been taken into account, a researcher still cannot be certain that the characteristics hypothesis is not the explanation; the differential might disappear after just one more socioeconomic variable has been taken into account.

I shall not discuss relations of regional or cultural factors that disappeared completely after the authors of the monographs in the European Fertility Project took socioeconomic variables into account, that is, those that are clearly explained by the characteristics hypothesis. The findings discussed here fall under the headings: region and terrain, religion, religiosity, ethnicity, and language. "Region" refers to regional differences that remain after various socioeconomic differences among regions have been taken into account, whether or not the authors had a convincing explanation of the sources of the regional differences. "Terrain" refers to mountainous areas, as opposed to valleys. "Religion" refers to differences among religious groups or to the proportion of an area's population belonging to a particular religious group when a substantial number of members of other religious groups are present in the country. For countries such as Portugal and Belgium, where the vast majority of the population subscribe at least nominally to Roman Catholicism, if they claim any religious affiliation at all, the proportion of the population declaring itself Catholic or the proportion voting for Catholic parties is a measure of religiosity, since the major alternative is not adherence to another religion but rather less involvement in the Catholic religion.

Table 7.1 presents the countries in the order in which the studies were done. Over time, cultural and regional factors have increasingly been taken explicitly into account. In the earlier studies, cultural factors were often treated as contaminating influences to be controlled away. In the studies of Switzerland and Great Britain, explicit socioeconomic versus cultural models were tested as well as combined socioeconomic and cultural models. For both Switzerland and Great Britain, a combined model was superior to both the wholly socioeconomic and the wholly cultural models.

Livi-Bacci's (1971) study of Portugal led the project in recognizing the importance of cultural and regional factors. There were great differences in the date of the onset of the decline of marital fertility between the north and the south of Portugal. Fertility declined first in the south, although the north was more industrialized. A positive partial correlation was found between the percentage of the population declaring itself Catholic in 1960 and the level of marital fertility in 1960. Also, marriages were more likely to be performed in a Catholic service in the north than in the south. These findings led Livi-Bacci to the conclusion that the difference in religiosity between the north and the south was a major cause of differences in the timing of the decline of Portuguese marital fertility.

Livi-Bacci's argument is a version of the particularized ideology hypothesis. The particularized ideology hypothesis contends that cultural differences are not proxies for socioeconomic differences. It states that the source of behavioral differences is the group's ideology. For example, it contends that Catholics have higher fertility than Protestants because Catholic religion (culture) places a higher value on children and places more severe sanctions against the use of contraception than does Protestant religion (culture).

The particularized ideology hypothesis also implies that within a group, differences should be related to the degree of religiosity. The more completely the particularized ideology is accepted, the greater should be the effect of that ideology on behavior.

A problem with the particularized ideology hypothesis is the characterization of a group's ideology. It is not adequate to say that Catholics have higher fertility than Protestants because Catholic ideology encourages high fertility to a greater extent than does Protestant ideology. The particularized ideology approach can lead to tautological statements that a group acts the way it does because that is how it acts, unless the ideology is characterized and can be measured in some independent way.

It may appear that the particularized ideology hypothesis is at work when other processes are operating instead. Stycos (1968) points out that low levels of use of birth control in parts of Latin America may seem to be due to moral reservations by Catholics to use birth control. However, sometimes the process operates through the Catholic Church hierarchy in the country working to inhibit the spread of information about birth control. He notes that surveys often showed no more negative attitudes toward controlling fertility in Latin American countries in which fertility control was rare than in countries in which it was more common. Rather, the position and strength of the Church hierarchy was related to the extent of influence of the Church on state population policy.

It was not possible with the Portuguese data available to Livi-Bacci to test whether more religious Catholics had higher fertility than less religious Catholics or nonbelievers or whether all people in a highly religious area tended to have high fertility. Thus, it could be either that areas with a high proportion of very religious people had high fertility due to the compositional effect of the higher fertility of the more religious, or that general fertility norms or the social structure differed according to the proportion of the population that was very religious. The observed pattern in Portugal would not be likely to be explained by differences in relative levels of economic development operating through the characteristics hypothesis, since the level of industrial development in Portugal was *positively* related to marital fertility.

In Germany, Knodel (1974) found that regional differences, related to linguistic differences among areas, were strongly related to the maximal level of marital fertility reached. These regional effects did not disappear when socioeconomic differences among regions were taken into account. However, the separate contribution of the regional factor to the explanation of the variance in marital fertility was not explicitly calculated. It is not clear whether the relation of differences in the level of fertility to linguistic areas was due to differences in the ease with which information could spread (it would be more difficult for information to cross a linguistic boundary), whether linguistic differences stood for differences in receptivity to the idea of the control of marital fertility, or whether these differences were related to differences in the social structure.

Knodel (1974) also found that the percentage of an area that was Catholic was positively related to the maximal level of marital fertility. It was not known whether the fertility of Catholics *and* non-Catholics was high in heavily Catholic areas or whether the relation of fertility to proportion Catholic was due to compositional averaging.

The finding of differences in the maximal level of marital fertility recorded are difficult to interpret. They could result either from longstanding differences in practices that influence the level of natural fertility (Henry,

1961), such as the duration of breast-feeding, or they could result from the timing of earlier fertility declines—before the existence of the vital records that Knodel used.

Knodel also showed that areas with a large proportion of non-Germans differed from predominantly German areas in the level of marital fertility: those areas with a high proportion of Danes had lower fertility, and those areas with a high proportion of Poles had higher fertility. It was not possible, from the data employed, however, to determine whether the fertility of Germans within the Danish or Polish areas differed from the fertility of otherwise similar Germans elsewhere in Germany. Thus, it is not known whether differences in fertility among areas that are related to ethnic composition were the result of a compositional effect or whether local fertility norms or some aspect of the social structure related to fertility varied among areas.

Forrest (1975) found that differences in the ethnic composition among areas were important in Austria. Areas in which over 90 percent of the population were Poles or Ukrainians had higher fertility and a later fertility decline, while areas in which over 90 percent of the population were Austrians and Czechs or Germans and Austrians had lower fertility and earlier fertility decline. These differences remained even after differences in the average levels of socioeconomic variables were taken into account.

Since the areas differed both in ethnic composition and in the level and timing of socioeconomic development—the Ukrainian-Polish areas were less developed—it was difficult to determine the source of the difference. Forrest observes that Austria at that time was a country whose population did not have a well-developed sense of national identity. It may be that the Polish-Ukrainian areas and the rest of Austria were a part of different social systems. That is, the regions may have been so different that it would be more appropriate to view them as separate countries.

Why does this not simply reduce to the characteristics hypothesis? It does not reduce to the characteristics hypothesis if the same values on socioeconomic variables in different regions do not lead to the same behavior. Direct ways of dealing with this issue have been suggested by a number of scholars. They usually involve controlling for the group mean or lagging the dependent variable (Blau, 1960; Davis et al., 1961; Erbring and Young, 1979; Firebaugh, 1979; Schwirian, 1973).

Along the same line, Livi-Bacci (1977) also found that regional differences in Italian marital fertility remained after important socioeconomic variables were taken into account. Although the north, center, and south differed in the level and timing of socioeconomic development, a characteristics hypothesis argument about the effects of socioeconomic development does not adequately explain the differences in the timing of fertility decline. Rather, the fact that the south as a region had a low level of socioeconomic development seemed to delay the control of marital fertility more than could be explained simply by the values of indicators of socioeconomic development.

Dependency theorists point out that the context in which a country or region develops affects its course of development. Countries or regions that develop early have better market opportunities than those that develop later. Later-developing countries or regions are often exploited by those that developed earlier. Thus, achievement of a given average level on a socioeconomic variable, if attained relatively late, may not lead to the same behavioral changes that it led to in countries and regions that reached that same level earlier (Wallerstein, 1974; Evans, 1979). Livi-Bacci's (1977) argument that the different position of Italy and the rest of Europe by the time southern Italy reached a given level of socioeconomic development affected the behavioral options of people in southern Italy (in this case for fertility decline) is a dependency-theory argument.

A counter to the dependency-theory argument is the argument of the "preconditions of modernization," which contends that often there are differences among regions or among countries in their pre-modern social structures that differentially facilitate later change, including behavioral changes, such as a rise in the age at marriage or decline of marital fertility. These differences in pre-modern social structure often arise due to idiosyncratic factors, such as climate or the nature of the soil (Black et al., 1975; Rozman, 1973). The explanation of the relation of female literacy and female age at marriage in late nineteenth-century European Russia by Coale, Anderson, and Härm (1979) is an example of a "preconditions of modernization" argument.

Livi-Bacci also suggested that religiosity operated similarly in Italy and Portugal. The positive relation of marital fertility in 1931-1961 to the proportion of voters in a province who supported the liberalization of the Italian divorce law in 1961 bolstered Livi-Bacci's contention that differences in religiosity affected differential acceptance of control of marital fertility. Again, it is not known whether behavior was related to religiosity through a compositional or contextual effect.

Livi-Bacci found that Jews as a group experienced an earlier marital fertility decline than Italians generally, although he did not determine the extent to which this was due to socioeconomic characteristics of Italian Jews. Since the vast majority of Italian Jews lived in urban areas, the observed distributions of Italian Jews and non-Jewish Italians do not allow analysis of whether rural-urban residence affected Italian Jewish fertility behavior in the same manner in which it affected the fertility behavior of other Italians.

Livi-Bacci's argument about early Italian Jewish fertility decline is an example of the "minority group status hypothesis," which is one kind of social milieu hypothesis. All of the social milieu hypotheses relate the behavior of a given group to the social context in which the group exists. There are two kinds of social milieu hypotheses.

The first kind of social milieu hypothesis is concerned with the way the behavior of members of a given group varies according to the social context in which group members find themselves. Usually the concern is with minority groups. For this kind of hypothesis, the behavior of members of the majority group or of the dominant group in society is assumed to be unaffected by the presence of minority group members.

The minority group status hypothesis contends that the fact of being a minority group in a society can affect the fertility behavior of the minority group's members (Goldscheider and Uhlenberg, 1969; Goldscheider, 1971). Goldscheider writes that minority group members will have lower fertility than they would otherwise if:

> . . . 1) acculturation of minority group members has occurred in conjunction with the desire for acculturation; 2) equalization of social and economic characteristics occurs and/or social and economic mobility is desired; 3) no pro-natalist ideology is associated with the minority group and no norm discourages the use of effective contraception (Goldscheider, 1971, p. 297)

It might be possible to characterize a group in a particular temporal and geographical setting according to these three characteristics. Participation in nonethnic organizations, intergroup marriage rates, or other intergroup contact measures could be examined as indicators of a desire for acculturation. This has been attempted with good results for Hispanics in New York City (Cooney and Ortiz, 1979), but clearly is more difficult for research on the past. A comparison of intergenerational mobility rates for minority group members and for majority group members who had similar initial socioeconomic characteristics could indicate whether or not social mobility was possible. Measurement of the third condition is the most difficult. Content analysis of written work could be done, but it is very risky to generalize from stated ideology to working ideology.

In Belgium, Lesthaeghe (1977) found that social processes operated so differently in the Flemish and Walloon areas that Flemish areas had to be analyzed separately from Walloon areas. Not only were there differences in the level and timing of the decline of marital fertility, but many *socioeconomic* variables operated differently in the two areas. Thus, differences in the level of economic development, operating through the characteristics hypothesis, could not be the explanation.

For example, in the Flemish area, the percentage of the population that was literate was positively related to fertility, while in the Walloon area, it was negatively related. Apparently in the Walloon area, education acted as an agent of modernization, while in the more religious Flemish area, it acted to reinforce Catholic values. The phenomenon in the Flemish area is similar to the finding for the United States in the 1950s that among Catholic women who obtained all of their education in Catholic schools, the higher the level of education, the larger the number of children desired (Westoff et al., 1961). The relation between Catholic religiosity and later control of marital fertility in Belgium was also supported by the finding that the proportion voting for non-Catholic parties in 1910 was negatively related to marital fertility in 1910, even after various socioeconomic factors had been taken into account.

The difference in the timing of the onset of fertility control in relation to religiosity was not the *direct* result of the extent to which people in different parts of the country followed explicit, contemporary church policy and teaching. The Catholic Church in Belgium did not start to make explicit pronouncements against the control of marital fertility until after that control was well under way in some parts of Belgium.

Just as Knodel found differences in fertility behavior according to the linguistic composition of areas important in Germany, Lesthaeghe found that the linguistic composition of districts in Brussels was related to fertility behavior. Behavioral differences according to linguistic characteristics are often interpreted as the result of differences in the ease of information flow. If groups differ in language, then information originating in one linguistic group will flow more easily to those who understand that language than to people who do not understand the language. Thus, fertility control may spread along linguistic lines because of differential access to knowledge about how to control fertility. This point of view is in keeping with work on the diffusion of innovations (Rogers, 1962).

It is important, however, not to assume immediately that behavioral differences along linguistic lines are exclusively due to the information flow argument. *Knowledge* of a language and *identification* with a linguistic group are not the same. In multilingual societies, typically many people are multilingual. Identification with a linguistic group may indicate a person's adherence to that group's norms or his commitment to a particular set of social relations, rather than his inability to understand the language in which an idea originated.

For example, Silver (1978) found that among non-Russians in the Soviet Union in 1970, the determinants of whether a large proportion of a non-Russian group knew Russian well were very different from the determinants of whether a large proportion of the non-Russian group claimed Russian as their native language. A high educational level and a high proportion of the group having attended schools where Russian was the main language of instruction were positively related to a high proportion of non-Russians knowing Russian well. These socioeconomic characteristics were unrelated, however, to whether a high proportion of non-Russians claimed Russian as their native language. For this aspect of linguistic identification, a cultural difference—whether the traditional religion of the group was Islam or not—was much more important.

Lesthaeghe (1977) found that in the parts of Brussels where many people understood both French and Flemish there was a later fertility decline than in those parts of Brussels where people tended to understand only French. This suggests that in Brussels the connection between fertility decline and language was more closely related to differences among linguistic groups in norms or social structure than to differential access to information about fertility control due to language knowledge.

Blau (1977) agrees that behavior of different groups all of whom reside in the same locality can be influenced by local norms. But he argues that these norms are established through social exchange and interaction on the *community* level. He further argues that it makes a great difference whether ethnic heterogeneity in a society stems from ethnic differences within or among communities. One would expect that the behavior of all groups in an area would only be influenced by the ethnic composition of an area through local norms affecting everyone if the different ethnic groups were mixed within the same communities.

Coale, Anderson, and Härm (1979) found that for European Russia in 1897, for most groups the average age of female marriage for members of a given ethnic group across provinces had a strong positive relation to the average age of female marriage of all nongroup members living in the same province. The one case in which this relation did not hold was for rural Jews. Rural Jews tended to have a similar average age of female marriage regardless of where they lived and regardless of the average age of female marriage of rural non-Jews in the same province. If Blau's argument is correct, the different pattern for rural Jews might result from a greater concentration of Jews in totally Jewish villages than was true of other ethnic groups, or a greater degree of separation between Jews and non-Jews than between other groups.

Coale, Anderson, and Härm (1979) also found that the set of European Russian provinces that had experienced a substantial decline in marital fertility by 1926 was virtually identical to the set of provinces in which Great Russians constituted less than 50 percent of the population. These provinces were geographically contiguous on the western side of European Russia and collectively differed from the rest of European Russia in several ways. For instance, they had low infant mortality in 1926, and a low proportion of the population was Orthodox in religion. Thus, it is difficult to determine what factors *caused* the difference in the timing of the decline of marital fertility between this region and the rest of European Russia.

It is clear, though, that the low marital fertility in the western provinces was not the result of an averaging of high Great Russian marital fertility and low non-Great Russian marital fertility. For almost every province within the region of reduced marital fertility in 1926, Great Russian marital fertility was as low or lower than the marital fertility of the remainder of the population of the given province.

It also does not seem that differences between Great Russian fertility and the fertility of the rest of the population within provinces in the low fertility part of western European Russia were due to relative differences in the social status or level of development between Great Russians and others. Rural Great Russian women in some western provinces were more likely to be literate than other rural women, and in some western provinces they were less likely to be literate than other rural women; whether Great Russian rural women were literate more or less often than other rural women was unrelated to whether rural Great Russian women had higher or lower fertility than other rural women. The fertility of other ethnic groups, such as Ukrainians and Poles, was similarly strongly related to the marital fertility of the remainder of the population.

In European Russia in 1959, Coale, Anderson, and Härm (1979) found that differences in marital fertility were again related to the ethnic composition of provinces. At that time, those provinces in European Russia in which a high proportion of the population consisted of eastern Finns or Turkic peoples had high rural marital fertility. These areas were not distinguished by particularly low levels of education or a lack of medical facilities. However, in 1959, the fertility of Russians in rural parts of the ethnically distinct, high fertility provinces did not differ substantially from the fertility of Russians in rural areas elsewhere in European Russia. Rather, the high marital fertility in these provinces was due to high fertility among the eastern Finns and Turkic peoples.

Although it was possible to determine that differences in marital fertility in European Russia were not the result of compositional averaging in 1926 but were the result of compositional averaging in 1959, a number of questions remain. It was not possible too determine from the data used whether the findings were the result of ethnic mixing within communities in 1926 but of little ethnic mixing within communities in 1959. Even if it were found that the fertility of all ethnic groups was affected only when communities were ethnically mixed, as Blau (1977) suggests, it still would not be known whether the findings in 1926 were the result of differences in the social structure of differences in norms about fertility.

The findings for European Russia in 1926 are consistent with the second kind of social milieu hypothesis. Like the first kind, the second kind admits that the behavior of minority group members can be influenced by the social setting in which they find themselves. But this second kind of hypothesis goes further to contend that members of the majority group also can be affected by the social composition of the area and that, in fact, members of *all* groups in an area are influenced by the social setting in which they find themselves.

The ecological fallacy points to the difference between the two kinds of social milieu hypotheses. It contends that if aggregate characteristics of the populations of areas are found to be related to differences in the behavior of these populations, this does not necessarily mean that people who differ with respect to the differentiating characteristic are more or less likely to behave in a given manner (Naroll, 1968).

For example, imagine that two regions differ in the proportion literate. Imagine that the region with the higher proportion literate has lower fertility. The ecological fallacy points out that from this finding it would not be justified to conclude that literate people have lower fertility than illiterate people. The observed pattern would also occur if both literate and illiterate people in the more literate region had lower fertility than people in the same literacy category in the less literate region.

The second kind of social milieu hypothesis falls under the general heading of the study of contextual effects, also called structural effects or compositional effects (Blau, 1960; Coleman, 1968). Freedman (1974) points out that there are two kinds of contextual variables: (1) those based on the aggregate occurrence of a characteristic among the individuals in the population (such as the proportion literate), and (2) those that are global, that is, they affect all members of the population equally (such as the distance from the capital city).

There has been much controversy about whether and when contextual effects are "real," especially when the first kind of contextual variable is studied. For example, consider an ongoing debate about whether if a high proportion of students in a high school drink alcoholic beverages, this leads other students to consume alcohol (Barton, 1968, 1970; Bowers, 1968; Hauser, 1970a, 1970b, 1974). The controversy is about how to make the argument in a nontautological way. In their study of fertility in the Russian Empire and the Soviet Union, Coale, Anderson, and Härm (1979, p. 73) wrote: "A conclusion that marital fertility was especially low in Latvia in 1897 and 1926 because the province was full of Latvians would not be our first choice as the final product of our research. . . ." In 1926, where western ethnic groups, such as Latvians, were a high proportion of the population, all ethnic groups in the area tended to have low fertility. Thus, whatever it was that caused Latvians to have low fertility when there were few non-Latvians around also led non-Latvians to have low fertility in the presence of Latvians.

It is also important to note that neither geographic nor ethnic boundaries are impassible. In the Soviet Union between 1959 and 1970, Karelians and members of several other small ethnic groups were changing their self-identified ethnic group membership to Russian at a high rate (Anderson and Silver, 1983; Coale, Anderson, and Härm, 1979). If these former minority group members had lower fertility than Russians and retained the lower fertility after reidentification, then measured Russian fertility later would be lower than if ethnic boundaries had remained fixed. The selectivity of migration, whether geographical or in terms of group membership, can complicate any analysis of fertility differentials over time.

In Switzerland, F. van de Walle (manuscript) found that regions were important for marital fertility, whether the regional classification was along linguistic or along religious lines. Within the religious classification, the percentage of the district that was Protestant significantly contributed to the explanation of fertility, while within the linguistic classification, the percentage of the district that was German-speaking also contributed significantly. Within each classification, the percentage of the population living at a low altitude was related to a low level of marital fertility, perhaps due to unmeasured aspects of social organization, although this relation remained after various socioeconomic variables were taken into account.

F. van de Walle (1975) found that fertility was low in one part of Switzerland, even though it was unlikely that many people in that area were intentionally controlling their marital fertility. Rather, fertility was low because a large proportion of the adult men were absent as labor migrants much of the time, thus reducing the exposure of their wives to the risk of pregnancy. The social structure of this area led to particular demographic patterns—a large amount of temporary out-migration and low marital fertility—that were the result of a combination of the development status of the area and the situation elsewhere.

For Great Britain, Teitelbaum (1984) found that the date of marital fertility decline was related to the percentage of the country that was Catholic for England and Wales, and to the proportions of county population born in various other countries: for England and Wales, fertility was lower the higher the proportion of the population that was born in France; for Scotland, fertility was higher the higher proportion of the population that was born in Ireland; for Great Britain as a whole, fertility was lower the higher the proportion of the population born in England or Wales and higher the higher the proportion of the population born in Ireland.

It was not determined whether these patterns were the result of compositional differences or whether the behavior of all people in an area was affected by the religious or nativity composition of the area. The finding that fertility was lower the higher the proportion born in France and higher the higher the proportion born in Ireland would seem to directly result from fertility behavior in those countries: early fertility decline in France and very late fertility decline in Ireland. Perhaps people born in those countries brought the fertility behavior of their native lands with them.

However, studies of migration and fertility often show that those who migrate are not representative of all people at the origin in fertility behavior—often they have lower fertility than those at the origin (cf. Simmons et al., 1977; Connell et al., 1974). The finding of high fertility in those areas with a high proportion of people born in Ireland raises three unanswered questions: (1) Did the Irish-born people simply bring high Irish fertility with them, or did their fertility differ significantly from the fertility of otherwise similar people still in Ireland? (2) Was the high fertility in heavily Irish areas due to high fertility only among the Irish-born part of the population or did all people in heavily Irish areas tend to have high fertility? (3) Did the relation of the behavior of people to the composition of the area in which they lived depend on whether their community tended to be exclusively Irish-born or whether Irish-born people lived in communities with a large proportion of non-Irish-born people?

Maps of the date of marital fertility decline suggest that the Lowland-Highland division of Scotland was important. However, the proportion of the population who were Celtic speakers (the indicator chosen for this division) had an insignificant effect on fertility after socioeconomic variables were taken into account. This finding seems to be a simple illustration of the characteristics hypothesis accounting for differences between areas with a high proportion and a low proportion of Celtic speakers. But the actual explanation may not be so simple. Hechter (1975), using a dependency-theory argument, contends that England practiced internal colonialism within the British Isles, and that the relatively low level of economic development in the highly Celtic areas of the British Isles and their ethnic composition were causally linked. If Hechter's argument is correct, then if high fertility were related to relatively low economic development, the Celtic composition of an area and the level of fertility of that area are not as unrelated as the characteristics hypothesis would suggest.

Implications for Further Research

The European Fertility Project showed that the relation of cultural and regional variables to marital fertility decline cannot be completely explained away by spurious association with socioeconomic characteristics at the individual level. A number of mechanisms have been proposed through which forces leading to differences in the level and timing of decline in marital fertility could be manifested through regional or cultural variables.

Kuhn (1962) points out that the way in which science progresses and better theories are formulated is through a recurring process of theory formulation, theory testing, exploratory research, and theory reformulation. When a theory is tested, it is never *completely* supported. For those parts of the proposed theory with which the empirical data are not consistent, the research changes from being theory testing to being exploratory. In the exploratory stage, an *after the fact* explanation of the inconsistent findings is proposed that leads to theory reformulation and retesting. The process then begins again.

Since the Theory of the Demographic Transition in a simple form was not strongly supported, a large part of the European Fertility Project quickly moved from the theory-testing stage of science to the exploratory stage. No fully articulated, reformulated theory seems justified yet. But the findings of the European Fertility Project do suggest that behavior does not change directly and simply as the result of differences among individuals on the basis of socioeconomic variables or the aggregation of those differences. Although differences in regional and cultural variables among groups were sometimes found to be the result of compositional differences in behavior, they often were not.

Further work with the help of regional experts should be pursued in three areas: (1) collection of data to distinguish among groups of alternative hypotheses; (2) insight into the choice of valid indicators and in the interpretation of variables in the particular time and place; and (3) questions of the effects of timing and earlier social and historical conditions on the interaction between the place considered and the rest of the world.

The problem of obtaining adequate data has already been mentioned. Most of the European Fertility Project studies used national, aggregate data. Often data at that level were not available in sufficient detail to allow the determination of whether an observed difference according to the composition of an area was in fact due to compositional averaging or whether a contextual effect was present. Rarely were data available that would allow determination of whether a relation of fertility to ethnic composition in an area as large as a province were related to the settlement patterns of ethnic groups.

Determination of whether a relation between marital fertility and a cultural or regional variable was due to a compositional or contextual effect would not *solve* the problem, but it would certainly limit the range of plausible alternative hypotheses in any given situation. Data at the level of detail required would often be available only for smaller areas.

The kinds of problems and patterns found at the aggregate level in the European Fertility Project should help researchers to target what data to collect. For example, a question suggested by Knodel's (1974) work is whether Germans in predominantly Danish areas had fertility that was different from the fertility of Germans in predominantly German areas. Teitelbaum's (1984) finding that fertility in Great Britain differed according to the proportion of the population from France or from Ireland also suggests the value of detailed research comparing fertility of French-born, Irish-born, and native-born people within areas of Great Britain as well as comparison of the fertility of migrants with the fertility of those in their homelands.

Regional experts can help with the validity/inverse validity question. For example, they might suggest interpretations of the meaning of findings such as F. van de Walle's (manuscript) discovery for Switzerland that marital fertility declined earlier at higher altitudes. Any suggested difference in the social structure between high and low altitude areas could then be tested through determination of whether the presence or absence of that type of social structure also related to marital fertility level or decline in other settings.

Both the dependency theory explanations and the preconditions of modernization explanations require a long-term historical perspective. Without information about pre-decline conditions, theories of this type cannot be tested. Also without information about the pre-decline society, researchers can easily be misled into believing that simple socioeconomic explanations hold when they do not.

Much of the criticism of research on the effect of cultural variables and of research on contextual effects has assumed that explanations of such findings were necessarily vague or mystical or that they essentially relied on drawing erroneous causal inferences from residuals because of failure to include the "right" socioeconomic variables. This chapter has argued that the effects can be real and are not mystical. However, to make progress it is necessary to pursue what Verba (1967) has called a "disciplined configurative approach." What is needed to understand marital fertility decline is not a unique theory or explanation of the decline in marital fertility for each different time and place, but particular knowledge of the culture and history and detailed data for small areas combined with the discipline inherent in a theoretical approach.

Chapter 8: Regional Patterns of Nuptiality in Western Europe, 1870–1960

Susan Cotts Watkins

Introduction

In 1953 John Hajnal noted that a marriage boom had recently occurred in a number of European countries, resulting from a sharp decline in the average age at marriage among women and an increase in the proportion who had married by the end of their childbearing years.

> The present situation is thus largely unprecedented in recent western history. It is not only the level of proportions single in the last few years that deserves special notice. The reduction has taken place with unparalleled suddenness. No one examining the trend of proportions single up to the early 1930's—or the trend of any other statistical index for marriage—could have predicted the recent change. Reductions in the proportions single were indeed occurring in some of the countries before 1930, but they were slow in comparison with what has occurred in the last two decades. (Hajnal, 1953b)

The change consisted in the abandonment, in all countries of Western Europe except Ireland, of the late age at marriage for women and the widespread spinsterhood that had characterized the nuptiality of Western Europe in 1900. At that date, in much of Asia and Africa the average age at marriage was under 20, and 98 percent or more of the female population had married before the age of 50. In Western Europe, the average age at marriage was 23 or older, and at least 10 percent of the female population remained unmarried throughout their childbearing years (Hajnal, 1965; Coale, Anderson, and Härm, 1979). Although the marriage boom described by Hajnal occurred between 1930 and 1960, the increase in proportions married at each age had begun by 1860 in most of the *départements* of France, as well as in individual provinces in other countries. By 1960, the widespread abstention from marriage that was common earlier persisted only in many of the counties of Ireland and in a handful of provinces in the other countries.

This paper was first published in *Population Studies* 35(2) (1981).

The existence of measures of nuptiality for almost all the provinces of Europe permits the examination not only in changes in level but also of changes in variation between the provinces as well as between larger regions of each country during the last century. In many of the countries, there was less variation in nuptiality in 1930 than at the first date for which the necessary data are available (usually around 1870), and less variation in 1960 than in 1930. Differences between provinces in 1870 may reflect recent departures from an earlier homogeneity of nuptiality; the variation from county to county in 1870 may correspond to longstanding differences in other aspects of the society. If, as has been said, there is a tendency toward convergence in modernized societies such as those of Western Europe in 1960, one would expect to find smaller variation in the proportions married by age in 1960. This chapter will examine the change in variation in nuptiality between the provinces of most of the countries of Western Europe during a period from roughly 1870 to 1960.

Change in Level

Table 8.1 shows the course of the median and the mean level of I_m for the provinces of most countries of Western Europe for selected census dates between 1870 and 1960.

I_m is a summary measure of the proportions married at each age. A succinct definition is:

> The index of proportion married (I_m) is defined as the number of children married women would produce, relative to the number all women would produce, if both sets of women experienced the Hutterite fertility schedule. It is a fertility-weighted aggregate index of marriage that gives more weight to the proportions married at the prolific ages (less than 30) than at the less prolific older ages . . . it is confined to the interval zero (no women married) to one (all women 15 to 50 married). (Coale, Anderson and Härm, 1979)

The index is calculated from the proportions of women reported as currently married in the census:

$$I_m = \frac{\sum m_i F_i}{\sum w_i F_i},$$

Table 8.1. Mean and median I_m, selected dates.

		1850	1860	1870	1880	1890	1900	1910	1920	1930	1940	1950	1960
Belgium	Mean				.427	.425	.464	.502	.477	.577		.605	.697
	Median				.420	.414	.452	.490	.468	.566		.611	.695
Denmark	Mean	.424	.473	.456	.462	.476	.478	.498	.505	.518			.677
	Median	.418	.483	.464	.467	.478	.483	.500	.505	.518			.681
England and Wales	Mean	.482	.499	.504	.496	.471	.468	.472	.485	.507			.703
	Median	.482	.496	.501	.495	.462	.469	.474	.483	.511			.709
Finland	Mean				.495	.499	.483	.462	.393	.397	.460	.575	.608
	Median				.504	.504	.469	.449	.374	.404	.452	.573	.601
France	Mean	.534	.540	.543	.553	.556	.560	.605	.541	.616			.645
	Median	.546	.547	.550	.563	.567	.569	.611	.552	.626			.655
Germany	Mean			.468	.502	.495	.509	.523		.527			.686
	Median			.467	.495	.492	.517	.526		.533			.686
Ireland	Mean			.398	.364	.329	.316	.330		.361			.498
	Median			.387	.361	.326	.312	.324		.359			.4925
Italy	Mean		.560	.567	.545	.548	.551	.535	.497	.515	.522	.539	.581
	Median		.554	.571	.546	.540	.539	.537	.501	.516	.528	.542	.589
Netherlands	Mean		.408	.440	.468	.449	.454	.475	.488	.506			.636
	Median		.419	.448	.480	.456	.463	.473	.482	.500			.632

Norway	Mean		.411		.424	.425		.421	.411			.664
	Median		.410		.420	.423		.427	.418			.672
Portugal	Mean		.451		.462	.466	.488	.468	.486	.495	.524	.561
	Median		.458		.471	.461	.484	.475	.486	.495	.522	.562
Scotland	Mean	.398	.398	.398	.379	.383	.390	.403	.419			.658
	Median	.393	.391	.382	.362	.363	.377	.400	.428			.659
Spain	Mean				.591	.573	.566	.517	.513	.424		.556
	Median				.622	.597	.582	.528	.520	.431		.545
Sweden	Mean			.420		.423			.429		.633	.629
	Median			.419		.420			.434		.628	.629
Switzerland	Mean	.374	.411	.444	.428	.438	.459	.413	.427	.471	.517	.564
	Median	.388	.412	.439	.419	.434	.457	.420	.435	.471	.523	.569

Notes:

1. Belgium 1947 data are cited as Belgium 1950.
2. Germany 1933 data are cited as Germany 1930. Germany 1960 data include both the Federal Republic of Germany and the Democratic Republic of Germany.
3. Italy 1936 data are cited as Italy 1940.
4. Norway 1875 data are cited as Norway 1870.
5. Portugal 1864 data and Portugal 1878 data are averaged and cited as Portugal 1870.
6. Spain 1887 data are cited as Spain 1890.
7. Switzerland 1888 data are cited as Switzerland 1890.

where for age group i, m_i is the number of married women, w_i is the total number of women, and F_i is the marital fertility rate taken from the Hutterite schedule, one of the highest fertility schedules on record.[1]

The I_m's were calculated as part of the Princeton European Fertility Project from published census distributions of marital status by age or census-derived estimates. Census coverage and accuracy may be presumed to have varied from country to country and to have improved over time; but during the period under discussion, gross inaccuracy of reporting either age or marital status was not common. The existence of a national statistical office in all of these countries reduces the likelihood that regional differences in the indexes of nuptiality result from different procedures of census taking; only in Germany after 1945 and Ireland after 1921 was the information used to calculate I_m gathered by separate administrations.

Table 8.1 shows that the low level of nuptiality indicated by an I_m of 0.500 or less was typical of most countries at the first date for which data are available. Between that first date and 1930, I_m fell in some countries and rose in others. The lowest mean and median I_m in each national sequence are italicized in Table 8.1.

In Spain, Italy, and Finland, I_m fell from the comparatively high levels at the date for which data are first available to levels close to those found in the other countries of Western Europe before 1930. In most other countries, the overall trend between the first date and 1930 was an increase in I_m, although the rise was usually very gradual until 1930, after which it became more rapid—sometimes much more rapid. Only in France was the percentage increase in I_m greater before 1930 than after.

Unlike the changes in marital fertility during this period, which appear to have been irreversible once a significant decline had occurred, the rise in I_m was frequently interrupted. Before 1930, changes in the level of I_m

[1] Although fertility is not the focus of this study, it is not a disadvantage that I_m is weighted by fertility. The prime childbearing ages with greatest weights are also the prime ages of marriage; thus, I_m predominantly captures changes in the timing of marriage. The correlation of I_m with proportion married at 20–24 is always above 0.876 in Belgium (see Lesthaeghe, 1977). Since I_m is a period measure, however, and includes the past marital history of several cohorts, changes in I_m can be expected to be more gradual than changes in measures between successive censuses that describe only the experience of younger cohorts. Women who were married between the ages of 15–19 are 45–49 years old, thirty years later; thus their experience appears twice in the calculation of I_m at thirty-year intervals.

were dissimilar in different Western European countries. After 1930 (1940 in Spain), however, the proportions married increased in each of the countries under consideration. The rise affected every province in every country, even the counties of Ireland: in 1960, I_m in Donegal county was 0.442, the lowest in Europe, but well above the value of 0.315 in 1931. In most countries, the increase in the median between 1930 and 1960 exceeded 25 percent. The highest value of I_m in Western Europe in 1960, however, either for a country or a province, was still below the maximum recorded levels: in no country was I_m as high as it had been in China, Taiwan, or Korea before 1935.

Change in Variation

At the first date for which data are available, variation between the provinces of a country was substantial. In Belgium, for example, in the *arrondissement* of Tielt in 1880 the average age at marriage was 28.4, and 30.5 percent of women at the age of 50 were still single, while in the *arrondissement* of Charleroi the average age at marriage was 25, and only 9.2 percent of the women were still single at 50. In Portugal in 1864, 15.5 percent of the women aged 20–24 in the northern province of Viano do Castelo were married, compared to 42.7 percent of the women of this age in the southern province of Faro; in Viano do Castelo, 37.8 percent of women aged 50-54 had never married, while in Faro only 11 percent were still single.

Table 8.2 shows the change in variation over the period; the maximum variation attained is underlined. Two measures, the midspread and the standard deviation, are presented; within each country, the details of the change in variation differ according to the measure used to describe it.

The midspread or interquartile range, the difference between the upper and lower quartile, is less sensitive to changes in the extremes of the distribution than the standard deviation. In any analysis of changes in approximately five hundred province-level units over a period of one hundred years based on censuses of varying coverage and accuracy, the robustness of the midspread is a desirable quality, since it reduces the effect of extreme values. On the other hand, some of the genuine change in the distribution of provincial I_m's within each country occurred in the tails of the distributions. In this case, the sensitivity of the standard devia-

Table 8.2. Midspread and standard deviation of provincial I_m, selected dates.

		1850	1860	1870	1880	1890	1900	1910	1920	1930	1940	1950	1960
Belgium	S.D.				.043	.045	.056	.060	.065	.066		.058	.045
	Mid				.053	.060	.059	.055	.078	.080		.060	.064
Denmark	S.D.	.043	.030	.034	.024	.037	.023	.024	.023	.023			.033
	Mid	.087	.025	.043	.025	.037	.029	.032	.033	.028			.022
England and Wales	S.D.	.034	.035	.037	.039	.040	.040	.041	.035	.029			.035
	Mid	.043	.038	.050	.055	.055	.054	.054	.041	.038			.048
Finland	S.D.				.041	.040	.051	.047	.045	.036	.020	.018	.018
	Mid				.060	.047	.067	.073	.063	.040	.028	.016	.033
France	S.D.	.071	.074	.074	.074	.070	.067	.059	.051	.054			.037
	Mid	.118	.116	.110	.122	.115	.104	.098	.077	.075			.049
Germany	S.D.			.041	.035	.043	.045	.039		.061			.058
	Mid			.068	.051	.072	.061	.053		.084			.088
Ireland	S.D.			.047	.030	.022	.019	.021		.028			.033
	Mid			.062	.043	.031	.028	.011		.030			.038
Italy	S.D.		.018	.025	.038	.037	.041	.039	.045	.048	.047	.036	.044
	Mid		.025	.018	.040	.061	.064	.055	.064	.076	.055	.040	.069

Netherlands	S.D.	.037	.035	.037	.039	.042	.039	.035	.031			.028
	Mid	.049	.051	.046	.043	.049	.059	.051	.049			.034
Norway	S.D.		.034		.035	.032		.042	.037			.043
	Mid		.022		.027	.044		.044	.051			.040
Portugal	S.D.		.068		.062	.056	.057	.057	.047	.044	.046	.048
	Mid		.091		.080	.086	.077	.067	.061	.063	.073	.058
Scotland	S.D.	.058	.058	.059	.057	.061	.061	.049	.044			.030
	Mid	.058	.058	.062	.059	.082	.091	.067	.055			.032
Spain	S.D.				.079	.076	.075	.067	.062	.045		.042
	Mid				.098	.107	.099	.086	.090	.055		.060
Sweden	S.D.			.049		.048			.030		.027	.025
	Mid			.082		.066			.036		.027	.015
Switzerland	S.D.	.074	.058	.039	.042	.026	.022	.027	.035	.041	.040	.037
	Mid	.086	.072	.044	.051	.039	.021	.044	.050	.061	.056	.050

Notes:
1. Belgium 1947 data are cited as Belgium 1950.
2. Germany 1933 data are cited as Germany 1930. Germany 1960 data include both the Federal Republic of Germany and the Democratic Republic of Germany.
3. Italy 1936 data are cited as Italy 1940.
4. Norway 1875 data are cited as Norway 1870.
5. Portugal 1864 data and Portugal 1878 data are averaged and cited as Portugal 1870.
6. Spain 1887 data are cited as Spain 1890.
7. Switzerland 1888 data are cited as Switzerland 1890.

tion to outlying values may also be a desirable quality, since it tells a part of the story that would otherwise go unnoticed.[2]

There is no single pattern to the change in either the midspread or the standard deviation, nor is the trend in any country monotonic; the universality of the increase in nuptiality between 1930 and 1960 is not matched by a unidirectional change in variation. If we compare the midspread at the first date for which data are available with that at the start of the marriage boom in 1930, we can see that variation increased in Belgium, Germany, Italy, and Norway; decreased in Denmark, England and Wales, Finland, France, Ireland, Portugal, Scotland, Spain, Sweden, and Switzerland; and remained the same in the Netherlands. If we make the same comparison between 1930 and 1960, variation increased in England and Wales, Germany, Ireland, and Switzerland; decreaseed in Belgium, Denmark, Finland, France, Italy, the Netherlands, Norway, Portugal, Scotland, Spain, and Sweden; and remained the same in Switzerland.

In a majority of countries, then, there was less variation between the provinces in 1930 than the first date for which data are available, and in a majority of countries there was less variation between the provinces in a country at the end of the marriage boom than when it began. Whatever the sources of variation in nuptiality in the countries of Western Europe around 1870, or the specific course of change afterwards, there was less variation in 1960, when they can all be considered modernized, than either at the first date for which data are available or in 1930.

Although this recent relative homogeneity of nuptiality is compatible with theories of convergence in relatively modernized societies, it may well prove to be temporary. For example, if the trend in the future is toward cohabitation without marriage, as seems to be the case in some Scandinavian countries, an increase in variation in I_m could be expected

[2] Two other measures of variation were considered but not used: the coefficient of variation (the standard deviation divided by the mean) and the midspread of the logit (a re-expression of a proportion into $1/2 \log_e p/1 - p$). Taking the mean into account, through a measure such as the coefficient of variation, biases the results toward smaller variation—a bias that is sometimes acceptable. In this case, however, we were particularly curious whether there was a decrease in variation in nuptiality or not: since we felt that the use of the coefficient of variation might bias our results toward a finding of reduced variation, we decided against its use. Re-expression into the logit is often used in situations where the fact that a proportion is limited to a range between 0 and 1 may be important—that is, when the actual values fall near the upper or the lower boundary . A bunching of cases near the extremes (saturation points) should represent more variation than the same differences near the center. In our case, since I_m was never below 0.200 or above 0.800, this re-expression was not considered necessary.

as these new patterns are adopted more readily in some provinces than in others. It should be noted, however, that abstention from marriage accompanied by cohabitation without marriage differs from the type of abstention widespread in Western Europe in the past, when unmarried women did not appear to be regularly exposed to the risk of childbearing.

In general, during the early part of our period, around 1870, when the level of I_m in a province differed greatly from that in other provinces of the same country, it tended to be high, whereas exactly the opposite was true in 1960. The distributions of I_m within countries during the early part of the period are positively skewed while by 1960 most of the extreme values are in the lower end of the distribution.

Most of the provinces with unusually high values of I_m in 1870 and 1900 were those of precocious industrialization: Durham, Renfrew, and Staffordshire in England; East Lothian, Kinross, and Midlothian in Scotland; Glarus, Appenzell-Ausser Rhodes, and Appenzell-Inner Rhodes in Switzerland; and Charleroi, Thuin, Mons, Soignies, and Philippeville in Belgium. Examination of the distributions of I_m shows that the early change to higher nuptiality in these provinces was responsible for a considerable part of the variation in 1870 (1880 in Belgium) in these four countries; with the exception of the Swiss cantons, these provinces remained in the top part of the distribution at least until 1930.

In 1960, the provinces that were unusual were those in which nuptiality was low. A number of these are provinces that are coterminous with, or dominated by, large cities. In an examination of differences in urban and rural nuptiality in Imperial Germany, Knodel and Maynes found that nuptiality in urban areas was often lower than in rural areas because of what they summarized as "intricate links between marriage, migration and economic opportunity" (Knodel and Maynes, 1976). There is some evidence that this situation may not have changed by 1960. In 1960, nuptiality in cities, especially capital cities, was often considerably lower than in the other provinces. In the four Scandinavian countries and in England, France, and Germany, I_m was lowest in the province that includes the capital city or is coterminous; in Italy, Scotland, and Spain, the province that includes the capital was in the lowest quartile of the distribution. In both Norway and Denmark, the increase in the standard deviation noted previously was caused by the failure of nuptiality in the province containing the capital city to rise as much as in the other provinces of the country during the marriage boom; in both countries, there was a decrease in variation between 1930 and 1960, if it is measured by the midspread or by the standard deviation when the capital city is excluded.

Other provinces that were unusual in 1960 were unusual in respects other than nuptiality as well; several of these were areas that may have been prevented by geography or language from being fully integrated into the culture and economy of the nation. Funchal and Corsica, for example, are both islands: Funchal is 650 miles from the mainland of Portugal; Corsica is nearer Italy than France, and its ties with Italy have often been closer. It was estimated that in 1975, 200,000 of the 220,000 Corsicans spoke the native language, which is only understood with difficulty by French speakers (Stephens, 1976). The persistence of Gaelic in the highlands of Scotland and of Welsh in some areas of Wales, like the persistence of Corsican in Corsica, may be a sign of the continued isolation of these areas, an isolation that is likely to be both generally cultural and specifically economic. Ross and Cromarty, Inverness, Dunbarton, and the Shetland Islands, all in the Highlands, have different religious, political, and linguistic traditions from those of the Lowland Scots. That Breconshire and Carnavonshire are among the most distinctively Welsh of the counties of Wales was as true in 1971 as in 1891; in 1971, 55 percent or more of the population of these counties could read, write, and speak Welsh (Verdery, 1976).

It would seem, then, that during the early part of the period, when nuptiality was still low in most of the provinces of Europe, many of the unusual areas were either provinces of precocious industrialization or large cities; in 1960, many of the unusual provinces were either dominated by large cities or were regions which may have been less than fully integrated into the nation. The suggestion that unusual values of nuptiality may be related to relatively incomplete integration finds some support in the failure of the midspread to decline in Germany and Ireland; if homogeneity in nuptiality in 1960 reflects a tendency toward convergence in other aspects of these relatively modernized societies, then the lack of increased homogeneity in Germany and in Ireland between 1930 and 1960 may be related to their division into separate countries.

Regional Patterns of Nuptiality

There is no reason to expect that the first date at which we can measure variation in nuptiality between the provinces represents the situation with respect to provincial differences before that time. The first date is merely the first date for which I_m was calculated in the Princeton European

Fertility Project; it was usually the first date for which marital status by age was published in the census. Variation at this date could be due to a recent departure from an earlier homogeneity, or represent differences of longer duration.

Most of the theories formulated to explain the age patterns of marriage in Western Europe consider age at marriage to be a function of the age at which men can achieve an independent living. Malthus wrote that it was wages that would either check or encourage early marriages (Malthus, 1830). Because the joint family household seems rarely to have been the ideal or the practice in Western Europe, an independent living was likely to have been a prerequisite to marriage. A careful summary of the relation between the economy and marriage is that of Hermalin and E. van de Walle: People want to get married, they need a material basis for marriage, and thus,

> it follows logically that they *will* get married, provided dwellings and jobs are available. We assume, on the basis of these premises, that the extent of nuptiality reflects the availability of a material basis of marriage . . . . On the whole, and all other things being equal, the proportions ever married and the age at marriage will be influenced by the ways in which the new generation gains access to worldly possessions. (Hermalin and E. van de Walle, 1977)

In the peasant economies of much of Western Europe, access to the material basis of marriage was likely to depend on the inheritance of land, a cottage, a workshop, or something equivalent. Those who inherited earlier—or who could make a living that did not depend on inheritance—would marry earlier; those who could not inherit nor find another source of income could not marry.

These theories, after implicitly or explicitly accepting the importance of the rules of household formation for the age pattern of marriage, proceed logically to link change in marriage to change in the economy (Habakkuk, 1955 and 1974; Eversley, 1965; Levine, 1977). In detail, this approach takes into account specific nonagricultural occupational groups in which rates of marriage may be low (domestic servants, apprentices, or military recruits) or whose continued ties to the land may keep their age at marriage high (Knodel and Maynes, 1976; Lesthaeghe, 1977). In general, however, the argument may lead to the conclusion that nuptiality of population aggregates will be determined by the occupational composition of the population, and that the decrease in the mean age of marriage and the increase in proportions ever marrying in Western Europe during the nineteenth and twentieth centuries were the result of economic changes that increased the demand for labor in the nonagricultural sectors of the economy.

Although the body of theory linking nuptiality change to occupational changes in the population is impressive, we can raise some questions. There are clearly limits to the amount of change possible. Age at marriage falls in Europe to an average that was below 23 in 1960 but is still well above the levels found in traditional African and Asian societies; the amount of definitive celibacy has been greatly reduced, but in no European country has it fallen below five percent. Social rules concerning marriage—either the appropriate age at which marriage begins or the prerequisites for family formation—may have been modified, but they do not appear to have been discarded.

The timing of the changes in the level of I_m also raises questions about the link between the economy and marriage: that the age at marriage should decline in France before England makes it difficult to use obvious changes in the economy as a general explanation.

It is also not clear that an emphasis on the demand for labor as a stimulus to marriage, in the context of a society in which relatively few women participated in the labor market, is entirely appropriate as an explanation for women's age at marriage. Unless there is evidence that age differences between men and women at first marriage remained constant over the period, hypotheses that more directly consider the nuptiality of women might be preferable. In Nakahara, Japan, the mean age at marriage for men born after 1716 and married before 1831 was 27.1, which is not very different from the mean age of 26.5 for men in Colyton between 1770 and 1837; the average age at marriage for women, however, was 19.6 in Nakahara, while in Colyton it was 25.1 (Smith, 1977; Wrigley, 1966). A theory that emphasizes the demand for labor, *ceteris paribus*, as a stimulus to marriage would not seem directly to explain the differences in women's age at marriage between Nakahara and Colyton.

The basis of Hajnal's typology of marriage patterns is geographical: three different marriage patterns are associated with three large geographical areas. Other studies have presented evidence that marriage patterns may vary with geographical region. Examining age at marriage and proportions ever married in Russia, Coale, Anderson, and Härm found that the relation between geography and nuptiality could be made precise:

when the Russian provinces are classified into a number of regions, each region being farther from the Baltic than the preceding, the linear correlation between region number (which the authors note can be considered an index of distance from the Baltic) and the nuptiality of the rural populations in 1897 is 0.92 (Coale, Anderson, and Härm, 1979). Although nuptiality changes between 1897 and 1970 were impressive—the age at marriage fell in the western parts of European Russia—the relative levels in 1970 reflected the previous traditions of marriage in these regions.

Quételet, looking at a much shorter period during the middle of the nineteenth century in Belgium, was also struck by the regional patterns of marriage, and by the regularity within these regions of proportions married by age. Just as the explanations for marriage in terms of access to the material conditions of life are explanations of individual decisions to marry, Quételet considers the decision to marry to be an individual act *par excellence*. Yet he notes that mortality, which is not under the voluntary influence of the individual, varies substantially from year to year, while marriage does not. "One can say that the Belgian people pay their tribute to marriage with greater regularity than they do to death; one does not, however, consider whether to die in the same way as one considers whether to marry." He concludes,

> in the actual state of things . . . everything happens as if, from one side of the kingdom to the other, people tried to conclude the same number of marriages, each year, distributed in the same fashion among the different provinces, among the cities and the countryside, among men, women, widows and widowers. (Quételet, 1848)

Geography as an explanation for age at marriage ranks with "biology is destiny" as an explanation for women's roles. On the other hand, the suggestion that marriage patterns differ by region is intriguing, for it presents the possibility of an alternative hypothesis to the effect of occupational structure on nuptiality. People who live in the same region may marry in a similar fashion because they are part of the same organization of economic production; on the other hand, they may marry in a similar fashion because they share common ideas about the appropriate age at marriage or, more probably, about the appropriate circumstances under which a marriage should take place. If it is found that regional differences in nuptiality within the countries of Western Europe were as strong in the nineteenth century as they appeared to Quételet to be in Belgium and as they were in Russia in 1897, there would be reason for trying to specify more closely what *region* signifies, and for examining more closely the course of change in these regional differences.

The regions used in the analysis that follows are geographically contiguous provinces that can be seen to share a common culture. An acceptable description of regional culture is given by Homans:

> When a people has lived together generation after generation, sharing a common history, answering often to a common name, it tends to develop distinctive institutions, a distinctive way of life, adapted of course to its physical environment and technology. When faced with new circumstances, the people may well adjust its institutions to meet them, but the adjustment will start from the old traditions, and recognizable continuity will be maintained. (Homans, 1969)

A common history is fundamental to this concept of culture; the marks of a common history were usually a longstanding political integrity, as well as the existence of other institutions that would tend to separate one group from another, such as a distinctive religion or language.

In some countries the designation of regions was obvious: in Austria and Spain, regional boundaries correspond closely to well-accepted and long-established political divisions, and usually to different languages or dialects (Kann, 1950 and 1957; Leasure, 1962). In France, the pre-Revolutionary provinces, most of which had had a previous existence as a separate area before incorporation into the lands of the Crown, were designated as regions; again, some of these provinces were marked by a regional dialect or language.

In other countries the boundaries of the regions were not so obvious. In England, there is general agreement upon what counties constitute the various regions of the country, although they are not distinguishable by language, religion, or a recent separate political history. Portugal is divided into three regions—north, central, and south—following Livi-Bacci (1971). The regions of Germany were taken from Knodel, who based them on the regions used in the census of 1925, the census of 1933, and the dialect regions of Germany. Italy was more difficult: the meaningful division is between the south, which formed a state before unification and where linguistically similar dialects are spoken, and the rest. Following Livi-Bacci, we have used south, north, and center (Livi-Bacci, 1977). The usual division of Switzerland is on the basis of language, between French-speaking and German-speaking cantons. Because the six cantons that joined together in 1393 to form the Everlasting League, the basis of the Swiss Confederation, have a distinct tradition from that of the other German-speaking cantons, they were considered to be a separate region (Mayer, 1952). The division of Belgium into nine provinces and Ireland into four is usual; the grouping of the counties of Scotland into six regions follows Flinn (1977).

In earlier sections of this paper I showed that provinces within a country differed from one another, sometimes considerably, in the proportions of women married at each age, at the first date for which calculations of the index I_m are available. If the provinces are grouped into regions that attempt to capture some of the elements of a common culture, do the differences in nuptiality correspond to these regions?

The usual statistical test for differences between groups is the comparison of means: if the means of each region differ from one another by more than could be expected by chance, one can with some confidence reject the null hypothesis that there are no differences among the groups. The F-statistic allows us to make this comparison at a given level of confidence.

Table 8.3 presents this F-statistic calculated for several countries in 1870. All the values are significant, most of them at the 0.001 level: that is, we can with a considerable degree of confidence reject the null hypothesis that there is no difference in nuptiality between the regions of these countries. Within the countries of Western Europe, then, it would appear that regions, in this case contiguous provinces that can be seen to share a common culture, differ significantly in nuptiality in 1870.

Although regional differences often reflect differences in economic organization, including differences in occupational structure that are theoretically relevant for nuptiality, the statistical relation between region and nuptiality shown in Table 8.3 does not seem to be simply the result of these economic differences. Two examples should suffice.

Using statistics from Germany in 1871, a regional measure of nuptiality was compared to a regional measure of occupational distribution. The former measure was the mean of the I_m's of the administrative units in each region, and the latter was the regional mean of the proportion in each administrative area that was dependent on the secondary sector. There was little correspondence between the two measures. In a regression of I_m on the regional mean of the occupational variable, the coefficient was 0.000013 and not significant; the value of R^2 was 0.01. It may be the

Table 8.3. Analysis of variance: F-ratios.

	1870	1900	1930	1960
Austria	19.07 ***	17.11 ***		
Belgium	4.59 ***	7.29 ***	7.72 ***	4.77 ***
England and Wales	3.07 ***	2.51 **	1.45	3.66 ***
France	4.76 ***	4.00 ***	3.46 ***	2.52 *
Germany[a]	7.80 ***	12.57 ***	10.93 ***	
Italy	1.26	6.90 ***	5.19 **	1.77
Portugal	20.65 ***	13.97 ***	5.41 *	1.52
Scotland	8.97 ***	7.30 ***	5.86 ***	3.83 **
Spain	3.89 **	3.27 **	5.21 ***	5.19 ***
Switzerland	5.32 *	6.54 **	3.61 *	0.66

*** Significant at the .001 level.
** Significant at the .01 level.
* Significant at the .05 level.

Notes: a) No analysis of variance was done for Germany in 1960 because of the change in the number of administrative areas from 68 before World War II (Alsace-Lorraine is excluded) to 26 after the war.

case that so gross an occupational classification is not the appropriate measure of the influence of the economy on marriage; it is, however, a measure that corresponds closely to the way this influence is depicted in the literature.

Lesthaeghe found that when distinctions between occupations in Belgium were made more precisely, different aspects of the occupational structure were important for nuptiality in Flanders and in Wallonia. In his regression of the proportion of women who had been married by ages 20–24 on the occupational index specific to Wallonia, the residuals clustered geographically. Between 1890 and 1910, the two areas of greatest industrial development in Wallonia were in the province of Hainaut, on the border with France, and in the province of Liège, on the border with Luxembourg and Germany. In the *arrondissements* of Hainaut, next to early-marrying France, nuptiality was higher than would be predicted on the basis of occupational structure; in Liège, it was lower,. In this case, region seems to include ties with a culture across a boundary (Lesthaeghe, 1977).

It is easier to delimit regions, and to show that they are not always a surrogate for differences in occupational structure, than it is to determine what else about them in 1870 was relevant for nuptiality. Some geographical coincidences suggest directions in which to proceed. In France, the regions characterized by particularly low nuptiality during the nineteenth century—the Alps, the Pyrenees, the Massif Central, and Brittany—were, with the exception of Brittany, areas of male emigration at least since the end of the eighteenth century (Hufton, 1974; Chatelain, 1977). They were also areas in which the adherence to Catholicism was particularly strong (Le Roy Ladurie and Dumont, 1971; Boulard, 1960). The same overlap between provinces of emigration, comparatively devout Catholicism, and low nuptiality is found in the northern provinces of Portugal and in the contiguous and linguistically similar provinces of Galicia to the north, in Spain. In Scotland, the sex ratio in the traditionally Catholic Highlands was consistently lower than in the Protestant Lowlands (Flinn, 1977). In Belgium, East Flanders and West Flanders had the lowest levels of nuptiality in 1880, the highest levels of emigration in 1901–1910, and the most devout Catholics (Damas, 1964).[3]

There is also a geographical coincidence between regions that tended to be homogeneous with respect to nuptiality and those that tended to be homogeneous with respect to language, where the basis for the choice of regions was a common political history. In France, several of the pre-Revolutionary provinces, the predecessors of contemporary *départements*, were areas in which Catalan, Basque, Breton, and other non-French languages or dialects were spoken before the Revolution and remained current until the last part of the century; many of the inhabitants in these areas spoke no French as late as 1863 (Weber, 1976). In Scotland, the people of the Highlands spoke Gaelic, the people of the Lowlands, English; Welsh was also widespread in Wales, especially in the counties on the

[3] Further findings of a correspondence between the proportions of women married at certain ages and Catholicism are presented in Wrigley (1966), Knodel and Maynes (1976), and Watkins (1984). Note that few of the unmarried women in Catholic areas are members of religious orders. In 1886 in France, of the 19 million women in the population, about 13 per cent, or 2.5 million, were spinsters, of whom only about 64,000 had taken vows of chastity in joining a religious order (see E. Levasseur, 1892).

west coast, until the twentieth century (Verdery, 1976). Flemish dominated in the northern half of Belgium, and French dominated in Wallonia.

A plausible hypothesis within which these coincidences might be considered is that the regions, which we have found to be significantly different with respect to nuptiality, correspond to the outer limits of the marriage market, the circle within which people seek a spouse. The actual market may have been smaller: in France, it appears to have often been a *pays* as small as a cluster of villages. The outer limits of the marriage market may have been coterminous with geographical or linguistic barriers to communication with other groups: within the region, factors relevant to the proportion married by age, such as the supply of marriageable men, may have been affected by regional solutions to regional economic difficulties.

It was noted previously that in Russia there was a tendency toward convergence between 1897 and 1970; the regions kept their relative positions with regard to nuptiality during that period. The same tendency toward regional persistence in marriage patterns was found in a number of the countries considered here before 1930: in regions in which women married relatively early at the beginning of the period, this pattern often persisted until 1930; in several countries, the regional ordering persisted throughout the marriage boom and was still evident in 1960.

In Austria, Portugal, Scotland, and Switzerland, the relative order of the regions remains unchanged between the first date for which statistics are available and 1930 (1910 in Austria). In Belgium, England, France, and Spain, the order is quite similar. In all these countries except England in 1930, regional differences are statistically significant both at the beginning of the period and in 1930.

The persistence of regional differences and the stability of regional patterns of marriage in these countries are not the result of unchanged nuptiality. Although the percentage increase in the median was nowhere as great during this period as it was after 1930, some change in nuptiality occurred in all of them, and substantial change in several. It is this persistence of regional patterns before 1930 that provides some evidence for taking the regional differences among regions in 1870 to be the continuation of earlier traditions of nuptiality differences, rather than a result of recent departures from a previous homogeneity.

One would expect that the regional differences in nuptiality during the nineteenth century would be muted by 1960, either because the regional economies were replaced by a national economy that facilitated access to the material requisites of marriage at about the same age throughout the country, or because the growth of a national culture replaced the local marriage market with a national one, and a local consensus on the requisites for marriage with a national one. Where there were barriers to interdependence in 1960—for example, in Germany, Belgium, and Ireland—one would expect the regional differences to remain.

Table 8.3 shows the F-ratios for 1870, 1900, 1930, and 1960. Regional patterns of nuptiality remained statistically significant in most countries until 1930. After 1930, regional differences are weaker: in half the countries considered, they are not statistically significant.

Relatively nonmodernized societies are characterized by a considerable degree of regional autarchy; economic production is usually local, and most regions are self-sufficient in most goods (Levy, 1966; Black, 1976). In Europe, difficulties of transport hindered exchange among areas during the middle of the nineteenth century, and regional isolation sometimes extended to the use of local currencies and local weights and measures (Weber, 1976). In France, the maintenance of a local language as the sole language spoken by many in a region, despite high levels of administrative and judicial centralization, may be taken as a sign of lack of contact with other regions. The regional nuptiality patterns in 1870 and the findings of Sutter and his colleagues that the zone of intermarriage was smaller in traditional societies than in relatively modernized ones permit the speculation that this relative regional self-sufficiency may not have been irrelevant for nuptiality (Sutter and Tabah, 1951; Sutter, 1968).

If pre-modern societies are characterized by regional autarchy, relatively modernized societies are characterized by specialization and interdependence (Moore, 1974; Smelser, 1959; Levy, 1966). Measures of interdependence, such as merchandise carried by rail and road and issues of national newspapers, showed great increase. The systems of transport and communication expanded dramatically in Europe during the second half of the last century. In most countries, a national press, a broadcasting system, and a television system replaced earlier, more local centers of communication, and a single market, with standard weights and measures, began to determine the price of goods, calculated in a single currency.

Correspondingly, there has been a decline in regional cultures, a decline that is marked by the disappearance of regional languages. In a survey by the Ministry of Public Instruction in 1863, it was found that 25 percent of the total population of France spoke no French; by the end of the First World War, there were few monolingual speakers of languages other than French left in France (Levasseur, 1882; Bloch, 1921; Brun, 1923a, 1923b, 1927; Dauzat, 1927; Weber, 1976; Helias, 1978). The same holds for the disappearance of Welsh as a single language in Wales and Gaelic in the Highlands of Scotland, of Basque in the Basque areas of France and Spain, of Piedmontese in Italy, and of Corsican in Corsica (Stephens, 1976).

Where regional differences remain statistically significant, regions with characteristic nuptiality patterns in 1960 are those in which earlier differences in other aspects of society—what Homans has called "the precipitates of different past histories"—have persisted. Some of these are captured by linguistic differences, which reflect the persistence of regional cultures and may inhibit the further integration of these areas into the larger society. The same idea was expressed more elegantly by Samuel Johnson, who said: "There is no tracing the connection of ancient nations but by language, and therefore I am always sorry when a language is lost, because languages are the pedigrees of nations." In Belgium, language differences represent enduring cultural differences between the two parts of the country, many of which have been deliberately preserved. Wales, and especially those counties that have been slow to give up their adherence to the Welsh language, have long been culturally distinct from the other parts of England, and it is not surprising to find this distinctiveness reflected in their marriage patterns. In Ireland, six of the nine provinces of Ulster constitute the whole of Northern Ireland, which maintained its links with Great Britain when Eire became independent: some of the barriers to full integration between these two areas are well known. In Scotland, the use of Gaelic has not yet disappeared (though it seems to be declining) from the Highlands, the only region of the country that is marked by unusual nuptiality. And in Spain, the continued use of Catalan by many of the inhabitants of the provinces that once formed the kingdom of Aragon is likely to have hindered closer ties between these regions and the rest of the country.

If at least part of the explanation for the reduction in significant differences among regions by 1960 is the growth of a national culture, facilitated by such things as a national school system, by the development of national media, and by the mobility made possible by a developed system of transport, we would expect regional differences to continue to be significant in countries where part of the population does not share in the same school system or communications network, and where mobility among the regions was hindered.

In Belgium and Ireland, linguistic differences and political differences separate the populations, inhibiting communication and mobility. In Belgium, the French-speaking population of Wallonia and the Flemish-speaking population of Flanders have different newspapers, different broadcasting systems, and different school administrations. In Ireland, the separation of the Irish Republic and Northern Ireland has been matched by the development of separate national media: in both countries political divisions are marked by regional differences in nuptiality. The F-ratios are significant in every year at the 0.001 level in Belgium, and in 1931 and 1961 in Ireland.

Conclusions

In Western Europe between 1870 and 1960, the traditional Western European pattern of marriage was abandoned: increases in the proportions married by age—and especially the rapid increases after the early 1930s that Hajnal described as a marriage boom—occurred in every province. In addition, there was a tendency in many but not all of these countries toward a reduction of differences in provincial nuptiality: in 1960 there was less variation in nuptiality within most countries than there had been either at the first date for which figures are available or in 1930.

There is evidence that in 1870 nuptiality was similar in geographically contiguous provinces in the same region, but differed, sometimes substantially, from region to region within the same country. These regional patterns of nuptiality seem to correspond to different cultures, to what have been called "the precipitates of different past histories." During the course of the changes in the proportions married at each age that occurred between 1870 and 1930, the relative level of nuptiality among the regions of most countries remained much the same. After 1930, however, differences among regions were muted, and the relative order often changed. Where significant regional differences persisted longest, the patterns of nuptiality in 1960 appeared to be the residue of cultural differences in the previous century.

There is no reason to believe that the different past histories of these regions will not become even less relevant over time: it may have been true that in the past, geography was destiny for provinces, but we may speculate about its predictive value for the future. Nevertheless, the persistence of regional variation in some countries until 1960, and the correspondence of regional differences then to those of the previous century, as well as the significant differences in nuptiality in countries where obvious barriers to a more complete cultural integration exist, suggest further speculations. Short of complete homogenization, variation appears likely to remain a function of initial differences, just as increasing homogeneity appears to be a function of aspects of modernization. Modernization may be a universal solvent in many areas, but it does not appear always to dissolve persistent differences in nuptiality.

CHAPTER 9: Demographic Transitions in German Villages

John Knodel

ACKNOWLEDGMENTS

The helpful research assistance of Sara Millman and Ik-Ki Kim is gratefully acknowledged. I am also grateful to Sara Millman and Albert Hermalin for many useful discussions during the preparation of this paper. Albert Köbele, Rudolf Manger, Friedrich Sauer, and Lorenz Scheuenpflug kindly answered, through personal correspondence, a large number of questions concerning their village genealogies. The research on which the paper is based has been in part sponsored by Grants 1-R01-HD10178-01 and R01-HD14938 from the National Institutes of Health and from a research fellowship provided by the Rockefeller Foundation.

INTRODUCTION

Although the concept of the demographic transition was formulated half a century ago, our understanding of this phenomenon both historically and as it is now taking shape in the developing countries remains incomplete, particularly with respect to the secular decline in fertility. The extensive research efforts comprising what is known as the Princeton European Fertility Project have recently increased significantly our knowledge of the historical fertility decline in the industrialized world. The studies sponsored by this project, as well as most studies inspired by it, have been based primarily on macro-level data derived from census and vital statistics reports referring to administrative areas such as nations, provinces, or districts rather than to individuals or individual families per se. Thus, much of the description and analysis of the demographic transition as it took place in the past has been limited to those aspects that can be appropriately addressed by data for such aggregate units.

At the same time that the European Fertility Project initiated the first detailed examination of macro-level data on the European fertility decline, the analysis of micro-level data based on the technique of family reconstitution was rapidly expanding within the field of historical demography. Most of this work, however, has been restricted to periods prior to the onset of the secular decline of fertility and therefore has only made a limited contribution to our understanding of the demographic transition. Those few studies of this variety that have analyzed the fertility decline have been limited largely to elite groups of the population, such as the Geneva bourgeoisie and the French peerage (for exceptions, see Andorka, 1979; Imhof, 1975; Weir, 1980 and 1981; and Lachiver, 1973). The purpose of the present paper is to help redress this situation by tracing the demographic transition through the initial onset of fertility decline in a sample of German villages for which reconstituted family histories are available. Because the data refer to individual couples, the analysis can explore aspects of demographic behavior that have had to be largely ignored by previous aggregate-level studies. Moreover, since the village genealogies are based on parish records, the present analysis can extend considerably further into the past than is possible for studies based only on published vital statistics reports and census results. Since the social and economic lives of the rural population for the most part were rather locally circumscribed for much of the eighteenth and nineteenth centuries, the village is a particularly appropriate context in which to explore the demographic behavior of individuals.

The total sample consists of fourteen different villages, although for the purpose of analysis some villages, particularly the four located in the area of the former principality of Waldeck and the three in Bavaria, are frequently combined into single composite data sets to avoid problems associated with small numbers of cases. The reconstituted family histories on which this study is based come from village genealogies (*Ortsippenbücher*), a source unique to Germany.[1] Consideration is limited to couples mar-

[1] Unlike usual genealogies that trace vital events of a particular family line regardless of where the various branches may have moved, *Ortsippenbücher* encompass all families that have ever resided in a particular village. They are limited largely to the events that are recorded in the local records, particularly the parish and civil registers, and generally do not follow families that move away from the village. Thus with the exception of a small number of families that happen to move between villages that each have village genealogies available, families that migrated from the village are generally lost to observation. For families that migrated into the village from elsewhere, some limited information about events occurring prior to their moving into the village is sometimes available, since selected background information was sometimes recorded in the parish or civil registers of the village after their arrival. For example, the birth date of a bride or groom born elsewhere might be recorded in the marriage register at the time of the wedding. The nature and quality of these genealogies have been discussed at length elsewhere (Knodel, 1975; Knodel and Shorter, 1976), as has been the process for selecting families appropriate for inclusion in an analysis of fertility (Knodel, 1978c, Appendix).

ried during the eighteenth and nineteenth centuries. However, obvious problems with deficiencies in the death registration require that couples married during part or all of the eighteenth century in several of the villages must be excluded from some of the analyses. Although reproductive histories of couples married from 1900 on are also excluded, births occurring after 1899 to couples married before 1900 are not. Hence the time period covered by the study does extend into the early part of the twentieth century with the exception of one village (Werdum), where the genealogy was based only on records up to 1900.[2] There is ample evidence from aggregate-level data that both fertility and mortality had begun to decline by the end of the nineteenth century in much of Germany (Knodel, 1974). Thus while our data do not cover the demographic transition in its entirety, they do capture its early phases, including the onset of the secular decline in fertility. Given the apparent irreversibility of both mortality and fertility decline, these initial stages of the demographic transition are the most interesting and challenging to understand.

Descriptive information on the villages is summarized in Table 9.1. They range in population size from only a few hundred to close to two thousand at mid-nineteenth century. One of the places listed (Herbolzheim) gained legal status as a town in 1810 and in fact has the largest population, of the fourteen places included in the sample, since the beginning of the nineteenth century. For the sake of convenience, we refer to Herbolzheim as a village, although from 1810 onward it is technically a small town. Information on population size at around the start of the

[2] Although most of the genealogies include information about couples married during the twentieth century, these couples are excluded from the present analysis for several reasons. Information such as the death dates of the spouses is often lacking, and this information is essential for determining whether or not the couple is in observation during their entire reproductive span. By stopping with couples married before 1900, we also largely eliminate problems of interpreting individual reproductive histories that could result from disruptions associated with two world wars.

The fact that the village genealogy of Werdum was based only on vital events occurring up to 1900 means that for most analyses very few couples in Werdum who were married toward the end of the nineteenth century will be included, since complete information about them will be lacking. Because results for the combined sample of all villages represent self-weighting averages of the individual villages, these compositional shifts with respect to relative importance of individual villages occur over the period under observation. Thus toward the end of the period under observation, Werdum contributed much less to the combined sample results than it does for much of the rest of the period. Also, since relatively complete parish registers begin at different times for the different villages, considerable compositional shifts occur during the first half of the eighteenth century. This should be kept in mind when interpreting the results for the combined sample.

Table 9.1. Descriptive information on the villages selected for analysis.

Village	State or Area	Predominant Religion	Predominant Inheritance Pattern	Number of Families Available for Analysis[b]	Population Size[a]				
					About 1700	About 1800	About 1850	1900	1933
Grafenhausen	Baden	Catholic	partible	1276	201	1272	1462	1438	1406
Herbolzheim	Baden	Catholic	partible	2213	480	1746	1988	2018	3141
Kappel	Baden	Catholic	partible	1029	118	670	1373	1297	1485
Rust	Baden	Catholic	partible	1562	n.a.	1394	1926	1786	1844
Öschelbronn	Wurttemberg	Protestant	partible	842	n.a.	n.a.	886	1051	954
Anhausen	Bavaria	Catholic	impartible	287	n.a.	n.a.	290	305	341
Gabelbach	Bavaria	Catholic	impartible	256	170[c]	227	264	311	362
Kreuth[e]	Bavaria	Catholic	impartible	210	n.a.	n.a.	220[e]	400[e]	500[e]
Braunsen	Waldeck	Protestant	mixed	265	n.a.	239	267	233	228

Höringhausen	Waldeck	Protestant	mixed	627	450[d]	700[d]	762	730	892
Massenhausen	Waldeck	Protestant	mixed	460	n.a.	n.a.	463	413	358
Vasbeck	Waldeck	Protestant	mixed	503	300	n.a.	429	459	465
Middels	East Friesland	Protestant	mixed	695	n.a.	n.a.	n.a.	n.a.	906
Werdum	East Friesland	Protestant	mixed	1468	n.a.	n.a.	n.a.	n.a.	698

Notes:

a) Derived from various sources including data provided in the introductions to the village genealogies.

b) Couples for which all of the following are known: exact date of marriage, the wife's birth date at least to the year; the exact death date of at least one of the two spouses; and the exact birth dates of at least all but one child. Most analyses included in the present study are based on more restrictive criteria and thus are based on somewhat smaller numbers of cases than indicated here. The exact number depends on the particular analysis.

c) Estimated from the number of communicants.

d) Estimated from the number of houses.

e) The village genealogy refers only to the parish of Kreuth, which is smaller than the Gemeinde to which civil census statistics refer. In 1939 the parish included 516 persons while in 1933 the Gemeinde's population was 1325. Based on these figures, the population of the parish has been estimated from censuses at the dates shown.

f) Located geographically within the boundaries of the Waldeck area but administratively an enclave of Hesse-Darmstadt and later Hesse-Nassau.

n.a. = not available.

eighteenth century is provided for several of the villages in the village genealogies. The accuracy of this information is unknown and in several cases appears to be suspect. In particular, the rapid population growth indicated by a comparison of the population sizes at the beginning and end of the eighteenth century indicated for Grafenhausen and Kappel is not confirmed by an examination of changes in the number of marriages taking place.[3] Since there is less reason to doubt the accuracy of the early nineteenth-century statistics, the earlier figures for both may be serious underestimates.

The villages are located in five different areas of Germany. All four villages in Baden are within 15 kilometers of each other and all but Herbolzheim share common boundaries. They are on the Rhine Plain and close to the western edge of the Black Forest. The village of Öschelbronn is in the state of Württemberg on the eastern edge of the Black Forest. The two Bavarian villages of Anhausen and Gabelbach are located within 25 kilometers of each other and in an administrative district where longstanding traditions proscribed breast-feeding (Knodel and E. van de Walle, 1967). The third Bavarian village, Kreuth, is located about 100 kilometers away in a different district where breast-feeding was also thought to be uncommon, although internal evidence from the village genealogy suggests breast-feeding was probably more extensive in Kreuth than in the other two Bavarian villages.[4] The four villages located within the boundaries of the former principality of Waldeck in central Germany are all located within 20 kilometers of each other, although Höringhausen was an enclave that was administratively not part of Waldeck. The two villages in East Friesland, in the northwest corner of Germany, are also relatively close to each other, being separated by less than 20 kilometers.

[3] The first two population figures given for Grafenhausen refer to 1692 and 1813 and thus indicate over a 6-fold increase in population during a 125-year period (Köbele, 1971). In contrast, the total number of locally recorded marriages increased from 75 in 1690–1709 to 173 in 1800–1819, or only by 2.3-fold. In neighboring Kappel, the first two population figures refer to 1692 and 1803 and thus indicate almost a 6-fold increase in 115 years; but the number of local marriages increased only by 14 percent, from 132 during the first two decades of the eighteenth century (the extant parish registers date from 1700) to 151 during the first two decades of the nineteenth century. In nearby Herbolzheim, the first two population figures that refer to 1692 and 1810 point to a 3.6-fold increase in a 118-year period (Köbele, 1967), while a sample check of local marriages points to doubling of local marriages between the first two decades of the eighteenth and nineteenth centuries, respectively.

[4] For example, the difference between birth intervals following infant survivals and intervals following infant deaths is larger in Kreuth than in Anhausen and Gabelbach, but shorter than in other villages in the sample (see Knodel, 1982, p.4).

The four villages in Baden and the three in Bavaria are Catholic, while the other seven are Protestant. The villages also represent different inheritance patterns.

Additional information on the character of the sample villages is provided in Table 9.2, which shows summary information on the occupational distribution of the husbands for couples included in the present study. Also indicated is the percentage of couples for which occupational

Table 9.2. Percentage of couples married 1700-1899 for which husband's occupation is known and the percentage distribution of known occupations.

	% with Occupation Known[a]	% Distribution of Known Occupations[b]				
		Farmers	Artisans, Businessmen, Professionals	Laborers, Cottagers, Unskilled	Mixed, Other	Total
Grafenhausen	99	46	28	20	6	100
Herbolzheim	97	23	40	27	10	100
Kappel	99	29	28	27	16	100
Rust	94	19	41	25	15	100
Öschelbronn	93	33	35	16	16	100
Anhausen	85	14	21	51	14	100
Gabelbach	77	9	37	46	8	100
Kreuth	76	28	22	28	22	100
Brausen	89	20	33	32	14	100
Höringhausen	65	24	38	28	10	100
Massenhausen	62	22	25	36	17	100
Vasbeck	91	46	22	23	10	100
Middels	98	34	8	44	14	100
Werdum	96	24	19	51	7	100
All villages	92	28	30	30	12	100

Notes: Based only on couples included in the analysis (see footnotes to Table 9.1). Persons with two occupations in different groups were assigned to the mixed category.

a) As percentage of couples with known and unknown occupations.

b) As percentage of couples with known occupations only; the total may not add exactly to 100 because of rounding.

information is available among those families selected for analysis. For most of the villages, at least some information on the husband's occupation was available for the large majority of couples, although for several data sets, information was lacking for a substantial proportion of the couples, particularly during the eighteenth century. For several reasons, these tabulations can be considered only very rough indicators of the occupational distribution of the entire population. Men who never married are not included. Moreover, it is unlikely that husbands for whom occupational data are missing as well as husbands in couples who did not meet the criteria necessary for inclusion in the present study are randomly distributed with respect to the overall occupational distribution of the village. In addition, the groupings are crude and involve a fair amount of arbitrary judgment.[5] Nevertheless, it seems reasonably safe to assume that the diversity in occupational structures evident in the results reflects genuine diversity among the villages included in the sample.

No claim can be made that the fourteen villages included in the present study form a representative sample of the rural population of Germany in the eighteenth and nineteenth centuries. Nevertheless, as the information provided in Tables 9.1 and 9.2 make clear, and as information on intervillage differences in child mortality, marital fertility levels, and age at marriage presented below will indicate, the samples represent an interesting variety of social and economic settings in which to explore the onset of the demographic transition.

Infant and Child Mortality

The demographic transition model attributes central importance to the timing and interdependence of the secular declines in fertility and mor-

[5] The occupational classification scheme differs from that used in previous analyses of the village genealogies by the author. The new scheme is described in detail in an appendix of a monograph in preparation. The category labeled "Farmers" contained persons with titles indicating that they owned or leased a farm. Presumably they were self-sufficient and did not need to hire themselves out to earn a living. The group labeled "Artisans, Businessmen, and Professionals" is comprised largely of artisans or craftsmen but also includes some local businessmen and professionals. The category labeled "Laborers, Cottagers, and Unskilled" is intended to represent the rural proletariat. Although cottagers typically owned small tracts of agricultural land, they generally hired themselves out as laborers as well, or had some home-industry activity to supplement their incomes. Persons for whom more than one occupation was listed and for whom the first two listed occupations fell into different categories were placed in a residual category and not shown in the results except in their inclusion in the total for all categories.

tality. In particular, reductions in infant and child mortality are assumed to serve as an impetus for reductions in fertility. National level life tables providing detailed information on age-specific levels of mortality are available for Germany only after 1870. Several German states produced life tables for earlier years, although only exceptionally for periods prior to the mid-nineteenth century. Likewise, estimates of infant mortality at the national level do not start until the last third of the nineteenth century, although infant mortality rates for individual German states for earlier periods are somewhat more numerous than are full life tables. In general, the available official statistics indicate little evidence of any sustained decline prior to the end of the nineteenth century and in some states not until even later (Knodel, 1974; Kintner, 1982). In a review of time-series data on infant mortality based on local studies of cities, towns, and villages, covering in many cases the eighteenth century and even earlier, Kintner (1982) finds that the average level of infant mortality in these locations either increased or remained roughly constant until the late nineteenth century, when a decrease is first noticeable (see also W. R. Lee, 1979). Information on child mortality above age one is considerably scarcer. A steady and substantial decline is evident during the last third of the nineteenth century, when the first national-level life tables were compiled (Knodel, 1974). There is little evidence available from official statistics to determine how long this trend had been under way. Given the different implications of alternative sequences in fertility and mortality decline for understanding the demographic transition, and given the real possibility that infant and child mortality trends may have differed, information on long-term trends for years prior to the period covered by official statistics takes on added significance (Matthiessen and McCann, 1978).

The probabilities of dying before age 1 (${}_1q_0$) and before age 15 (${}_{15}q_0$), as well as between ages 1 and 5 (${}_4q_1$) and between ages 5 and 15 (${}_{10}q_5$) are shown in Figure 9.1 from the mid-eighteenth century to the early twentieth century for the combined sample.[6] Results indicating the

[6] Several features of a sample of births and the methodology used to compute the mortality risks are worth noting because they undoubtedly introduce some biases into the results. Since the results are based only on children born to the families selected from the village genealogies for analysis in the present study, illegitimate children other than those born to couples who marry later are excluded. Also, births occurring from 1900 on in the present study are only those to couples married before 1900 and thus are to women who undoubtedly are older than are all mothers giving birth during the same years. Moreover, these births are concentrated in years immediately following 1900. [Note continues on p. 347.]

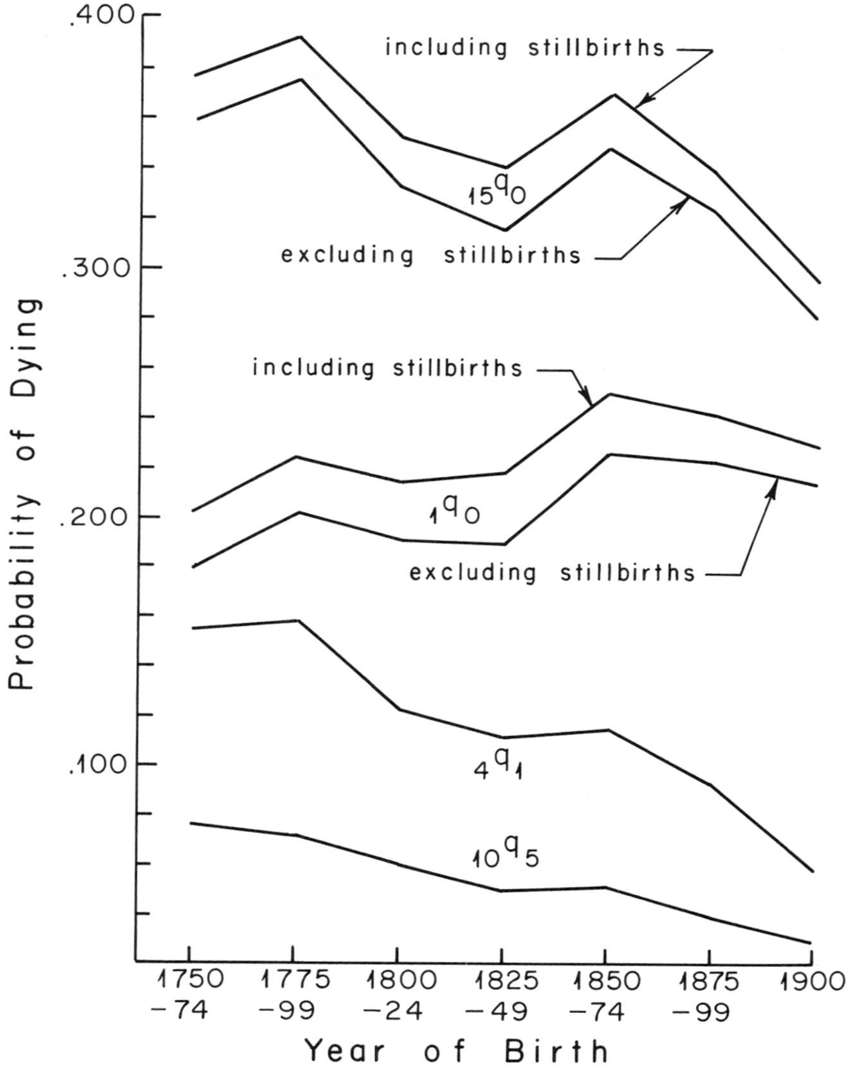

Figure 9.1. Trends in infant and child mortality, combined sample of 14 villages.

probability of dying before ages 1 and 15 are shown both including and excluding consideration of stillbirths which averaged about 3 percent of all births recorded in the genealogies during most of the period, but which fell to 2 percent of all births starting at the end of the nineteenth century. While the combined sample is clearly composed of a nonrandom selection of German villages, the levels of infant and child mortality indicated for the end of the nineteenth century correspond reasonably closely to the national levels indicated by official statistics.[7] Perhaps of greatest relevance for understanding the demographic transition is the indication that infant and child mortality follow divergent paths from the end of the eighteenth century to the beginning of the twentieth. While infant mortality reaches its highest level during the third quarter of the nineteenth century and declines only moderately by the start of the twentieth century, the probabilities of dying between ages 1 and 5 and between ages 5 and 15 decline almost steadily from the mid-eighteenth century on. One possible factor contributing to the decline of child mortality particularly at early ages immediately following infancy was the introduction of smallpox inoculation, which was made compulsory in a number of German states very early in the nineteenth century (W. R. Lee, 1979 and 1980).

The tardiness in the decline in infant mortality relative to improvements in mortality at older ages appears not to be unique to Germany but is rather a common feature of the demographic transition in much of Europe (Wrigley, 1969; Matthiessen and McCann, 1978). A realistic assessment of the linkages between the changes in mortality and fertility associated with the demographic transition clearly needs to incorporate measures of

---

Some compositional shifts occurred in the relative contribution of different villages, especially during the early periods when several villages are excluded due to obvious incompleteness in death registration and also toward the end of the nineteenth century when births included from Werdum decline sharply and are totally eliminated after 1900 (the genealogy of Werdum is based only on events occurring through 1900).

In calculating the mortality risks, children in the selected families for whom a birth date but no death date or additional information was provided were assumed to survive past age 15. Some of these children may actually have died before age 15 without their deaths having been registered in the parish records, perhaps because the family migrated. Given the way in which families were selected for analysis, this bias is probably minimal. See Knodel (1979, footnote 4) for a fuller discussion of this issue.

[7] For the period 1875–1899, our combined sample yields the following values: ${}_1q_0$ (excluding stillbirths) = 0.223; ${}_4q_1$ = 0.093; and ${}_{10}q_5$ = 0.039. This compares to an unweighted average of the three decadal estimates at the national level for the period 1871–1900 as follows: ${}_1q_0$ = 0.226; ${}_4q_1$ = 0.117; and ${}_{10}q_5$ = 0.053.

Table 9.3. Probability of dying before age 5 ($_5q_0$) by year of birth and village of residence, and the probabilities of dying before age 1 ($_1q_0$) and between age 1 and age 5 ($_4q_1$) by village of residence.

	$_5q_0$ by Year of Birth							All Years of Birth	
Village of Residence	1700-1749	1750-1799	1800-1824	1825-1849	1850-1874	1875 1899	1900+	$_1q_0$	$_4q_1$
Grafenhausen	.414[a]	.365	.350	.325	.374	.309	.310	.254	.123
Herbolzheim	.424[b]	.358[c]	.375	.370	.377	.333	.258	.236	.163
Kappel	--	--	.268[d]	.265	.326	.285	.244	.204	.102
Rust	--	.388[e]	.289	.268	.319	.371	.414	.243	.120
Öschelbronn	.403	.382	.430	.377	.399	.395	.240	.300	.129
Anhausen[h]	--	.482[f]	.371	.419	.472	.458	--	.381[m]	.083[m]
Gabelbach[h]	--	.405[g]	.377	.381	.458	.398	(.310)	.348[m]	.085[m]
Kreuth	--	.260	.244	(.219)	(.233)	(.235)	--	.211	.039
3 Bavarian villages[h]	--	.380	.342	.362	.426	.397	.311	.321[m]	.069[m]
Braunsen	.330[i]	.342	.215	.315	.314	.206	--	.171	.136
Höringhausen	.315[j]	.343	.241	.313	.288	.276	.188	.175	.142
Massenhausen	--	.354	.302	.346	.337	.178	--	.194	.147
Vasbeck	.276	.362	.351	.310	.321	.228	--	.208	.135

4 Waldeck villages	.297	.351	.285	.321	.314	.237	.181	.188	.142
Middels	--	.208	.185	.160	.182	.189	.111	.122	.067
Werdum	.327[k]	.278	.182	.238	.238	.212	--	.167	.108
All villages[l]	.362	.342	.311	.307	.337	.317	.279	.228	.124

<u>Notes</u>: Results in this table are based on locally born children of couples for whom the end of marriage occurred locally and the date of the end of marriage is known with certainty. Results based on fewer than 50 children or for periods of obviously deficient registration are omitted; results based on 50-99 children are shown in parentheses. The 1900+ category refers to children born in 1900 or later to couples married before 1900. The calculations of ${}_1q_0$ and ${}_5q_0$ include stillbirths in both numerator and denominator.

a) 1740-1749.
b) 1726-1749.
c) Excluding 1760-1766.
d) 1810-1824.
e) 1764-1799.
f) 1765-1799.
g) 1766-1799.
h) Deaths to children that were indicated by a cross without an exact date of death are distributed to age groups under 10 proportional to the age distribution of known deaths under 10 during 1800-49 in Anhausen and Gabelbach combined.
i) 1707-1749.
j) 1731-1749.
k) 1710-1749.
l) Weighted average for all villages for which data were available for each particular time period.
m) Excluding periods (in Anhausen and Gabelbach) when a cross without an exact date of death was used to indicate a child death.

mortality that go beyond just the first year of life. However, in the case of Germany, judging from the combined sample of villages, decreases in child mortality may have been largely canceled out by rising infant mortality during parts of the eighteenth and nineteenth centuries. The probability of surviving to age 15 appears to fluctuate within a relatively narrow range until the beginning of the twentieth century.

Trends in the probability of surviving to age 5 during the eighteenth and nineteenth centuries are shown in Table 9.3 for the individual villages along with summary information on infant and early child mortality for the entire period combined. Because of probable differences in the way stillbirths were treated in the parish records or by the compilers of the village genealogies, they are included in the mortality rates. In most villages, the risk of dying before age 5 fluctuated within a relatively narrow range during most of the period under observation. With the exception of Rust, and to a lesser extent, Kreuth and Middels, child mortality declines between the last two quarters of the nineteenth century and, where sufficient data area available, continues to decline during the early twentieth century. In most villages, the risks of death for young children were quite high, even at the end of the nineteenth century, and the improvement during the last half of the nineteenth century was quite modest.

Substantial differences in the levels of infant and child mortality for the various villages are also evident. One factor that was undoubtedly an important determinant of these differences, especially in infant mortality, was the prevailing practice of infant feeding. The highest infant mortality rates are found for two of the three Bavarian villages, both located in areas where breast-feeding was known to be relatively rare, at least during the nineteenth century. The lowest infant mortality was found for Middels and Werdum, both of which are located in East Friesland, an area where breast-feeding was apparently common and of relatively long duration (Bluhm, 1912; Röse, 1905).[8] Interestingly, the risk of dying in the first four years following infancy is relatively low in the Bavarian villages, perhaps reflecting a selection process in which only the hardier infants

[8] Further support for the important role of infant feeding practices in accounting for the observed differences in infant mortality levels is provided by the high negative correlation between the village infant mortality levels and the *difference* between the average intergenesic interval following an infant survival and following an infant death in the villages. The latter measure can be considered an indirect indication of the extent of breast-feeding in the village. A negative correlation coefficient of −0.86 is indicated based on the infant mortality rates in Table 9.3, and data on the difference between intergenesic intervals according to the survival of the child is provided in Knodel (1981, Table 3).

survived the high mortality before age one. Moreover, since many children in the Bavarian villages were not breast-fed at all and the rest were weaned at early ages, by the time infants passed their first birthday, weanling diarrhea would no longer be an important factor leading to death. In other villages where a substantial proportion of children might have been breast-fed longer than a year, the increased risk of mortality following weaning might contribute to the early child mortality rate.

Age at Marriage

As in most of Western and Northern Europe, entrance into marriage occurred relatively late in Germany during the eighteenth and nineteenth centuries. The ages at first marriage for both men and women are presented in Table 9.4. All villages clearly fall within the range of European late marriage. Age at first marriage for men averaged around 28 or 29 for the two-century period in most cases, with the main exception being the Bavarian villages where marriages began at even later ages. On the average, women entered their first marriage two to three years younger than their husbands. Their age at first marriage generally averaged close to 26 during the two-century period. The main exceptions are the Bavarian villages, where women were noticeably older at first marriage, and in Middels, where women were somewhat younger. There is no major change in age at marriage during the period although for both men and women a pattern of gradual increase followed by a sharper decline at the end of the nineteenth century is evident for most villages. In some cases, this reduction was probably related to the repeal of restrictive marriage legislation that had been passed in much of Germany earlier in the century (Knodel, 1967; Matz, 1980). In any event, these results for the villages at the end of the nineteenth century are generally consistent with those for Germany as a whole and, indeed, for much of Europe in indicating that nuptiality changes had only a minor impact on the trend in overall fertility at that time. If anything, nuptiality changes were counteracting the emerging pattern of fertility decline rather than contributing to it (Knodel, 1974; E. van de Walle, 1968).

The pattern of late marriage that characterized the village populations as a whole was also true for different socioeconomic groups, as evident in Table 9.5, which presents age at first marriage according to the occupational group of the husband. Perhaps the most striking feature of the results is the similarity in age at first marriage across occupational categories,

Table 9.4. Age at first marriage for men and women, by year of marriage.

	1700-1749	1750-1799	1800-1824	1825-1849	1850-1874	1875 1899	1700-1899
Grafenhausen							
men	27.0	27.7	28.0	28.1	28.1	27.6	27.8
women	26.3	25.9	27.1	26.6	25.4	24.4	25.8
Herbolzheim							
men	26.3	26.7	29.2	29.3	29.3	28.0	28.2
women	24.4	24.7	27.1	26.2	27.4	26.1	26.0
Kappel							
men	26.6	27.3	27.0	27.7	28.8	28.3	27.7
women	25.2	25.0	24.8	26.6	26.0	26.1	25.6
Rust							
men	27.1	27.7	27.1	29.4	29.2	27.6	28.1
women	25.5	26.0	26.3	27.2	26.6	25.5	26.1
Öschelbronn							
men	26.4	26.5	27.7	28.9	28.7	28.6	27.8
women	24.6	24.7	25.8	26.7	27.4	26.9	26.0
3 Bavarian villages							
men	(28.4)	30.5	30.3	33.7	33.3	32.1	31.8
women	27.7	28.9	29.3	30.9	30.4	28.1	29.0
4 Waldeck villages							
men	29.1	27.5	27.6	29.9	29.9	27.8	28.6
women	26.2	26.8	26.4	27.4	27.6	24.8	26.6
Middels							
men	--	28.9	27.6	29.4	29.6	28.4	28.8
women	(23.7)	22.8	23.4	25.2	24.7	23.5	23.9
Werdum							
men	29.8	29.6	29.2	29.6	29.9	(30.1)	29.6
women	24.3	25.7	25.1	26.8	26.8	(24.4)	25.7
All villages							
men	27.8	28.0	28.3	29.4	29.5	28.3	28.6
women	25.3	25.7	26.2	26.9	26.9	25.5	26.1

Note: Results based on fewer than 20 cases are omitted; results based on 20-49 cases are shown in parentheses.

particularly for men. To the extent that any consistent pattern is apparent, the laborer group and their wives appear to have married later than other villagers. This holds true both for the eighteenth and nineteenth centuries. Wives of laborers are characterized by later-than-average marriage ages in virtually all the villages, while for men the only exception is Werdum, where laborers enter their first marriage at a slightly younger age on the average than the rest of the villagers. There is little consistency in the difference between men in the farmer category and men in the predominantly artisan category with respect to age at first marriage but a rather consis-

Table 9.5. Age at first marriage for men and women, by year of marriage and occupational category of husband.

	Men				Women			
	Farmers,	Artisans, Businessmen, Professionals	Laborers, Cottagers, Unskilled	All (including unknown)	Farmers	Artisans, Businessmen, Professionals	Laborers Cottagers, Unskilled	All (including unknown)
Grafenhausen								
1700-1799	27.1	27.4	28.3	27.5	25.4	25.8	27.2	26.0
1800-1899	27.9	27.5	29.3	28.0	24.9	26.3	27.9	25.8
Herbolzheim								
1700-1799	26.3	26.6	27.4	26.6	23.4	24.3	25.7	24.6
1800-1899	28.9	28.6	29.5	28.9	25.5	26.3	27.7	26.6
Kappel								
1700-1799	26.8	26.8	27.6	27.1	23.8	24.6	26.7	25.0
1800-1899	27.6	27.7	28.9	28.0	24.4	25.2	28.4	25.9
Rust								
1700-1799	27.1	26.5	28.4	27.6	23.7	25.3	27.1	25.8
1800-1899	27.2	28.1	30.6	28.4	24.1	25.9	29.3	26.2
Öschelbronn								
1700-1799	25.8	25.6	(28.8)	26.4	23.0	24.6	(26.4)	24.7
1800-1899	28.6	28.2	29.9	28.5	25.9	27.4	28.1	26.8
3 Bavarian villages								
1700-1799	--	(27.9)	(30.9)	30.1	--	(27.0)	(38.1)	28.5
1800-1899	34.2	31.0	32.6	32.4	29.6	27.2	30.3	29.6
4 Waldeck villages								
1700-1799	27.3	28.1	28.1	28.1	25.7	26.7	27.6	26.6
1800-1899	28.3	28.8	29.6	28.9	25.1	26.6	27.6	26.6
Middels								
1700-1799	28.6	--	29.2	29.0	21.7	--	(24.1)	23.0
1800-1899	28.6	(28.3)	29.3	28.8	23.8	(24.0)	24.7	24.2
Werdum								
1700-1799	30.5	29.7	29.2	29.6	24.0	25.1	25.9	25.3
1800-1899	31.1	29.8	28.8	29.6	24.0	26.5	26.7	26.1
All villages								
1700-1799	27.6	27.3	28.6	27.9	24.1	25.3	26.4	25.6
1800-1899	28.6	28.5	29.7	28.9	25.0	26.3	27.7	26.4

Notes: Results in parentheses are based on 20-49 cases; results based on fewer than 20 cases are omitted. Husbands, and wives of husbands, with two occupations in different groups were coded in a separate mixed category. This category is not shown but is included in the results which refer to all husbands or wives.

tent difference is apparent for their wives. With the sole exception of the Bavarian villages, wives of farmers were characterized by an earlier age at first marriage than wives of men in the artisans' group. Moreover, without exception farmers' wives married younger than laborers' wives. Thus, despite the small magnitude of differences in age at first marriage associated with husband's occupation, for women the nature of these differences is both fairly consistent across villages and persists between the eighteenth and nineteenth centuries.

It is generally accepted that the key mechanism underlying the relatively late age at marriage characteristic of the Western European marriage pattern was the socially imposed link between ability to establish an independent livelihood adequate to support a family and entry into a marital union (Hajnal, 1965). Thus it is noteworthy that men's age at first marriage in our sample of villages appears to be less closely linked to their occupational category than is their wives' age at first marriage. While such a finding might seem inconsistent with our understanding of the traditional European marriage pattern, it agrees with observations by Wrigley (1961) based on late-nineteenth-century data that female nuptiality patterns were much more variable than male patterns. The mechanism through which men's occupations affect their wives' ages at marriage is an intriguing one and clearly deserving of further investigation.

The results from the German villages are also interesting in light of the recent discussions of the demographic impact of the proletarianization process that accompanied the transformation of Europe from a peasant to an industrial society (Tilly, 1978 and 1979). While the arguments linking proletarianization to population growth involve various dynamics, they generally assume the rural proletariat, most closely approximated by our category of laborers, cottagers, and unskilled workers, married earlier than the rest of the population, both because they were relatively freer from the preindustrial social controls that regulated marriage and because their maximum earning capacity was reached at a young age. Clearly, the results from the present sample of German villages do not conform with this expectation.

In sum, data on age at first marriage for our sample villages suggest that changes in nuptiality over the eighteenth and nineteenth centuries were fairly minor and thus cannot have had much impact either on trends in overall fertility for the village populations as a whole, or for fertility differentials among the major occupational subgroups. While the data from the village genealogies shed no light on changes in proportions married—

an aspect of nuptiality that could potentially change independently of the age at marriage—analysis of census data in the latter part of the nineteenth century indicates that the proportion of the population remaining permanently single was relatively stable on the national and provincial levels (Knodel, 1974; Knodel and Maynes, 1976). Thus it is the marital fertility component of overall fertility that is the proper focus of the study of the onset of the demographic transition in Germany.

Marital Fertility

Trends

To summarize trends in marital fertility, a modified version of the I_g index developed by Ansley Coale for use in the European Fertility Project has been adopted. Unlike the original, this modified version (labeled I_g') incorporates a direct standardization for age using the number of married women by five-year age groups for Germany as a whole as recorded in the 1871 census. Since in practice the value of I_g' does not differ greatly from that of I_g, for most purposes values of the modified index can be directly compared with values of the original index utilized in other studies.[9]

Table 9.6 shows the trends in marital fertility for the sample villages based on the age-standardized index of marital fertility. In this table, as in others that refer to fertility, data are presented by year of marriage and hence correspond to marriage cohorts rather than to year of birth of the

[9] As defined by Coale,

$$I_g = \frac{B_L}{\sum_f m_i F_i},$$

where B_L is the annual number of legitimate births in the specified population, m_i is the number of married women in each five-year age interval in the reproductive span in the specified population, and F_i is the fertility of married Hutterite women in each age interval.

The modified version is defined as follows:

$$I_g' = \frac{\sum f_i M_i}{\sum M_i F_i},$$

where F_i is the same as above, f_i is the observed fertility rate of married women in each five-year age interval in the specified population, and M_i is the number of married women in each five-year age interval in the reproductive span in the standard population, which in this case is the number of German women as recorded in the 1871 census. A comparison between I_g and I_g' for the village populations in our sample indicates that the effect of direct standardization is small and that the two measures are typically quite close.

Table 9.6. Age standardized index of marital fertility (I_g'), by year of marriage.

	1700-49	1750-99	1800-24	1825-49	1850-74	1875-99
Grafenhausen	.77	.87	.80	.75	.67	.53
Herbolzheim	.83	.82	.80	.72	.75	.74
Kappel	.77	.79	.75	.83	.82	.84
Rust	.80	.79	.84	.85	.85	.89
Öschelbronn	.72	.77	.85	.96	.91	.98
3 Bavarian villages	(.89)	.99	.90	.90	1.01	.90
4 Waldeck villages	.70	.77	.76	.83	.85	.70
Middels	--	.70	.64	.70	.63	.64
Werdum	.74	.73	.60	.67	.66	--
All villages	.77	.80	.77	.79	.79	.76

Notes: Results in this table are based on couples for which both the wedding and the end of the marriage occurred locally and the date of the end of the marriage is known with certainty. Results in parentheses are based on an average of 100-199 woman-years per five-year age groups from 20-49; results based on fewer than 100 woman-years are not shown.

children. Based on official statistics, the national level of I_g fluctuated between 0.76 and 0.73 for the late 1860s and the 1870s, the earliest period for which it can be calculated, and thus agrees well with the level of I_g' found for the 1850–1874 marriage cohort in the combined sample of fourteen villages (Knodel, 1974). There is substantial variation across villages in the level of fertility as measured by I_g'. Women in the three Bavarian villages experienced the highest fertility for most marriage cohorts. The 1850–1874 marriage cohort in these villages experienced fertility that even exceeded slightly the Hutterite standard underlying the marital fertility index. Women in Werdum and Middels, two villages in East Friesland, typically experienced the lowest fertility, rarely exceeding 70 percent of the Hutterite fertility level for any marriage cohort. As noted above, Bavarian villages were also characterized by the highest infant mortality and the East Friesland villages by the lowest. As with the case of mortality, the differences in marital fertility levels between these sets of villages is probably related to the differences in infant feeding practices with a relative absence of breast-feeding contributing to the high fertility in the Bavarian villages, and the much longer breast-feeding that characterized East Friesland contributing to the lower fertility there. Moreover, age at first marriage is considerably younger in the two East Friesland villages than in the three Bavarian villages. As a result of the younger age at marriage and the lower mortality, completed family size, when measured in terms of the average number of children surviving to age 15 who are born to women by the end of the reproductive span, was actually larger for the two East Friesland villages combined than for the three Bavarian villages combined, despite the much higher marital fertility in the latter.[10] This should caution one against interpreting differences in marital fertility alone as an indicator of average number of children actually raised per family.

Variation in trends in marital fertility among the villages are also evident. The decline in fertility so distinctly evident at the end of the nineteenth century in national and provincial level statistics (Knodel, 1974) shows considerable variation on the village level. In Grafenhausen, a sustained fall in fertility appears to have started considerably earlier than the end of the nineteenth century, with I_g' declining for each successive marriage cohort during the entire century. In nearby Herbolzheim a fertility decline early in the nineteenth century also appears to have taken place, but the level of marital fertility remains practically unchanged during the last half of the century. In contrast, in Kappel, Rust, and especially in Öschelbronn, marital fertility generally increased throughout the nineteenth century, reaching its highest level for the 1875–1899 marriage cohort. In the Bavarian and Waldeck villages, fertility drops fairly sharply in the last quarter of the nineteenth century but not to levels distinctly below those of all earlier cohorts. In the East Friesland villages of Werdum and Middels, it is more difficult to judge if a fertility decline is under way in the nineteenth century, both because I_g' fluctuates considerably and, in the case of Werdum, because there are insufficient data for the cohort married at the end of the century. Thus in terms of trends in the level of marital fertility, the village data indicate considerable diversity in the onset of the fertility transition.

[10] For example, for the couples married 1750–1849 whose marriages remained intact until the wife reached at least age 45, the average number of children surviving to age 15 per couple was 3.1 for the three Bavarian viillages and 3.6 for the two East Friesland villages.

Natural Marital Fertility Levels and Fertility Control

The trends in the observed age-specific marital fertility rates for the combined sample of the fourteen villages are presented in Table 9.7 for couples married between 1750 and 1899 grouped into marriage cohorts by quarter-century periods. Rates for married women 15–19 in late-marrying populations, such as those in the German villages in our sample, are typically difficult to interpret and thus little can be safely read into their changes. The results for the other age groups, however, are of considerable interest and indicate two distinct trends: toward higher fertility among younger married women and toward lower fertility among older women. The latter trend, particularly pronounced among women in their forties, undoubtedly reflects an increasing practice of deliberate family limitation, which is expected to have a disproportionate impact at older ages when women are more likely to have already borne all the children they wish to have. The steady increase in fertility among women 20–24 and the less regular increase among women 25–29 are more difficult to interpret in

Table 9.7. Age-specific marital fertility, Coale-Trussell indexes of natural fertility level (M) and marital fertility control (m), and mean square error (MSE) of estimates of M and m, by year of marriage, combined sample of 14 villages.

Year of Marriage	15-19	20-24	25-29	30-34	35-39	40-44	45-49	M	m	MSE
1750–74	384	439	425	374	303	173	26	.95	–.03	.001
1775–99	376	455	426	376	301	155	25	.99	.05	.000
1800–24	482	463	412	362	285	151	18	.99	.08	.000
1825–49	473	503	430	379	286	141	15	1.07	.18	.000
1850–74	486	533	450	362	288	128	15	1.14	.27	.001
1875–99	483	547	462	353	247	104	6	1.20	.46	.000
Percent change	+26	+25	+9	–6	–18	–40	–75	+26	--	--

Notes: Marital fertility rates are expressed per 1,0000 married women. The Coale-Trussell indexes are based on the age groups 20-24 through 40-44. Results are based on couples for whom wedding and end of marriage occurred locally and the date of the end of the marriage is known with certainty.

terms of volitional control because it is generally assumed that deliberate limitation of fertility is least likely at younger ages when the family building process is still at an early stage, and it seems particularly unlikely that any such tendency would be strongest among the earlier marriage cohorts and weakest among the later cohorts.

The increase of marital fertility of women in their twenties plus the rising levels of marital fertility in general as measured by the I_g' index for several of the village populations raises the possibility that the underlying level of natural marital fertility might have increased during the period under observation.[11] Fortunately, family reconstitution data that serve as the basis of the present study not only permit the calculation of age-specific marital fertility rates but also of a number of other measures that permit us to explore this issue in some depth.[12]

Coale and Trussell (1974) have proposed an analytical model of marital fertility, which, when applied to an observed schedule of age-specific marital fertility rates, permits the estimation of both the extent of fertility control within marriage and a scale factor of fertility level. The index of fertility control, designated as *m*, indicates the extent to which the age-pattern of observed marital fertility deviates from an empirically derived standard age-pattern of natural fertility in a way that increases with age, as is thought typical of populations practicing deliberate family limitation. It is predicated on the concepts of natural fertility and fertility control as originally proposed by Henry (1961): voluntary control refers to behavior affecting fertility that is modified as parity (and hence age) increases, while natural fertility exists when such parity-dependent behavior is absent. The index is constructed so that it will equal 0 if the shape of the observed fertility schedule in question is identical to that of the

[11] The concept of the "underlying level of natural marital fertility" refers to the level of marital fertility that would or does prevail in the absence of volitional attempts to control family size. This term is used rather than fecundity since the latter is sometimes viewed as determined narrowly by only biological determinants while natural fertility is determined both by biological and behavioral factors, provided the latter are independent of deliberate family size limitation. The concept has been operationalized by Bongaarts (1978) as the total natural marital fertility rate. For a fuller discussion of the concept, see Knodel (1982).

[12] The following discussion is based largely on analysis presented in greater detail in Knodel and Wilson (1981). In the present study, the small number of couples in the Werdum village genealogy during 1875–1899 that meet the appropriate restrictions imposed in particular analyses are included in results presented for that cohort, while in the Knodel and Wilson article they were usually excluded and thus account for some slight differences in results for the 1875–1899 marriage cohort.

standard natural fertility schedule. The faster fertility falls with age, the greater the amount of fertility control implied and the higher the value of the m index. Since m is determined entirely by the age-pattern of fertility, it is independent of the level of fertility.

The scale factor of fertility level, designated as M, is intended to be independent of the extent of voluntary control as defined above and thus can serve, under some circumstances, as an indicator of the underlying level of natural marital fertility.[13]

Because in the Coale-Trussell model voluntary control has been defined in the more narrow sense of parity-dependent behavior, deliberate efforts to extend birth intervals that are independent of the number of children already born can complicate the interpretation of both indexes. Where deliberate spacing of births independent of parity is common, the m index seriously underestimates the extent of voluntary control in its broader sense, which would include to space children as well as to stop childbearing at some chosen family size. Moreover, in such situations the level of M will be depressed, lowering the estimated level of underlying natural fertility. Thus if birth spacing efforts were increasing over time, the trend in M would understate any increases in the underlying natural marital fertility level that might be taking place.

Values of the M and m indexes are included in Table 9.7. They have been estimated by a technique proposed by Coale and Trussell (1978) utilizing ordinary least-squares regression. This procedure yields a value of the mean square error of the regression that serves as a measure of how well the observed age pattern of marital fertility fits with the Coale-Trussell fertility model. For all marriage cohorts of the combined sample of villages, the mean square error is extremely low, indicating an excellent fit. The increase in marital fertility among younger married women is reflected in the substantial increase in M in successive marriage cohorts, particularly during the nineteenth century, while the shift in the age pattern of marital fertility toward a more rapid decline with age, indicative of increasing practice of family limitation, is reflected in the rising values of m. The M index increased in value by more than one-fourth between the first and last marriage cohort while the m index rose from a level just slightly below zero, indicative of natural fertility, to a level substantially

[13] The M index is constructed so that it will equal 1.00 when the underlying level of natural fertility is the same as the level embodied in the standard natural fertility schedule. Deviations from one indicate the proportionate deviation from that level.

above zero, suggestive of at least some voluntary fertility control within marriage.

The relative constancy of the achieved level of overall marital fertility (as summarized by I_g') in Table 9.6 for successive marriage cohorts stands in marked contrast to the almost steady increase in the *M* index and is apparently the result of substantial but countervailing increases in family limitation at older ages and in fertility levels at younger ages. Only between the last two marriage cohorts is the increase in the practice of family limitation large enough to more than compensate for the increasing fertility in the early years of marriage and result in a modest decline in overall marital fertility.

These results indicate that a movement away from natural fertility toward deliberate family limitation began at least in some parts of rural Germany considerably before the end of the nineteenth century, the period that generally has been accepted as marking the onset of the fertility transition in Germany on the basis of measures of aggregate fertility derived from census and vital statistics reports. Insofar as our sample of fourteen villages is typical of rural Germany, it appears that the earlier onset of voluntary fertility control was masked in the measures of observed fertility by a substantial and concurrent rise in the underlying level of natural marital fertility.

A potential source of distortion of changing levels of marital fertility, particularly among younger married women and thus of the trend in the *M* index, is in the changing patterns of premarital sexual behavior. Prenuptial pregnancies leading to postnuptial births artificially inflate marital fertility rates at ages where newlyweds make up a large proportion of married women.[14] Thus the increase in the proportions of brides that were pregnant at marriage—from about 15 percent for couples married in the last half of the eighteenth century to about one-fourth by the end of the nineteenth century for the combined sample (Knodel and Wilson, 1981)—could be responsible for at least some portion of the observed increase in the *M* index.

[14] The reason for this is that in the calculation of marital fertility rates, brides who are pregnant at the time of their wedding are treated as if they were at risk of conceiving only from the date of the wedding, when in fact they were obviously exposed to the risk of pregnancy for some period prior to marriage. Given the way in which the *M* index is calculated, any circumstance that disproportionately increases marital fertility rates at younger ages will *ceteris paribus* increase the value of *M*.

In order to eliminate the influence of changing prevalence in prenuptial pregnancy on the *M* index, we have recalculated *M* on the basis of age-specific marital fertility schedules adjusted for prenuptial pregnancies. The adjustment consisted of attributing to the denominator of the age-specific marital fertility rate the same number of woman years of exposure prior to the first legitimate birth for women who were pregnant as brides as was found for nonbridally pregnant women in that marriage cohort.[15] The adjusted values of the *M* index are shown in the first column of Table 9.8. As expected, the effect of adjustments is to reduce the level of the *M* index for each marriage cohort and also to reduce the amount the *M* index increases over successive cohorts. Nevertheless, the amount of increase remaining is still substantial: the 26 percent increase in *M* between couples married during 1750–1774 and couples married during 1875–1899 prior to adjustment is reduced by only 3 percentage points, to 23 percent, after adjustment. Thus a real increase in the natural marital fertility level remains to be explained.

Natural Marital Fertility Components

While broader explanations in terms of changing social, economic, or cultural patterns are beyond the scope of the present study, it is possible with the family reconstitution data at hand to explore the components of the observed changes in the underlying level of natural marital fertility and thus contribute to an understanding in terms of the underlying proximate determinants (Bongaarts, 1978). In particular, we can examine changes in primary sterility, fecundability, and the length of the post-partum nonsusceptible period through a variety of indirect measures.

In any population of reasonable size, at least a small proportion of couples is unable to bear any children because of physiological impairments in either the husband, the wife, or both. If we assume that voluntary childlessness was negligible in our sample of German villages during the period under observation, then the extent of primary sterility can be approximated by the proportion of married women who remained childless through to the end of the reproductive span. A measure of childlessness is included in Table 9.8 and indicates no consistent trend. Some

[15] The effect is to reduce the fertility rate in all age groups in which bridally pregnant women married. The reduction is disproportionately large in the younger age groups, where bridally pregnant newlyweds represent a substantially higher proportion of all married women than in older ages.

Table 9.8. Coale-Trussell index of natural fertility level (M) adjusted for prenuptial pregnancies, percentage of married women remaining childless by age 50, estimated mean fecundability, and two alternative estimates of the duration of the postpartum nonsusceptible period, by year of marriage, combined sample of 14 villages.

Year of Mar	Adjusted M	Percent Permanently Childless	Estimated Mean Fecundability	Estimated Duration (in Months) of Postpartum Nonsusceptible Period: Estimate 1	Estimate 2
1750-74	.92	11	.21	9.6[a]	12.3[b]
1775-99	.97	11	.22	10.7[a]	12.3[b]
1800-24	.95	14	.26	11.8[a]	11.5 (12.0)[c]
1825-49	1.01	12	.27	11.1	10.6
1850-74	1.08	10	.28	9.9	8.8
1875-99	1.13	10	.28	7.5	5.8

Notes: M values are based on couples for whom wedding and end of marriage occurred locally and the date of the end of the marriage is known with certainty. Results indicating the percentage permanently childless are further restricted to marriages which remained intact until the wife reached at least age 45. Mean fecundability and both estimates of the postpartum nonsusceptible period are based on couples married locally with no record of a birth occurring prior to nine months after marriage. Both the percentage permanently childless and the estimated mean fecundability are standardized for age at marriage based on the distribution by age at marriage for the combined 1750-1899 marriage cohort. Estimate 1 of the postpartum nonsusceptible period represents the difference between the interval to first birth and the interval between the first and second confinements for women with at least three confinements and for whom the first birth survived; estimate 2 represents the difference in the average birth interval following the birth of a child dying within the first month of life and the birth of a child surviving at least one year, excluding intervals between the penultimate and ultimate births.

a) Excluding couples in villages and during periods when registration was obviously deficient.
b) Excluding Kappel and the three Bavarian villages due either to obvious deficiencies in death registration or problems in distinguishing exact age at death.
c) The figures not in parentheses only exclude births in part of the cohort in Kappel due to obvious deficiencies in death registration; the figure in parentheses excludes all births to couples in Kappel and the three Bavarian villages to facilitate comparison with the estimates for the two earlier marriage cohorts.

decline from the unusual peak for the 1800–1824 marriage cohort is evident but only to a level slightly lower than prevailed during the last half of the eighteenth century. These results suggest that changes in primary sterility were not an important contributor to the rise in the natural marital fertility level.

Fecundability, the probability of conception during a menstrual cycle in the absence of contraception, can be estimated indirectly from data on the interval between marriage and first birth. More precisely, an estimate can be derived from the proportion of legitimate first births that occur during months 9, 10, and 11 after excluding births that occur earlier than nine months following marriage. These proportions are converted into estimates of fecundability based on a model proposed by Bongaarts (1975) and slightly modified by Knodel and Wilson (1981, Appendix 1). Because the estimate is derived from intervals between wedding and first birth (and couples with illegitimate births have been excluded), it is independent of the influence of breast-feeding. The values it yields, however, refer to fecundability immediately following marriage; if fecundability declines with the duration of marriage, as is often assumed, then the level of fecundability in the population at large could be substantially below that which is estimated here. Results of this measure are included in Table 9.8 and point to a substantial rise: estimated fecundability increases by about a third between couples married in 1750–1774 and those married during the last quarter of the nineteenth century.

The final determinant of the natural marital fertility level examined in Table 9.8 is the nonsusceptible period following birth during which a woman is not at risk to conceive. It is now widely accepted that differences in breast-feeding practices are the major determinant of the nonsusceptible period (Van Ginneken, 1978). One simple way to estimate the mean duration of nonsusceptibility from reproductive histories is to compare the interval between marriage and first birth (excluding intervals involving a premarital pregnancy) with the following interval between first and second births (excluding intervals following an infant death).[16] The difference should reflect the extent to which the first to second birth interval is extended by nonsusceptibility. For several reasons, the estimate is only a rough approximation. Declining fecundability with increasing duration of marriage will tend to lengthen the waiting time to conception and thus lengthen the interval following first birth relative to the interval following marriage, biasing the estimate of the nonsusceptible period upward. Attempts to postpone either the first or second birth would also influence the estimate. A further drawback with a simple comparison is that the interval before a woman's last birth tends to be distinctly

[16] Results in the present study differ from those in the Knodel and Wilson (1981) article because the latter included intervals following infant deaths.

longer than other intervals, even in the absence of deliberate birth control. Where a woman has only two children, this interval may yield a poor estimate of the nonsusceptible period. This problem, however, can be easily avoided by basing estimates only on women with at least three legitimate confinements.

Results obtained by this method are included in Table 9.8 as "estimate 1" of the nonsusceptible period. They indicate an increase in nonsusceptibility peaking for the 1800–1824 cohort, followed by a steady decline in the duration for cohorts married during the remainder of the nineteenth century. It is important to note that the extent of the decline, as well as the apparent increase for couples married during the latter half of the eighteenth century, is very much determined by the unusually long estimate found for the cohort of 1800–1824. While we have no reason to believe the estimate for this cohort to be less reliable than for others, the only approximate nature of the estimation techniques should be borne in mind.

A second way of estimating the length of the nonsusceptible period is to examine the relationship between the length of birth intervals and the age at death of the child born at the beginning of the interval. An interval following the birth of a child who survived beyond the age of weaning will reflect the full influence of breast-feeding, while an interval following the death of a child who dies before being weaned will, on average, be shorter. The strength of this relationship in the aggregate depends on the proportion of infants breast-fed and the average duration and intensity of breast-feeding. As with the previous estimate of the nonsusceptible period, intervals between the penultimate and ultimate births are best excluded from consideration.

Results based on this second method are presented in Table 9.8 as "estimate 2" and support a considerable decline in the nonsusceptible period, especially during the nineteenth century. A minor problem of comparability across marriage cohorts is created by the necessity to exclude Kappel and the Bavarian villages due to death registration problems when calculating this measure for couples married during the eighteenth century. Since the prevalence and duration of breast-feeding was probably unusually low for the Bavarian villages, their exclusion in the estimates referring to couples married prior to 1800 creates a compositional bias when examining trends. To facilitate comparison, results for the 1800–1824 marriage cohort are shown both for all villages and for only those villages that served as the basis of estimates for the earlier cohorts.

When this problem is taken into consideration, there appears to be little change indicated between the 1750–1774 and 1800–1824 cohorts. A problem for interpreting the results arises from the fact that the decline in the estimate during the nineteenth century is due in part to increasing intervals after an early death, which should logically be independent of changes in breast-feeding habits, and not only to decreasing intervals following child survival. About two months of the almost six-month decline comes about in this puzzling way. Even if the increase in intervals following infant deaths is discounted, however, the estimates still indicate that a decline of three to four months in the length of the nonsusceptible period during the nineteenth century remains.

Although the two estimates of the nonsusceptible period are not consistent with each other regarding changes during the last half of the eighteenth century, both point to substantial decline during the nineteenth century. Perhaps the most likely explanation for such a change, if is it indeed genuine, is a reduction in the prevalence and duration of breast-feeding. It is also possible that breast-feeding patterns changed little but that their impact on the nonsusceptible period increased because of improved nutrition. Although this idea is still controversial, some scholars argue that there is a substantial negative association between levels of nutrition and the extent to which breast-feeding delays the return of ovulation (Frisch, 1982; but see also Bongaarts, 1980, and Menken, Trussell, and Watkins, 1981). Direct information on breast-feeding is rare for periods before the latter part of the nineteenth century in Germany. It is noteworthy that annual statistics on breast-feeding collected from midwives in Baden during the last quarter of the nineteenth century and the early years of the twentieth century indicate that in the area where the four Baden villages in our sample are located, there was virtually no change between 1882 and 1905 in the proportion of mothers reported as not having breast-fed their children. Unfortunately, data for earlier years are not available.

More on Family Limitation

The fertility transition has been characterized as a shift from a system in which fertility behavior was largely controlled through social institutions and customs to a system where the private choice of the individual couple plays the major role. Thus the modernization of reproductive behavior consists of a process whereby the predominant mechanisms for fertility control moved from the societal level to the family level (Wrigley,

1969 and 1978a). While a variety of factors influenced the level of marital fertility prior to its secular decline, the shift to deliberate couple-level control appears to be associated with a new pattern of behavior that can conveniently be labeled family limitation. It is useful to distinguish this pattern not only from societal-level control, which often operates by controlling entrance into marital unions, but also from deliberate birth control in general. Family limitation refers specifically to deliberate attempts to limit the number of offspring through terminating childbearing before the end of a couple's reproductive span. It assumes that attempts are made to stop having children once the couple feels they have a sufficient number. Family limitation thus refers essentially to stopping behavior and assumes that fertility control is parity-dependent. Birth control is a more general concept which refers to any deliberate spacing or stopping behavior.

Family reconstitution data lend themselves fairly readily to a variety of measures that are designed to indirectly detect the extent to which couples practiced family limitation. Most of these measures are based on the observation that couples terminate childbearing earlier and marital fertility declines more rapidly with age in populations where family size is deliberately limited than in populations characterized by natural fertility, the term used to describe fertility in the absence of family limitation.

The Coale-Trussell index of fertility control (m), discussed above, is one such measure and conveniently summarizes the extent to which family limitation is implicit in the age structure of any marital fertility schedule. Values of the m index for the individual villages are presented in Table 9.9. The low values of m characterizing couples married during the eighteenth century in all the villages suggest that little if any parity-dependent control was being exercised at this time.

Noticeable contrasts in the trends in m values over time are apparent in the different villages. Of particular interest is the diversity of experience represented by the four villages in Baden, all of which are located quite near each other. Couples in both Grafenhausen and Herbolzheim show signs of adopting modern reproductive patterns well in advance of other villages. In Herbolzheim, a steady rise in m is evident for each successive marriage cohort, starting with couples married in the first quarter of the nineteenth century; in Grafenhausen a steady rise is indicated for couples starting with those married in the second quarter of the nineteenth century. In nearby Rust, m also increases steadily but at a more modest rate for cohorts married after the first quarter of the nineteenth century.

Table 9.9. Coale-Trussell index of fertility control (m), by year of marriage.

	1700-49	1750-99	1800-24	1825-49	1850-74	1875-99
Grafenhausen	.13	.05	.01	.34	.59	.79
Herbolzheim	-.11	-.11	.10	.37	.51	.67
Kappel	-.03	-.09	.15	.10	.17	.19
Rust	.07	.11	-.07	.09	.32	.51
Öschelbronn	.28	.18	.28	.17	.13	.27
3 Bavarian villages	(-.08)	-.04	.22	.08	.28	.41
4 Waldeck villages	.00	-.05	.02	-.02	.03	.44
Middels	--	.04	.10	.12	.21	.46
Werdum	.03	.23	.25	.29	(.31)	--
All villages	.04	.01	.08	.18	.27	.46

Notes: Results in this table on couples for whom both wedding and end of marriage occurred locally, and the date of the end of marriage is known with certainty. Values in parentheses indicate the results are based on an average of 100-199 woman-years per 5-year age group from 20-44; results based on fewer woman-years are omitted. Values of m shown underlined indicate that the mean square error of the regression used to estimate m exceeded .005.

In contrast, in Kappel there is a noticeable absence of any substantial increase in *m* for couples married throughout the nineteenth century. While the increase in the *m* index in Kappel between couples married at the end of the eighteenth century and the 1800–1824 marriage cohort may signal some early spread of family limitation, the trend clearly does not continue to any substantial extent for subsequent marriage cohorts. The striking contrasts among these four neighboring or nearby villages in Baden underscore just how localized important differences in demographic patterns could be during the preindustrial era.

Contrasts among the other villages in the sample are also evident. In Öschelbronn the trend in *m* is even less decisive than in Kappel, and the value of this index even for couples married at the end of the nineteenth century does not rise above values characterizing earlier cohorts. In other villages, the value of *m* is typically higher for the 1875–1899 marriage cohort than for any of the previous ones (excluding Werdum, for which data for this cohort are missing). Some fluctuations in the value of *m* are to be expected when calculations are based on small numbers of couples, such as in the present study, making it difficult to distinguish genuine changes in the underlying fertility pattern from random movements. Thus it is difficult to interpret increases in *m* that are not part of a trend, such as between the 1700–1749 and 1850–1899 marriage cohorts in Werdum and the 1750–1799 and 1800–1824 cohorts in the Bavarian villages. Changes of this magnitude can neither be taken as conclusive evidence of family limitation nor dismissed out of hand. We can be more confident that the increases in *m* values characterizing the fertility of couples married at the end of the nineteenth century reflected an increase in the practice of family limitation because in most cases they were distinctly higher than previous values and often represented a continuation of a rising trend.

The experience of several villages demonstrates even more clearly than results for the sample as a whole that the onset of the transition to modern reproductive patterns as signaled by increased family limitation may be obscured in data representing trends in marital fertility levels under circumstances where the underlying level of natural marital fertility may be increasing, as is the case for our sample of German villages. Perhaps the most striking example is provided by Rust. The level of marital fertility as measured by I_g' actually increases across successive cohorts married during the nineteenth century (see Table 9.6), while at the same time the *m* index indicates that family limitation efforts were steadily if slowly increasing. Herbolzheim also provides an interesting example. In spite of the leveling off of marital fertility as measured by I_g' in the second half of the century, the *m* index continues the trend toward higher values already established among earlier cohorts. Of course, if the natural marital fertility level is not changing or the increase in family limitation is sufficient, marital fertility will decline as attempts at fertility control increase. Grafenhausen is a clear case of concurrence in these two trends. In addition, a number of the increases in *m* between the last two marriage cohorts in several villages were also accompanied by noticeable declines in marital fertility.

The wide range in the level of marital fertility in the absence of any substantial practice of family limitation (as evident for cohorts characterized by low values of the *m* index) underscores the importance of societal-level influences on fertility in the pretransition situation. For example, among couples married in 1750–1799, the *m* index is virtually identical for the Bavarian and Waldeck village populations, despite a large difference in marital fertility levels. While it may be convenient to infer the practice of family limitation from the levels of marital fertility, it can also be quite misleading. Very low levels of fertility usually do involve deliberate birth control of a parity-dependent nature, but moderate or high levels do not necessarily rule out family limitation as indicated by examples from several of the Baden villages. In both Rust and Herbolzheim, for example, even the cohort married at the end of the nineteenth century is characterized by I_g' levels that are moderately high but also by values of the *m* index that clearly point to some family limitation. In contrast, I_g' in Middels for cohorts married between the mid-eighteenth and mid-nineteenth centuries is considerably lower but associated with very low levels of the *m* index.

Another measure that should be particularly sensitive to family limitation is the age at which women bear their last child. In populations where family limitation is common, women bear their last child at an earlier age than in populations where no deliberate attempts to stop childbearing are made. Table 9.10 presents this measure for couples in which the marriage remained intact until the end of the wife's reproductive span. One striking feature of these results is the similarity in the age of mother at last birth across different villages for the earlier marriage cohorts. Prior to declines in this measure associated with the fertility transition, the average age at which women terminated childbearing was generally around 40. This closely corresponds to the results from other family reconstitution studies from Europe from populations assumed to be characterized by natural fertility (D. S. Smith, 1977).

The trends in age of mother at last birth are reasonably consistent with trends in the values of the *m* index. For most villages, the age of mother at last birth is rather similar for the cohorts during the first and second halves of the eighteenth century. Sharp declines in the age of mother at last birth for the cohorts married at the end of the nineteenth century are evident for both the Bavarian and the Waldeck villages, paralleling corresponding increases in the *m* index. Some divergence between the trend in family limitation given by the age of mother at last birth and the *m* index is apparent for Grafenhausen and Herbolzheim. In Grafenhausen, the age of mother at last birth declined steadily for each successive cohort from the end of the eighteenth century, suggesting an earlier onset of family limitation than was apparent from the *m* index. In Herbolzheim,

Table 9.10. Age of mother at last birth in completed unions, by year of marriage.

	1700-49	1750-99	1800-24	1825-49	1850-74	1875-99
Grafenhausen	40.0	40.2	39.9	38.5	37.3	35.2
Herbolzheim	40.8	49.9	39.7	37.7	37.2	37.5
Kappel	40.2	41.1	40.2	40.4	39.2	38.9
Rust	40.1	40.1	41.4	39.8	39.2	38.6
Öschelbronn	39.1	39.1	38.3	39.0	39.3	38.6
3 Bavarian villages	(41.1)	41.2	(39.8)	40.0	40.2	38.4
4 Waldeck villages	39.9	41.0	40.2	41.0	40.7	37.5
Middels	--	40.4	(39.1)	40.4	39.1	37.8
Werdum	39.7	39.3	38.7	39.1	(37.7)[a]	--
All villages	40.0	40.3	39.8	39.3	38.8	37.7

a) Includes a small number of couples married betweeen 1875 and 1899.

Notes: Results in this table are based on couples for whom the end of marriage occurred locally and the date of the end of the marriage is known with certainty. Completed unions refer to marriages in which the wife reached at least age 45 by the time the marriage ended. Results in parentheses are based on 20-49 women; results based on fewer than 20 women are not shown.

the age of mother at last birth, after declining substantially for the cohorts married in the first half of the nineteenth century, levels off for cohorts married in the second half while the *m* index indicates a continuing increase in family limitation for these cohorts. Even so, the age of mother at last confinement for the 1875–1899 marriage cohort in Herbolzheim is substantially below the level experienced for cohorts married in the eighteenth century or early in the nineteenth century. Some irregular downward movement in the age of mother at last birth is even evident for Kappel for couples married during the nineteenth century—not so different from the trend observed for Rust—although far less decisive than the decline observed for the neighboring village of Grafenhausen.

The two measures of family limitation examined—the Coale-Trussell index of fertility control and the age of mother at last birth—are not independent of each other. Trends in both of these measures reflect the disproportionate decline in fertility at older ages that characterized most of the villages at some point in the nineteenth century, although in different ways. In addition, the age of mother at last birth is based exclusively on completed unions, while the *m* index is based on couples whether or not their union ended before the wife completed her reproductive years. Furthermore, they can and do give somewhat different pictures of the emergence of family limitation in our sample villages. Taken together, however, they provide somewhat more information than either one of them does alone. Both underscore the fact that the decline in fertility at the end of the nineteenth and early twentieth centuries, evident in the macro-level statistics for Germany and reflected in some of the sample villages, was the result of a fundamental transformation of reproductive behavior from a pattern characteristic of natural fertility to one indicative of deliberate attempts to stop childbearing before the end of the wife's reproductive years. Even in those villages where little or no decline in the level of marital fertility was evident at the end of the nineteenth century, there were signs that the underlying behavioral pattern was also beginning (or continuing, as in the case of Herbolzheim) to change, and that the behavioral mechanisms that were eventually to reduce fertility to much lower levels were already emerging. Beyond this, the village data reveal interesting differences in the onset of the trend toward family limitation. At the one extreme, data for Grafenhausen, Herbolzheim, and, to a lesser extent, Rust—all near each other—show evidence of increasing couple-level control very early in the nineteenth century. At the other extreme, Öschelbronn and perhaps even Kappel (a neighbor of both Grafenhausen and Rust and near to Herbolzheim) both show no evidence of fertility decline and only minimal evidence of increasing family limitation even by the end of the nineteenth century. Previous analysis of aggregate data shows substantial regional variation in fertility transition (Knodel, 1974). Even greater variation appears to exist among villages, including nearby ones.

Fertility and Family Limitation by Occupational Grouping

Was the diversity observed in the changes in reproductive behavior among populations matched by a similar diversity within villages among different socioeconomic groups? In an effort to shed some light on this question, the measures of marital fertility and family limitation examined for the village populations as a whole are reproduced in Table 9.11 according to the occupational category of the husband. In order to avoid problems associated with small numbers of cases in each category, results are presented for only two broad marriage cohorts, couples married between the mid-eighteenth and mid-nineteenth centuries, and couples married in the latter half of the nineteenth century. In addition, the two East Friesland villages as well as the three Bavarian and four Waldeck villages have been combined into single data sets.

It is difficult to summarize occupational differentials in marital fertility since there appears to be little consistency among different villages. Perhaps the most striking feature for couples married between 1750 and 1849 is the general lack of substantial occupational differentials. For the villages of Herbolzheim, Kappel, and the two East Friesland villages, virtually no differences in the level of marital fertility are evident for the different occupational groups and in the other villages there is rarely as much as a 10 percent difference between the occupational groupings with the highest and lowest rates. Clearly, occupational differences in fertility within villages are less than the differences found in the average fertility between villages. Occupational differentials are more pronounced for couples married after 1850 because of the differences in the extent to which the various occupational groupings participated in the onset of fertility decline toward the end of the nineteenth century, but again these contrasts defy clear-cut generalizations. In addition, since the 1850–1899 cohort generally involved smaller numbers of cases, random fluctuations are more likely to affect the results. Occupational differentials with respect to changes in fertility between the two marriage cohorts also show little consistency among the different villages.

The changes in reproductive behavior that were emerging during the nineteenth century in the German villages are less evident in measures of the level of marital fertility than in the measures of family limitation, since fertility trends were confounded by the increase in the natural marital fertility level as discussed above. Among the couples married prior to 1850, occupational differentials as revealed by the index of fertility control and by the age of mother at last birth are generally minimal. For most occupational categories, the *m* index is quite low and the age of mother at last birth is quite close to age 40. The most noticeable exception is the laborer category in Öschelbronn, which is characterized by the highest *m* value and, together with artisans in the East Friesland villages, the lowest age at last birth, but which may suffer from being based on a small number of cases.

Table 9.11. Age standardized index of marital fertility (I_g'), index of fertility control (m), and the age of mother at last birth, by year of marriage and occupational category of husband.

	I_g' Index			m Index			Age of Mother at Last Birth		
	1750–1849	1850–1899	Change	1750–1849	1850–1899	Change	1750–1849	1850–1899	Change
Grafenhausen									
Artisans, etc.	.85	.62	-.23	.15	.81	+.66	39.6	36.6	-3.0
Farmers	.77	.57	-.20	.18	.72	+.54	39.3	35.7	-3.6
Laborers, etc.	.84	(.76)	(-.08)	.16	(.29)	+.13	40.0	(39.4)	(-0.6)
Total, inc. unknown	.81	.60	-.21	.13	.67	+.54	39.6	36.3	-3.3
Herbolzheim									
Artisans, etc.	.78	.75	-.03	.14	.61	+.47	39.2	37.2	-2.0
Farmers	.74	.66	-.08	.08	.79	+.71	39.6	36.4	-3.2
Laborers, etc.	.77	.80	+.03	.12	.59	+.47	39.3	38.0	-1.3
Total, inc. unknown	.78	.74	-.04	.08	.60	+.52	39.6	37.5	-2.1
Kappel									
Artisans, etc.	.80	.77	+.03	.00	.17	+.17	41.0	38.1	-2.9
Farmers	.77	.82	+.05	.07	.25	+.18	39.9	38.8	-1.1
Laborers, etc.	.79	(.87)	(+.08)	-.04	(.29)	+.33	40.9	39.8	-1.1
Total, inc. unknown	.79	.83	+.04	.03	.18	+.15	40.6	39.1	-1.5
Rust									
Artisans, etc.	.83	.86	+.03	.04	.32	+.28	40.4	39.3	-1.1
Farmers	.83	.84	+.01	-.10	.61	+.71	40.4	38.3	-2.1
Laborers, etc.	.77	.88	+.11	.11	.46	+.35	40.4	38.8	-1.6
Total, inc. unknown	.82	.87	+.05	.05	.42	+.37	40.4	38.9	-1.5
Öschelbronn									
Artisans, etc.	.89	1.00	-.11	.23	.11	-.12	38.8	39.4	+0.6
Farmers	.79	.84	+.05	.15	.33	+.18	38.6	38.1	-0.5
Laborers, etc.	(.84)	--	--	(.36)	--	--	(38.5)	(40.1)	(+1.6)
Total, inc. unknown	.84	.95	.11	.19	.20	+.01	39.1	39.0	-0.1

3 Bavarian villages									
Artisans, etc.	(.94)	(1.02)	(+.08)	.31	.37	+.06	39.9	(39.5)	(-0.4)
Farmers	.79	(.85)	(+.06)	-.01	(.31)	(+.32)	(40.5)	(39.3)	(-1.2)
Laborers, etc.	.91	.97	+.06	.08	.33	+.25	40.1	39.1	-1.0
Total, inc. unknown	.95	.95	+.00	.05	.33	+.28	40.5	39.3	-1.2
4 Waldeck villages									
Artisans, etc.	.83	.74	-.09	-.07	.28	+.35	41.1	38.7	-2.4
Farmers	.83	.81	-.02	-.13	.22	+.35	40.9	38.9	-2.0
Laborers, etc.	.77	.83	+.06	.03	-.01	-.04	40.7	39.7	-1.0
Total, inc. unknown	.78	.78	-.00	-.03	.19	+.22	40.9	39.5	-1.4
2 East Friesland villages									
Artisans, etc.	.66	--	--	.21	--	--	38.5	(39.1)	(+0.5)
Farmers	.68	.64	-.04	.18	.71	+.53	38.9	37.6	-1.3
Laborers, etc.	.69	.64	-.05	.15	.20	+.05	39.9	38.6	-1.3
Total, inc. unknown	.68	.65	-.03	.18	.30	+.12	39.6	38.4	-1.2

<u>Notes</u>: I_g and *m* are based on couples for whom both wedding and end of the marriage occurred locally and the date of the end of marriage is known with certainty.

Values of I_g and *m* are based on less than an average of 100 woman-years per five-year age group from 20-44 are omitted; values based on an average of 100-199 woman-years are shown in parentheses.

Values of *m* shown underlined indicate that the mean square error of the regression used to estimate *m* exceeded .005.

The average age of mother at last birth is based on couples for whom the end of marriage occurred locally, the date of the end of marriage is known with certainty and the wife reached at least age 45 by the time the marriage ended.

Results for the age of mother at last birth based on fewer than 20 women are omitted; results in parentheses are based on 20-39 women.

The category "Artisans, etc." includes businessmen and professionals; the category, "Laborers, etc." includes cottagers and other unskilled workers.

Somewhat more consistency is evident in the changes in the indexes of family limitation for couples married before and after 1850 than was apparent for changes in the level of marital fertility. Increases in family limitation are indicated by increases in the *m* index and decreases in the age of mother at last birth. The most common pattern was for farmers to show the greatest increase in the practice of family limitation. There were exceptions, most notably in Kappel but also elsewhere. While occupational differentials in the increase of family limitation practices are reasonably consistent, it is also worth noting that in those villages where at least a moderate increase in family limitation is indicated for the total population, all three occupational categories seem to have participated at least to some extent in altering their reproductive behavior in a manner consistent with parity-dependent control.

Birth Spacing

The measures of fertility control that have been examined so far are designed to detect attempts to stop childbearing more or less permanently and reveal little if anything about birth-spacing patterns. In historical demography studies, the average length of the last birth interval is sometimes used as an indicator of fertility control (see, for example, Wrigley, 1966). The last birth interval is probably more sensitive to attempts at stopping childbearing than to attempts to space children deliberately, however, particularly in populations where family limitation is just being initiated. When the practice of family limitation is increasing, the last birth interval is expected to rise because even after couples reach the number of children they consider sufficient, additional births occasionally occur due either to accidental pregnancies, changes of mind, or desires to replace a child who has died. On the other hand, contemporary observers in the eighteenth and nineteenth centuries in Europe have sometimes expressed the opinion that some women deliberately prolonged breast-feeding to postpone the next birth. More recently, several historical demographers have suggested that birth spacing was an important element of fertility control in the populations they have studied (for example, Gaunt, 1973; Lachiver, 1973). The spread of any such spacing behavior could have contributed to a decline in fertility.

In order to examine if changes in spacing behavior were part of the changing reproductive patterns in the sample villages, trends in the average legitimate birth interval in completed unions are shown in Figure 9.2. Since changes in the last birth interval may reflect stopping behavior

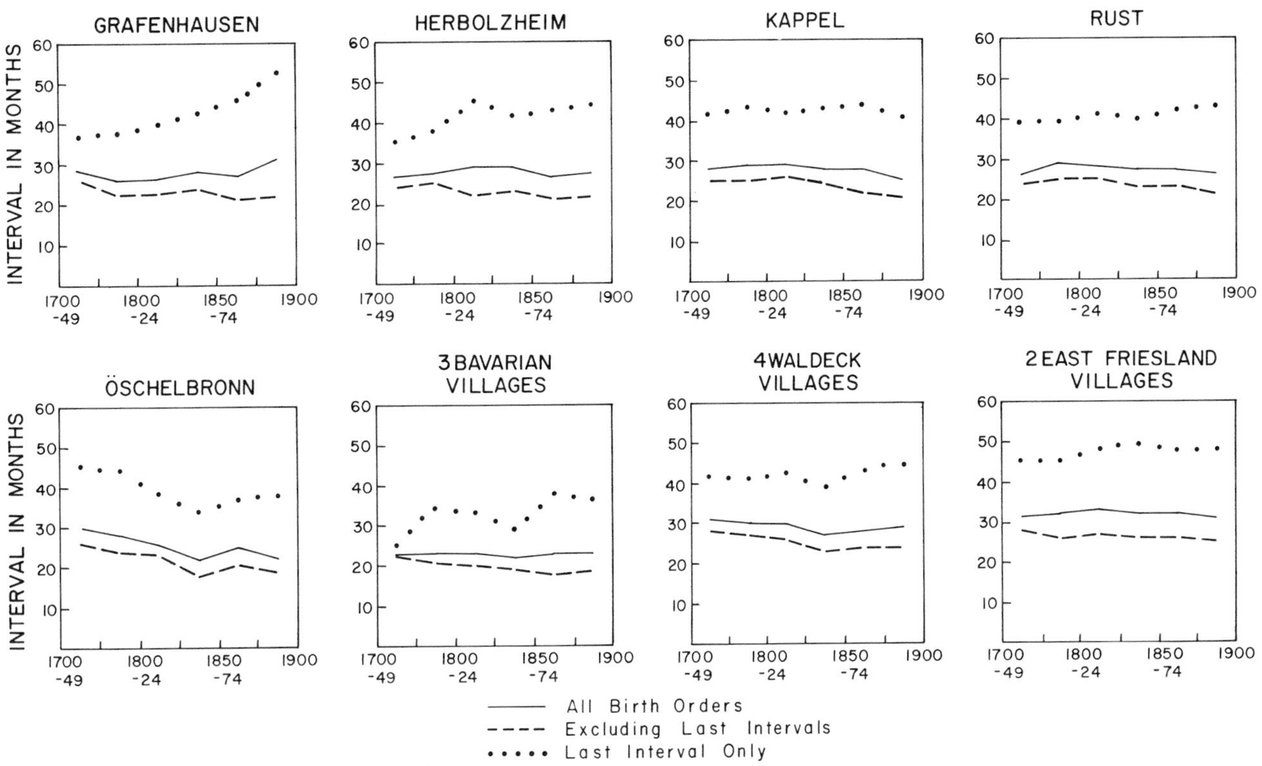

Figure 9.2. Average legitimate birth interval per married woman with two or more legitimate births in completed unions, by year of marriage. Solid lines and broken lines include the interval from marriage to first birth.

more than spacing behavior, results are shown separately for the last interval, for intervals excluding the last, and for all birth orders together. Again, the results for the four villages in Baden are particularly interesting. In Grafenhausen, where the previous results indicated a continuous fertility decline associated with increasing family limitation throughout all or most of the nineteenth century, the average birth interval follows a slightly irregular trend toward higher levels for successive marriage cohorts from the end of the eighteenth century. This is entirely attributable, however, to an increase in the last birth interval. The average birth interval excluding the last shows no consistent tendency to lengthen, and in fact is slightly lower for couples married at the end of the nineteenth century than for most earlier marriage cohorts. In neighboring Rust, where a steady but more modest increase in family limitation was indicated throughout the nineteenth century but where marital fertility rose slightly, a less pronounced but clear trend toward longer last intervals is evident. This is accompanied, however, by shorter birth spacing prior to the last interval and thus by a decline in average of all intervals. In Herbolzheim, which also has indications of increasing family limitation throughout most of the nineteenth century, the results are somewhat different. An increase in the average last interval apparent for the earlier marriage cohorts levels off for couples married after the first quarter of the nineteenth century. In part because of offsetting changes in birth intervals excluding the last, the interval for all birth orders remains rather constant across the entire period under observation. In nearby Kappel, where there is little evidence of family limitation and fertility rises during the nineteenth century, no evidence of a lengthening in the last interval is apparent and the average of all intervals declines.

The other villages show no indication of increasing attempts to prolong birth intervals. Although the last interval fluctuates, it follows no consistent trend. Even among couples married at the end of the nineteenth century, there is no apparent increase in the interval between the last two births. This is rather surprising in view of the other evidence that family limitation was emerging in a number of the villages. It implies that those couples who were deliberately stopping childbearing before the end of the wife's reproductive period were remarkably efficient in their practice of birth control, as failures would have lengthened the average birth interval, particularly the last interval. The results are somewhat confounded, however, by the apparent improvements in fecundity noted above, which would have acted to decrease birth intervals. Nevertheless, it seems unlikely that the improving fecundity would have been sufficient to offset the effect of failures in birth control practice on the last interval if the method being used was not reasonably efficient. Possibly during the early stages of the fertility transition, at least in some of the sample villages, couples relied more on abstinence to terminate childbearing than on coitus interruptus or other methods that would seem to have higher inherent failure rates. In any event, the initial phase of the fertility transition does not seem to be characterized by attempts to increase the spacing between births. This finding underscores the importance of stopping behavior and hence parity-dependent control as the crucial factor underlying the modernization of reproductive behavior.

Comparisons of the length of the average birth interval across villages reveal substantial variations that persist throughout the entire period under observation. The two East Friesland villages are characterized by intervals averaged over all birth orders that exceed 30 months for each marriage cohort shown, while the Bavarian villages are characterized by birth intervals that are consistently below an average of 24 months. In both the Bavarian villages and the East Friesland villages, the average birth interval fluctuates only within a very narrow range. This is generally true for the other village populations with the exceptions of Grafenhausen, where the average interval increases as a result of the lengthening of the last interval, and Öschelbronn, where a pronounced although somewhat irregular trend toward shorter birth intervals for successive marriage cohorts is evident. In the case of Öschelbronn, this was reflected in the rather pronounced increase in marital fertility observed above.

Although a wide variety of factors influence the average length of the birth interval, including deliberate attempts to space births, differences in breast-feeding practices are undoubtedly an important influence on the differences observed across the sample village. As indicated above, breast-feeding was least common in the Bavarian villages and probably most common and extensive in the East Friesland villages. Since breast-feeding can prolong birth intervals substantially (Knodel, 1977a), it seems likely that much of the difference observed between these two sets of villages can be attributed to differences in their breast-feeding practices. Other factors undoubtedly are also at work. For example, fecundability as indirectly measured from the distribution of intervals between marriage and first birth is generally, if not consistently, higher for the Bavarian villages than for Werdum or Middels (Knodel and Wilson, 1981). However, the contribution of this factor is probably minor since the length of the average birth interval remains fairly constant despite considerable change in the index of fecundability. The persistence of fairly constant birth intervals in most of the villages over time suggests that the differences across villages are probably in large part determined by practices entrenched in longstanding custom. Infant feeding practices are probably among the most important of these.

Child Mortality, Fertility, and Family Limitation

The relationship between mortality and fertility is at the heart of the demographic transition model. The proposition that reduced mortality, followed by some appropriate time lag, should lead to reduced fertility is assumed by some to be almost self-evident. As mortality improves and greater proportions of children survive, it is expected that couples will reduce their fertility since fewer births are required to achieve any given desired family size. To the extent couples attempt to ensure the survival of at least some minimum number of offspring, the reduction in fertility as the result of lowered child mortality could be substantial even in the absence of reductions in family size targets, since the number of additional children needed as insurance is considerably higher at high mortality levels than at low mortality levels. In addition, reduced mortality increases population size both on the aggregate and at the household level and may thereby result in pressures to reduce fertility.

Considerable effort has been made by participants in the Princeton European Fertility Project to assess, on the basis of macro-level statistics, the role of decreased infant and child mortality in precipitating and maintaining the secular fertility decline (F. van de Walle, Chapter 4.) All in all, the results have been mixed, with no clear-cut conclusions emerging either for Germany or for Europe in general (Knodel, 1974; Matthiessen and McCann, 1978). Trends in child mortality and marital fertility, as measured by the probability of surviving to age five ($_5q_0$) and the marital fertility index (I_g'), are shown in Figure 9.3 for the sample villages. The child mortality measure has been calculated to correspond to the experience of the marriage cohorts as does the marital fertility index, rather than referring to the year of birth of the child. The results do not indicate any clear-cut association between the timing or extent of fertility and mortality changes on the aggregate level in the villages. In particular,

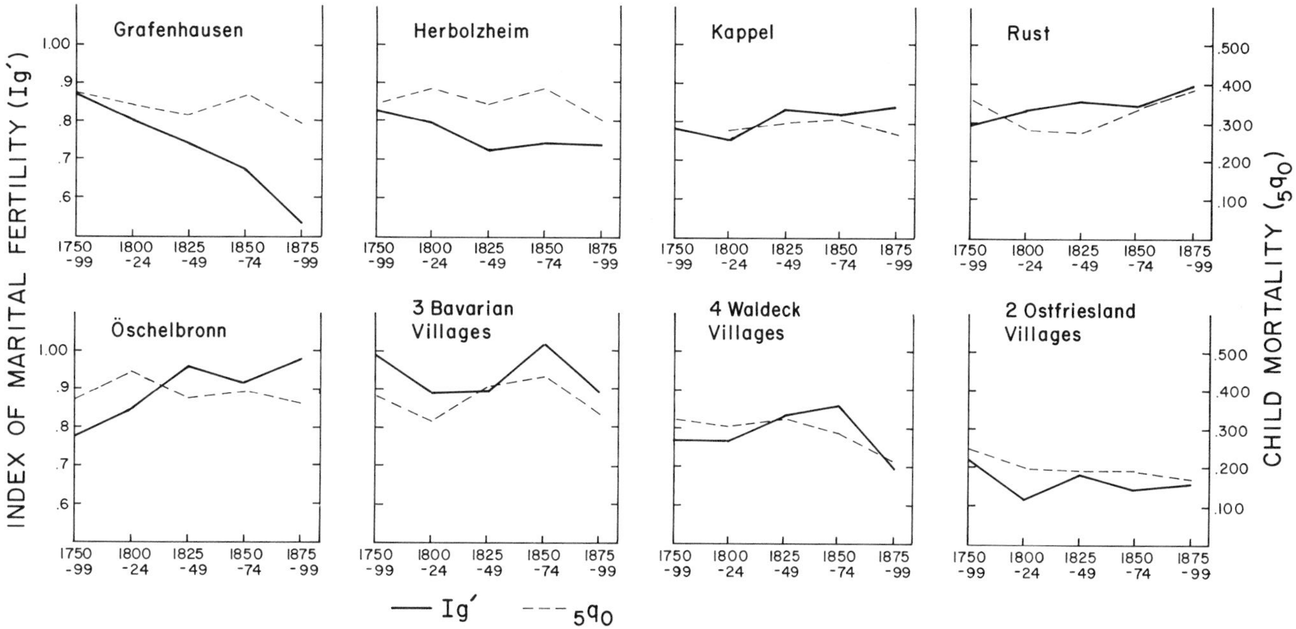

Figure 9.3. I_g' and child mortality ($_5q_0$) by year of marriage.

there is no consistent association of a prior decline in child mortality with a subsequent decline in marital fertility. Generally, the village data suggest substantial local variation in the relative timing of fertility and child mortality declines.

The experience of the villages characterized by early declines in fertility and increases in family limitation are of special interest. In Grafenhausen, where the decline of fertility and increase in family limitation was both early and pronounced, there is no sustained decline in child mortality experienced by marriage cohorts prior to the end of the nineteenth century. Likewise, in Herbolzheim, where early although somewhat less pronounced changes in fertility and family limitation are evident, there is no decline in the child mortality experienced by couples married prior to the last quarter of the nineteenth century. Moreover, in both of these villages the level of child mortality remained substantial throughout the nineteenth century at the same time as reproductive patterns were changing.

Despite the fact that the aggregate trends in marital fertility and child mortality in the sample of villages do not support the usual expectation based on the demographic transition model that a decline in child mortality will precede and indeed precipitate a decline in fertility, such data do not tell us whether or not at the micro-level experience with child mortality was associated with the extent to which couples participated in the spread of family limitation and the onset of the fertility transition. It is possible to examine this issue with family reconstitution, and it is to this task that we now turn.

Results contained in Figure 9.4 show, for the combined sample, the trends in the number of children ever born, the age of mother at last birth, and the percentage of couples continuing childbearing for successive marriage cohorts according to their experience with child mortality (defined as death before age 5) among the first two or three children. All women who married prior to 1825 are grouped together, since family limitation, as measured by the *m* index and the age of mother at last birth, was very low, and little change took place for cohorts married before the second quarter of the nineteenth century. In addition to being limited to couples whose marriage remained intact until the wife reached the end of the childbearing span, the results are adjusted by multiple classification analysis for several possibly confounding influences: (a) the remaining period of reproductive exposure, as measured by the age of the wife at the time of attaining the given parity (modified slightly to allow for the shorter nonsusceptible period following an infant death in cases where the child

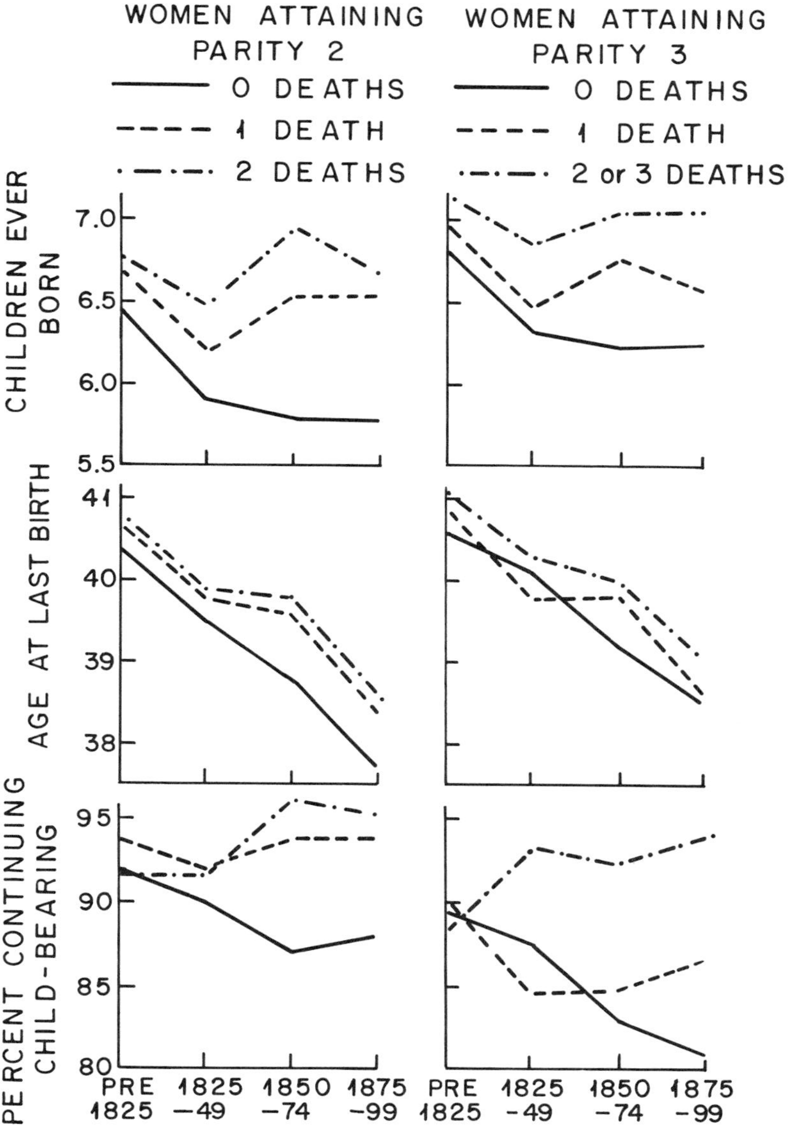

Figure 9.4. Children ever born, age at last birth and percent continuing childbearing among women attaining parities 2 and 3, according to the number of deaths among children already born, by year of marriage.

born at attainment of the given parity dies as an infant); (b) fecundability, as measured by the interval between marriage and first birth; (c) the occupational category of the husband; and (d) the village of residence. Details of these adjustments are explained elsewhere (Knodel, 1981).

Interpretation of the results is complicated somewhat by the underlying level of natural marital fertility and the shift in the age at marriage during the period under observation. Nevertheless, the results seem reasonably clear. Focusing first on the number of children ever born, the largest declines are experienced by couples whose first two or three children all survived, and the least decline is indicated for couples who lost two or more children in the first two or three births. Indeed, for those couples who did experience some child loss, there is virtually no consistent trend in children ever born evident across successive cohorts. The leveling off of the number of children ever born for couples married during the third and fourth quarters of the nineteenth century who had experienced no child loss among their first few children may reflect the counterbalancing effects of increasing family limitation on the one hand and higher underlying natural marital fertility levels combined with a lower average age at marriage on the other.

The increasing family limitation between cohorts married in the third and fourth quarters of the nineteenth century is illustrated by the decline of the age of mother at last birth, not only for couples with no child deaths among their first few children, but also among couples with less favorable child mortality experience. The general trend toward lower age at last birth across successive marriage cohorts in the nineteenth century is evident for women regardless of their experience with child mortality. Among women attaining parity 2, this decline is more pronounced among those whose first two children both survived. Among women attaining parity 3, there appears to be little difference in the extent of the decline in age at last birth according to child mortality experience; but the decline is more consistent, affecting each successive marriage cohort, for those with no prior child deaths.

Results based on the percentage continuing childbearing agree quite closely with those based on children ever born. Among women attaining parity 2, only those with no child deaths among the first two births show a lower proportion continuing childbearing among the cohort married at the end of the nineteenth century compared to the pre-1825 cohort. For women attaining parity 3, only those with no child deaths show a consistent decline in the percentage continuing childbearing across successive marriage cohorts. The trends are most likely affected by the rising underlying level of natural marital fertility and changing age at marriage, particularly in the age at first marriage for women married during the last quarter of the nineteenth century (see Table 9.4).

These results suggest that at the level of individual couples, a relationship between child mortality and changing reproductive behavior did exist, despite the fact that child mortality remained relatively constant during the nineteenth century when the new reproductive patterns were emerging. Within this context of relatively unchanging overall child mortality level, a couple's experience with the survival of its own children appears to have influenced its chances of participating in the adoption of family limitation and the reduction of fertility associated with the early stages of the fertility transition. Thus favorable child mortality experience apparently facilitated a couple's adoption of family limitation, leading to lower fertility, while unfavorable experience with child mortality seems to have impeded, if not totally prevented, such efforts.

Summary and Conclusions

The present study has examined the early stages of the demographic transition as it occurred in rural Germany, based on micro-level, family reconstitution data for a sample of fourteen villages. Analysis of such data clearly provides a useful complement to the more conventional approach, such as the one followed by the Princeton European Fertility Project, that focuses on published macro-level data from census and vital statistics reports covering the broader population. Micro-level, local studies have two important advantages: (1) they permit a more detailed examination of the behavioral changes involved in the demographic transition, and (2) since they are typically based on parish registers, they can extend converage further into the past for periods when census and vital statistics data are generally not available. Most findings that have emerged from the present analysis would not have been possible to obtain from conventional data sources or from the usual micro-level approach. A review of the principal results not only serves as a useful conclusion to the present study, but also underscores the unique contribution micro-level, reconstitution data for local populations can make to our understanding of the demographic transition as it occurred historically.

The results strongly suggest that the underlying level of natural marital fertility significantly increased between the end of the eighteenth century and the onset of the twentieth century. The analysis of the proximate determinants responsible for the increase, while not conclusive, is clearest with respect to an increase in fecundability. The evidence, although not entirely consistent, was also suggestive of a reduction in the nonsusceptible period following birth. Least clear was evidence concerning a reduction in primary sterility; apparently changes in this component were relatively unimportant.

Examination of the average interval between births reveals that changes in birth spacing generally did not play an important role in the initial stages of the fertility transition in rural Germany. Rather, the modernization of reproductive behavior appears initially to consist largely of a shift toward parity-dependent control of fertility rather than a deliberate extension of birth intervals. The emergence of parity-dependent control is evident in the shifting age pattern of marital fertility and the declining age of mother at last birth, both of which were clearly evident for the combined sample.

There is substantial variation across villages with respect to the demographic experience during the period under observation. Indeed, this has given rise to the reference to plural demographic transitions in the title of this study. The range in village levels of fertility and mortality is considerable. The trends in fertility also differ. But perhaps the most striking aspect of the diversity among the small sample of villages is in terms of the timing and emergence of family limitation. In all villages, couples married during the last half of the eighteenth century appear to be characterized by predominantly natural fertility. However, in some family limitation emerges shortly after the turn of the nineteenth century while in others natural fertility persists until close to or even through the end of the century. Moreover, such differences can be extremely pronounced even between two neighboring villages, underscoring just how local the process of fertility transition could be in the past. The results also demonstrate that cross-sectional or over-time differences in overall levels of marital fertility—the type of information typically available from conventional sources and relied upon heavily by the Princeton European Fertility Project—are not always sensitive to differences in the patterns of childbearing indicative of parity-dependent control. In at least one village, the increasing level of natural marital fertility was sufficient to lead to an increase in observed overall marital fertility despite clear indications that attempts at family limitation were also increasing.

In contrast to the considerable differences across villages, occupational differentials in marital fertility and the extent of family limitation within villages were minimal for couples married prior to 1850, when the setting was predominantly one of natural fertility. Some consistency with respect to occupational differences in the increase in family limitation among couples married in the second half of the nineteenth century is evident. In most villages, above-average increases generally characterized couples in which the husband was a farmer.

Nuptiality trends for the villages generally indicate that changes in the age at marriage played little part in the secular decline of fertility associated with the demographic transition, although a decline in the average age at first marriage for women was evident for most villages toward the end of the nineteenth century. This would have counteracted to varying degrees any decline in marital fertility that occurred. Occupational differentials in levels and trends of age at marriage were not pronounced. The generally later-than-average age at marriage for wives of landless laborers contradicts the view espoused by some that rural proletarianization led to early marriage.

In general, reductions in child mortality above age one preceded improvements in infant mortality. The latter evidenced little decline until the end of the nineteenth century in most villages. These differences suggest that a somewhat biased picture is given from simply examining infant mortality alone, as has been common in much of the analysis undertaken by the Princeton European Fertility Project. It bears pointing out, however, that throughout the period under observation infant mortality was an extremely important component of mortality under age 15, often accounting for over half of all the deaths. Moreover, a moderate rise in infant mortality during the third quarter of the nineteenth century sufficiently counteracted the improvements in mortality risks above age one to the extent that the overall probability of dying before age 15 was little different than it had been at the end of the eighteenth century.

On the village level, there is a little evidence to support the central tenet of demographic transition theory that prior declines in child mortalty are necessary for or precipitate declines in fertility and increases in fertility control. In those villages where family limitation emerged earliest and proceeded furthest during the nineteenth century, it did so in a context of relatively high child mortality and in advance of any sustained improvements. Thus, based on a macro-level comparison of trends in child mortality and fertility for the sample as a whole, or for the separate villages, we can conclude that a reduction in child mortality was clearly not necessary to precipitate changing reproductive patterns. However, exploration of the relationship between fertility and mortality at the micro-level indicates that a link between reproductive behavior and child mortality is indeed evident. Those couples with the most favorable child mortality experience were most likely to adopt family limitation and to reduce their fertility. Unfavorable experience with child mortality seems at least to have impeded, if not totally prevented, such efforts. Thus, although changes in reproductive behavior occurred during a period when the general level of child mortality remained moderately high throughout, for the individual couple participation in the early stages of the fertility transition was apparently enhanced by favorable child mortality experience. This places the macro-level finding of little association in fertility and mortality trends in quite a different perspective.

The present study demonstrates the value of analysis of local, micro-level data for expanding our knowledge of the behavioral processes underlying the demographic transition. Such studies clearly serve as a useful complement to the more usual macro-level analysis, such as is characteristic of the Princeton European Fertility Project. The substantial diversity of demographic experience of the villages included in the sample also caution against generalizing extensively from the experience of any single village, as is sometimes done in the field of historical demography. While the findings of the present study raise at least as many questions as they answer, the ability to open up new issues is testimony to the value of such micro-level analysis. We hope that these many unanswered questions will contribute to a broader agenda for future research on the demographic transition.

Village Genealogies Used As Data Sources

Brezing, Karl. 1963. *Dorfsippenbuch Öschelbronn.* No publisher given.

Hauf, Franz. 1975. *Ortsippenbuch Gabelbach.* Frankfurt: Zentralstelle fur Personen- und Familiengeschichte.

Janssen, Ludwig. 1961. *Die Familien der Kirchengemeinde Werdum.* Teil I. Aurich: Verlag Ostfriesische Landschaft.

———. 1966. *Die Familien der Kirchengemeinde Middels.* Aurich: Verlag Ostfriesische Landschaft.

Janssen, Ludwig, and Manger, Hans Rudolf. 1975. *Die Familien der*

Kirchengemeinde Werdum. Teil II. Aurich: Verlag Ostfriesische Landschaft.

Köbele, Albert. 1967. *Sippenbuch der Stadt Herbolzheim*. Grafenhausen bei Lahr: Selbstverlag des Herausgebers.

———. 1969. *Dorfsippenbuch Kappel am Rhein*. 2d ed. Grafenhausen bei Lohr: Selbstverlag des Herausgebers.

———. 1969. *Ortsippenbuch Rust*. Grafenhausen bei Lahr: Selbstverlag des Herausgebers.

———. 1971. *Ortsippenbuch Grafenhausen*. Grafenhausen bei Lahr: Selbstverlag des Herausgebers.

Sauer, Friedrich. 1975. *Höringhausen*. Arolsen: Waldeckischer Geschichtsverein.

Scheunpflug, Lorenz. 1961. *Ortsippenbuch Anhausen*. Frankfurt am Main: Deutsche Arbeitsgemeinschaft genealogischer Verbande.

Verein für bäuerliche Sippenkunde und bäuerliches Wappenwesen e.V. 1938. *Dorfsippenbuch Kreuth*. Goslar: Blut und Boden Verlag.

———. 1939. *Dorfsippenbuch Vasbeck*. Goslar: Blut und Boden Verlag.

Wetekam, Robert. 1956. *Massenhausen*. Arolsen: Waldeckischer Geschichtsverein.

———. 1971. *Braunsen*. Arolsen: Waldeckischer Geschichtsverein.

Chapter 10: Lessons from the Past: Policy Implications of Historical Fertility Studies

John Knodel and Etienne van de Walle

The implication most frequently drawn for current population policy from the historical record of European fertility can be summed up in the slogan, "Development is the best contraceptive." It is easy to understand how a cursory reading of western experience can lead to such a conclusion. Over the long run and at the highest level of generality, broad developmental changes that transformed Europe from a predominantly rural-agrarian to a predominantly urban-industrial society accompanied the transition from high to low levels of fertility. In the world today, there is a broad inverse relationship between the degree of development and the level of the birth rate. Much of the fertility decline in Europe took place before modern contraceptive methods or safe medical abortion were readily available, and thus couples who limited their family size must have done so through withdrawal or abstinence, that is, through methods theoretically available to everyone. If abortion was important—and there is some evidence that there were many abortions in certain countries by the beginning of the twentieth century—it was such a dangerous procedure that women probably resorted to it only in cases of extreme need, and mostly outside of wedlock.

Such impressions of the European experience, in combination with the cross-sectional differences in fertility apparent today between the developed and developing countries, have been used as evidence to support arguments that organized family planning programs in the developing world are unlikely to contribute much to the precipitation or acceleration of fertility declines.[1] With socioeconomic development, motivations to reduce family size will emerge and fertility decline will take care of itself. Moreover, modern birth control methods are not necessary for it to take place. "There is ample historical evidence . . . that fertility can be greatly reduced without access to modern contraception. There is no reason to

This paper was first published in *Population and Development Review* 5(2): 217–245 (June 1979).

[1] See, for example, Blake and Das Gupta (1975, p. 245), and Demeny (1975b).

assume that the same thing would not happen anywhere in the contemporary world if that is what people really wanted" (Demeny, 1975a). Or so the argument goes.

There has recently been a marked increase in the number as well as the breadth and depth of historical studies of European fertility. As a result, a much more detailed picture of the historical record is available today than just a decade ago. Two quite different types of demographic studies have been largely responsible for the recent expansion of our knowledge of historical trends: European micro-level family reconstitution studies, which typically refer to village populations during the pre-industrial and generally pre-fertility decline period; and macro-level studies of the secular decline in fertility on the national and provincial levels. The first type of study is based on the reproductive histories of individual couples reconstituted usually from the church registers of baptisms, burials, and marriages. Also included in this genre are studies based on genealogies of special subgroups of the population, particularly social elites, for whom previously compiled genealogies are readily available. Although the French developed both the technique of family reconstitution and the methodology to analyze the resultant data just two decades ago, scholars elsewhere have been quick to follow their lead. By now such studies are available from most European countries, although they cover, even in France, only a minuscule proportion of the total population. Usually such family reconstitution studies span long periods of time, extending back well before the general secular decline of fertility. They provide detailed information on reproductive behavior that can be used to test a variety of hypotheses within the framework of the family.

The second type of study is labeled macro-level because such studies are based largely on published census and vital statistics data that are typically already aggregated in the source on the basis of such administratively defined geopolitical units as districts, provinces, or states. A study of the European fertility decline based on this kind of data has been undertaken by staff and associates of the Office of Population Research at Princeton University under the direction of Professor Ansley Coale. As a result of this project, considerable information has been unearthed on the demographic trends over the last century or so at the provincial level, as well as on the general socioeconomic context in which they occurred.[2]

[2] An excellent summary of some of the results of this project is given by Coale (1973).

In addition to the contributions made by these two types of studies, both of which provide extensive quantitative evidence, our understanding of reproductive behavior in the past is also being increased by a third group of studies that are largely qualitative in nature. Such studies stem more out of the tradition of social history than of demography and are based on literary evidence, including letters and novels, and on commentaries by contemporary observers such as nineteenth-century statisticians' interpretations of vital statistics and county and small-town medical doctors' reports on their patients and on local health-related conditions. These studies shed light on the extent of knowledge of birth control and attitudes toward reproduction and children in the past and help place the newly emerging quantitative results in their social, psychological, and cultural context.

Formerly, interpretations of the European fertility experience were based on a combination of hazy empirical impressions and theoretical preconceptions. As a result of the substantial increase in the amount of information available, we can no longer be content with such an approach. If policy implications are to be drawn from the European experience, they must rest on generalizations based on the wealth of detail that has newly emerged.

Our own reading of the historical evidence leads us to several observations that we believe have relevance for current discussions concerning population policy, in particular for the debate over the potential contributions of family planning programs:

1. Fertility declines took place under a wide variety of social, economic, and demographic conditions.
2. The practice of family limitation was largely absent (and probably unknown) among broad segments of the population prior to the decline in fertility, even though a substantial proportion of births may have been unwanted.
3. Increases in the practice of family limitation and the decline of marital fertility were essentially irreversible processes once under way.
4. Cultural setting influenced the onset and spread of fertility decline independently of socioeconomic conditions.

What is the evidence behind each of these conclusions, and what are their implications for current population policy in the developing world? In answering these questions, we will present what we feel are the most plausible interpretations, but we acknowledge that other interpretations are possible and that extrapolations from historical experience to the present are necessarily speculative. We also wish to underscore that most of our discussion of the historical record is based primarily on the European (especially Western European) experience. Although less numerous, historical studies of fertility are also emerging for North America, Japan, and other areas. Our focus on Europe stems from the more extensive research on Europe and our greater familiarity with it.

One important difference between the Western European demographic experience and that of developing countries today, as well as non-Western European countries in the past, should be borne in mind: the difference in nuptiality patterns. Western European populations during at least the seventeenth through nineteenth centuries were characterized by relatively late ages of marriage and high proportions remaining permanently single in comparison with other populations historically and certainly in comparison with most current developing-world populations (Hajnal, 1965). The unique Western European marriage pattern played a crucial part in the larger demographic regime of pre-industrial Europe, keeping overall birth rates typically below the levels experienced in most developing countries today. Our focus is mainly on marital fertility and thus does not address this difference. Although this adds somewhat to the problems of extrapolating from the historical experience to the situation in the developing world, we do not feel that this seriously compromises the applicability of the particular lessons we draw.

The Socioeconomic Context of Fertility Decline

The most striking finding to emerge from the recent upsurge of research on the fertility transition in Europe is that it occurred under remarkably diverse socioeconomic and demographic conditions.

Evidence

Table 10.1 lists a series of indexes of socioeconomic development at the time of the onset of the fertility decline for seventeen countries of Europe and four countries in the developing world. Onset of fertility decline is defined as the year marital fertility had declined by an estimated 10 percent from its maximum recorded level in the course of a continuous decline to a much lower level.

Table 10.1. Demographic and socioeconomic indexes at onset of fertility decline for selected countries.

	Date of Decline in Marital Fertility by 10 Percent	Marital Fertility before Decline (I_g)	Index of Proportion Married (I_m)	Overall Fertility (I_f)	Infant Mortality (per Thousand)	Percentage of Male Labor Force in Agriculture	Percent Rural[d]	Percentage in Cities over 20,000 Population	Percentage Illiterate[e]
France	ca. 1800	.70	.51[a]	.30[a]	185[c]	70	81	7	High
Belgium	1882	.82	.44	.35	161	30	56	22	30
Switzerland	1885	.72	.44	.29	165	33	78	9	Low
Germany	1890	.76	.50	.39	221	38	68	21	Low
Hungary	ca. 1890	.63	.70	.45	250	73	84	11	49[f]
England and Wales	1892	.68	.48	.31	149	15	28	57	Low
Sweden	1892	.71	.42	.31	102	49	81	11	Low
Scotland	1894	.75	.42	.31	124	13	27	49	Low
Netherlands	1897	.85	.45	.35	153[c]	29	26	42	Low
Denmark	1900	.68	.47	.32	131	42	61	23	Low
Norway	1904	.75	.42	.30	76	37	72	18	Low
Austria	1908	.68	.51	.36	205	40	--	19	21

Finland	1910	.70	.46	.31	114	66	85	9	44
Italy	1911	.68	.54	.36	146	46	38	28	39
Bulgaria	1912	ca. .70	ca. .74	ca. .45	159	70	82	7	60
Spain	1918	.64	.51	.30	158	66	45	26	46
Ireland	1929	.71	.35	.23	69	48	73	20	Low
Costa Rica	1962	.89[b]	.50[b]	.57	74	58	66	20	14
Taiwan	1963	.70	.70	.42	49	47	42	31	30
Chile	1964	.65[b]	.50[b]	.39	103	37	29	53	15
Thailand	ca. 1970	ca. .75	.75	ca. .51	77	75	85	12	18

Source: Adapted with additions and corrections from Etienne van de Walle and John Knodel, "Demographic Transition and Fertility Decline: The European Case," in Contributed Papers: Sydney Conference, International Union for the Scientific Study of Population, 1965, p. 55.

Notes: Country borders are of the date of decline. All figures refer to the year estimated as the date of a 10-percent decline in marital fertility except the index of the level of marital fertility before decline. Estimates were obtained by interpolation or extrapolation when data were not directly available for the year indicated.

a) In 1831.
b) Excluding consensual unions.
c) Children dead after registration only.
d) In communities of fewer than 5,000 or legal definition.
e) Both sexes, aged 10+ or 15+; high refers to percentages of young adults unable to sign their name on the marriage certificate or of illiterate army recruits, exceeding 50 percent; low refers to percentages under 10 percent.
f) 6+.

Noncontracepting populations exhibit a broad span of fertility levels, in part because of differences in proportions married, but also because of the variability of marital fertility, even in the absence of deliberate family limitation. On a scale giving the value of 1.0 to the highest marital fertility ever recorded reliably, that of the Hutterites of North Dakota married in the 1920s, national populations are scattered at various levels between 0.6 and 0.9. This is the meaning of the index I_g in Table 10.1. The index I_f has a comparable structure, but refers to all women rather than only to married women, and reflects the additional effect of I_m, the proportion married, on overall fertility. It is always lower than I_g because in all populations some women in the reproductive ages are unmarried, and these women virtually always experience lower fertility than married women.

The date of decline of marital fertility can be identified from a time series of I_g. Pre-decline fluctuations are typically moderate, and the change in trends, from a more or less level plateau, is sudden and unambiguous, so that an approximate date can be assigned to it (see, for example, Figure 10.1).

Although the fertility decline began in England only after considerable urbanization and industrialization had taken place, it occurred at about the same time in Hungary, which was at a substantially lower level of development as measured by conventional socioeconomic indexes. Indeed, the first country to show signs of fertility decline was France, where birth rates started to fall around the time of the French Revolution. France could hardly be considered very advanced at the time in terms of any standard definition of development. In addition, recent research has revealed several examples of local populations outside of France where the fertility transition began in rural settings long before there was evidence of socioeconomic development (Andorka, 1972; Knodel, 1978b).

Differences in the level of literacy reached by the western countries at the time of their fertility declines were also considerable. And within each country, no consistent relationship has been found between education and fertility. Fertility itself varied greatly in pre-decline Europe. Not only did very diverse combinations of birth and death rates make for a wide range of growth rates at the time of the transition, but also variations in the proportions married—typically low in Western Europe and high in Eastern Europe—influenced the pre-decline levels of overall fertility.

The decline of infant and child mortality has often been singled out as a decisive factor that influenced the perceptions of parents about the

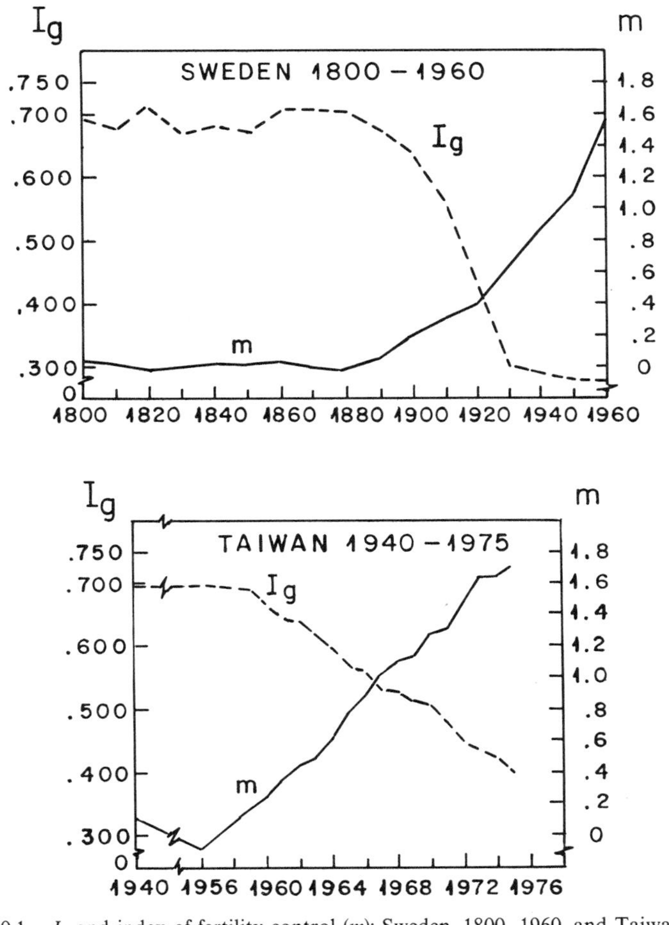

Figure 10.1. I_g and index of fertility control (*m*): Sweden, 1800–1960, and Taiwan, 1940–1975.

desirable size of the family. It has been argued that parents revise their demand for births downward when the supply of living children (the combined result of fertility and mortality) increases. Yet fertility declined under a wide variety of infant mortality conditions, as is apparent not only from the cross-national comparison in Table 10.1 but also from provincial comparisons within countries (Knodel, 1974; Lesthaeghe, 1977). In Germany there was actually a tendency for marital fertility to decline earlier in areas with higher infant mortality than in areas with lower levels.[3] In most instances, the decline of child mortality (but not necessarily infant mortality) had started before marital fertility dropped. But before a causal link can be established, the extraordinary differences in the lags between the two declines will have to be explained. For instance, infant mortality in Ireland had reached comparatively low levels when marital fertility I_g started to decline, while in Belgium and Germany it was still quite high. In addition, in some areas infant mortality, if not child mortality, dropped either at the same time as or later than fertility (Knodel, 1974; Lesthaeghe, 1977).[4] At this stage, no definitive conclusion can be reached on the role of declining mortality in the fertility transition in the West. Moreover, whereas many European countries experienced fertility decline before infant mortality had fallen significantly, in most countries of the world today infant mortality has fallen substantially. There is little evidence that this fall has been sufficient in itself to initiate a drop in the birth rate.

In general, an examination of the social, economic, and mortality conditions at the time of the onset of the fertility decline in various European countries reveals no consistency in the level of development. Of course, it would be unrealistic to expect absolute consistency in these measures, even if some threshold of socioeconomic development were the critical prerequisite for fertility decline. The measures are crude and suffer from varying degrees of noncomparability across countries. Also, varying combinations of development might be interchangeable with respect to initiating the fertility transition. It seems highly unlikely, however, that such

[3] For the 71 administrative areas of Germany, the predecline level of infant mortality correlates -0.32 with the year that I_g declined by 10 percent.

[4] There are several sources of difficulty in interpreting the historical record of the relationship between declines in infant and child mortality and declines in fertility. First, there is considerable evidence that child mortality (say above age 1 but under age 15) dropped before infant mortality, and thus the latter may not accurately reflect the change in the supply function of births for parents. This point of view is argued by Matthiessen and McCann (1978). Second, it is not always as easy to establish a clear "take-off" for the decline of infant and child mortality as it is for the decline of marital fertility. In some countries, such as Germany and Austria, available evidence suggests infant and child mortality remained fairly constant and high before the late nineteenth century, when it started to decline; however, in other countries, such as Sweden and France, existing series in infant *and* child mortality indicate earlier declines in the eighteenth and early nineteenth centuries. A priori arguments would lead us to expect a noticeable impact of the widespread use of smallpox vaccinations after 1800, although the French infant and child mortality decline is already marked before that time (see Blayo, 1975). However, if there was a causal link in France between the early decline in mortality and the onset of the fertility transition, why then did the parallel decline of mortality in Sweden not produce similar results?

considerations could explain away the remarkable extent of diversity evident in Table 10.1. In an extreme case, such as Bulgaria, fertility began to fall at a time when the population was almost entirely rural, agrarian, and largely illiterate. Clearly, large genuine differences in the level of development existed among European populations at the start of their fertility declines. It seems safe to conclude that no obvious threshold of social and economic development was required for the fertility transition to begin.

Table 10.1 also gives several examples of recent fertility declines outside of Europe. Countries undergoing the demographic transition since 1960 show a diversity in socioeconomic levels of development (according to the indicators used in the table) similar to that which characterized the western nations in the nineteenth century. Moreover, it would not be difficult to cite countries that are now considerably more industrialized and urbanized and have lower illiteracy and infant mortality than many nineteenth-century European countries, but where marital fertility has not yet started to decline. A particularly interesting example is provided by the non-European republics of the Soviet Union, especially the central Asian republics, where high levels of marital fertility have persisted and even increased, at least until quite recently, despite major advances in the level of development over the previous half-century (Coale, Anderson, and Härm, 1979).

Implications

Although a high level of social and economic development (as measured by the usual indexes) may often accompany a fall of fertility, it is clearly not a precondition. Thus, the introduction of a family planning program in a developing country at an early stage of development does not necessarily foreclose its success. After all, the initiation of fertility decline based on voluntary use of relatively inefficient means of fertility control occurred in some European populations at a time when their level of socioeconomic structural development was remarkably low. Whether or not a family-planning program will meet with success will be determined by how receptive couples are to reducing their fertility once the knowledge and means of birth control are available. Their motivations in this respect are apparently only loosely linked to the level of development, at least as conventionally defined.

Conversely, the mere attainment of a certain threshold of socioeconomic development appears an uncertain predictor of the trend of fertility.

Apparently the level of development necessary to provoke a change in reproductive behavior is so variable that there is no telling, except after the fact, whether modernization was advanced enough for fertility to decline. Thus, the historical record provides little assurance that efforts to reduce fertility or hasten a decline through raising the level of socioeconomic development will meet with early success.

Pre-transition Fertility Behavior

Three propositions are advanced concerning fertility behavior in Western Europe prior to the onset of decline: the practice of family limitation was largely absent; it was probably unknown to large segments of the population; and there was latent motivation for reduced fertility among substantial portions of the population before fertility began to fall.

Evidence

Direct evidence on the use of birth control is generally lacking for historical European populations. One of the important advances in modern historical demography has been the development of indirect techniques to determine whether couples were practicing some form of family limitation within marriage.[5] These techniques involve measures that can easily be derived from family reconstitution data, such as age-specific marital fertility rates and the age of mother at last birth. They are based on the observation that couples generally terminate childbearing earlier and marital fertility declines more rapidly with age in populations in which family size is deliberately limited than in populations characterized by natural fertility, the term used to describe fertility in the absence of family limitation. The reason for this difference is that most married couples who wish to limit their family size concentrate their childbearing in the earlier part of the wife's fertile period. Once the number of children considered sufficient is reached, efforts are made to stop childbearing, thereby reducing marital fertility rates disproportionately at older ages and lowering the average age of the mother at last birth.

[5] Family limitation as used here refers to behavior intended to stop childbearing at some particular number of children and is thus a special case of birth control, an expression that refers to both stopping and spacing behavior. Deliberate attempts to space births may also have been absent in the pre-decline period, but most of the indirect techniques developed so far are capable of detecting only the absence of stopping behavior.

Recently, Ansley Coale and James Trussell (1974, 1978) have developed an index of family limitation, called *m*, based solely on the age structure of marital fertility and independent of the level of fertility. It is calculated by comparing the age pattern of the observed marital fertility schedule with a "standard" natural fertility schedule, based on a series of populations that are presumed to practice little or no contraception. The more the observed age pattern deviates from that of the standard schedule in a predicted fashion (that is, proportionately more at older ages), the higher the value of *m*. In addition, *m* is constructed so that it will equal zero if the shape of the observed fertility schedule is identical with that of the standard natural fertility schedule. The greater the value of *m*, the greater the deviation of the schedule in question from the standard, and hence the greater the amount of fertility control implied.[6]

Application of this technique to the results of the many family reconstitution studies, as well as to official statistics when available, indicates that family limitation in Western Europe was either absent or quite minimal (perhaps limited only to special segments of society, such as the social elites) prior to the onset of the long-term decline in marital fertility. When the index *m* of fertility limitation can be computed prior to the secular decline of fertility, it is usually close to zero and unchanging. When *m* begins to increase, the change is typically marked, as is the change in the trend of fertility (see, for example, Figure 10.1). Whenever age-specific marital fertility rates are available, for countries or provinces as a whole, *m* indexes can be calculated. It is, however, with micro-level data that the study of the patterns of fertility using this index has most applications.

Family limitation emerges among some groups of the population much earlier than among others and long before any urban-industrial transformation is evident. This is especially true among certain groups of social

[6] Small differences in the value of *m* are not necessarily meaningful indications of differences in the extent of family limitation. For example, among the ten empirical fertility schedules that served as the basis for determining the standard shape of natural fertility, the values of *m* ranged from -0.15 to 0.24. On a cross-sectional basis, some range of differences is to be expected even when little or no family limitation is being practiced. On the other hand, modern populations in which contraception is widespread are typically characterized by *m* values well over 1.0. Thus, moderate or large cross-sectional differences or consistent trends over time in a series of *m* values can be interpreted with reasonable confidence as reflections of differences in the degree of fertility control (Coale and Trussell, 1978). Since *m* is determined entirely by the age pattern of marital fertility rates, it is independent of the level of fertility and therefore insensitive to any attempts to space births that are independent of the wife's age and, presumably, her parity.

elites, such as the Genevan bourgeoisie or the French and Italian nobility, although early signs of family limitation are found in some village populations as well, especially in France, where it is common to detect family limitation in the rural population by the end of the eighteenth century (Henry and Houdaille, 1973). The same populations that are characterized by early evidence of family limitation also experience early fertility decline, and when the data extend back to the pre-decline period in these populations, signs of family limitation are lacking. In other words, the evidence does not suggest that family limitation was practiced at some moderate but constant level prior to the secular fall in marital fertility rates. Instead, its incidence seems to have been quite minimal and in many cases completely absent.

Evidence that family limitation was not practiced to any great extent prior to the fertility decline does not necessarily mean that it was unknown. It is possible that couples had little motivation to use birth control techniques to limit childbearing because desired family sizes were large and typically exceeded the number of surviving children actually achieved. Indeed, the lack of motivation to reduce fertility is often given as the reason why fertility remained high for as long as it did. Although such an interpretation cannot be definitely ruled out, indirect evidence leads us to conclude that family limitation was not a form of behavior known to the majority prior to the fertility transition period and thus was not a real option for couples. Moreover, additional evidence suggests that births were frequently unwanted, especially among women, and thus at least latent motivation to reduce fertility existed.

First, in pre-transition populations, couples did not adjust their reproductive behavior to their own experience with infant and child mortality (Knodel, 1978a, 1978c). Couples whose children all survived continued childbearing just as long as couples whose children had died early. Thus, couples who would seem to have had the greatest incentive to practice family limitation—those whose children all survived—did not do so.

Second, a comparison of trends in marital and nonmarital fertility indicates that both declined more or less simultaneously in most European countries (Shorter, Knodel, and E. van de Walle, 1971). It seems unlikely that motivation to avoid out-of-wedlock births was absent before the fertility decline period and that by mere coincidence such motivation emerged at the same time as married couples were deciding to have fewer children in response to new social, economic, and demographic conditions.

The large number of foundlings apparently deserted by unwed mothers in the eighteenth and nineteenth centuries underscores how unwanted many illegitimate births were (Langer, 1974). A more plausible interpretation is that birth control practices were not widely diffused prior to the parallel declines in legitimate and illegitimate fertility and that the spread of the knowledge and skills to avoid unwanted births enabled both married and unmarried couples to reduce their fertility simultaneously.

Two arguments have been invoked to demonstrate that methods of birth control were widely available to the population at large before the onset of fertility decline. First, reference to such methods has appeared in many different cultural contexts since antiquity. Second, the technique that is most likely to have been responsible for the decline of fertility in the West, withdrawal, requires no special knowledge or implements and is available to every couple having the barest understanding of the mechanism of reproduction. These two arguments are formidable, and we shall discuss them in turn.

References to birth control methods, ranging from the magical to the potentially effective, abound in the literature prior to the contemporary era (Himes, 1963). Forms of intercourse that might reduce fertility are presented as perversions that aim at heightening sexual pleasure; the loss of fertility is often presented more as a penalty for the perversion of nature's ends than as an intended goal. References to birth control, moreover, are far more numerous than references to family limitation; that is, extramarital relations are the privileged locus of contraception. This is not necessarily because motivations to avoid the child did not exist within wedlock, as we shall argue below. Rather, contraception is presented as the specialized knowledge of rakes and seducers, who advertise their skills as a way to persuade their intended partners.

We see no reason to believe that withdrawal was widely acceptable or even known before the onset of fertility decline, or that it can be "reinvented by every couple" when need arises. References to withdrawal are scarce in the West before 1700 (although they abound in Islam from medieval times). Although the Bible makes reference to "the sin of Onan," onanism had come to assume a different meaning, that of masturbation. Withdrawal is often referred to as learned behavior in the literature.[7]

[7] For an extensive review of the evidence supporting this point, see E. van de Walle (1980); see also Stone (1977, Chapter 9).

While it seems likely that abstinence was generally recognized as a means of avoiding pregnancy, this is a uniquely costly technique requiring great self-control. Permanent abstinence for the purpose of limiting family size requires the repeated denial of immediate pleasure for the much more distant benefits that may be perceived in connection with avoiding childbirth. In brief, it seems unrealistic to assume that just because people may know "where babies come from," they automatically have a viable means of family limitation at their disposal (Demeny, 1975a).

Analysis of literary evidence and other qualitative material also supports the contention that the very concept of family limitation was alien to the mentalities of much of the population in the pre-transition era. Either techniques of birth control were unknown or the use of them, particularly within marriage, was simply "unthinkable."[8] Malthus, for one, believed that restrictions on marriage were the only means to reduce fertility. Of allusions to contraception made by the French writer Condorcet, Malthus (1798) said, "I profess not to understand . . . he alludes, either to a promiscuous concubinage, which would prevent breeding, or to something else as unnatural." Although he had missed the exact meaning of Condorcet, Malthus said that this would "destroy virtue and purity of manner" and was clearly to be rejected. Other writers shared his belief that fertility could not or should not be controlled within marriage. For example, Diderot wrote:

> The act of propagation is so much in conformity with the wish of Nature, and she invites to perform it by such a powerful, such a repeated, such a constant attraction, that it is impossible for the largest number of people to evade it. . . . In spite of all the contrary resolutions and systems, it is impossible for men to cheat the wish of Nature in such a way as to influence population ever so little. (Grimm and Diderot, 1813, pp. 318–319)

It is the many references to Nature, in such texts, that have led to the use of the term natural fertility to refer to a mode of behavior, common in those times, and still common in many developing parts of the world today, in which couples make no deliberate attempt to control marital fertility.

[8] The "unthinkability" of birth control has been argued by Philippe Ariès. See, for example, Ariès (1960) and Stone (1977).

Can we assume that family limitation was not practiced prior to the decline in fertility because couples welcomed as many children as natural fertility would bring? Is it true that "the age-old attitude toward high fertility was always similar to the attitude toward longer life: high fertility was considered a blessing" (Demeny, 1974)? The answer seems to be no, especially when viewed from the mother's vantage point. Direct evidence on the motivations of couples in centuries past is at least as difficult to come by as is evidence on the practice and knowledge of birth control. Nevertheless, accumulating indirect evidence suggests that in many areas of Europe during the eighteenth and nineteenth centuries significant numbers of legitimate as well as illegitimate births were unwanted, especially by their mothers.

The lay and religious literature of the time contains frequent references to economic motives for small families and even more to noneconomic motives (as for example, to preserve the health and beauty of the wife) to avoid excessive childbearing within marriage; but such references do not usually mention the need for fertility control. In his classical discussion of the subject, Norman Himes (1963) concluded that the health (or medical) motive for birth control was very old.[9] But it was the woman who had a stake in avoiding the dangers of childbearing and the debilitating effects of closely spaced pregnancies, whereas intercourse was traditionally thought of as the husband's prerogative. For women, there was no real option to practice family limitation since viable methods were either unknown, considered unacceptable for use within marriage, or required initiation by the husband.

The contemporary literature on infant mortality and child rearing sheds light on underlying attitudes toward reproduction and family size during the period prior to the fertility transition. Abusive child-care practices and general neglect appear to have been commonplace in much of Europe, suggesting that children were not necessarily welcome additions to the household. While outright infanticide was not unknown, especially among unwed mothers, far more common were traditional practices of infant hygiene and child rearing in various parts of Europe that led to what social historians today label "concealed infanticide" or "infanticide by neglect." Such practices included sending the baby out to a wet nurse; dosing the infant with gin or opiates to keep it quiet; having the baby sleep in the

[9] For an extensive review of the lay and religious literature, see E. van de Walle (1980).

same bed with the parents, thus risking "overlaying" and consequently suffocating it; leaving the infant unattended lying in its own filth—often in stifling swaddling clothes—for hours on end; feeding the baby unwholesome "pap" from an early age instead of breast-feeding it; and rocking the infant violently in its cradle until it was virtually knocked into a sleep of insensibility. Not all these practices were common everywhere, of course, but collectively they surely contributed to the high infant and child mortality that characterized much of Europe in the eighteenth and nineteenth centuries (Shorter, 1975, Chapter 5, and 1978a; Langer, 1972, 1974; Piers, 1978; Stone, 1977; Sauer, 1978).

Even more to the point, contemporary observers report that parents, particularly mothers, were frequently indifferent to the departure or loss of a child and in some cases welcomed the death of a child as an easing of their burden (Shorter, 1975, 1978; Braun, 1978, pp. 318–319; Stone, 1977; W. R. Lee, 1977, p. 282). They appear not to be describing isolated incidents but rather pervasive attitudes among a poverty-stricken populace. Such evidence is hard to reconcile with the contention that couples declined to use birth control because they wanted to maximize their family size. Rather it suggests that many women continued having unwelcome births because there was little option to do otherwise.

The custom of hand-feeding, rather than breast-feeding, young infants was common through much of central Europe and had a devastating effect on infant mortality, given the deficient nutritional content of the infant's food and the appalling hygienic conditions of the day (Knodel and E. van de Walle, 1967). It is not difficult to understand why mothers chose such a course within the context of a society where women were expected to labor all day alongside their husbands as well as to have primary responsibility for child care, and where the loss of infants was met with ambivalence or indifference. Paradoxically, for areas where breast-feeding was common and prolonged there is scattered evidence that in some cases this was also related to the fact that children were not always welcome. A number of contemporary observers mention that women purposely prolonged breast-feeding in order to delay their next pregnancy. Indeed, this is one of the few actions women themselves could take to reduce their fertility, however ineffective and inconvenient it was (Shorter, 1975, p. 176; Livi-Bacci, 1977, p. 256; Knodel, 1978b).

In some respects, it seems reasonable to argue that negligent child-rearing practices and the resulting infant and child deaths served as a way to limit family size in the absence of birth control, particularly in view of the apparent unwillingness of parents to change their ways, despite the frequent decrying of these practices by authorities. From this perspective, the high infant and child mortality rates found in much of Europe prior to the fertility decline can be considered as much an accommodation to high fertility as the opposite. In other words, the conventional argument that couples maintained high fertility in part to counteract high infant and child mortality may have the causal ordering reversed.[10] High mortality among the very young may have in part reflected couples' reactions to unwanted births. Such an interpretation helps explain why a prior decline in infant mortality was not a necessary precondition for marital fertility to start to decline in a number of areas of Europe.

Literary evidence and scattered commentaries by contemporary observers are an unreliable basis for establishing facts about fertility in the past. But there is little else to go on. For whatever it is worth, this evidence is consistent with the idea that family limitation was not widely available or acceptable prior to a radical change in attitudes; and although such a change cannot be dated with precision, the statistical record is consistent with the suggestion that the adoption of contraception within marriage occurred suddenly, and massively, in large segments of the population where its use had been previously extremely limited because it was either unknown or objectionable.

Implications

If family limitation was an innovation in Europe at the time of the onset of the fertility transition and its diffusion contributed to the pace of fertility decline there, the same process can occur in developing countries today, where in many cases family planning also represents a new type of behavior. Organized family planning programs that provide information and services, as well as propaganda efforts designed to legitimate family planning practices, may well help initiate or accelerate the adoption of family planning practices. The "legitimation" function of a government program may be of considerable importance if existing birth control techniques are primarily associated with extramarital sex, as they appear to have been for a long time in Europe and reportedly are in parts of Africa today, possibly contributing to their unacceptability or "unthinkableness"

[10] See, for example, W.R. Lee (1977, p. 69). Based on a review of anthropological evidence Susan Scrimshaw (1978) comes to a similar conclusion regarding present-day developing countries; indeed, there appear to be remarkable similarities in the historical and present-day situations.

within marriage. Naturally, the success of a family-planning program depends on the receptivity of the couples to fertility reduction. But the absence of practice prior to campaigns to disseminate information and services does not necessarily indicate the lack of such receptivity. It may just as well reflect an unfamiliarity with the concept and methods of family limitation.

If we are correct that women were more receptive to birth prevention than their husbands, then the methods of birth control available are also of some importance. The argument that withdrawal is always an option not only ignores the real possibility that it may be unknown or culturally unacceptable, but also overlooks the possibility that it may be the wife who is most interested in preventing births. The fact that a variety of modern methods are promoted by family planning programs today, including many "female methods," such as the pill, IUD, injection, and tubal ligation, should contribute to an acceleration of fertility decline.

Finally, the historical evidence suggests that high infant and child mortality may have been as much a reaction to high fertility as vice versa. If, in the absence of birth control, dissatisfaction with excessive fertility led to significant numbers of infant deaths through neglect or abusive child care, this suggests that high infant and child mortality rates are not necessarily contraindications to readiness for family planning programs, as has been generally assumed. Indeed, just the opposite may be true.[11]

The Irreversibility of Family Limitation and Fertility Decline

Increases in the practice of family limitation and the decline of marital fertility were largely coincident and, once under way, were largely irreversible and gained momentum.

Evidence

Examination of the time series of the index of family limitation (*m*) and the index of the level of marital fertility (I_g) for Sweden, a country that entered the fertility transition in the late nineteenth century, and for Taiwan, a country in which fertility began to fall only two decades ago,

[11] Scrimshaw (1978) makes the same point based largely on evidence from present-day developing countries: "High mortality, when looked at in the context of family formation patterns, may point to a readiness for family planning rather than the opposite" (p. 397).

reveals remarkable similarities, as shown in Figure 10.1.[12] In both countries, once the m index starts to rise above a minimal level and once the I_g index starts to fall below the pre-decline level, these trends continue virtually uninterrupted until radically different levels are achieved. Although the pace of these changes was far more rapid in Taiwan than in Sweden, both countries show the same irreversibility in the fall of marital fertility and the concomitant increase in the practice of family limitation.

The association of rising m values with the decline in marital fertility helps confirm that the fertility transition results from a new form of reproductive behavior rather than from an extension of previously established patterns. Recall that the m index is based solely on the age pattern of marital fertility and is entirely independent of the fertility level. The rising m values associated with the fertility transition indicate that an earlier termination of childbearing and a disproportionate reduction in fertility at older ages contributed to the fall in fertility. In contrast, any deliberate control of marital fertility prior to the transition must have been through lengthening the period between births. We know this from the results of a large number of family reconstitution studies, which make clear that, historically over long periods of time and across diverse populations, the average age of women at last birth was remarkably consistent prior to the fertility decline, generally being close to 40. It seems reasonable to assume that this average was largely biologically determined. Thus, the substantial differences in pre-decline levels of marital fertility are attributable to differences in the average birth interval, whether due in part to deliberate spacing or otherwise, and not to differences in the age at which couples stopped having children. Not only was stopping behavior new for most couples; its increasing practice appears to account almost entirely for the initial phase of the fertility decline, since the average birth interval remained fairly constant as fertility started to drop.[13] Only later in the transition do increases in the average birth interval make an important contribution to lower fertility levels. Thus, whether or not deliberate birth

[12] The values of the m indexes plotted in Figure 10.1 differ somewhat from those published earlier (in Knodel, 1977b), since they are calculated by a method different than recommended by Coale and Trussell (1978). More specifically, a regression equation based on the values of marital fertility for the six five-year age groups, 20–24, . . . , 45–49, was employed to estimate m. Somewhat higher values of m, ranging from 0.06 to 0.26, are found for Sweden prior to the fertility decline if the age group 45–49 is excluded from the regression.

[13] Increases in the last birth interval are sometimes evident, but this can best be interpreted as a reflection of attempts at stopping rather than spacing per se. See Knodel (1978b).

spacing was practiced prior to the decline, a new and different type of fertility control—stopping behavior, or what we call family limitation—was responsible for precipitating the fall of fertility to modern levels.

While the *m* index is an indirect measure of family limitation, direct evidence from a series of surveys in Taiwan substantiates the increasing use of birth control during the period of rising *m* values in that country (Sun, Lin, and Freedman, 1978). Direct historical evidence on the prevalence of birth control for Sweden or other Western countries during the equivalent stage of the fertility transition does not exist, but it seems safe to conclude that the shifts in the age pattern of marital fertility reflected by the rising values of *m* similarly signified a major increase in the deliberate practice of birth control there as well. The particular mix of methods practiced would naturally have been quite different, with withdrawal and possibly abortion assuming major importance. Indeed, the difference in the type of methods used may have contributed to the strikingly different pace at which family limitation was adopted in Sweden and Taiwan. But the main point is that the trend toward terminating childbearing at increasingly earlier ages was similar despite the differences in the methods of birth control used and the pace at which they were adopted.

Sweden is not an isolated case in the historical record. Examination of the changes in the age pattern of marital fertility in European populations over time, evident in both official statistics and family reconstitution studies, indicates that throughout Europe once the practice of family limitation rose above minimal levels, it continued to increase in a virtually uninterrupted fashion until much higher levels of control prevailed. Likewise, examination of time series of the level of marital fertility indicates that once a decline began, it continued steadily until much lower fertility, typically well below 50 percent of the pre-decline level, was achieved. This irreversibility is apparent on the national, provincial, and even village levels, as well as for special subgroups such as the social elites covered in some family reconstitution studies. Moreover, the trends in increasing family limitation and declining marital fertility are largely coincident. This generalization holds for virtually all populations, including those that experienced unusually early signs of family limitation and fertility decline, although in such cases the pace of change was generally slower. The evidence from Taiwan, and indeed from an increasing number of other developing nations (most of which are at an earlier stage of their fertility decline), suggests the same experience is being repeated in present-day developing countries but at a greatly accelerated pace (see Knodel, 1977b; Knodel and Debavalya, 1978). In brief, the increase in the practice of family limitation and the decline of marital fertility seem to be one-way processes that generate a "momentum" of their own.[14]

Implications

The steady and irreversible increase in the practice of family limitation under a diversity of social and economic conditions in Europe suggests that the idea of controlling the number of children born rather than leaving it to fate has a wide appeal, once the possibility of control is realized. The steady decline in marital fertility may reflect a combination of increasing efficiency in the practice of family limitation and falling desired family sizes. Indeed, these two factors may interact. Only after the possibility of effectively limiting childbearing becomes a reality and its advantages become fully appreciated does it make sense to couples to aim for even smaller family sizes.

If our hypothesis is correct, the high and relatively constant fertility that characterizes pre-decline societies corresponds essentially to a period in which it is not widely acknowledged that reproduction can be manipulated by individual couples within marriage. Couples do not have target family sizes. They accept, in some cases reluctantly, as many children "as God sends." Questions on desired family size asked in surveys taken in Tropical Africa often elicit giggles and meaningless responses, presumably because people believe it is not in their power to affect the outcome of a natural process (Caldwell, 1977). In the absence of a choice, societies often have characteristics that accommodate high fertility: large families are welcomed or at least unquestioned. The appearance of articulated desires concerning family size may coincide with or shortly precede the realization that reproduction can be manipulated; and once methods are on hand by which smaller and smaller family sizes can be attained by successive cohorts of couples, the norm about size starts to evolve downward.

The pattern of steady increase in family limitation and steady decline in fertility is indicative of a "diffusion process." Once some couples in a community adopt the new behavior patterns, it becomes relatively easy

[14] One well-known exception to this generalization has been indicated for the English village of Colyton, where E. A. Wrigley (1966) found some evidence of family limitation in the seventeenth century, following a plague epidemic; fifty years later the villagers apparently reverted to uncontrolled fertility. However, the finding is best treated as a rare exception, based on a rather small number of cases. Even the validity of this exception is under debate. See Morrow (1978), and Wrigley (1978d).

for other couples to imitate. In addition, the cost of going against religious proscriptions or other norms that may have served as barriers to the use of family limitation in the pre-transition period rapidly diminishes as couples become aware that others in the community are violating the old norms as well.

This interpretation of the European experience clearly contradicts the assumption sometimes made that family planning programs can only skim the cream off the top and that after initial success, demand for their services will dry up.[15] The historical record suggests that, once started, the decline of fertility does not stop easily.

The Influence of Cultural Setting

Cultural setting influenced the onset and spread of fertility decline independently of socioeconomic conditions. Proximate areas with similar socioeconomic conditions but dissimilar cultures entered the transition period at different times, whereas areas differing in the level of socioeconomic development but with similar cultures entered the transition at similar times.

Evidence

Despite the great diversity of their socioeconomic characteristics, the countries of Europe had one striking factor in common when fertility declined: time itself. This is the main finding emerging from Table 10.1. With the exception of the forerunner, France, and a few stragglers, such as Ireland and Albania, the dates of decline were remarkably concentrated. The momentous revolution of family limitation began in two-thirds of the province-sized administrative areas of Europe during a thirty-year period, from 1880 to 1910. Moreover, the fertility decline took hold at much the same time in areas of Western culture overseas, from English-speaking Canada to New Zealand. We doubt this remarkable homogeneity can be explained by the influence of economic development on the independent motivations of millions of couples. Instead, we see this as evidence that some diffusion of information on contraception as well as some communi-

[15] Evidence from an increasing number of developing countries confirms sustained demand for family-planning programming services. Despite this, some still argue that "acceptors . . . are the cream skimmed off the top." See Petersen (1978).

cation of normative beliefs must have occurred within the larger European (or Western) cultural sphere.

There are, of course, differences of timing among areas. A persistent finding of the recent research on fertility decline in Europe is that the onset and spread of the fertility decline appears to cluster regionally in a way that cannot be explained through common socioeconomic characteristics. There is greater similarity in fertility trends among provinces within the same region but with different socioeconomic characteristics than is true among provinces with similar socioeconomic characteristics but located in different regions. Provinces within regions typically share similar cultural characteristics, such as a common dialect or common customs. Regional boundaries often coincide with cultural boundaries, which in turn impede the flow of information and the process of diffusion. In addition, there are undoubtedly differences between cultures in terms of traditions, customs, and values that can either impede or facilitate the adoption of family limitation behavior and small-family norms.

The importance of cultural and language boundaries in differentiating the timing and pace of the fertility transition is made starkly clear by the historical experience of Belgium, which is divided into Walloon (French-speaking) and Flemish (Dutch-speaking) areas. Maps plotting fertility during the transition period make clear that "the areas with high marital fertility and a late decline are nearly all on the Flemish side, and those with an early and faster decline are on the Walloon side" (Lesthaeghe, 1977, p. 110). Moreover, physical proximity was of no importance in areas where the two cultures met. An examination of a sample of paired communities, never more than 10 kilometers apart but on opposite sides of the language border, reveals that although there were no significant measurable social and economic differences between the communities, the language boundary was "a real demarcation line between two obviously noninteracting demographic regimes" (Lesthaeghe, 1977, p. 112).

While the Belgian experience is impressive in indicating how the existence of a language border within even a small country can serve as a cultural barrier to the spread of the fertility transition, the experience of English-language countries overseas demonstrates the importance of language and culture in the fertility transition in a different way. The "extraordinary similarity between the course of birth rates in Australia and the United States, and the similarity between the fertility of these two societies over time and those of Britain, New Zealand, and English-speaking Canada" serve as one of the most striking manifestations of "the diffusion of fertility control practices within single language groups" despite the quite different social and economic situations that characterize these countries (Caldwell and Ruzicka, 1978, p. 81).

Recent analysis of the fertility decline in Russia also underscores the importance of culture and tradition in determining the fertility response of a population to social and economic change (Coale, Anderson, and Härm, 1979). The persistence of customs and attitudes unfavorable to family limitation and reduced fertility appears to be the most likely explanation of why Eastern minorities in European Russia were so slow to reduce their fertility despite many decades of postrevolutionary social change, including the extension of education, the reduction of mortality rates, and massive indoctrination efforts. Similarly, longstanding cultural features seem to underlie the continuing persistence of high marital fertility and the absence of family limitation in the rural populations of Central Asia. Although a direct connection remains to be established, the subordinate position of women, which appears to be an entrenched part of the dominant Muslim culture of Central Asia, is probably a factor (Coale, Anderson, and Härm, 1979).

Implications

Cultural setting and tradition are likely to exert an independent influence on the response of populations to organized family-planning efforts as well as to general development. While family-planning programs may elicit a very favorable response in some populations even at quite low initial levels of development, in others we might expect such efforts to be quite unsuccessful at considerably higher levels of development. Under the latter circumstances, it is hard to be optimistic about the potential of either organized family planning or general development efforts for lowering population growth until these cultural barriers are broken down. Family planners would be offering their message and wares to an unreceptive, even, perhaps, largely inaccessible audience (particularly in situations where women's roles are highly segregated and male domination is extreme), whereas general development programs would be most likely to increase population growth by reducing mortality while fertility remains high.

Matters would be far simpler if those particular cultural characteristics that are favorable or unfavorable to family limitation were readily identifiable. If the presence of certain characteristics in a society were a sure indication of a special receptivity to policy efforts, this society could then be singled out for special programs. If, on the contrary, a particular cultural trait were identified as counter to the diffusion of contraceptive practice or the small-family norm, the focus of information and propaganda campaigns might especially address this point. Unfortunately, there is very little firm knowledge concerning the cultural factors that have facilitated the acceptance of family limitation.

One cultural feature that we believe the historical record suggests is particularly important is the status of women. We regard this more as a cultural characteristic than a socioeconomic or structural one since the extent to which women participate in the broader socioeconomic system beyond the home and extended family appears to be determined more by religious and other cultural values than by socioeconomic development per se. Of course the two are related, but the point is that the success of both family-planning programs and more general development efforts designed to affect fertility may be quite dependent on the cultural beliefs regarding the appropriate role of women. This implication is consistent with the evidence suggesting that women may be more receptive than men to the limitation of family size, at least in circumstances where fertility is quite high. In cultural settings where the female role is subordinate to the extreme and where women are isolated from the broader communication network, policies designed to alter the status of women may be more conducive to reduced fertility than either family planning alone or more general development efforts.[16]

Sociological theory has attempted to describe both cultural and structural factors that sustain high fertility. These include the role of the kinship group as the locus of decision making in the area of reproduction and the means by which individuals can further their interests within kinship groups. John Caldwell (1976) suggests that in present-day circumstances, the onslaught and popularity of media material that reflects Western attitudes and value systems, if they could be measured, would also reflect the breaking down of cultural barriers and the diffusion of universal fertility norms. The identification of social and cultural indicators that would reflect receptivity to family limitation has lagged behind measurement of

[16] For an example of how the subordinate status of women plays a semi-autonomous role within the broader framework of social and economic organization in a contemporary developing country, see Arthur and McNicoll (1978, especially pp. 52–53). For evidence that in some developing countries there is a greater receptivity to birth control among women than men, see Huston (1978). Ruth Dixon (1978) argues that general development efforts in developing countries often have little impact on the status of women.

the more readily identifiable socioeconomic characteristics. Such indexes would be of considerable value to social scientists and policymakers alike. More effort needs to be made in this direction.[17]

Conclusion

It may be helpful to rephrase the argument of this paper using the general framework developed by Richard Easterlin (1975). The determinants of fertility must work through (a) the demand for children, as determined by income, prices, and tastes; (b) the supply or potential output of children in the absence of fertility limitation, a function of natural fertility and the survival of children; and (c) the cost of fertility regulation, both psychic and objective. We believe the historical record suggests the relative lack of importance of income and prices in determining the demand for children prior to or during early stages of the fertility decline. In fact, the typical situation in the past seems to have been one in which the demand function is indeterminate and in which, to repeat Coale's expression, fertility is not "within the calculus of conscious choice" (Coale, 1973, p. 65).

When target family size begins to be articulated, the dominant factor may be tastes, which may reflect external influences as much as or more than socioeconomic conditions specific to the society in question. In contrast to those who postulate a role of declining infant mortality in hastening the resort to contraception to regulate the size of families, we note that the decline of fertility occurred among countries with very different supply functions, both in terms of overall fertility and in terms of childhood survival. Finally, we believe that what is understood by the "cost of fertility regulation," a term that covers a variety of factors including sheer famil-

[17] The particular indexes that may be most appropriate for identifying readiness to decline in the historical setting may not always be the same as those appropriate for developing countries today. In general, however, it is not implausible that, independent of the overall level of development, countries where the education and labor participation of women does not lag much behind that of men, where women are integrated into the modern communications and transportation networks, or where the cost of children exceeds their value to the family as an economic unit are candidates for an early and rapid decline of fertility. In addition, the generalization of Western standards of public health, with their strong component of maternity and child-care programs, seems likely to be a harbinger of successful family planning. Indexes measuring these factors might prove far more predictive of fertility decline than conventional development indexes.

iarity with the concept and means of family limitation, is an extremely important component of an explanation of the secular fertility decline, as it occurred in Europe and as it will occur in many other parts of the world where high fertility now prevails. Here, too, the diffusion of attitudes toward and knowledge of contraception, and of contraceptive techniques and implements themselves, may trigger or accelerate the decline of fertility. The model Western nations provide of family limitation and small family sizes may be among the most important factors in contemporary fertility declines in a number of developing countries.

If our interpretation of the European transition from high to low fertility is correct, some of its early features can only be explained by a change in tastes or a decline in the cost of fertility regulation or some combination of the two. These features include the variety of social, economic, and demographic conditions under which the decline of fertility occurred; its remarkable concentration over time; the apparent coincidence of the decline with the sudden adoption of family limitation practices; the rapid generalization of such practices, once they appeared; the resultant drastic change of reproductive regimes; and finally, the importance of cultural factors among those that appeared to influence the onset and the spread of the fertility decline.

Although the European experience confirms a loose relationship between socioeconomic modernization and fertility decline, it also suggests that there was an important innovation-diffusion dimension to the reproductive revolution that swept the continent. This suggests that the introduction of the concept of family limitation (along with the means of effective fertility control), particularly in combination with the diffusion of tastes for modern consumer goods, higher material aspirations, and an awareness of alternative roles for women, can have a substantial impact on populations today. Indeed, given the nature of modern communications existing in much of the developing world today, the potential for rapid diffusion of birth control practice is considerably greater than it was historically in Europe. At the same time, the historical record does not suggest success will necessarily be immediate. Even within Europe there were cultural clusters particularly resistant to the modernization of reproduction.

One of the more important implications of our interpretation of historical fertility studies is that current recommendations to shift the emphasis away from family-planning programs and toward development efforts as a means of reducing fertility should be viewed with considerable caution.[18] Stressing the importance of general development programs or the selective restructuring of such programs at the expense of programs aimed at disseminating both knowledge and methods of birth control is politically popular at the moment.[19] Our interpretation of the historical record, however, casts doubt on the assumption that such shifts in policy will often be expedient in hastening declines in birth rates. In many cases a greater payoff might well result from concentrating efforts on improving and extending existing family-planning programs.

Of course, it would be unrealistic to assume that either family-planning programs or development efforts designed to influence fertility will be successful everywhere immediately, especially if no attention is paid to the long-established cultural values regulating fertility in specific societies. In particular, the historical record indicates special heed must be paid to those cultural features that determine the status of women and their ability to assert their own wishes regarding childbearing. In addition, the success of organized family-planning efforts depends on programmatic factors such as program content, strategy, organization, and administrative structure—factors about which the historical record cannot tell us much since the fertility transition in the West occurred while most governments, rather than enacting programs to encourage fertility decline, remained staunchly pronatalist.

Although it would be foolish to expect that all the critical policy issues of today can be effectively addressed by looking into the past experience of the West, anyone familiar with the richness of the findings emerging from the large number of in-depth studies of the historical fertility experience now under way will be quick to realize we have far from exhausted their implications for current policy. Moreover, we recognize there is sufficient room for genuine disagreement with those implications we have drawn. Too often, however, interpretations of the historical record are

[18] For various versions of arguments for deemphasizing family-planning programs, see Demeny (1975b), Demerath (1976), Petersen (1978) and Davis (1977, 1978).

[19] As, indeed, it has been since the 1974 World Population Conference at Bucharest. A central recommendation of the World Population Plan of Action passed at Bucharest is contained in paragraph 31: "... that countries wishing to affect fertility levels give priority to implementing development programmes and educational health strategies which, while contributing to economic growth and higher standards of living, have a decisive impact upon demographic trends, including fertility" (*Population and Development Review* 1 [1]: 163-181.)

based more on theoretical preconceptions derived from the present than on an empirically grounded familiarity with what actually went on in the past. We hope we have made clear that recent research has expanded our knowledge of the historical record to a point where such an approach can no longer be acceptable. We also hope we have helped form a basis from which a more informed debate can continue.

CHAPTER 11: Conclusions

Susan Cotts Watkins

INTRODUCTION

The *Decline of Fertility in Europe* summarizes the results of a study of the population change of nations in modern times, largely by means of a decade-by-decade examination of the decline of fertility in the provinces of Europe over the past century. In the late nineteenth and early twentieth centuries, the populations of most of these provinces experienced what can only be called a social revolution. The revolution consisted in the widespread adoption of a particular mode of fertility regulation—the termination of childbearing in marriage before the woman's physiological capacity to reproduce was exhausted—a reduced reliance on the variety of community customs that had controlled fertility in the past, and, eventually, the descent of marital fertility to very low levels indeed. A societal transformation of such magnitude and consequence inevitably called for precise description and for explanation.

The classic description of the demographic transition is given stylized presentation in a familiar picture that depicts the transition as tripartite. In the past, the picture shows, both mortality and fertility were high and approximately equal over the long run, thereby generating extremely slow population growth. The line representing mortality is irregular and interrupted by periods of crisis, while fertility is shown as unchanging. In the second stage, the time of transition, mortality falls while fertility remains high, generating a period of population growth until fertility begins to descend as well. In the third stage, those countries that have completed the demographic transition are depicted with low and approximately equal levels of both mortality and fertility, once again indicating little or no population growth over the long run. Now, however, it is the fertility line that is interrupted by the baby boom and bust, while the mortality line is straight. The stylized presentation is obviously imprecise; neither measures of fertility or mortality, nor the scale, nor the length of the lag were consistently specified. To the extent that this stylized presentation was based on more than casual observation, evidence consisted of trends in crude birth rates and crude death rates in the countries of Europe and European settlement for a relatively brief period of history.

The form this description took, particularly the emphasis on levels and lags, and the appeal of the explanation offered for the decline in fertility owed much to the circumstances of the post-World War II period. Mortality declines had been steep and swift in those countries in which death rates were high at the beginning of World War II. No more than simple calculations were needed to show that even if mortality fell no more, but especially if its decline continued, in the absence of a fall in fertility population growth rates would be very high, higher than those that had ever been recorded in countries that had experienced all three stages of the transition. Population growth was considered by some a dominant threat to human welfare.

The postwar period also saw a surge of enthusiasm for exporting development, political but especially economic, to those countries that had not yet been transformed along the lines of the West: it was the heyday of modernization theories in political science, sociology, and economics. The two concerns were sometimes combined—it was suggested that unimpeded population growth would retard or even doom attempts at modernization but that development would bring lower fertility in its train. The view that falling infant or childhood mortality would stimulate declines in fertility was particularly appealing, since mortality declines had already occurred in many developing countries, and further declines were seen as desirable even by those who were not enamored of Western-style modernization.

In 1953 Notestein succinctly outlined the emerging theory of the demographic transition:

> The new ideal of the small family arose typically in the urban industrial society. It is impossible to be precise about the various causal factors, but apparently many were important. Urban life stripped the family of many functions in production, consumption, recreation, and education. In factory employment the individual stood on his own accomplishments. The new mobility of young people and the anonymity of city life reduced the pressures toward traditional behaviour exerted by the family and the community. In a period of rapidly developing technology new skills were needed, and new opportunities for individual advancement arose. Education and a rational point of view became increasingly important. As a consequence the cost of child-rearing grew and the possibilities for economic contributions by children declined. Falling death rates at once increased the size of the family to be supported and lowered the inducements to have many births. Women, moreover, found new

> independence from household obligations and new economic roles less compatible with childbearing. (Notestein, 1953)

The narrative was persuasive. Part description and part theory, what came to be called the "Theory of the Demographic Transition" expressed previous explanations of the fertility decline in the idiom of post-war concerns with population and development. Yet, just as the stylized description of levels and lags in the transition from high to low mortality and fertility was still imprecise, to the degree that the narrative could be shaped into a testable theory, one suitable for export, it was largely untried.

Attention turned to Europe as a suitable area in which to assess the determinants of fertility decline, for it was there that both revolutions had occurred. It was not difficult to read the record of social change in nineteenth-century Europe in such a way that the engine of demographic change appeared to be just the processes that were considered such valuable exports to the developing world, such as in increases in life expectancy, productivity and literacy, or, more generally, escape from the dead hand of the past. It did not seem coincidental that profound demographic change had occurred precisely in the cluster of countries that had already undergone the vast societal transformations that, to nineteenth-century observers as well as in retrospect, formed a watershed between the world we had lost and modern times. The results of such an examination would be of general significance, however, because it was believed that ". . . the principles drawn on for the account of Europe would be widely transferable under appropriate circumstances" (Notestein, 1953, p. 21).

The European Fertility Project was an attempt to document the narrative in detail and to provide empirical verification or refutation of specific explanatory hypotheses. The aims of the project are summarized by Coale and Treadway in the opening paragraphs of Chapter 2:

> The Project was designed with two principal purposes—to create a detailed quantitative record of fertility in each of the several hundred provinces of Europe, during the period of major decline, and to determine the social and economic conditions that prevailed when the modern reduction in the rate of childbearing began.

An important aspect of the Project was to make both the description and explanation of the decline comparative. If Europe was to be a source of lessons from the past that would provide instruction for the developing world of the present, generalizations about the fertility decline would have to hold for all, or at least most, of Europe. The project was therefore extensive in scope and required the contributions of many individuals.[1] Comparative analysis also required consistent strategies both of description and explanation. Although these strategies make comparison among countries and provinces possible, they also place constraints on the interpretation of the results; thus, it is useful to consider them in some detail.

Strategies of Explanation and Description

Early discussions of the fertility decline often ignored the distinction between nuptiality and marital fertility, though either could predominate in changes in common measures of fertility such as crude birth rates. Yet by the early twentieth century, many researchers had pointed out that the decline in birth rates was due in part to the limitation of births within marriage (National Birth-Rate Commission, 1916); by the time of the European Fertility Project it was widely accepted that the predominant mode of fertility control in modern countries was control within marriage.

Demographic measures that permitted a distinction between nuptiality and marital fertility were developed for the project, using the most widely available data, vital registration of births by the marital status of the mother, and census information on the distribution of women by age and marital status. The index of marital fertility, I_g, expressed the level of marital fertility as a proportion of a standard, the reliably recorded fertility of the prolific Hutterites. Thus the births to married women in the particular population are compared to the births that population would have had had they reproduced at the rate of married Hutterite women. Similarly, the index of illegitimate fertility, I_h, compares the births to unmarried women in the particular population to the same Hutterite standard. The

[1] The seven monographs that present the results of research on the fertility of a particular European population are: *A Century of Portuguese Fertility* and *A History of Italian Fertility During the Past Two Centuries* by Massimo Livi-Bacci; *the Decline of Fertility in Germany, 1871–1939* by John Knodel; *The Decline of Belgian Fertility, 1800–1970* by Ron Lesthaeghe; *The Female Population of France in the Nineteenth Century* by Etienne van de Walle; *Human Fertility in Russia since the Nineteenth Century*, by Ansley J. Coale, Barbara Anderson, and Erna Härm; and *The British Fertility Decline: The Demographic Transition in the Crucible of the Industrial Revolution* by Michael S. Teitelbaum. Three further volumes are in preparation: on Switzerland by Francine van de Walle, on France by Etienne van de Walle, and on Denmark by Poul C. Matthiessen. In addition, numerous articles have been published, many of which are cited in the bibliography to this volume.

index of nuptiality, I_m, compares the births to married women in the population to births to all women, if both groups were subject to Hutterite fertility, and is thus a fertility-weighted measure of the proportions married. Overall fertility, I_f, combines the effects of marriage, marital fertility, and illegitimate fertility.[2]

A working assumption of the project was that at the early stages a decline in I_g was due to parity-specific control. Parity-specific control (also called family limitation) had been defined by Henry to mean that the timing of the cessation of childbearing is conditional upon the couple's previous fertility history (Henry, 1961; Knodel, 1977b). The concept of parity-specific control emphasizes the importance of the number of children already born in the couple's decision to terminate childbearing; those with more children will stop childbearing earlier than those with fewer. Since higher parities occur at older ages, family limitation should also be evident in an earlier age at the birth of the couple's last child and thus in steeper declines in fertility by age relative to the age pattern of fertility in populations that do not practice parity-specific control (called natural fertility populations by Henry).

Because neither parity nor the age of the mother at the birth of her children was widely recorded in nineteenth-century Europe, it was usually not possible to calculate directly either measures of parity-specific control or presumed approximations, such as deviations from the age-specific fertility schedule of a natural fertility population. I_g, which is based on births at all ages and parities, is an imperfect measure of parity-specific control. Since variations in I_g across units may be due to variations in the many determinants of the length of birth interval, such as breast-feeding (see Coale, Chapter 1), a declining sequence of I_g's was used to identify the initial stage of the fertility transition.

In the few places where appropriate data exist to calculate both a measure of family limitation and I_g, there was evidence of a long plateau of marital fertility and no evidence of family limitation, and when the decline in I_g began it was paralleled by an increase in control at the older ages.[3] Once a pattern can be identified, it is possible to use much sparser data in situations where more detailed information is not available. The European Fertility Project relied upon the characteristic configuration of levels of I_g

[2] The calculation of these indexes is described in detail by Coale and Treadway in Chapter 2 of this volume.

[3] The evidence is discussed more fully by Coale in Chapter 1 of this volume, by Knodel in Chapter 9, and by Knodel and van de Walle in Chapter 10.

and of measures of family limitation where full information is available to support the interpretation of declines in I_g as evidence of parity-specific control.[4] Nonetheless, more work utilizing individual-level data to examine variations in birth intervals would clarify not only the relative importance of stopping behavior in the fertility transition, but also the significance of parity for this behavior.

The unit of analysis was to be geographic. The choice was in large part pragmatic, for the data were consistently collected by geographic area. To consider the whole country would not have permitted detailed comparison; to consider individuals, villages, or parishes would have greatly restricted the universe of observation. Each of the countries of Europe had the requisite data available for at least some category of administrative unit smaller than the entire country, but larger than a village or the parish; the names of these units vary from country to country (counties in England, cantons in Switzerland) and are here called provinces. The four indexes discussed earlier were calculated for every province in Europe for most years in which a census provided a distribution of women by age and marital status, and vital registration provided birth by marital status. The indexes, published as Appendix A to Chapter 2 of this volume, constitute one of the major accomplishments of the Project.[5]

[4] Even this, however, may be imperfect: (1) A level sequence of I_g's may mask compensatory increases in the level of fertility at younger ages and increases in parity-specific control at the older; and (2) in principle, a declining sequence of I_g's may be due to deliberate attempts to lengthen the interval between births rather than to deliberate attempts to terminate childbearing. Thus the assumption that a declining sequence of I_g's represents the adoption of parity-specific control—or that a level sequence represents its absence—needs to be justified.

This can only be done by using information on the timing of births (for example, from family reconstitution studies using parish registers or genealogies). Knodel's careful examination of birth intervals in a sample of German villages showed, first, that increases in the underlying level of natural fertility sometimes balanced an increase in control at the older ages. Thus a level sequence of I_g's cannot unambiguously be interpreted as evidence that the transition to parity-specific control had not yet begun. Secondly, although birth intervals at the younger ages sometimes declined in the initial stages of the transition, they rarely lengthened (Knodel, Chapter 9). Even if they were to do so, however, attributing longer birth intervals to deliberate attempts to space births would be difficult. Since the most common techniques of fertility control in marriage in nineteenth-century Europe appear to have been abortion, abstinence, and withdrawal, it seems likely that couples would be inclined to practice these methods later in marriage rather than earlier.

[5] A tape containing this and other data was created by Roy Treadway and is available from the Office of Population Research, Princeton, New Jersey. The available data were generally good: both censuses and vital registration at a reasonable level of accuracy were available for most countries of Europe since at least the last quarter of the nineteenth

There are obvious constraints on the interpretation of the findings of the European Fertility Project, constraints that arise not only from the imperfect correspondence between I_g and the parity-specific behavior it is meant to measure, but also from the choice of the level of aggregation. While provinces permit more detailed comparison than would be possible if the entire country were the unit, they may still mask considerable demographic heterogeneity among smaller geographic regions.[6] Thus, the findings for a province might indicate only an aggregate pattern produced by what may have been quite different patterns of decline.

As explanations of the transition were formulated in the period following World War II, they abandoned physiological debility; they questioned the importance of innovations in birth control technology in view of the evidence that the early stages of the decline were accomplished by some mix of abortion, abstinence, and withdrawal—methods thought to have always been available; and they emphasized the correspondence between the structures of the material world in which everyday life is lived and the social rules that regulate reproduction. Explanations of the fertility decline were usually phrased in terms of the differential characteristics of leaders and laggards: leaders would differ from laggards in reasonable and predictable ways.

century. Although the calculations of the indexes were usually straightforward, insufficiencies in the data sometimes required elaborate estimation techniques, for example those used by E. van de Walle (1974) for France. The period covered is between the time of the first census, generally around 1870, and 1960. In some provinces it was found that the first date for which data are available well precedes the beginning of the fertility decline, while in others the decline was already underway. The boundaries of the countries and the provinces remained relatively consistent over time, changing primarily as the result of an exchange of territory following a war or the dismemberment of one national unit into several. For some countries, especially those of the former Austro-Hungarian Empire, it was thus impossible to calculate a long historical series of indexes. The number of provinces for which indexes were calculated was 588 in 1870; 589 in 1900; 626 in 1930; and 617 in 1960.

[6] Chaunu has argued that the *départements* of France consisted of a wide variety of microdemographic regimes, each a combination of different levels of nuptiality, fertility and mortality, and Smith has documented this using evidence from parish-reconstitution studies in France, England and Germany (Chaunu, 1972; D. S. Smith, 1977). Where it was possible to calculate the indexes for lower levels of aggregation (such as *circondarios* in Italy and districts in Switzerland), provinces were found to be relatively homogeneous. Knodel, however, found considerable diversity among villages in the timing of the initiation of family limitation; neighboring villages in the same administrative area of Germany were separated by nearly a century in the initiation of their decline in marital fertility (Knodel, Chapter 9).

Certain features of the material landscape were brought into high relief in the explanatory framework: the change in occupational structure attendant on the transformation of production caused by the widespread substitution of inanimate for animate sources of energy and the use of ever more refined tools to multiply effort; the concentration of these productive processes in urban areas and migration from the country to the city; and an increase in educational attainment. However modernization is defined, these processes are among the cluster of expected changes.

The stories that linked modernization to new patterns of childbearing were sometimes brief and crude, but their logic is appealing. Many of them trace paths by which the great transformations in the work place and in education would increase the price and diminish the returns of children to their parents. The altered distribution of occupations from farm to factory would, it was argued, restrict the opportunities for children to contribute to the family economy at an early age and increase the opportunity costs of time spent in domestic activities for women, and the passage of laws restricting children's participation in factory labor and requiring their enrollment in school would reinforce this shift in economic incentives. The focus on economic considerations and on individual couples was supplemented by drawing on major strands in sociological inquiry, particularly the transformation from *Gemeinschaft* to *Gesellschaft*. For example, the migration of populations from rural to urban areas would permit those who wished to do so to abandon old customs or adopt new forms of family life free from the social control that constrained their behavior in small rural villages; education would weaken the force of traditional beliefs and authority while promoting the notion that life chances could be improved through individual effort. A parallel argument proposed that declines in infant mortality would stimulate declines in marital fertility because families preferred having surviving children rather than new births; even if they had not been performing such rational and individualistic calculations, a greater probability of survival to adulthood could, as Freedman has noted, play havoc with social structures such as inheritance systems designed to accommodate a lower level of survival (Freedman, 1961–1962).

The logic embedded in the usually more elaborate versions of these stories was persuasive to many. It did not, however, account for differences between France and the other countries of Europe: in France, fertility began to fall around the time of the French Revolution, well before the onset of the decline elsewhere. Even if France is considered a special case, however, there are other points of tension between the explanations for fertility decline that drew on modernization and the data used in the European Fertility Project to support or contradict them.

The first point of tension derives from the level of aggregation. Because the decision to limit fertility is more easily visualized as an individual rather than a group decision, it is tempting to emphasize individuals ceaselessly revising their calculations of the value of children. When, however, the data refer to provinces (or any other spatial unit), individuals are hidden behind proportions, and the findings are more appropriately interpreted as speaking of social solutions to social problems. Second, most of the stories take as an *explicandum* the desired number of children. If this is so, then the relevant measure of fertility is I_f, overall fertility, for it would be irrelevant whether that number is achieved by aggregate variation in marriage or in marital fertility; only if the timing of marriage is considered a decision distinct from its fertility implications are measures of marital fertility appropriate. Last, most of the tests of explanation that attempt to distinguish leaders from laggards examine differentials in I_g in a given year. Because, however, levels of marital fertility can vary substantially in the absence of parity-specific control, such a comparison need not directly reflect the differential adoption of family limitation. Although a substantial and progressive decline in I_g is unlikely in the absence of family limitation, cross-sectional variation in marital fertility may be the result of differences in the many other determinants of fertility. Thus it is difficult to infer differential adoption of family limitation from variations in marital fertility in a single year.

Further constraints upon interpretation arise from the measures of modernization. The scarcity of data dictated the reduction of complex concepts to simple measures of occupation, of literacy, or of urbanization. Although the demographic indexes are uniform across provinces and dates, the other measures are not always comparable. Furthermore, despite the fact that the authors of the monographs and the chapters in this volume were addressing similar questions, the direction each took was determined not only by the availability of data—sometimes richer, sometimes sparser—but also by idiosyncratic theoretical predilections, and, increasingly, by the findings of the previous monographs.

In summary, then, the strategies of description and explanation required to overcome limitations in the data and to permit comparability also impose constraints on the interpretation of the results. Particularly, the lack of fit between the stories told about the mechanics and the motivations behind the fall in marital fertility and the measures available to support or contradict these stories caution against facile interpretation, comparison, and generalization of the results. Given these caveats, however, the findings are impressive.

Findings

Descriptions

The province-by-province analysis covering a period of about a century has added considerable detail to our knowledge of the demographic transition. Some of the tenets of demographic transition theory were confirmed by these studies; others were contradicted.

The findings of the European Fertility Project have modified the stylized description of the demographic transition in several ways. In the first stage, before the transition had begun, overall fertility, which combines the influence of proportions married by age and marital fertility, was found to be lower than the classic description suggested. Mean overall fertility (I_f) was, at the national level, about 30 to 50 percent of the Hutterite standard, and there was considerable geographic variation among provinces. Excluding France, in 1870 12 out of 501 provinces had an I_f of over 0.590, while 29 provinces had an I_f of under 0.275, less than half as much (see Coale and Treadway, Chapter 2, Table 2.4). Overall fertility was as low as it was partly because in most provinces less than half of the women of childbearing age were married, and fertility among the unmarried was low.

More significantly, the level of *marital* fertility was not as high as would have been expected had married women been reproducing at the Hutterite level. In 1870 the mean I_g of the provinces of Europe (excluding France) was 0.723, slightly more than 25 percent below the Hutterite standard. Geographical variation in marital fertility was also substantial: in a few Belgian *arrondissements*, the I_g in 1870 was above the Hutterite level, while in 30 provinces it was below 0.600 and in 7 provinces below 0.530 for the first few decades for which data were available to calculate I_g (Coale and Treadway, Chapter 2, Table 2.2).[7] Despite the many accounts

[7] If provinces in which I_g at the first few dates for which data are available are in descending sequence are set aside, the distribution of the I_g's of the remaining provinces closely approximates a normal distribution, with about 6 percent of the provinces below 0.600 both in the actual distribution and the fitted normal. The low but unchanging I_g's could be the result of nonparity-specific factors that affect fertility or of the practice of contraception or abortion by a substantial but unchanging proportion of couples (see Coale and Treadway, Chapter 2).

of various social supports for high fertility in populations in the past, fertility in Europe was by no means as high as either biological capacity or well-recorded maxima would suggest; everywhere, other practices modulated overall fertility, and usually marital fertility as well.

Overall fertility was not stable, but could and did fluctuate. These movements can usually be attributed to changes in I_m rather than in I_g, for the latter shows only slight fluctuations during the brief pre-transition period for which data were available to calculate the indexes. Wrigley and Schofield have demonstrated substantial shifts in another measure of overall fertility, the Gross Reproduction Rate, in England between 1541 and 1871; the GRR reached a minimum of 1.81 in 1661 and a maximum of 3.06 in 1816 (Wrigley and Schofield, 1981, p. 230). They concluded that variations in nuptiality rather than in marital fertility produced the fluctuations in overall fertility, since evidence from the parishes for which family reconstitution techniques permitted the calculation of age-specific marital fertility rates showed that marital fertility remained quite stable over time (Wilson, 1982; Wrigley and Schofield, 1983).

These findings suggest that the stylized depiction of fertility during the pre-transition period needs to be clarified. Levels of both overall and marital fertility were lower than they would have been had either populations or married couples exploited their full reproductive potential. If the fertility line is drawn to represent overall fertility, substantial fluctuations are possible, and they have been documented for three centuries of English history. If the fertility line is drawn to represent marital fertility, there is reason to believe that it was relatively stable over time. Thus the adaptations of reproduction to the economy and society seem to have been expressed through marriage rather than through marital fertility.

The classic graphic presentation of post-transition levels of mortality and fertility was generally confirmed. Mortality is both lower and more stable than it had been in the past, and, apart from war-time, has rarely risen. Both overall and marital fertility can and do fluctuate in response to economic conditions and social fashion (Stolnitz, 1964, p. 32); but the magnitude and duration of such fluctuations is slight in absolute terms, usually much less than the change in overall fertility in England between 1661 and 1816.

With respect to the transition itself, a number of important findings were precisely documented for provinces outside of France: (1) Between 1870 and 1960, declines in marital fertility were usually greater than declines in overall fertility; (2) the decline in overall fertility was unambiguously due to changes in marital fertility, rather than nuptiality; (3) once the decline in a province had begun, it almost always continued monotonically—that is, it was not reversed—until very low levels were reached; and (4) the initiation of the decline spread like an epidemic across Europe, so that by 1930 very few provinces remained untouched.

First, if the fertility line is drawn to represent overall fertility, I_f, the changes between 1870 and 1960 are less striking than changes in I_g. Mean I_f (excluding France) falls from 0.379 to 0.223; among the individual provinces, I_f is sometimes higher in 1960 than it was a century earlier. If one takes child survivorship into account as well, it becomes obvious that, on average, couples did not raise many more children to maturity in 1870 than they did in 1960. If, however, the measure is I_g, the discrepancy between past and present is greater. Mean I_g (excluding France) falls from 0.723 to 0.352, and in every individual province it is lower, usually by 50 percent or more, in 1960 than it was in 1870.

Second, the decomposition of overall fertility into measures of nuptiality and marital fertility made it possible to distinguish between the effect of I_m and I_g on the declines in I_f. Between 1870 and 1930, there was relatively little change in nuptiality. With the exception of France (where I_m rose during the nineteenth century), Ireland (which had a sharp drop in I_m after the famine), and Russia after the turn of the century, changes in nuptiality consisted of gentle falls in the proportions married in some countries (Spain, Italy, and Finland) and gentle rises in the proportion married in most others (Coale and Treadway, Chapter 2; Watkins, Chapter 8). During the marriage boom after 1930, sharp changes occurred in I_m in most provinces; however, since I_m rose, the effect was to counteract the effect on I_f of continued falls in I_g between 1930 and 1960. Trends in provincial levels of illegitimate fertility were similarly inconsistent between 1870 and 1930; because the amount of childbearing outside of marriage was usually low, the effect of changes in I_h on I_f was generally negligible. Thus marital fertility was clearly the predominant influence on the fall in overall fertility between 1870 and 1930. Although this conclusion is not surprising, it was nevertheless useful to document precisely the relative importance of changes in marriage and in marital fertility during the transition.

The third finding shows that remarkably small initial changes in I_g herald the transition. In virtually all of the provinces of Europe, once I_g had declined by 10 percent it continued downward.[8] In some provinces the descent was unequivocal and precipitous, in others hesitant and gentle; but in all but a handful of provinces I_g never again reached the level of the pre-decline plateau once it had fallen by 10 percent. Subsequently the only substantial and widespread rises in marital fertility were during the baby boom following World War II. Not only did these increases fall far short of reaching 1870 levels, but they in no way indicated an abandonment of family limitation. It would appear from the experience of the provinces in Europe that once a decline in I_g of 10 percent is achieved, populations continue to exert ever more stringent fertility controls. They may loosen these controls, but they do not abandon them. If this is true for populations outside of Europe as well, it is an important finding of the European Fertility Project.

The fourth, and perhaps most startling, finding is the speed with which the initiation of family limitation spread throughout the provinces of Europe. Before 1870, low fertility indicating parity specific control, a 10-percent decline in I_g, or other more direct measures of family limitation has been convincingly documented only in some *départements* of France or adjacent provinces and for unusual social groups elsewhere, such as the aristocracies, the Jews, and some urban populations (Livi-Bacci, Chapter 3). Although some of these forerunners showed signs of family limitation by the seventeenth century, similar behavior was apparently not adopted by their neighbors.

After 1870 the timing of the initiation of the decline is highly compressed. The post-1870 declines began primarily in the heart of Europe: after 1920, the decline was initiated in Ireland and in the extreme southern and eastern peripheries of Europe (Russia, Rumania, Albania, southern Italy, Spain, and Portugal). If France is excluded, 59 percent of the provinces of Europe experienced the beginning of the transition during the three decades between 1890 and 1920 (Coale and Treadway, Chapter 2). Within countries, family limitation spread rapidly: all of the provinces of Switzerland experienced a 10 percent decline in I_g in 78 years; in Italy in 60 years; and in Germany in 33 years. England and Denmark were

[8] Most of the provinces in which marital fertility subsequently rose are in France. Elsewhere, only in a few provinces in Italy and one in Portugal did I_g fall by 10 percent and then rise to pre-decline levels before falling again. The fluctuation in Italy and Portugal can be attributed to heavy emigration rather than to family limitation or, as in the Papal States, to a shift in some births from the legitimate to the illegitimate category after civil registration of births was made mandatory (Livi-Bacci, 1971, p. 61; Livi-Bacci, 1977).

even more rapid—Denmark in 25 years, England in 16. As a result, national levels of I_g descended swiftly, in most countries declining from 90 to 60 percent of their pre-decline levels in 18 to 30 years (Coale and Treadway, Chapter 2). If levels of marital fertility before 1870 were shaped by longstanding social customs, it would appear that the cake of custom crumbled rather rapidly.

These detailed descriptive findings gain significance when considered against the tapestry of fertility control before the beginning of the demographic transition. Although knowledge of the past is not as detailed as knowledge of the present, it is more extensive than the pleasingly symmetrical but abbreviated depiction visually suggested in the usual graphic presentation (which gives equal time to pre-transition, transition, and post-transition populations). In the long period of the recorded past, a variety of checks to population growth regulated either the stream of deaths or the stream of births. Mortality interrupted population growth, as did out-migration; migration from Europe to the United States and South America was especially significant in the late nineteenth and early twentieth centuries. Fertility was restrained by a diversity of controls: among these the most consequential were widespread abstention from marriage and extended breast-feeding following the birth of a child. These restraints on fertility seem to have been primarily the result of customs that had the effect, if not the intent, of limiting fertility; fertility was under social rather than individual control (Wrigley, 1978a; Lesthaeghe, 1980). Recorded marriages and births are the precipitates of reproductive arrangements in the past, but the intimate behavior of which they are a consequence was and is rarely open to view. Variation in coital frequency due to passion, distaste, or the separation of spouses can affect the frequency of births, as can nongenerative forms of intercourse such as withdrawal, or a resort to abortion. All of these controls affected either the time at which childbearing started or the spacing between births. What is striking is the lack of evidence, for the majority of the populations of Europe, that any of these practices were deliberately used by married couples to stop childbearing before the onset of physiological sterility.[9]

Though community customs, such as those that determine the proper circumstances for marriage or the acceptable duration of breast-feeding, may be slow to change, custom does not preclude flexibility. The systematic

[9] An ambiguous exception may be the attempt in some societies to avoid concurrent childbearing by two generations of women in the same family: in Nepal and Bangladesh, for example, women are supposed to stop childbearing after the marriage of a daughter.

response of one demographic parameter to change in another or to change in resources, is central to the notion of a homeostatic equilibrium that has been used to interpret pre-modern demographic regimes (Wrigley and Schofield, 1981; Dupâquier, 1972). Moreover, it seems sensible to assume some tolerance for the violation of ordinary conventions by individuals in the face of extraordinary circumstances such as unusual illness, or untoward economic hardship. Nor did the customary practices that determined fertility preclude the attainment of rather low levels of aggregate fertility: an estimated Gross Reproduction Rate of 1.8 in England in 1661 or an I_g of 0.519 for rural populations of Central Asia in 1926 is low compared to the Hutterite standard.

During the initial stages of the demographic transition this diversity of behavior was replaced by a single approach, the earlier termination of childbearing. Only later, it would appear from what is known so far, did the deliberate spacing of children within marriage become important. Although women today may delay marriage, nurse their children for long periods, and behave in other ways that have the effect of delaying or hastening the birth of the next child, these are not important determinants of the level of marital fertility compared to the use of contraception. And even the adoption of modern contraceptives that permit a wide variety of spacing patterns to achieve low levels of marital fertility did not alter the new pattern by which, for most women, childbearing was increasing confined to a relatively few years of their married lives; in virtually all European populations today marital fertility rates are very low for women older than 35.

The emphasis on levels of fertility—either in the aggregate as in the classic description of the demographic transition, or at the level of the individual couple where hypotheses are often phrased in terms of the number of children that the family desires—has obscured what may be the most distinct break with the past: the ever-earlier termination of the woman's childbearing years. Although this is usually explained by a reduction in desired parity and thus by an earlier achievement of desired parity, it is also necessarily related to age and to marital duration. Thus, just as smaller family sizes may have become more desirable, so also may earlier stopping—the devotion of fewer rather than more years of life, or years of marriage, to child-rearing—have come to be seen as preferable, perhaps as women's time or family leisure were given a greater value. In other words, although number, age, and marital duration are intertwined in the family-building process, considerations of number need not overwhelm considerations of time.

Once the pattern of earlier stopping was adopted in sufficient measure to depress I_g by 10 percent, it spread through virtually the entire population. It does not ever seem to be relinquished, and it obviates the need for the previous diversity of social controls, though it may be combined with the use of contraception during other intervals in the reproductive years. It is hard to imagine the circumstances under which populations of Europe would return to a pattern of childbearing in which the first birth is closely associated with marriage and the last with menopausal sterility.

In Europe, the adoption of earlier stopping was paralleled by a fall in fertility, though it is obvious that the two need not move together. Parity-specific control, like pre-transition controls, is consistent with a variety of levels of fertility. Very low levels of fertility, however, such as those common in Europe today, may not be attainable without parity-specific control, and as Coale notes (Chapter 1) once such control is adopted, very low levels of childbearing may become irresistible.

The initiation of family limitation was achieved by some mix of abortion, abstinence, and withdrawal; although condoms and devices to block the entrance to the uterus were known before the nineteenth century, they do not seem to have been effectively manufactured or widely distributed until well into the twentieth century.[10] Compared to modern methods of fertility control, abortion, abstinence, and withdrawal required sacrifices; their effective use in marriage bespeaks a considerable degree of determination by one or both spouses. Moreover, family limitation often spread in the face of direct opposition from, or at best the silence of, public spokesmen. In England, the strenuous efforts of the tiny Neo-Malthusian League to promote the use of contraception were met with hostility from the church hierarchy and medical profession and with disinterest from the labor and socialist parties and even from the Victorian advocates of women's rights (Soloway, 1982). It may be said that the adoption of parity-specific control was a revolution accomplished with primitive technology and without generals.

Explanations

During the nineteenth century the landscape in which the family was formed and dissolved altered dramatically. Given the rough coincidence of modernization and the demographic transition, and the persuasiveness

[10] Many birth-control techniques were probably known by at least some societies for centuries (Himes, 1963). In his review of early modern French sources, however, E. van de Walle (1980) notes that they are usually mentioned in the context of illicit rather than marital relations.

of the stories that were told to explain their relation, it is surprising that, in country after country, the tests of the hypotheses embedded in demographic transition theory produced no certain confirmation of the theory.

As noted earlier, the relation between infant mortality and marital fertility was expected to be particularly significant. According to the theory, a decline in infant mortality should stimulate and therefore precede a decline in marital fertility. One of the more surprising discoveries was that this expectation was often upset. In Switzerland, the decline in infant mortality preceded the decline in I_g almost everywhere. In Denmark and Germany (where Knodel had found that at the national level trends in the infant mortality rate closely paralleled trends in I_g) only about half the provinces followed the expected sequence, while in the other half marital fertility had begun its decline before infant mortality fell. In most of the provinces of Belgium and in England, marital fertility fell before infant mortality (F. van de Walle, Chapter 4; Matthiessen, 1985).

When the test of the relation is the degree of association between the level of infant mortality and the level of I_g, for all the provinces considered together the correlation coefficient was 0.156 in 1870 and 0.383 in 1900; in 1930 the correlation was smaller and not statistically significant (at conventional levels). Within individual countries, the correlations were significant and positive for only two countries in 1870, Germany and the Netherlands, and two in 1930, Sweden and Switzerland. The low correlations in 1870 would be expected if most provinces at that time had not yet abandoned natural fertility—if, in other words, fertility was not yet within the calculus of conscious choice (F. van de Walle, Chapter 4). Van de Walle's findings suggest that the correlations are likely to be significant at one stage of transition—when it has well begun but is not yet over.

It may be true that couples require time to adjust their childbearing to changed levels of infant mortality; yet when change in the infant mortality rate and change in I_g were examined together, in only three countries was the correlation coefficient significant and in the right direction. When the correlation was between the infant mortality rate and a lagged change in I_g, in no country was the coefficient significant and in the right direction; and when the test was the date the infant mortality rate reached 100 and the date I_g reached 0.600, in only four out of the eight countries was the coefficient statistically significant and in the right direction.

The preceding battery of tests showed little association between I_g and the infant mortality rate during the late nineteenth and early twentieth centuries. The correlation coefficients that measure this relation are usually not statistically significant and often have the wrong sign. When the relation between marital fertility and infant mortality was examined in a multivariate context, the results were neither stronger nor more consistent.

Matthiessen and McCann, among others, have noted that it would be more appropriate to consider childhood rather than infant mortality. If parents are trying to adjust the size of their family to some desired number of children, they presumably are more interested in surviving children than in births. Since in Europe mortality in childhood usually declined before infant mortality (Matthiessen and McCann, 1978; Wrigley, 1969), the relation between mortality and marital fertility might be better examined using measures of mortality during childhood. Even aggregate measures of infant or childhood mortality may be misleading, however, for the relation between mortality and fertility could be expected to be more evident for families than for provinces. Using data from German villages, Knodel found that for couples married after 1825, those who had no infant deaths were more likely to adopt family limitation after their second or third child than were couples who had experienced the death of a child (Knodel, Chapter 9). Interestingly, this relation was not evident among couples married before 1825. Knodel's findings suggest not only that relations that are obscured at the aggregate level may become evident when individuals are considered, but also that family calculations based on surviving children may not be a timeless behavior.

Industrialization has been defined in a number of different ways and is less easily collapsed to a single measure than is infant mortality. Most tests of demographic transition theory, however, interpret it to involve at least a reduction in the proportion of the population engaged in agriculture and a corresponding increase in employment in the industrial and service sectors of the economy. The monographs of the European Fertility Project usually showed evidence of a correspondence between these measures and I_g, although the relation was often so weak as to be statistically insignificant either in bivariate or multivariate contexts.

If different occupational groups received different economic benefits from children, the relevance of industrialization for fertility is primarily in the changed distribution of individuals in occupational categories. But as Lesthaeghe and Wilson have argued in Chapter 6, the commonly used measure of this change, the proportion in agriculture, does not adequately capture the economic benefits of children to the family, for household production to which children can contribute at a relatively early age is characteristic of cottage industry as well as of agriculture. When these occupational groups were combined, they found a much stronger relation between increased industrialization and decline in marital fertility. In a parsimonious multivariate model that included only one additional measure (of secularization, measured by votes for nontraditional parties in elections in the early twentieth century), the proportion of variation (R^2) explained by the two variables together is generally quite high: Italy 0.739, Belgium 0.837, Germany 0.626, Switzerland 0.862, The Netherlands 0.299, and Denamrk 0.855. The influence of the occuptational structure in the regression equation is measured by the multiple regression coefficient, and in their regressions that coefficient is usually substantial (Lesthaeghe and Wilson, Chapter 6, Table 6.6). Although it is not possible to compare directly the coefficients in the multiple regression equations used by the authors of the monographs with those from the equations used by Lesthaeghe and Wilson, it would seem that their theoretically appropriate combination of agriculture and cottage industry is preferable to a strict division between agricultural and industrial sector. The importance of secularization, which they take to represent the expanding domain of activity in which individual rationality could legitimately play a part, is emphasized in their findings, as well as in subsequent work by Lesthaeghe (1980, 1983), Caldwell (1976, 1982), and Ryder (1983).

The changing roles of women have received considerable attention in examinations of fertility differentials in developing countries. In the European Fertility Project, consideration of women's roles was limited only to participation in the labor force and was examined only in the monographs on Germany, on England, and on Switzerland. For England, the measure "proportion in the nondomestic, nonagricultural labor force" was not statistically significant (Teitelbaum, 1984). In Germany, Knodel found a zero-order correlation of -0.43 between change in nonagricultural female employment and the date of a 10-percent decline in I_g (Knodel, 1974, p. 234). In Switzerland, the correlation between I_g and the proportion of women in industry was -0.334 (F. van de Walle, manuscript). These analyses of the role of women in the demographic transition do not permit generalization, but they do support further inquiry; in particular, it would seem fruitful to explore definitions of the role of women more ample than are expressed by the simple measures of their participation in the labor force used here.

Although urbanization is not an inevitable concomitant of industrialization, in most countries industrial occupations were concentrated in cities. Just as industrialization presents a complex of concepts that might be related to marital fertility, so also does urbanization. In his examination of forerunners of the fertility decline, Livi-Bacci showed that urban populations may have begun the transition well before their country cousins (Chapter 3); because the measures available are usually crude birth rates, however, it is not possible to separate the effect of different marriage patterns in urban and rural areas from variations in marital fertility. When better data make it possible to do so, Sharlin (Chapter 5) finds that urban marital fertility is almost always lower than rural marital fertility. At the time of the decline, if there is a difference in the date of the decline it begins first in urban areas. The larger urban areas have an earlier and swifter decline than the smaller areas; Sharlin also proposes that the specific occupational structure of cities (industrial versus administrative, for example) could well affect the timing and pace of their declines.

Like industrialization and urbanization, education is not a simple concept and is usually crudely measured by illiteracy. The statistical analysis of the correspondence between literacy and marital fertility often shows the relation to be quite weak. Some findings were perverse: in Belgium, for example, Lesthaeghe found that literacy was negatively correlated with marital fertility, as expected, in Wallonia, but positively correlated with marital fertility in Flanders (Lesthaeghe, 1977), and Livi-Bacci had found literacy to be positively correlated with marital fertility in Portugal (Livi-Bacci, 1971). In Switzerland, where F. van de Walle calculated correlations between the proportion of recruits in the Swiss army with the highest scores on an examination of reading, writing, and composition, and the date of 10-percent decline in I_g, the zero-order coefficients were usually between 0.64 and 0.68, suggesting that education rather than literacy may show a stronger relation to the timing of the fertility decline than simple illiteracy (F. van de Walle, 1980).

The analyses reviewed above isolated several of the central relations postulated in the various versions of the demographic transition theory. The relations were, as we have seen, usually weak and often statistically insignificant. Yet bivariate analyses may be misleading. Since changes in the processes that were taken to represent modernization did not occur in isolation, statistical analyses should attempt to take into account the additive and interactive effects of these processes.

In the country monographs, simple multivariate statistical techniques were used to relate provincial variation in I_g to several (usually only three or four) independent variables. More sophisticated statistical techniques may prove to be more fruitful (see, for example, Richards, 1977). Many of the regression equations used the level of I_g at a given time as the dependent variable rather than change in I_g over time, which would have been preferable, since level confounds the influence of nonparity-specific factors with the increasing family limitation that corresponds to a change in I_g. (The few analyses that used change in I_g as the dependent variable did not, however, show markedly different statistical effects.) Although other independent variables, such as the estimates of income and prices often favored by economists, may in retrospect seem more attractive, the variables used were central to the explanations of the fertility transition that were given widespread credence in the post-World War II period.

In many countries and time periods the conventional measure of variance explained, R^2, was over 50 percent. Whether a given R^2 is little or large depends on the level of aggregation, the parsimony, and specification of the equation, and, perhaps most crucially, on the eye of the beholder. Since the specification of the multiple regression equations differed by country and sometimes, as in Belgium, between parts of the same country, a comparison of coefficients among countries is hazardous; the coefficients were ordinarily not large, however, although in some cases relations that had been perverse in the bivariate analyses reverted to the expected direction. Although the measures of modernization used in the European Fertility Project do not well predict provincial differences in marital fertility at any time during the late nineteenth and early twentieth centuries, the differences in level were usually in the expected direction. In general, relatively urban and industrialized provinces with low levels of illiteracy and infant mortality were the leaders in the transition, as seen in their usually lower levels of I_g at a given date.

It is also possible to ask if there was a threshold of change that stimulated a decline in I_g; if there was, one would expect to find that the decline in fertility began when each country was about equally transformed. Knodel and E. van de Walle compared the date of a 10 percent decline in I_g at the level of the country with the infant mortality rate, the percentage of the male labor force in agriculture, the percentage in cities of 20,000 or more, and the percentage illiterate, at that date. They found a wide range of doses at the time of the response: for example, infant mortality rates ranged from 250 deaths per 1,000 live births in Hungary to 69 in Ireland; the percentage in agriculture varied from 70 in France to 13 in Scotland; the percentage in rural areas ranged from 85 in Finland to 26 in the Netherlands (Knodel and E. van de Walle, Chapter 10). Date, it would appear, is a better predictor of the onset of the fertility decline than were these measures of development.

Knodel and E. van de Walle have proposed one solution to this puzzle by gathering evidence to suggest that the emphasis in demographic transition theory on measuring motivation with modernization is misplaced. They propose that there may have been a considerable degree of unwanted childbearing well before there was substantial change in the usual measures of modernization, but that the prevention of births was not considered acceptable within marriage (Knodel and E. van de Walle, Chapter 10). Since motivation did not depend on modernization only, it would follow that once marital fertility was accepted as being within the calculus of conscious choice, deliberate birth control could spread rapidly.

In the course of these attempts to explain differentials in levels of fertility during the period of transition and variations in the timing of the decline, it became evident that clusters of continguous provinces could be viewed as going through the transition together despite what were sometimes significant differences in the extent to which modernization had occurred (Coale, 1973; Anderson, Chapter 7). In country after country it was found that after controlling for the level of modernization, those provinces that were contiguous, and especially those that could be said to share a language, religion, or ethnic identification, or more generally a cultural as well as a spatial location, were similar to each other in initial levels of I_g, in the time of the onset of the transition, and in the speed of decline. Most of the variation in I_g was among regions: within regions, fertility was relatively homogeneous. What was true of marital fertility was also true of nuptiality: when regional boundaries were drawn to conform to longstanding historical divisions (sometimes based on language, sometimes based on administrative convention that presumably reflected cultural differences that were no longer specifiable), I_m was homogeneous in virtually every country within the regions, while the regions differed substantially from one another until at least 1930 (Watkins, Chapter 8).

Although a common language appears to have sometimes facilitated the spread of innovative patterns of fertility control (Lesthaeghe, 1977), it is unlikely that regional boundaries merely represent geographical or linguistic barriers to the diffusion of information or attitudes toward family limitation. Outside of France and some nearby provinces, early fertility declines occurred in two Danish provinces, in Latvia, in St. Petersburg, in the Swedish island of Gotlands, in a few countries in Hungary and in one province in East Serbia (Coale and Treadway, Chapter 2). These areas are not obviously related to France by geography or language, making a simple explanation of diffusion from early-declining France unlikely.

Regional differences in infant mortality, marital fertility, and nuptiality in several of the countries, especially the larger ones, are often notable before the beginning of the demographic transition. If different groups (defined perhaps by religion, ethnicity, or a common way of life) that shared the same regional location behaved differently in ways that affected their demography and if the various regions consisted of different proportions of these groups, then regional differences can be attributed to the variety of social groups in these regions. Similarly, during the transition some groups adopted the new forms of fertility behavior more rapidly than others, and again the composition of the region would affect the timing of the transition for the entire province (Anderson, Chapter 7).

The effect of a group need not, however, be limited to its simple weight in the calculation of the aggregate measures. In European Russia, variation in rural I_g in 1926 (when some provinces had already experienced a 10-percent decline in I_g) was substantial. Provinces that were exclusively Great Russian had higher rural marital fertility than provinces that which contained substantial proportions of "Western" groups, such as Latvians, Estonians, and the Poles of White Russia and the Ukraine. Yet within these provinces, marital fertility was low not just among the Western nationalities but among all. "Apparently, the Western nationalities are not themselves especially prone to low marital fertility; rather, where there are Western nationalities present, conditions were such that marital fertility was relatively low for everyone" (Coale, Anderson, and Härm, 1979, pp. 75–78).

Those who share a common territory are likely to share at least a minimal agreement on a set of conventions. Some of these conventions may appear trivial, such as, in our own society, consensus on rules for motor traffic, or a medium of exchange; others are more profound, such as rules for the acceptable distribution of scarce but valued goods such as medical care. The sway of some, such as those summarized by the Western European marriage pattern, may encompass a large area, while others may be more local. These patterns of preference are persistent, handed down from generation to generation rather than reevaluated or renegotiated by each new cohort. Moreover, specifically demographic conventions encompass many aspects of reproduction, such as the acceptability of extramarital sexual relations or extramarital births, the circumstances determining the initiation or termination of childbearing, the spacing of births, and the relative importance of male and female children; the priorities given to each of these may vary from society to society.

In regions that seem to represent longstanding cultural demarcations within a country, it is reasonable to suppose that provincial similarities in fertility and marriage represent common solutions to the problem of societal reproduction in the context of a particular environment. All societies must maintain a flow of generations and transfer material goods and social values from one generation to another: patterns of reproduction, modes of production, rules of inheritance, and conventions about household formation and dissolution are likely to be central to societal continuity. Thus, childbearing and marriage will be articulated with other aspects of the society, though the specific links themselves as well as the strength of the social commitment to these links may vary from one group to another.

Some social rules that govern behavior may be meant to regulate reproduction, while others may have unintended consequences for mortality, nuptiality, or marital fertility. Migration to early industrial cities often implied a reduced probability of infant and child survival, surely unintended. The age at first marriage (often closely followed by the birth of the first child) will have consequences for completed family size, but the consequences may be unintended if the age at first marriage is determined by the age at which resources to set up an independent household are achieved. Breast-feeding may be determined by (or at least compatible with) the patterns of women's work, while coital frequency may reflect shared perceptions about the appropriate intensity of relations between husbands and wives as compared to the relation between parents and children, or shared perceptions of proper masculine and feminine behavior.

Changes in the environment may have consequences for reproduction even when the rules themselves remain unchanged. Thus, protoindustrialization appears to have been accompanied sometimes by an earlier age at marriage, with consequences for completed fertility (Levine, 1977; Mendels, 1972). That women are responsible for the nourishment of infants will mean breast-feeding when there is no alternative to mother's milk, but it may mean the substitution of bottled milk when it becomes available; the diminution in the proportion of women breast-feeding or the shortening of its duration will, all other things being equal, lead to a rise in fertility. Such rises in marital fertility preceded a 10-percent decline in marital tility in a number of provinces of Europe, and need not be interpreted as the result of a desire for more births.

Moreover, as the environment changes, the rules themselves may be stretched or abandoned: for example, some places in early industrial England saw a temporary relaxation of longstanding preferences for nuclear family households (Anderson, 1972). Just as the rules that regulate reproduction vary from culture to culture, the tenacity with which these rules are maintained when the environment changes is likely to vary; attitudes toward household formation and dissolution may be more flexible and more responsive to immediate circumstances than conceptions of the proper roles of men and women. It has been argued that modernization is a universal social solvent (Levy, 1966) destroying old patterns of social relations and replacing them with new ones: the immediate effect of the solvent, however, is likely to vary as the medium into which it is introduced varies. Thus, region may be seen as summarizing shared conventions linking pretransition modes of production and reproduction which retarded or hastened the effect of modernization on previous patterns of reproduction.

The attempts to distinguish between the leaders and laggards in the fertility decline that have been briefly summarized above are part of a long tradition of interest in fertility differentials in demography. Yet a concern for differentials should not obscure the similarities.

Eventually, the effect of modernization on fertility is much as the theory predicted, for in all relatively modernized societies overall fertility is low. Summarizing the preliminary findings of the European Fertility Project in 1973, Coale wrote that if a relatively modernized society is defined as one which in 1960 had over 50 percent of its population in urban settlements of 20,000 or more, if under 30 percent of the active male population was in agriculture, fishing, or forestry, and if 90 percent of the women between the ages of 6 and 13 were in school, then total fertility in 1960 was low (Coale, 1973).

Coale's findings can be given considerably more detail by focusing attention on provinces, on marital fertility, and on the timing of the initiation of the decline of marital fertility. In all countries except Ireland and Albania, all provinces went through the transition in marital fertility, even those with relatively high levels of illiteracy and infant mortality, and those with relatively low levels of industrialization and urbanization. In most countries, the lag between the date of the 10-percent decline in the first of the leaders and the last of the laggards was relatively short, compared to the long periods in the past during which there is reason to believe that marital fertility was rather stable. Thus, even though urban provinces did experience a 10-percent decline in I_g before the rural provinces in the same country, the rural provinces followed within a few decades. In Denmark, the lag between provincial towns and urban was more than two decades in only one province; in all of the others it was less than fifteen years (Matthiessen, 1985). The similarities in rural-urban timing may be the result of the diffusion of either ideas or birth control techniques, or of subtle changes in rural socioeconomic structures attendant on proximity to urban places. It is likely that migrants or rural dwellers who visited the city brought back new ideas and/or techniques that may have been adopted even though the socioeconomic circumstances in the rural areas had not yet changed in the ways postulated by demographic transition theory. Proximity to a city, however, also means proximity to urban markets for rural produce, and may have changed the context in which families lived without a change in occupations or residence.

It also appears that the different occupational groups may have begun the fertility transition within a relatively short period of time. In Prussia the fertility rates of agricultural workers were higher than those of workers in three other large occupational groups between 1882 and 1907, but fertility rates in all four occupational groups declined during those years (Knodel, 1974, p. 115). Similarly, in most of the German villages analyzed there was an increase in family limitation in each of the three occupational groups (artisan, farmer, and laborer) during the period 1850–1899 (Knodel, Chapter 9, Table 9.11). When consideration is extended to groups characterized on the basis of religion, there are also similarities in the timing of the onset of the transition. Again in Germany, while predominantly Catholic provinces had consistently higher fertility levels than provinces with few Catholics, the differences in the dates at which the transition was initiated were small (Knodel, 1974, pp. 133 and 136).

These findings suggest that the effect of modernization need not be confined to those individuals who adopt new occupations, who move to the city, who learn to read. Education facilitated the spread of new attitudes and techniques even to the uneducated. The establishment of centers of industrial production within a province not only affected those who entered the factory, but also altered the context of work for those who remained in traditional occupations. Relations between town and country took on new forms and intensities as production developed, thus changing the nature of rural agricultural production. The environment of the city may have rearranged the relative values of investments in children and in other goods, but its bright lights were also reflected far beyond its boundaries, in tales told in the hinterland. The new ways of making a living that were adopted by some surely expanded the horizons of the possible for others, offering avenues of opportunity—either escape or negotiation *in situ*—that were not perceived earlier.

The evidence that would permit assessment of similarities and differences in the timing of the transition in marital fertility in groups such as these is still quite sparse, for much research has concentrated on levels of fertility rather than on the timing of the change. The timing of the onset of the transition is, however, particularly significant in view of the findings of the European Fertility Project that once a 10-percent decline in I_g occurred, further decline invariably followed. Seen against the centuries of apparent stability in marital fertility, these similarities in timing are impressive. They are also puzzling. Demographic transition theory had predicted that some individuals or groups would be expected to find an advantage in having fewer children, while others would continue to find more children valuable; there is some support for this in the analysis of leaders and laggards during the transition, although the statistical relations are usually weak. Curiously, however, even those who could be expected to find continued child-bearing advantageous or family limitation unacceptable adopted family limitation rather soon after the leaders.

Conclusions

Where, then, do our descriptions and explanations stand after two decades, eleven volumes, hundreds of tables, figures, and maps, and thousands of words of the European Fertility Project?

The sheer accumulation of data, particularly the calculation of indexes of demographic change for the approximately six hundred provinces of Europe at ten-year intervals over the last century, has permitted a more detailed description of the demographic transition than was possible when using cruder measures and larger aggregates, and a more comprehensive one than that based on town or village. Although these dry numbers by no means tell the whole story, they do provide a setting into which the subtle understandings of social historians, economists, anthropologists, and others can be placed. They are also enough to require that the classic descriptions and explanations of the demographic transition in Europe be modified.

The indexes have given a scale to the usual schematic depiction, and make it clear that aggregate fertility in the past was high only relative to the present. Against a scale derived from well-recorded fertility levels rather than anecdotal evidence of the social supports to high fertility, both overall and marital fertility in the past appear as relatively moderate. Overall fertility (I_f) was about a third to a half of what it would have been had women married at the beginning of their reproductive years, and borne children at the rate of the prolific and reliably recorded Hutterites; marital fertility (I_g) was about three-quarters of that standard. It may be true, as Notestein wrote in 1953, that "peasant societies in Europe . . . are organized in ways that bring strong pressures on their members to reproduce," but these pressures were muted by community customs that had the effect of limiting births. The distinction between measures of overall fertility, marital fertility, and nuptiality also permitted demonstration that the social control of fertility could vary substantially from province to province.

The fall in the level of fertility sketched out in the usual descriptions of the demographic transition in nineteenth-century Europe was not in itself unprecedented, for a decline of comparable magnitude had occurred previously in England. This earlier decline, and the subsequent rise, were but an extreme version of the effect on births of fluctuations in nuptiality, which Wrigley and Schofield have traced to variations in the economy (Wrigley and Schofield, 1981). What was apparently new in the nineteenth and early twentieth centuries was the responsiveness of marital fertility. Pre-transition levels of marital fertility varied from parish to parish or province to province, but the levels were stable over time. Once the transition began, flexibility in reproduction was achieved by marital fertility as well as, or often instead of, by marriage.

Before the transition the rich tapestry woven by the biological and behavioral determinants of overall fertility did not include, for any significant proportion of couples, the termination of childbearing between marriage and menopause. Now, in contrast, there are few couples who do not deliberately end childbearing before the onset of physiological sterility. Thus merely measuring changes in the level of marital fertility does not adequately capture the revolution in reproductive arrangements. The transition consisted not only of a reduction in the average number of children born to a couple—a fall which, after all, had occurred before—but also in the adoption of behavior by which childbearing terminated at an earlier stage in the couple's reproductive years.

This innovative behavior was adopted with great rapidity, compared to the long periods in the past when marital fertility was stable. Within a province, once marital fertility had fallen by 10 percent, the decline almost always continued—albeit sometimes slowly and hesitantly, sometimes quickly and precipitously—until very low levels of marital fertility were reached. In most provinces, marital fertility had not begun to decline by 1870; by 1930, I_g was at half of pre-decline levels almost everywhere. A comparison of the dates of the 10-percent decline in I_g shows that the initiation of the decline was highly compressed, both temporally and spatially. If France is excluded, more than half of the provinces of Europe began their sustained decline during a period of three decades, between 1890 and 1920. The declines generally occurred first in the provinces of northwest Europe, and somewhat later in the peripheral areas of southern and eastern Europe. Nevertheless, although there were provincial leaders and laggards in the transition, seen against the backdrop of centuries the gap between them was relatively short; in most countries less than a century separated the first provincial decline from the last. In one, England, the lag was no more than sixteen years.

Classic statements of demographic transition theory led to expectations that the leaders in the fertility transition would be provinces in which few infants died and in which many adults were literate, worked in industrial occupations, and lived in cities. In general these simply stated and crudely measured expectations were upheld, although the statistical relations were usually weak. Some of the analyses suggested that substituting measures of childhood for infant mortality and education for illiteracy, combining occupations in agriculture with those in cottage industry, and including a measure of secularization would improve our ability to distinguish between leaders and laggards.

The decline in marital fertility can precede significant modernization, simply defined, as it did in France and among some forerunners elsewhere: the European experience suggests that modernization is sufficient but not necessary. Nor is the response of fertility to the changes that define or accompany modernization always immediate: the lag may be quite variable and seems to be associated with longstanding cultural differences. The findings that contiguous provinces that shared a cultural as well as geographical location had similar levels of nuptiality and fertility and similar patterns of decline give reasons to believe that the set of preexisting regional conventions by which reproduction is articulated with other social arrangements may mute for one group of provinces or enhance for another the impact of changes associated with the usual measures of modernization.

Although the goals of the European Fertility Project were primarily to describe and explain differentials in the fertility transition, a concern for differentials should not obscure the similarities. To be sure, the details of pre-transition circumstances and the pattern of decline differed from province to province, region to region, and country to country, and roughly comparable measures of modernization do explain some of the differences in the initiation of what was to be an irreversible decline in marital fertility. Although relatively modernized provinces usually began the transition earlier, those with relatively high infant mortality and illiteracy and relatively low levels of industrialization and urbanization followed within a few decades, well before they had reached the same threshold of social and economic change as the pioneers.

It would appear that the new ways of living adopted by some change the landscape for all. In the context of a concern for lessons that can be exported from nineteenth-century Europe to contemporary countries elsewhere, it is tempting to emphasize diversity; in the context of the history of fertility in Europe, the similarities, in the end, seem the most likely to be instructive.

References

Anderson, Barbara A. 1978. Some Factors Related to Ethnic Reidentification in the Russian Republic. In *Soviet Nationality Policies and Practices*, edited by Jeremy Azrael. New York: Praeger.

Anderson, Barbara A., and Silver, Brian D. 1983. Estimating Russification of Ethnic Identity of Non-Russians in the USSR. *Demography* 20(4): 461–489.

Anderson, Michael. 1972. Family Structure in Nineteenth-Century Lancashire. Cambridge, Eng.: Cambridge University Press.

Andorka, Rudolf. 1971. La prévention des naissances en Hongrie dans la région Ormansag depuis la fin du XVIIIe siècle. *Population* 26(1): 63–78.

———. 1972. Un exemple de faible fécondité légitime dans une région de la Hongrie. *Annales de Démographie Historique* (1972), pp. 25–53.

———. 1978. *Determinants of Fertility in Advanced Societies*. New York: The Free Press.

———. 1979. Family Reconstitution and Types of Household Structures. In *Time, Space and Man*, edited by Jan Sundin and Erik Soderlund, pp. 4–33. Atlantic Highlands, N.J.: Humanities Press.

Ariès, Philippe. 1960. Interprétation pour une histoire des mentalités. In *La Prévention des naissances dans la famille: Ses origines dans les temps modernes*, by Hélène Bergues et al., pp. 311–327. Institut National d'Etudes Démographiques, Travaux et Documents, Cahier No. 35. Paris: Presses Universitaires de France.

Armengaud, André. 1973. L'Attitude de la société à l'égard de l'enfant au XIXe siècle. *Annales de Démographie Historique* (1973), pp. 303–312.

Arthur, W. Brian, and McNicoll, Geoffrey. 1978. An Analytical Survey of Population and Development in Bangladesh. *Population and Development Review* 4(1): 23–80.

Bachi, Roberto. 1981. Marriage and Fertility in Jewish Traditional Society. Jerusalem: Israel Academy of Science and Humanities.

Barclay, George W.; Coale, Ansley J.; Stoto, Michael; and Trussell, T. James. 1976. A Reassessment of the Demography of Traditional Rural China. *Population Index* 42(4): 606–635.

Bardet, Jean-Pierre. 1974. La Démographie des villes de la modernité (XVIe–XVIIIe siècles): Mythes et réalités. *Annales de Démographie Historique* (1974), pp. 101–126.

Barton, Allen H. 1968. Bringing Society Back In. *American Behavioral Scientist* 12: 1–9.

———. 1970. Comment on Hauser's "Context and Consex." *American Journal of Sociology* 76(3): 514–517.

Bellet, Daniel. 1900. La Vie économique. In *Le Portugal*, by Brito Aranha et al. Paris: Librairie Larousse.

Beltrami, Danièle. 1954. *Storia della popolazione di Venezia dalla fine del secolo XVI alla caduta della republica.* Padua: CEDAM (Casa Editrice Dott. Antonio Milani).

Berger, Peter L. 1973. *The Social Reality of Religion.* Harmondsworth, England: Penguin University Books.

Bergues, Hélène, et al. 1960. *La Prévention des naissances dans la famille: Ses origines dans les temps modernes.* Institut National d'Etudes Démographiques, Travaux et Documents, Cahier No. 35. Paris: Presses Universitaires de France.

Black, C. E., editor. 1976. *Comparative Modernization.* New York: Free Press.

Black, Cyril E.; Jansen, Marius B.; Levine, Herbert S.; Levy, Marion J., Jr.; Rosovsky, Henry; Rozman, Gilbert; Smith, Henry D. II; and Starr, Frederick. 1975. *The Modernization of Japan and Russia.* New York: The Free Press.

Blake, Judith, and Das Gupta, Prithwis. 1975. Reproductive Motivation versus Contraceptive Technology: Is Recent American Experience an Exception? *Population and Development Review* 1(2): 229–249.

Blalock, Hubert M., Jr. 1968. The Measurement Problem: A Gap between the Languages of Theory and Research. In *Methodology in Social Research*, edited by Hubert M. Blalock, Jr., and Ann B. Blalock. New York: McGraw-Hill.

Blau, Peter M. 1960. Structural Effects. *American Sociological Review* 25: 178–193.

———. 1977. *Inequality and Heterogeneity.* New York: The Free Press.

Blayo, Yves. 1975. La Mortalité en France de 1740 à 1829. *Population*, vol. 30, Numéro Spécial, pp. 123–142.

Bloch, Oscar. 1921. *La Pénétration du français dans les parlers des Vosges méridionales.* Paris: Librairie Ancienne Honoré Champion.

Bluhm, A. 1912. Stillhaufigkeit und Stilldauer. In *Handwörterbuch der Sozialen Hygiene*, edited by A. Grotjahn and J. Kaup. Vol. 2, pp. 570–591. Leipzig: F.C.W. Vogel.

Bongaarts, John. 1975. A Method for the Estimation of Fecundability. *Demography* 12(4): 645–660.

———. 1978. A Framework for Analyzing the Proximate Determinants of Fertility. *Population and Development Review* 4: 105–132.

———. 1980. Does Malnutrition Affect Fecundity? A Summary of the Evidence. *Science* 208: 564–569.

Boserup, Ester. 1970. *Women's Role in Economic Development.* London: Allen & Unwin.

Boulard, F. 1960. *An Introduction to Religious Sociology.* London: Darton, Longman and Todd.

Bourgeois-Pichat, J. 1965. The General Development of the Population of France since the Eighteenth Century. In *Population in History: Essays in Historical Demography*, edited by D. V. Glass and D.E.C. Eversley, pp. 474–506. Chicago: Aldine.

Bouvier, Leon F.; Macisco, John J., Jr.; and Zarate, Alvin. 1976. Toward a Framework for the Analysis of Differential Migration: The Case of Education. In *Internal Migration: The New World and the Third World*, edited by Anthony H. Richmond and Daniel Kubat. Sage Studies in International Sociology 4. Beverly Hills, Calif. Sage Publications.

Bowers, William J. 1968. Normative Constraints on Deviant Behavior in the College Context. *Sociometry* 31(4): 370–385.

Braun, Rudolf. 1978. Protoindustrialization and Demographic Changes in the Canton of Zurich. In *Historical Studies of Changing Fertility*, edited by Charles Tilly, pp. 289–334. Princeton: Princeton University Press.

Brezing, Karl. 1963. *Dorfsippenbuch Öschelbronn.* No publisher given.

Brun, Auguste. 1923a. *L'Introduction de la langue française en Béarn et en Rousillon.* Paris: Librairie Ancienne Honoré Champion.

———. 1923b. *Récherches historiques sur l'introduction du français dans les provinces du midi.* Paris: Librairie Ancienne Honoré Champion.

———. 1927. *La Langue française en Provence de Louis XIV au Félibrige.* Marseille: Institut Historique de Provence.

Burgière, André. 1972. De Malthus à Max Weber: Le Mariage tardif et l'esprit d'entreprise. *Annales E.S.C.* 4–5: *1128–1138.*

Caldwell, J. C. 1979. Variations in the Incidence of Sexual Abstinence and the Duration of Postnatal Abstinence among the Yoruba of Nigeria. In *Natural Fertility Patterns and Determinants of Natural Fertility:*

Proceedings of a Seminar, edited by H. Leridon and J. Menken. Liège: Ordina Editions.

Caldwell, John C. 1976. Toward a Restatement of Demographic Transition Theory. *Population and Development Review* 2(3-4): 321–366.

———. 1977. The Economic Rationality of High Fertility: An Investigation Illustrated with Nigerian Survey Data. *Population Studies* 31(1): 5–27.

Caldwell, John C. 1982. *Theory of Fertility Decline*. New York: Academic Press.

Caldwell, John C., and Ruzicka, Lado T. 1978. The Australian Fertility Transition: An Analysis. *Population and Development Review* 4(1): 81–103.

Carlsson, Gösta. 1966. The Decline of Fertility: Innovation or Adjustment Process. *Population Studies* 20(2): 149–174.

Chatelain, Abel. 1977. *Les Migrants temporaires en France de 1800 à 1914: Histoire economique et sociale des migrants temporaires des campagnes françaises au XIXe siècle et au début du XXe siècle*. 2 vols. Villeneuve-d'Ascq, France: Université de Lille III.

Chaudhury, Rafiqual Huda, and Ahmed, Nilufer Raihan. 1979. *Female Status in Bangladesh*. Dacca: Bangladesh Institute of Development Studies.

Chaunu, Pierre. 1973. Reflexions sur la démographie normande. In *Sur la population française au XVIIIe et XIXe siècles*. Paris: Société de Démographie Historique.

Coale, Ansley J. 1965. Factors Associated with the Development of Low Fertility: An Historic Summary. In *United Nations World Population Conference, Belgrade, 1965*, vol. 2, pp. 205–207. New York.

Coale, Ansley J. 1969. The Decline of Fertility in Europe from the French Revolution to World War II. In *Fertility and Family Planning*, edited by S. J. Behrman, Leslie Corsa, and Ronald Freedman. Ann Arbor, Michigan: University of Michigan Press.

———. 1971. Age Patterns of Marriage. *Population Studies* 25(2): 193–214.

———. 1973. The Demographic Transition Reconsidered. In *International Population Conference, Liège, 1973*, vol. 1, pp. 53–72. Liège: International Union for the Scientific Study of Population. Also published in *The Population Debate: Dimensions and Perspectives. Papers of the World Population Conference, Bucharest, 1974*, vol. 1, pp. 347–355. New York: United Nations, 1975.

Coale, Ansley J.; Anderson, Barbara A.; and Härm, Erna. 1979. *Human Fertility in Russia since the Nineteenth Century.* Princeton: Princeton University Press.

Coale, Ansley J., and Demeny, Paul. 1966. *Regional Model Life Tables and Stable Populations.* Princeton: Princeton University Press.

Coale, Ansley J., and Trussell, T. James. 1974. Model Fertility Schedules: Variations in the Age Structure of Childbearing in Human Populations. *Population Index* 40(2): 185–258. Erratum, *Population Index* 41(4): 572.

———. 1978. Technical Note: Finding the Two Parameters That Specify a Model Schedule of Marital Fertility. *Population Index* 44(2): 203–213.

Coleman, James S. 1968. The Mathematical Study of Change. In *Methodology in Social Research,* edited by Hubert M. Blalock. New York: McGraw-Hill.

Connell, John; Dasgupta, Bislab; Laishlay, Roy; and Lipton, Michael. 1974. *Migration from Rural Areas.* Delhi: Oxford University Press.

Cooney, Rosemary S., and Ortiz, Vilma. 1979. Labor Market Areas and Hispanic Females in the Labor Force. A paper presented at the annual meeting of the American Sociological Association, Washington, D.C.

Damas, H. 1964. Population de la Belgique: Les Migrations intérieures. *Population et Famille/Bevolking en Gezin,* no. 4, pp. 31–62.

Dauzat, Albert. 1927.*Les Patois.* Paris: Librairie Delagrave.

Davis, James A.; Spaeth, Joe L; and Huson, Carolyn. 1961. A Technique for Analyzing the Effects of Group Composition. *American Sociological Review* 26: 215–225.

Davis, Kingsley. 1977. World Population Growth and United States Foreign Policy. Statement prepared for hearings before the Committee on Appropriations of the House of Representatives, March 31, 1977.

———. 1978. Population Growth and Policy in the Less Developed World. Testimony before the House Select Committee on Population, February 9, 1978.

Day, Lincoln. 1968. Natality and Ethnocentrism: Some Relationships Suggested by an Analysis of Catholic-Protestant Differentials. *Population Studies* 22(1): 27–50.

Demeny, Paul. 1968. Early Fertility Decline in Austria-Hungary: A Lesson in Demographic Transition. *Daedalus,* pp. 502–522.

———. 1974. The Populations of the Underdeveloped Countries. *Scientific American* 231(3): 149–159.

———. 1975a. Letter to the Editor. *Scientific American* 232(5): 6.

———. 1975b. Observations on Population Policy and Population Program in Bangladesh. *Population and Development Review* 1(2): 307–321.

Demerath, Nicholas J. 1976. *Birth Control and Foreign Policy: The Alternatives to Family Planning.* New York: Harper and Row.

Dixon, Ruth. 1978. *Rural Women at Work.* Baltimore: Johns Hopkins University Press.

Dumond, D. E. 1975. The Limitation of Human Population: A Natural History. *Science* 187: 713–721.

Dupâquier, Jacques. 1972. De l'Animal à l'homme: Le Mécanisme autoregulateur des populations traditionelles. *Revue de l'Institut de Sociologie, Université Libre de Bruxelles,* no. 2, pp. 177–211.

———. 1979. Etude comparative des données concernant la fecondité dans 25 monographies concernant le bassin Parisen à la fin du XVIIe siècle et au début du XVIIIe siècle. In *Natural Fertility,* edited by Henri Leridon and Jane Menken, pp. 409–439. Liége: Ordina.

Dupâquier, J., and Lachiver, M. 1969. Sur les débuts de la contraception en France ou les deux Malthusianismes. *Annales—Economies, Sociétés, Civilisations* 24(6): 139–1406.

Easterlin, Richard A. 1975. An Economic Framework for Fertility Analysis. *Studies in Family Planning* 6(3): 54–63.

———. 1976. Population Change and Farm Settlement in the Northern United States. *Journal of Economic History* 36(1).

Erbring, Lutz, and Young, Alice A. 1979. Individuals and Social Structure: Contextual Effects and Endogenous Feedback. *Sociological Methods and Research* 7(4): 396–420.

Evans, Peter. 1979. *Dependent Development: The Alliance of Multinational, State, and Local Capital in Brazil.* Princeton: Princeton University Press.

Eversley, D. E. C. 1965. Population, Economy and Society. In *Population in History: Essays in Historical Demography,* edited by D. V. Glass and D. E. C. Eversley, pp. 23–69. Chicago: Aldine.

Finlay, Rager P. 1981. *Population and Metropolis: The Demography of London, 1580–1650.* Cambridge, Eng.: Cambridge University Press.

Fahlbeck, Pontus E. 1903. *Der Adel Schwedens (und Finlands): Eine demographische Stüdie.* Jena, German Democratic Republic: G. Fischer.

Firebaugh, Glenn. 1979. Assessing Group Effects: A Comparison of Methods. *Sociological Methods and Research* 7(4): 384–395.

Flinn, Michael, editor. 1977. *Scottish Population History: From the Seventeenth Century to the 1930s.* Cambridge, England: Cambridge University Press.

Forrest, Jacqueline E. D. 1975. Fertility Decline in Austria, 1880–1910. Ph.D. dissertation, Princeton University.

Freedman, Ronald. 1961–1962. The Sociology of Human Fertility: A Trend Report and Bibliography. *Current Sociology/La Sociologie Contemporaine* 10–11(2): 35–119.

———. 1974. Community-Level Data in Fertility Surveys. Occasional Papers No. 8, World Fertility Survey.

Freud, Sigmund. 1930. *Civilization and Its Discontents.* Translated and edited by James Strachez. New York: W. W. Norton & Co., Inc., 1961.

Friedlander, Dov. 1969. Demographic Responses and Population Change. *Demography* 6(4).

———. 1973. Demographic Patterns and Socioeconomic Characteristics of the Coal-Mining Population in England and Wales in the Nineteenth Century. *Economic Development and Cultural Change* 22(1): 39:51.

———. 1977. The Effect of Child Mortality on Fertility: Theoretical Framework of the Relationship. In *International Population Conference, Mexico, 1977*, vol. 1, pp. 183–203. Liège: International Union for the Scientific Study of Population.

Frisch, Rose E. 1978. Population, Food Intake, and Fertility. *Science* 199: 22–30.

———. 1982. Malnutrition and Fertility. *Science* 215: 1272–1273.

Galbraith, J. K. 1971. *Economics, Peace and Laughter.* Harmondsworth, England: Pelican Books.

Garden, Maurice. 1977. La Démographie des villes françaises du XVIIIe siècle: Quelques approches. In *Démographie urbaine, XVe-XXe siècle: Actes des troisièmes rencontres Franco-Suisses, Lyon, 23–24 Avril* 1976, pp. 43–85. Lyon: Centre d'Histoire Economique et Sociale de la Région Lyonnaise, Université de Lyon II.

Gaunt, David. 1973. Family Planning and the Preindustrial Society: Some Swedish Evidence. In *Aristocrats, Farmers and Proletarians: Essays in Swedish Demographic History*, edited by Kurt Agren et al., pp. 28–59. Uppsala: Almqvist and Wiksell Informationsindustri.

Gautier, Etienne, and Henry, Louis. 1958. *La Population de Crulai, Paroisse Normande: Etude historique.* Institut National d'Etudes Démographiques, Travaux et Documents, Cahier No. 33. Paris: Presses Universitaires de France.

Goldscheider, Calvin. 1971. *Population, Modernization and Social Structure.* Boston: Little, Brown.

Goldscheider, Calvin, and Uhlenberg, P. R. 1969. Minority Group Status and Fertility. *American Journal of Sociology* 74: 361–372.

Goldstein, Alice. 1981. Some Demographic Characteristics of Village Jews in Germany: Nonnenweier, 1800–1931. In *Modern Jewish Fertility,* edited by P. Ritterband. Leiden: Brill.

———. 1985. Determinants of Change and Response among Jews and Catholics in a Nineteenth-Century German Village. New York: Conference of Jewish Social Studies.

Greppi, A. 1970. Indagine demografica sull'aristocrazia Genovese nei secoli XVII-XVIII. Ph.D. dissertation, Università di Genova.

Grimm, Baron de, and Diderot, Denis. 1813. *Correspondance Littéraire, Philosophique et Critique.* Vol. 5. Paris.

Habakkuk, H. J. 1955. Family Structure and Economic Change in Nineteenth-Century Europe. *Journal of Economic History* 15(1): 1–12.

———. 1974. *Population Growth and Economic Development since 1750.* Leicester, England: Leicester University Press.

Haines, Michael. 1979. *Fertility and Occupation: Population Patterns in Industrialization.* New York: Academic Press.

Hajnal, John. 1953a. Age at Marriage and Proportions Marrying. *Population Studies* 7(2): 111–136.

———. 1953b. The Marriage Boom. *Population Index* 19(2): 80–101.

———. 1965. European Marriage Patterns in Perspective. In *Population in History: Essays in Historical Demography,* edited by D. V. Glass and D.E.C. Eversley, pp. 101–143. London: Edward Arnold.

Hauf, Franz. 1975. *Ortsippenbuch Gabelbach.* Frankfurt: Zentralstelle fur Personen- und Familiengeschichte.

Hauser, Robert. 1970a. Context and Consex: A Cautionary Tale. *American Journal of Sociology* 75(4): 645–679.

———. 1970b. The Author Replies. *American Journal of Sociology* 76(3): 517–520.

———. 1974. Contextual Analysis Revisited. *Sociological Methods and Research* 2(3): 365–375.

Hechter, Michael. 1975. *Internal Colonialism: The Celtic Fringe in British National Development*. Berkeley: University of California Press.

Helias, Pierre-Jakez. 1978. *The Horse of Pride*. New Haven, Conn.: Yale University Press.

Hélin, Etienne. 1973. Une Sollicitude ambigué: L'Évacuation des enfants abandonnés. *Annales de Démographie Historique* (1973), pp. 225–229.

Henry, Louis. 1956. *Anciennes familles genevoises. Etude Démographique: XVIe–XXe siècle*. Institut National d'Etudes Démographiques, Travaux et Documents, Cahier No. 26. Paris: Presses Universitaires de France.

———. 1961. Some Data on Natural Fertility. *Eugenics Quarterly* 8(2): 81–91.

Henry, Louis, and Houdaille, Jacques. 1973. Fécondité des mariages dans le quart nord-ouest de la France de 1670 à 1829. *Population* 28(4–5): 873–924.

Henry, Louis, and Levy, Claude. 1960. Ducs et pairs sous l'ancien régime: Caractéristiques démographiques d'une caste. *Population* 15(5): 807–830.

Hermalin, Albert I., and van de Walle, Etienne. 1977. The Civil Code and Nuptiality: Empirical Investigation of a Hypothesis. In *Population Patterns in the Past*, edited by Ronald D. Lee, pp. 71–111. New York: Academic Press.

Herman, Jan. 1980. The Evolution of the Jewish Population in Prague, 1869–1939. In *Papers in Jewish Demography, 1977*, edited by U. O. Schmelz, P. Glikson, and S. Della Pergola, pp. 53–67. Jerusalem: Institute of Contemporary Jewry, Hebrew University of Jerusalem.

Hersch, Liebman. 1948. Jewish Population Trends in Europe (Prior to World War II). In *The Jewish People: Past and Present*, vol. 2, pp. 1–24. New York: Jewish Encyclopedic Handbooks, Central Yiddish Culture Organization.

Himes, Norman E. 1936 and 1963. *Medical History of Contraception*. New York: Gamut Press.

Hofstee, E. W. 1972. Enkele opmerkingen over de ontwikkeling van de huwelijksvruchtbaarheid in Nederland. *Mens en Maatschappij*, pp. 43–91.

———. 1978a. *De Demografische Ontwikkeling van Nederland in de Eerste Helft van de Negentiende Eeuw: Een Historisch-Demografische en Sociologische Studie*. Deventer, Netherlands: Van Loghum Slaterus.

———. 1978b. Paper presented at the 50th Anniversary Conference of the Nederlandse Vereniging voor Demografie, Utrecht.

Holbing, M. 1845. Baranya varmegyenek orvosi helyirata (Medical Description of the Country of Baranya). Pecs.

Hollingsworth, T. H. 1964. The Demography of the British Peerage. Supplement to *Population Studies* 18(2).

Homans, George C. 1969. The Explanation of English Regional Differences. *Past and Present* 43: 18–34.

Hufton, Olwen. 1974. *The Poor of Eighteenth-Century France, 1750–1789.* Oxford: Clarendon Press.

Huston, Perdita. 1978. *Message from the Village.* New York: Epoch B. Foundation.

Imhof, Arthur E. 1975. Die namentliche Auswertung der Kirchenbücher. Die Familien von Giessen 1631–1730 und Heuchelheim 1691–1900. In *Historische Demographie als Sozialgeschichte*, edited by Arthur E. Imhof. Darmstadt: Selbstverlag der Hessischen Historischen Kommission Darmstadt und der Historischen Kommission für Hessen.

Janssen, Ludwig. 1966. *Die Familien der Kirchengemeinde Middels.* Aurich, Federal Republic of Germany: Verlag Ostfriesische Landschaft.

———. 1971. *Die Familien der Kirchengemeinde Werdum.* Part 1. Aurich, Federal Republic of Germany: Verlag Ostfriesische Landschaft.

Janssen, Ludwig, and Manger, Hans Rudolf. 1975. *Die Familien der Kirchengemeinde Werdum.* Part 2. Aurich, Federal Republic of Germany: Verlag Ostfriesische Landschaft.

Kann, Robert A. 1950. *The Multinational Empire: Nationalism and National Reform in the Habsburg Monarchy, 1848–1918.* 2 vols. New York: Columbia University Press.

———. 1957. *The Habsburg Empire: A Study in Integration and Disintegration.* New York: Praeger.

Katz, J. 1959. Family, Kinship and Marriage among Ashkenazim in the Sixteenth to Eighteenth Centuries. *Jewish Journal of Sociology* 1: 4–23.

Kintner, Hallie. 1982. The Determinants of Infant Mortality in Germany from 1871 to 1933. Ph.D. dissertation, Department of Sociology, University of Michigan, Ann Arbor.

Kirk, Dudley. 1946. *Europe's Population in the Interwar Years.* New York: Gordon and Breach Science Publishers.

Knodel, John. 1967. Law, Marriage and Illegitimacy in Nineteenth-Century Germany. *Population Studies* 20(3): 279–294.

———. 1968. Infant Mortality and Fertility in Three Bavarian Villages: An Analysis of Family Histories from the Nineteenth Century. *Population Studies* 22(3): 297–318.
———. 1970. Two and a Half Centuries of Demographic History in a Bavarian Village. *Population Studies* 24(3): 353–376.
———. 1974. *The Decline of Fertility in Germany, 1871–1939.* Princeton: Princeton University Press.
———. 1975. Ortsippenbücher als Quelle für die historische Demographie. *Geschichte und Gesellschaft* 1(2–3): 288–324.
———. 1977a. Breast-Feeding and Population Growth. *Science* 198(4322): 1111–1115.
———. 1977b. Family Limitation and the Fertility Transition: Evidence from Age Patterns of Fertility in Europe and Asia. *Population Studies* 31(2): 219–249.
———. 1977c. Town and Country in Nineteenth-Century Germany: A Review of Urban-Rural Differentials in Demographic Behavior. *Social Science History* 1(3): 356–382.
———. 1978a. European Populations in the Past: Family-Level Relations. In *The Effects of Infant and Child Mortality on Fertility*, edited by Samuel H. Preston, pp. 21–45. New York: Academic Press.
———. 1978b. Fertility Transition in Rural Germany: An Analysis of Family History Data. Paper presented at the Social Science History Association Meetings, Columbus, Ohio, November 3–5, 1978.
———. 1978c. Natural Fertility in Pre-Industrial Germany. *Population Studies* 32(3): 481–510.
———. 1979. From Natural Fertility to Family Limitation: The Onset of Fertility Transition in a Sample of German Villages. *Demography* 16: 493–521.
———. 1981. Child Mortality and Reproductive Behavior in German Village Populations in the Past: A Micro-Level Analysis of the Replacement Effect. Research Report No. 81–1. Population Studies Center, University of Michigan.
———. 1982. Natural Fertility: Age Patterns, Levels, Trends. In *Determinants of Fertility in Developing Countries*, edited by Rudolfo A. Bulatao and Ronald D. Lee. New York: Academic Press.
Knodel, John, and Debavalya, Nibhon. 1978. Thailand's Reproductive Revolution. *International Family Planning Perspectives and Digest* 4(2): 34–49.
Knodel, John, and Kintner, Hallie. 1977. The Impact of Breast-Feeding

Patterns on the Biometric Analysis of Infant Mortality. *Demography* 14(4): 391–409.

Knodel, John, and Maynes, Mary Jo. 1976. Urban and Rural Marriage Patterns in Imperial Germany. *Journal of Family History* 1(2): 129–168.

Knodel, John, and Shorter, Edward. 1976. The Reliability of Family Reconstitution Data in German Village Genealogies (Ortsippenbücher). *Annales de Démographie Historique* (1976), pp. 115–154.

Knodel, John, and van de Walle, Etienne. 1967. Breastfeeding, Fertility and Infant Mortality: An Analysis of Some Early German Data. *Population Studies* 21(2): 109–131.

Knodel, John, and Wilson, Chris. 1981. The Secular Increase in Fecundity in German Village Populations. *Population Studies* 35(1): 53–84.

Köbele, Albert. 1967. *Sippenbuch der Stadt Herbolzheim im Breisgau, Landkreis Emmendingen in Baden.* Grafenhausen bei Lahr, Federal Republic of Germany: Selbstverlag des Herausgebers.

———. 1969. *Dorfsippenbuch Kappel am Rhein.* 2d ed. Grafenhausen bei Lahr, Federal Republic of Germany: Selbstverlag des Herausgebers.

———. 1971. *Ortsippenbuch Grafenhausen.* Grafenhausen bei Lahr, Federal Republic of Germany: Selbstverlag des Herausgebers.

Koebel, W. H. 1909. *Portugal: Its Land and People.* London: Archibald Constable.

Kollmann, Wolfgang. 1976. Bevölkerungsgeschichte 1800–1970. In *Handbuch der Deutschen Wirtschafts- und Sozialgeschichte.* Vol. 2, pp. 9–50. Stuttgart: Klett.

Konner, M., and Worthman, C. 1980. Nursing Frequency, Gonadal Function, and Birth Spacing among !Kung Hunter-Gatherers. *Science* 207: 788–791.

Kuhn, Thomas S. 1962. *The Structure of Scientific Revolutions.* Chicago: University of Chicago Press.

Lachiver, Marcel. 1973. Fécondité légitime et contraception dans la région parisienne. In *Sur la population française au XVIIIe et au XIXe siècles. Hommage à Marcel Reinhard*, pp. 383–401. Paris: Société de Démographie Historique.

Langer, William L. 1972. Checks on Population Growth: 1750–1850. *Scientific American* 226(2): 92–99.

———. 1974. Infanticide: A Historical Survey. *History of Childhood Quarterly* 1(3): 353–365.

Leasure, J. William. 1962. Factors Involved in the Decline of Fertility in Spain, 1900–1950. Ph.D. dissertation, Princeton University.

Lee, R. 1980. Lactation, Ovulation, Infanticide, and Woman's Work: A Study of Hunter-Gatherer Population Regulation. In *Biosocial Mechanisms of Population Regulation*, edited by Cohen, Nealpase, and Klein. New Haven, Conn.: Yale University Press.

Lee, W. R. 1977. *Population Growth, Economic Development and Social Change in Bavaria, 1750–1850.* New York: Arno Press.

———. 1979. Germany. Chapter 4 in *European Demography and Economic Growth*, edited by W. Robert Lee, pp. 144–195. London: Croom-Helm.

———. 1980. The Mechanism of Mortality Change in Germany, 1750–1850. *Medizin Historisches Journal* 15: 244–268.

Le Roy Ladurie, Emmanuel, and Dumont, Paul. 1971. Quantitative and Cartographical Exploitation of French Military Archives, 1819–1926. *Daedalus* 100(2): 397–444.

Lesthaeghe, Ron J. 1977. *The Decline of Belgian Fertility, 1800–1970.* Princeton: Princeton University Press.

———. 1980. On the Social Control of Reproduction. *Population and Development Review* 6(4): 527–548.

———. 1983. A Century of Demographic and Cultural Change in Western Europe: An Exploitation of Underlying Dimensions. *Population and Development Review* 9(3): 411–436.

Levasseur, Emile. 1892. *La Population française.* Vol. 3. Paris: Arthur Rousseau.

Levine, David. 1977. *Family Formation in an Age of Nascent Capitalism.* New York: Academic Press.

Levy, M. J., Jr. 1966. *Modernization and the Structure of Societies.* Princeton: Princeton University Press.

Litchfield, Robert B. 1969. Caratteristiche demografiche delle famiglie patrizie fiorentine dal sedicesimo al diciannovesimo secolo. In *Saggi di Demografia Storica*, pp. 17–34. Florence: Dipartimento Statistico-Matematico, Università di Firenze.

Livi, Livio. 1918 and 1920. *Gli ebrei alla luce della statistica.* 2 vols. Florence: Libreria della Voce (vol. 1); Vallecchi (vol. 2).

Livi-Bacci, Massimo. 1968a. Fertility Changes in Spain, 1887–1950: Summary Report. Paper presented at the Bellagio Conference on European Fertility, Bellagio, Italy.

———. 1968b. Fertility and Nuptiality Changes in Spain from the Late 18th to the Early 20th Century. *Population Studies* 22, Part 1 (March): 83–102, and part 2 (July): 211–234.

———. 1971. *A Century of Portuguese Fertility*. Princeton: Princeton University Press.

———. 1977. *A History of Italian Fertility during the Last Two Centuries*. Princeton: Princeton University Press.

———. 1980. Demography of a Rural Community in the Nineteenth Century: Pitigliano, Italy. In *Papers in Jewish Demography, 1977*, edited by U. O. Schmelz, P. Glikson, and S. Della Pergola, pp. 33–52. Jerusalem: Institute of Contemporary Jewry, Hebrew University of Jerusalem.

McKeown, Thomas. 1976. *The Modern Rise of Population*. London: Arnold.

Malthus, Thomas R. 1798. *Population: The First Essay*. Ann Arbor, Mich.: University of Michigan Press, 1959.

———. 1830. A Summary View of the Principle of Population. In *Three Essays on Population*, pp. 13–59. New York: New American Library, 1960.

Matthiessen Poul C. 1985. *The Limitation of Family Size in Denmark*. Copenhagen: The Royal Danish Academy of Sciences and Letters.

———, and McCann, James C. 1978. The Role of Mortality in the European Fertility Transition: Aggregate-Level Relations. In *The Effects of Infant and Child Mortality on Fertility*, edited by Samuel H. Preston, pp. 47–68. New York: Academic Press.

Matz, Klaus-Jurgen. 1980. *Pauperismus und Bevolkerung*. Stuttgart: Klett-Cotta.

May, R. M., and Rubenstein, D. Forthcoming. Reproductive Strategies. In *Reproductive Fitness*, edited by C. R. Austin and R. V. Short. Cambridge: Cambridge University Press.

Mayer, Kurt B. 1952. *The Population of Switzerland*. New York: Columbia University Press.

Mendels, Franklin. 1972. Protoindustrialization: The First Phase of Industrialization. *Journal of Economic History* 32(1): 241–261.

Menken, J. 1979. Seasonal Migration and Seasonal Variation in Fecundability: Effects on Birth Rates and Birth Intervals. *Demography* 16(1): 103–119.

Menken, Jane; Trussell, James; and Watkins, Susan. 1981. The Nutrition

Fertility Link: An Evaluation of the Evidence. *Journal of Interdisciplinary History* XI(3): 425–44.

Mols, Roger. 1954, 1955, and 1956. *Introduction à la démographie historique des villes d'Europe du XIVe au XVIIIe siècle.* 3 vols. Louvain: Editions J. Duculot.

Monnier, Alan. 1981. L'Europe et les pays développés d'outre-mer. *Population* 36(4–6): 883–896.

Moore, Wilbert E. 1974. *Social Change.* 2d ed. Englewood Cliffs, N.J.: Prentice-Hall.

Morrow, Richard B. 1978. Family Limitation in Pre-Industrial England: A Reappraisal. *Economic History Review* 31(3): 419–428.

Mosk, Carl. 1978. *Rural-Urban Differentials in Swedish Fertility, 1880–1960.* Working Paper No. 123. Berkeley, Calif.: Department of Economics, University of California.

Muret, J. L. 1766. *Mémoire sur l'etat de la population dans le pays de Vaud.* Yverdon, Switzerland.

Nahon, Gerard. 1976. Demographie des Juifs portugais à Saint-Esprit-les-Bayonne (1751–87). *Bulletin de la Société des Sciences, Lettres et Arts de Bayonne*, no. 132, pp. 155–202.

Naroll, Raoul. 1968. Some Thoughts on Comparative Method in Cultural Anthropology. In *Methodology in Social Research*, edited by Hubert Blalock and Ann Blalock. New York: McGraw-Hill.

National Birth Rate Commission. 1916. *The Declining Birth Rate: Its Causes and Effects.* London: Chapman Hall.

Notestein, Frank W. 1953. Economic Problems of Population Change. In *Proceedings of the Eighth International Conference of Agricultural Economists*, pp. 13–31. London: Oxford University Press.

Ohlin, G. 1961. Mortality, Marriage, and Growth in Pre-Industrial Populations. *Population Studies* 14(3): 190–197.

Page, Hilary J. 1973. Age, Marriage Duration and Fertility: An Analysis of Cross-Sectional Data. Ph.D. dissertation, Princeton University.

Page, Hilary J., and Lesthaeghe, Ron, editors. 1981. *Child-Spacing in Tropical Africa: Traditions and Change.* London: Academic Press.

Pantelides, Edith, and Coale, Ansley J. 1979. Two Sets of County Boundaries, and Erroneous Figures for County Vital Rates in Nineteenth-Century Ireland. In *The British Fertility Decline: Demographic Transition in the Crucible of the Industrial Revolution* (1984), by Michael Teitelbaum. Princeton: Princeton University Press.

Peller, Sigismund. 1965. Births and Deaths among Europe's Ruling Families since 1500. In *Population in History: Essays in Historical Demography*, edited by D. V. Glass and D.E.C. Eversley, pp. 87–100. Chicago: Aldine.

Perrenoud, Alfred. 1974. Malthusianisme et Protestantisme: Un Modèle démographique Weberien. *Annales—Economies, Sociétés, Civilisations* 29(4): 975–988.

———. 1979. *La Population de Genève du seizième au début du dixneuvième siècle: Etude démographique.* Vol. 1. Genéva: Société d'Histoire et d'Archéologie de Genève.

Petersen, William. 1978. The Effects of Government Policies on the Fertility of Less Developed Countries. Paper presented at the annual meeting of the American Association for the Advancement of Science, Washington, D.C., February 14, 1978.

Piers, Maria. 1978. *Infanticide.* New York: Norton.

Preston, Samuel H., editor. 1978. *The Effects of Infant and Child Mortality on Fertility.* New York. Academic Press.

Quételet, Lambert Adolphe J. 1848. *Du Système social et des lois qui le régissent.* Paris: Guillaumin et Cie.

Rashin, A. G. 1956. *Naselenie Rosii.* Moscow.

Richards, Toni. 1977. Fertility Decline in Germany: An Econometric Appraisal. *Population Studies* 31(3): 537–553.

Rogers, Everett M. 1962. *Diffusion of Innovations.* New York: Free Press.

Röse, C. 1905. Die Wichtigkeit det Mutterbrust für die körperliche und geistige Entwicklung des Menschen. *Deutsche Monatsschrift für Zahnheilkunde* 23: 129–176.

Rozman, Gilbert. 1973. *Urban Networks in Ch'ing China and Tokugawa Japan.* Princeton: Princeton University Press.

Ryder, Norman B. 1983. Fertility and Family Structure. *Population Bulletin of the United Nations,* no. 15. New York: Department of International Economic and Social Affairs.

Sardi Bucci, Deanna. 1976. La Comunità ebraica di Firenze durante la prima metà del XIX secolo: Caratteristiche demografiche, economiche e sociali. *Genus* 32(3–4): 75–115.

Sauer, Friederich. 1975. *Höringhausen.* Arolsen, Federal Republic of Germany: Waldeckischer Geschichtsverein.

Sauer, R. 1978. Infanticide and Abortion in Nineteenth-Century Britain. *Population Studies* 32(1): 81–93.

Savorgnan, F. 1923. Nuzialità e fecondità delle case sovrane d'Europa. *Metron* 3.
———. 1925. La fecondità della aristocrazie. *Metron* 4.
Scheunpflug, Lorenz. 1961. *Ortsippenbuch Anhausen.* Frankfurt am Main: Deutsche Arbeitsgemeinschaft Genealogischer Verbande.
Schmelz, U. O. 1971. *Infant and Early Childhood Mortality among the Jews of the Diaspora.* Jerusalem: Institute of Contemporary Jewry, Hebrew University of Jerusalem.
Schultz, T. Paul. 1980. An Economic Interpretation of the Decline in Fertility in a Rapidly Developing Country: Consequences of Development and Family Planning. In *Population and Economic Change in Developing Countries*, edited by Richard A. Easterlin. Chicago: University of Chicago Press.
Schwirian, Kent P. 1973. Some Analytical Problems in the Comparative Test of Ecological Theories. In *Comparative Social Research: Methodological Problems and Strategies*, edited by Michael Armer and Allen Grimshaw. New York: John Wiley.
Scrimshaw, Susan C. M. 1978. Infant Mortality and Behavior in the Regulation of Family Size. *Population and Development Review* 4(3): 383–403.
Sharlin, Allan. 1978. National Decrease in Early Modern Cities: A Reconsideration. *Past and Present*, no. 79, pp. 126–138.
Shorter, Edward. 1975. *The Making of the Modern Family.* New York: Basic Books.
———. 1978. The Great Transformation of Mother-Infant Relations, Eighteenth to Twentieth Centuries. Manuscript prepared for UNESCO's commemoration volume for the International Year of the Child.
Shorter, Edward; Knodel, John; and van de Walle, Etienne. 1971. The Decline of Non-Marital Fertility in Europe, 1880–1940. *Population Studies* 25(3): 375–393.
Siampos, George, and Valaoras, Vasilios G. 1960. Long-Term Fertility Trends in Greece. International Population Conference, London.
Silver, Brian D. 1978. Language Policy and the Linguistic Russification of Soviet Nationalities. In *Soviet Nationality Policies and Practices*, edited by Jeremy Azrael. New York: Praeger.
Simmons, Alan; Diaz-Briquets, Sergio; and Laquian, Aprodicio A. 1977. *Social Change and Internal Migration: A Review of Findings from*

Africa, Asia and Latin America. Ottawa: International Development Research Centre.

Singarimbun, Masri, and Hull, Terence H. 1977. Social Responses to High Mortality Which Act to Support High Fertility. In *International Population Conference, Mexico, 1977*, vol. 1, pp. 225–240. Liège: International Union for the Scientific Study of Population.

Smelser, Neil. 1959. *Social Change in the Industrial Revolution.* Chicago: University of Chicago Press.

Smith, Daniel Scott. 1977. A Homeostatic Demographic Regime: Patterns in West European Family Reconstitution Studies. In *Population Patterns in the Past*, edited by Ronald D. Lee, pp. 19–51. New York: Academic Press.

Smith, Thomas C. 1977. *Nakahara: Family Farming and Population in a Japanese Village, 1717–1830.* Stanford, Calif.: Stanford University Press.

Soboul. Albert. 1977. De l'Ancien régime à la révolution: Problème régional et réalités sociales. In *Régions et régionalisme en France du XVIIIe siècle à nos jours*, edited by Christian Gras and Georges Livet, pp. 25–54. Vendôme, France: Presses Universitaires de France.

Soloway, Richard Allen. 1982. *Birth Control and the Population Question in England 1877–1930.* Chapel Hill, N.C.: The University of North Carolina Press.

Stengers, J. 1971. Les Pratiques anticonceptionnelles dans le mariage au XIXe et au XXe siècle: Problèmes humains et attitudes religieuses. *Revue Belge de Philologie et d'Histoire* 49(2): 403–481 and 49(4): 1119–1174.

Stephens, Meic. 1976. *Linguistic Minorities in Western Europe.* Llandysul, Dyfed, Wales: Gomer Press.

Stolnitz, George J. 1964. The Demographic Transition. In *Population: The Vital Revolution*, edited by Ronald Freedman. Garden City, N.Y.: Anchor Books.

Stone, Lawrence. 1977. *The Family, Sex and Marriage in England 1500–1800.* New York: Harper and Row.

Struve, C. A. 1802. *A Familiar Treatise on the Education of Children.* London.

Stycos, J. Mayone. 1968. *Human Fertility in Latin America: Sociological Perspectives.* Ithaca: Cornell University Press.

Sun, Te-Hsiung; Lin, Hui-Sheng; and Freedman, Ronald. 1978. Trends in Fertility, Family Size Preferences, and Family Planning Practice: Taiwan, 1961–76. *Studies in Family Planning* 9(4): 54–70.

Sündbärg, G. 1909. Maisons souveraines de l'Europe en 1841–1890. *Ekonomisk Tidskrift* 11, part 6.

Sutter, Jean, and Tabah, Léon. 1951. Les Notions d'isolat et de population minimum. *Population* 6(3): 481–498.

———. 1952. Effets de la consanguinité et de l'endogamie: Une Enquête en Morbihan et Loir-et-Cher. *Population* 7(2): 249–266.

———. 1955. L'Évolution des isolats de deux départements français: Loir-et-Cher, Finistère. *Population* 10(4): 645–674.

Switzerland. 1878. *Statistiques de la Suisse, mouvement de la population en Suisse en 1876, livraison 35*. Berne.

———. 1901. *Statistiques de la Suisse, mariages, naissances et décès, 1871–1890, livraison 128*. Berne.

Szajkowski, Zosa. 1946. The Growth of the Jewish Population of France: The Political Aspects of a Demographic Pattern. *Jewish Social Studies* 8(3): 179–196 and 8(4): 297–321.

Teitelbaum, Michael S. 1974. Birth Underregistration in the Constituent Countries of England and Wales, 1841–1910. *Population Studies* 28: 329–343.

———. 1984. *The British Fertility Decline: Demographic Transition in the Crucible of the Industrial Revolution.* Princeton: Princeton University Press.

Tilly, Charles. 1976. *Sociology, History and the Origins of the European Proletariat.* CRSO Working Paper, no. 148. Ann Arbor, Mich.: Center for Research on Social Organization.

———. 1978. The Historical Study of Vital Processes. In *Historical Studies of Changing Fertility*, edited by Charles Tilly, pp. 3–55. Princeton: Princeton University Press.

———. 1979. Demographic Origins of the European Proletariat. CRSO Working Paper, no. 207. Ann Arbor, Mich.: Center for Research on Social Organization.

Ulmer, Henri. 1927. La Mortalité infantile en France de 1871 à 1926. *Bulletin de la Statistique Générale de la France* 17: 65–108.

Vandenbroeke, C. 1977. Caractéristiques de la nuptialité et de la fécondité en Flandre et en Brabant aux XVIIe–XIXe siècles. *Annales de Démographie Historique* (1977), pp. 7–20.

van de Walle, Etienne. 1968. Marriage and Marital Fertility. *Daedalus* 97(2): 486–501.

———. 1974. *The Female Population of France in the Nineteenth Century: A Reconstruction of 82 Départements.* Princeton: Princeton University Press.

———. 1979. Urban–Rural Differences in Fertility. Manuscript.

———. 1980. Motivations and Technology in the Decline of French Fertility. In *Family and Sexuality in French History*, edited by Robert Wheaton and Tamara K. Hareven. Philadelphia: University of Pennsylvania Press.

van de Walle, Etienne, and Preston, Samuel H. 1974. Mortalité de l'enfance au XIXe siècle à Paris et dans le département de la Seine. *Population* 29(1): 89–107.

van de Walle, Etienne, and van de Walle, Francine. 1972. Allaitement, sterilité et contraception: Les Opinions jusqu'au XIXe siècle. *Population* 27 (4–5): 685–701.

van de Walle, Francine. 1975. Migration and Fertility in Ticino. *Population Studies* 29(3): 447–462.

———. 1980. Education and the Demographic Transition in Switzerland. *Population and Development Review* 6(3): 463–471.

———. *One Hundred Years of Decline: The History of Swiss Fertility from 1860 to 1960.* Manuscript.

Van Ginneken, Jeroen K. 1978. The Impact of Prolonged Breastfeeding on Birth Intervals and on Postpartum Amenorrhoea. In *Nutrition and Human Reproduction*, edited by W. Henry Mosley, pp. 179–198. New York: Plenum Press.

Van Heek, F. 1973. *Van Hoogkapitalisme naar Verzorgingsstaat. Een Halve Eeuw Sociale Verandering, 1920–1970.* Meppel, Netherlands: Boom.

Van Praag, Ph. 1978. The Development of Neo-Malthusianism in Flanders. *Population Studies* 32(3): 467–480.

Verba, Sidney. 1967. Some Dilemmas in Comparative Research. *World Politics* (October): 370–385.

Verbist, H. 1971. *Les Grandes controverses de l'eglise contemporaine de 1789 à nos jours.* Verviers, Belgium: Marabout Université.

Verdery, Katherine. 1976. Ethnicity and Local Systems: The Religious Organization of Welshness. In *Regional Analysis*, vol. 2, edited by Carol A. Smith. New York: Academic Press.

Verein für Bauerliche Sippenkunde und Bauerliches Wappenwesen. 1938. *Dorfsippenbuch Kreuth.* Goslar, Federal Republic of Germany: Blut und Boden Verlag.

———. 1939. *Dorfsippenbuch Vasbeck.* Goslar, Federal Republic of Germany: Blut und Boden Verlag.

Wallerstein, Immanuel. 1974. *The Modern World-System: Capitalist Agriculture and the Origins of the European World Economy in the Sixteenth Century.* New York: Academic Press.

Ware, Helen. 1977. The Relationship between Infant Mortality and Fertility: Replacement and Insurance Effects. In *International Population Conference, Mexico, 1977,* vol. 1, pp. 205–223. Liège: International Union for the Scientific Study of Population.

Watkins, Susan Cotts. 1984. Spinsters. *Journal of Family History* 9(4): 310–325.

Weber, Eugen. 1976. *Peasants into Frenchmen: The Modernization of Rural France, 1870–1914.* Stanford, Calif.: Stanford University Press.

Weir, David. 1983. Fertility Transition in Rural France, 1740–1829. Ph. D. dissertation, Stanford University.

———. 1981. Contraception, Infant Mortality, and Breastfeeding in Rural France, 1740–1830: Statistical Inference from Family Reconstitution Data. Working Paper No. 9, Stanford Project on the History of Fertility Control.

Westoff, Charles F.; Potter, Robert G., Jr.; Sagi, Philip C.; and Mishler, Elliot G. 1961. *Family Growth in Metropolitan America.* Princeton: Princeton University Press.

Wetekam, Robert. 1956. *Massenhausen.* Arolsen, Federal Republic of Germany: Waldeckischer Geschichtsverein.

———. 1971. *Braunsen.* Arolsen, Federal Republic of Germany: Waldeckischer Geschichtsverein.

Wilson, Chris. 1982. Marital Fertility in Preindustrial England, 1550–1849. Ph.D. dissertation, Cambridge, England.

Wolf, J. 1912. Kinderzahl und Sozialdemokratie in Deutschland. In *Die Volkswirtschaft der Gegenwart und Zukunft.* Supplement 1. Leipzig.

World Population Plan of Action. 1975. *Population and Development Review* 1(1): 163–181.

Wrigley, E. A. 1961. *Industrial Growth and Population Change: A Regional Study of the Coalfield Areas of North-West Europe in the Later Nineteenth Century.* Cambridge, England: Cambridge University Press.

———. 1966. Family Limitation in Pre-Industrial England. *Economic History Review* 19(1): 82–109.

———. 1969. *Population and History.* New York: McGraw-Hill.

———. 1978a. Fertility Strategy for the Individual and the Group. In

Historical Studies of Changing Fertility, edited by Charles Tilly, pp. 135–154. Princeton: Princeton University Press.

———. 1978b. Marital Fertility in Seventeenth-Century Colyton: A Note. *Economic History Review* 31(3): 429–436.

Wrigley, E. A., and Schofield, R. 1981. *The Population History of England 1541–1871: A Reconstruction.* Cambridge, Mass.: Harvard University Press.

———. 1983. English Population History from Family Reconstitution: Summary Results 1600–1799. *Population Studies* 73(2): 157–184.

Zanetti, Dante E. 1972. *La Demografia del patriziato Milanese nei secoli XVII, XVIII, XIX, con una appendice genealogica di Franco Arese Lucini.* Annales Cisalpines d'Histoire Sociale, série 2, no. 2. Pavia, Italy: Università de Pavia.

Index

Library of Congress Cataloging in Publication Data

Conference on the Princeton European Fertility Project (1979)
The decline of fertility in Europe.

"This book is the summary volume in a series on the Decline of fertility in Europe"—Half. t.p.
Bibliography: p.
Includes index.
1. Fertility, Human—Europe—Congresses.
2. Europe—Population—Congresses. I. Coale, Ansley J.
II. Watkins, Susan Cotts, 1938–. III. Title.
HB991.C66 1979 304.6'32'094 85-42682
ISBN 0-691-09416-0 (alk. paper)
ISBN 0-691-10176-0 (pbk.)